THE INTERNATIONAL LEGAL ORDER

The International Legal Order

Ingrid Detter

D.Phil. (Oxon); Jur.Dr. (Stockholm),
Lic. en Droit (Paris); Dipl. Eur.Law, CHEE (Turin);
sometime Fellow of Lady Margaret Hall and of St. Antony's College, Oxford
Barrister-at-Law of the Middle Temple and Lincoln's Inn
Adviser on International Law to the Holy See
Honorary Associate Professor at Åbo Academy in Finland
Professor of International Law in the University of Stockholm

Dartmouth

Aldershot • Brookfield USA • Singapore • Sydney

Published by
Dartmouth Publishing Company Limited
Gower House
Croft Road
Aldershot
Hants GU11 3HR
England

Dartmouth Publishing Company
Old Post Road
Brookfield
Vermont 05036
USA

British Library Cataloguing in Publication Data
Delupis, Ingrid
  International Legal Order
  I. Title
  341.01
Library of Congress Cataloging-in-Publication Data
Detter Delupis, Ingrid, 1936-
    The international legal order / Ingrid Detter.
      p.   cm.
    Includes index.
    ISBN 1-85521-580-2
    1. International law. I. Title.
JX3695.S8D484   1994
341–dc20   94-19948
                                                                    CIP

This book can be ordered from:
The Economist Bookshop, Houghton Street, London WC2A 2AE

ISBN 1 85521 580 2 Hbk
ISBN 1 85521 590 X Pbk

Printed in Great Britain at the University Press, Cambridge

To my son Lawrence

Table of Contents

CHAPTER IV
Sources of International Law: Soft Law
The Legal Value of Recommendations
of International Organisations

CHAPTER VII
Distributive Rules: Objects of Sovereign Functions:
Persons

CHAPTER IX

Abbreviations

ACJG	*Acta Scandinavia Juris Gentium*
AD	*Annual Digest*
AF	*Annuaire français de droit international*
AJIL	American Journal of International Law
AV	*Archiv des Völkerrechts*
BSFP	*British and Foreign State Papers*
BYIL	*British Year Book of International Law*
CD	United Nations Conference on Disarmament
CECA	Communauté européenne du charbon et de l'acier
CEE	Communauté économique européenne
CEEA	Communauté européenne de l'énergie atomique
CERN	Organisation européenne pour la recherche nucleaire
CML	*Common Market Law Review*
CL	*Current Law*
CLJ	*Cambridge Law Journal*
DGVR	Deutsche Gesellschaft für Völkerrecht
EBRD	European Bank for Reconstruction and Development
EC	European Community
ECOSOC	Economic and Social Council
ECTS	*United Kingdom European Community Treaty Series*
EHRR	*European Human Rights Reports*
ESA	European Space Agency
FAO	Food and Agriculture Organisation of the United Nations
GA	General Assembly
GATT	General Agreement on Tariffs and Trade
GJIL	*Georgia Journal of International Law*
HarvILJ	*Harvard International Law Journal*
IBRD	International Bank for Reconstruction and Development
IBS	*International Boundary Series*
ICAO	International Civil Aviation Organisation
ICLQ	*International and Comparative Law Quarterly*
ICJ	International Court of Justice
IISL	International Institute for Space Law
ILA	International Law Association
ILC	International Law Commission

ILO	International Labour Organisation
ILR	*International Law Reports*
IMF	International Monetary Fund
IMO	International Maritime Organisation
IndJIL	*Indian Journal of International Law*
IS	*International Studies*
ItYBIL	*Italian Yearbook of International Law*
ITU	International Telecommunications Union
JDI	*Journal du droit international*
LJ	*Law Journal*
LNTS	League of Nations Treaty Series
LQR	*Law Quarterly Review*
MLR	*Modern Law Review*
NATO	North Atlantic Treaty Organisation
NedTIR	*Netherlands International Law Review*
NorTIR	*Nordisk Tidskrift for International Ret*
OJ	*Official Journal of the European Communities*
ÖJZ	*Österreichische Juristenzeitung*
ÖZöR	*Österreichische Zeitschrift für öffentliches Recht*
PCIJ	Permanent Court of International Justice
RBDI	*Revue belge de droit international*
RCADI	*Recueil des cours de l'Académie de droit international*
RDISP	*Revue de droit international et de science politique*
RGDIP	*Revue générale de droit international public*
RIAA	*United Nations Reports of International Arbitral Awards*
RivDI	*Rivista di diritto internazionale*
SAYIL	*South Africa Year Book of International Law*
SC	Security Council
TIAS	*United States Treaties and other International Acts*
UKTS	*United Kingdom Treaty Series*
UNCED	United Nations Conference on Environment and Development
UNCLOS	United Nations Conference on the Law of the Sea
UNCTAD	United Nations Conference on Trade and Development
UNESCO	United Nations Educational Scientific and Cultural Organisation
UNTS	*United Nations Treaty Series*

UNYB	*United Nations Year Book*
UPU	Universal Postal Union
USTS	*US Treaties and Other International Agreements*
WHO	World Health Organisation
WMO	World Meteorological Organisation
Yale JIL	*Yale Journal of International Law*
ZaöRVR	*Zeitschrift für ausländisches öffentliches Recht und Völkerrecht*
ZLW	*Zeitschrift für Luft und Weltraumrecht*
(Ö	see *supra* under O)

Bibliography

The following are textbooks by the foremost international lawyers. There appears to be three distinct periods of prolific and solid writings on international law: towards the end of the last century; in the '30s; and between 1955-1970. For the *classics*, which are still useful guides, see my *Bibliography on International Law*, New York, 1976.

For my own theories on various topics of international law see, *i.a.*, my works

> *Law Making by International Organisations*, 1965.
> *Essays on the Law of Treaties*, 1967.
> *Finance and Protection of Investments in Developing Countries*, 1973; 2nd ed., 1987.
> *International Law and the Independent State*, 1974; 2nd ed., 1987.
> *The Law of War*, 1987.
> *The Concept of International Law*, 1987; 2nd ed., 1994.

For leading works see,

Accioly, *Tradado do direito internacional público*, 3 vols., 2nd ed., 1956-7.

Alvarez, *Le droit international nouveau dans ses rapports avec la vie actuelle des peuples*, 1959.

Alvarez, *Le droit internatonal nouveau*, 1960.

Anzilotti,*Corso di diritto internazionale*, 2 vols., 1928.

Balladori-Pallieri, *Diritto internazionale pubblico*, 8th ed., Milan, 1962.

Bastid, S., *Cours de droit international public*, 1976-1977.

Bedjaoui, *Le droit international: Bilan et perspectives*, 2vols, 1991.

Berber, *Lehrbuch des Völkerrechts*, 3 vols., 1964.

Bluntschli, *Das moderne Völkerrecht der civilizierten Staaten*, 3rd ed., 1878.

Brierly, *The Law of Nations*, 6th ed., 1963.

Briggs, *The Law of Nations*, 1953.

Brownlie, *Principles of Public International Law*, 4th ed., 1991.

Bowett, *The Law of International Institutions*, 1975.

Calvo, *Le droit international théorique et pratique*, 6 vols, 5th ed., 1896.

Carreau, *Droit international*, 3rd ed., 1991.

Cavaré and Quénéduc, *Le droit international positif*, 2 vols., 3rd ed., 1967-1969.

Carillo Salcedo, *El derecho internacional en un mundo en cambio*, 1984.

Colliard, *Institutions des relations internationales*, 9th ed., 1990.

Conforti, *Diritto internazionale*, 3rd ed., 1987.

Dahm, *Völkerrecht*, 3 vols., 1961.

Delbez, *Les principes généraux du droit international public*, 1964.

Diez de Velasco, *Instituciones de derecho internacional publico*, 2 vols., 1985.

Dupuy, R.J., *Cours général*, 179 RCADI 1979.

Dupuy, P.M., *Droit international public*, 1992.

Fauchille, *Traité de droit international public*, 4 vols., 1921-1926.

Giuliano, Scovazzi and Treves, *Diritto di diritto internazionale*, 1983.

Gonzales Campos & Sanchez Rodriguez & Paz Andrés Sàens de Santa Maria, *Curso de derecho internacional publico*, 1990.

Guggenheim, *Traité de droit international public*, 2 vols., 1967.

v.d. Heydte, *Völkerrecht*, 1960.

Jimenez de Arachaga, *Curso de dercho internacional publico*, 1960.

Kelsen, *Principles of International Law*, 1966.

Korowicz, *Introduction to International Law*, 1959.

LeFur, *Précis de droit international public*, 1939.

Manin, *Droit international public*, 1979.

Merle, *Sociologie des relations internationales*, 1988.

Miaja de la Muela, *Introducción al derecho internacional publico*, 1960.

Monaco, *Manuale di diritto internazionale*, 1960.

Morelli, *Nozioni di diritto internazionale*, 5th ed., 1958.

Navarro, *Derecho internacional publico*, 1954.

Nguyen Quoc Dinh & Dallier & Pellet, *Droit international public*, 3rd ed., 1987.

Oppenheim, *International Law*, 9th ed. by Jennings and Watts, 1992.

O'Connell, *International Law*, 2nd ed., 2 vols., 1976.

Planas-Suarez, *Estudios de derecho internacional*, 1959.

Reuter, *Droit international public*, 5th ed., 1976.

idem, Institutions internationales, 8th ed., 1975.

Idem, Institutions et relations internationales, 4th ed., 1988.

Rousseau, *Droit international public*, 5 vols., 1970-1983.

idem, Droit international public, 11th ed., 1991.

Seidl-Hohenveldern, *Völkerrecht*, 5th ed., 1984.

Scelle, *Précis de droit des gens*, 2 vols., 1932-1934.

Schätzel, *Internationales Recht*, 3 vols., 1962.

Sibert, *Traité de droit international public*, 1951.

Sierra, *Tratado de derecho internacional publico*, 1955.

Sperduti, *Lezioni di diritto internazionale*, 1956.

Starke, *An Introduction to International Law*, 8th ed., 1989.

Thierry & Combacau & Sur & Vallée, *Droit international public*, 1984.

Ulloa, *Derecho internacional publico*, 1957.

Verdross, *Die Verfassung der Völkerrechtsgemeinschaft*, 1926.

Verdross and Simma, *Universelles Völkerrecht*, 3rd ed., 1984.

Wengler, *Völkerrecht*, 2 vols., 1964.

Preface

There is great need for a modern textbook of international law, especially one that would be useful to students and practitioners of both international law and of international relations. International realities warrant a new test of the traditional approach to international law. Rule making within international society deserves fresh analysis as does the impact of international rules on and within States. Not least the new political framework of the world, with the greatest political changes since the Congress of Vienna after the debâcle of communism, makes it imperative to re-consider what many thought was an *accepted* or *acceptable* system of international law, allowing for competing ideologies, many of which are now defunct. It may be that any system of law exists to preserve and defend the interests of *individuals* rather than those of States, something which was often obscured by political theories which enhanced the 'State' at the expense of its citizens.

Naturally, it is important to defend and uphold the prerogatives of the legitimate State of international society, as the State forms the ultimate *power structure* of international society. But the time has come for bold statements as to the duties of a State vis-à-vis individuals, both its own citizens and others who find themselves in its territory. International law must also, or perhaps primarily, cater for the interests of individuals and of groups.

Modern topics in international society, such as questions regarding the role of non-governmental organisations, the NGOs, are scarcely mentioned in traditional textbooks although the NGO impact is formidable in modern international society. Other questions, concerning the exact way that rules come into being, or concerning the value of General Assembly Resolutions, receive only summary treatment in the usual textbooks.

There is a marked tendency of authors of current textbooks to view topics, even though treating each one with admirable scholarship, in isolation from each other. There is little effort to synthesise the issues and relevant problems into one *coherent theory*. The need for a new optique appears to be particularly pressing to analyse problems against a coherent theoretical background. It is less fruitful to study isolated 'parallel' topics, like, for example, the law of the sea, use of force and immunity of diplomats, in various segments which are not set in relationship with each other. There are textbooks, both in the Anglo-Saxon world, and on the Continent, where topics are studied in almost watertight compartments without considering any links whatever between them. Many traditional textbooks have adopted an almost blue print type classification of rules.

Another important point concerns a *consistent* approach. In the textbooks commonly used, authors may appear to adopt a theory, say on States and international organisations as the only subjects of international law, and then find themselves unable to explain why individuals also have rights and duties. Others may adopt a theory that individuals are the true subject of the international legal system and then find it hard to explain why, in other chapters in their books, individuals cannot always exercise their rights as such subjects. Most traditional textbooks contain, as a consequence of a fragmented focus of inquiry, numerous contradictions. Many traditional textbooks also put forward propositions which are unrealistic and incompatible with the actual political behaviour of States which ought to be of prime concern when the international lawyer analyses the international legal system.

The aspiration to tackle modern - and neglected - topics may be one reason for this book. Another, and naturally a much more important one, is to treat international law as a coherent, developed and sophisticated legal system, where topics are treated in a consistent contextual framework. Questions like terrorism and environmental rules, hardly mentioned in traditional textbooks, and other topical subjects, must be put in their conceptual context within the rule system.

By relating topics to classifications in my work on *The Concept of International Law* (1987), I shall attempt to demonstrate the coherence of various rules on international law, and vigorously defend a thomistic approach relying on natural law, as furnishing the clearest and most appropriate guidelines for the behaviour of States and other actors in international society.

It cannot be that international law is allowed to be viewed, as it has in some totalitarian regimes, as *dangerous* to the powers of the State. The international legal order is *founded* on notions of independence, interdependence and interaction of States. On the other hand, States must not forget that they are mere conglomerates of *individuals* and it is the individual that international law ultimately protects. It is also on the consent of individuals that the legitimacy of States depends and it is therefore the duty of States, and indeed in their self interest, to protect the interests and rights of individuals. It is therefore of some concern that some countries still deny any efficacy of rules on Human Rights in their own territory, unless converted into domestic legislation; this work may be in some way instrumental in drawing international attention to this anomaly, no doubt based on a misunderstanding that subjection to international general rules would, in some way, diminish the political power of the State.

It is the hope of the author to remedy the present deficiency of theoretical basis of the international legal system by adopting a new approach to the study of international law. Every event must somehow be susceptible to application of international legal rules. International law pervades every corner of international relations and there cannot be areas which we may leave out of our study.

Yet, certain topics are more important than others. In this work we shall concentrate more on the *emergence of rules* and the *actors* who contribute to rule formation. We shall also, but with less emphasis and detail, set out relevant rules for territorial and jurisdictional delimitation and for settlement of disputes: with regard to these subjects we shall limit ourselves to what is relevant to comprehend the framework for international rule making. For it is international rule making that is of the greatest importance and, surprisingly, it is that topic which is least treated in current textbooks on international law.

It has been a challenge to write the book in a way intended to spur students to take interest in the subject and to make those who equate international law with power politics change their attitude to the subject. The work also seeks to encourage researchers to look further into the links I have proposed, and to serve practitioners by suggesting new and different points for argument. As far as the author is concerned, this ambitious target will have been achieved if this work inspires only one student to continue his studies to do research in international law.

Both coherent theory and rigorous analysis of practice is required if a work of international law is to be useful to fellow scholars, to students, as well as to statesmen and practitioners. As Leonardo da Vinci is alleged to have said, theory may represent the leaders in battle, the generals and colonels - but practice represents the soldiers; and you cannot win a battle unless you have both.

London, 1st March 1994

Ingrid Detter Doimi de Lupis Frankopan

CHAPTER I

The Limits of the Discipline

i. Identification of International Law

a. Definition

Most textbooks claim that international law is a system between States and/or international inter-governmental organisations. By this definition, writers draw the conclusion that States and/or international organisations are the 'subjects' of international law. Yet, few have noticed a vicious circle: we do not find out anything about the contents of the law by referring to the 'subjects' of a legal system. So, by saying that international law applies between States and/or international organisations, or that these are the 'subjects of international law', we find out nothing more, neither about the contents nor the limits of the international legal system.[1] The only limits we know are those we have drawn ourselves: that States (and intergovernmental organisations) are 'subjects' of the international legal order.[2]

It would be unacceptable to use such parameters for a national legal system. No one would seriously suggest that *French law* is what applies between *Frenchmen*, for this is not correct. French law is better defined as a system which emanates from the French legislature to regulate matters of French concern. There is thus an *organic connection* between the legislature and the legal system as well as a criterion of *interest*.

It is impossible to use the organic criterion for the international legal system as we cannot say that international law emanates from, for example, *States*. Much else *emanates* from *States* - their own

---

[1]   See, in detail, *infra* Chapter III on Subjects of International Law and, on the argument, my *Concept of International Law*, 1987, *passim.*

[2]   Further on this proposition, see my *Concept of International Law*, 1987, 40 *et seq.*

national legal systems for example. But the *interest* criterion remains valid: international law does regulate matters of *concern and interest* to international society.

Therefore, I suggest,[3] that international law should be defined as a set of rules regulating matters of international relevance. This legal system includes rules of both public and private international law. If we base ourselves on actual practice rather than on what previous textbooks have claimed, international law may be said to be *a system of international legal rules applicable to situations of international relevance.*

b. The Historical Dimension

The adopted definition of international law also applies to earlier phases in history, before, during and after the rise of the Nation States in the 16th century.[4] From an early age, it was not only the relationships *between* States which were regulated by international law, but also some *internal* matters of States: thus, under the early *jus gentium* as elaborated also *slavery* was forbidden, and this prohibition could only be effective if it had immediate application inside States.[5]

Naturally, the international legal system developed rapidly after the rise of the Nation States: only then were there strong independent units which wished to establish contacts with each other, in, for example, the form of diplomatic missions and treaties. However, most writers during this time re-iterated that international law consisted both of one branch that applies *between* States,[6] as well as in *internal*

---

[3]   *Cf.* my *Concept of International Law, op. cit.* 88-91; *cf.* 41-43; and, *infra* for my doctrine of legal relevance and 129.

[4]   See my *Bibliography of International Law*, 1975, for sections of Material of Historical Interest, 13-14, for the Classics, 49-51, and for History of International Law, 51-54. On the development of *jus gentium* as the law common to pilgrims and all peoples in the conception of Gaius (*quod vero naturalis ratio inter omnes homines constituit, id apud omnes populos peraeque custoditur vocaturque jus gentium, quasi quo iure omnes gentes utuntur*), *Institutiones*, 1,1.

[5]   Isidore of Seville, *Etymologiae* V:6.

[6]   This is the *jus inter gentes*, as decribed by Suarez, *De legibus*, 1611, II:19:8.

sphere of States.[7]

After the rapid expansion of international law during the 16th and 17th centuries, States normally relied on the theories of *natural law,* according to which law is what is *necessary* in a society.[8] States thus accepted certain fundamental rights, such as, for example, self-preservation, equality and social interdependence as necessary. Writers like Vitoria (1480-1546),[9] Suarez (1548-1617),[10] Grotius (1583-1642)[11] and Vattel (1714-1767)[12] elaborated various versions of the natural law theory, all more conscious than many contemporary writers that the State is a member of a whole, a member of international society, and must therefore adapt its behaviour accordingly to the needs of this larger *society.*

Gradually, basic legal precepts were amplified in international agreements between States, treaties and other undertakings and, occasionally, by consistent behaviour, especially in territorial contexts where certain use could give rise to prescription.[13]

From the time of the French revolution, other ideas about the nature of international law were occasionally put forward. One theory of *positivism,* implying that law properly so called has to be enacted (*positivism* from *pono, positum* = put, enact). Using this test, only rules which were drafted and accepted could form part of international law. But what about all unwritten rules? These, according to the extreme positivists, did not exist at all.

A special threat to the international legal order were the assertions this century of the so called Uppsala School which regarded international law as 'superstition' with religious overtones and as a

---

4

subject dangerous to the sovereignty of the State. This doctrine, following earlier trends in Swedish legal and philosophical thought,[14] was most acutely put forward by Lundstedt some sixty years ago,[15] was a special version of *exaggerated positivism*. The nihilistic theory of Lundstedt was adopted by the Swedish authorities as giving ample lee-way and legitimacy to any internal excesses. Such excesses may be perpetrated by either the extreme left or by the extreme right (as Hegel had indeed inspired both Marx and Hitler). In the event of Sweden, Lundstedt's ideas were eagerly adopted as, by relying on such views, the (then left wing) Swedish Government pretended to be able to dispense with *any* rule of international law in the internal sphere, a view which appeared to strengthen the short term interests of State power. The theory was taken most seriously by Swedish jurists who are still affected by this extraordinary view; two or three generations of Swedish law students have thus been taught that a *State has the power to do anything* in its own territory.

Positivism in this extreme form, inspired by Hegel's totalitarian views and adopted by jurists like Jellinek,[16] and Triepel,[17] has now been utterly discarded elsewhere, although there are persistent remnants in Swedish legal thought in many fields.

In other countries, there are some international lawyers who may be called *moderate positivists* as they largely rely on enacted rules, in the form of treaties and/or customary rules,[18] *but* regard these as heavily circumscribed and limited by certain *general principles*,[19] especially in the field of Human Rights. Thus, virtually all international lawyers (outside Sweden, Norway, China, Serbia and Cuba) accept that the sovereignty of a State is severely limited with regard to action taken against its own nationals: whether or not the

---

14   Hägerström, *Stat och rätt, en rättsfilosofisk undersökning, 1904*; cf., Boström, *Satser om lag och lagstiftning*, 1845;

15   Lundstedt, *Law of Nations: Superstition of the Peoples*, 1930; cf. scathing criticism by, for example, Walz, *Das Wesen des Völkerrechts und Kritik der Völkerrechtsleugner*, 1930.

16   Jellinek, *System der subjektiven öffentlichen Rechte*, 1905.

17   Triepel, *Völkerrecht und Landesrecht*, 1899.

18   On the intricacies of customary rules and their true nature, see *infra* Chapter III.

19   *Cf. infra*, Chapter III, under General Principles.

State has acceded to a treaty, or whether it has enacted a national law on the matter, *the State is bound to respect basic Human Rights.*[20] This position is always taken by the natural law adherents; but it also taken by lawyers who call themselves *positivists*, in the sense that they place paramount importance on the written word and firm customary rules[21] but *also* allow other principles to operate.

Thus, many modern international lawyers, who think of themselves as moderate positivists, may place special emphasis on written law - as such written rules are clearly more reliable and more accessible - but few would deny the wealth and importance of unwritten rules. They then claim that such rules are part of *customary rules*[22] or of *general principles,*[23] accepted in some way by States. Above all, most such moderate positivists acknowledge that certain *compelling* rules,[24] operate within the territory of all States.[25]

Parallel to such ideas, there is also now a considerable revival of *natural law* in many countries of the world.[26] The adherents of natural law in the international field claim that certain rights and duties are *inherent*[27] in mankind and that whatever rules are necessary for the survival of international society must be inferred.[28] In the forceful revivals of natural law,[29] in which its proponents show that it is a system compatible with both common sense and

---

[20]   'Basic' is here used to indicate the most fundamental Human Rights and illustrated in consistent case-law, thus the right *to avoid* genocide, torture, slavery and, at least during the last few decades, apartheid. The *freedom of expression* probably forms an important ancillary right as deviations and violations of Human Rights in other fields may otherwise not be known. See, in detail, *infra*, in Chapter IV.

[21]   *Cf. supra*, note 9.

[22]   See *infra* under Customary Rules.

[23]   See *infra* under General Principles.

[24]   On *jus cogens*, see *infra*, under Chapter III.

[25]   See *infra*, Chapter III, on the misconceived theories of monism and dualism.

[26]   *E.g.* Verdross & Köck, Natural Law: The Tradition of Universal Reason and Authority, in Macdonald & Johnston, ed., *The Structure and Process of International Law, Essays in Legal Philosophy, Doctrine and Theory,* 1983, 17 *et seq.*

[27]   *Cf.* Verdross & Simma, *Universelles Völkerrecht,* 3rd ed., 1984, 3 *et seq.*

[28]   *Cf.* my *Concept, op. cit., passim* and at 37 for the Hypothetical Goal.

[29]   See, for example, Finnis, *Natural Law and Natural Rights,* Oxford, 1981.

State practice, it is made clear that much criticism of natural law is based on misunderstandings (and often lack of first hand reading) of authorities like St. Thomas Aquinas. Thus, the claim that natural law 'cannot be changed' is one such allegation which indicates the superficial studies of the critics. It is obvious that the law *necessary* for a society will adapt to the needs of that society.

Another misconception, that may explain the hostility among certain scholars who have not studied natural law theories in detail, is that natural law adherents claim that *the whole legal system* includes *only* natural law rules. On the contrary, natural law rules *supplement* rules that States have agreed on in treaties, and numerous other rules which have a different origin. However, it becomes most difficult to explain certain rules of international law, especially in Human Rights and in humanitarian law without recourse to *some* natural law rules.

As any society needs law - *ubi societas ibi jus*[30] - so does international society need a legal system. As law in general, international law *'has the object of assuring the co-existence of different interests which are worthy of legal protection'*.[31] Many such interests would appear to be *natural* or *inherent* in international society. But this does not mean that such interests are unchanging or static. On the contrary, interests that merit protection are part of an ever fluctuating structure, as the needs of the Third World amply illustrate today.

The most eminent and comprehensive work on international law in the contemporary world,[32] recognises that natural law must play an important role as *supplementing* the contractual law made by treaties or custom of States. The authors read into the formulation of article 38 of the Statute of the International Court of Justice,[33] when it refers to *general principles*, that this recourse implies a rejection of

---

[30] Where there is a society, there will also be a legal system. The saying is often attributed to Aristotle and was absorbed by the Roman law system, hence its common Latin form. For reference, see Aristotle, *e.g. The Politics*, III.16.iii (1287 a 16-18) 143: *cf.* EN V.6 (1134 a 26-30).

[31] Huber in *The Palmas Island Case*, ii RIAA 870.

[32] i:1 Oppenheim, 9th edition by Jennings and Watts, 1992, 25.

[33] On this *infra* under Sources of Law in Chapter III.

the earlier positivist view.[34] However, it may also, in the opinion of these authors, imply a rejection of a *complete* 'naturalist' view, according to which natural law is the *primary source* of international law.[35] In our own work, however, we find it unnecessary to weigh, against each other, the value of natural law and contractual law, as natural law rules are, in any event, *primordial* to the development of the whole international legal system: no legal system can develop without the general principles upon which conditions and effects are founded. What do contractual rules matter if there is not a general rule, derived from inherent common sense and binding on the ground of social necessity, that agreements are binding (*pacta sunt servanda*).[36] We therefore take the view that natural law rules which are truly *natural* and *inherent* in international society are fundamentally *necessary* to any legal system.[37] On the other hand, there is no question that international law has developed, and is still developing, on the basis of the *consent of States* and that, therefore, the legal system is clearly anchored in will of States. We are thus back to what Grotius suggested several hundred years ago when he accepted the role of natural law as coupled with the will of States[38] or, better still, at the views of St. Thomas Aquinas or Aristotle, representing a wide time span, who both accepted the twin development of law by the branches founded on nature and on the will of States.

It is worth underlining that international law is a *dynamic system*[39] and, as such, it is flexible and adaptable to new circumstances and to new actors in international society. It may be that the definition adopted in this work is designed to absorb also such dynamic changes in international action.

It is also important to stress that, although it may be interesting to note what theories international lawyers put forward to explain

---

34   *Ibid., op. cit., loc. cit.* See *infra*, under General Principles: Natural Law.

35   *Ibid., op. cit., loc. cit.*

36   See, in detail, my *Concept, op. cit.,* 49-51 and 122.

37   See further *infra* under General Principles: Natural Law.

38   *Ibid., op. cit., loc. cit.*

39   For references to writers on the Dynamic Nature of International Law, see my *Bibliography, op. cit.* 60-61.

their view of the international legal order (as indeed I seek to do myself), it is not for lawyers to change the contents of the law. Thus, it is immaterial if lawyers in Sweden and Norway deny the existence of certain basic Human Rights: it can be shown in State practice, as we shall demonstrate,[40] that there are such binding rules with regard to basic protection of individuals. Any State, which is not anxious to figure in Nuremberg or Tokyo-like proceedings, is wise to accept the limits of its competence in its own territory.[41]

c. The Hallmarks of International Law

International law is *different* from national (or what is often called *municipal* law). There is no *central legislature* in international society, nor is there any *central executive* or any *central courts* that are competent for all matters. These differences, however, are not necessarily shortcomings and certainly do not imply that international law is no legal system. On the contrary, it appears that international law may be a particularly sophisticated and complex legal system with an extremely refined (but *different*) rule making machinery.[42]

Austin[43] emphasised that *law is the command of the sovereign.* On that score, international law - not emanating from a *sovereign* - would not be *law.* Yet, nowadays it is generally conceded that there was a misunderstanding of words and Austin may not have been a hostile as assumed.[44] At any rate, anyone who observes States in practice will notice that States indeed behave *to obey and comply with international legal rules* and when they deviate, or when they assume they deviate, from these rules they issue *explanations, statements or excuses* and other States or organisations may in such cases resort to *sanctions.*

---

[40] See, *infra*, Chapter III, under General Principles and under Human Rights.

[41] See, *infra*, Chapter VI and VII, on Fettering of a State's sovereignty in its own territory, and *cf.* my *International Law and the Independent State*, 2nd ed., 1987, *passim.*

[42] See, in detail, my *Concept, op. cit., passim.*

[43] See Austin, *The Province of Jurisprudence Determined*, 1832.

[44] *Cf.* Hart, *The Concept of Law*, emphasising that international law does not emanate from a 'legislature'. This obviously is immaterial since rules are formed in other ways, see my *Concept of International Law*, 1987, *passim.*

We may thus agree with the French scholar Scelle who pointed out that, although there is no legislature, no executive and no general courts in international society, there is still a *legislative, executive and judicial function*, which is exercised in a different way from what we are used to in the internal law of States.[45] As I have pointed out, the way such *functions* are exercised may indicate that far from being any 'primitive' law, international law is a highly sophisticated legal system.[46]

Everyday events amply illustrate that there is a clear network of international rules which States and others observe in every detail. The more technical the rules, the more indispensable they appear to be and the more they prove the existence of a viable international legal system. These are the rules on technical communications, for example those of the Universal Postal Union (UPU)[47] or the International Telecommunications Union (ITU),[48] without which no one would be able to send letters from one country to another or make international telephone calls.

d. The Doctrine of International Relevance and International Concern

International relevance implies that a matter touches the interests of more than one State. A number of issues only affect one State; much is of mere domestic concern. But as States become more interdependent, the spheres of activities that States may claim as their own is shrinking. Internal policies may no longer be conducted as before without regard to other States. Yet, there is certainly still an area which a State may claim as its reserved domain and, under the rules of article 2(7) of the Charter of the United Nations this is a field where other States may not interfere. Article 2(7) thus provides that:

'Nothing contained in the present Charter shall authorise the United Nations to intervene in matters which are essentially within the domestic jurisdiction of any State or shall require the

---

[45] Scelle, *Droit international*, 1949.
[46] See my *Concept, op. cit., passim.*
[47] See *infra.*
[48] See *infra.*

members to submit such matters to settlement under the present Charter; but this principle shall not prejudice the application of enforcement measures under Chapter VII.'

This article reflects the so-called doctrine on *non-intervention* in the *reserved domain:* no other State or organisation may intervene in the domestic affairs of another State.[49] Matters within the reserved domain are generally not of immediate international relevance. It is important, however, to recognise that the ambit of article 2(7) is nowadays interpreted much more narrowly than when it was drafted in 1945. In other words, the area of the reserved domain is constantly shrinking as various matters within a State, especially in the area of Human Rights, are scrutinised by outside actors. Furthermore, the rule of reserved domain was always, and is still, subject to a number of reservations. These reservations may be of different types.

First of all, by concluding an *agreement* on any matter, even one which otherwise would have been within the reserved domain, a State may *make* a matter *internationally relevant* and thus relevant to other States. One such agreement is the Charter of the United Nations, the very instrument which contains the aforementioned article 2(7). This agreement expressly permits intervention in domestic affairs *under Chapter VII*, in other words if there is a threat to international peace and security.[50]

Secondly, a State is bound by a number of rules under general international law,[51] that is to say outside treaties and specific agreements, to allow for certain minimum *transit traffic* by, for example, land-locked States,[52] innocent passage in territorial

---

[49]   See *infra* in Chapter V in detail about the limitations of the Use of Force and of Intervention.

[50]   See *infra*, in Chapter IX *et seq.*, on Peaceful Settlement of Disputes.

[51]   We prefer to use the expression *general international law* to *customary international law*, as the latter term is not always warranted. On the misuse of the term 'customary' law to indicate rules which have not been formed by 'custom', see *infra* under Customary Law *latu sensu*.

[52]   See my *International Law and the Independent State*, 2nd ed., 1987, 60 *et seq.* and *infra*, 419 *et seq.* under Territory, Passage over Land.

waters[53] and certain passage through its air space.[54]

Thirdly, and perhaps most importantly, a State is bound by *general rules of international law,* accepted by all nations, to grant immunity to certain foreign agents,[55] as well as to provide certain *minimum treatment and Human Rights* to all individuals in its territory, certainly including its own nationals.[56] These rules are binding *whether or not they are embodied in a treaty or in a general convention.* Some, but not all, of these rules are so compelling that they are *indispositive* and they can thus not be set aside by treaty. This last mentioned body of rules is generally referred to by international lawyers as *jus cogens* and we shall have reason to revert to this important concept on several occasions.[57]

The above mentioned rules on obligations under a treaty, on rules of transit, and on treatment of agents and individuals, entail restrictions of a State's territorial sovereignty and appear as *exceptions* to the aforementioned article 2(7). Thus, the restrictions regard areas where international law *is concerned* with events inside the frontiers of a State, *i.e.* within the domestic jurisdiction of a State.

Any infringement of rules regarding territory, for example on borders, or on treatment of diplomats or concerning Human Rights, are consequently of immediate international relevance and may cause two types of reaction: if national frontiers are violated, the *territorial State* may become entitled to use force to retaliate.[58] If the case came before a Court or a tribunal the territorial State would be in the position of a *plaintiff.* If, on the other hand, rules on treatment of

---

53   *Ibid.,* 29 *et seq.* and *infra* 453 *et seq.* under Waters and Shelves, Passage Through Water.

54   *Ibid.,* 79 *et seq.* and *infra* 466 *et seq.,* under Air Space, Innocent Passage in Air Space and Outer Space.

55   *Ibid.,* 101 *et seq.* and *infra* 510 *et seq.,* under Jurisdiction, Immunity.

56   *Ibid.,* 125 *et seq.* and *infra* 366-368, Prophylactic Rules and Human Rights.

57   See, further, *infra.*

58   See, further, *infra* in Chapter V under The Prohibition of Force, Self-Defense. The legitimating factors are analysed in my *The Law of War,* Cambridge, 1987, 71-84, where special attention is paid to what I have called *patronising intervention,* the type of action known both to the United States and to the ex-Soviet Union, and by which the intervenor considers himself to be *entitled* or even *under duty* to act, see *ibid.,* 80-81.

aliens and/or nationals are concerned, this may also give rise to an international case before a tribunal or court[59] but here the territorial State would be in the position of a *defendant.*

When we consider action, or reaction, of other States, in the latter case, we perceive a *principle of legitimate intervention* in domestic affairs, as an important *exception* to that *notion of the reserved domain.* All such instances reflect a certain degree of *international relevance:* the acts in question are not limited, in their operation or in their effects, to the territorial State.

International relevance is enhanced and may be appropriately called *international concern*[60] if an issue has a wide ambit. For example, if two States regulate a matter of interest to them, the matter of agreement becomes one of international relevance. The agreement between the States so to speak lifts out the matter on to the international stage. If then numerous States conclude a multilateral convention on a specific matter, one could say that this matter becomes one of international concern, which indicates a heightened level of relevance. There may be occasions when, again, a convention between States reflects an already existing situation of international concern. For example, there was widespread discontent with the rule of apartheid among individuals and groups of individuals in some countries when States acted, largely within the United Nations, to attempt to remedy the situation by international political pressure and economic sanctions.[61]

The last example illustrates that law making[62] by States may be

---

[59] See, for example, the Nuremberg or Tokyo War Trials, and my *Law of War, op. cit.,* 352 *et seq.* There might be other sanctions: see *infra,* 598 *et seq.*

[60] *Ibid.,* 42.

[61] The form such pressure should take may be discussed: there is wide disagreement among scholars whether sanctions constitute any effective remedy. See my paper on Typology of Sanctions, BISA Conference, Aberystwyth, December 1987, and *infra* 595-618 on Sanctions.

[62] 'Law making' and 'legislation' can have many meanings and obviously we must here distinguish between national and international law making: see Gihl, *International Legislation,* Oxford, 1937. International law does not emanate from any specific legislature or any single 'source', see, *infra,* on *Sources of International Law.* Yet, although there is no formal and centralised way of assessing rules, there is often overwhelming evidence that certain rules operate and are recognised by States as effective, *infra* 193-320 on *Sources of*

caused or accelerated by activities of other actors. Those who make the law are thus not necessarily the same as those who cause the law to be made, nor is there necessarily any identity between those who make the law and those who are governed by the rules.[63]

As has been mentioned, most traditional textbooks suggest that international law is a system that applies between States, between States and inter-governmental organisations and/or between such organisations themselves. Such a narrow concept is not compatible with a realistic analysis of contemporary practice in international society. Other entities are also governed by international legal rules and a useful test is often whether their activities are *internationally relevant*.

Non-State bodies governed by international law, and of great importance in contemporary international society, are, as we shall see in detail later,[64] for example, liberation movements: the recognition of the Palestine Liberation Organisation on 13th September 1993 is a timely reminder to the many international lawyers who had excluded the PLO from their textbooks on the ground that it was not an international *subject*.[65] It is difficult to agree with the traditionalists, that, before the acts of recognition, PLO was devoid of any status at all under international law. One compelling argument for considering liberation movements subject to international law is obviously that a war-like situation may otherwise result in the State party - but not the liberation movement - being bound by the Laws of War.[66]

In our opinion, supported by further State practice, activities of other non-governmental organisations are also often governed by international law if they are of some size or importance (such as the Red Cross). Other examples are international Human Rights

---

International Law. For acts of international organisations, see my *Law Making of International Organisations,* Stockholm, 1965, *passim*; on recommendations of international organisations, for example, those on apartheid, see, *infra*, under Soft Law.

[63]   See *infra* 232 on the distinction Creators/Actors/Subjects.

[64]   See *infra* 59 *et seq.* under Subjects of International Law.

[65]   See on subjectivity and personality, *infra* in Chapter II on the Structure of International Society.

[66]   See my *Law of War*, Cambridge, 1987, 361 *et seq.*

movements (such as Amnesty), minority groups within States (such as the Tamils), or neglected majority groups of nationals (such as the blacks in South Africa), as well as individuals not forming part of groups.

Even multinationals, or transnationals, cannot be relegated to exclusive municipal jurisdiction but are, in some of their activities, governed by international law.

Many of the non-governmental organisations are not only governed by the international system but also *contribute* to its development: there is an important inter-change with these agencies. The view that international law is a wide system applicable to numerous international relationships is gaining increasing foothold in modern doctrine. Only if such a comprehensive notion forms the basis of our studies is it possible to understand the network of international rules. The practice of States and other actors in international society provides much material which enables us to establish certain types of rules.

ii. The Notion of Comity

a. Definition

The term *comity* is occasionally used to denote a rule which is not legally binding but only forming part of the courtesy (*courtoisie*) between nations. In this sense the term is often used to describe various non-binding rules with regard to the treatment of diplomats, for example rules on protocol which are observed in practice. Such rules are respected in the daily life of States, not on the basis of any legal obligations and not as part of the important compulsory rules on diplomatic rights, such as immunity,[67] but as *courtesy*; sometimes the term *comity* is used to denote such courtesy.

Most often, however, the term *comity* is used by practising lawyers, especially in the Anglo-Saxon world, to mean something else: it is taken to mean the mutual respect States show each other with regard to the application of their respective laws. As such,

---

[67]   See, *infra* 519 *et seq.*, under the section on Diplomatic Immunity.

comity can be a very useful term.

In *Hilton v Guyot* the term comity in this sense was succinctly defined as a form of *recognition*[68] of other legal systems. The Court said that

> ''Comity', in the legal sense, is neither a matter of absolute obligation, on the one hand, nor of mere courtesy and good will, on the other. But it is the recognition which one nation allows within its own territory to the legislative, executive and judicial acts of another nation, having due regard both to international duty and convenience, and to the rights of its own citizens or of other persons who are under the protection of its laws'.[69]

Comity is a most important concept in international law. It explains both certain consequences of the sovereignty of States, such as that of equality and of mutual respect. It crystallises numerous aspects of the *interdependence* of nations. Comity also lies at the very root of conflict of laws solutions. The Supreme Court of the United States expressed this connection clearly in *Lorenzen v Lydden*[70] where the Court said that

> 'International or maritime law in such matters as this[71] ... aims at stability and order through usages which considerations of comity, reciprocity and long-range interest have developed to define the domain which each will claim as its own. Maritime law, like our municipal law, has attempted to avoid or resolve conflicts between competing laws by ascertaining and valuing points of contact between the transactions and the states or governments whose competing laws are involved'.

---

[68] *Recognition* is a term which can be used in numerous different ways: in this context we are speaking of *acknowledging the existence, viability and efficacy of a specific legal order*. *Infra*, the term, in relation to the *acknowledgment of the existence of States*, will be studied in Chapter II.

[69] (1985) 159 US 113 233 per Mr Justice Gray.

[70] (1953) 345 US 571.

[71] The case concerned claims for injuries sustained in Cuba by a Danish seaman who had boarded the ship in New York. (Footnote added).

The technique of applying principles of comity leads, *inter alia* to what in conflict of laws is called the search for the *proper law of the contract*.[72] The Court in *Lorenzen v Lydden* said that the criteria that the Court should use

> 'appear to be arrived at from weighing the significance of one or more connecting factors between the shipping transaction regulated and the national interest served by the assertion of authority'.[73]

The concept of comity is thus closely connected with notions like sovereignty, extraterritorial application of laws and party autonomy. The reference to such broad notions needs to be explained.

b. Comity and Sovereignty

A State is, as a matter of principle, sovereign in its own territory and therefore decides what laws and rules apply to its citizens and other persons in its territory. This sweeping statement has, as we already indicated and which we shall investigate in greater detail, several serious limitations: it is certainly not true that a State can do what it pleases in its own territory. The most important limitations to its power are in the field of *Human Rights* and of *immunity* of certain agents of other States, like members of foreign government and diplomats. There are also other important limitations with regard to rights of *transit* and with regard to activities that may cause transboundary, or probably even only national, *pollution*.[74]

A State's power may furthermore be severely limited in its own territory by virtue of *treaties and agreements* which extend the powers of others or limit the powers of the territorial State in certain respects. The treaties of the European Community may illustrate this

---

[72] It is this technique which, in Scandinavia, with a less adequate term is called the 'individualising method'.

[73] (1953) 345 US 571.

[74] See, *infra*, under sections on Human Rights, Immunity, Transit and Environmental Rules.

point as here national legislative measures are demoted by Community legislation.[75]

These *limitations* of a State's sovereignty in its own territory can, in many situations be construed to correspond to *rights* of other States and can, in a sense, represent a form of recognition of the legal system of other States.

When we speak of comity we are no longer thinking of the clear limitations of a State's power by general rules or by treaties but we have in mind the *attitude* of one State to the legislative and judicial machinery of another State.

c. Comity and Jurisdiction

National Courts have certain attitudes to legislation and judicial decisions of other States when such matters becomes relevant in any one case. The term comity then tends to imply that a national Court gives effect, or refuses effect, to a *foreign law* or accepts the facts underlying a *foreign judgment* on the basis of respect for another State. There is often a considerable element of reciprocity in handling certain matters and a Court may, for example, often consider how and to what extent it is important that its own legislation or judgments of similar type are accepted elsewhere. Comity thus has a meaning of reciprocal respect that a State has for another State's legislative, executive and judicial structure, and for measures and acts emanating from its organs, such as for its laws, decrees and judgments.[76]

We shall later[77] investigate the practical implications of the *respect* that States have for the legal system of other States. However, it may here be mentioned that the root of that respect is based on comity and entrenched and secured by the safest basis of obligation of all, that of *reciprocity*.[78]

---

[75]   See, *infra*, under Organisations, The European Community.

[76]   See, further, *infra*, under Distributive Rules: Jurisdiction: Territoriality.

[77]   See *infra*, Chapter VII, under Extraterritorial Application of Judgments, Laws and Decrees.

[78]   See, further on this, my *Concept, op. cit.*, 122-128.

d. Comity and Extraterritorial Application of Foreign Rules

We shall later investigate to what extent foreign rules are applied in another State. However, it is useful to place that practice, carried out by many courts and authorities of the world, in the context of *comity*. Since comity implies the respect for the existence of another State's laws, it could be said to be a term which is applied at 'the receiving end': a court, for example, asks itself whether or not it shall apply a foreign law out of this respect for another country. At the 'sending end', the other State thus asks itself whether its own laws will have extraterritorial effect.

Contrary to what is claimed in many textbooks on international law, numerous laws, decrees and administrative decisions *are* applied in other States.

(i) Comity and the Act of State Doctrine

The question of extraterritorial application of the laws and decrees of one country in another, forms part of the problem concerning *division of competence* between States with regard to persons. We shall analyse these situations later in this treatise, especially in the light of the so called *Act of State doctrine*, which pretends to limit the power of courts to pronounce on incompatibility with international law, and in the light of nationalised assets, a previously[79] much debated topic.[80]

(ii) Comity and Recognition of Foreign Judgments and Awards

Older textbooks on Conflict of Laws, especially in Scandinavia, tend to treat recognition of judgments as something which can only have practical importance if a State has ratified a treaty obliging it to give effect to judgments of foreign States. Yet, as clear expression of respect for the judicial power of other States, such judgments are

---

[79] The importance is now overshadowed by intense and costly attempts to reverse nationalisations by re-privatisation in Eastern Europe.

[80] See, *infra*, under Chapter VII, on Extraterritorial Application of Laws, Decrees and Judgments.

often in practice enforceable in other jurisdictions.[81]

e. Comity and Refusal to Hear Cases

Devices like *blocking statutes,* adopted to accommodate the legitimate interests of other States, are sometimes used to ensure that a case, out of respect for comity, is taken to another more appropriate jurisdiction.[82] The power of a court to consider itself as inappropriate or as a *forum non conveniens* is also an expression for the respect of comity and that other courts, in other jurisdictions, are more apt to deal with a particular case.[83]

f. Comity and Public Policy

A Court may refrain from applying certain foreign public laws, on the basis of the argument that it is not for the courts of one State to enforce the public law of another (equal) State. However, in numerous cases courts do apply such foreign public laws and hesitation on the part of scholars in this respect are not, outside the realm of collection of taxes or fines, normally not warranted.[84]

g. Comity, Conflict of Laws and Public International Law

It has been thought useful to set out above the basic rules concerning comity for several reasons. In the first place, textbooks on international law rarely even refer to the notion of comity which is undoubtedly of primordial importance in the relationship between States.

Secondly, the notion itself illuminates the intricate and overlapping relationship between conflict of laws and public international law, the two major disciplines between which no rigid or sensible demarcation can be drawn.

Thirdly, the notion clarifies many attitudes of States and their

---

[81]   See *infra* in Chapter VII.
[82]   See in detail *infra* in Chapter VII.
[83]   See on this doctrine, *infra* in Chapter VII.
[84]   See in detail *infra* in Chapter VII.

courts and States are, as we shall see, the most important power bases in international society. Although there are also many other subjects and actors in the world, there is no doubt that States are the prime law creators and the main contributors to the setting of norms in international society. The way States contribute to the development of the international legal system will be studied later in this treatise, once the role of respective subjects and the general structure of the international society have been briefly explained.

Because of the comity between nations[85] one State may, in a number of matters, respect and give effect to rules of another national legal system, that is to say the internal law of another State. It is therefore useful to retain the distinction that, along one avenue of development, there has for some time be attempts to harmonise provisions of substantive internal law, whereas along another avenue, attempts are made to unify the more formal conflict rules themselves.

On the other hand, it is *because* of public international law that the conflict rules are generally held and respected. The systems thus intertwine and are thoroughly interdependent. Without understanding of this relationship we cannot appreciate the operation of rules in international society.

iii. Public International Law and Municipal Law

There is an ever increasing application of public international law in States. Foreign ministries are daily *practising* international law. Whenever a State takes action which in any way may be considered to deviate from international law, announcements are made, usually by a foreign ministry, by a Prime Minister or by a Head of State, to the effect that the State *has the right* under international law to take the *action* in question, or, that there has been action by others *justifying a reaction*. Occasionally, it is said by States that there has been a 'misunderstanding', a 'provocation' or other circumstances which entitles certain action. If, at times, States unwillingly concede that there has been breach of international law, it is often argued that the breach is 'deplorable' and that there are 'extenuating

---

[85]   *Infra* 499-502, 549-551 on public and private international law.

circumstances', which makes the action 'excusable' or, at least, 'understandable'. Such arguments are designed to preempt outright condemnation of the action by other States or by the United Nations. Incidences like the invasion of Grenada, 'assistance' to the government of Afghanistan or, conversely, 'assistance' to the groups which, in the opinion of the United States *ought* to have formed the government of Nicaragua, show a pattern of behaviour of States, justifying their decisions under a clear set of international rules.

National courts apply international legal rules in numerous situations. The *Tin Council Cases* in England bear recent proof of the importance of substantive international legal rules in domestic courts.[86] However, in certain increasingly isolated countries, like Sweden and Norway, judges are under the impression that nothing but enacted laws can be applied in domestic courts. Erroneously, they tend to rely on doctrines like that of *dualism* in their efforts to contend that not even international rules on Human Rights have effect unless incorporated by national laws. If that argument was correct, there could not have been any War Crimes Tribunals at Nuremberg or Tokyo.

The background is the following. A now almost historical aspect of international law that concerns the discussion on the merits of various conceptual views that internal state law, or the *municipal* law as it is usually called, belongs to (or does not belong to) *the same legal system* as international law. This is commonly referred to as a problem of *monism* and *dualism*.

By considerable simplification of the problem and by inadequate knowledge of the underlying theoretical arguments, it has sometimes been suggested in Sweden, even in government reports, that monism and dualism would be something that a State is free to choose for itself *in order to avoid direct international obligations*. This is not correct and it may be wise to discard such propositions at the outset of this work, although we shall have occasion to revert to the problem of monism and dualism.

With regard to monism and dualism one can safely say that the discussion of these schools to-day is largely of historical interest: at

---

[86]   [1988] 3 All E.R. 257; [1989] 3 All E.R.

least little new fuel has been added to the virtually extinguished flame of discussion (except in Sweden where the topic mistakenly has been thought to be crucial to the adherence of Sweden to the European Community).

A question regarding the specific relationship between international law and municipal law and the *efficacy* of international law in the internal law of States concerns the field of *jus cogens*, that is to say international rules which are so compelling, that States and others may not deviate from them by agreement nor set them aside by their behaviour in their territory. In some countries, for example in Sweden, such rules are familiar from national rules on contract under the name *indispositive* rules. A State can thus not, by referring to some theoretical system, avoid obligations under international law by referring to its national constitution or to its national laws.[87] A State can thus not, by any theoretical system, avoid the most compelling obligations as laid down in peremptory norms, that is to say compelling rules,[88] forming part of a body of rules called *jus cogens*, which we shall study in some detail later.[89]

The *efficacy* of international law inside States is an area which naturally is of the greatest practical importance. It is important at this early stage to remember that *any internal matter otherwise within the reserved domain* can become uplifted to one of international relevance or to the heightened degree of international concern. This can thus be done either by *specific undertaking* by treaty between States or a *special pledge* to international organisations or another outside body. Similar *uplifting* to the level of international law may occur by various types of *outrageous action* of States in their own territory, for example in the field of Human Rights, such as treating nationals in a manner deviating from the minimum accepted norm,[90] thus

---

[87] See *The Alabama Arbitration*, (1872) Hudson 6.

[88] Swedish students would be used to the term *indispositive* rules, for national rules with similar legal force.

[89] See, *infra* under *jus cogens* and under Law Making and Consent of States in Chapter III. The field of international compelling rules from which there is no contractual or treaty right of derogation can also better be studied in the context of the right of States to consent to international law rules.

[90] See *infra* in Chapter V under Prophylactic Rules: Human Rights.

violating *fundamental* Human Rights, harbouring terrorists or permitting other activity violating the legitimate rights of other States,[91] or using resources in violation of acceptable behaviour in international society.[92] In any of these situations, other States and other actors in international society may, as amply demonstrated in practice, resort to forceful measures such as sanctions[93] to compel a deviating State to turn back to comply with accepted rules of international law.

iv. Public International Law and Conflict of Laws

The system of international legal rules regulating situations of international relevance includes rules on both public and private international law, or, as the latter subject is usually called in the English-speaking world, conflict of laws. These two disciplines are difficult to distinguish unless we adopt completely artificial and unrealistic criteria.

Public international law is traditionally said to concern *relationships between States* (or States and inter-governmental organisations) and is said to be an *international system.* Private international law or conflict of laws is said to concern *relationships between individuals* and, at the same time, form part of the *national law.* That this distinction does not hold true is shown by the fact that a large part of public international law concerns relationships between individuals, especially in the field of Human Rights, and also by the fact that rules of conflict of laws have become increasingly *international* and *uniform* and are no longer merely national in character.

Thus, public international law has, as a legal system, much in common with private international law, or conflict of laws, which also regulates situations with international connections. However, we can also concede that conflict of law rules are *largely* rules belonging to national systems, whereas rules of public international law are *essentially* international in character.

91	See *infra* in Chapter V under Terrorism.
92	See *infra* in Chapter V under Environmental Rules.
93	See *infra* in Chapter IX under Consequential Rules: Sanctions.

It is useful to underline that private international law is not a specific branch of internal law, like, for example, the law of contract. It regards and touches every field of internal law and is concerned with solutions when there is a *conflict* with a foreign competing law.

There are many emerging rules of conflict of laws which have taken on an increasingly international stamp - such as, for example, the rule of habitual residence. The difference between such a rule, which is *internationalised* in the sense that it is *derived* from the substantive laws of numerous countries, and one which is *international* by itself, is indeed a fine one. Yet, the distinction, with regard to source of derivation, is some importance as a matter of principle.

A word may have to be said about the adjective *private* as a distinction between *private* and *public* law is not always easy to draw. The term *private law* is designed to convey that we are concerned with rights and duties of individuals *as between themselves* whereas *public law* concerns the organisation of the State itself, its organs and administration, as well as the relationship between the individual and the State, or, as in criminal law, with the sanctions imposed by the State for certain undesirable behaviour of individuals.

On the international scene, therefore, international public law denotes the relationship between States themselves, or with and between international organisations. However, as we shall see, individuals and other subjects often have direct rights and duties under the system.

A most important area which essentially concerns *individuals* but is more appropriately classified under public international law is that of Human Rights. In this field, there is general consensus on the requirement to protect interests by internal rules.[94] Public international law thus also includes rules regulating the relationship between individuals and the *system itself*. It is this *system* of international law which in international society replaces the laws of a State in so far as it is this system which lays down norms for

---

[94]   On the acceptance of fundamental Human Rights as forming part of general principles of EC law, see Hartley, *The Foundations of European Community Law*, 2nd ed., 1988, 132 *et seq.*

acceptable or undesirable behaviour.

Private international law is commonly taken to mean the rules in every State which govern conflict situations with other national legal systems. Typical situations involve precisely rights and duties of individuals, often derived from actions within different jurisdictions. Borderline situations arise which concern the relationship of aliens and a foreign government, as, for example, in an investment dispute, or those which bear on immunity; these may appropriately be considered to belong to either pubic or private international, or to both areas of law.

Private international law consists of several types of rules: *jurisdictional rules* which will depend which national court, if any, is competent to hear a specific case; *procedural rules* which will determine the way the case is handled; *substantive rules* which will decide the merits of the actual case.

Naturally, any rules belonging to *procedure* will be entirely *national rules* of the *forum* State, that is to say the country where the court is and where the dispute is heard. To such *procedural* rules we may count those which select a specific national court to hear a case, *i.e.* certain types of *domestic jurisdictional* rules, concerning which specific national court is competent, belong to this category. All such rules thus tend to be entirely national.

However, certain other types of *international jurisdictional rules*, which claim jurisdiction for a specific national legal system in general terms, cannot be entirely national: here the national systems must yield to demands of international comity to avoid overlapping claims of jurisdiction.[95]

Rules of private international law can be harmonised in two ways: either by unification of the internal laws themselves and, secondly, unification of private international law rules.[96] Both these avenues will reduce the possibility of conflict between laws. In recent years much work along these lines have been made and it is now clear that private international law rules applied in most countries are strikingly

---

[95] See, *infra* in Chapter VII under Distributive Rules: Object of Sovereign Functions: Jurisdiction and Conflict of Laws.

[96] *Cf. e.g.,* Cheshire and North, *Private International Law,* 11th ed., 1987, 9 *et seq.*

similar.[97]

It is not the fault of international law when lawyers face a problem: their difficulties are more often caused by *varying internal rules* on important issues. National legal systems have adopted radically different rules on, for example, *good faith acquisitions* well known in Europe but not generally admitted in English law; or on *common property of spouses*, again a rule not applied in English law; or on procedural matters like on *hearsay evidence*, not known in many countries in Europe; or even on basic precepts like *natural justice*, not known even to academic lawyers in Sweden.[98]

As we shall see,[99] substantive laws in many countries have now been extensively harmonised, a process which naturally limits the number of occasions when we find ourselves in conflict of law situations.

On the other hand, it is not only conflict of law rules which largely emanate from internal legal systems: public international law also consists, to some extent, of rules which are derived from a number of national legal systems. Among such rules, distilled from a number of different but convergent national sources, there are those which concern, for example, obligations like *pacta sunt servanda* (agreements should be kept), and on procedural matters like the rule

---

[97] Of course, an exception always had to be made for the former Soviet Union, and, so far, for its main successors of the CIS and the other recently independent States which used to be part of the USSR; on the Russian system, see Bogoslavski, *Private International Law: the Soviet Approach*, 1988. Exception must still be made for Cuba, for the Belgrade regime of what is left of Yugoslavia, that is essentially Serbia-Montenegro, and for China, virtually the only socialist States that are left after the great reversal of communist/socialist policies in the world 1988-1990. On the Chinese system *cf.* Chiu, Contemporary practice and judicial decisions of the Republic of China, *Chinese Yearbook of International Law*, 1987-1988, 225 *et seq.*

[98] When Professor Wade, a celebrated expert on administrative law and Master of Gonville and Caius College, Cambridge, gave the 1989 Cassel lecture in Stockholm University several questions from members of the Law Faculty indicated that in this university the term 'natural justice', as technical procedural notion, implying that both parties must always be heard and that no one must be judge in his own case, a notion used in the whole Commonwealth and in the United States, is largely unknown among lawyers in Sweden where some appeared to confuse it with *natural law*.

[99] See *infra* in Chapter VI.

audiatur est et altera pars (a court should hear both sides in a dispute) or the rule *nemo iudex in causa sua* (no one should be a judge in his own case).[100] As the Latin form of these maxims indicate they originate in Roman law. However, they have existed in many other previous legal systems and have subsequently been adopted in most modern legal systems we know. These are two principles which have brought together in a concept which in the English speaking world is known as *natural justice* as developed particularly in English administrative law. They are indeed rules which are essential to a fair hearing.[101] Such common maxims are thus founded on common rules derived from municipal law; conversely, many conflict rules are formed in the same way and are not dependent on the rules of only one State.

Furthermore, many other rules of public international law, for example on nationality or immunity are founded on parallel acceptance of rules in different jurisdictions. Consequently, public and private international law are two legal systems which may have more in common than what is usually accepted. In areas like nationality or immunity they are furthermore interconnected.

There are indeed tendencies to regard public and private international law as one and the same system.[102] Those who teach both subjects find it increasingly difficult to draw sensible limits between the two allegedly separate disciplines although the aforementioned guidelines may be useful. It is also difficult, and not always necessary, to distinguish between the two systems and the increasingly developed law of the European Communities, which, in a sense, represents a subsection of both public international law and of *international private law*.[103] This is not the same as *private international law* or *conflict of laws*. The term *international private*

---

[100]   On the role, contents and types of maxims in the rule structure of international law, see my *Concept, op. cit.*, 49-52.

[101]   See, for example, Wade, *Administrative Law,* 5th ed., 1985; Foulkes, *Administrative Law,* 1990.

[102]   *Cf.* Jessup, *Transnational Law,* 1956.

[103]   See, my *Law Making, op. cit.*, 271-274; for the notion of international private law in relation to operations of the World Bank see *ibid.*, 184-187; see my *Concept, op. cit.*, 75-79, for the notion *lex mercatoria* applying to commercial international transactions between, for example, States and private entities.

law is used to indicate a system of private law, common to several States. This is, in the EC, often achieved by Community legislation and, partly, by harmonisation of national rules.[104]

---

[104]   See further *infra* in Chapters II, III and IV.

CHAPTER II

The Structure of International Society

i. Characteristics of the International Legal System

International society has no constitution, no central legislature, no central executive organs, no central judicial body and no centrally administered sanctions. The lack of such backbones, known as essential in internal, national legal systems, is why some nihilists[1] doubt that international law is a *legal system* and why they seek to reduce it to devices of mere power struggle.

It is unnecessary to deny that the relative political strength of States is important in international society. It is also utopic to pretend that the international legal system sufficiently protects its weaker members, such as developing States or the formerly socialist States which now have severe financial and environmental problems. But if every legal system ideally had to be perfect in this respect, and had to consistently ensure the interest of all, then, the legal system of many States would be put in doubt.

We can thus establish that international law shares the shortcomings with many internal legal systems as far as fair protection of the weak is concerned. But we can also establish that the traditional mechanisms of law making, as known from internal systems, may not be the only ways legal rules come into being. We can by simple observation ascertain that there are some clear rules for the behaviour of actors in this society: those who do not follow such rules are often submitted to severe criticism or to military or economic sanctions.

It is clear that international law making is produced through

---

[1] For example, Lundstedt, *Law of Nations: Superstition to People,* 1929.

highly sophisticated mechanisms.[2] Although there is no world constitution, there are thus clear rules laying down the *structure* and the *distribution of powers and functions* of various actors.

Important framework for action is provided by the organisations like the United Nations, and, in Europe, the European Community. In a sense, the Charter of the United Nations, operating as it does on a global basis, does provide a form of international constitution, or at least a collection of coherent constitutional rules.[3]

Legislative functions are exercised both by States, through treaties,[4] and by decisions at international meetings and conferences.[5] Furthermore, legislative rules also emanate from international organisations, not only for their internal or administrative functions, but very often to bind their member States.[6] It is clear that, although there is no legislative power allocated to any central and specific organ/s, like the legislature of a State, there is, in the international society, a legislative *function*,[7] which is clearly exercised in an organised but decentralised manner.

To some the main stumbling block may be the absence of sanctions in international society: some students studying national law have been taught that a legal system *must* have such sanctions, and if the system does not provide such sanctions it is merely operating as a 'moral guide' as it lacks an essential qualifying hallmark of a system of law. But it is not correct to say that international society lacks sanctions. There are sanctions, but they do operate in a fractional manner to be imposed *in casu* when it is considered that a State, or other actors, are behaving in any way which is unacceptable to the international legal system. One need only think of economic sanctions imposed on South Africa, on Rhodesia[8] or military action

---

[2]   On the point that international law is *not* a 'primitive' system, see my *Concept, op. cit.*, 36.

[3]   So Verdross and Simma, *Völkerrecht,* 3rd ed., 1984, 66 *et seq.*

[4]   See, *infra* 235 *et seq.* under Sources of Law, Hard Law, Treaties.

[5]   *Cf. infra* 260-263 under Sources of Law, Hard Law, Unilateral and Parallel Declarations and Rules.

[6]   See, in detail, my *Law Making, op. cit., passim.*

[7]   *Cf.,* Scelle, *Droit international public,* 1949, *passim.*

[8]   See *infra* Chapter IX under Consequential Rules.

taken against Saddam Hussein,[9] to realise that the international society possesses tools to rectify misbehaviour in a way very similar to sanctions in internal law, that is it has methods to both restrain States from action or inaction, internationally or internally, as well as methods to punish ill-doers.

The rules of international society are evolved by various actors which also apply such rules in their mutual relationships. It is obvious that States play a primordial role in the international system: it is their consent, as we shall see, which underpins much of the system. But there are also other subjects and actors which contribute to the formation of the system and which, in turn, are governed by rules created by States and/or by themselves.

ii. Categories of Subjects of International Law

a. The Definition of a Subject

To say that an entity is a *subject* of international law means that the entity can assume rights and obligations under a legal system. One does normally not distinguish, in international law, between *subjectivity* and *personality*. In many national legal systems, *subjectivity* is the wider concept, whereas legal *personality* or *capacity* indicates the right to act, a right that not all subjects may have in all situations.[10] In international law, however, the terms *subject* and *persons* are normally used as synonyms.

Personality is, of course, mainly a formal concept which does not confer, by itself, any specific rights of duties. But it is a useful and, indeed, necessary notion in that it serves as a *focus of imputation*.[11] Acts are brought back, by such a link, to their originator, to the actor himself.

---

[9]   *Infra, ibid.*

[10]   One may here mention, for example, the restrictions usually imposed on minors.

[11]   *Cf.* Sereni, 2 *Diritto internazionale*, 1956, 258; Kasme, *La capacité de l'Organisation des Nations Unies de conclure des traités internationaux*, 1960, 30; *cf.* my *Concept, op. cit.*, 62-63 and *infra*, under Responsibility.

b. *Identification of International Subjects*

International law is, according to some textbooks, a system that applies between States themselves, or between States and inter-governmental organisations and/or between such organisations. As we have already mentioned, such a narrow concept is not compatible with a realistic analysis of contemporary practice in international society. Other entities are also governed by international legal rules.

The subjects of international law are manifold. They cannot be defined or identified *a priori* except in a general way. As history evolves, other and different entities may *become* subjects of the international system. International law is a legal system which has to adapt to what is needed in international society.

In national civil law systems the legislature normally decides which physical and legal entities enjoy legal subjectivity or personality. Not so long ago one could say that the government, or any State body, was free to decide on such matters. With the advent of democracy,[12] however, the *people* must have a say; the legislature is, in most countries, the only forum where the population of a State have a chance to have their voice heard and, therefore, it seems appropriate that a matter like legal personality should be settled by democratic means. As a result, restrictions on capacity to act as a subject, for example after bankruptcy, were modified. As a general rule, the *people* in civil law countries decide themselves, through their parliament, as to who shall enjoy legal personality.

In England, and in many countries of the Commonwealth, the Courts play an important role to decide on matters like legal capacity.[13] But such Courts form part of national systems where democracy is commonly assured and, therefore, the *people* can be reasonably certain that their interests will be looked after; they are

---

12 On the change, see my *Law of War*, Cambridge, 1987, 24-31; democracy may even be a condition for statehood; *cf. infra*, under States.

13 To be exact, there is a shared function between Courts and Parliament: Parliament may intervene, by a Private Act, for example, to widen the normal capacity to marry in special cases or to decide by Statute on the contractual capacity of a bankrupt. But the main duty to define legal capacity in general lies with the Courts.

relieved of an (albeit vicarious)[14] legislative, duty where they may have an interest in the result, but where they may be content not to have to take part in the formulation of legal rules.

In the international system there is no central legislature[15] and no Courts with general competence.[16] There are thus no functional or organic links between the law and the makers of the law, not even when it comes to the basic question as to who has *legal capacity* under international law. In such a situation it would be incompatible with logic to say that 'the subjects of international law are States'. We cannot know who the subjects are of a legal system unless we already know the contents of that law. Conversely, by saying that States, for example, are 'subjects of international law', nothing is clarified with regard to substantive provisions of the legal system.[17]

It may be more useful to say, as has been suggested in this work,[18] that international law governs matters of international concern or relevance. The sphere of its subjects must then, by necessity, remain flexible. This does not, however, make the *system* or *the legal rules* flexible: as in any legal system, it is of utmost importance that the rules are stable, clear, and, above all, *foreseeable*.

Only such element of *foreseeability* is compatible with *security of law*, a notion which is accepted by all legal systems and yet is difficult to express in English. The French all agree on the importance of the *sécurité du droit,* and the Germans accept *Rechtsicherheit* as being of paramount importance, and the Swedes (albeit in what has become a fairly fluid legal system) of *rättssäkerhet.* In the Scottish

---

14   The duty is vicarious in so far as the legislative function, in any event, is exercised through the intermediary of a Member of Parliament.

15   On the rule making process in international society in detail, see my *Concept, passim,* and *infra.*

16   The International Court of Justice obviously fulfills a most important function, see *infra* under Consequential Rules, Pacific Settlement; but it is not a compulsory Court for all States. Other Courts, like that of the European Community, may also fulfil important law making functions but then only within the system set up for those organisations. Naturally the decisions of all Courts may have informal impact beyond the parties and beyond the sphere for which they were created.

17   See, *supra* 1 *et seq.,* and in detail, my *Concept, op. cit.,* 40-43.

18   *Cf. supra* 1-9 under Identification of International Law.

legal system the notion of security of law is familiar to lawyers. Yet, in England one speaks of the notion of *the Rule of Law* which conveys connotations associated with foreseeability. Thus, although one does not speak about *security of law* in English law, its attributes of foreseeability and fairness pervade the whole English legal system.

A similar degree of stability, security and foreseeability is demanded of the international legal system. In order to ensure such qualities of the system it is, however, necessary to analyse the actual functioning of the system, so that we can describe what roles are assigned to different actors in practice. It is obvious that States do not always behave as they are supposed to in traditional textbooks and that other non-State actors are not content to be relegated to stay off the international scene altogether (as traditional textbooks contend).

There are thus numerous actors in international society who, at times, or for some purposes, function as subjects of international law and their role can, in many cases, be of importance to the development and the functioning of the international legal system.

iii. Types of Subjects

a. States

Kelsen, La naissance de l'état et la formation de sa nationalité, RDI 1929 613; Mouskhely, La naissance des états en droit international public, RGDIP 1962 469; Bluntschli, *The Theory of State,* 1895; Guggenheim, Les états comme sujets de droit des gens, in Les principes de droit international public, 80 RCADI 1952 80; Marek, *Identity and Continuity of States in Public International Law,* 1954; Arangio-Ruiz, *L'Etat dans le sens du droit des gens et la notion du droit international,* 1975; Mouskhely, La naissance des états en droit international public, RGDIP, 1962, 469; Münch, Staat und Völkerrecht, *Festschrift Doering,* 1989, 625; Strozzi, Recenti sviluppi nella disciplina dei rapporti tra Stati e regioni in materia internazionale, 1979; Crawford, *Creation of States,* 1979; Uibopuu, Gedanken zu einem völkerrechtlichen Staatsbegriff in Schreuer (ed.) *Autorität und internationale Ordnung,* 1979, 87; Plischke, *Micro-States in World Affairs,* 1977; Blair, *The Mini-State Dilemma,* 1968; De Smith, *Microstates and Micronesia,* 1970; Ehrhardt, *Der Begriff des Mikrostaats im Völkerrecht und in der internationalen Ordnung,* 1970.

For further literature, see, *infra,* under Recognition.

(i) The Role of States

The State is an important bearer of rights and obligations under international law. In this work, the functions of the State, with its substantial power base in international society, are examined.[19] Only States have permanently organised armed forces including an air force, and, except in the case of land-locked States, a navy. Liberation movements may have highly trained soldiers functioning under military command as an army; but the very nature of liberation wars, together with the limited financial resources of such movements, excludes other types of armed forces.[20]

Only sovereign States can join international inter-governmental organisations like, for example, the United Nations; only States have organised police forces, road networks or hospital services accessible for persons on a large scale beyond what companies can offer under employment contracts. Only States have, in theory, unlimited funds in the sense that they cannot go bankrupt. It is primarily States which conclude treaties.[21] Furthermore, certain privileges are reserved for States: for example, that of issuing passports and demanding allegiance of its citizens.

But the State has also important duties: if the State does not act in a way compatible with international law its responsibility will become engaged. The State may have to restore matters as they were before by restitution or the State may be liable to pay compensation and damages for harm caused. International responsibility may occasionally be engaged if the harm is caused to the State's own subjects. Sometimes, States may become responsible for breaking obligations under treaties, such as that of the European Convention of Human Rights or under the treaties of the European Community. In other cases States may be held responsible under general rules of international law. With regard to aggression, or genocide or torture, States have thus been held responsible. This has been amply shown by demands for war reparation after the First World War and in the

---

[19]   See further this Chapter and Chapters VI and VII.

[20]   See further, *infra*, Chapter V.

[21]   On the technique of other bodies adhering to treaties, see, my *Law of War, op. cit.*, 158 *et seq.*

judgments of the War Crimes Tribunals after the Second World War, when States and their leaders, and even other individuals, were held liable.[22]

(ii) The Criteria of a State

For literature see *supra* under a.

What is then a State? One usually claims that an entity must have three criteria to be a State. It must have a defined *territory*, a defined *population* and *organs* to control that territory and that population on the basis of some permanence.[23]

On the other hand, it has become clear that new conditions are imposed on candidates aspiring to be States. One such condition is that of *democracy*, which we will consider in some detail. A further condition appears to be that of *viability* of the State, which is a condition which goes to the size of a territory and/or of the population, or to the economy of the entity in question. Another condition, at least for recognition of other States, is that of *Security Council vetting* or approval, now when that body has taken upon itself to pronounce on the merit of various proclamations of statehood.

It is not always easy to identify a *State*. Some entities are undoubtedly in the process of *becoming* States and some writers have not hesitated to apply doctrines from Roman law such as that of *conceptus jam pro natu habetur* (to consider a conceived child as already born) to, for example, British Dominions.[24]

Although States are important subjects of international law, a fact

---

[22] On personal responsibility for international crimes, see, *infra*, under Human Rights and, in detail, my *Law of War, op. cit.*, 357-359 on the *respondeat superior* defence.

[23] *Cf.* The Montevideo Convention on Rights and Duties of States of 1933, article 1.

[24] See Fedozzi, Il concetto di personalità internazionale, in *Rivista internazionale di filosofia di diritto, i,* 1921, 100 and, further, on membership in League of Nations, my *Law Making, op. cit.*, 20 *et seq.*, and my *Treaty Making Power of International Organisations* (thesis), Oxford 1962, Chapter One.

emphasised both by writers[25] and tribunals,[26] they are not the only ones. The role and function of States are therefore better appreciated if viewed against the background of other entities which act in international society. However, States are undoubtedly the most powerful units in international life and merit therefore special attention with regard to their various attributes.

1. TERRITORY

It may be that States can exist without territory; the Holy See was treated as a State before the Lateran Treaty in 1929 which gave it territory.[27] The Palestine Liberation Organisation has proclaimed itself a State although it has no territory; but here the situation is complicated that its claim of statehood depends, in the end, on whether certain land is reclaimed from another State. Then, it may be that statehood, until recognition, is conditional and in abeyance.[28]

Borders do not have to be exactly defined: Israel was recognised and was admitted to the United Nations in 1949 before her borders had been clarified. It may even be said that frontiers of States are often not fully delimited nor defined.[29]

The territory does not have to be coherent. For example, Pakistan consisted, for a long time, of Pakistan and East Pakistan. Distances involved can, on the other hand, cause or facilitate the break up of such a State, as indeed happened when Bangladesh became independent.

Some States have incorporated extremely far away territories as

---

[25] *E.g.* Brierly, *The Law of Nations,* 6th ed. by Waldock, 1963, p. 41; Gihl, *The Legal Character and Sources of International Law,* 1957, 53; *idem, International Legislation, 1937;* Parry, The Function of Law in the International Community, in Sorensen, (ed.), *Manual of International Law,* 1968, 1; *idem, The Sources and Evidences of International Law,* 1946.

[26] The International Court of Justice emphasised in the 20's that international law regulates only relationship between 'independent' States: *The Lotus Case,* (1927), PCIJ, Ser. A., No. 10, 18.

[27] See, *supra,* under Subjects and the Holy See.

[28] Note recognition of PLO in September 1993.

[29] See, ICJ, *North Sea Continental Shelf Cases* (1969), *Reports,* 32. For the extent of State territory, see *infra,* in Chapter VI.

integral parts of the mother land. Tahiti is, for example, a *département* of France and thus forming part of France itself.

2. POPULATION

The requirement of a population of some permanence may pose problems in the case of *nomadic tribes*. However, The International Court of Justice has indicated that even such tribes may constitute, for the purposes of statehood, a *population*.[30]

Although the size of population may go to the question of *viability*, which will be discussed below, it must be mentioned here that many States, which are not normally considered 'small', have only few citizens. Iceland, for example, has only some 300,000 nationals. Other States, like China, have a population of such size, of over a billion citizens, without this necessarily being reflected in its political power or general influence on the international legal system.

The population of a State can, of course, be heterogenous and itself constitute a *nation* where members of a separate *people* are tied to each other by ethnic, religious, linguistic, historic or other bonds. It is such bonds which forms the best basis for a nation and it is such bonds which normally produce tension within a State containing several nations. Conversely, it is when a State contains several nations when tensions may arise. As recent events in Eastern Europe have shown, compared with successful federative in the Western world, *peoples of different nations* can only happily live together if they do so *by free will*, and not when they are forced to do so, for example by the shackles of an oppressive political system, such as communism.

A special problems arises when such nations spread over several States, such as the Kurds in Turkey/Iraq/Iran or the Tamils in Sri Lanka and in India.[31]

Nothing precludes the population of a State being *nomadic*, although one may require that the areas within which they move are defined when such a State is established, if there is no other fixed

---

[30]   *Western Sahara Case* (1975) ICJ *Reports* 1975 12.

[31]   On nations as separate subjects of international law, see *infra*, in this Chapter.

population. Later, once a State has come within existence, the right to leave and to come back, of all citizens, might even be construed as part of the basic Human Rights that a State must afford its citizens.[32]

However, a population alone will not secure statehood,[33] in the same way as any of the other criteria listed above and below will not, by themselves, lead to an entity being regarded as a fully fledged State.

3. ORGANS

A State should have an effective[34] government to control the territory and its population. This condition became crucial to Lithuania which declared itself independent from the Soviet Union in 1990. Yet, Lithuania was prevented, precisely by the Soviet Union, to exercise effective government and, therefore, it could for some time not achieve statehood.

The situation in Lithuania illustrated the tension which can arise between a *nation* and a mother *State*; in Lithuania there was, at the time of the declaration of independence, greater coherence in the nation than in the other Baltic States as the proportion of Russians, or other non-Lithuanians, in the territory was particularly low and that, therefore, the Lithuanians feel particularly united as a *nation*.

A similar situation arose in Croatia which exercised its rights under the Yugoslav Federal Constitution to secede from the Federation in June 1991, only to be invaded later that summer by Serbian-led Communist Federal armed forces. Croatia certainly had all organs of a State and had exercised its executive, legislative and judicial powers for some time under the Federal structure. This effective exercise was not prevented by the invading forces although the war obviously caused great difficulties.

---

[32] See, *infra*, Chapter V, under Human Rights.

[33] Tomuschat, Staatsvolk ohne Staat?, Festschrift Doehring, 1989, 985.

[34] By stating that a 'sovereign government' is a requirement for statehood, Jennings and Watts, in their edition of Oppenheim, *International Law*, 1992, 122, presumably mean that the government should be 'effective'. Sovereignty itself is, as we shall see, a consequence, rather than a condition of statehood, see *infra*.

In spite of misdirected efforts by the United States and by the European Community to force the Communist Federation to survive, it disintegrated rapidly by democratic forces and Croatia, and Slovenia, became recognised by an increasing number of States, including the European Community itself. By October 1992 Croatia had been recognized by the majority of States in the world and serves as a good example of a *nation* - which had existed as such for over a thousand years - re-emerging as a *State*.

These examples may show that traditional textbooks are not correct, and do not reflect actual state practice and the attitude of important international organisations, such as the United Nations and the European Community, when they demand that an entity to be a *State* must have fully functioning organs, controlling the population and the territory. What appears to be demanded, under actual international law, is that there are organs *capable* of exercising such functions, although they may be hampered in this exercise by outside factors.

In some cases, in times of war or armed conflict, there may be competing claims of government. It is not inconceivable that there is a duplication of governments as, for example, in the case of the Free French Government in England competing with the undoubtedly effective government of Vichy.[35] Also in Croatia, there were competing claims as the Federal Communists sought to maintain their sovereignty. But, as the initial civil war was transformed into an international war, as Croatia was recognised, first by Germany and then by numerous other States, the legitimacy of the Communist Federation for the liberated area was extinguished.[36]

We can therefore summarise what *organs* are required for an entity to be a State: it must be an *organised society* of a certain *permanence* where established organs have the *potential* to exercise their powers for *general purposes*, including executive, legislative and judicial functions. The claim that a *State* must have *effective organs* thus signifies that such organs are *potentially effective* to exercise general functions.

---

[35] See my *Law of War, op. cit.*, 110 *et seq.*

[36] On the importance of democratic will, see *infra*.

4. DEMOCRACY

Over the last few decades it has become obvious that no new unit
will be accepted as a State in international society unless it adopts the
fundamental rules of democracy. As we shall see in the context of
recognition,[37] units will not receive recognition until the requirement
of democracy has been fulfilled. On the other hand, States which have
already come into being, such as South Africa, or Iraq, or even
Kuwait, are currently under criticism precisely for not introducing a
more democratic regime. The condition of democracy thus appears to
operate as a bar to the formation of *new* undemocratic States[38] but
will not deny the actual statehood already achieved by earlier States,
which, however, may be the target of disapproving action, including
sanctions,[39] for their failure to adopt democratic rules.

Democracy - a notion against which no one argues nowadays as
much as in the days of Plato when it was by no means accepted that
the concept has only positive sides - is often used as a cloak for
politicising institutions. Thus, Courts and judicial tribunals in Sweden
have, in the last two decades, been thoroughly cleansed of the earlier
paramount decisive power of legally trained judges to give way to
democratic power. In the alleged name of democracy judicial power
in Sweden is now exercised by lay persons, politically elected for a
term of several years, who are now able to out-vote the judge even
in criminal matters, both with regard to guilt and with regard to
sentencing. Such tribunals, according to the dictionary *popular courts*,
have earlier only been known in totalitarian States, such as in the ex-
Soviet Union, and its satellite States.

True democracy demands decisive influence of the body which
represents the citizens, *i.e.*, Parliament. This power that Parliament
should have is nowadays undermined in many States. Any
membership of an international organisation obviously necessitates
that there is a review of how nationals of a State can make their voice
heard: often this is replaced by the influence exercised by
representatives of the government, its foreign ministry and other

---

[37]   *Infra*, under Criteria for Recognition.

[38]   See *infra*, on recognition, in this Chapter.

[39]   *Infra*, under Sanctions.

ministries and departments.[40]

Democracy can also be hampered by undue influence of ministries in other matters, without debates or decisions in Parliament. Such transfer of power to ministerial rule and rule by civil servants, similar to that in the former Eastern bloc, has, to a very large extent, taken place in Sweden where influence of Parliament is doubly reduced by the elimination of its First Chamber or Upper House; few countries have the single-tier parliamentary structure which Sweden has adopted and which renders parliamentary power more vulnerable and easier to displace, especially since numerous questions are never debated. As a recent example of these by-passing tactics one may mention the Treaty on the European Space (EES), which for a long time was even held *secret* to the Swedish Parliament, after the Government had already, in principle, accepted the agreement.

Democracy remains the lynch-pin of a properly constituted modern State and this is particularly reflected in the fact that no new State is recognised unless it complies with the requirements demanded by democracy. That democracy is demanded in this way,[41] is fully reflected in modern State practice on recognition.[42]

5. VIABILITY

The Montevideo Convention of 1933 on the Rights and Duties of

---

[40] See *infra*, in this Chapter, under the 'Normal Structure of International Organisations', for a discussion of shifting powers from Parliament to the Government by membership in an international organisation.

[41] But see the Statement of the Swedish Foreign Office, *Svenska Dagbladet* 29 August 1991, that 'democracy is the least important element for recognition', with regard to Sweden's recognition of Croatia and Slovenia. Sweden is almost alone in the world holding this anachronistic view, now virtually only embraced by China and Cuba.

[42] See *infra* in this Chapter on recognition. There is also, in that context a discussion of the fact that many already exisiting States have *ceased* being truly democratic, without for that reason losing their statehood. We must thus distinguish between *democracy* as a necessary element for *contemporary recognition* and *democrary* as an element, *de lege ferenda*, to be introduced or re-introduced in all existing States.

States, which is often cited as laying down the criteria of a State, adds that the entity should have the capacity to enter into relations with other States.[43] It could be argued that this last condition, *viability*, is, in effect, a consequence, rather than a condition of statehood.

Viability, however, may mean something else: if it is taken to mean the very ability of an entity to function as a unit it is surely relevant to the question as to whether a State exists.

A State does not have to be of any particular size and can indeed be very small.[44] States like Liechtenstein or San Marino, may even put their international affairs in the hands of another State to reduce the complications and expense of running their own diplomatic missions, but do not, by such delegation, lose their statehood. Some small States, like, for example, Andorra, are run as a condominium of which the administration is managed by two other States, in the event by Spain and France.

The question of *puppet States*[45] presents special problems with regard to recognition which is considered below.[46] In the context of recognition there are certain political overtones which would, at least at times, explain why recognition of a specific territory is not forthcoming.

Viability, however, often concerns the *will* of a nation or of a territory to become a State. The Falklanders undoubtedly realised that, with their minuscule population and their limited economy, it would be pointless to establish their own *State*. The Falklanders preferred to be linked to the United Kingdom.

The real test of viability lies in actual self-determination and independence of a *civitas perfecta* vis-à-vis other members of international society,[47] expressed in the *will* of an entity to achieve its own statehood.

---

[43]   165 LNTS 19.

[44]   See discussion in the judgment of the Administrative Tribunal of Cologne, Verwaltungsgericht Köln, 3rd May 1978, in the *Principality of Sealand Case*, DVBL, 1978, 510 *et seq.*

[45]   See, further, *infra.*

[46]   See *infra* under recognition in this Chapter.

[47]   *Cf.* Verdross and Simma, *Völkerrecht*, 3rd ed., 1984, 225.

(iii) The Essence of Statehood: Sovereignty

Carillo Salcedo, *Soberanía del estado y derecho internacional,* 1969; Ermacora, Uber die Souveränität, ÖZöR, 1953, 10; Kelsen, *Das Problem der Souveränität und die Theorie des Völkerrechts,* 1920; Sountausta, *La souveraineté des états,* Helsinki, 1955.

Sovereignty has traditionally been used as a concept to denote the collection of functions exercised by a State. Historically it implied at first the supreme power of a prince over his subjects and in that sense it was a concept which concerned primarily powers within the State. Later the concept gradually evolved to comprise also external aspects of State power. Jean Bodin wrote, in his *Six livres de la république* in 1577, that sovereignty has a double aspect: it means that the State or the prince has absolute power in his own territory and secondly, it implies that the State - or the prince - enjoys freedom from interference from other States and princes. Thus, there are both *internal* and *external* aspects of sovereignty. But the external aspects, concerned with relationships with other States, only became important after the rise of the Nation-States in Europe in the sixteenth and seventeenth centuries. When such States had become established, it became necessary to examine their inter-relationship.

Sovereignty, in its internal aspect, signifies the total power within the territorial framework and, also, the power to enlarge this power by what in French is called the *compétence de la compétence* or in German *Kompetenzkompetenz*: sovereignty is thus residual in organs which exercise the highest power inside the State and which can alter, increase or decrease, this power. It is this power that constitutes actual territorial sovereignty. It is this sovereignty which is transferred, for example, at State succession when a new State is formed or when certain power(s) is/are transferred or delegated to an international organisation.[48]

But sovereignty is never absolute: in its external aspects it is always limited by previously assumed obligations, for example, duties under numerous treaties or under general rules of international law accepted by States.

---

[48]   On relevant problems, see in greater detail, my *International Law and the Independent State,* 2nd ed., 1987, *passim.*

In its internal form, sovereignty is not limitless either for there are restrictions of the power of a State in its own territory derived from immediate duties to implement or respect certain rules of international law.[49]

(iv) Incidents of Sovereignty

1. GENERAL REMARKS

Sovereignty denotes, as mentioned, a collection of a State's functions. Sovereignty is an incident of statehood. On the other hand, it can itself be said to have certain incidents, or facets.

Sovereignty is thus commonly used to cover certain incidents of statehood which crystallised after the formation of a number of States. The concept thus covers the right of *equality,* the right of *independence* and the right of *self-determination.* The first of these incidents appears to be mainly concerned with the external relations of a State whereas the rule of independence regards both external aspects, as well as the power within the State in its own territory. Thus, in the *Island of Palmas Case*, the arbitrator Max Huber said that

> 'Sovereignty in the relations between States signifies independence. Independence in regard to a portion of the globe is the right to exercise therein, to the exclusion of any other State, the functions of a State.'[50]

Furthermore, he said

> 'Territorial sovereignty ... involves the exclusive right to display the activities of a State. This right has as corollary a duty: the obligation to protect within the territory the rights of other States, in particular their right to integrity and inviolability in peace and in war, together with the rights which each State may claim for

---

[49]   See *infra* Chapter III C iii under *jus cogens*, and Chapter VI C under Fettering of Sovereignty.

[50]   *Island of Palmas Case* [1928] Permanent Court of Arbitration ii 829.

its nationals in foreign territory. Without manifesting its sovereignty in a manner corresponding to circumstances, the State cannot fulfil this duty. Territorial sovereignty cannot limit itself to its negative side, *i.e.* to excluding the activities of other States, for it serves to divide between nations the space upon which human activities are employed, in order to assure them at all points the minimum protection of which international law is the guardian.'[51]

There is thus an inter-relationship between the concept of *equality* and that of independence and that inter-relationship appears to be one of causality: *because* all States are equal under international law, they all enjoy the rights of independence. Furthermore, self-determination appears to be part of the rule of independence but concerned mainly with the powers within the territory itself. In this sense the rule of independence represents the negative aspects, *i.e.* the right to remain free from foreign interference, whereas the rule of self-determination illustrates the positive elements, that is to say the right of the people to exercise the supreme power in the territory.

2. EQUALITY

Equality does not mean that all States have, in order to comply with the rule, to be *the same*. Some States will always be larger, stronger, richer or more influential than others. Some will have access to the sea, others will not have that advantage. Some will be rich in natural resources, others will not. Even if discrepancies in some fields were to be levelled out, States will still be subject to obvious geographical inequalities such as actual size, as to the fact whether or not they are land-locked, and with regard to their natural resources of which some States will have much and others little; some may even, like the oil States, have resources the financial potential of which, for a long time, was not realised.

Furthermore, even if aid to the Third World could be genuinely generous and effective, and even if, for the sake of argument, *poverty*

---

[51]   *Ibid., loc. cit.*

among States was abolished there will always be some States which are relatively poorer or more dependent and weaker than others. Thus, on the whole, the assets of States are highly disparaged, and in this sense they can never be *equal*.

Strength, in political terms, does not always depend on financial means, but often also on moral fibre in the government and among a State's citizens. Corruption can make a relatively rich State weak. Maladministration can dissipate natural resources of a potentially rich State. A change to an inadequate educational system can rapidly change a highly influential State to one of irrelevant mediocrity. Thus, the concept of equality does not prevent States from being factually different; they will always be unequal as far as political or economic strength is concerned.

Nor does it follow from the concept of *equality* that States have to obtain the same advantages in their treaties. Treaties, like contracts, will often give advantage to one State in return for another advantage from another. Multilateral treaties seem to do this to a lesser extent but there will still not be any exact equality for the mere reason that one advantage will be of greater practical significance to one State than to another. Let us merely think of adherence to the convention establishing the International Maritime Organisation (IMO): is membership of such an organisation going to mean more to Iceland, an important fishery State, than to Bolivia, which is land-locked (but which ratified the IMO convention in 1987)?

Niboyet has argued[52] that it is at least questionable whether the notion of equality is compatible with the practice not to give the same advantages to all under a treaty. But then Niboyet had only one special type of treaty in mind: those which concern conflict of laws. Such treaties often deal with rules concerning application of foreign laws, which perhaps demand some reciprocity as a matter of principle, or substantive rules which require uniform application.

There may be a case where there are important imbalances in a treaty so that one party does not receive any *quid pro quo,* that is to say, he does not receive anything in return for what he gives. Some

---

[52] Niboyet, La notion de la reciprocité dans les traités diplomatiques de droit international privé, RCADI 1935 ii 281.

have argued that this is an *unequal treaty* which should be void.[53] The consequences of such a general rule are far-reaching: I have suggested that a treaty should be void or voidable only if the treaty concerns limitation of sovereignty in a State's own territory; for such a treaty, a special rule requires *continuous consent*[54] enabling territorial States to denounce such a treaty when it no longer consents to the regime of the treaty. That this proposition corresponds to State practice is clear: numerous military bases have been dismantled precisely because a new government adopted a new policy and no longer wanted to consent to armed forces of another power.[55] Such a power of denunciation may apply even if there is a *quid pro quo* but lack thereof would certainly strengthen the argument of inequality.

The rule of international law which demands that all States are treated as *equal* implies that they are equally able to assume rights and obligations, in other words that they are fully equal in their freedom to act as well as fully equal before any impartial court or tribunal. This is then what McNair has called *forensic equality*[56].

3. INDEPENDENCE

A State is independent. This is then one of the external aspects or incidents of sovereignty. In the first instance, independence implies that one State must not interfere in the affairs of another State. Conversely, a State does not have to tolerate any interference from outside into its own affairs.

Independence is the *normal condition* of an established State,[57]

---

[53]   See my *Independent State, op. cit.,* 197 *et seq.,* for different organisations.

[54]   For my theory on *continuous consent* in detail, see my *International Law, op. cit.* 229-231. This theory is, I argue, to be preferred to the *rebus sic stantibus* doctrine which, as fluid and subjective and malleable to abuse, undermines the international legal system, allegedly permitting a State to denounce a treaty only because *fundamental circumstances* - as defined by that denouncing State! - have changed. Yet, it is clear that this doctrine, in its raw form, has not been accepted in State practice or by the International Court of Justice.

[55]   As a recent example, we may refer to the developments in Indonesia.

[56]   See further my article 'The Problem of Unequal Treaties', ICLQ, 1966.

[57]   See Separate Opinion of Anzilotti in *Customs Régime between Germany and Austria*, PCIJ A/B No. 41, 57 *et seq.*

designed to indicate that the State is not submitted to any other authority except that of international law.[58]

Independence does thus not mean that a State is free from external rules nor that it is relieved from legal rules of behaviour. Naturally, a State has to fit into its place in international society and obey the rules of that society. We need to presuppose that sociological needs to live together in a common world make certain minimum rules necessary. Some such rules of international law which do apply inside a State without any transformation or conversion into national rules concern, as we shall see, the right of passage. Other rules concern the treatment of individuals, such as granting immunity to diplomats or basic human rights to individuals.

Independence also means that a State must not be coerced into a treaty. It must not be forced to accept obligations by treaty unless it declares it wants to be bound by its own free will. As article 2(4) of the United Nations Charter prohibits force, at least military force,[59] so is this provision paralleled in the Vienna Convention on the Law of Treaties which now[60] attaches important consequences to the use of force in the treaty making process. Thus, the validity of a treaty concluded under military force is, under the Vienna Convention[61], void. In terms of State practice the legal force of any agreement concluded under military force is clearly questionable: it may not be as easy as it appears under the Vienna Convention on the Law of Treaties of 1969 that such a treaty is void. When the Vienna Convention was concluded there was considerable debate as to the problem of *past* treaties which had been concluded under force: would they now be declared void? The Conference solved this problem by referring only to treaties concluded after the Vienna Convention itself, but the main reason for this, which was to eliminate any discussion concerning the validity of Peace Treaties,

---

[58]   *Ibid.*

[59]   The Brazilian delegation at Bretton Woods suggested that the article should also cover economic force but this proposal was not adopted, see further, my *Independent State, op. cit.,* Chapter IV.

[60]   Under general international law, force used against an envoy or other person signing the treaty - as opposed to force against the State with which we are concerned here - was always illegal.

[61]   Article 39.

was not. It had seemed at the time of the Vienna Convention that since war was now 'forbidden', there would be no more Peace Treaties. Recent events demonstrate the ostrich attitude of the negotiators. Furthermore, how is the international legal system served by declaring Peace Treaties void? The Convention, by its unrealistic clause on invalidity of any agreement concluded under force, merely caused legal uncertainty with regard to numerous later settlements, in Vietnam, in Croatia, in Bosnia etc. On the other hand, it is clear that the most effective force of all, that of economic coercion, is probably not forbidden in international law.[62] An individual, who is poor, has a right, in most countries, to borrow at an exuberant interest rate; in the same way so have States the right to enter into treaties although they are only forced to do so by their financial or economic plight.

Independence implies, furthermore, a right to withstand foreign interference allegedly necessary in the interest of *regional security*. In the Grenada Crisis in 1983, and even more in the *Nicaragua Case* 1984-1985[63] it became obvious that the rule of independence is still threatened by regional security interests. The excuse in the Grenada incident was that humanitarian intervention provided legitimisation of the action. More likely reasoning would suggest that the United States sought to protect the supply of oil from Venezuelan ports or general protection against Cuban activities. In the case of Nicaragua it became apparent that United States action was based on security interests which were so prevailing that the independence of another State was made to suffer.

Independence implies a right not to be subjected to foreign interference. But, as underlined earlier, a State cannot avoid its general obligations under international law by claiming that its independence has been violated.[64] In other words, even if a State has been infiltrated or, as Iran claimed 'exploited', by another State, it commits a greater wrong by setting aside compelling rules of international law, for example rules on immunity of diplomats.

The Iranians abused the notion of independence to claim a right to hold hostages enjoying diplomatic immunity in Teheran in 1979.

---

[62] See, *supra,* under Prophylactic Rules, The Prohibition of Force.
[63] (1984) and (1985) ICJ *Reports.*
[64] *Supra.*

This incident gave rise to several cases, one before the International Court of Justice, the *Hostage Case*[65] and another large and complex case in the High Court of London, the *Frozen Assets Affair*, later settled when the frozen Iranian money was released in return for the freeing of the hostages; there were, and still are, literally thousands of cases later being settled by arbitration by a special tribunal in The Hague.

Iran's behaviour was particularly serious in this affair as this State violated some of the most fundamental rules of international society, that of immunity of diplomats, without which international relations cannot function. On the other hand, there is no question that intervention by military means is wrong under international law: the United States was condemned for trying to rescue the hostages with military force when Iran did not voluntarily release them in spite of the order of the International Court of Justice.

Although it is clear that intervention by military force is illegal this only applies if there is no prior consent by the government of the State where the intervention takes place. Consent may thus be a legitimising factor.[66] But even here there is an exception: if the consent was not democratically secured it will be inoperative. Thus, when the Kabul regime formally invited Russian troops to 'assist' in Afghanistan in 1979 this *consent* was not given by the *people* or by a *democratically elected government*. Consequently, the *consent* was void and the operation termed an invasion; there were even sanctions to show the disapproval of the world in that numerous nations stayed away from the Moscow Olympics in 1980.

A State's independence precludes the intervention of other States. But the reserved domain, as laid down in article 2(7) of the United Nations Charter is by no means as wide as it used to be when the Charter had been drafted. Since 1945 there have been significant inroads in the concept of the reserved domain; the expression is rarely used nowadays and few States resort to the concept to resist intervention.

When the concept of the reserved domain was revived during the

---

[65]   (1979) Interim Order 15 December 1979, ICJ *Reports* 1979, 7; (1980) Judgment 1980, ICJ *Reports*, 3.

[66]   See my *Law of War*, 75 *et seq.*

Spring of 1991, it was to criticize the United States for *not* intervening further in Iraq to protect the Kurds who were the victims of Saddam Hussein's savage persecution. Most of the commentators suggested that the Charter should not protect a ruler who resorted to what was considered to be a form of genocide. The stance by President Bush that these matters were within the exclusive jurisdiction of Iraq found little support in international society and the United States decided to intervene at least to establish *safe zones* for the Kurdish refugees.

International society has thus moved a long way from when intervention was thought to be implied in any talks or discreet criticism in any international fora of the regime in other countries. Not even the dying Soviet Union appeared to resent discussions and comments on for example, Human Rights in that country but rather sought to defend itself on the facts, *i.e.* meeting the argument and stating that the facts, on which reliance is placed, are either wrong/distorted/exaggerated or, occasionally, correct but the USSR had been unable to amend the situation. After the demise of communism, Russia has, of course, taken a different attitude to Human Rights problems.[67]

4. SELF-DETERMINATION

Before 1945 only two sovereign States in Africa enjoyed independence: South Africa, and on a much more modest scale - yet showing some military autonomy and resilience, especially in the Abyssinian war in 1936 - Ethiopia. Also Liberia, founded in 1847 as a haven for liberated slaves returning from America, was technically independent but, in practice, much of an American colony. In the 1960s the whole of the francophone colonies were given independence as well as the whole of British East and West Africa. There were some delays in the southern part, especially in Rhodesia where Zimbabwe emerged as an independent republic only in 1980. In 1991, Namibia, the last African dependent nation, became independent after UN supervision and South African rule has been

---

[67]   See *infra* under the Monist and Dualist School and under Human Rights.

dismantled.

In Asia, India had become independent in 1947, with Pakistan later splitting off and in turn dividing off the State of Bangladesh, formerly East Pakistan. In South East Asia Cambodia, later renamed Kampuchea, and Laos had been given their independence by France in 1949 and later there was a similar development in these areas with colony after colony being made independent; only the Vietnam war delayed some developments but even to this war there was an end.

It must be underlined that the time of salt water colonisation, *i.e.* colonies held by overseas mother countries, is over: hardly any such territories remain. A dot here and there, like Gibraltar and Hong Kong; but there is now a Joint Declaration on the latter colony to give the leased territories, together with the island, back to China in 1997. France is still holding islands like New Caledonia but not much more.[68]

Nor is there any number of trust territories left although many textbooks on international law faithfully still set out the system for their administration. One of the few remaining trust territories is Micronesia, designated as a strategic area under article 82 of the Charter, subjected to administration by the United States. Even this territory has had its right to self-determination affirmed and the trusteeship Agreement is due to be terminated in due course under a Compact of Free Association of 1982.

An interesting development is that many Third World Nations, through their tremendous debts to the industrialised world, have *reduced* their full independence: they are not free to do what they wish in many cases as they must be guided by what the lender States, lender international banks and other financial institutions, stipulate. So, for example, has the huge debt of Brazil been used as a bargaining argument in the persuasive efforts to restrain cutting of the Amazon Forest. It may be that Brazil has certain duties in this respect anyway, as a general environmental obligation,[69] but *debt for nature swaps* (which is now a fashionable topic) do involve the deliberate

---

[68]   Tahiti is an integral 'département' of France and is therefore not a 'colony'.

[69]   See, *infra*, under Environmental Rules.

reduction of sovereignty in return for a reduction of the debt.[70] The whole idea reflects, to some extent, the patronising attitude of the industrialised States towards the Third World.

This attitude is also amply demonstrated by *ineffective* aid to the Third World, aid which is given in many cases to be *seen* to be given, that is for a State to be able to announce that a certain proportion of the GNP[71] is given as Third World Aid, whereas *how* this is done is of lesser interest. Much is wasted as it is not of general concern what proportion actually reaches those who need it most rather than corrupt leaders.[72] Often aid is tied to conditions of purchasing goods or machinery from the donor nation, or machinery is given with a view to maintain spare part sales in the receiver country. Other types of imposing policies can be discerned, as for example, systematic interference with the right to form a family or sterilisation projects, with obvious racial connotations. Those who most profess non-racial views, like the Swedish government, often devote themselves to the most heavy-handed family planning policies in the Third World.

Furthermore, organisations, like, for example, the World Bank, which now profess to be guardians of the environment, are responsible for numerous environmental disasters by the numerous irrigation projects, which in India depopulated numerous viable villages to create severe urbanisation. Many of these projects were to the detriment of both the population, which had to leave their villages to the environment, as dams ruined the natural ecology, and to natural resources, as the dams often failed to provide energy after a short time period. India and other countries in the Third World even incurred great debts to the World Bank for these mismanaged 'helping' projects.

We can thus perceive that the rule of self-determination, has developed to dismantle the old colonial rule and to dismantle the

---

[70] On this complicated mechanism, see my work *Debt for Nature Swaps and Brazil*, Rio de Janeiro 1992.

[71] As is the case in, for example, Sweden.

[72] Even a year after the new non-socialist Swedish government came into power in September 1991, aid is still given to a number of totalitarian regimes in the Third World.

mandate and trust regimes. However, former colonial powers, joined by other industrialised States, have reverted to exercise considerable *control* of the Third World by financial measures, unimpeded by vague efforts to introduce *New Economic Order* (NIEO) in the seventies to help the Third World. Industrialized States were not too keen, however, to share their benefits with the poorer countries, as is demonstrated by the refusal of most important sea-faring nations to ratify the 1982 Law of the Sea Convention which would have given certain benefits to Third World countries, especially in the form of transfer of technical knowledge. The self-determination of Third World countries, in effective terms, is therefore often a mere lip-service by developed States.

The question of self-determination of nations within States still presents the greatest problem. That right, which, on the one hand, is one of the incidents of statehood and sovereignty, implies a right of a nation to have its own government. But what is a nation? Surely one cannot endorse fragmentation *in absurdum*?

In 1792 the French National Assembly declared that it would help and support *all peoples* wanting to recall their freedom. But it is unclear what groups the Assembly had in mind. If it concerned suppressed *French people(s)* the problem, and its solution, was within its borders. If it concerned *peoples* in other States the declaration may have conflicted with another statement by the Assembly that it would not interfere in the affairs in other States.

Relevant statements on self-determination are found in article 1(2) of the United Nations Charter where it is said that the organisation shall seek to

'develop friendly relations among nations based on respect for the principle of equal rights and self-determination of peoples and to take relevant measures to strengthen universal peace.'

The juxtaposition of *self-determination* and *peace* indicates that, in the mind of the drafters of the UN Charter, there is a link between these two concepts, and that promotion of self-determination will serve peace. It may be suggested that the inverted relationship also follows: if self-determination is neglected as a principle, there will be a risk of conflict and war.

Article 55 of the Charter reiterates this link between self-determination and peace, and adds another one between self-determination and social conditions, and states that

'With a view to the creation of conditions of stability and well-being which are necessary for peaceful and friendly relations among nations based on respect for the principle of equal rights and self-determination of peoples, the United Nations shall promote higher standards of living, full employment and conditions of economic and social progress and development.'

However, the drafters of the Charter had not foreseen the post-war colonial crisis and the rapid dismantling of the colonial empires. There was nothing in the Charter to cater for the need of handling the decolonisation process. It could be argued that Chapter XI, XII, XIII of the Charter which deal with non-self governing territories reflect international concern for colonial territories. But when a number of colonial crises arose, they were dealt with by the UN, as in the case of Indonesia, Morocco, Tunisia, Algeria and Cyprus, not under these Chapters, but either under articles 10, 11 or 14 by the General Assembly or under Chapter VII - as threatening peace and security - by the Security Council.

The silence of the Charter on self-determination as a legal rule was soon replaced by a string of important General Assembly Resolutions. The Universal Declaration of Human Rights took up the question.[73] Then came the now historic Declaration on the Granting of Independence to Colonial Countries and Peoples 1514 (XV) of 1960 which had considerable influence on the attitude of the great powers in the ensuing decolonisation process.[74] To implement the Resolution 1514 (XV) the General Assembly established a committee which made recommendations to the Assembly, after having heard petitioners.[75]

The next land-mark Resolution was probably the so called Friendly Relations Resolution in 1970, 2625 (XXV). In this

---

[73]   Article 21.

[74]   *Cf.* GA Res 637 (VII) of 1952.

[75]   GA 1654 (XVI) of 1961.

Declaration Concerning Friendly Relations and Cooperation among States in Accordance with the Charter of the United Nations, the General Assembly elaborated what is required for self-determination and suggested that alien subjugation, domination and exploitation constitutes a major threat to international peace and security.

The resolution stated that

> 'all peoples have the right freely to determine, without external interference, their political status and to pursue their economic, social and cultural development, and every State has the duty to respect this right in accordance with the Charter.'

But such a statement concerns more the right of independence as we have analysed earlier. However, self-determination involves, under this Resolution, also a right to elect a government representing *the whole people*. Thus, by this Resolution the notion of democracy, demanded sometimes as a new criterion in the case of recognition,[76] implies a *right* enjoyed by the citizens in a nation. But the core of self-determination, which surely concerns the right to rule one's own nation even if this implies secession from another is curtailed by the concluding final paragraph of the Resolution which states:

> 'Nothing in the foregoing paragraphs shall be construed as authorising or encouraging any action which would dismember or impair, totally or in part, the territorial integrity or political unity and independent States ...'

It may be that the right of secession still follows from the general notions of independence and self-determination; but it is also easy to see how it could be abused and how it could lead to fragmentation. Self-determination should technically be accorded to any *nation* of sufficient unity and coherence.

It is interesting to consider whether the right of self-determination entails a right not only to secede from a country but one to affiliate with another. This right had earlier been denied in the *Åland Affair*

---

[76]   See, *infra,* under Recognition.

where an overwhelming portion of the population wished to be linked to Sweden but a decision of the League of Nations compelled an affiliation of the Ålanders with Finland. Sweden was 'invited' to conclude an agreement drafted to this effect concluded in 1920 between the Great Powers, Sweden, Finland, the Baltic States and Denmark (but not the Soviet Union).[77]

The Advisory Opinion in the Case of Western Sahara in 1975 also indicates that the rule of self-determination is a double rule implying either a right for peoples to govern themselves or a right to affiliate themselves with another existing State. The Court also elaborated the notion of affiliation and ties of allegiance which must exist for there to be a link between a State and a nation.[78]

The requirement of democratic consent was noted in the Haiti crisis in 1986 when Jean-Claude Duvalier was deposed. But here, as later that year in the Philippines when President Marcos was deposed, the role of democratic self-determination was largely undermined by heavy-handed outside support.

The important right of self-determination is entrenched in the 1966 Covenants on Human Rights. Apart from the aforementioned characteristics of the rule it was here added, in both Covenants, that self-determination implies permanent sovereignty over the nation's natural resources. This had also been emphasised in the earlier 1961 resolution on Permanent Sovereignty over Natural Resources 1803 (XVII) where is was said that such sovereignty forms 'a basic constituent' of the right of self-determination.

(v) Recognition

Verhoeven, *Reconnaissance en droit international,* 1975; Dugard, *Recognition and the United Nations,* 1987; Chen, *The International Law of Recognition,* 1951; Charpentier, *La reconnaissance internationale et l'évolution du droit des gens,* 1956; Lauterpacht, *The International Law of Recognition,* 1947; Bindschedler, R., Die Anerkennung im Völkerrecht, DGVR, 1962; Menon, Some aspects of the law of recognition, RDISP, 1989, 161; Blix, Contemporary aspects of recognition RCADI, 170 ii 587.

---

[77]   See, in more detail, my *Independent State, op. cit.,* 183-186.
[78]   (1975) ICJ Reports 12.

1. GENERAL RULES

Once a unit fulfills the conditions of statehood it ought to be entitled to be recognised as a State. The conditions are, as we have seen before, that the entity has a territory, a population and effective organs to control that territory and that population; there may even be exceptions to these special conditions.[79] The additional criterion of *democracy*,[80] that only recently is demanded in international society, takes on special importance in the context of recognition. Recognition thus often depends on whether there is *democracy* in the candidate's territory.[81]

There have been numerous units in the world fulfilling the criteria of statehood without having been treated as States by the rest of international society. What is then the role played by recognition?

Recognition can, first of all, either mean the acknowledgement that certain facts exist. Such facts may be essential to the existence of a State, for example with regard to the extent of its territory. When the International Court speaks of the parties, in the *Temple of Preah Vihear Case*[82] as having 'recognised', by their conduct, the line indicating the demarcation, the Court is referring to physical facts underlying recognition of another State.

Used in another sense, recognition can imply the submission of a certain territory under the sovereignty of a specific State. In the *Right of Passage Case*[83] the Court found that the sovereignty of Portugal over certain villages in India was *recognised*; but this did not mean that the State of Portugal was recognised. This State had *already* been recognised; what was now at issue was the extent of Portuguese sovereignty and the extent of its territory. So, in the same way as in the *Temple Case*, we are here considering physical facts or actual exercise of power.

In this sense, recognition can concern an *acknowledgement* of the

---

[79]   See, *supra* 61 *et seq.,* under Definition of a State.

[80]   See, *supra* under Definition of a State, and under the special section, *supra*, on Democracy and *infra* on The Requirement of Democracy.

[81]   See further under The Requirement of Democracy in this Chapter.

[82]   (1951) ICJ *Reports*, 139.

[83]   (1960), ICJ *Reports*, 39.

rightfulness that a whole State has been swallowed up by another: this was the situation when Sweden, as one of few States, expressly recognised the incorporation of the three Baltic States, Estonia, Latvia and Lithuania, into the Soviet Union after the Second World War. It is important to recognise that such recognition can only have legal effect vis-à-vis the recognising State in the event that other States take exception to the political implications.[84]

It is important to underline, in that context, that such recognition cannot affect the *actual rights* involved, in other words, such recognition can only express the *subjective* attitude of a government but cannot alter what is *objectively* a State under international law; the statehood of the three Baltic States was probably *latent* or *dormant* during the time when they were unable to exercise sovereign functions having been absorbed by the Soviet Union.

Sweden was thus one of the few, and the first, countries to recognise the absorption of the three Baltic States into the Soviet Union. Many other States, including the United Kingdom and the United States, never recognised the incorporation. Vis-à-vis these States, the Baltic Republics also remained *States*. This attitude and recorded refusal to accept the aggression of the Soviet Union, became important when in the early '90s the question arose about *return of deposited gold.* Some countries had returned gold deposited in their banks on the condition that should the statehood of the three Baltic States revive, there would be no claims due against the country where the deposit was made, but against the Soviet Union. Sweden made no such *caveat*, but had handed the Baltic gold to the Soviet Union outright, without any conditions, and consequently became liable for returning the value of the gold in full as soon as demands from a Baltic republic were made.

Most commonly, in international doctrine, however, recognition is not taken to concern the acknowledgment of annexation, but rather *the existence of another State* and it is on this form of recognition we shall concentrate.

---

[84]   None of the Great Powers recognised, for some time, and some never, the incorporation of the Baltic Republics in the USSR.

2. RECOGNITION OF STATES AND RECOGNITION OF GOVERNMENTS

A State deals with another State and its people as represented in the international field by specific organs. It is therefore of little consequence if the government changes. A new *government* does not normally have to be recognised.

Yet, there may be room to keep international relations with a government in exile, or with an otherwise deposed government. It may be that, here too, certain requirements of effectiveness may be made. The United States claimed that, until 1933, it would only deal with the pre-Bolshevik government in Russia. In war situations serious problems have been caused by recognition (or non-recognition) of governments which have not been effectively in charge of a territory; it may then be questionable whether an act of recognition has any relevance in international law.[85]

Many States have hesitated to recognise States which allegedly have been formed in violation of international law. Thus, the South African Republics of Venda, Ciskei, Transkei, and Bophuthatswana have not been recognised as their creation violate the rule of non-racial discrimination. On the other hand, it is not clear whether such a rule is part of binding international law or not merely an expression for a reluctance to recognise a *puppet State*.[86]

Recognition of a government is not the same as recognition of a State. In their practice, States rarely issue specific statement of recognition of a government for the simple reason that the international *person* has not changed by the mere change of executive power.[87] After all, most States have periodic elections. There is even a claim that such elections are a duty under international law[88] and no one would expect new statements on recognition of governments on any regular basis.

---

[85] See my *Law of War, op. cit.*, 35 *et seq.*

[86] See *infra* in this Chapter.

[87] *Lehigh Railroad Ltd v Russia* [1927] 21 F 2d 396 Circ Ct App 2d Circ. *Cf. Gur Corp. v Bank of Africa,* [1986] 3 WLR 583.

[88] *Cf. supra* on The Requirement of Democracy, and, further, my *Law of War,* 24 *et seq.* on the democratisation of international society and the rule of democracy in general.

On the other hand, States are anxious to issue precisely such statements of recognition of a government if there has been a *dramatic change* over of government. Thus, in the case of a *revolution* one would expect a statement to clarify the situation. In such cases, the recognition of a new government probably coincides with the recognition of the new State as such; it is difficult to separate the two issues. The same often applies even when there is a less dramatic change from a socialist/communist socio-economic system to a more liberal form of government. Thus, the United States was quick to recognise the new government after the fall of Allende in Chile in 1973.

Many maintained for a long time the fiction that recognition of the Peoples' Republic of China concerned 'merely' the recognition of a government: there was thus one country but the *wrong* government, that in Taipei, had been recognised, and this could be rectified by an act of recognition of the *rightful* government in Peking, now commonly called Beijing. It must be stressed that if one applies the tests for statehood furnished above there are probably two Chinas; one fully-fledged State on the mainland, now recognised by virtually all other States, and another one, admittedly smaller but equally fully fledged, with its territory and government located in Taiwan.

Yet, in political terms one must concede that mainland China *claims* Taiwan as a Province (and includes it in the country's Weather Reports as a Province). Conversely, Taiwan claims to be the rightful government of mainland China.

Control of territory and the effective holding of authoritative power is, as when it comes to recognition of States, relevant in deciding on recognition of government. It was primarily on this ground that recognition of the government of the Republic of Vietnam was effected. But as the last example may indicate, the political element is even more pronounced when it comes to recognition of governments than of States in general.

For these reasons, the British government decided in 1980, quite rightly, to dispense with acts recognising governments, especially to avoid the equation of an act of recognition with that of approval.[89]

---

[89]   See 51 BYIL 1980, 367.

The new line will contribute to greater stability and, which is important, to greater uniformity since few other States accord recognition specifically to governments.

3. THE MAIN THEORIES

Most States do use the act of recognition to clarify their attitude to other States. There are two main theories as to the legal effects of such an act. According to the the the so called *declaratory* theory, which is put forward in most textbooks as the correct one, a State does not have to be recognised in order to exist. But this does not tally with State practice according to which recognition is of the greatest practical significance. Others argue, therefore, that recognition by other States has precisely the effect of constituting a State, *i.e.* they adhere to the *constitutive* theory.

The latter theorists[90] seek to reduce the implications of their views by arguing, at the same time, that there is a duty to recognise another State. Yet, it is contrary to the practice of States to let the creation of a State depend on an act of recognition.

Those who adhere to the declaratory theory, on the other hand, underestimate the fact that, although a State acquires legal personality from its inception, *i.e.* from when it fulfills the criteria of a State,[91] but that all new States depend, to some extent, on recognition for their *effective functioning*. Therefore, recognition is best seen as involving both constitutive and declaratory elements: it is declaratory in so far as it merely notes, or clarifies, that a State has come into being (which may have occurred earlier than the act of recognition); and it is constitutive in so far as it implies a willingness to enter into diplomatic relations with the new State on a bilateral, and/or multilateral, basis.

4. IMPLIED RECOGNITION

Recognition can validly be given by implicit behaviour. As just

---

[90]   For example, see the work by Lauterpacht, *The International Law of Recognition*, 1947.

[91]   See, *supra* 61 *et seq.*, under Definition of a State.

demonstrated, however, the fact that an entity is allowed to obtain membership of an organisation does not mean that other members of that organisation implicitly recognise the entity as a State. The reason for this is that recognition operates on a bilateral rather than on a multilateral basis.

On the other hand, recognition may be implied in many other acts. For example, if a State, without any act of recognition, enters into diplomatic relations with a new State, or if it concludes treaties with that State, it recognises, implicitly, the new State. Reservations in a treaty to the effect that the process of concluding a treaty will not imply any act of recognition are probably ineffective, partly because such clauses cannot operate as genuine reservations to a treaty, partly because of the contradictory implications of such statements.[92]

Acts of recognition only operate on a bilateral footing:[93] the membership of an organisation, for example, in the United Nations, does not amount to any act of recognition by other member States. Yet, the membership of the Federal Republic of Germany and the German Democratic Republic in 1973 clarified, to some extent, their position in the international society.

5. *DE JURE* AND *DE FACTO* RECOGNITION

Earlier many considered there to be a special form of recognition given *de facto*, implying a provisional act of recognition. Contrary to a *de jure* recognition - the formal type of final recognition - a *de facto* recognition can be revoked. In some instances, a State could then recognise *two* governments, one *de facto* and the other *de jure*.[94] It can be questioned whether such a category is useful. It has, furthermore, hardly been used in State practice in recent times.

---

[92]   See my *Essays on the Law of Treaties*, 1967, 116.

[93]   But recognition can be effectuated by several States *collectively*, as was done when the European Community recognised Croatia on 15th January 1992.

[94]   *The Arantzazu Mendi* [1939] AC 256. On the effect of *de facto* recognition, see *Haili Selassie v Cable & Wireless Co. (No. 2)* [1939] Ch. 182; on the effects of *de jure* recognition in terms of retroactivity, see *Gdynia Ameryka Linie v Boguslawski* [1953] AC 11; *Civil Air Transport v Central Air Transport* [1953] AC 70.

Some important cases, however, like *Luther v Sagor*,[95] show the unhappy results[96] when courts take the position that *de facto* control is sufficient: it nearly always benefits revolutionary coups and other disruptive acts in international society.

6. RECOGNITION *SUI GENERIS*

On the other hand, although there is little use of the *de jure/de facto* type distinction there has recently been a conditional or an atypical form of recognition. The Basic Agreement between the Federal Republic (FRG) and the German Democratic Republic (GDR) of 1972 (*Grundlagenvertrag*) provided that both States would enter into normal relations on the basis of equality, on the basis of the prohibition of force of the UN, respect for Human Rights and respect for the borders of each other. However, this agreement probably does not imply any act of recognition in the ordinary sense of the word. The conditions imposed are none other than what general international law imposes in any event on any State, whether or not a member of the UN. Yet, this could perhaps be called an act of recognition *sui generis*. That at least the Federal Republic did not regard DDR on the same footing as other foreign States was marked by the special use of permanent representatives rather than diplomats in the mutual relations of the two countries.

These remarks have no more than historical significance now that the two Germanies have merged, as they did on 3rd October 1990. Numerous agreements were concluded during the time of division and numerous other issues can only be understood against the background of the earlier legal regime in the two parts of Germany, of which each was a fully constituted State.[97]

---

[95]   [1921] 3 KB 532 and *supra* under Comity and the Act of State Doctrine.

[96]   In the event, English Courts recognised acts of the Bolshevik Revolution.

[97]   It was proposed, at regular intervals, in the International Law Association, that a Committee should be established to study 'Divided States'. Yet, any such notion is a contradiction in terms, there is either one State, or two States.

7. RETROACTIVE RECOGNITION

Once a State is recognised the question may arise whether the act of recognition will operate retrospectively and apply to measures taken *before* the date of recognition.

In some cases English Courts have not shown the same reluctance, or abhorrence, as one would expect in European Courts, to the question of retroactivity or to the possibility of a rule operating retrospectively. It may be that the principle of non-retroactivity is more securely entrenched in civil law thinking as a paramount principle, essential to the *security of law* without which there can be no rule of law.[98]

The question of retroactivity of recognition has been discussed in several well known cases, especially in connection with recognition *de jure*.[99] In *Luther v Sagor*[100] and in *Princess Paley v Weiss*[101] the High Court in London had no problems in allowing retrospective operation of recognition and even of bare *de facto* recognition although this led to the deprivation of privately held property of the plaintiffs.

The House of Lords, on the other hand, came to different results in two later cases: *The Gdynia Ameryka Linie v Bogloslawski*[102] concerned the Polish merchant marine under control of the Polish exile Government in London, and the *Civil Air Transport Inc. v Central Air Transport Corp.*[103] concerned aircraft that, in violation of local law, had been transferred from Hong Kong to the People's Republic of China. Although the English House of Lords discussed the question of retroactivity, which civil law Courts would probably have found abhorrent as violating fundamental rules of law, the House of Lords came to the conclusion in the *Bogloslawski Case* that recognition may operate retrospectively but in then only to spheres of actual control, which precluded the operation of the principle in the

---

[98]   *Cf. infra* 254-257 on General Principles, Security of Law.

[99]   See *supra* under recognition *de jure*.

[100]   [1921] 3 KB 532. For criticism of this case *cf. infra*.

[101]   [1929] 1 KB 718.

[102]   [1953] AC 11.

[103]   [1953] AC 70.

case. In the other case concerning *Civil Air Transport*, the House of Lord considered that recognition should not apply retrospectively to validate unlawful acts. In all these cases, however, there may have been considerable political elements, not in any way improperly taken into account by the Courts but inevitably forming the *setting* for their decisions.[104]

8. PREMATURE RECOGNITION

Ijalaye, Was Biafra at any time a State in international law? AJIL 1971, 551.

Some claim that premature recognition can amount to illegal intervention in the affairs of another State, *i.e.* most often in the affairs of a mother State. One of the most recent examples of complaints about such premature recognition was in the case of France, which protested that some States had prematurely recognised the regime in Algeria.

Another example occasionally listed as an example of premature recognition, is that of Bosnia, after its secession from the communist rule of the former Federation of Yugoslavia. Although Bosnia was rapidly recognised by a number of countries, by the European Community and immediately accepted as a Member of the United Nations, there were soon signs that recognition may have been forthcoming too soon, before the State had fully established itself. There is little ground for such assumptions which rather reflect political opportunism and a clear wish of the Great Powers to determine the fate of a small country. What may have been questionable, however, are the borders of the new State, which presumably should have allowed for a greater influence of the wishes of the inhabitants: there was, for example, clear indications that the Croats of Hercegovina, a nearly totally Croatian region, would have preferred to associate themselves with Croatia, rather than being absorbed by Bosnia. In this respect there was little *democracy*[105] when decisions were taken.

It may be questioned whether in these post-colonial days there is

---

[104]   *Cf. infra* 89 *et seq.*, under Political Nature of Recognition.
[105]   See *supra* under Democracy as a notion in international society.

any need to speak of premature recognition as giving rise to any well-founded right of complaint under international law. Yet, it must be remembered that some States that recently became independent have, as already mentioned, fragmented into new States, such as Pakistan/East Pakistan - Bangladesh. When uprisings are not successful, as in the case of Biafra seeking to form a new State independent of Nigeria, there may still be problems caused by premature recognition.

On the other hand, States should be able to recognise any new entity which *appears* to fulfil the normal criteria for statehood without threats of possible ensuing responsibility for premature recognition, at most, premature recognition is, if an entity does not survive into an established State, a *nullity*, devoid of any legal consequences in terms of responsibility.

9. CRITERIA FOR RECOGNITION

(a) The Effectiveness Criterion

Cavaré, La reconnaissance de l'état et le Manchukuo, RGDIP, 1935, 5; Eekelaar, Rhodesia: the abdication of constitutionalism, MLR 1969, 191; Fischer, La non-reconnaissance du Transkei, AF, 1976, 63.

In order to exist as a State there must be some independence of the unit vis-à-vis other States. Independence, as an effectiveness criterion, has a two-fold character: it is a condition of potential statehood although, at the same time, it flows as a consequence of statehood and is an incidence of statehood. Viewed in this light, the Peoples' Republic of China, or Croatia and Slovenia, existed long before they were recognised. So did the German Democratic Republic.

To ignore the factual powers of a State and to rely too heavily on absence of recognition produces unrealistic results. It would appear, for example, that for all intents and purposes, Taiwan is a State and the fact that she has claims to represent the 'whole' of China[106]

---

[106] The Peoples' Republic of China has similar claims of representation and, to make a point, includes Taiwan on the national weather forecast map on daily TV broadcasts as part of the Peoples' Republic.

cannot vitiate her legitimate existence; nor can the absence of recognition be relevant in this respect, especially bearing in mind that it was Taiwan, and not Mainland China, that *was* a Member of the United Nations and exercised her active and passive right of legation all over the world.[107] On the other hand, the Peoples' Republic is *also* a State; the relationship between the 'two Chinas' cannot be reduced to simplistic right of representation of the 'legitimate' government. It may be that a future agreement between the *two States that no doubt exist now* to resolve relevant problems.

(b) Puppet States

We have already seen that States may be fully constituted under international law although they are very small.[108] But if they place their foreign affairs in the hands of another State this must be done by their own free will and with their full consent. In other words, they must not be fully controlled by another State.

Still, a certain *viability*[109] is required. Some small nations may, as mentioned earlier, fall short of this as their territory *and* their population is too small. Other States do not fulfil the criterion of viability because they are controlled by some other State. Those who claim that recognition is merely declaratory fail to pay sufficient heed to the practice of States which, apart from the fulfilment of required criteria of statehood (territory, populations, effective organs) also demand a certain degree of international *effectiveness*. It is on this basis that some puppet States have been excluded from the circle of genuine States. Manchukuo, set up by Japan in the 1930s on the mainland of China, was such a State. Other examples are Ciskei,[110]

---

[107] *Contra*, Shaw, *International Law*, 2nd ed., 1986, 148-149.

[108] *Supra*, under Subjects of International Law.

[109] See *supra* on this condition for statehood.

[110] This country formed the object of a court inquiry to the Foreign Office in 1986 where the FCO declined to answer as to whether Ciskei was a State, insisting that the HM Government no longer recognises governments and that the 'attitude of Her Majesty's Government can be inferred from the nature of its dealings with the regime concerned and in particular whether (it) deals with it on government to government basis', *Gur Corp. v Trust Bank of Africa* [1986] 3 WLR 583, a phrasing which left the court with little guidance.

Transkei or the South African homelands.[111]

(c) Satellite States and Regional Hegemony

An earlier special category of puppet States were the so-called *satellite States*, controlled, to a lesser or higher degree, by the former Soviet Union. These - Poland, East Germany (DDR), Hungary, Bulgaria, Rumania, and Czechoslovakia - were usually called *satellites*, in the sense that they had little or no control over their own affairs. Much of the espionage activities of the Soviet Union was furthermore carried out through these satellites, to earn them some suspicion in the West.

It is to be noted that the term *satellite* always apply to those States which are *geographically adjacent* or *near* the ex-Soviet Union. The USSR also controlled numerous other countries, particularly in the Third World, but in this respect one did not use the term satellites. Nor has that been done with regard to States geographically near the United States although there was undoubted American influence, if not control. In this respect it has been preferable to speak of *regional hegemony*.[112]

(d) Conflicts with Prohibiting Rules

There may be a conflict between recognition and the rules prohibiting for example the use of force. In this sense there is an enhanced political element in any act of recognition and this political aspect affects the effectiveness of a country aspiring to be a State.

Earlier, before the use of force to enlarge one's territory was unequivocally forbidden, there were cases where the taking of territory resulted in the recognition of another State being *in control* of a country. Thus, it is in this historic light we must read cases like

---

[111]   *Cf. infra* on the element of democracy.

[112]   Note that the United States would not tolerate the positioning of any atomic weapons within its region, as clearly illustrated by the *Cuban Quanrantine* in 1962. The USSR was not, on the other hand, able to prevent the positioning of similar weapons in West Germany, within missile range of the USSR.

Haili Selassie v Cable and Wireless Ltd. (No. 2)[113] which concerned the recognition by the United Kingdom of the King of Italy as Emperor of Ethiopia after the Italo-Abyssinian war. It is, however, impossible that this could happen now, in this day and age, when it is impossible to expand State territory by annexation.[114] Still, efforts are made, sometimes accompanied by armed force: this happened when the Belgrade regime sought to annex parts of Bosnia even after Bosnia had been internationally recognised.

(e) Security Council Vetting

Similarly to the situation when there is a conflict between the aspirations of recognition and violations of the rules prohibiting the use of force, there can also be a conflict between recognition and obligations to implement policies laid down by the Security Council of the United Nations. The rules prohibiting force and UN Resolutions may, obviously overlap, as Resolutions repeat the wording or in other ways give effect to prohibitive rules under article 2(4).

Rhodesia, under Ian Smith after UDI (the unilateral declaration of independence), certainly appeared to fulfil all criteria of statehood even though there was a constitutional problem with regard to its relationship with the United Kingdom. The problem here is largely historic after the emergence of Zimbabwe, a new State, which having a majority black government became immediately adopted in international society. While the Smith regime lasted, however, the attitude of the Security Council as to the legitimacy of the white government precluded its recognition by other States.

The Turkish Republic of Northern Cyprus (TRNC) is another example where a State appears to be fully constituted but unable to obtain recognition from other States, largely because of Security Council Resolutions[115] supporting the integrity of the island as a whole and the nowadays entirely Greek government in Nicosia. The Turkish Republic of Northern Cyprus (TRNC) set itself up in the

---

[113]   [1939] Ch. 182.

[114]   See, *infra*, under Territory.

[115]   SC Res 541 1983, 550, 1984.

northern part of the island with its own government in northern Nicosia, a part of the city now called Lefkoša. TRNC has not been recognised by any other State except Turkey which helped it to be formed. It has well defined borders, even patrolled by United Nations Forces, a population as well as effective organs. Its legislature enacts laws modelled upon those in Turkey but its Courts follow also decisions of the House of Lords in the United Kingdom, the former colonial power.

In the case of Northern Cyprus, the territory is still subject to Security Council Resolutions which apparently cause reluctance among UN members to recognise an already functioning State. In the case of Cyprus, there is also a fear that recognition could be prejudicial to a possible re-unification of the island, of the Greek part, which now on the international level claims to represent the whole of Cyprus, and the northern Turkish break-away part. However, it is important to remember that the northern part has now functioned as a State in practice during the past twenty years.

Security Council Resolutions may not only influence the attitude to seceding countries and induce other States from refraining to grant such countries recognition. In the case of Kuwait, the attitude of the Security Council effectively precluded any recognition of the annexation by Iraq, as Resolution 678 of 1990 authorised force to protect the independence of Kuwait. Already Resolution 661 of the Security Council had *determined* that Iraq had 'usurped the authority of the legitimate Government in Kuwait' and consequently ordered far reaching sanctions against Iraq. Two years later the power to take resolute action and history might one day question for what motives a similarly forceful declaration was not issued against the Government of Belgrade, committing a very similar annexation effort against Bosnia, as Iraq had committed against Kuwait.

Sweden declared in 1973[116] that it always seeks to recognise any State whose authorities exercise *factual control* over the territory of the State and exercise, in this area, sovereign functions; such recognition does not imply any political support. Yet, Sweden does not always act along those proclaimed lines, for example, if there is

---

[116]   *Utrikesfrågor* 1974, 295.

any conflict between recognition and obligations under Security Council Resolutions. Here, Sweden has taken the view that Security Council resolutions prevail - as they were interpreted, by Sweden, to preclude recognition of Smith's Rhodesia or of Northern Cyprus - although such resolutions do not always explicitly prohibit recognition.[117]

(f) The Requirement of Democracy

It is increasingly clear that in addition to the basic criteria of a State - territory, population and effective organs - there is also a requirement, beyond that of independence, of democratic rule.[118] As mentioned above,[119] the condition of democratic rule may not be a prerequisite to the existence of a *new* State but merely to its subsequent relationship to the external world. Thus, a State may have come into existence but, unless it abides with the requirement of democratic rule, other States, and the United Nations itself, may refuse to have any dealing with it and may subject it to sanctions. As far as concerns recognition of new States, democracy is clearly an important, or even the most important, condition.

There were earlier attempts in Latin America where there were attempts under the so called *Tobar doctrine*[120] in 1907 to link the recognition of revolutionary governments to a condition of free elections. But this doctrine has to be seen in the light of the later *Estrada doctrine*[121] of 1930 which claimed that any recognition (or non-recognition) can amount to illicit interference in the internal affairs of another State.

It has sometimes been argued that a treaty is void if *the people* have not accepted it although the government has given its consent. One such category which would be subjected to special rules would,

---

[117]   In the case of Rhodesia members of the UN were asked specifically by Resolution 2946 (XXVII) of 1972 to refrain from any act that might lend 'legitimacy' to the Smith regime.

[118]   See *supra* under Criteria of a State, Democracy.

[119]   See Under Criteria of a State, Democracy, in this Chapter.

[120]   AJIL 1908 Suppl. 229.

[121]   AJIL 1931 Suppl. 203.

74

according to some, be treaties concerning secession of territory,[122] and thus immediately relevant to recognition of a new State unit. However, it is difficult, for any contracting party, to assess whether *popular support* has been forthcoming; in such cases, *democracy* and *popular support,* may be a strong indication that the legislative body, for example, Parliament, where the citizens of a State are represented, should have debated the treaty. On the other hand, a contracting State must be able to rely on consent as expressed by authorised organs, normally the *government,* or one of its representatives.[123] However, there is certainly a marked tendency to make territorial settlements dependent on popular support. For example, the draft settlement in Rhodesia in 1971 was made dependent on the acceptance of 'Rhodesians as a whole'.

To claim nowadays that States, like recently Rhodesia, and now South Africa, must have some form of democratic rule in order to avoid sanctions is therefore quite a new development and, on the face of it, contrary to the wording of article 2(7) of the United Nations Charter which would appear to guarantee that the internal affairs of a State is truly a *reserved domain* where other States, or organisations, may not interfere.

In the Rhodesia settlement, as in the question of recognition of the Republic of Vietnam, the acquiescence of the population was thought essential by other States.

The development towards such a condition for recognition and for continued relationship with a regime is amply illustrated by the attitude to South Africa, an already recognised State. Unless it is admitted that democracy, involving some form of at least moderate majority rule, forms a condition for normal relationship between States it is impossible to understand the reaction to the internal policies of South Africa and of other nations which have recently emerged as States. How can a State be subjected to international sanctions for failing to introduce some form of democracy - as was also Ian Smith's Rhodesia - unless the rule of democracy is now a compelling rule in international relations?

---

[122]   Hyde i 366; *cf. idem* ii 1399.

[123]   Any person in sufficient authority possess what may be called *ostensible authority* to conclude treaties, see Blix, *Treaty Making Power*, 1960, *passim.*

The situation in law was amply illustrated by the attitude to countries like Lithuania where most States deplored the bloodshed caused by efforts to quash the independence movement. By 1990 there was widespread resentment that democratic rule was suppressed by Moscow's autocracy and shortly afterwards, the three countries consolidated their constitutional structure to merit recognition by other States. A strong element which favoured early recognition was undoubtedly the established system of democracy in these countries.

Another recent example is Croatia which in June 1991 announced its independence from the artificial communist construction of Yugoslavia. The State of Yugoslavia was formed as a kingdom in 1918 when six diverse nations, Croatia, Slovenia, Bosnia, Herzegovina, Montenegro and Serbia were joined together, much by the pressure exercised by the Great Powers. Serbia soon usurped power by a dictatorial regime of King Alexander I, assassinated in 1934 as a tyrant. After the Second World War the State of Yugoslavia was transformed into a Peoples' Republic under staunch Communist rule by Marshal Tito who, however, clearly marked his independence of Moscow.

In 1990, Croatia invoked the provisions in the Federal Yugoslav Constitution which permitted the different republics to leave if they so wished. But rather than accepting Croatia's democratic decision, the Belgrade regime invaded Croatia and sought to hold the Communist Federation together by force. To the surprise of many, the European Community through the mediator Lord Carrington, and the United States, tried for a long time to defer recognition and to prop up the old artificial federation, in spite of clear democratic signals. Eventually these democratic forces became too pronounced to be contained by outside domination and Croatia and Slovenia were recognised by a number of foreign States.[124]

The cultural, ethnical and religious differences are substantial between the Catholics in the north and the Orthodox and Muslim communities in the south. Tensions produced by these differences were aggravated by the rejection of Communist rule in Slovenia and Croatia, with considerable support from Bosnia and Herzegovina.

---

[124] By April 1992 over fifty States had recognised the new republics.

Again, it was the clear democratic order of the northern countries, Croatia and Slovenia, that enabled a speedy recognition by the majority of the countries in the world.

Serbia and Montenegro, however, are preserving the Communist system as a very lonely socialist regime in the international society of 1992. The Belgrade regime was much assisted in the war efforts by the fact that the federal army consisted of largely Serbian officers and soldiers as well as by the fact that Belgrade, the capital of Yugoslavia and of Serbia, controlled the central bank and the funds of the previously federal State.

10. THE DIMENSION OF TECHNICAL COOPERATION

Life for a new State or of a break-away territory can be very difficult it it is not admitted to certain international organisatons. In this context it is not the United Nations which is of the greatest importance. But it is essential that a new State is allowed to participate in technical organisations like the Universal Postal Union (UPU) and in the International Telecommunications Union (ITU).

A territory does not have to be a State to be a member of these organisations.[125] Yet, it was precisely the refusal to admit the State of Manchukuo to these organisations which made it wither away. And it is the refusal to gain admission to the UPU and the ITU which is now causing considerable difficulties to Northern Cyprus. Participation in such organisations thus form another limb of the effectiveness criterion. The means to be admitted to membership is clearly by first obtaining recognition by other States which, again, proves the practical importance of recognition and its important constitutive elements.[126]

11. VERIFICATION OF RECOGNITION

Recognition is relevant for a number of issues. One problem concerns, for example, diplomatic immunity which is only granted to envoys from recognised States. Another matter of great practical

---

[125]   See my *Law Making, op. cit.* 217 *et seq.*
[126]   See *supra* under Recognition.

importance is immunity in the courts.

A court will often have to know whether a State is recognised or not in order to decide on the aforementioned consequences. It will, in most States, consult the Foreign Office or the Foreign Ministry to check if the territory in question has been given formal recognition by its own executive. A court does thus not normally go into the question whether the relevant territory actually fulfills the normal requirements of statehood.

Even if this is the normal procedure some cases show that a court, or at least some independently minded judges, may proceed to examine whether a territory, *prima facie,* is, or is not, a State. Lord Denning, the Master of the Rolls, stated in *Hesperides Hotels Ltd. v Aegean Turkish Holidays Ltd.*[127] that the Foreign Office Certificate on non-recognition of the Turkish Federated Republic of Northern Cyprus only provided some evidence as to the status of this territory but was not conclusive. For example, German courts have also freely assessed whether a State exists even in the absence of specific recognition.[128]

12. THE POLITICAL NATURE OF RECOGNITION

Recognition is often coloured by political perceptions[129] and, since no State is forced to recognise another, there is a large measure of political discretion in any decision to recognise another State. The non-recognition of the Peoples' Republic of China until 1978 may illustrate the political dimension.

In a sense then, recognition may be perceived to pronounce on the legitimacy of another State. According to the *Estrada doctrine,* formulated by the Mexican Minister for Foreign Affairs by that name in 1930, some States, like Mexico at that time, may refrain from recognising other States precisely to avoid any affront to the *dignity* of other States. However, since the opening of diplomatic relations themselves implies a decision on recognition, it is difficult to see how

---

[127]   [1978] QB 205 CA; [1979] AC 508.

[128]   RG 29.6.1920.

[129]   On the problem of retrospective operation see *supra* under 7 and on the question of impartiality see *infra* under 13.

States can avoid pronouncing, even by implication, on their attitude to another entity as a functioning State.

Recognition has nearly always considerable political overtones which dictate, in each individual case, whether States *ought* to recognise a unit as a State. This is clearly illustrated in the case of liberation movements.

There has been much discussion of the *recognition* of liberation movements. Recognition, in this context, has often meant the same as *approval* and not necessarily the same as *recognition as a State*. Yet, it is clear that, at least in some cases, forms of *approval* might ultimately lead to *real* recognition on the assumption that the recognising State encouraged the aspirations for statehood of a particular liberation movement. Some have thus mistakenly believed that any contact with such organisations would imply some form of *recognition*. It may be that by allowing liberation movements to take part in international fora one emphasises also their duty to abide by international humanitarian (and other rules) but by ignoring them one may find that States, alone, bear the burden of obligations[130] as subjects and liberation movements, for example, are let off duties imposed by international agreements.

Any *contact* with liberation movements does not amount to condoning their actions. If this had been so, the negotiations with the Mao Mao guerilla, whose leader later became the President of Kenya, would not have been possible in the wake of independence of that country. But if statesmen worry that contacts imply approval, they may furthermore jeopardise the situation of hostages held by liberation movements. It cannot be correct to approach an intermediary merely to avoid any allegation that direct contact would *recognise* the liberation movements. This is, however, what the Swedish Prime Minister Carlsson did when he asked President Reagan to inquire at the UNITA Headquarters in Angola about three missing Swedes rather than making a direct demand when the three development aid workers had gone missing. It was stated that the reason for this action was reluctance to 'recognise' UNITA by direct contact, a consequence on which the Prime Minister cannot have

---

[130] On this point, see my *Law of War, op. cit.*, 361 *et seq.*

obtained accurate advice.

Contacts clearly do not lead to any *recognition* nor to any *approval* but it is, on the other hand, the *duty* of a government to protect its nationals.[131] Indirect contacts - especially through a country with which Sweden, at the time, had few political links - are less forthright. There is a further danger connected with such indirect contacts also in that a message may be distorted; and in this situation the intermediary was not even any close ally of the country whose nationals had been taken hostage.

When we speak of *recognition* of liberation movements, it is clear that normal rules for recognition of States apply; by referring to the candidate entity as a liberation movement we merely indicate that it *may* be a particularly well organised and probably motivated unit. On the other hand, the fact that certain other States view such movements sympathetically - or with hostility - has little to do with their becoming fully constituted States. Yet, the paramount effect of informal alliances of attitude, in this respect, is difficult to overlook and tends to enhance the *political* perspective of recognition in the case of liberation movements.

Another political aspect of recognition is the effect of a decision of one of the Great Powers. Once, for example, the United States had decided to recognise, the Republic of Red China, it was not long before a number of other States followed suit, by the domino effect,[132] and not long before China took its seat in the United Nations. This case may also illustrate the hollowness of the claim that recognition is merely declaratory: the fact that the 'other' China, Taiwan, still existed, was ignored by all and the Peoples' Republic was entitled to replace this State in every organisation. Surely, it would have been more in congruence with actual realities to admit that there were two Chinas, both fully constituted as States.

---

[131]   See *infra* on Allegiance and its consequences.

[132]   The syndrome of following the lead of the United States is paramount in international law: we may merely refer to the effect to the sudden *volte-face* of the United States in the Law of the Sea negotiations which abruptly precluded the ratification of the 1982 Law of the Sea Convention by *any* major sea-faring nation.

13. THE RULE OF IMPARTIALITY

Bearing in mind the political setting of recognition it is important to emphasise that recognition does not *per se* involve any political decision endorsing any *type* of regime. It is thus important to realise that the acknowledgement of the existence of a State does not imply any approval of its policies. Although the United Kingdom treated Hitler's Germany as a fully constituted State without any doubt of its statehood, the UK disapproved sufficiently of Germany's policies to declare war against this country in 1939. It is significant that war is, in fact, only declared against States; so animosity might even *prove* that an entity is a State.[133]

Recognition of a State and the maintenance of this recognition does thus not imply any value judgement as to the merits of its government. Recognition is thus, as a matter of principle, an impartial act. States often fail to treat recognition in this functional way by lending it overtones of approval, with regard to the type of regime, that should not accompany the act of recognition.

14. DUTIES FLOWING FROM RECOGNITION

Once a new State has been created and has been recognised, other States come under duty to *respect* the existence of the new State, *i.e.* to grant it the privileges of *equality*, *independence* and *self-determination* as set out earlier as *criteria of statehood*.[134]

The attitude of other States must be to support, on the one hand, the right of a State to preserve its integrity but, at the same time, respecting the right of self-determination, in the sense of definitely refusing to condone any use of force of the new government to quash further independence movements in the country. The ambit of article 2(7) of the UN Charter which guarantees the reserved domain of a State is thus limited by the reduced right a State nowadays has to use

---

[133]   Note the persistent criticism of entities which undoubtedly are/were States: Hitler's Germany; the USSR; South Africa; Amin's Uganda; Pol Pot's Kampuchea.

[134]   See *supra*.

force in its own territory against its own subjects.

States which take a passive role, as many have done with regard to Serb atrocities in Bosnia, effectively allowing, by their passivity, violations of Human Rights as civilians are deliberately attacked, raped or ethnically cleansed, are themselves guilty of violations of international law: third States are bound to *uphold* what the International Court has called *fundamental rules of international law*.[135] Other States, even those which are non-members of the United Nations,[136] are thus under duty to *recognise* the illegality of a situation created by violations of international law and are under duty to *refrain* from any assistance which may prolong such illegality.[137]

The State which has violated *fundamental rules* of international law, on the other hand, is *precluded* from arguing that it has been acting in self-defence or has any other justification for its action.[138] If a State thus commits gross violations of Human Rights or of humanitarian law, it cannot exculpate itself by claiming any *rights* to action with such consequences.

A gentle formula of intervention has also been found by other signatories of the Helsinki Protocol to guarantee that the provisions of the Conference on Security and Cooperation in Europe, the CSCE,[139] are upheld, especially with regard to the obligation to refrain from the use of force as well as with respect to the protection of Human Rights.

15. EFFECTS OF NON-RECOGNITION

Verhoeven, Relations internationales de droit privé en absence de reconnaissance, RCADI, 1985 iii 9; Frowein, *Das de facto Regime im Völkerrecht*, 1968.

If an entity is not recognised as a State it may have severe

---

[135]   *The Namibia Case, Advisory Opinion*, (1971), ICJ *Reports* 56. On the duty of *solidarity*, see my *Concept, op. cit.* 124-128 and *infra*.

[136]   *Ibid.*, 53, 56.

[137]   *Ibid.*, 54.

[138]   See to this effect *Hostages in Teheran Case*, (1980), ICJ *Reports*, 26.

[139]   On the CSCE see *infra*, in this Chapter.

implications for individuals seeking remedies in local courts in another State: for if a State is not recognised nor is its acts, decisions or legislation. Nor can a non-recognised State appear as plaintiff in a law suit, at least not in Anglo-Saxon courts which are tied to the same attitude as the executive with regard to the State in question.[140]

On the other hand, a State which is fully recognised enjoys sovereign immunity[141] and may thus escape being brought to court as a defendant in at least non-commericial disputes. Such immunity attaches to both *de jure* and *de facto* recognition,[142] as illustrated by the *Aranzazu Mendi*[143] where the nationalist government of Spain was held to be recognised as it exercised control over a large portion of Spain.

Furthermore, the acts taken by the *government* in a *State* which is not recognised will themselves not be taken in account in a non-recognising State. In other words, if a law has been enacted in a territory which is not recognised as a State by another State, this law will not have any effect in the State which opposes recognition. There are many cases from the time of the Russian Revolution on this point. *Luther v Sagor*[144] is the leading case; the Soviet Union was recognised by the United Kingdom *de facto* during the litigation in the English Courts in 1921 and it was held that this *de facto* recognition operated to validate the taking of the plaintiff's stock of wood in 1918 as Soviet power dated to the end of 1917 and the

> 'acts of that government must be treated by the courts of this country with all the respect due to the acts of a duly recognised foreign sovereign State'.[145]

---

[140]   *USSR v Cibrario* [1923] AD 1923-1924.

[141]   *Infra* under Immunity of States.

[142]   *Cf. supra* under the heading Recognition *de jure* and *de facto*.

[143]   [1939] AC 256.

[144]   [1921] 1 KB 456; [1921] 3 KB 532.

[145]   *Ibid., per* Lord Justice Banks. For critical comments on this case, see, *supra*, under Comity and the Act of State Doctrine.

The ruling in *Luther v Sagor*[146] has been modified by another case, the *Carl Zeiss Stiftung Case,* which concerned the specific situation in East Germany. Here was a State, for long unrecognised by the United Kingdom, but where the unrecognised authorities undoubtedly acted under the authority of the Soviet Union, a recognised State. Because of this situation the laws of the East German authorities could be recognised as coming from *subordinate bodies* of the Soviet Union.[147]

Non-recognition will not necessarily preclude international claims[148] as non-recognition is *evidence,* or even strong evidence, of statehood but this evidence which does not oust factual efficacy in international law.[149] Therefore, non-recognition does not preclude that a court in another State accepts as valid laws enacted by the non-recognised State.[150]

b. Groups of States: The Commonwealth

Fawcett, *The British Commonwealth in International Law,* 1963; de Smith, *The New Commonwealth and its Institutions,* 1964; Rousseau, *Le Commonwealth dans les relations internationales,* Cours, 1957/1958.

States can group together and then form a separate international person. This is, as we shall see, the case when State found international organisations.[151] However, before an entity achieves the consolidation that is necessary to form an organisation, States may more loosely group together in an association which enjoys separate or even *parallel* international subjectivity under international law. This is the case of the Commonwealth which consists of States which are more closely associated than those in an alliance,[152] and less tightly

---

146   See the previous note.

147   *Carl Zeiss Stiftung v Rayner & Keeler Ltd. No. 2,* [1966] 3 WLR 125; [1966] 2 All ER 536 (HL).

148   But see *City of Berne v Bank of England* 9 Ves. 347.

149   *Tinoco Arbitration* (1923) 1 RIAA 369.

150   *Hesperides Hotels v Aegean Turkish Holidays* [1978] QB 205 (CA) *per* Lord Denning.

151   See in the following section, *infra.*

152   On Alliances, see my *Law of War,* Cambridge, 1987, Chapter I.

bound together than States in an international organisation.

The Commonwealth Secretariat prepares important conferences by which the various States coordinate their policies and their laws. The Queen is the Head of the Commonwealth and symbolises the personal bonds between the member States.

c. Fettered States

Certain territories may be *potential* States but they have not reached their full degree of independence. Other entities are, or have been actual States, but, for political reasons they are submitted to restricting international measures that appear to deprive them of their statehood.

These bodies, which are also subjects under the international legal order, range from protectorates,[153] mandates,[154] trust territories[155] to territories submitted to 'internationalisation' under, for example, like Tangier under the Act of Algeciras of 1907,[156] like Danzig[157] or the Saar region under the Treaty of Versailles,[158] or Trieste under the Peace Treaty with Italy after the Second World War.[159]

---

[153] See *Rights of the United States in Morocco* (1952) ICJ *Reports* 1952 176;

[154] *The International Status of South West Africa* (1950) ICJ *Reports* 1950 128. See, Diena, Les mandats internationauz, RCADI 1924 iv; Rolin, La pratique des mandats, RCADI 1927 iv.

[155] See, Vedovato, Les accords de tutelle, RCADI 1950 i; Toussaint, *The Trusteeship System of the United Nations*, 1960.

[156] See, Rouard de Card, *Le statut de Tanger d'après la Convention du 18 décembre 1923*, 1925.

[157] See, Hostie, Le statut international de Danzig, RDILC 1933 512.

[158] Coursier, *Le statut international du territoire de la Sarre*, 1935. The region was atteched to Germany after a plebiscite in 1935, and to France after the Second World War. It was proposed to give the region, administered by France, a 'European status' in 1954, a proposition which was rejected by a vast majority. The Luxemburg Agreement of 1956 provided for a return of the area to Germany, see, Colliard, *Institutions des relations internationales*, 9th ed., 1990, 129. On *demilitarised areas*, see my *Law of War, op. cit.,* 142 *et seq.*

[159] This regime lasted from 1947 until 1954. On the details of administration, see Leprette, Le statut international de Trieste, 1948.

There are, at present, only one protectorate[160] and hardly any trust territories.[161] There are some *condominia*, for example, Andorra.[162] These territories, are, or were, considered in international law as being international persons capable of assuming rights and obligations, and may be considered to enjoy *residuary sovereignty*.[163] However, the types of these internationally administered territories furnish ample examples of the refined mechanisms of international law.

d. International Organisations

See my own work on *Law Making by International Organisations*, 1965; Reuter, *Institutions internationales*, 1975; Abi-Saab, (ed.), *The Concept of International Organisations*, 1981, and his own article by the same name, *ibid.*; Colliard, *Institutions des relations internationales*, 9th ed., 1990; Valticos, International Organisations and International Law, JAIL 1986 1; Dehousse, *Les organisations internationales, Essai de théorie générale*, 1968; Virally, *Définition et classifications des organisations internationales*, 1951; Seidl-Hohenveldern, *Das Recht der internationalen Organisationen einschliesslich der supranationalen Gemeinschaften*, 4th ed., 1984; Carillo Salcedo, *El derecho internacional en un mondo de cambio*, 1984; Merle, *Les acteurs dans les relations internationales*, 1986: Monaco, *Scritti di diritto delle organizzazioni internazionale*, 1981; Diez de Velasco, *Instituciones de derecho internacional publico*, 1986; Dupuy, R.J., (ed.), *A Handbook of International Organisations*, 1988; Schermers, *International Institutional Law*, 2nd ed., 1980; Bowett, *International Institutions*, 4th ed., 1982; Shin-Tsai Chen, *The Theory and Practice of International Organisations*, 1973; Panebianco, *Introduzione al diritto della organizzazione internazionale*, 1987; Ribbelink, *Opvolging van internationale organisaties*, 1988; Taylor and Groom (eds.), *International Institutions at Work*, 1988; Partsch, 1989; Bokor-Szegö, International Organisations of Universal Character and the Domestic Legal Order of States, in *eadem, Questions of International Law: Hungarian Perspectives*, 1988.

(i) Traditional Criteria

160 On previous examples, see the detailed survey in I.i Oppenheim 9th ed. by Jennings & Watts, 270-274.
161 See *infra* under the Trusteeship Council.
162 Administered since 13th century by 'two princes', the Spanish Bishop of Urgel and the French Head of State, see Colliard, *Institutions des relations internationales*, 9th ed., 1990, 65.
163 *Cf.* I.i Oppenheim 9th ed., by Jennings & Watts 1992, 316.

Just as any other juridical person can be distinguished from its founders under various systems of municipal law, so can an international organisation be distinguished from its members. In other words, once an entity is sufficiently consolidated in the international sphere, it can act in its own name and assume its own rights and duties. Such an entity is considered to have *international personality*.[164] If it is devoid of such personality we are dealing with a mere *association* of States.[165] If, on the other hand, the organisation is sufficiently consolidated, it will constitute a separate international person which will override and overshadow the duties of its Member States, in the case when the organisation acts in its own right. The consequence is that there can be no piercing of the veil[166] and that the organisation must be liable for all duties assumed; no recourse can be made to the individual member States.[167]

An organisation where the members are States, are usually called *inter-governmental*. This term is used to emphasise that governments, or States, are members rather than private bodies or individuals. For some time many writers insist that organisations must be inter-governmental in order to qualify as international subjects, *i.e.* consist of *State* members.

Some inter-governmental organisations are, at closer analysis, not consisting only of States: the two oldest Specialised Agencies, the Universal Postal Union and the Telecommunications Union,[168] both include also *administrations*, that is to say either postal or telecommunications administrative units in areas which are not fully

---

[164]   *Cf. supra* and my *Law Making by International Organisations, op. cit.* Chapter One. See, *e.g., Re European Transport Agreement* (1971) 22/79 CMLR 335.

[165]   The name is obviously irrelevant. Thus, there is no question that the European Free Trade Association (EFTA) is an organisation, amply demonstrated by its treaty making practice alone. See, *infra*, and on EFTA as an organisation under international law, for example, my Association Européenne de Libre Echange (AELE/EFTA), in AF 1960.

[166]   With regard to companies, see the *Barcelona Traction Co.,* (1964) ICJ *Reports* 6.

[167]   *International Tin Council* 3 [1990] 2 AC 418; *Maclaine Watson v DTI [1988]* 3 All ER 257.

[168]   See *infra*, in this Chapter, under section b.

constituted States.[169] This illustrates the demands of writers that organisations must be truly inter-governmental are, consequently, at variance with State practice itself. In exceptional cases, other organisations may be allowed to join as members but this would be very rare. However, there is now a recent trend for the European Union to join organisations as a full members, sometimes in their place and sometimes doubling up with its own members; in this latter case the voting strength of those States is thus re-enforced by an additional, as it were, corporate vote in the name of the EU.

The most important organisations, such as the United Nations and the European Union are all of the *inter-governmental* type, although the latter organisation to a large extent controls and regulates the behaviour not only of States but also of individuals.

In order to exist as an international organisation, it is necessary for an entity to possess permanent *organs* and, furthermore, that such organs have a more or less *permanent* character, and that the entity is sufficiently *consolidated* to be able to act in its own name.[170]

That such criteria are useful and accepted in international society is clear, at least since the important Advisory Opinion of the International Court of Justice in the *Reparations for Injuries Case*[171] was delivered in 1949. After this important Opinion of the World Court, few writers, except for isolated academic opinion,[172] denied that also international organisations are subjects of international law. There was, for a while, a tendency in Soviet writings[173] to deny the personality of international organisations. There is now, however, overwhelming authority that the inter-governmental organisations are important bearers of rights and obligations in international society. Apart from the important case concerning the UN, we can refer to other authorities for the international personality of the European

---

[169]   See, in detail, my *Law Making, op. cit.,* Chapter Four.

[170]   *Ibid.,* Chapter One, and my *Treaty-Making Power of International Organisations,* (Thesis), Oxford, 1962, Chapter One.

[171]   (1949) ICJ *Reports* 174.

[172]   Jenks, The Legal Personality of International Organisations, BYIL, 1945, 267.

[173]   See, my *Concept, op. cit.,* 22-24. Note the insistance of the USSR to replace the Secretary General by a Triumvirate, in order to dilute his influence.

Union (EU),[174] and it is clear that numerous other bodies enjoy international personality under the international legal order.[175]

In the past, many international organisations have exercised functions within specified, limited - often technical - fields. Discussions about the European Community, or now, the European Union,[176] concern, at times, its alleged *supranationality*: it is said to be even more than states and thus above its members. This largely exaggerated argument often misses the point that the Community actually lacks a territorial base for any statehood. The European Community certainly represent a further step in terms of organisational development and enjoy a large measure of legislative power, often replacing that of the member states. As their legislation is directly applicable in the member states, the Community do, in a sense, have its *subjects*, enhanced by the projected Maastricht Treaty, which speaks of *citizens of the European Union*.[177] These subjects are then persons beyond the sphere of the civil servants working for the organisation and comprise, apart from the member states themselves, also their citizens. But however developed the Community may be as an international organisation there is one criteria for statehood which it does not fulfil: it does not have a territory over which it exercises *general* functions.[178]

Considering the criteria of *permanence, organs* and *consolidation*, in turn, it may be useful to point out that it is not always necessary that the original founder-members had the *intention* of creating a permanent structure with proper organs. It can be that an entity

---

[174] *Re European Road Transport Agreement*, (1978) 22/70 CMLR 335; *Maclaine Watseon v DTI* [1988] 3 All ER 257.

[175] See *Arab Monetary Fund v Hashim (No. 3)* [1991] 1 All ER 871 concerning the right to sue, allowed, on appeal to the House of Lords but only as they could show that the plaintiffs could show that they were incoporated as a company in Abu Dhabi. This is too restrictive a view.

[176] See further *infra*.

[177] Under the Treaty original nationality of the Member States will be retained but will be supplemented by the overriding citizenship of the Community of all nationals. That this would be unconstitutional was alleged by Lord Reese-Mogg, a former editor of the *Times*, who in July 1993 took legal action in the High Court in London to preclude ratification by Britain of the Maastricht Treaty.

[178] *Cf. supra* in this Chapter under Criteria of a State, Organs.

develops into such a permanent entity. Once an entity have permanent organs, it becomes academic to argue that they do not *exist*. Efforts to create a Multilateral Trade Organisation (MTO) are currently being discussed. Although its founders may have intended organs or regimes to be *provisional*, such intentions may be overtaken by time itself: to say that GATT is not an international organisation is to say the least absurd to anyone who has walked past its huge building in Geneva where it was established as a temporary and transitional measure 43 years ago, awaiting the coming into being of an International Trade Organisation (ITO) which still does not exist. Efforts to establish a trading organisation, now called multilateral, (MTO) are still being discussed. GATT has established rules on trade which are followed *de facto* by its 89 members and by a further 29 States, representing together about 4/5ths of the world trade and can for all practical purposes be said to be an international organisation.[179]

The requirement that the entity must be sufficiently *consolidated* to be able to act in its own name implies that the members have endowed the entity with some minimum powers vis-à-vis the founders themselves. Such powers need, of course, not at all imply any right to take binding decisions, although some resolutions, for example concerning staff matters and headquarters may always entail obligations for the founders.[180] Even when an organisation is inter-governmental, and clearly active in the international field, the question can thus arise as to whether it is sufficiently consolidated to be an international subject. This was answered, not surprisingly, in the affirmative in one of the recent *Tin Council Cases*.[181]

The fact that an organisation can conclude *treaties* has by some been thought to be relevant to the question concerning its specific consolidation.[182] But capacity to conclude treaties may well flow from the fact that the organisation has international personality, and thus be a *consequence* rather than a *precondition* of such personality.

---

[179]   *Cf.* similarly, Verdross and Simma, *Völkerrecht*, 1984, 213.

[180]   *Cf.* my *Law Making, op. cit., passim* and *infra* under The Legal Value of Recommendations of International Organisations.

[181]   *Rayner (Mincing Lane) v DTI*, [1989], 3 WLR 879.

[182]   *Cf.* First Report by Waldock to the International Law Commission, *ILC Yearbook*, 1962, ii, 31 on the Law of Treaties.

The fact that an organisation like NATO was not even a party to its own Headquarters Agreement may indicate lack of personality but, naturally, there are other ways that an entity can manifest its independence of its members.

The distinction between an organisation and an association of States is paramount. The main question concerns the *imputation* of acts to the organisation or to the members, a question which is of basic importance to the question of legal responsibility for acts.[183]

Some[184] suggest that the difference between 'limited functional independence' and legal personality is merely a matter of degree. There is little truth in this statement as it is not always necessary, or appropriate, to conceive personality as having substantial meaning, of which you can have 'more' or 'less'; it is more useful to consider personality merely as a formal concept, serving to apportion and allocate responsibility by simple imputation process;[185] an act is thus 'led back' to an actor, which, in the case of an organisation is that entity itself rather than its member States. Questions concerning transparency and lifting the corporate veil, familiar from company and banking law, then become relevant. Whether or not responsibility is assumed by the *organisation* or its *members,* and whether there is any subsidiary responsibility for members with regard to undertaking of an organisation, can be a crucial question of financial or other type of burden.[186] On the other hand, secrecy or confidentiality is obviously less of a problem in an international intergovernmental organisation than in company law.

Some international organisations are founded by treaties, and one may perhaps say that a ratified treaty is the normal basis of an inter-governmental organisation. But there are exceptions. The General Agreement on Tariffs and Trade was only ratified by one State; the entity which is now known as GATT, and which, at least *de facto,* is

---

[183] *Cf. supra* under Traditional Criteria.

[184] *E.g.*, Brownlie, *Principles, op. cit.* 682.

[185] Brownlie denies the usefulness of this important notion on which, for example, criminal law and, to a large extent, tort relies, see, his *State Responsibility,* 1983, 36-37.

[186] *Cf., supra,* the *Tin Council Cases,* for example *Rayner (Mincing Lane) v DTI,* [1989], 3 WLR 879.

a fully fledged international organisation,[187] relies for its functioning on a provisional Protocol of 1947.[188] The European Space Agency was originally formed under French law as a company but was converted in 1975 to an inter-governmental organisation.[189] The conversion, however, was carried out by Treaty. The way an organisation is established is not necessarily relevant; what is essential is how and in what way the organisation actually acts and functions in practice.

As we shall see, there is little difference, in terms of legal consequences or political influence, or position in international society, between so called inter-governmental organisations of the traditional type and the increasingly important non-governmental organisations (NGOs)

(ii) Normal Structure of International Organisations

International Organisations have commonly a *plenary organ*, often called an *Assembly* or a *Conference*,[190] where all Member States are represented. Such a plenary organ is not appropriate to take care of day to day affairs so normally there is an *executive organ*, often called *Council*, or *Board*, to attend to such matters.

In addition, some organisations may have a Court of Justice.[191] In nearly all cases, there is a large number of *subsidiary organs* to which matters may be delegated on certain conditions.[192]

It is important to underline the effect organisational structure has on constitutional division of power in Member States. The fact that it is the Government of a State, or its Ministries and Departments, that send delegates to international organisations, contributes to a *shifting of power* in Member States *from the legislative, i.e.* from

---

[187] See further *infra* under Economic Organisations.

[188] See, *supra.*

[189] The conversion was, however, carried out by treaty.

[190] In an organisation with comparatively few Members, like the European Community, the plenary organ may be called a 'Council'.

[191] As, for example, the Council of Europe, the European Community or the United Nations.

[192] See my *Law Making, op. cit.,* 57 *et seq.*

Parliament, *to the executive,* that is to say the Government and its departments. This development has been going on nearly unchecked and nearly unchallenged especially since the end of the Second World War and yet this decline of parliamentary participation is a serious threat to democratic influence on the work of international organisations.

In Sweden, this shifting of power is particularly serious, partly because it has been overlooked and given rise to little public debate, partly because parliamentary power has already dwindled by massive delegation of functions to the government and its ministries.[193]

(iii) Normal Powers of International Organisations

Much of the law of international organisations concerns details and administrative matters which may change from time to time. Lawyers should attach more attention to the broad picture of the function of organisations and it is therefore useful to mention, briefly, what their main powers and functions are in contemporary international society.

Organisations may always carry out what I have called *primary acts.*[194] These are acts which concern internal matters such as staff and headquarters and rules of procedure, as well as some external matters such as budgetary matters. *Primary* matters may be a better term than 'internal' affairs as most of such primary matters are those which have to be attended to *before* an organisation starts working for the specific aims it is supposed to further. Many such matters are 'internal' (such as staff, headquarters and minor matters of procedure), but all acts do not merely concern internal functioning: the budget, involving decisions immediately directed to the Member States, being one notable exception.

Organisations do not have to be specifically authorised to decide on primary matters as it is in the nature of their normal work to decide on such questions. Some of the acts are taken from time to time, or yearly, but most of them will have to be decided on, in

---

[193]   This unchecked situation is aggravated by the lack of a constitutional court, and by the existence of popular courts, with politically nominated laymen with equal votes of the Judge.

[194]   See my *Law Making, op. cit., passim.*

general, *before* the organisations take up the work for which they were created.[195]

When the organisations start work towards the objectives for which they were created, they will take *operative acts,*[196] that is to say acts which are to further their special aims of particular organisations.

It is then in the nature of things that *primary acts* will be *the same,* or *similar,* in all organisations, whereas *operative acts* will *differ* from organisation, to organisation, and will depend on for which purposes the organisation was created.[197]

There is a wide scope for *implied powers,*[198] to enable organisations to achieve the aims for which they were created and these powers include also considerable rights of delegation, as well as a right to establish numerous subsidiary organs, with the budgetary consequences this may have for the Member States.[199]

The *voting pattern* of an organisation also reflects what power its Member States enjoy and to what extent the rule of sovereign equality is maintained. A system with weighted voting, by which States have different voting power, is employed in the European Community where the actual *economic power* of States is mirrored in voting strength. In most organisations, however, there is equal voting power although majority votes are often used; qualified majority decision being reserved for 'important' matters and unanimity for 'very important' issues, such as revision of the basic treaty and other far reaching measures.

Speaking of majority votes in an organisation like the United Nations, it may be worth remembering the watering-out effect that the increase of membership has had on the voting strength of a founding State which was an initial signatory to the Charter in 1946: its vote in 1946 was worth 1/50th and now, in 1992, it has been diluted to 1/170th, or what the current ever increasing membership of the UN has reached.

---

[195]   See my *Law Making, op. cit., passim.*
[196]   This is the term I chose to distinguish these acts, *ibid., passim.*
[197]   See further my *Law Making, op. cit.,* Chapter One.
[198]   See my *Law Making, op. cit.,* 24 *et seq.*
[199]   See, in detail, my *Law Making, op. cit., passim.*

In this context, it is also relevant to note the shift of power in favour of some executive officers of organisations that was certainly foreseen by the States that founded the organisations. For example, the UN Secretary General has by far exceeded any power granted him under the Charter.[200]

(iv) Normal Privileges of Organisations

Bedjaoui, *Fonction publique internationale et influences nationales*, 1958; Kunz, Privileges and Immunities of international organisations, AJIL 1947; Cahier, *Etude des accords de siège conclus entre les organisations internationales et les pays où elles résident*, 1959; *Cf.* Bogdanov, *Pravovye vaprosi prebivanitya OON v SSHA*, 1962.

In order for organisations to be able to carry out their functions efficiently, they are also granted certain privileges usually in the form of *immunity* for their staff members (certain executives and delegates) as well as for their premises, much on the same line as diplomats. However, immunity is usually limited to acts taken on duty, as is normal in the case of consuls, and does not cover private transactions or acts.

There is a general Convention on Immunities and Privileges of the United Nations of 1946 and another Convention on Immunities and Privileges of the Specialised Agencies of 1948 (as revised). It is important to distinguish these Conventions, which are agreements *between the Member States* in favour of an organisation, and the Headquarters Agreements which are agreements concluded *by an organisation and a host State*.[201]

Organisations are usually tied to one particular host State where they have their headquarters. Headquarters Agreements[202] may specify and enlarge privileges and immunities, but, contrary to the general agreements on immunities which operate vis-à-vis *all* Member States, Headquarters Agreements only envisage privileges *in the particular host State*.

---

[200]   See further *infra* under United Nations, Secretary General.

[201]   See my *Law Making, op. cit.*, 124 *et seq.*

[202]   On the nature of such agreements, see my *Law Making, op. cit.*, 118-139.

(v) The Main Organisations

This is not the place for any detailed study of specific organisations. The reader will be well aware of, and specifically referred to, competent monographs on certain organisations.

However, this Chapter treats international organisations *qua* subjects of international law and also seeks to identify certain characteristics which are relevant to the study of international organisations in this respect. We shall therefore analyse, above all, the place of organisations alongside States in the structure of international society.

1. THE UNITED NATIONS

Virally, *L'organisation mondiale,* 1972; Kelsen, *The Law of the United Nations,* 1964; Goodrich, Hambro and Simons, *The United Nations,* 3rd ed., 1969; Jimenez de Arechaga, *Derecho constitucional de las Naciones Unidas,* 1958, Bindschedler, R., La délimitation des compétences des Nations Unies, 108 RCADI 1963 312; Higgins, *The Development of International Law Through the Political Organs of the United Nations,* 1963.

for recent literature, note:

Simma, *Charta der Vereinten Nationen, Kommentar,* 1990; Cot and Pellet, *La Charte des Nations Unies, Commentaire article par article,* 1985; Bardonnet (ed.), *L'adaptation des structures et méthodes des Nations Unies, Colloque,* The Hague, 1986; *Cf.,* Cot and Pellet, Les Nations Unies? Mais encore? *Monde diplomatique,* November 1990, 17.

The United Nations succeeded the League of Nations[203] as a World Organisation in 1945. The League had been formed in 1919, to be based in Geneva, after the First World War, and had also attempted to prevent another war. However, the provisions of the Covenant of the League were weak and deficient and did not effectively rule out

---

[203] Scelle, *La Pacte de la Société des Nations et sa liaison avec les Traités de Paix,* 1919; Rousseau, *La compétence de la Société des Nations dans le règlement des conflits internationaux,* thèse, 1927; Redslob, *Théorie de la Societé des Nations,* 1927; Guggenheim, *Der Völkerbund,* 1932; Andrassy, La soverainté et la Société des Nations, RCADI 37 iii.

the use of force.[204] Furthermore, the League of Nations was undermined by the fact that the United States was not a member, and to some extent, by the fact that the Permanent Court of International Justice (PCIJ), established at the same time as the League in The Hague, was not part of the Organisation.

The UN set out to remedy some of the faults of the League: article 2(4) of the Charter vigorously prohibits any military use of force;[205] the United States was to take an active part; the newly formed International Court of Justice (ICJ) in the Hague was to be a main organ of the Organisation.

The United Nations has, as its declared purposes, to maintain international peace and security, based on respect for equality of nations and for the self-determination of peoples. The Organisation also aims at achieving international cooperation to deal with certain economic, social cultural or humanitarian problems.

However, its powers do not match these aims. For one thing, the aims are vague and non-defined or, at least, too vast to be obtained through the machinery of the United Nations. The UN has, on the other hand, served as a useful platform for discussion, for diffusion of tension and has provided a valuable framework for diplomatic operations.

The six principal organs of the UN are the Security Council, the General Assembly, the Secretary General, the Economic and Social Council (ECOSOC), the Trusteeship Council and the International Court of Justice.

(a) The Security Council

Jimenez de Arechaga, Le traitment des différends internationaux par le Conseil de Securité, 85 RCADI 1954; Brugière, *La règle de l'unanimité des membres permanents du Conseil de Securité*, 1952; Bailey, *Voting in the Security Council*, 1969; Boyd, *Fifteen Men on a Power Keg: a History of the Security Council*, 1971; Flory, M., L'ONU et les opérations de maintien de la paix, AF 1965 446; Gentile, Competenza del Consiglio di Sicurezza el del Assemblea Generale in materia di manitenimento o ristabilimento della pace, *Comunicazioni e Studi*, 1953 285; Kahn, *Law, Politics and the Security Council*, 2nd ed., 1969; Kerley, The powers of

---

[204] See, further my *Law of War, op. cit.*, 54 et seq.

[205] See, in detail, *infra*, under Prophylactic Rules.

investigation of the Security Council, AJIL, 1961, 892: Schachter, The quasi-judicial role of the Security Council and the General Assembly, AJIL 1964 960; *Cf.*, Rousseau, Statistique des vétos au Conseil de Sécurité, RGDIP 1990 931 and preceding volumes.

The Security Council used to be of great importance during the time of the two superpowers but has now, after the collapse of the Soviet Union, declined in importance. It consists of fifteen member States of which five are *permanent members*, *i.e.* US, UK, France, China and the CIS, successors of USSR. There are ten[206] non-permanent members of the Security Council.

The most important power of the Security Council is undoubtedly to decide whether there exists a *threat* to international peace and security under article 39 of Chapter VII of the Charter. It can then also decide whether there has been an act of aggression[207] when it can take *emergency action.*

Some of the powers of the Security Council have been carried out with respect to the UN troops, who have been dispatched to maintain peace in troubled areas.[208]

A dramatic resolution in October 1992 on *seizure* of Iraqi funds which would be diverted to defray UN expenses may highlight the elastic limit of powers that the Security Council claims to have but which, without an most liberal interpretation, would not have the legitimate basis in the Charter.

Most of the decisions of the Security Council are, in essence, recommendations and, as such, non-binding.[209] However, if the Council sees it as important, it can make its decisions binding and if these are issued (which is rarely the case) under article 25 of the Charter, the Member States are obliged to carry them out as binding resolutions. Such *binding decisions* can be coupled with *emergency*

---

[206] The number was increased from six to ten after a revision of the UN Charter in 1966.

[207] See also the 1970 GA Resolution 2625 (XXV) Declaration on Friendly Relations of 1970 and the GA Resolution 3314 (XXIX) of 1974 on Definition of Aggression.

[208] See, on the UN forces, Higgins, *The United Nations Peace Keeping Forces,* 1969 - (numerous volumes).

[209] See, *infra*, on Recommendations.

action under Chapter VII.

The Security Council remains *a power organ* of the United Nations which, technically, can demand States to obey. The competence of the Security Council, however, has for years reflected the split between East and West at the expense of the promotion of respect for international law and for Human Rights.

The effective functioning of the Security Council has, above all, been impeded by the use of the *veto*, or by leaving the Council,[210] tactics which preempt the adoption of a valid decision.[211]

The limitations of the powers of the Security Council were clearly demonstrated in the Bosnian war. Only belatedly, when many innocent lives had already been lost, did the Security Council condemn the Serbian aggression and their abhorrent policy of *ethnic cleansing* whereby large groups were tortured and killed in obvious violation of the Genocide Convention and of general rules of international law on Human Rights.[212] The plight of the attacked nations, Bosnia-Herzegovina and Croatia, was made worse by UN sanctions which prohibited any purchase of arms to defend the attacked countries, in spite of these States having been internationally recognised by a vast number of other States.[213]

The functioning of the Security Council has, above all, been effectively impeded by the use of the *veto*, or the practice to leave the Council by walking out (*chaise vide*). These two practices preempt the valid adoption of decision.[214] Although the Security Council has the right to take *authoritative action*, the Members of the United Nations have an immediate interest in ensuring that this power is exercised *legitimately*. There is, as yet, no mechanisms to verify that

---

[210] The policy of what the French call '*la chaise vide*'.

[211] On this point with regard to the Korean crisis and the alleged invalidity of the attempted decision in the Security Council, see my *Law Making, op. cit.,* 60 with references. The action was probably better qualified as 'collective' international action under US command; *cf.* Bastid, Mme S., *Cours de droit international public,* Paris 1951-1952, 340.

[212] See further *infra* under Human Rights.

[213] There was specific and early recognition extended by the European Community,

[214] See discussion of this point in relation to the adoption of a decision relating to action in Korea, in my *Law Making, op. cit.,* 60, 71, 202.

this is the case. The United Nations should, it is suggested, provide its own Constitutional Court to examine compatibility of certain action with the Charter.

(b) The General Assembly

There is no recent comprehensive study of the General Assembly; Vallat, The competence of the UN General Assembly, 97 RCADI 1959; Brugière, *Les pouvoirs des Nations Unies en matière politique et de securité*, 1955; Bailey, *The General Assembly of the United Nations*, 1964.

The Security Council is the restricted executive organ of the United Nations. On the other hand, The General Assembly is, in a sense, the parliamentary body of the UN, composed by delegates from all the member States. However, the General Assembly is deprived of real power and has only, under the Charter, the power of making recommendations.[215] The Assembly *discusses* problems and is an important forum for debate and lobbying.

It is also to be remarked that, if the Security Council does not act in a time of crisis, the General Assembly can take over: this was demonstrated in the famous Uniting for Peace Resolution of 1950.[216] This Resolution stated that, if functioning of the Security Council is blocked by a veto, the General Assembly

'shall consider the matter immediately with a view to making appropriate recommendations to Members for collective measures, including, in the case of a breach of the peace or act of aggression, the use of force when necessary, to restore international peace and security'.

By this Resolution, a *de facto* revision of the UN Charter took place and the General Assembly assumed some of the Security Council powers in time of crisis. Applying the said Resolution in 1956 the General Assembly established and dispatched the UN troops to Egypt,

---

[215] On the legal force of such recommendations, see, *infra*, under Sources of Law, Recommendations, in Chapter IV.

[216] GA Res 377 (V) 1950. On this famous Resolution, see my *Law Making by International Organisations*, 1965, 37 *et seq.*

the United Nations Emergency Force (UNEP) - the first blue berets - during the time of the Suez crisis when the Security Council, much because of a Soviet veto, was unable to act.[217] The Uniting for Peace Resolution was also used in 1980 with respect to Afghanistan. However, action taken by the General Assembly is not to be categorised as *enforcement action*[218] as demonstrated in the *Expenses Case*.[219]

The normative function of the General Assembly[220] is most significant as the Assembly by various resolutions certainly contributes to the *crystallisation of international norms*, even if such resolutions are technically non-binding.[221]

(c) The Secretary General

Smouts, *Le Secretaire Général des Nations Unies*, 1971; Rovine, *The First Fifty Years, The Secretary General in World Politics*, 1970; Virally, Le rôle politique du Secretaire Général des Nations Unies, AF 1958 360; *idem*, Le testament politique de Dag Hammarskjöld, AF 1961 255; Schwebel, *The Secretary General of the United Nations, His Political Powers and Practice*, 1952.

The Secretary General is the head of the UN administration;[222] he is appointed by the General Assembly on the recommendation of the Security Council. The Secretary General is entitled to bring any question bearing on peace and security to the attention of the Security Council and he is expected to use his own initiative in this respect.

The importance of the office of the Secretary General varies according to the person who holds office: at times the Secretary General has been extremely influential in international politics, at times he has been ignored. The height of the office was presumably

---

217   See *supra*, previous page, on the Korean crisis. In the Suez affair there was never any question of alleged illegality of the decision as the General Assembly undoubtedly can take majority decisions under the Charter.

218   *Supra* under Security Council.

219   (1962) ICJ *Reports* 151.

220   See on this *infra* under The Legal Value of Recommendations.

221   See further *infra*.

222   Bastid, S., Statut juridique des fonctionnaires des Nations Unies, 1955; Langrod, Le secretariat de l'ONU, AV 1956; Bailey, *The Secretariat of the United Nations*, 1964.

during the time of Dag Hammarskjöld, a Secretary General who exercised his function with diplomacy and discretion. Recently, the office of Secretary General has been questioned and assumed less importance as there has been heavy-handed interference in matters outside the relevant latitude of competence as foreseen by the Charter.

The Secretary General has recently assumed power, not at all anchored in the Charter, and which surpasses what the members could expect to be warranted, and also despatches senior officers to control compliance with arms treaties which they have not ratified. Such excesses are bound to rebound in hostility against the increasingly patronising attitude of the United Nations.

The present Secretary General, Mr Boutros Boutros Ghali, a professor of international law, has also surprisingly demonstrated an ambition to extend the powers of his office in the Croatian crisis when the consent of the territorial power was given too little attention. Instead of protecting the invaded country, Croatia, from hostile communist forces, the Secretary General sought to *mediate* between what was called 'hostile factions', an attitude which appeared to many as unwarranted as there was clearly a case of aggression by a heavily armed organised Serbian army on defenceless civilians[223] in countries all outside Serbia, in turn a country where not one single shot had been fired. In this context, a clear condemnation of, for example, ethnic cleansing could have been forthcoming from a powerful Secretary General; but from Mr Boutros Boutros Ghali there was no such message.

There were questionable excesses of power when the Secretary General countermanded decisions taken by the United Nations High Commissioner for Refugees (UNHCR), Mrs Sadako Odako, with regard to Bosnia, indicating petty rivalry and personal splits in an organisation which should symbolise harmony and peace.

d. ECOSOC

Vellas and Inchaupse, *Les compétences du Conseil économique et social des Nations Unies,* 1950; Delbez, Les pouvoirs du ECOSOC des Nations Unies, in *Etudes Scelle,*

---

[223]   It may be noted that not a single shot in the war has been fired on the territory of Serbia or Montenegro, Serbia's only ally.

vol. 1; Sharp, *The United Nations Economic and Social Council*, 1969.

The Economic and Social Council (ECOSOC), an innovation beyond the organic structure of the League of Nations, consists of 54 States.[224] Eighteen members are elected by the General Assembly to serve for a three year term.

By Resolution 28847 (XXVI) the composition of the Council favours the Third World: 14 members represent Africa, 11 Asia, 10 Latin America; beyond these, there are six members representing what, in 1971, was Eastern Europe, and 13 represent the rest of the World, that is to say the developed or industrialised States.

The Council is the head of organs like the High Commissioner of Refugees and of the Technical Assistance Committee. It also co-ordinates the activities of the specialised agencies.[225]

Article 63 of the Charter of the United Nations allows ECOSOC to establish special Commissions for its work,[226] especially for economic questions and to ensure enhanced respect for Human Rights.

e. The Trusteeship Council

Chowdhuri, *International Mandates and Trusteeship Systems*, 1955; Parry, The legal nature of trusteeship agreements, BYIL 1950 164; Vedovato, Les accords de tutelle, 76 RCADI 1950 609.

The Trusteeship Council has lost its importance after previous trust territories have become independent or joined other States.[227] The Council may, however, retain importance in case a territory is placed under UN supervision in the future.

---

[224] ECOSOC had initially 18 members, increased to 27 in 1963 and to 54 by Resolution 2847 (XXVI) of 1971.

[225] See on these organisations, *infra*.

[226] The Council would probably have this power anyway as establishment of subsidiary organs are subsumed under the the so called *implied powers* with which every institutional organ is endowed, see my *Law Making, op. cit.*, 29 *et seq.*

[227] On the dismantlement of virtually all trust arrangements, except for the Pacific island of Palua, see I:i Oppenheim, 9th ed. by Jennings & Watts, 1992, 308-318.

It became clear, in 1993, that there is considerable pressure to retain the trusteeship mechanism precisely to apply in the case of Bosnia, a country which the Great Powers - in 1993 as in 1914 - consider unworthy of separate existence and which the United Nations wish to force into collective supervision.

(f) The International Court of Justice (ICJ)

For a bibliography see *infra* under Consequential Rules.

We shall deal with the ICJ in the context of Consequential Rules of international society.[228] Here we may only briefly point out that the predecessor of the ICJ, the Permanent Court of International Justice, the PCIJ, was not an organ of the League of Nations which reduced its role; the ICJ plays a greater role as part of the World Organisation, the United Nations.

The ICJ reduced its own importance during a number of years by limiting its function to act as an arbitrator in border disputes. Although such disputes may be important, they are not on the level of other matters of substance. Recently, however, the ICJ has resumed its important role as mediator in more substantial matters.

2. THE SPECIALISED AGENCIES: THE TECHNICAL ORGANISATIONS

For examples of law making in international society, we can find some fascinating material in the extensive practice of international organisations. States, surprisingly enough, are often unaware (unless we speak about EC) of the power exercised, with the original, but forgotten, consent of States, or what I have called *abstract consent* given at the rime of founding an organisation.[229]

Attached to the United Nations, by means of loose cooperation agreements, are the *Specialised Agencies*. Three of these existed before the creation of the United Nations, namely the Universal Postal Union (UPU)[230] and the International Telecommunications Union

---

[228]   See *infra*.

[229]   See my *Law Making, op. cit.*, 322.

[230]   On UPU's regulatory power see my *Law Making, op. cit.*, 217 *et seq.*

(ITU),[231] created over 130 years ago to facilitate international communications, and the International Labour Organisation, created after the First World War in 1919.

The rest of the numerous Specialised Agencies were all created after the Second World War, in 1945, or later. Among these we may note the World Health Organisation (WHO), empowered to issue important rules on vaccination and other measures to combat epidemics.[232]

Other organisations, like the International Civil Aviation Organisation (ICAO),[233] issue binding Regulations for the Member States, through a restricted body of the organisation where not all members are represented and which normally takes a vote by majority. Decisions bind not only those who vote against them, but also those who are not represented on that body.

Other specialised agencies with technical aims are the International Maritime Organisation (IMO), the World Meteorological Organisation (WMO), the Food and Agriculture Organisation (FAO), the United Nations Educational, Scientific and Cultural Organisation (UNESCO), and the International Labour Organisation (ILO). Of these, the UPU, ITU, WHO and ICAO, and to some extent IMO, may take binding decisions by majority votes.[234]

To the superficial scholars who assume that the European Community has introduced *majority voting* it is useful to remember that we have, for over a hundred years, accepted to be bound, as States, by such majority voting through various technical organisations, like the UPU and ITU, now tied to the UN as technical specialised agencies. Not only has voting been taken by a majority vote in such organisations, but the voting body has been one not representing all the members but one where only a selection of these members were present, that is to say by a restricted, or *executive* body of the Organisation.[235]

| 231 | On ITU's regulatory power see *ibid.*, 223 *et seq.* |

231   On ITU's regulatory power see *ibid.*, 223 *et seq.*

232   On its regulatory powers, see my *Law Making, op. cit.*, 1965, 234 *et seq.*

233   See *ibid.*, 247 *et seq.*

234   See, in detail, my *Law Making, op. cit.*, Chapter Four.

235   See further, my *Law Making, op. cit.*, 247 *et seq.*

3. THE SPECIALISED AGENCIES: THE ECONOMIC ORGANISATIONS: THE BANK AND THE FUND

Broches, International legal aspects of the World Bank, 98 RCADI 1959 301; Aufricht, *The International Monetary Fund: Legal Basis, Structure, Functions,* 1964; Fawcett, The International Monetary Fund and international law, BYIL 1964 32.

Some of the specialised agencies, created to form part of the *UN system* after the Second World War have *economic functions* and are best treated separately. These are The International Bank for Reconstruction and Development (IBRD) or, more popularly, The World Bank, and the International Monetary Fund (IMF) or *The Fund.*

Although much power has been given to the aforementioned specialised agencies with technical tasks, little decision-making power has been delegated to the global economic organisations. Thus, the World Bank, that is the International Bank for Reconstruction and Development (IBRD), and the International Monetary Fund (IMF), have no power of decision[236] unless their member States fully agree.

It is precisely because of the functional and technical character that it has been possible to grant considerable decision-making power to the technical specialised agencies. Conversely, it is precisely because of the economic aims of the World Bank and of the Fund that it has been difficult to endow these organisations with the power of decision and they are therefore in charge of perhaps considerable factual economic power but unable to formally bind their Member States by decisions or regulations. On the other hand, the mere refusal of loans and of drawing rights reflect by itself a different form of obligatory decision, from which there is no appeal.[237]

Naturally, these economic organisations have the power for

---

[236] Except in the field of *primary,* often *internal* matters, such as administration of headquarters, staff, etc., see further *infra* and my *Law Making, op. cit.,* Chapter One.

[237] An appeal to the General Assembly is not likely to be effective; the ICJ can be approached to give an Advisory Opinion, but only if the Security Council, the General Assembly or an organ empowered by the General Assembly, so demands; see *infra.*

internal regulation,[238] or the power for what I have called *primary matters* (as some of these matters are 'external' in the sense that they concern the Member States;[239] one example may be the budget, which is certainly not only an 'internal' matter.

Furthermore, their external power, often exercised in conjunction with their Member States, should not be underestimated. The Bank thus is an important instigator of development projects in the Third World. The Fund is an important lender of money and provides drawing facilities to numerous countries.

4. THE EUROPEAN UNION (EU)

Hartley, *The European Community*, 1987; Kapteyn and van Themaat, *Introduction to the Law of The European Community*, 1989; Plender and Usher, *Cases and Materials in the Law of the European Communities*, 1989.

(a) The Purpose of the EU

This is not the place to explain the complicated structure and powers of the European Community (EC), now called the European Union (EU), but only for some comments to place this organisation amidst other subjects of international law.

The European Coal and Steel Community (CECA or ECSC) was formed in 1952,[240] by the Paris or the *Montan* Treaty, to create a common market for the base industries of war, coal and steel. A common market implies a free market with tariff and quota-free circulation for manpower, goods and capital together with a common external barrier, which distinguishes it from a mere free trade area.

As a common market in the base industries of war would prevent a future war in Europe, especially between Germany and France, it was thought expedient to add, in 1958 nuclear energy as another type of base industry of war, and EURATOM was created.[241] The

---

238   See, my *Law Making, op. cit.* 42 *et seq.*, and *supra*, under Normal Powers of Organisations.

239   *Ibid., loc. cit.*

240   See, Reuter, *La Communauté Européenne du Charbon et de l'Acier*, 1952.

241   Pirotte *et al.*, Trente ans d'expérience: EURATOM, La naissance d'une Europe nucléaire, 1988.

general economic organisation, The European Economics Community (EEC),[242] was formed at the same time, in 1958, by the Rome Treaties.

The original six members, France, Germany Italy, and the Benelux countries (Belgium, Netherlands and Luxembourg) were joined by the United Kingdom, Ireland and Denmark in 1972, by Greece in 1981 and by Spain and Portugal in 1986.

The legal system of the European Union is part of international law as a sub-system of an international organisation. The inner law of the EU, however, is based essentially on French administrative law which inspired numerous provisions of the Paris and Rome Treaties.

The essential features of the European Union is that its organs can bind its Member States and *their companies and citizens,* its laws and regulations have force *superior to that of internal laws, including constitutional rules,* and its powers rely on constant and increasing *delegation of sovereignty.*[243]

Furthermore, the Union governs matters with a *European element*[244] and sets out to harmonise rules in Europe.

(b) The Institutions

Freestone and Davidson, *The Institutional Framework of the European Communities,* 1988; Läufer, *Die Organe der EG,* 1989; Capotorti, *Lo status giuridico del Consiglio europeo alla luce dell'Atto unico,* 1988.

---

[242] See, above all, Hartley, *The European Community, op. cit.* Note that most early literature about CECA (ECSC), CEE (EEC) and Euratom, was published in French and German, the prevailing official languages of the Community before the United Kingdom joined. See, for example, Reuter, *La Communauté Economique du Charbon et de l'Acier,* 1952; Everling, Glaesner & Sprung, *Die Europäische Wirtschaftsgemeinshaft,* 1960. (The other official languages before 1973 were German, Italian and Dutch).

[243] Such delegation is of a temporary and conditional character. Member States are undoubtedly entitled to *resume* this delegated sovereignty and leave the Organisation; that this would cause economic and political problems is obvious but the *legal right* to leave the organisation undoubtedly subsists.

[244] *Bulmer v Bollinger* [1974] Ch 401 *per* Lord Denning.

(1) The Commission

Louis, Le rôle de la Commission dans la procédure en manquement selon la jurisprudence récente de la Cour de Justice, in *Du droit international au droit de l'intégration*, 1987, 397; Mangas Martin, El Acta Unica Europea y las modalidades de ejercicio de las competencias de ejecución atribuidas a la Comisión, RevInstEur 1988, 789.

The EU consists of a Commission,[245] where seventeen members act in their personal capacity. The *personal capacity* implies that they may not take instructions or act on behalf of the Member States or on behalf of any other interests.

The Commission exercises different functions under the three treaties and has considerably more powers under the Coal and Steel Community Treaty than under the EURATOM and the general EC Treaty.

Numerous Regulations binding national companies and also individuals, as well as Member States, are issued by the Commission.

The Commission is the Union watchdog and often brings matters before the Union Court when a State, a firm or a Union institution has been at fault under the Treaties.

(2) The Council

Dewost, *Les pouvoirs discrétionnaires du Conseil des ministres*, 1988; Meier, Jahrbuch EurInt 1987/88, 51.

The Council of Ministers consists of one representative from each Member State and has, as such, great powers to bind the Member States, their firms and their citizens.

The Council acts by weighted voting, which implies that some of the twelve countries have *stronger voting power* than others. The voting power is assessed on the basis of the respective GNP of the

---

[245] The Commission, the executive of the Community, consists of the three special executives of the three Communities, the Coal and Steel High Authority and the EEC and EURATOM Commissions, *merged* into one Commission in 1965. See Maugius, *Le Traité de Bruxelles du 8 avril 1965 relatif à la fusion des institutions des Communautés européennes*, Centre doc., Faculté de Lyon, 1965.

country. France, Germany, UK and Italy have ten votes; Spain has eight, Belgium, the Netherlands and Portugal have five votes; Greece, Ireland and Denmark have three and Luxembourg two.

Normally the Council acts by simple majority; occasionally, there is qualified majority for which then 54 votes are needed, cast by at least eight votes. On some matters unanimity is still required although there is a trend away form such requirement in the EU.

One common way to bind Member States is by issuing Directives, which are binding with regard to the end to be achieved but leaves it free to each Member State to decide on the means to be used to implement the Directive.

To bind the companies and individuals directly, the Council normally uses Regulations or Decisions.

The Council is assisted by the Committee of Permanent Representatives which consists of ambassadors of the Member States to the EU.

(3) The European Parliament

Chauchat, *Le contrôle politique du Parlement européenne sur les exécutifs communautaires*, 1989; Grabitz and Schmuck, *Direktwahl und Demokratisierung*, 1988; Louis and Wahlbroeck, *Le Parlement européen dans l'évolution institutionnelle*, 1988; Monaco, El Parlamento en el marco institucional de la Comunidad Europea, RevInstEur 1988, 715; Santaniello, Atto unico e Parlamento europeo, AffSoc 1988, 21.

The MEPs, Members of the European Parliament, did not have much status before the United Kingdom joined the EC, but the power of the European Parliament has recently grown. It may be a reflection of the importance of national Members of Parliament in England, that the European Parliament soon acquired a more important role.

To-day the European Parliament exercises very important functions with regard to budgetary questions but, above all, with regard to new membership. The Parliament has thus decisive powers when the Union considers applications from new members. It can also, by a vote of censure, force the Commission to resign.

A dispute about the site of the European Parliament, at present in Strasbourg from where France is unwilling to move it, concerns the location of the new EU Environmental Agency; this Agency, now working as a task force, cannot take its own headquarters in an EU country before agreement has been reached with France on the Parliament.

(4) The Court of Justice

Schermers, *Judicial Protection in the European Community,* 1979; Tomuschat, *Gerichtliche Vorabentscheidung,* 1965; *Cf.* Wegmann, *Nichtigkeitsklage gegen EG,* 1967; Herrmann, Entwicklung des Rechtsschutzes in europäischen Gerichtsbarkeit, *Rabels Zeitschrift* 1981, 413.

There are no appeals from the Union Court. It is composed of thirteen judges and there are six Advocates-General. The procedural system is largely derived from French procedural law.

National Courts have important rights under the Treaties to send questions to the Court for preliminary ruling in case there is doubt of interpretation.

Individuals may be parties to cases before the Court and firms are frequently taken to the EU Court for failing to follow EU rules. Individuals had already been given *locus standi* in the European Court of Human Rights; thus the European Union *is not innovative* in this respect as is often claimed. The sophisticated and developed process of the EU Court is, however, impressive, both as far as concerns the respect for the rule of law[246] and as far as concerns efficiency and clarity of judgments.

(5) The Court of First Instance

To off-load the Union Court the great burden of minor cases, mainly concerning points on competition, a Court of First Instance was established in 1988.[247] This Court is particularly concerned with cases concerning *competition.*

---

[246] Note that Human Rights and general principles securing natural justice are specifically incorporated, see Hartley, European Community, *op. cit.* and *supra.*

[247] JO 24th October 1988.

(c) The EU Impact

The EU is the world's largest trading unit, responsible for almost 40 per cent of the world trade. The EU has, however, political roots,[248] and has recently re-assessed its political ambitions.

One of the main features of the EU is that it binds, by its rules and decisions, individuals and firms in the Member States and not only the States themselves. Furthermore, individuals and firms have a right of complaint to the EU Court, a right frequently exercised. The focus of the EU on the *individual* is furthermore reflected in the fact that the rules on Human Rights, developed by the Court of Human Rights in Strasbourg, under the European Convention on Human Rights, has already been taken over and *absorbed* by the EU Court.[249] Any new Member, for example Sweden, which is now a candidate, thus becomes immediately and directly bound by the jurisprudence of the EU Luxemburg Court which has incorporated the entire case law on Human Rights of the Strasbourg Court.

Clear rules as to the right of individuals under the Treaties of Paris and Rome have developed, such as that an individual may enjoy right *directly* under an EC Treaty.[250] Furthermore, clear rules show that there must be no discrimination between individuals in the EU.[251]

A strength of the EU is that, by definition, its rules have to prevail over the laws of the Member States, a mechanism which secures uniform treatment within the Union.[252]

In Eastern Europe it has acted with great courage and resolution to guide the ex-communist countries to more viable economic systems. However, in this context it has sometimes overstepped its competence. Some inquired from where the EU derived its

---

[248]   *Cf. supra.*

[249]   See *infra* on Human Rights in Chapter IV.

[250]   *van Gend & Loos v Nederlandse Administratie der Belastingen* (1965) ECR 1.

[251]   See efforts of Spanish ships to register under the UK Merchant Shipping Act of 1988, eventually given relief, *Factortame Ltd v Secretary of State for Transport* [1990] 3 WLR 818 (AC).

[252]   See, for example, *Costa v ENEL* (1964) 585.

competence to send observers to Croatia to monitor the truce between the invading communist Federal Army and Croatia. Until the Serbian communist army shot down an EU helicopter, the EU took the view that the Federation must remain in power, although many questioned both the EU attitudes and its mandate on these questions.

A number of States are waiting to become new Members of the European Union. Austria has applied without any reservations whereas Sweden is acting in a somewhat ambiguous way, hoping for an unrealistic transitional organisation, the EES.[253]

The Maastricht Treaty - drafted to speed up and deepen political co-operation in Europe - appears, in 1993, to be failing: the Danes accepted the agreement only by a second ballot and the French achieved too narrow a vote in a referendum to warrant democratic support. There is an increasing opinion against the Treaty in the United Kingdom where a former editor of the *Times,* Lord Rees-Mogg took the unprecedented step of seeking to preclude ratification by a High Court action, demanding a greater influence of Parliament on the decision.[254] The paradoxical situation has arisen that Sweden, which is not a Member of the EU, is supporting the Treaty more than what the Member States do; the British government appears to have failing support among its own party for the treaty.

What is certainly disturbing, from the point of view of democratic safeguards, is that the Maastricht Treaty is virtually inaccessible. It was eventually published in England under the title *The Unseen Treaty*[255] to enable a more open debate. Similarly, the Treaty establishing the European Economic Space (EES) is similarly inaccessible by the mere fact that it consists of 16,000 pages which cannot be easily purchased by individuals. Although Sweden is currently discussing adhesion to the EES, the Treaty has, in its details, not even been discussed in Parliament.

The relatively new policy of secret treaties is in stark violation of President Wilson's 'Points', after the First World War, that, from then

---

[253] See *supra.*

[254] *Cf. supra* under States, Democracy and under Recognition, The Requirement of Democracy, in this Chapter.

[255] *The Maastricht Treaty, The Unseen Treaty,* London, 1992.

on, States would only condone 'open covenants openly arrived at'.[256]

The Maastricht Treaty *incorporates* the West European Union, a powerful defence alliance, as an essential new part of the Union. Naturally, Sweden could hardly discuss conditions of *neutrality* once the Maastricht Treaty has become effective (if it ever does) as this Treaty couples the Union with a defence alliance, coordinates foreign defence policy, and integrates further any defence industries.[257] Such development is clearly incompatible with any individual defence policy pursued by Sweden and also with concepts of *freedom from alliance* or *neutrality,*[258] vital to Sweden's foreign policy.

It is clear that the European Union looks after the interests of its members at the expense of other States. In other words, it is *against* liberalisation of trade outside its own *customs union,* which protects internal manufacturing and trade, and as the cooperation within EU deepens from a customs union into a *political union*, the notion *Fortress Europe* is increasingly used to indicate that the EU is looking after its own affairs behind unpenetrable walls. The notion, currently dismissed as unwarranted by EU representatives like Jacques Delors, is often used by outside commentators, especially in the United States, as a pejorative invective against the Union: there have been times recently when this hostility against the selfish policies of the EU nearly caused trade wars with the United States. It is at least clear that any ambition to provide substantial assistance[259] to the

---

[256] See my *Essays on the Law of Treaties*, 1967 on Publication of Treaties.

[257] After Sweden becomes a Member of the Community, Bofors, and other Swedish war material manufacturers, important earners of foreign exchange, will be completely regulated by Brussels decisions, regulations and directives and not necessarily allowed to retain their production.

[258] Sweden's traditional and declared foreign policy rests, according to manifestoes of *all* the political parties, on *freedom from alliances in peace* and *neutrality in war*. This distinction and this policy cannot be conceptually or practically combined with membership in the European Community.

[259] Clearly, we are hear speaking about relative values. Of course, it is possible, as an EC Member, to give *some* help to the Third World and the EC itself provides much such assistance. However, it is not possible, as an EC State, to help the Third World in any *substantial* way as this certainly involves *allowing for import of goods* from the Third World and this the EC, because of its external tariffs and quotas, cannot allow.

114

Third World is difficult to conceive as compatible with the aims of the European Union.[260]

5. OTHER INTERNATIONAL ORGANISATIONS

(a) Military and Security Organisations

Other organisations of importance can be grouped as those with predominant interest in military matters and security as the North Atlantic Treaty Organisation NATO),[261] the West European Union (WEU);[262] other organisations of this type are sometimes watered out to concern only *regional solidarity* as in the Organisation of American States (OAS),[263] as restructured following the Punta del Este and the Buenos Aires Declarations.[264]

All these organisations are marked by a definite trend towards unanimity votes and complete agreement between the Member States for any action.[265]

Naturally, among the political and military organisations there has been a considerable shift of importance following the demise of communism in Eastern Europe. NATO, which had as its counterpart another military bloc, the Warsaw Pact,[266] suddenly finds itself alone in its field in the region. Looking back at historical precedents of alliances, it is to be expected that other States now regroup into different blocs although permanent or quasi-permanent bloc building

---

260 It will be interesting to hear the Swedish Government's explanation how this problem - so far not at all tackled by the Government - will be resolved, especially in view of the Swedish declared policy to provide help for the Third World.

261 See Moore, *NATO and the Future of Europe*, 1958.

262 Cavaré, L'Union occidentale, *Mélanges Scelle* 93; Vignes, L'Union de l'Europe occidentale, AF 1955, 490.

263 Gros Espiell, Le processus de la reforme de la Charte des Etats americains, AF 1968, 138; Robertson, Revision of the Charter of the OAS, ICLQ 1968, 346.

264 See Colliard, *Institutions et relations internationales,* 9th ed., 1990 nos. 399, 436 *et seq.*

265 On NATO see, for example, Bastid, S., L'obligation de consulter pour les Etats parties au Traité de l'Atlantique de Nord, AF 1955, 464.

266 Meissner, *Der Warschauer Pakt,* Cologne 1962; Lachs, Le traité de Varsovie du 4 mars 1955, AF 1955, 120.

of political-economic organisations like the European Union,[267] may restrict the freedom of States to enter into non/compatible alliances.[268]

The Conference on Security and Cooperation in Europe, CSCE, was becoming a security organisation with a planned institutional structure, when its own *raison d'être*, the East-West tension, suddenly disappeared. The Conference was responsible for introducing *confidence building measures* which were designed to lessen tension between the two military blocs, by, for example, giving advance warning about military manoeuvres and even inviting members from the opposite armed forces to watch. Under Basket III Human Rights was also to be a main concern of the CSCE.[269] After the demise of communism, however, the CSCE has changed shape altogether: Human Rights, from having been one of the ten principles on which the Final Act of Helsinki was based in 1975, is now the *first responsibility of governments*.[270] CSCE is, however, a converted organisation which has recently left its previously important task in the détente process between East and West and now, in a new political scenario, devotes itself to the enhancement of Human Rights. The CSCE recently emphasised that respect for Human Rights is an 'essential safeguard against an overmighty State'.[271]

To further its new functions, the CSCE has now *institutions* to assist it in the implementation of action, as specified by the Charter of Paris of 1990 and by the follow-up meeting in Berlin in 1991. A Council, consisting of Ministers of Foreign Affairs, meets regularly, assisted by a secretariat, and by a Committee of Senior Officials, who prepares all meetings, and a Consultative Committee, for special tasks such as arms control questions, a Conflict Prevention Centre, and an Office for Free Elections, to mark a special interest in democratic

---

[267]   For the political dimension of the European Community, see *supra*, under the European Community.

[268]   As mentioned above, the WEU is incorporated into the European Community by the Maastricht Treaty.

[269]   See *infra* in Chapter V under Human Rights.

[270]   See in detail on this dramatic development, Alting von Geusau, *Beyond Containment and Division*, 1992, 154 *et seq.*

[271]   See further, Alting von Geusau, *Beyond Containment, op. cit.*, 155 *et seq.*

processes. Precisely this focus on democracy and other Human Rights indicates that there is a strong *nexus* between security issues and Human Rights.

(b) Cultural and Human Rights Organisations

We could almost have discussed the CSCE under this heading considering the changes of its functions after the adoption of the Paris Charter.[272] However, there are some organisations which have always and exclusively devoted themselves to cultural work and to the promotion of Human Rights. One of the most important organisations in this context is the Council of Europe, which has also contributed to stability and security in Europe by enhancing respect for Human Rights.

(1) The Council of Europe

Sorensen, Le Conseil de l'Europe, RCADI 1953 ii; Robertson, *The Council of Europe*, 2nd ed., 1961; Jacobs, *The Council of Europe*, 1976; Carstens, *Das Recht des Europarats*, 1956.

Certain organisations, like the Council of Europe, are actively promoting the furthering of Human Rights in its Member States. We shall have occasion to revert later to the work of this organisation in connection with our study of Human Rights;[273] in this context we merely focus on its role in international society and its functions as the main organisation ensuring the respect for Human Rights in Europe.

The Council of Europe, too, has obvious political roots and should also be viewed as a potential framework for security cooperation.

After the Second World War, there were considerable forces to propose specific, clear rules, to prevent atrocities taking place by violation of human rights of individuals. As we shall see later,[274]

---

[272] See *supra* in the previous section.
[273] See *infra* in Chapter V under Human Rights.
[274] See *infra*.

such Human Rights, at least the most basic ones, are effective in the international legal system without any incorporation in national legal systems or in international treaties. This is, in spite of what is sometimes claimed in Swedish textbooks, overwhelmingly proved by international State practice, pronouncements of the International Court of Justice,[275] of the Court of Justice of the European Union and of the Court of the Council of Europe.

Initially, there had been plans to make this organisation the *main* organisation in Europe, that is to say, the Council of Europe, was, at one stage in the early fifties, designed to be what later became the European Community. Thus, in 1950 there were plans to introduce a common European passport, as well as other far-reaching measures to speed up European integration.

Of these plans came nothing and, instead, the Council of Europe became an international organisation with weak powers - except in the field of Human Rights.

The Organisation consists of a powerless Assembly, the Parliament, which seeks to exercise, with little success, some political influence in European affairs. There is also a Council of Ministers which, occasionally, plays a role in handling complaints of violations of Human Rights.

The most important organ, however, is the Commission, which examines at first hand, all complaints from individuals in States which have ratified the European Convention of Human Rights of 1950.

The Council of Europe has acquired substantial authority in Human Rights Affairs.[276] The importance of the judgments of the Court of Justice is enhanced by the fact that the Court may also add substantial damages to successful claims against a nationals home State.[277]

---

[275]   E.g., *The Namibia Case*, (1974) ICJ *Reports*; *The Hostage Case* (1980) ICJ *Reports*.

[276]   Flauss, L'activité conventionelle du Conseil de l'Europe relative à la Convention européenne des droits de l'homme, Bilan d'une décennie, AF 1989, 484.

[277]   *La semaine juridique*, 1 septembre 1992.

(2) The Nordic Council

Wendt, *The Nordic Council and Cooperation in Scandinavia*, 1959, Petrén, G., Les resultats de dix ans de coopération nordique, AE XI 27; Zorgbibe, *Les Etats/Unis scandinaves*, 1968.

Organisations which claim to have, as their main objective to promote cultural or other common interests, like the Nordic Council, can, if in the particular instance there are not serious political divergent views, provide a useful framework for cooperation in military and security matters. Alternatively, they can be useful in the promotion of Human Rights or other interests of individuals.

One organisation which appears to have failed under both headings is the Nordic Council which could have, and still can, provide a useful framework for Nordic cooperation. Hitherto, however, the Nordic Council has lived a somewhat lame and modest life, in total obscurity, away from any interests of the citizens in the Nordic countries, and away from the mainstream discussions on Human Rights in other fora.

(c) Economic Organisations

(1) Cooperation Frameworks: OECD

Hahn and Weber, *Die OECD, Organisation fur wirtschaftliche Zusammenarbeit und Entwicklung*, 1976.

Certain organisations are concerned, not with security or military matters but concentrate on economic cooperation. As we have demonstrated earlier, some such cooperation has also political roots or motivation, like the European Union.[278] Also the Organisation for Economic Cooperation and Development (OECD), formerly the Organisation for European Economic Cooperation (OEEC)[279] an organisation which was originally established to manage the so called Marshall Aid, given to Western Europe by the United States after the

---

[278] See *supra* on the European Community.

[279] Adam, *Organisation européenne de coopération économique*, 1949; Elkin, The OEEC, its structure and powers, AE, 1956, 96.

Second World War. The OECD now devotes itself to promote general economic cooperation.

(2) International Banks

Political aims are also promoted by the means of certain international Banks. It is worth noting that the World Bank,[280] too, was established after the Second World War as the IBRD, the International Bank of Reconstruction and Development. In a similar fashion, after the collapse of communism in Eastern Europe, a new international Bank was established in 1990 as the European Bank for Reconstruction and Development (EBRD), or the so called *London Bank*, named after its Headquarters, to distinguish it from the World Bank in Washington. The London Bank will assist in the transition in Eastern Europe to market economy, with special regard to environmental questions and to the privatisation process.

Other international Banks have as main objective to channel Third World Aid, such as the World Bank itself,[281] and also the African Development Bank,[282] the East African Development Bank,[283] the Arab Development Bank[284] the Asian Development Bank,[285] the Inter-American Development Bank[286] and the Islamic Development Bank.[287]

If economic cooperation is already at a sophisticated level, as in the European Union, an investment vehicle, like the European Investment Bank (EIB),[288] may facilitate the furthering of set

---

[280] See *supra*, on the IBRD.

[281] See *supra*.

[282] Created by the Treaty of Tunis of 1963.

[283] This is an interesting example of an international Bank which survived the death of its mother organisation, the East African Community, see my work *The East African Community and the Common Market*, 1969.

[284] Created by the Treaty of Cairo of 1974.

[285] Created by the Treaty of Manila of 1965.

[286] Created by the Treaty of Santiago of 1959.

[287] Created by the Treaty of Jeddah of 1974.

[288] Certain overseas aid is channelled through the EIB to the Lomé countries (in Africa, the Caribbean and the Pacific); the EIB also promotes ventures in Europe itself and takes an interest in environmental protection.

economic objectives; in a similar light we may view the EBRD[289] and the Arab Investment Bank.[290]

(d) Trade Organisations

Economic cooperation is naturally not only dependent on banking structures but also on other frameworks which facilitate trade. Certain trade organisations have been established to encourage and improve international trade.

(1) Regional Efforts

Certain economic cooperation is carried out either in the form of free trade organisations, like the European Free Trade Association (EFTA),[291] the Latin American Association for Free Trade, (LAFTA)[292] or the Carribean Free Trade Organisation, the so called (CARIFTA),[293] or as customs unions, or working towards such a target, like the Andean Pact;[294] such organisations are inevitably influenced by the development and the experiences of the European Community.[295]

In the area of economic co-operation, there has been considerable change following the political transformation in Eastern Europe. Thus,

---

[289] In spite of recent scandals which caused the premature leaving of the President Jacques Attali, under whose direction the Bank, during two years, had spent more on its London premises than on aid to Eastern Europe.

[290] Created by the Treaty of Rijadh of 1974.

[291] See my article on Aspects institutionnels de l'Association européenne de Libre Echange, AF 1960 791.

[292] See the Montevideo Treaty of 1960 and, for a general survey, Simmonds, International economic organisation in Central and Latin America and the Carribean, ICLQ 1970 376.

[293] Carnegie, Commonwealth Caribbean regionalism: legal aspects, YWA 1979 180.

[294] Based on the Treaty of Cartagena of 1960, see Rideau, La Cour suprème de Colombie et l'intégration économique latino-americaine dans le Groupe Andin, RIDC 1973 331; Salazar Santos, *Aspectos juridicos de la integración andina*, 1972;

[295] See *supra*, under the European Community.

the Council for Mutual Assistance (CMEA),[296] commonly called COMECON, has also been dismantled.

(2) GATT

See, Flory, T., *Le GATT, droit international et commerce mondial,* 1968; *idem,* L'évolution du système juridique du GATT, JDI 1977 787; Grainger, *GATT Disputes,* 1989; Hudec, *Developing Countries in the GATT Legal System,* 1987; Petersmann, *The New GATT Round of Multilateral Trade Negotiations,* 1988; Simmonds and Hill, *Law and Practice under the GATT,* 1987; Jaenicke, Das allgemeine Zoll und Handelsabkommen, AV 1959 301.

Of considerable contemporary importance is GATT, in a phase of international politics when trade wars may take the place of the previous East-West tension. In 1992 the United States is considering imposing trade sanctions against French goods in an attempt to fight *Fortress Europe,* the European Union's more hostile image.

GATT, the General Agreement on Tariffs and Trade, which is not supposed to exist as an international organisation (in spite of its imposing building in Geneva) but only as an *agreement* administered by States, has no power of actual decision but is actively contributing to liberalisation of world trade. As such, it is in direct opposition to the European Union which is striving to deepen its internal trade ties and to exclude other trade. GATT seeks to promote liberalisation of trade also to assist the needs of the Third World. It is important to underline that such a policy is in contrast with the proclaimed aims of the European Community/the European Union, an organisation which is clearly protectionistic.[297] Even the policies of GATT are viewed by some in the Third World as too protectionistic and too much in favour of the industrialised States.

However, GATT plays an important role in multilateral trade negotiations even if some desire a higher degree of liberalisation. GATT has an important set of panels for conflict resolution in trade disputes.

---

[296]   Caillot, *La CAEM, Aspects juridiques et formes de coopération économique entre pays socialistes,* 1971; Kaser, *COMECON,* 2nd ed., 1967.

[297]   On this point, see *supra,* under the Impact of the EC, in this Chapter.

(3) Commodity Organisations

Kahn, *The Law and Organisation of International Commodity Agreements*, 1982. For a survey of existing commodity agreements, see Colliard, *Institutions des relations internationales* 3, 1990, 784; *cf.* Fischer, les associations de pays exportateurs de produits de base, AF 1976, 528; Eisemann, *L'organisation internationale du commerce des produits de base*, 1982.

It is difficult to assess the work of GATT in the field of liberalisation of trade unless its efforts are set next to those of UNCTAD[298] and those of special commodity organisations, like the Sugar Council, the Wheat Council and other specialised organs for commodity trade. The vulnerable position of some of these commodity agencies was amply demonstrated when the International Tin Council was dismantled having exhausted its own funds.[299]

The special position of the Organisation of Oil Exporting Countries (OPEC),[300] which has undergone a considerable change in terms of actual influence and power, merit special attention.

(4) UNCTAD

El-Nagger, The UN Conference on Trade and Development, 128 RCADI 1969 241; Hagras, *United Nations Conference on Trade and Development, A Case Study in UN Diplomacy*, 1965.

The United Nations Conference for Trade and Development (UNCTAD) was created by Resolution 1707 (XVI) of the UN General Assembly in 1961 to provide a forum for international trade discussion with special regard to commodities. Decisions are taken by qualified majority which, at first glance, may indicate that the Conference has some power of decision. However, the resolutions taken by UNCTAD are all essentially *recommendations*, and, as

---

[298] See *infra.*

[299] See *Rayner (Mincing Lane) Case v DTI* [1989], 3 WLR 879 and *supra.* under Traditional Criteria of International Organisations, in this Chapter.

[300] See my *Finance and Protection of Investments in Developing Countries*, 2nd ed., 1987, 245; Fischer, L'Organisation des pays exportateurs de petrole, AF1 961 163; el Sayed, Etude d'une organisation internationale pour la defense des interets prives des Etats, 1967.

qualified majority is easy to obtain in UNCTAD where developing countries are amply represented, the effective force of resolutions adopted is technically not binding. On the other hand, it is precisely because of UNCTAD pressure that certain improvements, in favour, of developing countries, have been introduced by industrialised States by unilateral or collective concession.[301]

(e) Nuclear Organisations

Fischer, L'Agence internationale de l'énergie atomique, AF 1956, 616.

In the technical sphere, albeit with considerable political overtones, we may note the work of the Atomic Energy Agency in Vienna (IAEA).[302] The Agency was created under a resolution of the General Assembly in 1954 but it was thought useful to keep the organisation distinct from the United Nations system and the Agency was thus not made a specialised agency but given considerable autonomy.

The OECD[303] has also a special Agency for Nuclear Energy in order to coordinate various national efforts.[304]

The atomic agencies have frequent contacts with the European Community for Nuclear Energy, EURATOM.[305]

(f) Space Organisations

The important general organisation the European Space Agency (ESA) in Paris, is devoted to space research and to operational launching of satellites.[306] Apart from the headquarters, ESA has, as integrated agencies or centres that form part of the organisation, a research Centre, the European Space and Technology Centre (ESTEC) in Holland, the European Space Operational Centre (ESOC) in

---

[301] See, *supra*, on the Force of Recommendations.

[302] Created by the Convention of New York of 1957.

[303] See *supra*.

[304] The Agency was created by a decision of 1956 of the OEEC Council.

[305] *Supra*.

[306] See further *infra* in Chapter VIII on Space Law.

Germany and a European Space Research Information Network (ESRIN) in Italy. There are also launch bases for the Ariane project in Kouron in French Guyana, the Hermès project development division in Toulouse, and telescope sites in Baltimore and in Munich.

ESA are one international organisation which is cooperating with several national agencies, such as NASA in the United States, and has a permanent special liaison office with NASA in Washington. This is a type of cooperation which again illustrates the assymetry of actors: is it reasonable to accept the idea of traditional textbooks that ESA, but not NASA, is an international subject?[307]

A special type of organisation of an entirely new kind has mushroomed around new technical development, particularly concerning telecommunication in space. There are now organisations specifically for telecommunications like Intelsat,[308] Intersputnik,[309] Inmarsat,[310] Eutelsat,[311] Eumetsat,[312] and Arabsat.[313] It is clear, that satellite telecommunications play an ever increasing role in modern international society.

The present role of peaceful satellites has shifted the emphasis from the previous military scenario in Space involving the planned United States Strategic Defence Initiative (SDI), more popularly called 'Star Wars', by which the United States planned to install a deflecting mirror system above its national territory in order to divert enemy attack by laser beams.

An area of paramount interest today is the legal situation of commercial satellites, especially such satellites which are involved with telecommunications.[314]

---

[307] Cf. *supra* under Criteria of International Organisations, in this Chapter.
[308] Founded by the Treaty of Washington of 1964.
[309] Founded in 1971 by Decision of Supreme Soviet.
[310] Founded by Treaty of London 1976.
[311] Founded by the Treaty of 1977.
[312] Founded by the Treaty of Geneva in 1983.
[313] Founded by a Treaty of 1976.
[314] See further *infra* in Chapter VIII.

e. Non-Governmental Organisations

Bettati & P.M. Dupuy, *Les organisations non-gouvernementales et le droit international,* 1986; Wiederkehr, La convention du Conseil de l'Europe sur le statut des organisations non-gouvernementales, AFDI 1987, 749.

It is suggested that it is not correct to consider only intergovernmental organisations to be subjects as also non-governmental entities can be bearers of rights and duties under international law.[315]

Non-governmental organisations are mentioned by Article 71 of the Charter of the United Nations which provides that the Economic and Social Council of the United Nations (ECOSOC) may consult such organisations. NGOs, which are bodies of international membership but without lucrative aims, constitute a fruitful source of inquiry to the international lawyers wishing to assess their rights and duties, or overall role, in international society.[316]

The NGOs have multiplied over the years and some of them are considered as important power factors in international politics. Some suggest that, for example, Human Rights have developed in recent years largely as a result of the work of organisations such as Amnesty and other NGOs. Their work has been considerable; some claim that the recent expansion of Human Rights has been entirely due to activities by NGOs.[317]

Some NGOs have played an important role for some years, not only as subjects of international law but as actual originator of practices and of rules. One may, for example, consider the part played by the International Red Cross in numerous wars during the last hundred years,[318] the impact of Amnesty in certain Human Rights

---

[315]   *Cf. supra,* under Traditional Criteria of International Organisations, in this Chapter.

[316]   See, *e.g.* Institut de Droit international, Report by Mme Suzanne Bastid, 43 *Annuaire de l'Institut,* 1950 i 547 *et seq.* and ii 335 *et seq.*

[317]   *Cf.* Feld and Jordan, *International Organisation,* 1983, 250.

[318]   On the International Committee of the Red Cross, (ICRC) - and on the organisation of independent national branches - see, Pictet, La Croix Rouge et les Conventions de Gèneve, RCADI, 1950, I, 27 *et seq.;* Ruegger, The Juridical Aspects of the Organisation of the International Red Cross, RCADI 1953 i 481; Guggenheim & Bindschedler-Robert, 2 *Traité du droit international public,* 337. *Cf.* my *Law of War, op. cit.*

Affairs, or the effect of action by GreenPeace in environmental matters.

f. Individuals

Scelle, *Cours de droit international public,* 1947-1949; Dahm, *Die Stellung der Menschen im Völkerrecht unserer Zeit,* 1961; Sperduti, L'individu et le droit international, 90 RCADI, 1956 727; Korowicz, The problem of the international personality of individuals, AJIL, 1956, 533; Lapradelle, La place de l'homme dans la construction du droit international, CLP, 1948 140; Salvioli, L'individuo in diritto internazionale, RDI, 1956, 5; Norgaard, *The Position of the Individual in International Law,* 1962; Weugler, Die Stellung der Einzelpersonen im gegenwärtigen Völkerrecht, in *Festschrift Laun,* 1953, 431.

See also, *infra,* under Human Rights.

Individuals may also be subjects of international law. In a sense, they are always the *ultimate subjects* in the international system since States, organisations and entities consist of individuals. The State is nothing but an abstract agglomeration of individuals who have come together in a State for their own convenience. This is a question of fact which is not dependent on political theory. It is thus the State which exists for the individuals and not the individuals for the State.[319] Furthermore, it may be noted that the function of the State is to serve the individuals, rather than *vice versa.* This is a vital proposition to all States who wish to protect the Rule of Law. It is also being increasingly emphasised in the restructuring of the socialist, or formerly socialist, countries of Eastern Europe and only denied by some extremist regimes.

Naturally, there may be a question of allegiance that individuals owe their home State.[320] But a government of a State that does not wish to disintegrate is wise to remember that it is ultimately the individuals of the State that actually make up the State itself; and the government is a mere agency of these individuals.

The question of individuals as subjects of international law is closely linked to that of democracy and the power of people in their

---

[319]   *Cf.* my *Concept, op. cit.,* 62-63.
[320]   See, *infra,* under Nationality.

own State[321] as well as to the question of the rights of minorities[322] or, indeed, majorities.[323]

Individuals may, of course, be given certain rights and duties under a treaty. Individuals enjoy rights of action under several Human Rights treaties, for example under the European Human Rights Convention.[324] Individuals also enjoy important rights of action under the Treaties of the European Community, now the European Union; they have also, under the EC Treaties, important obligations. Outside EC/EU law, individuals are subjected to obligations under general international law and have special duties especially with regard to treatment of other individuals. It is thus important to note that individuals enjoy personality under general international law.

If an individual is an agent of the State, such as a Head of State, member of the government, or a diplomat, consul, customs officer or member of the armed forces,[325] he is not normally responsible, on the international level, for his actions: they are imputed to his home state which, so to speak, takes over the responsibility of the agent. However, an exception is made for crimes against basic Human Rights: if the acts of a State agent violate such basic rules he will himself have to answer for his acts.[326] Violations of *basic Human Rights* thus engages the personal responsibility of individuals.[327]

The Nuremburg Court ruled clearly that individuals may have direct international duties,[328] for example in the field of crimes of aggressive war - the individuals were leaders of a State - or in the

---

[321]   On democratisation of international society, see my *Law of War, op. cit.* 24 *et seq. Cf., infra*, Nations and under Hallmarks of States.

[322]   See further, *infra*, under Minorities.

[323]   *Cf., infra*, under Majorities.

[324]   See, further, *infra*, under Human Rights.

[325]   Numerous persons and entities may be agents of the State. See *Krajina v Tass Agency* [1949] 2 All E.R; *Dexter & Carpenter v Kungl. Järnvägstyrelsen*, 1930 43 F 2d 705; *Bacchus S.R.L. v Servicio Nacional del Trigo*, [1957] 1 QB 438, [1956] 3 All E.R. 715. *Cf.* also *Carl Zeiss Stiftung v Rayner & Keeler Ltd (No. 2)* [1967] 1 AC 853, [1966] 2 All E.R. On the role of a Central Bank and on later limitations, see *e.g.* the *Trendtex Case* [1977] QB 579.

[326]   Wright, Q., War Criminals, 39 AJIL 1945, 271.

[327]   *Cf.* my *Law of War, op. cit.*, 353 *et seq.*

[328]   Judgment 1 October 1946, 1 Nuremberg Trials, 222; 41 AJIL 1947, 220.

field of crimes against humanity, such as genocide or torture, as well as in the case of espionage.[329] Conversely, individuals enjoy certain clear and specific Human Rights, directly under international law.[330] In February 1993 the United Nations Security Council confirmed this by specific Resolutions in the Bosnian crisis.

g. Classes

See my *Concept of International Law,* 1987, 22 *et seq.* for more references to writings in Russian.

Soviet writers used to insist that international law involves actors others than States.[331] However, rather than looking to the individual, the Marxist-Leninist approach has been to emphasise the role of *classes.* International law is, by Marxists, considered to form a super-structure above world economic relations which exist between States and in which *dominant classes* are antagonists.[332] *Classes* are, according to Marxist theory, involved in a struggle between two systems.[333]

However, according to Marxist theory, international law is mainly a system between sovereign States. The notion of sovereignty, which may not have the same meaning as in the West,[334] is central to Marxist thought.[335] On the one hand, sovereignty, in Marxist theory,

---

[329]   *Cf.* my article on Foreign warships and immunity for espionage, in AJIL, 1984, 1079.

[330]   See, *infra,* under Monist and Dualist Schools and, *infra,* under Human Rights.

[331]   Tunkin, *Law and Force in International Society,* 1983, 25; *Pravo i sila v mezdunarodnogo sistema,* 1981.

[332]   Durdenevski, V.N., and Krylov, S.B., *Mezhdunarodnoe Pravo,* Soviet Academy of Sciences (ed.), Moscow, 1947, 5. Cf. Tunkin, G.I., *Droit international public,* 1965, 244.

[333]   Pashukanis, *Ocerki po mezhdunarodnoe pravo,* 1935, 5.

[334]   Bystricki, R., *Le droit de l'intégration économique socialiste,* 1978, 13; Tunkin, G.I., *Teoria, op. cit., loc. cit.*

[335]   *Cf.* views of writers such as Korovin, E,A., *Mezhdunarodnoe pravo pereshodnogo vremini,* 2nd ed., 1924, 37.

is clearly subordinated to the socialist objectives.[336] On the other hand, it is possibly of greater doctrinal importance than the notion of class struggle.[337] Sovereignty implies, in Marxist thought, considerable power of the State over the individual.

Events are rapidly transforming values and previously accepted notions in the States which used to be part of the former Soviet Union, and in the other former communist/socialist States. The Soviet Union reintroduced, already before its disintegration, laws allowing private property[338] and a new market economy. It is probable that the new developments in Eastern Europe will wipe out the theories on classes as separate subjects of international law. We have already seen[339] that the Soviet Union accepted that international law, as a system, is superior to internal law. It is reasonable to expect further revision of the Soviet doctrine on *classes* as subjects of international law by the successors in titles, the CIS and the other new States which used to form part of the former Soviet Union.

In previous years one could talk about the *Western approach* and the *Marxist approach* to international law. Today, the polarity has disappeared: there are no more Marxist States, apart from China, Cuba and Serbia. It is indeed difficult to fathom the incredible speed with which Communist regimes crumbled in Poland, in East Germany, in Czechoslovakia, (now the Czech Republic and Slovakia), in Roumania, Bulgaria, and then in the USSR itself, as well as in Albania, one of the last bastions in Europe.

No doubt other theories on international law will evolve in new, different blocs in the world. But so far we have only the Western view left; China's attitude is pragmatic as one of a nation which has as its tradition to accept moral, rather than law, as a guide for behaviour in society.

---

[336] See Koshevnikov, Sovetskoe Gosudarstvo i Revoluziya Prava, No. 3., 149 and Ratner, L., Mezhdunarodoe Pravo v Marksistkom Osvecenii, in Sovetskoe Gosudarstvo No. 6, 1935, 131; cf. the emphasis given to sovereignty in the Constitution of the Soviet Union of 7th October 1977, article 29. Note The Law of Amendments and Additions to the Constitution of 1988.

[337] See *e.g.* Levine, I.D., *Suverenitet,* 1948, 64.

[338] Adopted for scrutiny in November 1989 and enacted in February 1990.

[339] *Infra,* under Monism and Dualism.

130

h. Nations

See my *International and the Independent State,* 2nd ed., 1987; and further under Individuals, *infra.*

Nations are units which share ethnic or other coherent features, like language, culture or religion. A nation is not the same as a State although one often speaks of *Nation-States.* The Nation-States were, generally speaking, the entities of established or consolidated in the 16th century and some subsist to this day: as far as these are concerned, a *nation* and a *State* coincide. In other words, the whole State consists of a people with the same or similar language, history, culture etc.

Sweden may be one such Nation-State. Or are the Laps a separate nation? They possibly could be a separate nation but their nomadic life reduces their stable affiliation of specific territory within the state. Numbers too may be important: the role of the Laps may be too small to warrant us speaking of a Lap nation. If there is that problem of size and strength, a group of people may still have the special protection of international law as *minorities.*[340]

A State that hosts more than one nation inside it is prone to suffer tension. There are occasionally cases where a reasonable *modus vivendi* can be obtained, like in Belgium.[341] The reason for success in this State is probably dues to the *absence of force*: once peoples live together and choose to continue this arrangement, there are strong bonds that unite them. When, on the other hand, they are *forced* to live together, either under a dictator or under a political system which itself incorporates *force*, such as communism or socialism, the different peoples are, as soon as that force is removed, likely to wish to go their different paths.

It is thus normally true to say that a nation within a State may itself be a potential new State. The tension that ensues is amply illustrated by the declaration of independence of Lithuania in 1990; this declaration was caused by the fact that there were several nations

---

[340]   See *infra.*

[341]   But see the *Belgian Language Case* before the Court of the Council of Europe 1966, and *infra,* under minorities.

within the Soviet Union. The consolidation of Lithuania, as a nation, was also assisted by the fact that in this country there are less Russians than in the other Baltic Republics: the national unity was thus more easily achieved.

It will depend on many factors whether the nation secedes from the mother State: Does it want to? Is it too small? Is is viable on its own? (All these questions were considered by the Falklanders to establish whether they wanted continued affiliation with the United Kingdom). Will it encounter political hostility and not be recognised by many other States? (These questions were relevant, although not entirely foreseen, by the Republic of Northern Cyprus.) Is the government sufficiently effective to be recognised by others? (This question was asked in 1990 by Lithuania.)[342] Does it actually wish to be *fully independent* or does it wish to affiliate itself to another unit? (This question was asked by the Falklanders in 1984. It is also a question which had been asked by the Ålanders in the 1920's when they decided, by 99.9%, to affiliate themselves to Sweden - which they were not allowed to do by the Great Powers). Is it possible to be a *nation* if there is no territorial coherence but members of a group (based on race, creed or defined by other criteria) live in different areas? (This question was asked in Pakistan when East Pakistan - now Bangladesh - wished to secede. Similar questions have been asked by both Catholics and Protestants in Northern Ireland.)

Nations may wish to secede from a mother State and they may achieve their objective by means of exercising a right of self-determination.[343] But to allow the principle of self-determination without restriction would lead to unacceptable fragmentation of the international society.[344] There are also numerous countries, like the United Kingdom and Belgium, which amply illustrate the possibility of multinational societies within a democratic system.[345]

---

[342] See, *supra*, on Recognition.

[343] *E.g.* GA Resolution 637 (VII) of 1952 and, especially GA Resolution 1514 (XV) of 1960 on the Granting of Independence to Colonial Countries and Peoples and GA Resolution 2625 (XXV) of 1970. See further for the historical background my *Independent State, op. cit.*, 6-18.

[344] See my *Independent State, op. cit.*, 17.

[345] On the prerequisite of democracy, as opposed to the coercive communist system, for such structures, *cf. supra*.

The test, however, would normally be the *consistent and determined will* of a unit to form its own State. Since it is the citizens who make up the State, such a test would appear to be useful to test legitimacy on the basis of democratic consent.

Such a will to secede is likely to prosper and crystallise itself more readily in politically oppressive systems, as can be observed in the transformation of Eastern Europe.

j. Minorities

For literature, see also under Human Rights.

Claude, *National Minorities*, 1955; Modéen, *International Protection of National Minorities in Europe*, 1961; Sabelli, *Nazioni e minoranze etniche*, 1928; Langenhove, Le problème de la protection des populations aborigènes aux Nations Unies, 89 RCADI 1956 321; Lanning, *Il problema delle minoranze nazionali*, 1946; Kunz, The present state of international law for the protection of minorities, AJIL 1954, 282;

Some minorities are protected by treaties. Individuals may have been given the right of complaint before international or national tribunals to protect their specific rights under such treaties.[346] Even outside treaties it appears that minorities may enjoy some protection. For example, the State may have bound itself by a specific unilateral declaration[347] to respect certain minorities in some particular way. Furthermore, general rules may also protect minorities as some relevant rules coincide with, or are sumsumed under, general rules on Human Rights.[348] Rights of minorities must be finely balanced against the rights of the State to decide in its own territory[349].

---

[346] See *e.g. Polish Nationals in Danzig* (1931), PCIJ, Ser. A/B, No. 44, 24. For specific treaties see Treaties of Versailles, Neuilly, Trianon, Lausanne and St. Germain after the First World War in 1919 and the Treaty of Dorpat of 1920, of Riga of 1920, of Brunna of 1920 and Upper Silesia of 1922. Cf. also the 1947 Peace Treaty which in parts deals with South Tirol/Alto Adige as well as the Austrian State Treaty of 1955.

[347] For unilateral declarations see my *Concept, op. cit.*, 105-106.

[348] See my *Independent State, op. cit.*131 *et seq.*

[349] On this power and its limitation see my *Independent State, op. cit.*, passim.

k. Majorities

For literature, see under Human Rights, *infra*.

In the case of South Africa, there is a question of a *majority* - not a minority - which does not have its voice reflected in the ruling of the country. There, too, the action of groups is important and relevant to international society. The novel rules of *democracy*[350] would appear to ensure that a majority group is always guaranteed influence in the running of the country. But, as seen from ample practice around the world, this is not always so. At present, South Africa is obviously the most flagrant example. In due course, the aim must be to ensure a one man - one vote situation in South Africa. This cannot be achieved immediately, although some faraway countries seem to perceive no problems: much is needed in terms of education and information before such policy can be effectively introduced so that every man and woman knows for what they are voting in open elections.

Majorities enjoy, however, already rights and duties, as coherent groups, under international law and accordingly, majorities are subjects of the international legal order. They are, for example, assured a general right of self-determination, even if this cannot always be immediately realised.

They also enjoy a right not to be subjected to apartheid or degrading treatment. Any State which exposes them to such a system is immediately responsible for a serious violation of international law. This is clearly indicated by Article 19 of the Draft of the International Law Commission on State Responsibility. Offending States may be subjected to economic sanctions[351] or other forms of disapproval.

On the other hand, the black majority in South Africa is itself under duty, when its political influence increases, to respect the rights of white and other minorities.

As majorities tend to be naturally more powerful because of the numerical superiority, they have an important duty to, in turn, respect

---

[350]   See my *Law of War, op. cit.*, 24 and *supra* under Criteria of a State, and *supra*, under Individuals.

[351]   Sanctions are not the most effective way of dealing with an unwanted situation in international society, see, *infra*, under Sanctions.

and safeguard the interests of minorities, particularly with regard to their safety under the law.

l. Belligerents and Insurgents

See my own *Law of War*, 1987; Ijalaye, Was Biafra ever a State in international law?, AJIL 1971, 551.

Rules of war may allow insurgents to be recognised as belligerents. There are strict conditions how insurgents qualify as such.[352] Belligerents may conclude certain agreements with the other belligerent party/parties, just as if they were States.[353] Should, however, they fail to win the civil war they are fighting, the personality of the group will dissolve.[354]

m. Liberation Movements

Tomuschat, Staatsvolk ohne Staat, *Festschrift Doering*, 1989, 985; and *supra* under Recognition.

There is a fine line, if any, between insurgents and liberation movements. The latter movements may be more organised and, at any rate, there is an inlaid element of potential success, or concrete hope of success, in the term liberation movement.[355]

Liberation movements have recently been given special standing in international negotiations. Not so long ago liberation movements were accepted as observers in international organisations. Their role has now rapidly changed and they now occasionally have voting rights and right to enter into international agreements.[356]

They often, however, occupy a fluid position in international society as they usually attempt to form their own States. In other

---

[352] See further my *Law of War, op. cit.*, 36 *et seq.*

[353] See further my *Law of War, op. cit.*

[354] See, in detail, *ibid.*, 37. It is important to add that there are also other types of belligerents as this term by itself merely indicate an entity, such as for example a fully constituted State, which is waging a war.

[355] It is left open here if such 'hope' is subjective or objectively warranted.

[356] See my *Law of War, op. cit.*, Ch VI.

words, the term liberation movement is synonymous with that of a *temporary subject* in international law: a liberation movement may *qua* subject of international law assume rights and obligations.[357]

Some entities become States, like Algeria, after their Liberation Wars have been successful; others, who fail to win such wars, are extinguished as States, like the insurgent/liberation movement in Biafra.

Even if terrorist movements sometimes can act as subjects of international law, and would, as a rule be subjected to numerous obligations of international law, especially in the context of armed conflict,[358] their rights may be limited in times of national unrest. Thus, the right to broadcast, another entrenched Human Right,[359] has, at times, been limited in the United Kingdom.[360]

After the spectacular recognition of the Palestine Liberation Organisation, PLO, by Israel on 13th September 1993, it may be useful for international lawyers to recognise that liberation movements cannot be relegated outside the textbooks as 'non-subjects'[361] of international law. In one sense, the development with regard to such movements and their emergence into statehood is more significant than the sometimes modest position assumed by some States in the international legal order.

n. The Holy See

Le Fur, *Le Saint Siège et le droit des gens*, 1930; Verdross, Die Stellung des Apostolischen Stuhles in der internationalen Gemeinschaft, ÖAKR 1952, 54; Falco, *The Legal Position of the Holy See Before and After the Lateran Agreements*, 1935; Cardinale, *The Holy See and the International Legal Order*, 1976; Van der Heydte, Die Stellung und Funktion des Heiligen Stuhls im heutigen Völkerrecht, ÖZöR 1950 572; Oechslin, *Die Völkerrechtssubjektivität des Apostolischen Stuhls under der*

---

[357] On the importance of the submission of liberation movements to standards of humanitarian law, see my *Law of War, op. cit.,* 271 *et seq.*

[358] See my *Law of Law, op. cit.,* Chapter IV.

[359] See *infra* in Chapter IV.

[360] *Ibid., loc. cit.*

[361] See also the US legislation curtailing the activities of the PLO at the UN Headquarters, *Obligation to Arbitrate on UN Headquarters Agreement* (1988) ICJ *Reports,* 12.

136

Katholischen Kirche, 1974; Nuccitelli, *Le fondement juridique des rapports diplomatique entre le Saint Siège et les Nations Unies,* 1956.

There is common agreement that the Holy See is a subject of international law, not only after 1929, when it was given a territorial base under the Lateran Treaty,[362] but that it was such a subject also much earlier in history.[363] The position of the Pope is regulated in canons 321 *et seq.* of the *Codex Juris Canonici* of 1983, as revised, which confirm the Pope's temporal and spiritual authority. The Vatican has now a well defined two-fold function, both as a temporal State which conclude treaties and receives and sends ambassadors as well as being the authority over the world-wide Catholic Church.

One may remark that the international role played by the present Pope John Paul II confirms the role of the Holy See as both actor/subject, and as a temporal State, creator of rules in international society.[364]

Apart from the traditional role played by the Holy See as a subject of international law, Pope John Paul II *himself* is probably one of the charismatic leaders that is acting as a subject of international law in his own right. We note that international law reports now include commentaries on the Pope's travels as relevant to the development of international law.[365]

o. International Orders

Monaco, Osservazioni sulla condizione giuridica internazionale dell'Ordine du Malta, 64 RCADI 1981, 14; de Fischer, L'Order souverain de Malte, 163 RCADI 1979 ii 1.

The Order of Malta is a good example of a subject of international law which is functioning very well without a territorial base, receiving

---

[362]   1 Whiteman 587.

[363]   Bluntschli, Le droit international codifié, 1870, 137; Berber, Lehrbuch des Völkerrechts, Munich, 1975, i, 162.

[364]   For a survey of the Pope's speeches to the diplomatic corps, setting out the Holy See's views on international law, see, The Holy See at the Service of Peace, Vatican City, 1988.

[365]   Rousseau, Voyage du Pape, RGDIP 1989, 933; 1990, 148, 515, 806. *Cf.* de Montclos, *Les voyages de Jean Paul II,* 1990.

and sending ambassadors and doing most useful work in humanitarian law in armed conflicts all over the world[366] Forty-one States now have diplomatic relations with the Order.[367] The Order had earlier a territorial basis for its sovereignty, in Rhodes and, later, in Malta itself. Having turned down the offer of having Gotland, the Swedish island in the Baltic, for its own use, it established itself as a sovereign *sui generis*, within the territory of another State.[368]

p. Institutes

See my *Concept of International Law,* 1987, 27.

International research institutes may act in the international society and may conclude agreements with departments of States in their home country or with others with which they cooperate.[369]

q. National Public Bodies

The question whether an entity is an agent of a State has some bearing on the question of its own international personality. If it is not an agent of the State it may perhaps act on its own, assuming international rights and obligations. This is sometimes the case with National or Central Banks. It is not always easy to ascertain whether such banks act on behalf of a State.[370] Whether or not central banks act as such agencies, they often conclude agreements of considerable importance.

Ministries or departments may also conclude agreements with

---

[366] Maschke, *Der deutsche Ordensstaat,* 1935; Pflug-Harttung, *Die Anfänge des Johanniter-Ordens in Deutschland,* 1899; Bergstrand, *Johanniterordens historia,* 1922. *Cf.* my *Concept, op. cit.,* 25-26.

[367] *The Order of Malta, Yesterday and To-day,* Rome, *s.d.,* 4.

[368] Wienand, Der Orden auf Rhodos in Wienand, (ed.), *Der Johanniter-Orden, der Malteser Orden,* 1970, 145; Heritte, *Essai sur l'Ordre des hospitaliers de St. Jean et son gouvernement civil et militaire à Malte,* 1912. Engel, *Histoire de l'Ordre de Malte,* 1968, 311. *Cf.* my *Concept, op. cit.,* 25-26.

[369] See further my *Concept, op. cit.,* 27.

[370] See, the *Trendtex Case* [1977] 1 QB 529 (CA).

their opposite numbers in other States.[371] There are cases where their agreements are subsequently approved by States or where they had previous authorisation; there are also cases where they seem to act quite independently.[372]

Municipalities conclude numerous agreements, especially in Europe where transborder affairs are often of common concern. This practice also applies to Swedish municipalities although Sweden officially denies the right to conclude international agreements to other bodies than the government. As one example of current practice one may refer to the Agreement between the Mayor of Gdansk and the Municipality of Karlskrona of 31st March 1990 on a ferry link between Poland and Sweden.[373]

r. National Private Bodies

The British, Dutch and French East India Companies, The British North Borneo Company and the British South African Company represented their home States and even concluded agreements with other States on their behalf[374] and sent their own envoys.[375] The power of these companies was such that some considered them to enjoy *delegated sovereignty*[376] or even called them *mediate sovereigns*.[377] Nowadays numerous national private bodies conclude agreements of a kind which goes beyond what only private entities do. Thus, national airline corporations have concluded agreements like the General Agreement of 25th September 1956, with provisions *i.a.* on Meteorological Services and Telecommunications or the Interline Traffic Agreements within the framework of inter-State treaties registered by each State.[378]

---

[371]   Blix, *Statsmakternas förbindelser*, 1967, *passim*.

[372]   *E.g.* Carreau, *Droit international public*, 1986.

[373]   *Sydöstran*, 31st March 1990.

[374]   *Cf.* Terway, *East India Company and Russia 1800-1857*, 1977.

[375]   Vattel, *Droit des gens*, 7, iv, vii, 103; Bynkershoek, *Quaestionum juris publici libri duo*, ii ch. iii.

[376]   Alexandrowicz, *An Introduction to the History of the Law of Nations in the East Indies*, 1967, 15.

[377]   Westlake, J., *Collected Papers on Public International Law*, 1914, 197.

[378]   See *Multilateral Interline Traffic Agreements Manual*, 13th ed., 986.

Some agreements of national private bodies may thus be concluded with States and these may be similar to treaties. An interesting example of this technique is the Fishing Agreements in Japan between China and Japanese fishing corporations[379].

s. International Companies

Report by Seidl-Hohenveldern, 60 *Annuaire de l'Institut*, 1983 i, 1 et seq., 97; Adam, *Les établissements internationaux*, 1957; 4 Les organismes internationaux specialisés, 1977; Liebbrecht, *Entreprises à caractère juridiquement international*, 1972.

Some companies are set up under a treaty between States. Two or more States may participate in the equity of the companies. These international bodies have become important in practice and have clearly international personality to act. They are said to have an international position.[380]

There are many types of international enterprises incorporated under a national legal system, like common enterprises under the EURATOM Treaty,[381] the Bank for International Settlements Convention of 20th January 1930,[382] European Central Inland Transport,[383] the Bâle-Mulhouse Airport and the International Mosel Company,[384] EUROFIMA, *Société pour le financement de matériel ferrovière*[385] or *Eurochémie*.[386]

An enterprise created by treaty and incorporated under national law may change its status and become an international organisation.

---

[379]   See, Lee, L.T., *China and International Agreements*, 1969, 65.

[380]   Fiore, P., *Il diritto internazionale codificato e la sua sanzione internazionale*, 5th ed., 1915; *contra*, Phillimore, W., Droits et devoirs fondamentaux des Etats, RCADI, 1923, 64.

[381]   Article 45 *et seq.*

[382]   104 LNTS 441; 6 UNTS concluded under the 1951 Peace Treaty of 8 September 1951, 136 UNTS 45. See, further, Schloss, The *Bank of International Settlements*, 1958.

[383]   Cmnd. 6685, 1945.

[384]   Council of Europe, *International Public Enterprises in Industry and Commerce*, 1957.

[385]   See Sweden, Prop. 211/1955 and Prop. 59/1958.

[386]   Prop. 186/1959.

140

The European Space Agency (ESA)[387] is an example: it operated, originally, as a French société but is now an intergovernmental organisation.[388]

t. Multinationals

Angelo, Multinational Corporate Enterprises, RCADI, 1968, 447; cf. my Concept of International Law, 1987, 32; Kopelmanas, Application du droit international aux sociétés multinationales, 150 RCADI 1976 ii 114; Aramburu Menchaka, Multinational Firms and Regional Processes of Economic Integration, 150 RCADI 1976 ii 394; Czempel, Die Reprivatisierung der Weltwirtschaft. Die Vereinten Nationen und die transnationalen Unternehmen, UN, 1989, 149; Wallace, Legal Control of the Multinational Enterprise, 1983; Cf. Kolvenbach, Neue Rechtsprobleme für multinationale Unternehmen, Wettbewerb, 1989.

A multinational, or what is now, by some, called a transnational company,[389] is one with production and/or distribution services in several countries. The term multinational is probably a preferable term, because of its acceptance in usual language, although some discern nuances and distinctions between trans/ and multinationals. Multinationals usually spread their activities through subsidiaries and their transactions to a number of States and their economic power may be formidable with their budget exceeding the GNP of many small States and it is not out of place to compare their power to some form of sovereignty.[390]

Multinational companies are normally organised by private interests within a particular country according to the private law of that state[391] although there may be government participation, like in the case of British Petroleum.

It may be important to control the behaviour of multinationals especially in developing countries so that they do not abuse their

---

[387]   UNTS 1/2 15 241, 1962.
[388]   ESA succeeded, in 1975, the European Lauch Organisation (ELDO) and the European Space Research Organisation (ESRO). On ESA's Centres see *supra*.
[389]   For further bibliographical details, see my Concept, op cit., 30.
[390]   Cf. Timber, International Combines and National Sovereignty, Univ. Pennsylvania LR, 1947, 578.
[391]   Cf. Sereni, op. cit., p. 133.

powerful position.[392]

Which law applies to transactions of multinationals? Their contracts are, because of their power position, similar to State contracts.[393] It is a difficult, and often recurring, problem to establish whether international law or the national law of the home or of the host State shall apply to transactions of multinationals.[394]

Actions which took place before the multinational arrived in a host country should probably be governed by its home State, especially with regard to investments in countries affected by UN sanctions. Once the multinational has established a subsidiary company in another State, the laws of that host country should apply.[395]

Many agreements of multinationals are not expressly subjected to the municipal law of any country in their agreements. There is usually no indication of any law in the initial, often very friendly, agreements between a State and a multinational establishing itself in that State. As neither party is keen not to even think about conflict, nothing may be said about applicable law or arbitration at all: the parties do not visualise falling out with each other. The host State is, at this stage, usually keen for the multinational to establish itself. Conversely, the multinational is not in the position of suggesting much else than the host State's legal system, as the host state, because of the equality of

---

[392] See Institut de droit international, 57 Annuaire 1977 ii 338. For new Codes of regulation see, United Nations Code for Transnational Corporations E/C.10/AC.2/8 1978; 17 ILM 1978, 453; with numerous revisions, notably the issue of 1988, UN Centre on Transnational Corporations; The ILO Tripartite Declaration on Principles Concerning Multinational Enterprises and Social Policy of 1978 17 ILM 1978, 453, a set of OECD Guidelines for Multinational Enterprises 1976 15 ILM 1976, 969; 17 ILM 1527; Blainpain, *The Badger Case* and the OECD Guidelines for Multinational Enterprises, 1977, revised in 1979; the Council of Europe Draft Code on Multinationals of 1977 Doc. 3762 1976; the EEC Code of Conduct for Subsidiaries of Multinational Enterprises 1977 and 1986, concerning *i.a.* activities in South Africa; OJ C 118/15 1977; and OJ 1986; The Principles of the International Chamber of Commerce Regarding Multinational Enterprises 1974 191/83.

[393] See my *Concept, op. cit.,* 75 *et seq.*

[394] Department of Economic and Social Affairs, *The Impact of Multinationals in International Relations,* New York, 1974, 49-50.

[395] *Cf. ibid., loc. cit.*

States, cannot accept being bound by the municipal legal rules of any other State.

However, a conflict, if it comes to that, can be solved: this is an area where international law plays an important part. General international rules, supplemented by certain lowest-common-denominator rules from municipal systems, are merged into a viable legal system to apply to the agreement.[396] This set of rules is akin to a common *lex mercatoria*.[397]

u. Joint Ventures

Proceedings, IBA Conference on Joint Ventures, Warsaw, 21-25 April 1990; see my *Finance and Protection of Investment in Developing Countries,* 2nd ed., 1987; United Nations, ECE, *Joint Ventures,* 1989 with updating.

Joint ventures are popular in the Third World as a form of activity into which companies of the industrialised world are encouraged to invest, considering the relative protection they receive under the joint venture umbrella. The protection is derived from the simple fact that the ownership of the joint venture is shared between the foreign company and the Third World government, or one of its government controlled companies. As the ownership is partly in the hands of the Third World State, or controlled by it, there is less incentive to nationalise the venture than a completely foreign-owned enterprise.

As a host State is less motivated to nationalise a joint venture which it shares with an investor, the form of such joint ventures have, over the last two decades, provided a useful vehicle to protect foreign investment and yet ensure the interests of the host State as well. There has been an ever increasing trend to form joint ventures also in the States of Eastern Europe, particularly in those which have become de-socialised but still suffer from problems like fragile economy and relatively untried political conditions.

There are forms of joint ventures involving a local, private or public company, which is not owned or controlled by the State, but

---

[396] See my *Concept, op. cit.,* 75 *et seq.,* for Substantive Rules For All Types of Cooperation, a chapter which deals with the adaptation of rule sets to accomodate the adjudication of a specific dispute.

[397] See, further, *ibid.,* 75 *et seq.*

the common form of joint venture, however, is hall-marked precisely by government participation. The joint venture is different from other national and international companies: it is not designed to run or develop common services or other matters for the parties but rather acts as an umbrella for the exploitation by one party-expert in the territory of a party-host, for mutual benefit and profit.

Many types of joint ventures have been set up by multinationals. When this happens, there may be three subjects of international law acting together: The State, the multinational[398] and the joint venture itself.

The choice of law for joint venture contracts is a fruitful field of exploration for international scholars. In many cases, joint venture partners have to rely heavily on the law of the territorial State.[399] Should one partner thus need injunctive relief, it is to the Courts of this State he must address himself, and, both for procedure and substance, it is the law of the *forum* that the Courts in that State will apply. A number of choice of law questions arise with regard to the shareholders' agreement, the corporate relationship, third party suppliers agreements *et cetera* which cannot be solved by simple recourse to the *lex fori*. Ordinary conflict of laws solutions will then be applied.[400] In the first instance there is a search for the intention of the parties[401] and, if there is not such displayed intention as to which law is to apply, one resorts to a search for the proper law, that is to say the law with which the contract has its closest and most real connection. This law is not necessarily the one of the host State for all aspects of various relationships of the joint venture.

iv. The Latent Subjects of International Society

---

[398] See *supra*.

[399] For a survey of applicable laws, see, United Nations, ECE, *Joint Ventures, 1988* with updating; *cf.* Hobér, *Joint Ventures in the Soviet Union*, 1988.

[400] See further *infra*, in Chapter VI.

[401] *Hamlyn v Talisker Distillery* [1894] AC 202; *Vita Food Products v Unus Shipping* [1939] AC 277 (PC); *Tzortzis v Monark Line* [1968] 1 WLR 406 (CA).

144

We have seen that there is a great variety of subjects of international law. There are thus numerous entities and persons who may, in a given situation, be or become subjects of international law. The notion of a subject of law is thus relative and flexible and cannot, except as an outline, be laid down beforehand.

To be a subject of international law means that an entity or a person can exercise or be endowed with international rights and obligations: in other words, in a given situation an entity or a person will, for a particular purpose, be lifted out of his ordinary intra-state or national (municipal) law system to be protected, or given more far reaching obligations, under the international legal system.

However, the various entities we have seen *might* be subjects of international society, or, perhaps better said, are *potential subjects* in this system, do not always act in their *capacity of such subjects*. Even States which are the most important power structures in international society and the most important subjects, and, indeed, the prime law makers, are not always acting in their capacity of international subjects.

For example, when States are concerned with their domestic affairs, they act by virtue of their internal sovereignty. It is only when their action has international *relevance*, that their quality of *international subjects* becomes important. This may either occur if they take action outwards, towards the international sphere, by, for example, concluding treaties or acting in international organisations, or when their internal behaviour is circumscribed by international rules, such as, for example, duties they have in the field of Human Rights or with regard to the immunity of diplomats. Here, if they set aside what the international legal system imposes on States as their duties, their international responsibility will be engaged and they will be liable to damages, sanctions or other consequential effects.[402]

Actions of States are internationally relevant in cases rights and duties are *direct*, *i.e.* they are activated without any specific treaty or conventional[403] regulation. Examples of this is, for example, the

---

[402]   See *infra*, Chapter VIII.

[403]   Note that this adjective is used to mean regulation by treaty or 'convention' and does not imply any element of tradition, as in common parlance, nor of non-obligation, as in the usage of the term in the context of the practice of the

punishment of war criminals or the corresponding guarantees of basic Human Rights which concern certain individuals. Another example is the growing tendency to consider multinationals responsible, on an international level, for environmental damage.

In other cases, rights and duties are *indirect* in so far as they operate as the basis of a treaty system. This is, for example, the case when individuals are given the right to take action in international Courts against their own State, like under the European Convention on Human Rights or under the treaties of the European Communities.[404]

Other examples are furnished by treaty-making mechanisms allowing non-state parties to adhere to international agreements on the same footing, with similar rights and obligations, as States.[405]

Even in these cases, States may, in the event of violations of relevant rules, have their international responsibility engaged. On the other hand, there are numerous aspects of State action which does not concern the international legal action and when the State organises these affairs it is not for international law to limit or prescribe certain action.

It is thus not always that even States acts by virtue of their international personality. With regard to other subjects of international law, it is even more frequent that their action is determined by other parameters than international law, or, in other words, that their action has no international relevance.

Houses of Parliament.

[404]   See, *supra*, under individuals.

[405]   See my *Law of War, op. cit.*

CHAPTER III

Sources of International Law: Hard Law

A. IDENTIFICATION OF RULES

i. The Relationship Between Law Making, State Powers and Sources of Law

We have seen that States are the prime law makers in international society. In one form or another they give their consent to new rules that emerge in international society.[1] We have seen that there are many actors and subjects in international society.

We shall find that creation of international law is a highly complex and sophisticated process.[2] A network of rules results from the interaction of actors/subjects/creators in international society. We have seen that there are numerous entities and individuals that are *subjects* of international law, *i.e.* capable of *assuming international rights and duties.* On the other hand, there are a number of bodies that are merely *latent* subjects of international law. However, international law is not, in all its parts, necessarily *relevant* to all latent subjects.[3] But States are always, in their external relations, and increasingly with regard to their internal affairs, concerned with the operation of international law.

There is a *wider* circle of entities and individuals which are *actors* in international society and whose conduct may be important to the development of international law. There is, furthermore, a *narrow* circle of entities, normally only States, which are *creators* of international law. It is therefore important to consider, in detail, the position of the most important power structure, the *State*, in international society and investigate the limits of its power and of its

---

[1]   See, my *Concept, op. cit.,* 96 *et seq.*
[2]   See *ibid., op. cit., passim,* and *infra.*
[3]   *Ibid.* 129.

jurisdiction. It is necessary to analyse to what extent there are restrictions on the competence of the State.

It is also important to analyse, first, the sources of international law and to establish how rules emerge in international society. The mechanisms for rule creating are numerous. However, we may briefly review the basic categories of rules by which actors and subjects are bound in the international sphere.

ii. Definition of the Term Source

Verdross, *Quellen des Universellen Völkerrechts*, 1973; Finck, *The Sources of Modern International Law*, 1937; Parry, *The Sources and Evidences of International Law*, 1965; Scelle, Essai sur les sources formelles du droit international, 3 Recueil Gény, 1936, 400; Borchard, The theory and sources of international law, 3 Recueil Gény, 1936 328; Kopelmanas, Essai d'une théorie des sources formelles du droit international, RDI 1938 101; Gihl, The legal character and sources of international law, in 1 *Scandinavian Studies in Law*, 51; Fitzmaurice, Some problems regarding the formal sources of international law, *Symbolae Verzijl*, 1958, 153; Jennings, What is international law and how do we tell when we see it? SchwJIR 1981 59; *idem*, Recent developments in the International Law Commission: Its relation to the sources of international law, ICLQ 1964, 385; Bin Cheng, On the nature and sources of international law in Bin Cheng (ed.), *Teaching and Practice*, 1982, 203; StJ MacDonald & Johnston (eds.), *The Structure and Process of International Law: Essays in Legal Philosophy, Doctrine and Theory*, 1983; Sorensen, *Les sources du droit international, Etude sur la jurisprudence de la Cour permanente de justice internationale*, 1946; van Hoof, *Rethinking the Sources of International Law*, 1983; Meissner, Die sowjetische Bewertung der Völkerrechtsquellen, *Ost-Europa Recht*, March 1955, 2; Müllerson, New Thinking by Soviet Scholars, AJIL 1989, 494; Danilenko, *Obychai v sovremennom mezhdunarodnom prave*, 1988; *idem*, The Theory of Customary Law, GYIL, 1988, 9.

See also relevant chapters in the leading textbooks, particularly Rousseau, *Droit international public*, i, 1970, 55-443; Reuter, *Droit international public*, 1973.

For historical aspects, see Guggenheim, Contribution à l'histoire des sources du droit des gens, 94 RCADI 1958 1.

A *source* of law can mean the *ultimate* source of a law and in this sense be used synonymously with the *basis of obligation.*[4] Many

---

[4]   *Cf.* Berber, *Lehrbuch des Völkerrechts*, 1975, i pp. 37-40.

distinguish instead between a *formal* and a *material* source of law, then reserving the term *formal* for the mechanisms through which the law comes into being. These mechanisms are in any State the normal constitutional machinery. Some claim that the category of formal sources serves little purpose in international law for which there is no such constitutional machinery.[5] Yet, if the term *source* is used, as it often is, to denote the very ways that international law comes into being,[6] then it would seem to come very near the way we understand a formal source in municipal law.

But *source* can also be understood in the material sense of the word indicating where the legal rules come from, *i.e.* the factual framework where the rules are located.[7] However, if a *source* of international law is understood to mean the very material facts which state the law, we are saying nothing more than that the sources *are* the law and that the sources themselves comprise the whole material network of rules. It is therefore more useful to let sources of international law denote the *mechanisms* by which international law comes into being.

iii. Article 38 of the Statute of the International Court of Justice

Article 38 of the Statute of the International Court of Justice lists the sources of international law and indicates thus what the sources are, in the opinion of its drafters.

The Statute of the International Court of Justice enumerates the sources of international law in a somewhat illogical and deficient manner but, since sources cannot be discussed without reference to this by now well-established provision,[8] it is necessary to set it out

---

5 *Cf.* Brownlie, *Principles, op. cit.,* 1.

6 So Briggs 44. *Cf.* Maryan Green, *International Law, Law of Peace,* 2d ed., 1983, 1st ed., 1973, 15 *et seq.*

7 See further my *Concept, op. cit.,* 44-45.

8 Article 38 of the Statute of ICJ is specifically invoked in the Revised 1928 General Act for the Pacific Settlement of International Disputes of 28th April 1949, 71 UNTS 101, articles 18(2) and 28. It is a provision which is also commonly adopted in international arbitration treaties. Furthermore, although not specifically invoked, the predecessor of article 38, the article of the Permanent Court of International Justice of similar wording, has been applied

here.

1. The Court, whose function is to decide in accordance with international law such disputes as are submitted to it, shall apply:
(a) international conventions, whether general or particular, establishing rules expressly recognised by the contracting States;
(b) international custom, as evidence of a general practice accepted as law;
(c) the general principles of law recognised by civilised nations;
(d) subject to the provisions of Article 59, judicial decisions and the teachings of the most highly qualified publicists of the various nations, as subsidiary means for the determination of rules of law.

2. This provision shall not prejudice the power of the Court to decide a case *ex aequo et bono*, if the parties agree thereto.

It is not clear whether the drafters of this provision intended it to be exhaustive. Its obscure formulation is less of a problem than the obvious gaps.[9] For example, unilateral declarations and decisions and regulations of international organisations are not mentioned.

One major conceptual problem is, of course, that since article 38 *lists* the sources of international law, it cannot *itself* be a source.[10] Considering furthermore the other deficiencies - indicated above - of this article, it is useful to consider article 38, therefore, as a *guideline* to the sources of international law, providing information on the *main sources* of international law and not as any exhaustive list indicating all *fontes juris gentium*. Furthermore, the importance of article 38 must not be over estimated as the article itself constitutes part of the sources of international law to which it refers. It can therefore not

---

in numerous international arbitrations, *e.g.* in *The Naulilaa Case* (1928), 2 RIAA 1011, in *The Cysne Case,* [1930], 2 RIAA 1035 and in *The Case Regarding the Interpretation of Article 11 of the London Protocol* (1926), 2 RIAA 755.

[9] See, *infra*, under General Principles.

[10] See i:1 Oppenheim, ed. Jennings & Watts, 24 and Ross, *A Textbook of International Law*, 1947, at 83.

150

validate the legitimacy of other sources.[11]

iv. Hierarchy of Sources?

Maschke, *Die Rangordnung der Rechtsquellen,* 1932; Monaco, Observations sur la hiérarchie des sources du droit international, *Festschrift Mosler,* 1956, 599; Bos, The hierarchy among the recognised manifestations ('sources') of international law, 1 *Festschrift Miaja de la Muela* 363; Akehurst, The hierarchy of the sources of international law, BYIL 1974-1975, 273; Vallindas, General principles of law and the hierarchy of the sources of internaticnal law, in *Mélanges Spiropoulos,* 1957, 525.

Some have discussed whether there is a hierarchy of sources. Article 38 (1) of the Statute of the International Court of Justice does mention treaties first. It would seem that such instruments probably are the most *important* sources of law in international society for the simple reason that they are clear and often unequivocal, whereas other sources, by their nature, are bound to be more uncertain.

If there are two conflicting rules of international law one will usually give preference to a later rule (*lex posterior derogat juri priori*) and one will also allow a more specific rule to derogate from a general rule (*lex specialis derogat legem generalis*).[12] But such rules are difficult to apply unless rules of international law, from whatever source, are viewed as being on an equal footing.

Furthermore, there are cases where treaties are set aside by custom,[13] or displaced by general principles.[14] Consequently, sources mentioned in article 38 of the Statute of the International Court are better viewed as parallel and not as sources ordered in any hierarchy. Then, the two above mentioned presumptions of preference of date (the *lex posterior* case) or more specific rules (the *lex specialis* case) may operate as useful, modifying, mechanisms.

v. Codification of International Law

Zemanek, Die Bedeutung der Kodifizierung des Völkerrechts für seine Anwendung,

---

[11]   *Cf.* I:i Oppenheim, 9th ed. by Jennings & Watts, 1992, 24.

[12]   *Cf.* my *Law Making, op. cit.,* 275-290; *cf.* 25-41.

[13]   Karl, *Vertragsrecht und späteres Gewohnheitsrecht,* 1986.

[14]   For example, by the operation of *jus cogens* see, *supra.*

Festschrift Verdross, 1971, 565; Dhokalia, *The Codification of Public International Law,* 1970; Daudet, *Les conférences pour la codification du droit international,* 1968; Geck, Völkerrechtliche Verträge und Kodifikation, ZaöRVR 1976 96; Briggs, Reflections on the Codification of International Law by the International Law Commission and by Other Agencies, 126 RCADI 1969 i 233; Jennings, Progressive development of international law and its codification, BYIL 1947, 301.

Specifically on the International Law Commission, see Sinclair, *The International Law Commission,* 1987; Tomuschat, Die Völkerrechtskommission der Vereinten Nationen, VN 1988, 180; Jennings, Recent developments in the International Law Commission: Its relation to the sources of international law, ICLQ 1964, 385.

A rule of international law is more accessible, clear and often unequivocal if it is laid down in writing in an agreement. Numerous rules of international law may be codified in conventions or treaties. The work to embody more and more rules in such convenient written and binding form is actively encouraged by the International Law Commission, a body within the framework of the United Nations, which has drafted numerous specific conventions.[15]

However, codification need not be used in the strict sense of meaning, implying binding rules, laid down in a treaty. It can also be conveniently used to denote efforts to clarify the contents of international law in some other form of writing. In that sense, important codification work is also carried out by specialist and eminent research institutes, like the *Institut de droit international,* and by professional/academic associations, like the International Law Association. The value of statements, declarations and drafts of such bodies varies with their academic standing in international society.

If codification is understood in a loose, informal sense, we may also include here the writings of publicists, which under article 38(1) of the Statute of the International Court of Justice, constitute a supplementary source of international law. It is the works of jurists and commentators which provide the required evidence of 'customs and usages',[16] a notion too frequently distorted to imply some fictiously formed 'customary law',[17] but which probably, at the time,

---

[15] See list in United Nations, International Law Commission, 1989.
[16] *The Paquete Habana* (1900) 175 US SC Rep 677.
[17] For criticism of customary law theories, see *infra* in this Chapter.

referred to practice by States.[18]

Naturally, not everything what every international lawyer writes reflects international law. But if we turn to the most eminent publicists, and look for common agreement between them on some specific rule, we will find considerable guidance as to the contents of international law on a specific problem, although we, from time to time, require refreshing and sharp criticism of accepted authorities not to fall into blue print patterns.

In the same way, we could look at the judgments of the International Court of Justice and, occasionally, at judgments and awards of other courts and tribunals. Judgments and awards may well, in most cases, only operate between the parties. However, when a Court of some standing, particularly the International Court of Justice, expresses a view on a matter, we can be reasonably certain that this is an authoritative statement on what international law provides, at least what it provides at the moment in time when the judgment is pronounced. In one sense, the International Court of Justice in particular, codifies international law and, at the same time develops[19] the international legal system. The Court often takes *avant garde* views on numerous issues, for example on notions like *solidarity* or on notions like *jus cogens*.[20]

B. TYPES OF RULES

i. The Hypothetical Goal

My earlier work *The Concept of International Law* (1987) sought to classify rules of the international society in appropriate categories: if one uses an inductive approach to analyse the maze of rules that States appear to follow in their various relationships, it becomes clear

---

[18]   It is interesting to note that textbooks about the turn of the century did not speak much of customary law, but far more of treaties, conventions, general rules and State practice.

[19]   *E.g.* Lauterpacht, *The Development of International Law by the International Court*, 1958.

[20]   See my Concept, *op. cit.*, 94 *et seq.*, and *infra* in Chapter III.

that at least *modern*[21] international society and its agents behave *as if there were* a specific hypothetical goal for their various activities. This hypothetical goal I have, in my previous work, presumed to be that of *promotion of the welfare of international society*, thus indicating some minimum duty of positive action.[22] — Finnis ?

ii. Rules to Ensure the Hypothetical Goal

International relations scholars have often searched the *rationale* of rules in international society.[23] International lawyers have been more hesitant, overpowered as they have been by positivist doctrine,[24] refusing to attach any importance to rules which are laid down by States by their authority, and refusing to admit the obvious conceptual advantages of a thomistic approach which allows for *different layers of rules*, a clear *inherent duty* for subjects of the international legal order to respect notions of *independence* and *interdependence*.[25]

Once we assume that a goal to preserve and improve international relations exists, rules that we pragmatically see used become more readily identifiable. It is patently clear that modern international society has condemned *war and armed conflict* and States and others behave to show that there are certainly binding rules in this respect *outside the realm of treaties*. General rules also exist for the protection of a *minimum standard of Human Rights*, as well as to *outlaw piracy* and *terrorism*. States and other actors are also increasingly concerned about *environmental degradation* and do not hesitate to take steps to reverse the trend.

---

[21] Note that Artistotle emphasised that *every* society (*polis* or *koinonia*) is established for something 'good'. The 'true' koinonia (from the adjective *koinos* meaning something shared in partnership) will always pursue the 'true good', Aristotle, *Politics*, I.1.i (1252 a 1-7) 25 and for a commentary, see, for example, Mulgan, *Artistotle's Political Theory*, 1987 13.

[22] See my *Concept, op. cit.*, 46-47, and *supra*.

[23] See Bull, *The Anarchical Society*, 1977, 16 *et seq.* on the *preservation of the international society* as a viable goal; *cf.* similar expressions by Holsti, *International Politics*, 4th ed., 1983 129; Modelski, *Principles of World Politics* 1972, 288 on *survival*.

[24] But see 1 Hyde 2-3.

[25] Thomas Aquinas, *Summa theologica*, 1267-1273.

Action in these matters is not always taken by States in the form of treaties, but also by unilateral declarations and simple, but apparently binding, statements. States often see themselves bound to abide in certain rules, although they have not signed an international agreement to this effect. These rules are thus *general rules*, although not necessarily customary rules, as we shall see in a closer analysis.

States and other groups may *condemn* the way certain States resort to force, treat their own citizens, or damage the environment, and make corresponding pronouncements, and even instigate, sanctions for violation of certain standards of *Human Rights*.

The above mentioned rules appear to form the core of the international legal system as it is they which secure international and regional peace and well being: they are what I call the *prophylactic rules*, specifically designed to prevent any action which would obviate the hypothetical goal.

These rules are supplemented by rules on structure of international society, (*stabilising rules*),[26] rules on distribution and competence, (*distributive rules*),[27] rules on cooperation and contacts, (*promotional rules*),[28] as well as by rules on consequences for violation of international law, (*consequential rules*).[29] All these rules operate within a formal framework of necessary and intrinsic *maxims* and general principles.

iii. Intrinsic Rules: Maxims and General Principles

Certain rules are *formal* in the sense that they apply in procedure of courts or other hearings. They are *intrinsic* in so far as they are essential in the legal system of international society and they are, in fact, indispensable to any legal system. As we shall see,[30] maxims and general principles are formal pillars on which the efficacy of international law depends.

---

[26]   See my *Concept, op. cit.*, 57 *et seq.*

[27]   *Ibid.*, 58 *et seq.*

[28]   *Ibid.*, 68 *et seq.*

[29]   *Ibid.*, 79 *et seq.*

[30]   *Infra* in this Chapter under Natural Law.

iv. Entrenching Rules: Prophylactic Rules

Other rules in international society are less technical than the above
mentioned maxims and less general than the aforementioned general
principles. Some of these substantial rules are *entrenching* in the
sense that they pervade and secure the structure of the international
legal system.

We can distinguish here a group of rules which I have called
prophylactic rules, *i.e.* those which are designed to prohibit harm to
international society. To this group we can count rules which forbid
the use of force, between States, or, between groups, such as
insurgents, freedom fighters or terrorists, between such groups and
States, or between States and individuals by violating Human Rights.
Some prophylactic rules concern the protection of international
society from environmental damage or excessive waste of natural
resources.[31]

In a later Chapter[32] we shall investigate, in detail, the various
types of prophylactic rules that operate and are effective in
international society.

v. Entrenching Rules: Stabilising Rules

Entrenching rules secure, as has been mentioned, the very structure
of international society. There appears to be two further types of such
rules, beyond those which we have called prophylactic rules. These
other two types, analysed in detail below,[33] concern either division
of competence between subjects in international society, and are thus
distributive rules, or they concern communications, in which case we
may call them *contact rules*.

A special type of these rules thus concern distribution of
competence between States and between States and organisations.
Some distributive rules divide competence and functions within the
national space, others do so in common areas; a separate type of rules
concern, in this field, distribution of jurisdictional competence.

---

[31] See, *infra*, under Prophylactic Rules: Protection of the International Society.
[32] See *infra*, Chapter V.
[33] See *infra*, Chapters VI and VII.

Contact and cooperation rules, may concern communications international transactions, such as treaties, or warning mechanisms in case of disasters. Also the modalities of immunity of agents belong to this group.

vi. Promotional Rules

Other rules may be called *promotional* in the sense that they enhance the possibility or harmonious development of international society, by cooperation, sharing and setting of targets for development. However, although this group is of great practical importance, especially with regard to the Third World, these rules are rarely binding but often merely *programmatic*.[34]

vii. Consequential Rules

When States and other actors violate the binding rules of international law certain consequences ensue. *Consequential rules* thus deal with correction and sanctions, using general principles such as imputability, responsibility and foreseeability, to assess specific consequences of violations.

C. THEORY OF ACTS

The rule system sketched above has come into being by various *acts*, normally taken by States - which are the most important subjects of international law - and such *acts* may *recognise* existing necessary rules, or, on many occasions, *create* rules. Rules may be subject to *revision*; a coherent theory of acts may assist in distinguishing various categories of relevant legal acts.[35] It is by various *acts* that States *recognise* or *adopt* specific rules, especially on *ethical standards of behaviour*.[36]

---

[34]   See *infra* in the Chapter on Legal Value of Recommendations. Further, on programmatic rules, see my *Concept, op. cit.*, Chapter II.

[35]   See in detail my *Concept, op. cit.*, 85 *et seq.*

[36]   See, in detail, my *Concept, op. cit.*, 87-119 and *infra* under Natural Law.

D. LAW MAKING AND THE CONSENT OF STATES

i. Consent as a Law Making Factor

a. States and non-State Actors

It is important to stress the role of the State in the law making process of international society. There is, of course, no legislature to enact rules but one can clearly see States, the most important power bases, as originators of rules of international law.[37]

It is interesting to note that international lawyers are only now waking up to realise that there are other units than States of importance.[38] International relations scholars recognised this long ago when they abandoned the extreme State paradigm.[39] But we must not exaggerate and seek to replace the State with other actors: we must be aware of the importance of the State as a power base and regard other actors as supplementing the role of States. It is interesting to note that international relations scholars are now returning to acknowledge the importance of the State as the important unit.

In a sense, international lawyers, that is, most of them, have always been one step behind international relations scholars. Most international lawyers still only accept States, and inter-governmental organisations, as subjects of the international legal system while they ignore other actors. Yet, one must recognise the importance of the non-State actors alongside the formidable power base of the State. In other words, the assumption that the State provides a power base of paramount importance in the international system also holds true as

---

[37] For the proposition that States give their consent to rules of international law in one form or another and on various forms of consent, see my *Concept, op. cit.*, 96-105, on Basic and Enhanced Participation of States, on Permission Acts and Acts of Delegation; on Contractual Acts, Promissory Acts, Parallel Acts, Acts of Recognition and Authoritative Acts, and 123-124 for Consent of States as Basis of Obligation.

[38] 'Important' in the sense that they are influencial actors, see, *infra*, on Variety of Creators/Actors/Subjects and *cf.* my *Concept, op. cit.*, 129 *et seq.*

[39] For example, Burton, *Systems, States, Diplomacy and Rules*, 1968, *passim; Cf.* Aron, *Paix et guerre entre les nations*, 1962, 133.

158

far as international law is concerned. At the same time, we must be aware of the fact also that other subjects are important in the international legal system.[40]

b. The Requirement of Consent — *eroded*:

(i) General Aspects

States give their consent in clear and unequivocal form to a number of rules of international law. To others they consent by conclusive action, indicating that they accept the existence of specific rules.

In some cases, rules are so evident and of such basic importance that an entity, by the very fact of becoming a State, must be presumed to have consented to such rules. I have identified rules formed by *passive participation*, whereby the consent of a State is presumed - as no State can take part in international affairs without respecting such rules.[41] This is the group of rules that concern what I have called *prophylactic rules*,[42] that is to say the prohibition of the use of force, the promotion of respect of Human Rights, and the duty not to degrade the human environment.

One can also distinguish cases where States take very active part in the formulation of international rules and thus contribute by *active participation* to their creation by giving their clear consent by their very action. This may occur when a State concludes a treaty agreeing to certain general rules.

A distinct way of displaying definite consent by specific action is by creating an international organisation to perform certain duties or functions. The delegation of specific powers to an organisation is perhaps a third form of consent, implying especially clear and unequivocal State agreement that the organisation will be allowed to perform specific duties; this form of consent can then be called *enhanced participation*.[43]

These three types of acts of *consent* concern the *degree of*

---

40   See, *infra*, on Subjects of International Law.

41   See my *Concept, op. cit.*, 96-105.

42   See *supra* in this Chapter and, for different types, *infra*, Chapter V.

43   *Ibid.*, 98.

participation in the rule-making. One can also distinguish a different type of consent to rules when certain rules come into being because States *allow*, by their passivity, this to happen. The root of the rules is then based on the different degree of State control: by what can be called *permitting* acts, States may *allow* non-State actors to perform certain functions. Multinational companies or NGOs[44] may, for example, be permitted to exercise some function with special acquiescence of States. Alternatively, States may delegate power to international organisations to perform certain functions and then *allow* them to expand their competence beyond that of implied powers[45] to work on behalf of the States.

A further way of classifying types of consent to rules is according to the *form of consent* given. States may agree by concluding a *contractual* act, such as a treaty.[46] Such acts are binding on the basis of the fundamental maxim *pacta sunt servanda*, a rule without which no legal order can subsist.[47]

A further, and very common form, is to make a *promissory* statement. Contrary to what most textbooks claim, such statements are very important in State practice: States do attach binding force to such pronouncements which are given in unilateral,[48] or, occasionally, *parallel*,[49] form. Furthermore, other States consider themselves entitled to *rely* on certain promissory statements of others. If we disregard the effect of honourably keeping your word in international relations, we impute to States more Machiavellian techniques than they actually employ in State practice. There are thus, in international society, rules reminiscent of *estoppel*, implying that a party is not allowed to contradict the veracity of statements or facts made public by statements of authorised representatives or by his own behaviour, especially if others have taken acts relying on this

---

[44] *Ibid.*, 98.
[45] On implied powers see my *Law Making, op. cit.,* 29 *et seq.*
[46] This is also, as mentioned above, a form of active participation.
[47] *Cf. supra*, on Maxims.
[48] See, further, my *Concept,* 100 *et seq.*
[49] This is the case when a number of States jointly agree on common action. See, my *Concept, op. cit.,* 102.

160

behaviour.[50]

A third, and again a very common form of giving consent, is by *adoption:* here, States adopt pre-standards,[51] or provisional standards, and by their adoption they place a formal stamp of approval on such non-binding standards *to make them* obligatory by unilateral *adoption.*

By a fourth form of consent process States may recognise the existence of certain ethical rules[52] and other basic rules of essence to the international legal system. By *stating* the law in formal and clear pronouncements (including unilateral or parallel statements) States thus acknowledge, by this act of recognition,[53] that relevant rules exist.[54] In this way States indicate that they acknowledge that there are specific legal rules[55] and certain necessary ethical[56] standards,[57] binding in law, in international society.

The difference between *adopting* and *recognising* rules is that *adoption* involves a certain law making function whereas *recognition* implies that the rules in question have been created spontaneously from the legal framework and only require a stamp of recognition.[58]

A classification of types of consent like the one suggested above is useful to show that behind most rules in international society we

---

[50] See further, *infra* under Soft Law, Acceptance by Voting, Acceptance reinforced by Acquiescence: Estoppel, in this Chapter. *Cf.* Bowett, Estoppel before international tribunals and its relation to requiescence, BYIL 1957, 176 *et seq.*

[51] See *infra,* under Standards.

[52] *Cf. supra* on Ethics, under Customary Law *latu sensu* in this Chapter.

[53] Obviously, it is important to distinguish such acts of *recognition of rules,* implying recognising the *existence* of certain rules in the international system from acts of *recognition of States,* see *supra* under States, in Chapter II.

[54] See my *Concept, op. cit.,* 104.

[55] Such recognition may imply a re-confirmation of maxims, see *supra* in this Chapter.

[56] *Cf. supra,* on Ethics as Customary Law *latu sensu,* in this Chapter.

[57] In the context here we are concerned with *recognition of standards, i.e.* acknowledging that certain standards *exist.* This group of rules can also be enlarged by acts of *adoption,* whereby States agree to abide by further rules. *Cf. infra* on Adoption of Standards, under Soft Law, Types of Recommendations.

[58] Distinguish, from this form of *recognition* in the sense of *acknowledging* rules, the common process in international society of *recognising States,* (and, occasionally governments); see further *supra,* Chapter II, under Recognition.

can trace the *consent of States*. But this does not mean that States are the only subjects of international law: it only signifies that it is the States which are the *prime law makers* in international society.[59]

(ii) Abstract Consent

In many cases States delegate their right to create law to international organisations which then exercise a right of *delegated legislation*.[60] To such legislation States have given their consent in advance, thus they have given what I have called their *abstract consent*, by signing a treaty which created the organisation, a treaty which becomes the *Constitution* of the organisation.[61]

States may thus grant powers to international organisations to carry out certain functions. The legitimacy of action of organisations depend on whether they stay within the latitude of powers granted; acts which do not fall within this framework will be considered as *ultra vires*. There are, as often in a legal system, exceptions to this rule. When the Security Council was blocked by veto in 1950 during the Korean crisis, the General Assembly took the famous Uniting for Peace Resolution and exercised the powers otherwise reserved for the Security Council. The Uniting for Peace Resolution was later used as the basis for the General Assembly decision to form the first United Nations troop contingents, the United Nations 'Emergency Force (UNEF).[62]

The fact that State consent is at the root of delegated legislation implies that States can also *resume powers* lent to international organisations. It may be very costly, in economic and cultural terms,

---

[59] On the numerous types of international subjects, see, *supra*, Chapter II. Further, on the function of States as *prime law makers* in international society, see my *Concept, op. cit., passim*.

[60] See my *Law Making, op. cit., passim*. On the point of delegated power *cf.* my *Concept, op. cit.*, 73-75.

[61] See my *Law Making, op. cit.*, Chapter One, *passim* and 322.

[62] See my *Law Making, op. cit.*, 38, on the Resolution changing *de facto* the UN Charter. On the UN Forces see the series of volumes by Higgins, *The UN Forces*, 1976 -.

to leave the European Community, but, although the treaties[63] do not foresee any right to leave the organisations,[64] it would be absurd to contend that States could not do this, provided they compensated other member States if any losses were incurred as a result of the withdrawal from membership.

The notion of *abstract consent* can also be used to denote powers given to an international court for all future disputes, for example by signing the Optional Clause of the Statute of the ICJ.

(iii) Continuous Consent

State consent may, in some cases, have to be *continuous*. This is the case when a State permits restrictions of its territorial sovereignty by allowing another State, or an organisation, to exercise sovereign functions, for example, to legislate (like Member States allow the European Community to legislate), to adjudicate (as China allowed the Great Powers to exercise judicial functions[65]), or to keep military bases (as, for example, the Philippines and numerous other countries allowed the United States) which also implies the exercise of sovereign functions.[66]

Some claim that a State has the right to denounce a treaty under the rule *rebus sic stantibus* if it can prove that fundamental circumstances have changed. This rule implies that a treaty is always concluded on the (implied, or silent) condition that, should circumstances change, the treaty will not be operative. The change, say the traditional textbooks, must be *fundamental*.

This is a dangerous rule. Who decides on what is *fundamental*?

---

63 The Paris Treaty of 1952 creating the European Coal and Steel Community (CECA or ECSC), and the Rome Treaties of 1958, establishing the European Economic Community (CEE or EEC) and Euratom.

64 But note that the European Coal and Steel Community was created for a time of fifty years, a later amended article.

65 See my article on Unequal Treaties, ICLQ 1966, which deals in some detail with the Capitulations Treaties with China under which the Western Consuls were given the right to try cases involving their own citizens for crimes committed in China.

66 Further on my theory of *continuous consent* see my *International Law and the Independent State,* 2nd ed., 1987, 197-199 and 218-219.

It can be used as a political cloak to allow virtually any treaty to be denounced.[67] Instead of resorting to such questionable rules, it may be realistic to allow States a right to denounce treaties, including those establishing international organisations, if by such treaties States have restricted their territorial sovereignty. By being members of the European Community, States delegate powers to the organisation. The Community exercises a law making function granted to it by the Member States for the *convenience* of these States. The Member States obviously think this is for the better and for a purpose from which they all derive substantial advantages. By the EC treaties States delegate law making sovereignty to the European Community, *i.e.* the right to replace, for some purposes, the law making power in their own territory. But this power is not lost forever: such treaties, as well as those establishing military bases or other restrictions of territorial sovereignty, require what I have called *continuous consent* of the territorial State.[68]

(iv) Consent by Acknowledging Ethical Standards

In a few cases, mainly in the field of Human Rights and humanitarian law, law making in international society implies the enactment of certain legal rules with ethical contents. Here, States are law makers in the sense that they acknowledge or *recognise*[69] certain values as valid legal precepts. For these specific rules, which may be very few indeed, but always of some considerable importance to the individual, the consent of States is sometimes presumed:[70] if a vast majority of States adopt a certain level of treatment as binding, this may indicate

acquiescence again.

---

[67]   See, for example, Verzijl, Le principe *rebus sic stantibus* en droit international public, *Festschrift Schätzel*, 515; Granfelt, Striden kring *rebus sic stantibus*, självbestämmanderätten och minoritetsrätten: ett förspel till världskriget 1939, NTIR 1945, 20; Lissitzyn, Treaties and changed circumstances, AJIL 1967, 895; Kaufmann, *Das Wesen des Völkerrechts und die clausula rebus sic stantibus*, 1911.

[68]   See my *Independent State, op. cit.*, 197 *et seq.*

[69]   *Cf. supra*, on Recognition of ethical standards, and further, my *Concept, op. cit.*, Chapter II.

[70]   See, in detail, *ibid.*, 96-105 on State participation in the formation of rules and 116-117 on States as prime law makers.

164

an international *minimum standard*. A good example of such a standard of treatment is the prohibition of *apartheid*. Here, an isolated State is not allowed to lower a Human Rights standard below the accepted level acknowledged by most other States.

In the sphere of basic Human Rights, which may be limited to the very narrow field of prohibition of genocide, slavery, torture and apartheid, we are dealing with general rules which have an immediate impact in the internal law of States as the rules concern the treatment of individuals. The basic Human Rights, the prohibition of genocide, slavery, torture and apartheid, are thus general international rules which *break through* the sovereign walls of a State. The proof that this is a correct analysis lies in the fact that if these rules are violated other States criticise, or take sanctions against, an offending State. Its responsibility has thus become engaged. This is then the reason why Sweden is able to criticise South Africa for its *apartheid* policy inside the State: if one did not take this line it would be impossible to explain why States may criticise South African internal legislation on apartheid without violating article 2(7) of the United Nations Charter which speaks about the *reserved domain*.[71] These are the matters within a State's jurisdiction where any comments may be viewed as interference or intervention. In other words, it is clear that the *international minimum standard* prevails over article 2(7).

Certain Human Rights form part of international *jus cogens*,[72] that is the body of law which States recognise they are not entitled to *alter* or to *reduce*.[73] The requirement of *consent* of States to basic Human Rights, that is at least those concerning genocide, slavery, torture and apartheid - and more Human Rights of this basic type may be emerging - may be merely formal. One could safely say that this is an area where State consent must in all cases be *presumed*.

The act of acknowledging relevant ethical standards is taken by

---

[71] But *cf.*, *infra*, under Monist and Dualist Schools and under Restrictions of Sovereignty Over Property and Individuals, on the reluctance in Sweden to allow application of general rules on basic Human Rights in its own.

[72] See further, *infra*, under *jus cogens*.

[73] Clear recognition has been given in the universal Vienna Convention on the Law of Treaties which provides that treaties in conflict with such *jus cogens* are to be considered null and void; see further *infra*.

recognition or *adoption* of these rules, according to certain mechanisms provided in the international legal order.[74]

ii. The Monist and the Dualist Schools

Kelsen, *Das Problem der Souveränitet und die Theorie des Völkerrechts*, 1928; *idem, Reine Rechtslehre*, 1934, *General Theory of Law and State*, 1949, 363 *et seq; idem*, Les rapports des systèmes entre le droit interne et le droit international, 14 RCADI 1926 iv, 227; *idem*, 43 RGDIP 1936, 5; Verdross, *Die Einheit des rechtlichen Weltbildes und Grundlage der Völkerrechtsverfassung*, 1923; *idem*, 8 ZVR 1914, 329; *idem, Die Völkerrechtliche Kriegshandlung und der Strafanspruch der Staaten*, 1920; *idem*, RDI 1934, 1954, 219; *idem, Abendländische Rechtsphilosophie*, 1963; *idem* and Simma, *Universelles Völkerrecht*, 1974; Kunz 52 RDILC 1925, 556; *idem*, 1 WWR 1 787; *idem, Changing Law of Nations*, 1968; Lauterpacht, 25 *Transactions of the Grotius Society,* 1940 51; Scelle, *Droit international public*, 1949; Jellinek, *System der subjektiven öffentlichen Rechte*, 1905; *idem, Die rechtliche Natur der Staatenverträge*, 1880; Triepel, *Völkerrecht und Landesrecht*, 1899; *idem*, Les rapports entre le droit interne et le droit international, RCADI 1923, 77; v. Liszt, *Völkerrecht*, 11th ed., 1918; Walz, *Völkerrecht und Staatliches Recht*, 1933; *idem*, Les rapports du droit international et du droit interne, 61 RCADI 1937 iii 375; Anzilotti, *Il diritto internazionale nei giudizi interni*, 1905; Cavaglieri, *Corso di diritto internazionale*, 3rd ed., 1924; Quadri, *Diritto internazionale pubblico*, 1960; Balladori Pallieri, *Diritto internazionale pubblico*, 8th ed., 1962; Ross, *Theorie der Rechtsquellen*, 1929; Drost, *Grundlagen des Völkerrecht*, 1936.

There has, for a number of years, been discussion among scholars whether international law and national law form one or two systems of law. Monists maintain that international law and municipal law form part of the same legal system. A consequence of this theory would, to some of its proponents, be that, because of the unity of the two systems of law, the individual is a subject of international law. Most of the adherents to the school acknowledge, however, only an indirect role of the individual. Monists have favoured prevalence either of the international[75] or, more rarely, of the national[76] system.

Dualists, on the other hand, perceive the international legal

---

[74]   See *infra* in this Chapter, under Natural Law.

[75]   See the writings of Kelsen, Verdross, Kunz and Scelle in the above bibliographical references.

[76]   *E.g.* the writing of Jellinek in the bibliographical references.

system and municipal law as conceptually and functionally distinct.[77] According to the dualist school, there are thus two systems, international law and national law, each having its different subjects, its different law making processes and characteristics. The dualist theory has been adopted by a number of States, including the Scandinavian States, Italy, the Soviet Union and its satellites and successors. When the study of international law was re-introduced as an academic subject in the Soviet Union in 1924 after having been *abolished* after the 1917 Revolution,[78] the choice of system was influenced by the exaggerated importance that this school attaches to the notion of sovereignty.[79]

The dualist theory has become favoured by scholars, who, sometimes under the firm guidance of statesmen, reject any form of international law immediately applicable in the internal sphere. To these scholars it is ultimately for the State to decide what rules of international law will apply within its borders. Thus, the traditional view in Scandinavian countries such as Sweden and Norway, is a politically rooted aversion, often based on socialist doctrine, to allow any general rules of international law, even on Human Rights, apply within the national systems unless they have been properly *converted*, *transformed* or *incorporated* into national rules. At the same time, it is precisely these governments which insist that international rules forbidding apartheid apply directly within South Africa. These governments have been the most staunch supporters of sanctions while, on their own ground, they would, under the guise of the 'dualist school', prohibit any direct application of any rule of international law, even in the field of Human Rights.

It is abundantly clear that the *dualist* doctrine cannot exculpate a State for violating international law, as many of the supporters of the doctrine in Sweden have erroneously been led to believe. The theoretical construction is *irrelevant* with regard to the assessment whether a State has complied with its obligations under international

---

[77] See the writings of Triepel, von Liszt, Walz, Anzilotti, Cavaglieri, Quadri, Balladori Pallieri, Ross and Drost in the bibliographical references.

[78] See my *Concept, op. cit.*, 22-23, in some detail.

[79] *E.g.*, Krylov, Les notion principales du droit des gens, 70 RCADI 1947 i 445, and further, my *Concept, op. cit.*, 22 *et seq.*

law or with regard to assessing the width and depth of such obligation. Thus, general rules have been allowed to operate directly without a country thereby accepting to be bound more than any other country by general rules of international law. In other words, many such rules bind a country with regard to immediate, compelling and sanctioned operation inside the country, whatever its scholars pronounce on *dualism* or *monism*. Consequently, if Swedish Courts pretend, as they do, that they can dispense with any respect for Human Rights as Sweden is a 'dualist country', they are severely mistaken and, in due course, sanctions might well be imposed on Sweden for practical effects of such views. To pretend that sovereignty implies freedom to dispense with binding rules on, for example, Human Rights, are views hitherto only put forward by totalitarian countries, like Hitler's Germany or Stalin's Soviet Union.

In English law it is abundantly clear that general principles of international law apply directly as *law of the land*. It is even established that the *latest version* of such a general rule must be allowed immediate and direct application in the internal sphere and must be directly applied by the Courts.[80]

The Supreme Court of Canada has assumed that rules of customary[81] international law, *i.e.* general rules of international law, are adopted as part of Canadian law.[82] It has even indicated that changes in that law must be considered.[83] The Quebec Court has also recognised changes in general international law as effective in Canada.[84] But the Supreme Court has been more restrictive in applying new international law directly if such new rules extend the

---

[80] For authority of the main rule see *Triquest v Bath* [1764] at 1428. *Cf. e.g., R. v Keyn* [1876] 2 Ex D 63 CCR on admiralty jurisdiction. *Cf. The Phillipine Admiral* [1977] AC 373. On the point of *latest rule* see *Trendtex v Central Bank of Nigeria* [1977] QB 529.

[81] On the meaning of the term, see, *infra*.

[82] *Republique Démocratique du Congo v Venne* [1971] 22 DLR (3rd) 669.

[83] *Newfoundland Reference re Continental Shelf* [1984] 1 SCR 86 at 116, 5 DLR (3th) 385.

[84] *Penthouse Studios Inc. v Venezuela*, [1969], 8 DLR (Que CA) 686; *cf. Zodiak International Products Inc. v Polish People's Republic* [1978], 81 DLR (3rd) 656, 4 BLR 179 (Que CA).

competence of Canadian authorities.[85] For such matters, Canada would prefer to enact specific legislation. But this, in itself, does not show reluctance to allow direct application of international law but rather an interest to apportion duties between internal organs. The reason could thus well be the State's interest to ensure that its respective authorities are clear as to their respective competence.

Treaties, on the other hand, have to be converted in England to have effect in the country.[86] Similarly, under the Constitution of the Federal Republic of Germany,[87] general rules of international law also apply directly but treaties have to be converted. In numerous countries even treaties have immediate application, like under the French[88] or the Dutch Constitution;[89] in the United States, too, treaties may become *law of the land*.[90] Furthermore, in the United States general international law is also immediately applied by the Courts unless contrary to statute.[91]

There is, however, firm authority in case-law of courts and tribunals that a State cannot rely on the provisions or deficiencies of its own Constitution or its own municipal law to avoid its obligations under international law.

The *Alabama Claims Arbitration*[92] is a case in point. Ships were built in England for private buyers. The ships were unarmed but it was generally known that they were going to be converted into warships for the Confederate to fight the Union in the American Civil

---

85 See the *Newfoundland Reference re Continental Shelf Case, supra* and *cf., Re Dominion Coal Co. Ltd. v County of Cape Breton* [1963] 48 MPR 174, 40 DLR (2d) 593 (NSCA).

86 *E.g., British Airways v Laker Airways Ltd.* [1983] 1 All ER 779; *cf. Mortensen v Peters* [1906] 14 Scots. LTR

87 Article 25 GG.

88 Article 55 Constitution of 1958.

89 Article 66 of the Constitution of 1956.

90 Treaties adopted by two-thirds majority of the Senate have the force of law and override state and federal laws; the executive agreements made by the United States President also have the force of law, and override state laws, but yield, on the other hand, to Acts of Congress. See, article VI para. 2 of the Constitution; but the provision is limited to 'self-executing' treaties; on this, see Hackworth, v, 177.

91 *E.g. The Paquete Habana*, (1900) US 677.

92 (1872) Hudson, *International Tribunals*, 1944, 5.

War. The United Kingdom was neutral at the time and, by allowing the ships to sail, this country had, argued the United States, breached her obligations under the rules of War.[93] The arbitrators rejected the British argument that it had not been possible to prevent the sailing of the ships constructed under private contracts and said

'... the government of Her Britannic Majesty cannot justify itself for a failure in due diligence on the plea of insufficiency of the legal means of action which it possessed.
... it is plain that, to satisfy the exigency of due diligence, and to escape liability, a neutral government must take care ... that its municipal law shall prohibit acts contravening neutrality'.

This case illustrates that a State is *under a duty to make sure that its internal laws comply with international law* and, if they do not, the State may incur responsibility for consequences of the discrepancy between international law and municipal law.

Furthermore, the Permanent Court of International Justice stated in the *Case Polish Nationals in Danzig*[94] that

'It should ... be observed ... that a State cannot adduce as against another State its own Constitution with a view of evading obligations incumbent upon it under international law or treaties in force. Applying these principles to the present case, it results that the question of the treatment of Polish nationals or other persons of Polish origin or speech must be settled exclusively on the basis of the rules of international law and the treaty provisions in force between Poland and Danzig.'

When a case comes before an international tribunal or court, it is to be expected that tribunal or court will apply the above mentioned rules of hierarchy, whether or not the State claims to be adopting the dualist doctrine. It is thus a well settled international rule that will be applied in the international sphere to assess the obligations of a State in its own territory and with regard to its own laws. There is

---

[93]   See my *Law of War, op. cit.*, 139 *et seq.*
[94]   (1931) PCIJ Series A.

overwhelming support for this view, not only in international case law but also among scholars and statesmen. The principle of primacy of international law over municipal law applies to all aspects of the municipal law, to constitutional provisions, ordinary legislation and to decisions of its courts.

The primacy of international law is particularly important in the field of Human Rights. War crimes cases before the Nuremberg and Tokyo Tribunals provide ample evidence that no 'dualist' system can save States - and/or individuals[95] - from responsibility for infractions and violations of rules concerning minimum treatment of human beings.

It must be noted that the discussion on monism and dualism has faded, in most countries, over the last twenty-five years. Discussion has, however, recently flared up in Sweden, partly in connection with problems of allowing direct legislation of the European Community were the country to join this organisation, partly because of the anachronistic insistence that not even the most basic rules of international law reflected in, for example, the European Convention on Human Rights do not apply automatically in Sweden.

Thus, no general international legal rules are held to apply in Sweden. Furthermore, treaties also have to be *converted* into internal Acts.[96] Without much foundation in scholarly writings, discussions on treaties often refer to *transformation,* which then means the conversion of a treaty rules by rewriting and re-formulating, for example, the text of a treaty and *incorporation* which signifies a simplified system, converting a treaty, into internal law by a simple internal legislative 'order', providing that an annexed text will apply as municipal law. Occasionally, *transformation* is used to mean only informal adoption of rules. The distinction between 'transformation' and 'incorporation' is largely unknown in non-Scandinavian doctrine where the two terms are used synonymously and it is a distinction likely to cause misunderstanding, especially since neither term is well

---

[95]   See my *Law of War, op. cit.,* 353 *et seq.,* on individual responsibility and *infra,* Chapter VIII on Consequential Rules. On *minimum standards,* see infra in Chapter V.

[96]   On this, see SOU 1974:100.

defined.[97]

It is obviously in order for a State to demand *conversion of treaties* into internal law before the rules of such instruments operate inside a country. What is not in order, is to disallow the operation inside a State of the most basic general rules of international law reflected *either* in treaties, *or* those which exist in international law as a whole, independent of treaties. State may thus not claim that its internal law has nothing to do with such rules unless they have been *transformed.* Such a view, currently *en vogue*, both as the official attitude of the Swedish Ministry of Foreign Affairs and of numerous Swedish academics[98] and judges, is possibly resting on a series of misunderstandings both as to the nature of international law and of the practice and attitude of other States. For example, any political party which adopts, as a central part of its policy, the view that all international rules, even those on basic Human Rights, have to be converted into internal rules, must, together with their electorate, be aware that they are endorsing a constitutional system only operated by Hitler, Stalin and a few other totalitarian rulers. The view, that a State can evade the rules of international law by a dualist system, is misconceived and based on ignorance of important international practice and case-law. It is the result of an increasingly untenable position, isolated in the world, that sovereignty would imply complete freedom to interpret and implement rules of international law by sheer discretion.

It is thus a misapprehension that States adopting a dualist system could somehow evade the application, within their territory, of basic Human Rights. Dualism normally implies, in practical terms, that certain international rules, for example, those in a treaty, have to be converted or transformed into internal law. But, of course, being a dualist does not imply denial that basic rules on Human Rights, at least those covering genocide, slavery, torture and apartheid, apply within a State. Hardly any State claims that it is free to do what it likes in these matters and few would deny that such basic rights

---

[97] In English terminology, for example, *incorporation* implies automatic application in internal law, see Dixon, *Textbook on International Law*, 1990, 41.

[98] See *supra* in the Preface and in Chapter I.

constitute immediately compelling law for all States. One isolated objector to this rule of immediacy used to be South Africa but even there one can perceive a change of attitude.

The effect, in terms of State responsibility and in terms of individual responsibility,[99] of denial of application of basic Human Rights in a State's own territory, is amply illustrated in the judgments of the Nuremberg and Tokyo War Trials, as well as in the pronouncements of the Security Council on, for example, the Amin regime in Uganda.

A noteworthy statement was made by the then Soviet foreign minister Shevardnaze on 9th March 1989, in connection with the ratification, by the Soviet Union of the United Nations Covenants on Human Rights: also the Soviet Union - although it adhered to the dualist doctrine - admitted the supremacy of rules of international law on Human Rights. The document does not limit this supremacy to only basic Human Rights but states that, as a system, international law is higher than national laws. The Soviet Union notified the United Nations of the withdrawal of its earlier reservations concerning the compulsory jurisdiction of the International Court of Justice in respect of agreements relating to Human Rights. The Representative of the USSR asked, in an accompanying note, that the letter of Mr Shevardnaze be distributed as a document of the General Assembly and Mr Shevardnaze himself, who obviously attached considerable importance to the statement, asked the Secretary General, as depository of the relevant Human Rights treaties, to distribute his letter 'as an official document of the United Nations'. He wrote

'The Soviet Union, which attaches great importance in present circumstances to enhancing the role of the International Court of Justice in world affairs, has begun to consider the question of withdrawing the reservations which it made previously to a number of international treaties concerning the jurisdiction of that judicial organ. Given the importance of the further promotion of co-operation among States in the humanitarian sphere, it was deemed desirable to begin the process by dealing with Human

---

[99]   See, *infra*, under Human Rights.

Rights agreements.'

In the light of the above, on 10th February 1989, the Presidium of the Supreme Soviet of the USSR adopted a decree whereby the Soviet Union accepts the compulsory jurisdiction of the International Court of Justice in respect of the following international treaties: the 1948 Convention on the Prevention and Punishment of the Crime of Genocide, the 1949 Convention for the Suppression of the Traffic in Persons and of the Exploitation of the Prostitution of Others, the 1952 Convention on the Political Rights of Women, the 1965 International Convention on the Elimination of All Forms of Racial Discrimination, the 1979 Convention on the Elimination of All Forms of Discrimination against Women, and the 1984 Convention against Torture and Other Cruel, Inhuman or Degrading Treatment or Punishment.

The Soviet Foreign Minister then went on to underline the reasons for this change in Soviet acceptance of the compulsory jurisdiction of the International Court of Justice and commented on the revised attitude of the Soviet Union to international law in general. He said

'In taking this decision, the Soviet Union was guided by the desire to strengthen the international legal order, which upholds the primacy of law in political affairs. In advocating the primacy of international law, we take the position that *international legal norms and obligations of States take precedence over their domestic enactments.*'[100] (Emphasis added.)

This is a forceful statement which underlines the *primacy of international law.* The Soviet Union was one of the communist States which had earlier claimed that sovereignty implies full freedom of the State to act. But this indicates that, even if a State with such views on sovereignty, there are certain important basic rights in international law which must not be set aside in internal legislation. We may investigate what these rules are.

---

[100]   General Assembly document A/44/171, 9th March 1989.

iii. The Notion of *jus cogens*

Some, and very few, rules are of such a compelling nature that States cannot deviate from them by concluding a treaty. Those few rules which are so binding that they cannot be set aside are usually referred to as the rules of *jus cogens*, compelling law, or as peremptory norms of international law. The above mentioned rudimentary rules on basic Human Rights form part of this body of rules called *jus cogens*.

The concept of *jus cogens* has been entrenched in the Vienna Convention on the Law of Treaties which, in article 53, provides that all treaties concluded in violation of *jus cogens*, *i.e.* peremptory norms, are void.[101]

Article 53 of the Vienna Convention on the Law of Treaties thus provides

'A treaty is void if, at the time of its conclusion, it conflicts with a peremptory norm of general international law. For the purposes of the present Convention, a peremptory norm of general international law is a norm accepted and recognised by the international community of States as a whole as a norm from which no derogation is permitted and which can be modified only by a subsequent norm of general international law having the same character.'

Some basic Human Rights are certainly covered by the concept *jus cogens*.[102] However, there is no known case yet where the validity of a treaty has actually been disputed because of any alleged conflict with *jus cogens*.[103]

There is no common agreement on the exact ambit of the article or of the meaning of *jus cogens*; but there is overwhelming doctrinal support for the rule of *jus cogens*, of some substantial contents, as

---

[101]   On the extent of the prohibition, see my *Independent State, op. cit.*, 133-134. In the discussions of the article at the Conference, Sweden supported the concept strongly.

[102]   Robledo, Le *jus cogens* international, 172 RCADI 1981, 167.

[103]   Gaja, *Jus cogens* beyond the Vienna Convention, 172 RCADI 1981, 286.

constituting international *lex lata*.[104] There is also general consensus, among scholars as well as among States, that the notion of *jus cogens* covers at least the basic Human Rights, *i.e.* genocide, slavery, torture and apartheid, as well as the right to privacy and, probably, the prohibition of aggressive war. It may be submitted that there are now emerging rules on terrorism allowing universal jurisdiction[105] for the prosecution of terrorists; such rules would be *consequential*[106] as following logically infractions of the *jus cogens* rules on terrorism.

The International Court has pronounced itself on the question using the term *erga omnes* to signify rules binding for all in the international society regardless of their specific acceptance. The Court has mentioned rules on Human Rights, including slavery and racial discrimination, as well as the crime of *aggression*,[107] as typical examples of peremptory norms of international law.

Jus cogens cannot be explained in other terms than those of *natural law* so violently discarded by the Uppsala School[108] and by most Swedish lawyers. However, delegates of Sweden to international conferences have sometimes shown a different face to the outside world.[109] In other parts of the world, however, there is a marked

---

104 See, Hannikainen, *Peremptory Norms (jus cogens) in International Law*, Helsinki, 1988, *passim*.

105 On universal jurisdiction as one - in most cases - exaggerated ground for competence of courts, *infra*, Chapter VI.

106 See *infra*, Chapter IX on Consequential Rules in general, as defined in this work.

107 *Barcelona Traction (Second Phase)*, (1970) ICJ *Reports*, 3 at 32; *cf. Advisory Opinion on Namibia*, (1971) ICJ *Reports*, 52; *cf. Hostages Case* (1980) ICJ *Reports* 26 on diplomatic immunity as a fundamental rule of international law..

108 The Swedish nihilistic school led by Hägerström, a philosopher, and Lundstedt, a lawyer, whose book *The Law of Nations, Superstition of People*, 1927, was adopted as authoritative by Swedish Universities and by Swedish authorities.

109 See the discussions and statements on the article on *jus cogens* by States during the Vienna Conference on the Law of Treaties. It is noteworthy that Sweden was expressly in favour of the adoption of the article. *Cf. supra* under the Monist and Dualist Schools and *infra*, under Treaties, Definitions.

revival of thoughts and theories of natural law[110] and numerous international lawyers adopt natural law as a special category of rules, equated to or a euphemism of, *jus cogens*.[111]

iv. Variety of Creators/Actors/Subjects

There is not necessarily identity between *creators* of international rules, *actors* in the international sphere and *subjects* of international law. An example may clarify this proposition. A treaty may enable individuals to enjoy rights additional to those they already have under international law. For example, the European Convention on Human Rights gives the right to individuals to take legal action, in certain cases, against their own home State. Individuals would not enjoy such a right under general international law.[112] But the States which concluded the Convention were the *creators* of the right and of relevant legal rules in question. The groups, individuals and statesmen who encouraged the Convention to be adopted were the *actors*. And the individuals who now enjoy the right of petition to the European Commission and the European Court of Human Rights are the *subjects* of the rules.

We may distinguish numerous persons and bodies as actors in international society. International relations scholars identify charismatic leaders who may play a substantial role in development of both politics, for better or worse, and whose influence on law can not be denied. Few would doubt that the changes in attitude to international law and the international legal system have been due to the personality of the Soviet leaders Gorbachev and later, Yeltsin. However, many now question the motives for Gorbachev's so called liberal era which was interrupted by the repression of the independence movements in the Baltic States and which later led to the disintegration of the whole Soviet Union.

---

[110]   See books by the Oxford Professor of Jurisprudence, Finnis, for example, *Natural Law and Natural Rights*, 1984.

[111]   See, for example, Dixon, *Textbook, op. cit.*, 13, 17. *Cf. supra* under the Historical Dimension in Chapter I and *infra* on General Principles: Natural Law, in this Chapter.

[112]   See, *infra*, under Individuals.

Some would contribute some proportion of the changes in Eastern and Central Europe, accelerating the creation of numerous new international legal rules, to Pope John Paul II, Head of a very different State from that of Mr Gorbachev and Mr Yeltsin.[113]

Of course, actors on the international scene need not be Heads of State. Sometimes, single individuals can have a profound influence on the change of attitude of others and of States. Let us draw to attention the influence of Mahatma Ghandi on the rules on the use of force. Coming from a very different background, Bob Geldorf achieved more by single-handed action to help developing countries, than many international or State aid agencies and had some influence on projects to rationalise aid to developing countries.

Other important actors are large companies and private associations and groups. The importance of multinationals as actors in the world cannot be denied. Pressure groups, like Greenpeace, Friends of the Earth or Amnesty, show, in numerous ways, how actors can contribute to public opinion which, in turn, may produce changes in international law.

Actors in international society may thus contribute to the formulation of rules by internationally relevant acts,[114] but States are the prime law makers as they have to give their consent to applicable rules.[115]

Some thus appear to have rights and duties under international law and thus qualify as *subjects*; others only act,[116] and are consequently *actors*; some are both; and States appear to actually create or make the law, often by delegation to international organisations,[117] or, again, by giving their consent in clear and open ways through treaties, or in oblique ways by implicit acts, or by unilateral undertakings;[118] and in some situations States are

---

[113]   On the specific role of the Pope as temporal and spiritual leader, see *infra*, under Subjects of International Law, The Holy See.

[114]   *Ibid.*, 130.

[115]   *Ibid.*, 131. For situations where their consent to law making is presumed, see, *supra*, under Individuals.

[116]   But the acts must be internationally relevant, see, my *Concept, op. cit.*, 88-91 and 129.

[117]   See my Law Making, *op. cit.*, 1965, *passim.*

[118]   See my Concept, *op. cit., passim.*

themselves also *subjects* or *actors*, as well as *creators* of legal rules.[119]

There is a great variety of actors and subjects but States appear to be the ultimate law makers in international society. Other rule making activity can be derived back to States. It is they which have given, what I call, *abstract consent* to law making by international organisations.[120] It is also States which have the power to identify useful values and adopt them as binding rules of international law.[121]

E. HARD LAW

Many have recently distinguished the *ordinary* rules of international law and the *soft law* which in an ever increasing way appears to regulate international society. The difference is, according to the doctrine and state practice, that only *hard law* is technically binding whereas *soft law* reaches similar goals in other ways - although many international lawyers are not agreed as to how this process is achieved.

i. Treaties

Cf. my *Essays on the Law of Treaties*, 1967; Ago, Le droit des traités à la lumière de la Convention de Vienne, RCADI 1971, vol. 134, 297; Bastid, S., *Les traités dans la vie internationale*, 1985; Reuter, *Introduction au droit des traités*, 1972; *idem*, *Introduction to the Law of Treaties*, 1990.

Further see, Bittner, *Die Lehre von den völkerrechtlichen Vertragsurkunden*, 1924; Höjer, *Les traités internationaux*, 1928; Bergbohm, *Staatsverträge und Gesetze als Quellen des Völkerrecht*, 1873; Frangulis, *Théorie et pratique des traités internationaux*, 1934; Kraus, Système et fonctions des traités internationaux. RCADI 1934 iv 317; Starke, Treaties as a 'source' of international law, BYIL 1946, 341; Lachs, The law of treaties, Some general reflexions on the Report of the International Law Commission, *Festschrift Guggenheim* 1968 398; Vitta, *Studi sui trattati*, 1958; Parry, The law of treaties in Sorensen, (ed.), *Manual of Public International Law*, 1968; Triska & Slusser, Treaties and other sources of order in international relations,

---

[119]   *Ibid.*, *passim.*

[120]   See my *Law Making, op. cit., passim.*

[121]   See, *infra*, under Sources, Soft Law, in Chapter IV.

The Soviet view, AJIL, 1958 699.

On the Vienna Convention, see, Reuter, *La Convention de Vienne sur le droit des traités*, 1970; Sinclair, *The Vienna Convention and the Law of Treaties*, 1973; Maresca, *Il diritto dei trattati, La convenzione codificatrice di Vienna del 23 maggio 1969*, 1971; Nascimento e Silva, *Conferencia de Viena sobre o direito dos tratados*, 1971; Neuhold, Die Wiener Vertragsrechtskonvention 1969, AVR 1971-1972, 1; Capotorti, Il diritto del trattati secondo la Convenzione di Vienna in SIOI (ed.), *Convenzione di Vienna sui diritto dei trattati*, 1969, 1.

a. Definitions

Numerous old rules of international law are codified and contained in treaties. The codification of rules in international society in treaties is actively encouraged by specific bodies, for example, by the International Law Commission.[122]

Treaties are instruments concluded by States: the term is reserved for instruments between States, and in writing.

The Vienna Convention on the Law of Treaties of 1969, which was a 'treaty on treaties' clarified many earlier rules. But there were also some new controversial or ill-defined notions. One may be the blanket rule on peremptory norms: any treaty which violates such *jus cogens* (binding law) is void *ab initio*. Virtually all States accept that there exist such rules[123] but there is little agreement as to their contents. Yet, it is clear, as mentioned above, that at least basic Human Rights form part of *jus cogens*, *i.e.* rules prohibiting genocide, slavery, torture and apartheid.[124]

b. Types of Agreements

Many writers distinguish between law making treaties and treaty contracts, the difference being that agreements of the latter type, the treaty contracts, visualise transactions which are carried out within a certain time whereas the former type, the law making treaties, include

---

[122]   See, *supra*, under Codification.

[123]   Note the prominent exception of Sweden; see *supra* note and accompanying text; Sweden voted in favour of the article on *jus cogens* in the Vienna Convention.

[124]   *Cf. supra*, on *jus cogens*.

agreements which establish longer lasting rules. As an example of law making treaties one may mention the Convention on the Immunity of Diplomats or, indeed, the Convention on the Law of Treaties itself.

The distinction of the two types has little to do with the number of parties to the agreement although it is true to say that *most* law making treaties are multilateral instruments whereas *most* treaty contracts tend to be bilateral. There are, of course, numerous exceptions to this general rule: treaties on extradition are normally bilateral agreements but are also clearly law-making in the sense that they establish a lasting legal regime, applicable to a generality of cases in the future.[125] Conversely, multilateral agreements can, occasionally, be treaty contracts.

c. Treaty Making Techniques

Treaties may be concluded in various ways. More important treaties may be concluded by *long procedures*, entailing the use of specific mechanisms. Many treaties are thus subjected to *ratification,* a special form of approval. *Ratification* implies *the final approval of a State of the obligations contained in the treaty*. The procedure for ratification varies from country to country and depends on constitutional provisions and rules. Treaties that are to be ratified must thus receive final approval from a specific organ of the State, normally after some treatment in the legislature, *Parliament* or *riksdag*, or what the legislative body may be called. In many cases, ratification involves some degree of participation of the legislative body. Thus, in many States, a treaty is subjected to parliament (or the equivalent body) before the instrument of ratification is issued, often by the Executive, as the final approval.

Discussion in the United Kingdom in February 1993 on the Maastricht Treaty on European Union illustrated the difference when the ratifying body - under English law the government - is at odds with the legislative body, Parliament, on the merits of ratification of

---

[125]   On the meaning of the term regime, see my Concept, *op. cit.,* 38 *et. seq.*

a specific treaty.[126] There was a complicated situation in view of the fact that s. 6 of the European Assembly Elections Act, an English Act of Parliament, stipulates that the approval of (the) Parliament (of Westminster) must be sought for ratification of any treaty (or any annexed protocol) which provides for an increase in the powers of the European Parliament, *i.e.* the Parliament of EC. However, under the Social Policy Protocol annexed to the Maastricht Treaty, the Member States authorise an increase in the powers of the European Parliament.[127] Such an increase would thus, under English law, have to be approved by (the Westminster) Parliament.

Numerous treaties do not require ratification, and are only concluded by what I have called *short procedures*[128] whereby a signature of an envoy is sufficient to bind the State. That representative must have full powers to sign for the State but his position will suffice, as *apparent authority*[129] even without such a document. One distinguishes thus between treaties which are *ratified*, and those agreements which become effective after simple signature, normally called *agreements in simplified form.* The latter type is very common and account for numerous treaties in contemporary international society.

The agreements in simplified form can be signed by any agent of the State with apparent or ostensible authority. It may the Head of State himself, or the Foreign Secretary, another minister, or, as often is the case an ambassador or even another agent or envoy who has been given full powers.

However, agreements in simplified form imply a *risk* to democracy as here it is the *executive* of a State which takes upon itself to bind the State without reference to the legislature. If treaties become effective in the internal legal sphere, as they do in many countries, for example, in the United States, in France and in the

---

[126] In July 1993 Lord Rees-Mogg took legal action in the English Courts to stop the ratification of the Maastricht Treaty, alleging that the UK government had used royal prerogative to bypass Parliament, *The Times*, 20th July 1993.

[127] This view, put forward by Anthony Lester, QC, is supported by professor Hartley, an expert on EC law, and by professor Rudden of Oxford, see *Gazette*, 24 February 1993.

[128] See my *Essays on the Law of Treaties*, 1967, 24-27.

[129] *Cf.* Blix, *Treaty Making Power*, 1960, on 'ostensible authority'.

Netherlands, the executive thus *takes over* some of the functions which should be reserved for the legislature. It is wise for the parliamentary body to keep an eye on the shifting of power which undoubtedly circumscribes the power of the legislature by allowing certain treaties to be concluded, in simplified form, by the government alone in areas where the executive often would be deprived to act on its own by decree.

d. Treaty Making Power

The national State of each country decides who is entitled to contract on their behalf and conclude treaties and agreements with other States. However, anyone in sufficient authority is *deemed* to have what has been called *ostensible* or *apparent* authority[130] to conclude a treaty. This approach is largely approved by case law.[131]

In international organisations there is also a specific organ, or organs, charged with the power to conclude treaties.[132]

e. The Point of Obligation

Once a treaty has entered into force it *binds* the parties. The *chronological point of obligation* of a State *varies* according to whether or not the treaty requires ratification. If the treaty is one in simplified form it will become effective on *signature* (or at any other date specified in the treaty).[133] If, on the other hand, the treaty is to be ratified - according to its own wording, according to some other specific rule or some special understanding with the contracting party/parties, the point obligation will be deferred until ratification has been completed.

---

[130]   *Cf.* Blix, *Treaty Making Power*, 1960.

[131]   *Eastern Greenland Case* (1933) PCIJ Series A/B No. 53.; *cf. Rio Martin Case,* 2 RIAA 615.

[132]   See my article on Organs of international organisations exercising their treaty-making power, BYIL 1962, for an analysis.

[133]   See on the entry into force according to different formulae, my *Essays on the Law of Treaties*, 1967, Chapter III.

f. Validity

Occasionally States seek to displace and explain away obvious contractual undertakings they have entered into. Like businessmen, who sometimes regret having entered into a contract when prices have gone up or down, States seek legal formulae to rid themselves of an obligation.

A common avenue for such self interests is the *rebus sic stantibus doctrine*. The doctrine implies that every contractual undertaking, such as a treaty, has a *silent clause* which stipulates that the agreement is only concluded provided the circumstances stay (*rebus stantibus*) as (*sic*) they are at the time of conclusion. As everything changes and moves, this is the ideal clause for the crafty statesman who wishes to prove that the State finds itself in *different* circumstances than when the State entered into the treaty. The qualification that the change should have been *fundamental* does little to improve the hazards of the escape mechanisms of the doctrine as apparently only the State itself (the State which wishes to denounce the treaty) can decide what actually is fundamental.

I have suggested[134] that the doctrine of *rebus sic stantibus,* dangerous as it is to international stability of legal relationships, should be replaced by a doctrine of *continuous consent* applicable for *certain treaties*, namely those which restrict territorial sovereignty in the area of a State.[135]

Another escape avenue out of contractual bonds is to claim that a treaty was concluded *under force*. According to the Vienna Convention on Treaties[136] a treaty is invalid or *void* if it has been entered by force or under threat of force, in violation with the principles of the United Nations. Obviously - apart from cases of personal violence against a personal representative, a situation of which no on can find actual examples - the article causes more problems that it solves. Perhaps the drafters of the Convention were led to believe that, since war had been forbidden by article 2(4),[137]

---

[134]   In my *Independent State, op. cit*, 197-199, 218-219.
[135]   See *infra,* in Chapter VII on Fettering State Sovereignty.
[136]   Article 52.
[137]   See *infra* in Chapter V.

States would no longer need Peace Treaties. But any Peace Treaty is concluded under *military force*.[138] Even if we thus disregard treaties concluded *before* the Vienna Convention, to which it is said not to apply, and even if we disregard numerous cases of *economic force*,[139] there are numerous treaties that fall under the article which declare treaties void, and which yet should not possibly be affected, if we apply the minimum of common sense. The only solution is to disregard the wording of the Vienna Convention on Treaties, a technique that the Convention itself stipulates should guide interpretation of the text.[140]

A *mistake* is rarely occasion for the invalidity of a treaty,[141] nor are arguments that the treaty was concluded by a person not authorised under internal law.[142]

On the other hand, a treaty concluded in violation of *jus cogens*[143] is *void* under the Vienna Convention, that is if it violates what the Convention calls *peremptory norms* of international law.[144] As mentioned in the context of our analysis of *jus cogens* earlier in this Chapter, it is uncertain as to what is included under the heading of peremptory norms. However, there is universal agreement that the concept covers at least prohibition of genocide, slavery, torture, apartheid and terrorism.[145]

g. The Effect of Treaties

---

138   See further, my *Independent State, op. cit.,* 141-216.

139   *Ibid.,* 195 *et seq.*

140   On literal or textual interpretation, see *The Admissions Case* (1948) ICJ *Reports* 57; *Maritime Safety Committee of IMCO Case* (1960) ICJ *Reports* 150; *cf. Polish Postal Services Case* (1925) PCIJ Ser. B No. 11-.

141   *Temple Case* (1962) ICJ *Reports,* 6.

142   See *supra* on apparent authority.

143   See on this notion *supra* in this Chapter.

144   Article 52. The French text speaks about '*une norme impérative du droit international général*'. As mentioned earlier, the Swedish delegation spoke forcefully in favour of this article although Sweden does not recognise the efficacy of any rules of international law inside Sweden unless they are converted into Swedish law, see *supra* under Monism and Dualism, in this Chapter.

145   See *infra* also under Chapter V.

We have surveyed the effects of treaties earlier in this Chapter in the context of our investigations of the theories of Monism and Dualism. It is thus for the municipal law of each State to decide on the effects of treaties in the respective jurisdiction. As we have seen, numerous States, like France and the Netherlands as well as the United States, allow many treaties to operate *as law*. Others, who recognise all general principles of international law as *law of the land*, like the United Kingdom and Germany, demand conversion of treaties into domestic laws, unless they reflect such general rules. Few countries, like Sweden, accept neither general principles nor treaties in their domestic legal sphere.

ii. Customary Law

For a view that the term is used for numerous unidentified rules, see my Concept, *op. cit.*, 112 *et seq.*

In general see, Verdross, Das völkerrechtliche Gewohnheitsrecht, JapAIL, 1963, 4; Dupuy, R.J., Coutume sage et coutume sauvage, in *Mélanges Rousseau*, 1974, 75; Guggenheim. Les deux éléments de la coutume en droit international, in *Mélanges Scelle*, 1950, i, 275; *idem*, L'origine de *l'opinio juris sive necessitatis* comme deuxième élément de la coutume dans l'histoire du droit des gens, in *Mélanges Basdevant*, 1960, 479; Amato, *The Concept of Custom in International Law*, 1971; Thirlway, *International Customary Law and Codification*, 1972; Bin Cheng, United Nations Resolutions on Outer Space: 'Instant' international customary law, 5 Indian JIL 1965, 23; *idem*, Custom: the future of general state practice in a divided world, in St. Macdonald and Johnston (eds.), *The Structure and Powers of International Law*, 1983; Charpentier, Tendances de l'élaboration du droit international public coutumier, in *L'élaboration du droit international public*, 1975, 105; *cf.* my Concept *of International Law*, 1987, esp. 112-120.

a. Customary Law strictu sensu:

A Term Implying a Specific Law Making Technique

Customary law is held by most textbooks to be the prime source of international law. Rules of international society are said to emerge by custom, or usage, which represents a *factual* side, coupled with *opinio juris,* a *psychological* side. The first requirement, of usage, means that a certain number of States behave in a consistent manner over a certain long period of time. The second element, required for the formation of customary law, concerns the assessment of the usage as *law,* in other words a mental qualification of the material facts to upgrade the *usage* to *customary law.*

Rules formed in this two-fold way, by practice or usage, coupled with a subjective element of considering such rules as legally binding, could be said to constitute customary law *strictu sensu,* that is to say in the true, narrow and technical meaning of the term.

If we go back for more than one hundred years we shall find that works on international law do not commonly concentrate on customary law. Instead, writers refer to treaties, as the main source of international law, and to generally binding rules. It is thus relatively new to make customary law *strictu sensu* the predominant source of international law.

b. Problems with Customary Law strictu sensu

The problems with customary law *strictu sensu* are many. Article 38 of the Statute of the International Court[146] indicates, by its very formulation, that *some* customary law exists before the practice of States have even begun. Therefore, such law cannot be formed in the traditional way, of usage + *opinio juris* as the chronological order is inverted. The formula on 'custom, as evidence of a general practice accepted as law', has been much criticised as allegedly distorting that custom by itself is a source of law. However, the formula is useful precisely as it underlines that States follow a practice because they *already* consider it as binding. Thus, the source of law must precede and exist *before* that practice.[147]

Furthermore, there are other problems connected with customary law *strictu sensu.* If States gradually became bound by usage they might also become by 'bad' or undesirable usage. How do you explain how states become bound even by such undesirable past

---

146   See *supra* at the beginning of this Chapter.

147   i:1 Oppenheim, ed. Jennings & Watts, 26 n 5 and accompaning text.

See finnit also moral element? seems to be ignored here.

behaviour? Kelsen even found the ultimate basis of obligation of international law in that States *should behave as* they customarily had behaved.[148] If law is to have some beneficial effect on the society which it regulates one can wonder why this is so. The proposition is almost designed to slow down improvement of international standards.

It is clear in the modern world that we only encounter further problems if we rely too much on customary law *strictu sensu*: if every non-treaty rule has to have emerged, and be proved to have emerged, in the two-fold process that traditional textbooks consider necessary, (by usage + *opinio juris*), we have to resort to artificial fictions. The use of such fictions is never a healthy sign; it is preferable to improve and adapt the theory to realities.

+ slow The main problem with customary law *strictu sensu* is its uncertainty. Who is to prove these nebulous rules, that have emerged through a nebulous process? Who can, furthermore, contribute to *State practice*? Only the organs of the State in the narrow sense of the term or all civil servants? Does a professor of international law in Sweden, where he/she is a civil servant of the State, really contribute to *State practice* by *all* he/she says or does? Whose State practice is relevant? Who will, indeed, *know* about what various State organs and the mass of civil servants do? Who is to select from the maze of material which represents *State practice* what is relevant and essential? It is clear that, in this sense, a wide view of *State practice* can be used as a cloak to prove almost any rule.

Further problems are caused by uncertainty of the timing when a new rule is operative as binding. Thus, according to the standard view on customary law, States become bound by their own behaviour: if States behave in the same way for a long time and consider this behaviour as *the law*, they will become bound by their own action and by their own opinion. But at what moment in time does the new rule emerge? If it is necessary to act, for a long time, and then to introduce a psychological element of considering this action as *law*, there is no *new* rule; States look upon their own behaviour as if that already represented the law. But when did *that* law come into being? aspect of the fiction.

---

[148]   Kelsen, *General Theory of Law and State*, 1946, 369.

188

Furthermore, it is difficult to prove a rule by passivity. But this is what we have to do if we rely on customary law to show rules, for example, prohibiting *torture of prisoners of war*. Outside conventional frameworks and treaties there is held to be such a rule by most writers. But where does it come from? How can States become bound by what they have *not* done over a certain period of time?

How do we explain that there are rules for Outer Space exploration? Here, there was no practice *over a long time* but rules emerged at once. Nor were 'many States' involved in the process of creating new rules: in the late '50s and '60s only two States were able to send up satellites or rockets.

In most cases one can explain the emergence of new rules, or the consolidation of old rules, in other ways and without referring to customary law *strictu sensu*. With regard to torture one can, for example, refer to sociological needs and/or to reciprocity. Or, one could cling to the customary law paradigm and argue that States had consented to dispense with the requirement of usage or practice, and that, therefore, here was a *different type* of customary rule. Or, more appropriately, one could here refer to a rule, adopted by common consent of States, based not on custom but on common agreement on the level of treatment of individuals in the modern world. One could say that States are *presumed* to have consented to obvious rules forbidding practices like torture. Thus, there is a *general rule* in force by *mutual agreement*.

In the case of Outer Space law it would appear reasonable that States adopted, by their unilateral decisions,[149] rules for space exploration by common consent that such rules apply immediately to a new situation, without any practice or 'usage' and without the participation of any substantial number of States.

Above all, States do not, in practice, behave as if they considered themselves bound *only* by customary rules of international law based on the *consistent practice* by a *large number* of nations over a *long time*. That would be only one of many considerations States make when testing whether a rule is to be applied. The British Government, for example, does not necessarily make a general survey to ascertain

---

[149]   *Infra*, under Unilateral Declarations.

whether, say, Gambia, Venezuela and the Philippines, together with a certain number of other States, have adhered to a certain practice, applied consistently, over a long period of time. The Government would be more likely to apply criteria such as 'Is the rule useful?'; 'Would it be politically disadvantageous *not* to apply this rule?'; 'What future developments could be projected if we do/do not accept this rule?'; 'What would other States/public opinion say if we do/do not follow this rule?'; 'Have we indicated in some unilateral pronouncement that we adhere to this rule?' or similar, nearly extra-juridical, considerations. It is suggested that it is useful to bear such considerations in mind when we investigate whether *consent* has been given.

My earlier work on theory of international law[150] sought to explain the international legal system without relying on customary law except for cases where there is a clear territorial connection. Indeed, it appears that most times the International Court of Justice has explicitly applied 'customary law', it has been in situations where the customary rules, based on usage and *opinio*, were tied to specific rights in specific geographical areas and thus had *a territorial connection*.[151] It is also in such cases, where there is a territorial bond, that it is easier to prove the existence of a practice, or *opinio juris*, and consequently the existence of a rule.

The traditional requirement that *numerous* States should have respected the relevant rule by *long and consistent practice*, are conditions which are usually displaced, in both humanitarian matters where one would have to speak of *negative* practice[152] and in Space Law.[153] On the other hand, it appears that *another* requirement mentioned above, that of a *territorial connection* is *more important* as one that replaces the condition of substantial number. Thus, a rule respected by consistent practice - but by a *few* States - over a long

---

[150]   See my *Concept, op. cit., passim*.

[151]   *Ibid.*, 115-116.

[152]   Abstention cannot be equated to positive or active practice and it is, furthermore, impossible to *prove* extent of negative practice; see also my *Law of War, op. cit, passim*.

[153]   Here there has been *immediate* practice by *few* States, see *infra* in Chapter VI under Space Law.

time is often an undisputable rule of international law and one that constitutes a *customary rule strictu sensu*. Some rules in international society are thus actual customary rules *strictu sensu* but they are not as many and substantial as made out by traditional textbooks.

There are a number of rules in international society which are commonly referred to as *customary rules*. Most textbooks contain large chapters on numerous such rules and, in fact, often relegate *any* unexplained rule in international law to this category without any stringent analysis of their *method of creation*. In other words, a number of rules are often thought of as customary law, although the traditional conditions (long and consistent practice by a substantial number of States) for the coming into being of such rules are not fulfilled. It is useful to analyse and establish that the origin and characteristics of these rules which perhaps conveniently can be called *customary rules latu sensu*. Yet, it is important for students to recognise that none of these rules come into being through the process which creates the above mentioned limited category of *true* customary law.[154]

It may be that the term *customary law* is too entrenched in the vocabulary of international lawyers to be changed. However, if one retains the term it is important to underline that the term *customary* normally can be equated with *general* - or, occasionally, regional or local - international law. In other words, we may well use the term *customary rule* but we must then be aware that the notion covers any non-treaty rule which we identify as binding. Thus, the term *customary rule* does not necessarily mean that a certain rule has been formed in a specific way. It can also be used in a wide meaning, or *latu sensu*, to mean a *generally accepted rule*.

c. Specimen of a Customary Rule strictu sensu: Prescription

As emphasised already in this work, customary rules have an important role to play but for such rules to be *genuine customary law*

---

[154] International legal terminology is firmly entrenched to use the category of customary law for a number of rules. What I seek to do here, however, is to set out that the *formation* of certain rules are not compatible with traditional requirements of *customary rules latu sensu*.

there must usually be a *territorial connection.* This is often the case if long and consistent practice results in *prescription.*[155]

Prescription can operate to validate a full title to territory in international society.[156] Rules on territorial prescription[157] are true customary rules which develop out of usage and *opinio juris.* However, more often, usage is restricted to a few, or even two States. So the requirement that some insist on, the *substantial* number of States adhering to the rule is, almost by definition, not fulfilled.

Rules of this type, concerning prescription, are truly based on usage and connected to territory; these rules are often similar to those derived by prescription under national legal systems. The rights derived under these rules may concern land or water areas, passage or certain sovereign claims.

iii. Unilateral and Parallel Declarations of States

Many rules, which have not been created by the rigorous pattern prescribed for *customary law strictu sensu,* and which are not *inherently necessary* as some other rules analysed below,[158] appear to be formed by acts of adoption - by which States adopt, and formally approve of, provisional standards elaborated by, for example, NGOs.[159] Rules of the road[160] and rules on common areas[161] are formed by promissory acts[162] of States, combined with a parallel acts, that is, many States undertake to behave in a certain way, but in a co-ordinated parallel way, rather than by contractual means.

---

[155] For the benefit of Swedish students, the term in Swedish is *hävd.* The Swedish legal term *preskription* corresponds to what in English law would be called *limitation, i.e.* rules concerning time barring of claims or other time rules for actions.

[156] *Supra* under Acquisition of Territory.

[157] It may assist Swedish students to refer to the Swedish term *hävd,* to some extent equivalent to prescription.

[158] See *infra* under Natural Law in this Chapter.

[159] See my *Concept, op. cit.,* 103-104.

[160] But some are inherently necessary, see *infra* under d. Convenience (a) Traffic in this Chapter.

[161] See the previous note.

[162] *Ibid.,* 100-103.

There has, for some time, been a noticeable reluctance among international lawyers to attach any importance to unilateral statements or promises. Yet, it is such rules which provide intense international regulation on a number of topics although rules are clearly neither customary rules, nor laid down in formal treaties.

To attach legal consequences to unilateral or parallel statements, or behaviour, is not uncommon in legal systems. As is apparent from the English doctrine of estoppel, also known in international law.[163] It is not the interest of any Rule of Law to allow and encourage the acts of misleading others.

Furthermore, it is clear from State practice as international relations scholars readily accept, that the *political weight* of unilateral statements is such that it often overrides earlier apparent 'rules'.[164] Therefore, both unilateral and parallel acts of States form an important source of international law.

a. Unilateral Acts

See my *Law Making by International Organisations*, 1965, 17, 42. 154 *et passim* and my *Concept of International Law*, 1987, 87 *et seq.* and esp. 105 for a new theory of unilateral and other acts.

Jacqué, *Eléments pour une théorie de l'acte juridique en droit international public*, 1972; Venturini, La portée et les effets juridiques des attitudes et des actes unilatéraux des états, 117 RCADI 1964, 363; Suy, Les actes unilatéraux en droit international. 112 RCADI; Kiss, Les actes unilatéraux dans la pratique française du droit international, RGDIP 1961, 317; Virally, Cours de droit international public, RCADI, 1983 v 169; Rigaldies, *Contribution à l'étude de l'acte unilatéral en droit international public*, Thémis, 1980-1981, 417; Rubin, The international legal effect of unilateral declarations, AJIL, 1977, 1; Leutert, *Einseitige Erklärungen im Völkerrecht*, 1979.

On specific acts see, in general, Pfluger, *Die einseitigen Rechtsgeschäfte im*

---

[163] See, Bowett, Estoppel before international tribunals and its relation to acquiescence, BYIL 1975, 174; MacGibbon, Estoppel in international law, ICLQ 1958, 468.

[164] As an example, see the recognition of PLO by Israel on 13th September 1993, contrasted with *Tel-Oren v Libya* (1984) 726 F 2nd 774 where the PLO was equated to groups 'not bound by the dictates of international law' which, on that ground, could not sue or be sued.

Völkerrecht, 1936; for recognition, *infra,* under Recognition; for notification, see Cansacchi, *La notificazione internazionale,* 1943; for promise, Carbone, *Promessa e affidamente nel diritto internazionale,* 1967; Quadri, La promessa nel diritto internazionale, RDI, 1963, 91; for protests, MacGibbon, Some observations on the part of protest in international law, BYIL, 1953, 293; Kunz, Protest, ii WV 810; Rothmann, Der völkerrechtliche Protest, 1923; for renunciation, Tommasi di Vignano, La rinuncia in diritto internazionale, 1960; Cavaglieri, Alcune osservazioni sul concetto di rinuncia nel diritto internazionale, RivDI 1918, 3; for acquiescence, see MacGibbon, Customary international law and acquiescence, BYIL 1957, 115; Bentz, Le silence comme manifestation de volonté en droit international public, RGDIP 1963, 44.

Unilateral declarations may be the traditional forms of protest or notification; even recognition[165] is often listed under these acts. But the prime function of unilateral acts may not be these types. A state may bind itself by other clear one-sided statements to a certain behaviour. This happens with increasing frequency in international society and States do appear to respect their own previous unilateral undertakings.

In the *Case of the Ihlen Declaration,* the so-called *Eastern Greenland Case,* the matter was considered by the Permanent Court of International Justice.[166] Here, a representative of the Norwegian government had stated, in the Norwegian Parliament, the Storting, that Norway would no longer make any claims to Eastern Greenland. Denmark held Norway to this statement which may be construed as a unilateral declaration.[167]

As an example of the legal relevance of unilateral statements of *States* in international society, we may refer to the statements made by France that it would cease Nuclear Tests in the Pacific. This statement was taken by the International Court to have *binding legal consequences.*[168] It is probable that such legal consequences have to be limited to cases where the State *intends* to be bound.[169]

An important, and ever increasing, source of law is found in the

---

[165]   See, *supra,* under Recognition.

[166]   *Eastern Greenland Case* (1933) PCIJ A/B No. 53.

[167]   But the Court referred to an 'agreement' between Denmark and Norway, *ibid.,* at 71-72.

[168]   *Nuclear Test Case* (1974) ICJ *Reports* 253.

[169]   *Burkina Faso v Mali* (1986) 554.

unilateral decisions and regulations of *international organisations* which contribute to the expansion of international law. One important category are decisions of the Security Council which may, as illustrated in the Iraq-Kuwait affair, be binding under article 25 of the United Nations Charter.[170] Organisations also issue rules for their internal or primary[171] matters - that sector only forms a small proportion of their work - but they issue a number of rules and regulations for the Member States. The most interesting law making organisations are the technical specialised agencies of the United Nations. Here, for example, the World Health Organisation (WHO) is particularly interesting because of its contracting-out procedure.[172] Furthermore, the World Meteorological Organisation (WMO),[173] the International Civil Aviation Organisation,[174] the Universal Postal Union and the International Telecommunications Union all show interesting law making techniques.[175]

It is to the achievements of these organisations and to their unilateral rules that we must point when we are questioned about the *existence and binding force* of international law: without these organisations and their rules it would not be possible to send an overseas letter or to make an intercontinental phone call; nor would it be possible to apply international rules for cholera vaccinations.[176]

b. Parallel Acts

States may make unilateral *declarations,* in pairs, or in certain numbers. The numerical factor tends to reinforce the legal effect of such declarations. There are many situations when States make concerted, or *parallel* declarations,[177] particularly at international

---

[170]   See Resolutions 660-678/1990-1991 of the Security Council.

[171]   For the term see my *Law Making, op. cit., passim,* and, *infra,* under Types of Recommendations, Resolutions on Primary Matters.

[172]   See, in detail, my *Law Making op. cit.,* 1965, 234-245.

[173]   *Ibid.,* 228-244.

[174]   *Ibid.,* 247-255.

[175]   *Ibid.,* 217 *et seq.*

[176]   On the value of recommendations, see *infra* in the following sections.

[177]   *Cf. supra,* under The Requirement of Consent, in this Chapter.

conferences and they often regard such declarations as something more than mere policy statements.

One example is the Gleneagles Agreement, *i.e.* the 1977 Comnmonwealth Statement on Apartheid in Sport, which was strictly adhered to in practice although technically not a binding instrument. Another example is the so called Helsinki Act, the basic document of the CSCE; the Conference on Security and Cooperation in Europe; this document, as amended, has had considerable influence on the behaviour of States.[178]

(i) Standards

As we shall see later in this treatise, international organisations often provide certain technical *standards* by resolutions, modestly phrased as 'recommendations' although they may have some considerable legal force.[179] However, States may, outside the framework of organisations agree on certain *standards* that they will respect in their mutual dealings.

For example, unification of measures in modern times was held to be of paramount importance to technical development on the national level towards the 18th century when the Paris Academy proposed the measure of a kilogram in 1799, a measure adopted by law on 10th December 1799. In 1879 the Bureau of Weights and Measures was formed under the first Metric Convention of 20th May 1875, adopting the metre and the kilogram on the international scene.[180] A new Convention was concluded in Sèvres on 6th September 1921.[181] The Bureau - and later the International Committee of Measures, an organ under the Metric Convention[182]-establishes international standards and measurement scales of physical

---

178   On the process of confidence building measures, see my *Law of War, op. cit.*, Chapter II.

179   See *infra* under Soft Law in this Chapter.

180   The members of the Bureau comprises most European countries but, apart from India, Pakistan, Thailand, Iran and Egypt, there are few Third World countries.

181   LNTS 427. On the historical background, see further Guillaume, *La Convention du Mètre et le Bureau International des Poids et Mésures*, 1902.

182   560 UNTS 79.

size, determines fundamental physical constants and improves the International System of Units (SI).

National and international standardising organisations also promote other aspects of uniformity in technical matters. As mentioned, some of these organisations and agencies adopt standards in various resolutions, in which case the question of their legal effect is more conveniently analysed in the context of recommendations by international organisations.[183] However, when States themselves in this field, outside organisations, we can observe another example of parallel declarations which provides an important source of law in international society.

On the other hand, States do not merely adopt *technical* standards to be complied with in international relations for obvious convenience: they also adopt standards which concern substantive, fundamental matters, like the *minimum standard of Human Rights*, applicable at any given time.[184] These standards often converge on matters like ethical standards,[185] especially concerning behaviour towards *individuals*, in matters like *Human Rights*, in *humanitarian law*,[186] or in attitudes towards the Third World by certain *sharing formulae*[187] or specific *aid*. Once a proposed pre-standard,[188] is accepted as a guideline by other States, this is often converted into a parallel unilateral act, adopting a standard for action which is regarded as binding by States. Standards become, in this way, a main source for the development of international law.

(ii) Pre-Standards

Before rules on standards are formally or effectively adopted, they exist in a *pre-standard* form. Many actors, public and private, find it useful to comply with such pre-standards, not least for economic

---

[183]   *Infra* in this Chapter.

[184]   *Cf.* O'Connell, ii *International Law*, 2nd ed., 1970 943.

[185]   *Infra* in this Chapter. See also *supra* on the Theory of Acts.

[186]   See my *Law of War, op. cit*, 271 *et seq.*

[187]   On the absence of legal duty to share *everything*, see my *Concept, op. cit.*, 69-70.

[188]   See *infra* in the next section.

reasons. If proposals are likely to lead to binding rules it is obviously useful to have the foresight to comply with pre-standards.

As one example one may mention the MARPOL Convention which, *before its adoption* in 1973, was known to lead to new rules on, for example, slop tanks to prevent risk of marine oil pollution. Many found it convenient to construct ships to comply with the proposed standards before rules became binding at the entry into force of the Convention.

Similar behaviour, adopting standards not yet legally binding, is found among EC candidates, like Sweden which in 1992, long before it could expect to become a Member of the Community, modified *glögg*, a Swedish traditional Christmas drink allegedly not acceptable to EC standards; earlier still, specifications of Swedish lorries, and even the design of passports[189] were adapted to correspond to EC standards, long before such standards could in anyway become binding in Sweden.

Pre-standards are often *testing the water* and seeking re-assurance of other States that the proposed line of action meets with approval. We also note this technique in international organisations, as we shall see with regard to, for example, the Moratorium Resolution.[190]

iv. Natural Law

One can distinguish between various categories of *rules of international society*; only some rules, and probably very few, are actually formed according to the accepted formula of usage + *opinio juris*. The bulk of international legal rules are probably found in conventions and treaties to which States,[191] and others[192] give their clear and express consent and where rules are normally set out more or less clearly in writing. These rules have been examined earlier in this Chapter.

---

[189]   But not to the same non-forgeable standard, *cf. infra.*

[190]   *Infra* under Recommendations of International Organisations, Guidelines for Action.

[191]   On treaties see *infra* under (I) Hard Law i., in this Chapter.

[192]   On the right of liberation movements to accede to treaties, see my *Law of War, op. cit.*, 42 *et seq.*

Other international legal rules emerge in other ways and by different mechanisms, and could be called customary rules *latu sensu*. All that the adjective 'customary' signifies in the latter case is thus that these rules have been adopted, in some way, as legally binding rules in international society; the qualification that they are only customary rules *latu sensu*, however, signifies that they have *not* grown out of any usage + *opinio juris* but are the fruits of other methods of rule making. 'Customary' then, with regard to those rules, only means *common* or *general*.

Some rules, especially those on Human Rights, are only 'customary' *latu sensu*, *i.e.*, the very wide meaning of the term and gain validity by simple recognition by States by a collective convergence of conviction. Here, States accept the rules by stating them.[193] It is much simpler to speak of *natural law* in this context for it is obvious that the process of conceptual *recognition* of such rules implies that they are, more or less, *inherent in the international legal system*. The fear that many lawyers appear to have to recognise this category of rules is inexplicable, since those of us who do acknowledge the existence of natural law find ourselves in the good company of Plato,[194] Aristotle[195] or St. Thomas Aquinas[196] as well as with the 'father' of international law, Hugo Grotius,[197] the later Emer de Vattel,[198] or our own contemporary *nestor* of international law, Alfred von Verdross.[199]

The relevant natural law rules which are in this sense rooted in processes which are necessary or obvious in international society are

---

[193] See my *Concept, op. cit.*, 104.

[194] See the distinction between *nomos*, the law made by agreement or custom, and *phusis*, nature, which explained other rules more firmly rooted in divine or natural processes, see, Plato, *The Laws*, 624a.

[195] Aristotle, *Politics* 1.2.x (1253 a 928): law and justice are good for the proper development of human nature; neither is contrary to *phusis* which, in turn, is not opposed to *nomos*.

[196] *Summa Theologica*, 1968-1273.

[197] See his *De jure belli ac pacis*, 1625.

[198] *Le droit des gens ou principes de la loi naturelles appliqués à la conduite et aux affaires des nations et des souverains*, 1758.

[199] For example, in Verdross & Simma, *Universelles Völkerrecht*, 3rd ed., 1984; *cf.* Verdross, *Abendländische Rechtsphilosophie*, 1972.

of various types. Some concepts, like *justice* is clearly, in the Platonic sense, *immutable* in its essence but *variable* in its application. Numerous other rules, however, are highly *variable* and *dynamic*, depending on the actual needs of international society at any given time. On the other hand, they are not evasive or esoteric rules, as the adversaries claim, but far more succinct than the nebulous 'customary' rules to which so many refer without much foundation as to their coming into being according to the formatistic processes thought necessary for such rules. In a way, natural law may, as far as a large part of their contents is concerned, often be a euphemism of *common sense.*

Some of the natural law rules are binding because of logical necessity[200] and other rules are binding because of the social interdependance[201] which follows from the partnership of States, living side by side in an international society, governed by the Rule of Law.

a. General Principles

Bin Cheng, *General Principles of Law as Applied by International Courts and Tribunals,* 1953; Reuter, Le recours de la Cour de justice des Communautés Européennes à des principes généraux de droit, *Mélanges Rolin,* 1964, 263; Verdross, Les principes generaux du droit dans la jurisprudence internationale, 52 RCADI 1935, 195; Scerni, *I principi generali di diritto riconoscuiti dalle nazione civile nella giurisprudenzia della Corte permanente di giustizia internazionale,* 1932; McNair, The general principles of law recognised by civilised nations, BYIL 1957 1; Sereni, *Principi generali di diritto e processo internazionale,* 1955; Tunkin, General principles of law, 95 RCADI 1958, 9.

On gaps or *lacunae* in international law, see Siorat, *Le problème des lacunes en droit international,* 1959; Lauterpacht, *Private Law Sources and Analogies of International Law,* 1927, re-printed 1970; Donati, *Il problema delle lacuni dell'ordinamento giuridico,* 1910.

---

[200]   See my *Concept, op. cit.,* 121-122.
[201]   *Ibid.,* 122-123.

200

A national or international court may resort to *general principles*[202] to prove general acceptance of procedural rules, including rules on evidence. Thus, the International Court of Justice resorted to such general principles, common to *all systems of law*, on circumstantial evidence[203] or on situations when such evidence must be excluded.[204] Other formal rules which can be subsumed under the category of general principles, and which are often applied by international courts and tribunals concern matters like imputation,[205] proportionality,[206] duty of care and the obligation to pay reparation for incurred injury and damage.[207] Rules of reparation may, in some cases, take the form of a specific form of *apology*,[208] restitution[209] or compensation.[210]

Some formal rules of *calculation of territory* will have clear impact on the *extent* of certain rights, like the notion of *straight baselines* for the calculation of water territory, again a rule rooted in common sense.[211] Other general principles also exist in the international legal order, for example the rule on *good faith* in all international transactions. Similar general principles often fill out the *lacunae*,[212] or gaps, in the international legal system when there are

---

202   In the work *Concept, op. cit.*, I denied the existence of substantial 'general principles' on the ground that most can be reduced to formal maxims, and few other 'principles' appear to have much substance. On reflection I do not think this is right. I have therefore revised my theory to embrace also the notion binding of substantial general principles, beyond those incorporated in what I call *maxims*.

203   *Reparations Case* (1949) ICJ Reports, 4, at 41.

204   *The Corfu Channel Case* (1949) ICJ *Reports* 1949, 4.

205   I do not share the idea put forward by one isolated author, see Brownlie, *Responsibility of States*, 1984, that this would in any way be an unnecessary notion. On the contrary, it is a concept without which no legal system can operate.

206   *Lithgow Case* (1986), European Court of Human Rights, *Reports* 1986.

207   *Chorzow Factory Case* (1928) PCIJ Ser. A No. 17.

208   *The I'm Alone*, (1935) 3 RIAA 1609

209   *Temple Case* (1962) ICJ *Reports* 6; *Texaco v Libya* (1977) 53 ILR 389.

210   *E.g. Amoco Case* (1987) 15 Iran US CTR; *Lusitania Claim* (1923) 7 RIAA 32.

211   *Anglo-Norwegian Fisheries Case* (1951) 116.

212   See, *e.g.,* Siorat, *Le problème des lacunes en droit international*, 1959.

not sufficient substantial rules available.

Some important general principles concern what we have called *prophylactic rules*[213] without which the *hypothetical goal*[214] can be achieved, for example rules on *non-appropriation of parts of res communis.*[215]

Other general principles can also provide substantive rules, such as *e.g.* rules on the notion of *trusts,*[216] on *limited liability,*[217] or on the rule of *subrogation.*[218] General principles on substantive matters can also lead to the displacement of a rule that would otherwise apply. This can, for example, occur by the operation of *jus cogens*, which itself can be conceived as a general principle.[219]

Thus, a court can apply general principles to prove matters of substance, *i.e.* to prove that a legal rule concerning the merits exists in numerous States and that the rule, therefore, deserves to be lifted up onto the international level as an international general principle. This was done, for example, in the *Filartiga Case*[220] where a United States Court relied on torture being forbidden in 55 States to prove that there existed a general international rule on prohibition of torture.

Rules of international law may also, in many cases, be used by national courts in a case without transformation. The United States Restatement (Revised) provides that

> 'General principles common to the major legal systems, even if not incorporated or reflected in customary law or international agreement, may be invoked as supplementary rules of international law where appropriate'.[221]

In this context we are often concerned with common concepts like

---

213   See *infra* in Chapter V.

214   *Supra* in this Chapter and *cf.* my *Concept, op. cit., passim.*

215   *Cf.* Verdross & Simma, *Universelles Völkerrecht*, 3rd ed., 1984, 698.

216   *International Statute of South Africa* (1950), ICJ *Reports* 1950.

217   *Barcelona Traction* (1970), ICJ *Reports* 1970.

218   *Mavrommatis Case* (1925), PCIJ Ser. A No. 5.

219   See, *supra*, under *jus cogens.*

220   *Filartiga v Pena-Irala*, [1980], 630 F 2d 876 (2d Circ).

221   Restatement (Revised) 1985 para. 102(4).

202

imputation, duty of care and quantum of reparation, common to all legal systems[222] and, to the extent they are necessary, lifted up onto the international level to amplify the international legal system on specific matters. One very important general principle, to which international courts and tribunals have reverted repeatedly, is the rule that injury and damage must be followed by a basic duty of full compensation,[223] and that such compensation must be *adequate, prompt* and *effective*.[224] We can be reasonably certain, however, that these rules have not developed through any general usage + *opinio juris* process and that they, therefore, are only customary rules *latu sensu*.

Many of these principles will be derived from analogies with national laws and will often involve an element of comparative analysis: the court which is dealing with a dispute may, for example, accept the lowest common denominator as a viable rule for its procedure or for adjudicating on the merits. One good example is the *AM & S Case* before the Court of the European Communities,[225] where general principles on privileged communication were used as *gap fillers*.[226]

On the other hand, the rules cannot be *equated* with mere municipal rules. As Lord Asquith stated in the *Abu Dhabi Case*,[227] with regard to his mandate to decide, under an arbitration agreement, with 'good will and sincerity of belief' and in a fashion 'consistent with reason', such expression *prescribed*

'the application of principles rooted in the good sense and common practice of the generality of civilised nations - sort of modern law of nature'.

---

[222] *Cf. South West Africa Case* (1950) ICJ *Reports* 128.

[223] *Chorzow Factory Case* (1928) PCIJ Ser. A No. 17.

[224] This is a rule used in numerous expropriation and nationalisation cases, see - also for a summary of earlier practice - the *Lithgow Case*, (1986) European Court of Human Rights, *Reports* 1986.

[225] 2 CMLR 264.

[226] *Cf.* Janis, *An Introduction to International Law*, 1988, 49.

[227] ILR 1951, 149.

Such common sense rules, derived from the necessity of the international social order, cannot be equated to any *customary rules*, formed by fictitious conditions, as alleged by those who seek to reduce all rules to the vague category of customary law, used increasingly for the political self interest of States. The *practice* to which the award refers does not imply practice in the sense of usage, but rather practice in the sense of acceptance - a process by which States acknowledge, recognise and adopt general rules.[228]

b. Maxims

Maxims could be seen as a specific sub-section of general principles. There is some merit in keeping the two categories distinct, as a generic section of general principles which have a wider ambit, and restricting maxims to essential procedural aspects where they play their greatest part.

Certain rules embody maxims[229] which are dependent on neither practice nor on *opinio juris*. Some of these rules like, *nemo judex in causa sua* (no one may be a judge in his own case), *audiatur et altera pars* (let both parties be heard in a dispute),[230] are derived from Roman law as well as those which govern further basic rules on fair hearings, such as *ne bis in idem* (only hear the same case once), on *res judicata* (or the legal force of a judgment not to be uprooted after a certain time) or on the exclusion of circumstantial evidence.[231] Another maxim concerns the effcts of judgment and the stabilisation of the legal order by ensuring consistency of courts, such as the rule

---

[228]   See also *infra* under Ethics, in this Chapter.

[229]   See *ibid.* 49 *et seq.*

[230]   These two rules form what in Anglo Saxon law is called *natural justice*, essential in every case. See *supra*. Not application in practice in cases where one party has not attended, *e.g.* the International Court of Justice in the *Hostage Case* (1980), ICJ *Reports* 1980, where the Court examined *ex officio* certain points which one could have expected the non-attending State might have raised.

[231]   *Corfu Channel Case* (1949) ICJ *Reports* 1949, 4.

of *stare decisis* (that precedents should be followed),[232] These *jurisdictional maxims* are of different types and can be grouped according to whether they intervene before or after a dispute has arisen.[233]

Other maxims go to the core of *international security of law*, in the sense that they duplicate internal rules, again derived from Roman law, on *pacta sunt servanda*, (contracts should be kept) or, in the field of crime and responsibility, *nullum crimen sine lege*, (no one must be punished for an act which was not a crime when he committed it). Some have even thought the principle on *pacta sunt servanda* so essential that the whole network of international rules depend on this rule: it would thus be the *fundamental norm* or the *Grundnorm*.[234] In our opinion, the function of maxims is essential even if they, by themselves, do not explain the basis of obligation in international law.[235]

Maxims are thus obvious rules which are essential to the international legal system and without which the legal system cannot function. Indeed, as mentioned above, no legal system can operate without these minimum rules.

These rules are not customary rules in the strict sense of the word: they are not adopted after any *usage* and *opinio juris* procedure. On the contrary, they are adopted as binding rules by States by a simple and immediate acknowledgement process. Since all

---

[232] This is a rule of (Roman and) English law which exercises considerable influence in international law although it is, in international courts and tribunals, technically a question of a rebuttable presumption. Note the practice to *follow* a case, as in, for example, *The Exchange of Greek and Turkish Populations Case* (1925) PCIJ Ser. B No. 10, which expressly followed the earlier *Wimbledon Case* (1923) PCIJ Ser. A No. 1, and the practice to *distinguish* cases in later similar situations, *e.g.* as was done in the *Interpretation of Peace Treaties Case* (1950, ICJ *Reports* 1950, 65 where the earlier *Eastern Carelia Case* (1923) PCIJ Ser. B No. 5 was distinguished.

[233] See, further, my *Concept, op. cit.*, 49-51 on Initial, Conditional, Contingent, Stabilising and Consequential maxims.

[234] Kelsen, *Principles of International Law*, 1952, 417.

[235] It is necessary to rely on other rules to establish the reason why international law rules are binding. On the basis of obligation, which may vary according to the different types of obligation, see, in detail, my *Concept, op. cit.*, 121-128 and *infra*.

legal systems use such rules, there is not even any conscious process; States merely borrow such notions and concepts from their own internal system and convert them for use in the international legal order.

Most maxims have a procedural content and refer to aspects of due process or fair trial. *Pacta sunt servanda*, which refers to good faith in contract relationships, is an exception; it could perhaps be what I have called,[236] an *initial* maxim in the sense that it is, *per se*, relevant, *ab initio*.

It is the maxim *pacta sunt servanda* that *partially* obligations explains under international law, namely with regard to contractual undertakings, like treaties.[237]

c. Ethics

Other rules are neither localised, nor dependent on practice, nor mere logic maxims but form part of general basic ethics of international society. The obvious examples of legally binding ethical rules are substantive rules on the fundamental or basic Human Rights as well as rules on humanitarian treatment in armed conflict. Here, the rules depend on the consent of states, by what some have called *Rechtsüberzeugung* or conviction of law, to a certain level of individual, or group treatment.

To this group we may nowadays also count rules concerning prohibition of force, including prohibition to resort to aggressive war, rules which form a fundamental principle derived from basic considerations inherent in the international legal order.[238] This view has firm support in the judgment of the international Court of Justice in *The Nicaragua Case* where the Court said that

'... from having constituted a marked departure from customary international law which still exists unmodified, the Charter gave expression in this field (on prohibition of force) to principles already present in customary international law, and that law has

---

[236]   My *Concept, op. cit.,* 49.

[237]   See my *Concept, op. cit.,* 121 on a variable basis of obligation.

[238]   Rijkkema, 20 NYIL 1989, 91.

in the subsequent four decades developed under the influence of the Charter, to such an extent that a number of rules contained in the Charter have acquired a status independent of it. The essential consideration is that both the Charter and the customary international law flow from common fundamental principle outlawing the use of force in international re- lations.'[239]

Similar views were put forward in *The Hostages in Teheran Case*[240] where the Court underlined the duty to uphold fundamental rules of international law by third States not involved immediately in any dispute: the reason for such solidarity is founded on the basic or fundamental nature of the violated norm.[241]

An important question concerns the *identification* of relevant rules of this category. Here we need to resort to a *theory of acts*[242] which explains how States by, for example, *recognition*[243] or *adoption*[244] acknowledge the existence of an ethical standard. Such acknowledgement is not necessary for the existence of the rule but for its identification.

It is in the nature of this category that it can be *expanded* according to the needs and attitude of States. Here we are not concerned with *immutable* notions of natural law, like *justice* or a *hypothetical goal*.[245] A century ago aggressive war was not necessarily unethical; fifty years ago there were those who actively promoted apartheid without being criticised for breaking international law or for upholding unethical views.

The dynamic nature[246] of this category therefore suggests that

---

[239] ICJ, *Nicaragua v United States,* ICJ *Reports* 1986, Judgment para. 181.

[240] ICJ *Reports* 1980.

[241] Cf. my *Concept, op. cit.* 124 *et seq.*

[242] See in detail my *Concept, op. cit.,* 87-121, and *supra* in this Chapter for a summary of my views.

[243] *Ibid.,* 104.

[244] *Ibid.,* 103.

[245] See *supra* in this Chapter on *justice* under General Principles and further *supra* under the Hypothetical Goal.

[246] It is only those whose reading of natural law has been confined to the Sophists who may be under the misapprehension that natural law is exempt from any change. On the contrary, it is a flexible and dynamic notion, reflecting what

there may be future modifications of the substantive contents of this group. However, as has been observed with any Human Rights, it appears that rules that apply to the treatment of *individuals* can only be upgraded and it seems unconceivable that these rules, at least in the present sociological framework, could be abolished or diminished.[247]

d. Convenience *Also / comity – see p. 14 of this bk.*

(i) Traffic

Some rules, which are not localised to territory, but relate to the *use* of territory or water, form part of a body of law to which the international society, for some time, has expressed its general consent for *convenience*. Rules of this type concern, for example, traffic flow or separation lanes at sea. There may be usage, or practice, and general agreement as to the contents of a rule; but there is no procedure of usage + *opinio juris* before the rule is made. In other words, the usage and general agreement may, in this case, be a *consequence,* rather than a precondition to the operation of the rule.

Some of these rules are localised in the sense that they operate in a certain area, but they do not establish title but merely apportion traffic flows. These rules are not necessarily dependent on practice: they may concern rules of the road, either in waterways[248] or in space,[249] and will operate immediately, adopted by necessity, without the requirement of elapse of any time span or of practice of any substantial number of States. The rules are often indicated by an international organisation and may[250] be immediately *binding*.[251]

---

the needs may be *at any given time* in international society.

[247] This obviously does not mean that Human Rights would be effectively safeguarded but only that the *attitudes* in the contemporary international society would not tolerate a *legalised downgrading* of these now established rights.

[248] See *infra.*

[249] See *infra.*

[250] As is the case of the rules of the International Maritime Organisation on Traffic Separation.

(ii) Inter-State Contacts

Other types of customary rules appear to concern various forms of communication between States, in what one may generally call inter-state contacts. For example, rules on diplomats belong to the most respected and oldest branches of international law. There is no doubt that the various rules on diplomatic immunity developed out of custom, out of usage + *opinio juris*, although I would like to evade claims that there had been a maze of state practice to bring about formation of rules.[252] It was rather a matter of immediate social necessity, but one may agree that details and clarification came through later use.

To this group we can also count the rules on immunity of heads of State, of State organs in general, as well as rules on how treaties should be concluded. One example under the latter heading may be the power of an agent to bind the state by treaty.

For such rules concerning communication between States, custom, understood in a wide sense, may play an important role.

e. Apportionment

Other rules concern the division or apportionment of territory or resources. These are rules which are localised to certain types of areas but these rules are not always, as in the case of prescription, dependent on practice. These rules establish immediate agreement on non-use or the extent of use; here, we may consider rules on Antarctica, high seas or on the exclusive economic zone.[253]

f. Tort

Some rules, of quite a different character, concern the construction of

---

[251]   The *ground of obligation* in this case would be the *abstract consent* given by the States which founded (or later adhered to) the organisation, see my *Law Making, op cit.*, Chapter One.

[252]   *Cf.* my Concept, *op. cit.*, 118-119.

[253]   *Cf. infra*, under Waters and Shelves.

liability and responsibility. In this area we are concerned with concepts and notions, partly common or similar to the maxims discussed above.

Rules of this type are not localised but concern the responsibility and liability in, for example, environmental matters. Important notions and concepts,[254] such as that of imputation, proportionality and duty of care,[255] often imported from municipal systems, are used to assess liability.

g. Equity

Reuter, Quelques réflexions sur l'équité en droit international, 15 RBDI 1980 180; De Visscher, C., *De l'équité dans le règlement arbitral ou judiciaire des litiges de droit international public,* 1972; Bin Cheng, Justice and equity in international law, 8 CLP 1955 185; Degan, *Equity et le droit international,* 1970.

Equity is not a separate source of law but a mechanism for mitigating what the law would otherwise provide. It is useful to discuss the nature of equity in this context, however, as courts often take recourse to equity as a general principle of law, as those we have just analysed.

Equity, in international law, is, of course, quite different from the notion as used in English Chancery law.[256] In international law equity implies the power of a court to use equitable principles to mitigate the result of the application of the law or to fill gaps in the existing network of international rules. According to Aristotle the main rule is that equity means equality.[257] However, in the jurisprudence of international courts, the two notions have not always had the same meaning. The application of equitable principles has sometimes led to the division of water in an unequal way when the court found it 'fair' that the parties should have differently sized

---

[254] See *infra* under General Principles, in this Chapter.

[255] See *infra* under General Principles; *cf. supra* under Maxims.

[256] For the concept of equity in English law, see, for example, Pettit, *Equity and the Law of Trusts,* 8th ed., 1989.

[257] *Nicomachean Ethics,* bk. 5, ch. 10.

portions of water territory. Equity in international law does thus not always mean equality even if this sometimes may be the case.[258] In matters of maritime delimitation, the ICJ has stressed that it is not principle of *equidistance* but the *equitable result* that must be the guide light.[259] This *equitable result* can be achieved by *equitable criteria*.[260]

Using equitable principles thus means that the court or tribunal does what appears *fair* in the case.[261] In a sense this application of equity implies the use of a *general principle*[262] in the sense of article 38(1) of the Statute of the International Court of Justice,[263] as discussed above. This use of a general principle of equity must, if we are to be exact, be distinguished from the situation when a court is asked to judge *ex aequo et bono*, *i.e.* according to what the court finds 'fair' *regardless of formal provisions in the law*. Article 38(2) states specifically that the provisions in article 38(1), which lists the sources of international law,[264] does not preclude the ICJ from adjudicating *ex aequo et bono*, but only if the parties so agree. To leave a case for such adjudication is, for obvious reasons, more common in arbitrations when the parties are more ready to accept a wide discretion of the tribunal in deciding between the parties, than in formal court procedures.

Although it has been pointed out that adjudication *ex aequo et*

---

[258]   See *e.g.*, *The Anglo-French Continental Shelf Arbitration* [1979], 18 ILM 399; cf. *The Tunisia v Libya Case* [1982], ICJ *Reports* 1982, 18.

[259]   *North Sea Continental Shelf Case* (1969) ICJ *Reports* 3. On 'special circumstances' under the 1958 Continental Shelf Convention, see *Anglo-French Continental Shelf Case* (1979) 18 ILM 397.

[260]   *Libya v Malta* (1982) ICJ *Reports* 18; *Gulf of Maine Case* (1982) ICJ *Reports* 246.

[261]   *Diversion of Water from the River Meuse (Netherlands v Belgium)* (1937) PCIJ Ser. A/B No. 70; *Rann of Kutch Arbitration (India v Pakistan)* (1968) 17 RIAA 11; *Fisheries jurisdiction (United Kingdom v Iceland)* (1974) ICJ *Reports* 1974, 3; *Gulf of Maine Case* (1982) ICJ *Reports* 1982, 3 and 1984, 246; *Burkina Faso v Mali* (1986) ICJ *Reports* 1986, 554.

[262]   *Supra*, under General Principles.

[263]   See the *Diversion of Water from the River Meuse*, PCIJ, Series A/B No. 70, 76.

[264]   *Supra* under Sources.

bono is different from the application of equity as a general principle,[265] it is difficult to see the distinction as anything more than one of degree: when the International Court uses equity as a general principle it does so for *part of the case* or for a *part of an argument.* When the Court adjudicates *ex aequo et bono* - which it still has not done - the entire case will be dealt with according to what is found to be *fair.* It is clear that a tribunal, which lacks the agreement of the parties to adjudicate *ex aequo et bono,* may still allow the parties to rely on equity in their arguments.[266] Similarly, it is clear that lack of competence to adjudicate a case *ex aequo et bono* does not deprive a court the right to resort to equity as a set of general principles.[267]

The International Court emphasised in *Tunisia v Libya*[268] that equity as a legal concept, is *'a direct emanation of the idea of justice'*, a clear indication that the Court is not adverse to notion of natural law.[269] But the ICJ has underlined that it is not able, in the absence of a clear mandate by both parties to adjudicate *ex aequo et bono* and that, therefore, equity can only be used *infra legem*, that is to say to supplement, but not displace, the law.[270]

---

[265]   *E.g.,* Judge Hudson in the *Diversion of Water from the River Meuse Case,* (1937), PCIJ Series A/B, No. 70, at 73.

[266]   *The Rann of Kutch Arbitration* (1968), 17 RIAA 1 at 11.

[267]   See the *Diversion of Water from the River Meuse* (1937), PCIJ Series A/B, No. 70, 73. (Opinion of Judge Hudson).

[268]   (1982) ICJ *Reports* 18.

[269]   See *supra* under Natural Law, in this Chapter.

[270]   The Court refused the use equity *contra* or *praeter legem,* see *Burkina Faso v Mali* (1985) ICH *Reports* 6.

CHAPTER IV

Sources of International Law: Soft Law
The Legal Value of Recommendations of International Organisations

Tammes, Soft Law, in *Essays in Honour of Erades,* 1983, 187; Miehsler, Zur Autorität von Beschlüssen internationaler Institutionen, in Schreuer (ed.), *Autorität und internationale Ordnung,* 1979; Schreuer, Recommendations and the traditional sources of international law, GYIL 1977, 104; Schachter, Towards a theory of international obligation, VirJIL 1968-1969, 300; Schütz, Probleme der Anwendung der KSZE-Schlussakte aus völkerrechtlicher Sicht in Delbruck, Ropers & Zelletin (eds.), *Grünbuch zu den Folgewirkungen der KSZE,* 1977, 160.

On the force of recommendations see, especially, Verdross, Kann die Generalversammlung der Vereinten Nationen das Völkerrecht weiterbilden?, ZaöRVR 1966, 690; Skubiszewski, *Annuaire de l'Institut,* II:1977, 36-103; I:1985, 29-358; *idem,* BYIL, 1965-66; Vallat, The competence of the United Nations General Assembly, 97 RCADI 1959 ii, 230; Dupuy, R.J., Droit déclaratoire et droit programmatoire: de la coutume 'sauvage' à la soft law, SFDI, *Colloque de Toulouse, L'élaboration du droit international public,* 1974, 140; Seidl-Hohenveldern, International economic soft law, 163 RCADI 1979 ii, 176; Sloan, The binding force of a 'recommendation' of the General Assembly, BYIL 1948, 1; Schwager, *Empfehlungen internationaler Organisationen besonders auf den Gebiet der Europäischen Raumordnung,* 1990; Castaneda, *Legal Effects of the United Nations Resolutions,* 1969; *idem,* Valeur juridique des résolutions des Nations Unies, 129 RCADI 1970 i, 211; Golsong & Ermacora. Das Problem der Rechtssetzung durch internationale Organisationen, insbesondere im Rahmen der UN, 10 DGVR 1971, 1; Asamoah, *The Legal Significance of the Declarations of the General Assembly,* 1966; Falk, On the quasi-legislative competence of the General Assembly, AJIL 1966, 782; Elias, Modern sources of international law; *Essays in Honour of Jessup,* 1972, 51; and my *Law Making, op. cit.,* 207-213.

Rules supplementing international *hard law* (treaties and customary law *strictu sensu)* are useful to bring about a development of international law. These rules are often a form of unilateral acts but, occasionally, they emanate from multiple sources, sometimes in an almost contractual way.[1]

Some such supplementing rules[2] are truly optional and contain general binding obligations but improve on the given framework in international society by allowing promotional rules,[3] implying voluntary additional rules. Yet, in some cases the *soft law*, *i.e.* the apparently non-binding rules, entail certain legal consequences for States. It is an important focus of inquiry which has interested many scholars over the years.

It may be that, in some cases, the soft law merely reflects other binding obligations, assumed by States in other ways. In that case the situation is similar to that of a treaty and a third State: of course, a third State can never be bound by a treaty which to him is a *res inter alio acta*, *i.e.* a transaction between others. But if the treaty *reflects* another obligation, for example another binding treaty, the third State will be bound, not by the first treaty, but on another ground, by the underlying agreement. Similarly, we shall investigate whether such situations can arise in the case of soft law or whether there is any other grounds for assuming that legal obligations result from rules of soft law.

i. Recent Trends of Development

There have, in the last decade or two, been speculations that resolutions of certain international organisations, particularly those of the General Assembly would have more than recommendatory force. In the United Nations General Assembly this would be so because of the underlying basis of resolutions adopted by the 'representatives of the world'.[4] It has been suggested that recommendations of the General Assembly constitute a new type of *soft law*,[5] *droit flou* or

---

[1] See, further, on Parallel Acts my *Concept*, 102 *et seq.*

[2] See my *Concept, op. cit.*, 67 *et seq.*

[3] *Ibid.*, 68 *et seq.*

[4] *E.g.* Falk, On the quasi-legislative competence of the General Assembly, 60 AJIL, 1956, 788.

[5] Seidl Hohenveldern, International economic soft law, 163 RCADI, 1979 ii, 176.

droit vert.[6] One can distinguish various distinct forms of recommendations of international organisations and, below, there is an attempt to classify such acts. We shall investigate whether any of the categories include measures which entail legal obligations.

ii. Types of Recommendations

Recommendations fall into several distinct categories. Their impact on behaviour of States and the degree of obligation can only be ascertained by a close analysis of the nature and characteristics of the acts in question.

a. Resolutions on Primary Matters

Many recommendations concern matters like Headquarters arrangements, staff or finance matters, or what I have called *primary matters*.[7] These are matters which, for organisational and administrative reasons have to be dealt with before an organisation can set out to work towards the objectives for which it was established. Once established, the organisation will attain these objectives by what I have called *operative acts*.[8] Primary acts are particularly frequent at the beginning of the life of an organisation when first such matters are dealt with but measures relating to primary matters recur during the functioning years of an organisation. Budgetary questions, in particular, recur, of course, throughout the working life of an organisation. Precisely because budget questions form part of these acts, it is inappropriate to call such matters *internal* as all questions bearing on the budget must have immediate *external* impact, particularly on the Member States. A useful term may therefore be *primary* acts as such acts must be taken before any other *operative* act can intervene.[9]

---

6   Dupuy, R.J., Droit déclaratoire et droit programmatoire: de la coutume sauvage à la soft law, in Société française pour le Droit international, *Colloque de Toulouse, L'élaboration du droit international public*, 1974, 140.

7   See my *Law Making, op. cit.*, 42 *et seq.*

8   *Ibid., loc. cit.* and *supra*, under Normal Powers of Organisations.

9   *Ibid., loc. cit.*

Occasionally, acts of this type appear as 'decisions' rather than 'recommendations' but the latter term is not uncommon in this context. Whatever the heading of a resolution relating to primary matters, it entails immediate legal obligations both within the organisation and with regard to its member States. Budgetary measures thus effectively bind the member States. There is no question of doubting the legal force of other measures taken on primary matters for the administration of the organisation itself, such as staff or headquarters matters.[10]

b. Exhortations of Restraint of Specific Action

Certain resolutions of organisations, particularly those of the UN General Assembly, contain *exhortations* to states to *restrain action*. Such is the case, for example, with regard to resolutions concerning a war situation, such as for example, demands from the General Assembly of ceasefire in the Iran-Iraq war.[11] Resolutions by the Security Council 660-678 in 1990-1991 calling on Iraq to restore the *status quo ante* with regard to the illegal occupation of Kuwait, can be included in this category.

Other resolutions, for example, those on apartheid,[12] often contain a predominant *restraint element* even if occasionally coupled with requests for positive action. Resolutions of this type may be compared with jurisdictional measures of interim protection or injunctions in national or international courts. Such acts of injunctive relief often imply negative commands although in exceptional cases mandatory *injunctions* may be warranted.

There are similar resolutions of non-jurisdictional organs of international organisations requesting a *stand still* behaviour by a freezing Resolution, for example, as under the Resolution 1962 (XVIII) 1963 on extra-atmospheric activities. Similar resolutions or part of resolutions, concern stand still obligations with regard to the environment.

---

10   See further my *Law Making, op. cit., passim.*

11   GA Resolution 479, 28 September 1980.

12   *E.g.* Resolutions 37/69 B, 1982; for sanctions, see *e.g.* 36/172 N 1981 and *infra*, under Sanctions.

c. Programmatic Declarations on General Action

Other resolutions lay down *programmes for future general action* and often contain a detailed framework within which further implementing measures will have to be taken. A specific form of soft law results from the special sessions of the General Assembly dealing with topical issues, such as concern for the environment,[13] or the concern for the plight of the Third World.

One field of effort of the industrialised world concern precisely the improvement of conditions in the Third World. Soft law with a programmatic contents comprises, for example, the new international economic rules for the Third World. General Assembly Resolution 1701 (XVI) of 1961 concerns International Trade as the Primary Instrument for Economic Development. Another important resolution of the same type is Resolution 1710 (XVI) declaring the UN First Development Decade. Other important Resolutions of this type are those on the Establishment of the New International Economic Order (NIEO) 3201 (S-VI),[14] the Programme of action on the Establishment of the NIEO 3202 (S-VI),[15] the Resolution on Development and International Economic Cooperation 3362 (S-VII).[16] Resolutions of UNCTAD, formed in 1962[17] and made an organ of the General Assembly in 1964,[18] are also of this type.

Many rules in this field have come about because of the activities of Group 77 (now consisting of a larger number of States) which, for the first time, could encompass the developing states within one negotiating framework.[19] Some Resolutions lay down codes for economic behaviour which will be dealt with below.

---

[13]   *Cf. supra* on stand still.

[14]   13 ILM 1974 715.

[15]   13 ILM ILM 1974 720.

[16]   14 ILM 1975 1524.

[17]   ECOSOC Resolution 1917 (XXXIV); General Assembly Resolution 1785 (XXVII) 1962.

[18]   GA Resolution 1995 (XIX) 1964.

[19]   On the background see Sauvant, *Group of 77*, 1981.

d. Preferences

The attitude that all States drew benefits from the exploitation of colonies has led to some claims that all ex-colonial and other industrialised States are now obliged to 'pay back'.[20] Such general obligations presuppose a coherent notion of a true *community of nations*.[21] Yet, such a 'community' may not even exist: it may be more appropriate only to speak of an *international society*,[22] and international relations scholars are always quick to criticise international lawyers for the inappropriate and current use in international law of an international 'community' (for which all criteria are absent) instead of a society.

Under fragmented rules of international law, developing nations are given some preferences. For example, Part IV of GATT exempts non-reciprocal tariff preferences to developing countries from the general GATT rule on most-favoured nations.[23]

A special system of generalised and non-reciprocal and non-discriminatory preferences has also been adopted within the UN system[24] and in the European Community.[25] On the other hand, the highly protectionist policies of the European Community appear

---

[20]   Girvan, Expropriating the expropriators: compensation criteria from a third World viewpoint in Lillich, (ed.), 3 *Valuation of Nationalised Property*, 1975, 156. *Contra* (and possibly more convincingly): Seidl-Hohenveldern, Die Sozialpflichtigkeit des Eigentums und dessen Schutz im heutigen Völkerrecht, *Carl Heymann Verlag Almanach*, 1977, 86.

[21]   *Cf.* Dupuy, R.J., Droit déclaratoire, *op. cit.*, 13; Scheuner, Solidariätat unter den Nationen als Grundsatz in den gegenwärtigen internationalen Gesellschaft, *Festschrift Menzel*, 1975, 276.

[22]   See my *Concept, op. cit.*, 34.

[23]   Flory, T., *Le GATT*, 1968, 282; Jackson, J., *World Trade and the Law of GATT*, 1969, 854.

[24]   GA Resolution 2503 (XXIV) 1969.

[25]   The first EC system was adopted in October 1970 but, as it was largely unsuccessful, it was replaced by a new system in June 1972. This system was criticized by UNCTAD and as from 1st January 1977 the EC followed UNCTAD's recommendations and issued a new system, UN Chronicle October 1982, 42.

218

difficult to reconcile with the aims of GATT.[26]

e. Codes of Behaviour

Certain resolutions of the General Assembly contain *guides* of behaviour of States in primarily economic matters. One such example is Resolution 3281 (XXIX) on the Charter of Economic Rights and Duties of 1974.[27] Other *codes* for economic behaviour lay down rules of behaviour for non-State entities such as, for example, transnational corporations. There is now a preliminary United Nations Draft Code of Conduct of Transnational Corporations,[28] an ILO Tripartite Declaration on Principles Concerning Multinational Enterprises and Social Policy 1978,[29] the OECD Guidelines for Multinational Enterprises 1976[30] revised in 1979,[31] the EC Code of

---

26 On GATT in general, see *supra*, Chapter II, under International Organisations.

27 There is considerable literature on this important Resolution. See, for example, Virally, La Charte des droits et des devoirs économiques des Etats, Notes de lecture, AF, 1974, 75; Ladreit de la Charrière, L'influence de l'inégalité de devoirs des Etats sur le droit international, 139 RCADI 1973 ii, 253; Castaneda, J., La Chartre des droits et devoirs économiques des états, AF 1974 31; Petersmann, Völkerrecht und neue internationale Wirtschaftsordnung, 18 AVR 1978 35; Scheuner, *Solidarität, op. cit.*, 276; Tomuschat, Die Charta der wirtschaftlichen Rechte und Pflichten der Staaten. Zur Geltungskraft von Deklarationen der UN Generalversammlung, 36 ZaöRVR 1976, 458; Petersmann, Die Dritte Welt und das Wirtschaftsvölkerrecht, 36 *ibid.*, 510; *idem*, Internationales Recht und neue internationale Wirtschaftsordnung, 18 AVR, 1978, 35; Seidl-Hohenveldern, The Charter of Economic Rights and Duties of States, 2 Studi in onore di G. Balladori Pallieri, 1978, 550; Haight, The New International Economic Order and the Charter of the Economic Rights and Duties of State, 9 *International Lawyer*, 1975, 591; Kemper, *Nationale Verfügung über natürliche Resources und die Weltwirtschaftordnung der Vereinten Nationen*, 1976.

28 E/C.10/AC.2/8 1978; 17 ILM 1978, 453; there have been numerous revisions since then and there is by 1986 no firm final draft.

29 17 ILM 1978, 453.

30 15 ILM 1976, 969; 17 ILM, 1527; see Blanpain, *The Badger Case* and the OECD *Guidelines for Multinational Enterprises*, 1977, 1937.

31 OECD Dec. c (79) 102, the Council of Europe Draft Code of 1977, Doc. 3762, 1976.

Conduct for Subsidies of Multinational Enterprises 1977 and 1986,[32] and, finally, the International Chamber of Commerce Principles Regarding Multinational Enterprises 1974.[33]

UNCTAD has issued a general code for commodity problems as well as a draft international code of conduct on transfer of technology.[34] Transfer of technology has been held to be included under the general notion of the common heritage of mankind, particularly pertinent to the developing world.[35]

UNCTAD has also adopted a Code of Conduct for Liner Conferences.[36] The Andean Investment Code adopted under the Andean Pact[37] has been cited by authors as another example.[38]

Any effort to standardise and harmonise legislation also falls into the category of Draft Codes. Attempts to harmonise national rules by offering an international 'Code' for adoption was made by the Bustamante Code of Private International Law adopted by the Permanent Commission of Jurists in 1927 in Rio de Janeiro under the Third Inter-American Conference. The Inter-American Juridical Committee was initially the Standing Committee of the Inter-American Council of Jurists created by the Bogotà Charter in 1948 which set up the Organisation of American States (OAS). By

---

[32] These codes concern particularly activities in South Africa; *Keesings Archives*, 1977 21256; OJ c 118/15, 15 May 1977; EEC Information Offprint 1986; *cf.* Kukat, K., Verhaltungscodices für multinationale Unternehmen', 25 *Recht der Wirtschaft*, 1979, 297.

[33] No. 191/83. These principles were largely adopted in the OECD Code, see *supra* note 24.

[34] TD/CODE TOT/197; See *e.g.*, Kewenig, Technologietransfer aus völkerrechtliche Sicht in Kewenig, (ed.) *Völkerrecht und internationales wirtschaftliche Zusammenarbeit*, 1978, 71; Okolie, *Legal Aspects of Transfer of Technology to Developing Countries*, 1975.

[35] Pellet, *Le droit international du développement*, 1978, 118.

[36] 13 ILM 1974, 917. See, Grewlich, Die UN Konvention uber ein Verhaltungskodex fur Linienkonferenzen, 35 ZaöRVR, 1975, 742.

[37] 10 ILM 1971, 152; see my *Finance and Protection of Investment in Developing Countries*, 2nd ed., 1987, 7.

[38] Aramburu Menchaka, Multinational Firms and Regional Processes of Economic Integration, RCADI ii 1976, 394.

revision in 1967[39] the functions of the Council were transferred to the Committee. The Juridical Committee now advises on legal matters, promotes the development and codification of International Law, and studies legal ties of integration.

Important achievements in the field of harmonisation of national laws have been made by the codification work of the International Law Commission[40] and also under the Treaties of the European Community[41] as well as under the aegis of the Nordic Council.[42]

Suggestions made by harmonising bodies within international organisations often figure as *recommendations* to States.[43] In numerous cases, such bodies are not addressing themselves to States but to industry, to firms, companies and individuals. This is another example of the present cob-web system of international law, going beyond the State structures in the field of international co-operation.

f. Standards

Standards are similar to codes but have more technical contents. Uniform technical standards are adopted by numerous international organisations and bodies. Such entities are usually concerned with metrology and standardisation.

The International Organisation for Standardisation (ISO) in Geneva was formed in 1946. This organisation prepares international standards in some 2,300 working bodies covering most fields in technology. So far some 5000 standards have been issued. The members of this organisation are national standardisation bodies in 76 different countries. There is a General Assembly where all delegates of States and of other international organisations participate and a Council consisting of a president and 18 member bodies. A special information unit, the World Wide Information Network on Standards (ISONET), dissipates information of adopted and planned standards.

---

[39] Protocol of Buenos Aires of the Third Inter-American Specialised Conference, 1967.

[40] *Cf. supra.*

[41] *Cf. supra.*

[42] *Cf. supra.*

[43] See *e.g.*, EC Code, *Recommendations and Reports*, 1984, 21.

The International Organisation of Legal Metrology created in 1955[44] publishes, *i.a.*, international recommendations concerning measuring instruments subjected to or likely to be subjected to legal regulation.

The European Committee for Standardisation, formed in Paris in 1961 to promote standardisation in Europe. Like ISO, it has national standardisation bodies as members; it draws its members from 16 European States. This organisation operates as a company registered under Belgian law.[45]

There are also special European Standards on Nuclear Electronics (ESONE) adopted by the Central Bureau of Nuclear Measurement. The members of this organisation are five international and 42 national laboratories in 16 European countries. Standards adopted concern modular transistorised electronic equipment, and the so called Camac standard, an interface system standards (hard and software) for on-line computer automated measurement and control.

The Arab Organisation for Standardisation and Metrology was formed in 1965 by agreement approved by the Council for Arab Economic Unity as a specialised agency within the Arab League. This organisation sets the ASMO standards, unifies technical terms, and attempts to harmonise legislation related to metrology.

In the Scandinavian field there is, for example, the Scandinavian Pulp, Paper and Board Testing Committee which, since 1959 develops standard test methods (Scan Test) for Denmark, Finland, Norway and Sweden.[46]

Also the former Eastern bloc has its own regional standardisation, in particular the Institute of Standardisation formed in 1962 under the former, now defunct, CMEA or COMECON[47] and these standards have survived the disintegration and formal dismantling of political and economic alliances. The fact that technical standards, once adopted, override political barriers may show that they are designed to serve *convenience* rather than any particular political system. A

---

[44]   Treaty of Paris 12th October 1955.

[45]   *Cf. supra*, Chapter II, under Private Bodies.

[46]   Skandinaviska Kommittén för Prövning av Massa, Papper och Board, Stockholm.

[47]   6 *Recueil de documents*, Warsaw, 1962.

Convention on CMEA Standards was adopted on 21st June 1974 by Bulgaria, Cuba, Czechoslovakia, DDR, Hungary, Mongolia, Poland and USSR and, although CMEA is no more, the standards are still in operation.

Technical standards for literary works are elaborated by the International Standard Book Agency created in 1970. Its 62 State members have a central organisation to administer standardisation books by the ISBN system, originally intended to internationalise the book number system used in the United Kingdom. The Agency is advised by a Panel of Library Associations and Institutions (IFLA), the International Organisation for Standardisation (ISO), discussed above, the International Publishers Association and UNESCO.

In the food area there are specific standards, the ALINORM, adopted by the United Nations Food and Agricultural Organisation (FAO), often in collarboration with the World Health Organisation (WHO). Sometimes this type of standard is coupled with further specific *Codes* of behaviour.[48] The *Codex alimentarius* Commission under the FAO/WHO Standards Programme provides, for example, *recommendations of standards* of great importance to safety in food standards.[49] The Commission was formed in 1963 with a membership of 30 States which, by 1983, had increased to a membership of 122. The Commission thus develops standards, codes of practices and guidelines; it also promotes coordination of all food standards work undertaken by intergovernmental and non-governmental organisations. A Food Standards programme also helps to remove non-tariff barriers imposed by different national food regulations. Standards were adopted in 1968 and by 1983 some 190 international standards had been developed by the Commission and some 40 codes of practice had been adopted for food in international trade. A Code of Ethics for International Trade in Food has been issued to prevent countries with inadequate food control infrastructure from receiving hazardous, falsely labelled or sub-standard food. There is a special Guide to the Codex laying down Maximum Limits for Pesticide Residues in Food and a List of Recommended Maximum

---

[48] *Cf. supra*, under Codes of Behaviour.

[49] On the ALINORM, *e.g.* see *Report of the 15th Session* 1983, Appendix III, 100.

Contaminants in Food. There are also specifications for identity and purity of food additives.[50]

The Codex Standards are formally accepted by States by assurances that national legislation is forthcoming to provide for implementation. However, if this is not possible, Member States respond 'in an otherwise favourable manner'.[51] They may, for example, notify the Secretariat that products which do not comply with the Codex Standards may circulate in their territories.[52] Reservations are also allowed: Poland notified the Commission that most Standards 'with specified deviations' would be accepted.[53]

The GATT Code on Technical Barriers to Trade makes specific reference to the *Codex alimentarius* Commission and thus uses this instrument as a reference.[54] The Final Declaration of the Conference on Ministers of Foreign Affairs from Non-Aligned Countries in Delhi in 1981 welcomed the establishment of a working group from member countries to draw up a Programme for Action for Cooperation in the Sphere of Standardisation, Metrology and Quality Control.[55]

Another type of Standard is found in the *Standard Terms* used, for example, by the World Bank and the International Development Agency (IDA) in their transactions and in particular in relations to exceptions by the *Third Window Financing Facility* subsidised by the Interest Subsidy Fund.[56]

A further type of standard is used by the International Atomic Energy Agency for safety and protection of health under its article III A 6 of its Statutes. Such standards are not binding in the absence of specific agreement by the member States but such agreement becomes necessary if a project is to receive IAEA assistance.

---

[50] Guide to the Safe Use of Food Additives; *e.g.* Code of Marketing Breastmilk Substitutes; *Codex alimentarius Report* 1983, 99.

[51] *Report, op. cit.*, 102.

[52] *Loc. cit.*

[53] *Report, op. cit*, 5.

[54] ALINORM 83/43, Appendix III, 100.

[55] See *Report of the Working Group*, Havana, 1981; *cf.* Alinorm 83/43 Appendix V, 105.

[56] *UN Chronicle*, August-September 1975, 42.

g. Pre-Standards

As mentioned earlier, there are types of hard law which are adequately classified as pre-standards: they exist as a pool to draw on for specific approval by States and may have been elaborated at international conferences.[57] Recommendations of organisations may obviously fulfil a similar function. The 'softer element' however, is more pronounced when the suggestion of a pre-standard is embodied in a reocmmendation by an organisation: here, there must be unequivocal approval for a State to be considered to be legally bound.[58]

iii. Recommendations as a Source of Law

a. The Terminology

Recommendations of international organisations have been said to constitute a material source of international law.[59] Or, they have been said to occupy an intermediate place in the range of sources between material and formal sources.[60]

There is certain differentiation to be made, depending on the type of act and depending on the type of organ issuing and receiving it.

It may be useful to survey the types of alleged obligations and the grounds on which it is argued that recommendations, in certain cases, would be *binding* and to make some evaluation of the arguments.

---

[57]   See *supra* under Unilateral Acts, iii, b (ii) in Chapter III.

[58]   In the case of other pre-standards discussed above in Chapter III States have often directly participated in their formulation. It may be that there is only a slight difference between these categories; however, the concept appears useful for the classification of tentative or emerging rules.

[59]   Verdross & Simma, *Universelles Völkerrecht*, 1976, 332. *Cf. supra*, under Definition of the Term Source.

[60]   Bastid, S., Observations sur une 'étape' dans le développement progressif et la codification des principes du droit international, *Recueil Guggenheim*, 1968, 132 *et seq.*

b. Alleged Ensuing Obligations

It has been considered that General Assembly resolutions imply *the beginning of an obligation* for the Member States of the United Nations by creating an 'obligation to take them into consideration'.[61] According to this opinion, however, States would not, even if they had voted for the resolution, be bound to introduce any specific legislation.[62]

Others have taken a similar stand in the International Court of Justice: with regard to UN Resolutions States would have to 'take them into consideration' or to 'examine them in good faith'.[63]

In some organisations, like in the ILO, there are concrete obligations to this effect in the sense that members are obliged to *submit* ILO recommendations to their legislatures.[64] States are then under duty to report with regard to taken action.

The Secretary General of the United Nations may also *ex officio* make his own survey of implementation of recommendations.[65] A developed system with regard to duty to report has developed within the field of Human Rights. There are implementing measures under the European Conventions,[66] the European Social Charter,[67] the Racial Discrimination Convention,[68] the 1966 Covenants,[69] the ILO statute[70] and under UNESCO rules.[71]

---

[61]   A/C.3/SR 108, 1949 (Belgium) on the Draft Declaration of Human Rights.

[62]   *Ibid., loc. cit.*

[63]   Klaestad, Individual Opinion, *South West Africa Case,* [1955], ICJ *Reports* 1955, 88; *cf.* Lauterpacht, *ibid.*, 119.

[64]   See *e.g.* Morand, 'Réflexions sur la nature et des actes de planification', RGDIP 1970, 979.

[65]   See *e.g.*, GA 119, 1947 on Economic and Social Matters calling on the Secretary General and on ECOSOC to make reports on implementation, E/693 Adds 1-42.

[66]   Articles 19-59.

[67]   Articles 21-29.

[68]   Article 8-16

[69]   Articles 16-23 of the Economic Covenant; articles 28-45 of the Civil and Political Covenant. *Cf.* the Optional Protocol on Civil and Political Rights.

[70]   Article 22-34.

[71]   Article VIII.

Even under the non-binding Helsinki Act, the CSCE, there are provisions for implementation and review of implementing measures.[72] Such provisions are said to illustrate the *normative and institutional implications* of article 56 of the Charter and the joint and separate action of members which is necessary to achieve the aims of article 55 of the Charter concerning the universal respect for Human Rights.[73]

The non-implementation of recommendations may lead to certain disadvantages. The outright acceptance of IAEA standards becomes necessary if a project is to receive IAEA assistance, although the standards themselves are not obligatory.[74] Thus, in an indirect way, the 'recommended' standards are enforced by special advantages available to those which do comply. In other organisations, like EFTA, *sanctions* are introduced if recommendations are not implemented and yet the recommendations are *per se* facultative.[75] United Nations practice also shows examples of this type of *sanctioned recommendations*. Resolution 181 (II) 1947 on Palestine[76] provides that any attempt to modify the regulation of the recommendation by force may be regarded, by further assessment by the Security Council, as a threat to the peace.

c. Typology of Alleged Grounds for Obligation and Critique

(i) Interpretative Resolutions

Some claim that a General Assembly Resolution, although not in itself binding, may prescribe principles of international law: if it

---

[72]   See Principle IX and VII para. 6 on agreement on 'follow-up' whereby States will implement provisions of the Final Act (a) unilaterally; (b) bilaterally by negotiation or (c) multilaterally by 'meetings of experts of the participating States and also within the framework of international organisations'.

[73]   Arangio-Ruiz, Human Rights and Non-intervention in the Helsinki Final Act, 15 RCADI 1977 iv 234.

[74]   See, *supra*, under Standards.

[75]   See my Aspects institutionnels sur l'Association Européenne de Libre Echange (EFTA), Annuaire Français de droit international 1960, 793.

[76]   Brugière, *Les pouvoirs de l'Assemblée Générale des Nations Unies*, 233; Virally, *op. cit.*, 86.

'touches' on subjects in for example the UN Charter it may, they say, amount to an 'authoritative interpretation' of the Charter.[77] Examples of such Resolutions would, for example, be the Universal Declaration of Human Rights of 1948 and the important Resolution on Granting of Independence to Colonial Countries and Peoples 1514 (XV) 1060. Others call the interpretative activity *authentic interpretation*,[78] and for textual support this may be a better term.

The problem of the right to interpret has given rise to many interesting comments by writers. Many writers in former Eastern Europe considered it possible for an interpretative act of the Charter to acquire binding force provided the specific act receives general recognition.[79] Recognition could, said such writers, be expressed by voting.[80] These views reflect, to a large extent, attitudes of lawyers in the ex-communist States to underline the importance of the expressed views of every State: only the State itself could decide on its own obligations and, at the same time, pretending to be able to pronounce on which Resolutions are binding on other States, all in rather transparent effort to promote certain political views

Resolutions, which thus received such recognition, would, according to these writers, be sources of law and therefore constitute binding measures.[81] According to Soviet writers, acceptance could also be given by subsequent behaviour. Some claim this could be

---

[77]   *E.g.,* Brownlie, *Principles, op. cit.,* 696.

[78]   Schachter, Interpretation of the Charter in the Political Organs of the United Nations in Engel & Metall, (eds.), *Law, State and the International Legal Order, Essays in Honour of Hans Kelsen,* 1964, 271.

[79]   Lukashuk, I.I., *Istochniki mezhdunarodnogo pravo,* 1960, 92; Tunkin, G.I., *Teoria mezhdunarodnogo pravo,* 1974 171; Feldman, D., and Ianovskii, M.V., *General'naia assembleia OON,* 1968, 63 *et seq.,* 188 *et seq;* Radionov, P., 'Pravnata sila na aktovete na Obshchoto Sobranie na OON', 14 *Izvestiia na Instituta za pravni nauki,* No. 2, 1964, 80; Talalaev, A.N., *Iuridicheskaia priroda mezhdunarodnogo dogorova,* 1963, 150.

[80]   Kozhevikov F.I., *Obshchpriznannye printsipy i normy mezhdunarodnogo prava,* SGip, No. 12, 1959, 17.

[81]   Minasian N.M., *Istnochniki sovremennogo mezhdunarodnogo prava,* 1960, 1960, 112; 1966, 325; *idem, Pravo mirnogo sosushchestvovaniia,* 1966, 325. But see criticim by Tunkin of such views, *Teoria, op. cit.,* 163.

achieved by custom.[82] Some, like Morozov,[83] single out certain Resolutions having particular political and moral force, like the 1947 Resolution on Nuclear Weapons, which may qualify as a source of law. In the same vein, he refers to the Resolution on General and Complete Disarmament of 1959 and the Declaration on Granting of Independence of 1960 as binding.

One writer has suggested that States, which were in the voting minority when a certain decision was taken, may contest the validity of an interpretative act of the Charter while he, in the same breath, holds that the Uniting for Peace Resolution acquired immediately binding force for all.[84] Others have stressed that it is a question of adequate application rather than extensive or restrictive form of interpretation.[85]

Critique:

Instead of relying on any right of authoritative interpretation it may be argued that States may bind themselves by specific unilateral declarations.[86] It is more appropriate to view the situation, in law, as a case of unilaterally assumed obligations, rather than constructing a fictional situation of extended interpretation.

Lachs has pointed out that the Charter may need extensive interpretation in view of its contents and purposes[87] and this is undoubtedly true. But this does not lead to an assumption that interpretation of the Charter, by itself, is *binding*. Those who claim that interpretation of the Charter is *authoritative*[88] appear to imply that it is *obligatory*.

It is questionable whether the General Assembly has competence

---

[82]   *E.g.* Tunkin, G.I., *Teoria, op. cit.*, 171. Krylov, S.B., in Durdenevskii and Krylov, S.B., *Mezhdunarodnoe pravo*, 1947, 24

[83]   Morozov, G.I., *Organisatsiia Obedinennykh Natsii*, 1962, 217.

[84]   Degan, V.D., *L'interpretation des accords en droit international*, 1963, 23.

[85]   Shurshalov, V.M., *Osnovye voprosy teorii mezhdunarodnogo dogavora*, 1959, 428.

[86]   *Cf.* my *Concept, op. cit.*, 102 and 105.

[87]   Lachs, *op. cit.*, 1961, 209

[88]   See, *supra*, under Interpretative Resolutions.

to take any binding measures under the Charter.[89] In my view the Charter is a framework treaty, or a *traité cadre* and an interpretative act must primarily be conceived as an act that can be subsumed under the Charter, rather than one which extends or restricts its framework. Naturally, it is dangerous to assume that any *practice* by UN organ implies correct interpretation of the Charter.[90] Nor is it correct to equate *application* of the Charter to *interpretation* of the Charter.[91] An act of *interpretation* essentially *clarifies* the contents of the instrument.

(ii) Repetitive Persuasion

Some writers claim that recommendations acquire force if they are used by States in practice; these recommendations would thus give rise customary law *by repeated application*. Some attach considerable importance to citation of a resolution[92] and argue that a rule somehow emerges because of the *repeated statement*. Custom explains everything according to some: recommendations become absorbed in custom or contribute to form international custom.[93] On this ground, some thus argue that recommendations which are frequently repeated acquire some obligatory force through custom.

Critique:

Repetitive persuasion is certainly something that may *lead to the creation of law* or indicate what is *desirable de lege ferenda,* but the act of repetition does not represent law itself. Re-iterations may make

---

[89] Except, of course, in *primary matters*, see my *Law Making, op. cit.*, Chapter One.

[90] Tunkin, The Legal Nature of the United Nations, 99 RCADI i 1966 26 criticising views of Goodrich in his *The United Nations*, 1959 at 115.

[91] *Contra,* Brownlie, *Principles, op. cit.*, 696. *Cf.* Jessup, *The Modern Law of Nations,* 1949, 146; Kelsen, *Principles of International Law,* ed. Tucker, 2nd ed., 1967, 547 *et seq.*

[92] Johnson, D.H.N., The effect of resolutions of the General Assembly of the United Nations Law, BYIL 1955-1956, 97; Schachter, The quasi-judicial role of the Security Council and the General Assembly, AJIL 1969, 96.

[93] Tanaka, in the *South West Africa Case* [1966], ICJ *Reports,* 292.

disclaimers fade into oblivion but do not eliminate them.[94]

Custom may often *reinforce* the substantive contents of recommendations; or, alternatively, recommendations may be *evidence* of custom.[95] But all these are speculative arguments which do not explain what is binding and what is not. Such reasoning endangers the necessary line we must retain between *lex lata* and *lex ferenda* and undermines the security of law, which emphasises a constant need of foreseeability of the law[96]

(iii) Reflection of *lex lata*

Recommendations may repeat what the existing law already says. They are then binding not because of their own nature or quality; but their *root of obligation* is found outside the recommendation themselves.

Examples are the Declarations on Rights and Duties of States and the Friendly Relations Declaration.[97]

In the *Texaco Case* the Arbitrator Dupuy referred to certain recommendations with such underlying compulsory force derived from another ground. He spoke of recommendations which are binding because of an *opinio juris*: it was not the *opinio juris* which is the constituent part of customary international law that he mentioned, but *opinio juris* in particular indicating that body of customary law already existed. Thus he spoke of an *opinio juris*, in

---

94   Seidl-Hohenveldern, International economic soft law, *op. cit.*, 196.

95   Sloan, 'The binding force of a recommendation' of the General Assembly of the United Nations', BYIL 1948, 19.

96   Security of law is, in some other legal systems, called *Rechtsicherheit, sécurity de droit, sicurezza di diritto* or *rättssäkerhet*. The notion is not often used in English (but well in Scottish) law; in English law it comes near to the notion of *foreseeability*, see the *Lithgow Case*, European Court of Human Rights, (1986), *Reports* 1986. Yet, forseeability is only *one* element necessary for the security of law; therefore, it may often be more appropriate to equate security of law, which plays an important part in all civil law systems, with the English legal concept of *The Rule of Law*.

97   The Declaration on Principles of International Law Concerning Friendly Relations and Cooperations of States, 1970; on this, see, further, my *Finance and Protection of Investments in Developing Countries*, 2nd ed., 1987, 49.

a sense, reflecting the existence of customary law.[98]

Critique:

It may be correct to view recommendations, in some cases, as reflecting existing law; but then it is the law which is binding and the recommendations are only compulsory, not by their own merit but because of some *underlying source* of obligation.

Exhortations can only be binding if there is a clear constitutional basis for such obligations and then they are no *real recommendations.* They can thus be binding if they repeat as, in the case of use of force, obligations which States have already assumed by various previous undertakings. But then, again, recommendations are binding because of this underlying obligation and not, we submit, because they are recommendations.

The situation is much the same as in the case of treaties apparently binding third parties when they repeat provisions by which such parties are already bound.[99] In all these cases the acts in question merely reflect what binding rules already provide.

(iv) Expressions of the 'Views of the World'

Recommendations have also been conceived as examples of *collective unilateral acts of States.*[100] Some have even called certain resolutions *law making resolutions* by the virtue of them being adopted by such an august assembly.[101] The authority would be that General Assembly, as the principal organ of the United Nations, the World Organisation, entitled to represent the world. Resolutions of the General Assembly would be the principal instruments of elaboration of the wills of States and reflect the collective judgment

---

[98]   JDI 1977, 376, 379.

[99]   See my *Essays on the Law of Treaties, op. cit.,* 116.

[100]   *E.g.* the Bogotà Declaration of 1976, Marcoff, Sources de droit international de l'espace, 168 RCADI 1980 iii 79.

[101]   Brownlie, *Principles, op. cit.,* 14.

232

of the international community represented at the United Nations.[102] A Resolution could thus, according to some, be the *proof*, and constitute conclusive evidence as to the legal norm that the resolution has formulated.[103] A General Assembly Resolution would thus be half way[104] between custom and convention.

Critique:

The most problematic situation arises with regard to claims that recommendations are binding as *reflecting views of the world*. Here, it may be in order to answer the arguments with some force.

I submit that States can only speak for themselves and that they cannot, by forming part of an institutional body such as the General Assembly, transform their say into a conglomerate of State acts having a legislative effect. Their votes form part of an act of the organisation, and is imputable to the organisation, and not to the States. As a consequence, the legal effect of the act can only be decided in the light of the provisions of the Constitution of the organisation to which the act is imputed and to later practice by the organisation. Hence, it is clear that, on this ground, recommendations of the General Assembly cannot entail legal rights and duties as there is no constitutional basis for this in the Charter.

(v) Auto-Limitation

Another variation of construction of collective acts is to perceive the States in the General Assembly as limiting their own action by their own free will as co-authors of an act, similar to national plans supported by continuous consent.[105]

---

[102] Lauterpacht, Individual Opinion, *South West Africa Case*, [1955] ICJ, 1955, 122; Sorensen, Principes de droit international public, RCADI 1960 i 99.

[103] Sorensen, *op. cit.*, *loc. cit.*: 'une preuve concluante de l'existence de la norme juridique qu'elle formule'.

[104] *Ibid.*, *loc. cit.*,: 'mi-chemin'.

[105] Morand, *Réflexions*, *op. cit.*, 1974. *Cf.* similar suggestions regarding treaties, especially those restricting sovereign function inside the territory of a State, for example military base agreements, see my *Independent State, op. cit.*, 178 *et seq.*

Critique:

Is it really the recommendation which is binding in this case by auto-limitation? If a State chooses to bind itself unilaterally the basis of obligation does not lie in the recommendation but in the value of the State's own undertaking.[106] Similar critical remarks may be made with regard to estoppel.[107]

(vi) Specific Approval

Outright acceptance comes near to the problems relating to auto-limitation. There may be a contractual element which entitles us to qualify a recommendation as binding, but then not *per se* but as part of an agreement.

The first case concerns the outright and clear acceptance of an individual State, or a few individual States, by a clear act of acceptance *in casu*. One pertinent case is the acceptance by Austria of a League of Nation recommendation concerning the Hungarian border.[108] A similar case concerned acceptance of propositions by the Allied Powers regarding Silesia.[109]

Similar acceptances have been made within the trusteeship framework, for example by France[110] of recommendations (or conventions) by the UN or by the specialised agencies if such recommendations were *favourable* to the interests to the population in an administered territory and compatible with the trusteeship system.

In other organisations the common method is to specifically *approve* or to ratify relevant recommendations. This is, for example, the case in OPEC where recommendations are accepted by ratification

---

[106] On the legal effect of unilateral undertakings see my *Concept, op. cit.,* 100, 102, 105 and *supra.*

[107] See, *infra,* under Estoppel.

[108] 9 LNTS 209, Protocol of Venice. *Cf. The Mosul Case,* PCIJ No. 27, 122.

[109] League of Nations, Official Journal, 1921, 982. Sloan, Binding Force, *op. cit.,* 17.

[110] Special agreement 13 December 1946 article 6.

of individual States.[111] Recommendations are published only *after ratification* by the Member States.[112]

Critique:

Rather than using *fictions* to claim that a recommendation changes its optional character when it is *approved* of by a State, one could conceive the recommendation as an *offer* which is subsequently *accepted*. But this does not change the essentially facultative character of the recommendation. It will, in such a contractual situation only serve as *material* which enables the first limb, the *offer*, to be formulated.

(vii) Acceptance by Voting

There are two distinct questions regarding to voting. One problem is whether the sheer *number of votes* can produce a compelling or a facultative effect of a resolution. The second aspect concerns the question whether *individual voting* for a resolution produces any legal bond of compulsion.

There is a popular contention among other international lawyers that States voting for resolutions in international organisations somehow would incure legal obligations by the voting procedure.

1. RELEVANCE OF 'LANDSLIDE' FIGURES

When resolutions are qualified as 'law making' measures it is often done with reference to the *landslide voting figures*. Thus, typical examples include Resolution 951 (II) 1946 Reaffirming the General Principles of International Law Recommended by the Nuremberg Charter and Judgment; Resolution 1653 (XVI) 1961 on the Prohibition of Nuclear Weapons for War Purposes (55 to 20; 26

---

[111]   *E.g.* the acceptance and ratification of the official price set for *e.g.* Marker Crude Arabian Light 34 API ex-Ras Tanura at US $ 29 per barrel and ceiling for total OPEC production at 17,5 m. barrel per day within which members are allocated quotas, OPEC, *Annual Report,* 1982, 70-71.

[112]   *Ibid.,* 71, 73.

abstentions); Resolution 1514 (XV) 1960 Granting of Independence to Colonial Countries and Peoples (80 to nil; 9 abstentions); Resolution 1803 (XVII) 1962 on Sovereignty over Natural Resources (87 to 2; 12 abstentions); and Resolution 1962 (XVIII) of 1963 on Outer Space (unanimously adopted).

Some consider that a recommendation adopted by unanimity is a *declarative Resolution*. For example Resolutions 1721 and 1962 (XVIII) of 1963 on Outer Space have been said to have normative effect *sui generis*.[113] It is even suggested that a majority decision can create obligations if the minority is *insignificant*. Surprisingly enough these authors measure the 'insignificance' by the 'number' and the 'importance' of the relevant States.[114]

Certain writers claim that the *majority principle* - that a greater number can decide for a smaller number - is a universal rule as it is in many systems of constitutional and administrative law in parliamentary democracies[115] and that therefore recommendations in the General Assembly, taken by majority vote, have binding force.[116]

Critique:

The landslide argument is possibly the one put forward most forcefully by authors to support the allegation of a binding force of recommendations, particularly of recommendations of the General Assembly. The best way to tackle this argument is to underline the very simple fact that *when States vote they do not know the emerging voting pattern*. Therefore, States can hardly be bound by a vote which they only later discover to be a 'landslide' one. That is, if we respect the basic legal requirement of *foreseeability*,[117] we cannot allow

---

[113]   Marcoff, Droit international de l'espace, *op. cit.*, 79.

[114]   Sorensen, *Principes, op. cit.*, 1960 i, 100, 'nombre et l'importance des Etats'.

[115]   Elias, 'Modern sources of international law', in Friedmann & Henkin & Lissitzyn, (eds.), *Transnational Law in a Changing Society, Essays in Honor of Jessup*, 1972, 45.

[116]   *Ibid., loc. cit.*

[117]   See further *supra* on the requirement of foreseeability for the Rule of Law or for the *security of law*.

States to be bound on such loose grounds.

In using the landslide argument proponents argue that the minority is bound by what the majority says. But, for example, the Charter of the United Nations does not make any distinction between majority and minority votes. The Charter makes no distinction between resolutions adopted by majority of by unanimity and that the voting figures are not in themselves capable of changing the nature of obligation. Furthermore, how can the majority bind the minority when there is no support for this in the Charter? What happened here to the rules of sovereign equality? And all this in spite of the same authors caution that one must be careful to attribute, to the General Assembly, any legislating power.[118]

Other writers dispute that recommendations have any binding force and suggest that since the majority often consists of developing States,[119] the General Assembly is no longer representative of power distribution in the world and that the one State/one vote pattern would be outdated.[120]

Of course, the rule of majority has, for reasons of speed and efficiency, been adopted by international organisations. There are also some organisations, especially in the technical field, which operate exclusively on the majority principle and which sometimes do not even achieve that majority in a plenary but in a restricted organ of the organisation.[121] But unless the member States have given what I have called their *abstract consent*[122] to such far reaching powers of an organisation in the constituting *charter* an organisation cannot claim to bind members by majority votes. The obvious difference between international law and internal law in this respect is that the rule of democracy, demanding that the minority accepts the view of the majority by majority votes, can only operate if, at the same time,

---

[118] Sorensen, *op. cit., loc. cit.*: 'il faut se mettre garde contre toute tendance à attribuer à l'Assemblée Général un pouvoir legislatif'.

[119] *Cf.* Seidl-Hohenveldern, International economic soft law, 163 RCADI, 1979 ii 184.

[120] *Ibid., loc. cit.*

[121] See my *Law Making, op. cit.*, 217-317 on resolutions by UPU, ITU, WHO, WMO, ICAO and the European Communities.

[122] *Ibid.*, 322.

there are constitutional guarantees for minorities, at least for their *vital interests*.[123] To deny the binding force of recommendations on the basis that they lack constitutional support for such legal force appears to be preferable to political arguments such as contentions concerning power distribution in the United Nations.

Thus, not even a unanimous vote for a recommendation can create any legal obligations,[124] unless there is a constitutional basis for such obligation.[125] Unanimous decisions should be viewed within the framework of general international law,[126] as such decisions often reflect rules already binding with different bases of obligation. This is as far as one can stretch the legal implications in the absence of constitutional authorisation for binding force in the Charter of an organisation. Thus, the majority cannot bind the minority against their will without authorising constitutional provisions. The common use of majority rules in internal and in international law should not, by themselves, lead us to any other conclusions.

It is not possible to count votes and differentiate the legal obligation by voting figures. The main reason for this is, as already mentioned, that a voting State does not, at the time of casting its vote, know what the proportions will be. Thus, States have no knowledge of the outcome of a vote when they cast their own votes: it is not in the interest of international law to construe an obligation for States of which they, when they were voting, were not themselves aware by referring to *overwhelming* voting figures. Unless there are clear provisions in the Constitution of an organisation to take binding decisions, voting figures cannot by themselves produce obligations in law. Uncertainty of law is a considerable danger. But such uncertainty inevitably follows allegation of vague obligations which are difficult to ascertain and assess for the voting States themselves: at the time of voting they are not aware that they are voting to assume further obligations in law.

---

123   *Cf.* Tomuschat, *Die Charta, op. cit.*, 489.
124   Bastid, S., *Observations, op. cit.*, 144.
125   See my *Law Making, op. cit.*, 322.
126   See my *Law Making, op. cit.*, Chapter One; *Cf.* Tunkin, International Law in the International System, 147 RCADI 1975, 149.

2. CONSENSUS

Further complications have been caused by the new system of consensus. Some have emphasised that 'majority decisions seldom resolve controversial issues among sovereign States'.[127] Such views undoubtedly speeded up the now consolidated trend to prefer consensus decisions, especially within the framework of international organisations or international conferences for the negotiation of comprehensive multilateral conventions. There is now a marked trend towards consensus, particularly through pressure of Group 77 and other influences in UNCTAD.

It is now less important to count votes in favour and votes against a resolution. Consensus is achieved by bargaining mechanisms. The bargaining, risking a very watered-out text, goes on until consensus is reached. Consensus implies the *absence of any formal objections* and appears, in that sense, to be akin to unanimity. But consensus merely implies the absence of any *formal* objection[128] as the method is intended to avoid votes on questions which need the *unanimous decision* of States, either because they declare fundamental principles of international law such as the Friendly Relations Resolution 2526 (XXV) or because their realisation demand an effort of the whole international community, as does the implementation of the New International Economic Order (NIEO.)[129]

Critique:

The *united stand* created by the consensus method is effective in practice although it also indicates a compromise.[130] Either all parties concede points, which implies a substantial compromise, or only a very low common denominator is accepted. *Interest aggregation* may reduce the very number of interests to be reconciled.[131] But consensus also implies that the sharp contours of legal obligations

---

[127]   Sauvant, *The Group of 77, op. cit.,* 16.

[128]   *Cf.* Law of the Sea Convention 1982 article 161.

[129]   Bennouna, *Le droit du développement,* 1983, 85, who speaks about situations when 'un accord unanimine' is not necessary.

[130]   *Cf.* Sauvant, *The Group of 77, op. cit.,* 16-17.

[131]   *Ibid., loc. cit.*

have been diluted in the text. One example is the generalised system of preferences in UNCTAD adopted in 1970 which leave entirely the implementation to the donor States by further unilateral voluntary action.

Consensus is certainly not the same as unanimity[132] although no dissent is heard. That there is a distinction to be made between consensus and unanimity is clear from explanations that accompany resolutions where consensus was not obtained.[133] There have also been cases where parties have showed clear disagreement.[134]

The argument that a consensus overrides individual intentions is also questionable. However, consensus cannot produce obligations *ipso facto*[135] even though expressions of will and intention are naturally most important.

Consensus may be a new practice accepted, by superficial analysis, as producing law.[136] However, even when there is apparent unity of views this is not sufficient to create legal obligations by itself.[137]

Therefore, the value of consensus is limited. It may be a useful voting device to arrive at compromises. However, it does not *per se* lend obligatory force to a decision.

3. ACCEPTANCE BY INDIVIDUAL VOTING

The question arises whether *individual voting* for a Resolution can turn it into a binding instrument.

Some insist that a State which votes for a resolution in the General Assembly is bound by some *contractual* engagement created

---

[132] *Cf.*. Cassese, Consensus and some of its pitfalls, 58 RivDI, 1975, 760; Tomuschat, *Die Charta, op. cit.*, 488.

[133] *Cf.* Explanations to the NIEO declaration 3201 (S-VI) 13 ILM 1974, 715 or to the Resolution on the Programme of Action on the Establishment of the NIEO 3202 (S-VI) 13 ILM 1974, 720 *Cf.* Cassese, Consensus, *op. cit.*, 754.

[134] See Resolution 3362 (S-VII) on Development and International Economic Cooperation where there were 'reservations'. *Cf.* Cassese, *op. cit.*, 761.

[135] Bastid, *Observations, op. cit.*, 144.

[136] Lassan, Le consensus dans la pratique des Nations Unies, AF 1974.

[137] Bastid, S., Observations, *op. cit.*, 144.

by the vote in favour.[138]

Others have adopted the line that, although recommendations do not bind those in the minority, they generate a *justifying* effect for States which give *positive acceptance*. They maintain that a State that votes in favour of a recommendation absorbs obligations in so far as that State is deprived of any *right to complain*. For example, if a recommendation concerns prohibition of discrimination against imports from developing countries, a State that voted in favour cannot complain that it suffers because of lack of protection of trade as it gave its approval to the recommendation by voting.[139]

Critique:

What furthermore concerns the argument of *consent* by individual voting, it remains highly questionable that a State, which has expressed its support of a recommendation in the General Assembly, has actually expressed any such *consent* and that they, on the basis of such alleged *consent* would be in any way legally bound. As the constitution of the United Nations, the Charter, lacks provisions to make recommendations compulsory, no State can, by the mere fact that it has voted in favour of a Resolution be bound in law. To claim that individual voting entails legal obligations also means that foreseeability is discarded:[140] the State cannot *know* beforehand that it will be bound since the Charter is silent on the matter and no other clear rule imposes obligations on the State.

Assume that a State votes in favour of some proposal in an organisation where the constitution does not allow for any binding decision by the organ in which voting takes place. *The voting State is then quite unaware that its vote may bind it* and thus finds itself in a situation which is quite different from any contractual engagement: one cannot normally be bound in contract unless one is *aware* that a contract was *intended* and that a contract might result from one's behaviour.

---

[138]   Asamoah, The Legal Significance of the Declarations of the General Assembly of the United Nations, 1966, 70.

[139]   *Cf.* Seidl-Hohenveldern, Soft law, *op. cit.*, 195-196.

[140]   *Cf. supra* on land-slide votes.

The French Foreign Ministry has devoted special attention to the legal value of favourable votes in connection with the question of the extradition of Klaus Barbie. The French Government relied in its submissions to the Bolivian Government on Resolution 3074 and stated specifically that France had voted in favour of this Resolution. It had to concede, however, that Bolivia had abstained and to the conclusion that therefore the resolution was *not opposable to Bolivia*.[141] This formulation was later considered misleading by the French Government and was amended to state that Resolutions of the General Assembly of the United Nations are not *opposable to any State*.[142]

It is to be noted, however, that binding obligations *outside the voting process* may be achieved by contractual or unilateral mechanisms.[143] Thus, States may *proceed* to an agreement or a promissory statement *after* the decision. But, as in the case of consensus, the voting procedure itself does not endow a decision with any obligatory effect.

4. ACCEPTANCE BY VOTING REINFORCED BY ACQUIESCENCE: ESTOPPEL

Some writers, especially those who hold that voting in favour of a resolution is relevant, claim that further acts may *complement* the voting itself.[144]

Relying on *justifying effects* is reminiscent of the Anglo-Saxon doctrine of estoppel so eagerly adopted by some international lawyers to explain the legal effect of recommendations. This is the principle of self-exclusion which implies that a party is not allowed to contradict the veracity of statements or facts made public by statements of authorised representatives or by his own behaviour,

---

[141]   Minister of Foreign Affairs in a statement to Q.E. Barel, No. 22862, J.O.-A.N., 6th December 1975, AF 1976, 992.

[142]   *Ibid.*, No. 15934, J.O.-A.N. 23 November 1978, 7828, AF 1978, 1141.

[143]   See further my *Concept, op. cit.*

[144]   Marcoff, L'espace, *op. cit.*, 130.

especially if others have taken acts relying on this behaviour.[145] It has thus been suggested that for example the Resolution on the Principles of the Regime of the Ocean Floor and the Ocean Beyond National Jurisdiction[146] would create such estoppel.[147]

The doctrine of estoppel has also been said to be based on a certain element of reciprocity.[148] It has much in common with general rules on good faith,[149] again concepts imported from the Anglo-Saxon legal world. It can also be construed as being dependent on acquiescence,[150] but it is then perhaps preferable to search for a contractual relationship.[151] Finally, the doctrine of estoppel must be distinguished from the cases of unilateral promise, like the Ihlen declaration[152] or the French undertaking to cease nuclear tests in the Pacific.[153]

Critique:

The term estoppel is, in international law, not often used outright.[154] The bond of obligation which sometimes appears to exist as a result of estoppel can often be explained on the ground of a contractual[155] or unilateral[156] relationship. Estoppel, by itself, probably does exist as a ground for obligation in contemporary international law, but then as a special case of *unilateral behaviour.*

Unless the doctrine of estoppel is restricted to imply a precise unilateral undertaking by actual action or specific passivity, it is a

---

[145] Bowett, Estoppel before international tribunals and its relation to requiescence, BYIL 1957, 176 *et seq.*

[146] Resolution GA 2749, 1970.

[147] *Cf.* on the doctrine, Martin, A., *Estoppel en droit international public,* 1979.

[148] Vallée, Quelques observations sur l'estoppel en droit des gens, RGDIP 1973, 950.

[149] *Ibid.,* 992

[150] *Ibid.,* 983.

[151] *Cf. supra.*

[152] *Eastern Greenland Case,* [1933], PCIJ *Reports,* 1933, No. 53.

[153] *The Nuclear Test Cases, Australia v France,* [1974], ICJ *Reports,* 1974, 99.

[154] But see Alfaro in *The Temple Case* [1962], ICJ, *Reports* 1962, 39.

[155] See my *Concept, op. cit.,* 129.

[156] *Ibid.,* 102 and 105.

mechanism which appears somewhat retardive to those who prefer a more dynamic view of international law. If it is to serve a useful function in international law, it must thus be carefully distinguished from Kelsen's curious idea about the whole basis of obligation of international law that States ought to behave as they customarily always had behaved.[157] Such views of those relating to justified *expectations* have, by their lack of legal contents, only the value of prophecies and guesses but cannot furnish any firm legal guidance.

(viii) Convertible Acts

It may be that a recommendation, possessing only facultative legal value, can be converted into a compulsory one under the constitution of an organisation. This is the case if a situation before the General Assembly presents a threat to the peace and the matter is referred to the Security Council. In this situation a recommendation may appear to *obtain* compulsory force.

Critique:

If an act is *convertible* and another organ can effectively adopt the recommendation as a binding *decision*, there is no question of the recommendation being binding but rather of another measure, taken by another body, as having that effect.

The Security Council can, in many cases, intervene and take a binding decision when a matter has already been dealt with by the General Assembly by way of recommendation. But this does not convert the legal value of the General Assembly Resolution: it only indicates that such an act is potentially binding if and when converted into another act by another organ and subjected to another procedure.

(ix) Internal Decisions

Most writers agree that a recommendation which concerns the internal

---

[157]   Kelsen, *Principles, op. cit., loc. cit.*

order of an organisation is binding.[158]

Critique:

In this context, it may be useful to discern different bases of obligation and different categories of acts. As discussed earlier,[159] organisations take both *primary* and *operative* acts.

1. PRIMARY TYPE OF ACTS[160]

A recommendation on organisational matters may well be binding but this is not because the recommendation is *internal*. I have previously pointed out that the internal order is not an accurate expression to denote the sphere of such acts.[161] Instead, I have used the term *primary* acts for what others have called 'internal': all such acts concern what the organisation must do before it can set out to work towards its objectives. Typical acts thus deal with staff and headquarters questions. But, as mentioned earlier, certain issues, concerning, for example, financial matters cannot possibly be held to be 'internal' as they have an immediate impact on the member States which are 'external' to the core of the organisational set up.

Other acts that organisations proceed to take are, as I have called them, *operative* acts, in the sense that they envisage the attainment of the objectives for which the organisation was founded. The result of this important distinction between primary and operative acts is that primary acts are more or less the same in all organisations whereas operative acts vary, by necessity, from organisation to organisation.

Primary acts then are those which are currently obligatory within the organisation whether or not they are couched, in their own terms, as 'recommendations' or 'resolutions'. The reason for their legal

---

158 Most Western writers agree on this and even lawyers in Russia writing during the Soviet era, see, for example, Ignatenko, G.V., Souvorova, V.I., in Ignatenko, G.V., Ostapenko, D.D., (ed.), *Mezhdunarodnoe pravo*, 1978, 69 *et seq.*

159 See *supra* in Chapter II under Normal Powers of Organisations.

160 *Cf. supra*, on Resolutions on Primary Matters.

161 See my *Law Making, op. cit.*, 42 *et seq.*

obligation is derived from the organisational system itself which cannot function without a minimum degree of functional compulsion.

The legal force of such measures is explained by the theory of *implied powers:*[162] when States set up an international organisation they also, implicitly, grant sufficient powers for the minimum effective functioning of that entity.

2. HIERARCHICAL ORDER

The hierarchical relationship between the organ making the recommendation and the entity receiving it is highly relevant. If the recommendation emanates from an organ higher than the one to which it is addressed, it is generally binding due to the obligation inherent in any hierarchical relationship.[163] The reason for the obligatory nature is then reflected by the fact that the higher organ could instead, if it had wished, taken a decisive compelling measure itself: the term recommendation may then only be a euphemism for a binding decision.

Yet, the form and label of a recommendation are not irrelevant. In may be that even in such cases the measure is only *potentially binding* and that only *if* and *when it is converted* into a compelling measure by an act that the higher organ is entitled to take. Until such time the 'recommendation' may lack binding force or at least be only latently binding pending the contingency of conversion.

Thus, even in the field of primary matters,[164] a recommendation may not have binding force: only if it is the *clear intention* to create an obligation will an act be construed as having binding effect. The hierarchical order alone will not *ipso facto* lead to binding decisions. On the other hand, a hierarchical relationship of organs may lead to a *presumption* than a recommendation is binding if it is issued by a lower organ, and subsequently endorsed by a higher entity, endowed

---

162   See my *Law Making, op. cit.*, 29-33 and *supra.*

163   *Cf.* Virally, La valeur, *op. cit.*, 73.

164   See my *Law Making, op. cit.*, 42 *et seq.*, and *cf.* Cahier, Le droit interne des organisations internationales, RGDIP 1963, 503; Bernhardt & Miehsler, Qualifikation und Anwendungsbereich des internen Rechts internationalen Organisationen, 12 DGVR 1973, 7; *cf. supra.*

with power of decision. Yet, even here, it is then a matter of the endorsement, converting the recommendation into a decision, rather than the recommendation operating on its own.

It may be worth noting that the hierarchical relationship, within which the facultative character of a recommendation may be commuted into a binding one by a higher organ, only applies within one organisational unit. Thus, the United Nations cannot dictate to the specialised agencies as to what they are to do.

The relationship between the United Nations and the specialised agencies is not one of hierarchy: therefore resolutions by the United Nations cannot by themselves bind the specialised agencies.[165]

3. COMPLEX DECISION MAKING

In the European Community, for example, there is a highly developed system of *complex decision making*: an organ is often not entitled to act unless it has received the previous recommendation by another body.[166] Also the Council of Europe uses this technique.[167]

The Group of 77[168] take their own resolutions at special ministerial meetings and these resolutions often form the basis for further action by UNCTAD.[169] In such cases a *recommendation* is an essential ingredient in the subsequent decision; without the 'recommendation' the other organ may be unable to proceed. But the recommendation *itself* is nevertheless not legally binding albeit it may have such important legal *consequences*.

iv. The Varying Function of Standards and Recommendations

We may consider that, in the internal relationship of organisations, the term recommendation is sometimes used as a euphemism for decision; the same may be the case when an organisation deals with *primary*

---

[165] See my *Law Making, op. cit.*, 208-210.

[166] See my *Law Making, op. cit.*, 264.

[167] See *e.g.* Conseil de l'Europe, *Les Annales de l'Europe*, 1961.

[168] *Cf. supra*.

[169] Ministerial meetings have been held in Algiers 1967, Lima 1971; Manila 1974; Arusha, 1979 and New York, 1980.

matters, *i.e.* headquarters, staff and budgetary arrangements.[170]

In other cases the term recommendation is coupled with *sanctions* which makes it awkward to consider the act as optional. A recommendation may thus be technically facultative by itself but contingent effects are attached to it in the case it is not followed. It is important to retain the distinction between the recommendation and its effects: the effects are distinct and may be seen as pressure to encourage compliance, but they do not convert the recommendation into a binding act.

The vast majority of recommendations, however, concern suggested ways of action, in exhortations, or, even more commonly, suggested standards or codes of behaviour. The main role may, in fact, be played by *standards* which are forthcoming from different quarters as *suggestions*. Even States themselves may tentatively put forward provisional standards. One example is the new EEZ[171] which was elaborated during the negotiations of the 1982 Law of the Sea Convention, a Treaty which still has not entered into force. Yet, the EEZ, which was suggested by State delegates at the Conference, has been adopted in State practice, internal legislation and in notification to other States and seafarers.[172]

Standards, like recommendations, are thus mere suggestions, but they can be *adopted* by States.[173] However, these suggestions *remain* suggestions until they are adopted by States in some formal way as binding. Before that happens, standards and recommendations fulfil important *guiding functions* and we may identify some fields where they are useful instruments.

a. Unilateral or Parallel Agenda

Recommendations often contain suggestions with regard to future action. For example, when they concern individual, actual behaviour close in time, they are often *exhortations*, for a specific action; when they concern suggestions for future more general behaviour they may

---

[170] *Supra*, under Resolutions on Primary Rules.
[171] See, *infra*, under the Exclusive Economic Zone.
[172] See, *infra*, under the Exclusive Economic Zone, for how this was done.
[173] On the technique of adoptive acts, see my *Concept, op. cit.*, 103 *et seq.*

be *programmatic* recommendations.

Programmatic recommendations of organisations have only legal effect in so far as they produce *guideline effects*. They are similar in their legal value to certain figures we know from treaty law *pacta de contrahendo*. Thus they are not themselves binding but need further acts for implementation.

On the other hand, States may, individually, or jointly, issue *statements* which, in practice, are treated as binding.[174]

b. The Relevance of Convenience

With regard to technical standards it is obvious that parties will prefer to accept in practice, without any legal compulsion, a number of acts for their own convenience. Codes may also be considered for adoption by similar criteria. Members of the club using similar standards and codes will find international communication, trade and intercourse that much easier.

There has been considerable discussion in the United Nations on the binding force of international codes in connection with the drafting of codes for multinationals. The ICC has in its capacity of a private international body lobbied for a clear non-mandatory nature of the proposed code as business behaviour should be based on self-regulation rather than on obligatory rules. Furthermore, even if there was a need to have formally binding codes, this would not be done in the form of a resolution but in the form of a treaty.

Instruments are often elaborated by various bodies for the *convenience* of States. Yet, codes and standards are only binding if and when States adopt them by clear consent[175] and/or, with regard to entities subject to the jurisdiction of a State, if they are promulgated as national laws of that State. On the other hand, companies, firms and individuals are free to comply with such codes and often do so for their own business interests, or for other private motives. Convenience certainly constitutes a compelling motive for compliance.

---

[174]   *Supra* under Customary Law *latu sensu*, Parallel Declarations.
[175]   See my *Concept, op. cit.*, 123 and 99-105.

c. Guidelines for Action

Recommendations may also be guidelines for future action, a *cadre de référence* and clarify, as *lignes de conduite* goals within the framework of the constitution of an organisation.[176]

As well as States occasionally put forward *propositions for standards,*[177]so do international organisations, to investigate if the political climate is ready to *accept* a new rule in international society. This is what happened in the case of the Resolution on the Moratorium of the Sea-Bed[178] whereby States were requested not to exploit certain areas of the Ocean Floor and its Subsoil. International society was not ready for such rules and the rule on the Moratorium is clearly ineffective and *ultra vires* of the General Assembly which has no power to prescribe any such Moratorium, merely to *suggest* certain guidelines for States which States, may or may not accept. Similar comments may be made about other similar Resolutions, especially those on the vague notion of a *common heritage.*[179]

Recommendations of organisations may well be *adopted* in many cases where they elaborate provisional standards by States by acts of consent.[180] In other cases, where they embody specific programmatic declarations they may, as agenda, provide useful references for further voluntary action.

v. The Legal Impact of Recommendations in International Society

Outside the narrow band of *primary matters*[181] recommendations of international organisations usually denote a facultative measure that

---

[176]   Virally, La valeur, *op. cit.*, *loc. cit.*

[177]   See *supra* in Standards and Pre-Standards of States, in Chapter III.

[178]   GA Res 2574 D (XXIV), 1969.

[179]   *Cf.* Principles Governing the Sea Bed, Ocean Floor and Sub-Soil Thereof, GA Res 2749 (XXV) emphasising that the areas of the Ocean Floor and its sub-soil constitute a *common heritage of mankind.* For criticism of this notion, see *infra*, in Chapter VIII.

[180]   See my *Concept, op. cit.*, 73-75; 103; 129-130.

[181]   *Supra*, in this Chapter.

250

can be adopted or dismissed at will. The General Assembly of the United Nations has, for example, only power under article 10 of the Charter to formulate recommendations. According to the drafters of the Charter the term recommendation in that context means precisely a non-binding measure: proposals[182] to make the General Assembly a legislative organ with more far reaching powers of taking compulsory decisions had been rejected by a clear vote at the San Francisco Conference.[183]

Even if a General Assembly Resolution is called a *decision* it cannot, in view of obvious wording and practice, unless it deals with primary matters, be more than a recommendation.[184]

The term *recommendation* is, by definition, a non-binding measure:[185] such an act by an international organisation does not, in principle, entail any legal obligations or duties. Yet, as I have pointed out,[186] recommendations can have certain important legal consequences.

Recommendation may thus serve as *support* for future action[187] or they act as a *cadre de référence*[188] for such action. Thus, recommendations must be seen in their context as they are *proteiforme*.[189] It is, on the other hand, not possible to hold that States are bound by recommendations, which, however may be useful as *material*.

The important principle of security of law in international society is endangered if there is uncertainty of existing legal commitments. Therefore, the meaning of recommendations must not be distorted and

---

[182]   See 3 UNICIO 536 for the proposal by the Phillipines.

[183]   26 votes to one, see 9 UNCIO 70.

[184]   Arangio-Ruiz, The normative role of the General Assembly of the United Nations and the Declaration of Principles of Friendly Relations, 137 RCADI 1972 iii, 446.

[185]   *Cf.* the atypical way the term recommendation is used in the Treaty of the European Coal and Steel Community. See, Reuter, *La Communauté Européenne du Charbon et de l'Acier*, 1952.

[186]   See my *Law Making, op. cit.*, 207-213.

[187]   Flory, M., La troisième décennie pour le développement, AFDI, 1980, 605.

[188]   Virally, M., La deuxième décennie des Nations Unies pour le développement, Essai d'interprétation juridique, AF, 1970, 28.

[189]   Virally, La valeur, *op. cit.*, 94.

construed to entail obligations *per se.*

Yet, in specific cases, recommendations provide useful, *provisional norms* which, by the consent, and the convenience of States, can later be adopted as binding measures in a treaty or in some other obligatory form or instrument, or by way of clear, parallel unilateral undertakings.[190]

---

[190] See, my *Concept, op. cit.,* 102 *et seq. Cf., supra* under Customary Law *latu sensu,* Parallel Declarations.

CHAPTER V

Prophylactic Rules:
Protection of The International Society

According to the theory adopted in my earlier work, entrenching rules[1] lay down a relatively stable framework for action in the international society. Some of these rules are prophylactic[2] in the sense that they forbid certain harmful action. These rules are of primordial importance to the survival of international society. Some of these rules concern the prohibition of force; others concern human rights, in war and in peace, or humanitarian rules in armed conflicts; a third category relates to environmental protection.

i. Prophylaxis and the Hypothetical Goal

Let us thus assume that all legal rules of international society should be understood and interpreted in the light of a *hypothetical goal of international law and regulation*. Let us also assume that the hypothetical goal is the *promotion of the welfare of international society*.[3] It is then clear that certain acts that impede this goal will be

---

[1]   *The Concept of International Law, op. cit.*, 53 *et seq.*

[2]   *Ibid.*, 53 *et seq.*

[3]   See *supra* Chapter III and further, my work on the *Concept, op. cit.*, 66-67. Note that some writers have postulated *the preservation of international society* as an implicit goal. So, for example, Bull, *The Anarchical Society*, 1977, 16 *et seq.* Others have emphasised that what is really at issue is the *survival* of *mankind*: Modelski, *Principles of World Politics*, 1972, 288. To claim that regulation must *promote* such a goal appears to be thought abhorrent in a nihilistic legal system like that in Sweden (*cf.* ideas of Hägerström and Lundstedt that still prevail in legal education) but is part of mainstream legal philosophy, especially among writers in case-law countries, see, i Hyde, 2-3 and, for recent influential works, see Finnis, *Natural Law and Natural Rights, op. cit.*; occasionally writers who have left Scandinavia to teach elsewhere also hold similar views, see Holsti, *International Politics*, 4th ed., 1983, 288.

forbidden or discouraged and that other acts, which are deemed to be beneficial to the hypothetical goal, will be encouraged.

Prophylactic rules prohibit activities that would obviate the hypothetical goal. In other words, if we postulate the *promotion of the welfare of international society* to be an implicit goal of any regulation of international activities, then certain acts must be prohibited, like aggression and other harmful acts, violations of human rights or intentional or negligent damage to the environment.

The theory of a hypothetical goal, and of methods of interpreting rules in the light of such a goal, is certainly close to theories of *natural law*, which are now undergoing a forceful revival, both in the West and in Eastern Europe.

ii. Prohibition of the Use of Force

For my own views see my *International Law and the Independent State*, 2nd ed., 1987 and my work on *The Law of War*, 1987.

In general see, Wehberg, L'interdiction du recours à la force, 78 RCADI 1951 i, 1; Neuholdt, *Internationale Konflikte, verbotene und erlaubte Mittel ihrer Austragung*, 1977, 55; Randelshofer, Use of Force, 4 *Encyclopedia* 1982, 265; Bowett, *Self-Defense in International Law*, 1958; McDougal & Feliciano, *Law and Minimum World Public Order, The Legal Regulation of International Coercion*, 1951; see, also, Dahm, Das Verbot der Gewaltanwendung nach Artikel 2(4) der UNO-Charta und die Selbsthilfe gegenüber Völkerrechtsverletzungen die keinen bewaffneten Angriff enhalten, *Festschrift Laun* 1962, 48; Zourek, *L'interdiction de l'emploi de la force en droit international*, 1974; Stone, *Legal Controls of International Conflicts*, 1959; Wengler, *Das völkerrechtliche Gewaltverbot, Probleme und Tendenzen*, 1967; Brownlie, *International Law and the Use of Force by States*, 1963; Waldock, The regulation of the use of force by individual States in international law, 81 RCADI, 1952 ii, 451-517; Murphy, *The U.N. and the Control of International Violence. A Legal and Political Analysis*, 1982; Vincent, *Non-Intervention and International Order*, 1974; Ch. Rousseau, *Le droit des conflits armés*, 1983; D. Bindschedler-Robert, *La reconsidération du droit des conflits armés*, 1971; Q. Wright, *A Study of War*, 1942; Berber, 2 *Völkerrecht: Kriegsrecht*, 1977; Oppenheim, 2 *International Law*, 1952; Clausewitz, *Vom Kriege*, 1834, 18th ed., 1972; *idem, On War*, ed. Michael Howard, 1976.

a. The Historical Background

Force was for long not only permitted but encouraged in international society. War was the order of the day and any State which considered it needed more territory, or prestige, by a successful war effort, would wage war without any restrictions. There were attempts, some of which were successful, of limiting the right to war, the *jus ad bellum*,[4] to just wars, that is to those which appeared *justified*. That such qualifications were necessarily subjective is obvious. Both parties would often not agree whether a war was *just*.[5]

Nevertheless, theories on *just war* were, far from justifying certain wars as is sometimes claimed, important efforts to *limit the right to war*. The writings of St Thomas Aquinas, in turn much inspired by St Augustine, and writings of other scholars of the Church, had considerable impact in this respect.

Well into the last century, for example, even debts were often collected by armed force and it was thought quite in order to take reprisals, with armed force, for non-payment. Thus, when France failed to pay instalments on the spoliation claims under a Treaty of 4 July 1831, President Jackson stated, on 1 December 1834 that the United States should insist upon prompt execution of the Treaty and in the case of refusal *take redress into their own hands*.[6]

That the use of force is an unsuitable mechanism to recover monies due was made apparent by the naval blockade and the bombardment of ports in Venezuela in 1902 when this country had not paid certain debts to alien residents. The attacking powers, Italy, United Kingdom and Germany, found little excuse in that Venezuela had just suffered a major financial crisis as a result of a civil war.

Attempts were made in the Hague Convention II of 1907 to prohibit war, and, initially, the prohibition concerned precisely armed attacks to secure payments. The Hague Convention on Limitation of the Employment of Force for the Recovery of Contract Debts[7] thus

---

[4] From this *jus ad bellum*, *i.e.* the right to wage wars, must be distinguished the *jus in bello*, *i.e.* the legal rules, with regard to weapons, methods and humanitarian treatment, that apply once there is a state of armed conflict. See further, my *Law of War, op. cit., passim.*

[5] Walzer, *Just and Unjust Wars, op. cit.*; see further my work on the *Law of War*, 1987, 126 *et seq.*

[6] Richardson's *Messages* III 97, 106, and *ibid.*, 147, 152-161.

[7] 3 NRGT 3 série, 414.

prohibited force to secure payment of money.

The Treaty, the so called Drago-Porter Convention, prohibited States to resort to war in order to recover debts. The 1907 Convention may be seen as a direct result of the views of States that what had been done in the Venezuela affair a few years earlier had not been appropriate: debts must be recovered in other ways than by the use of military force.

Rules of restraining war and the use of force in international community are usually coupled with a positive duty to solve disputes by peaceful means. Such positive duties preceded the complete prohibition of war. The Hague Convention I 1899 on Pacific Settlement of Disputes[8] and the similar Convention I of 1907[9] obliged the parties to seek a peaceful solution to their disputes before resorting to hostilities. The Treaties for the Advancement of Peace, the so called Bryan Treaties of 1913-1914, prohibited declarations of war or the opening of hostilities until an arbitral commission had examined the merits of the dispute.[10] Czar Nicholas II proposed an arbitration procedure - a much ignored historical fact - three days before the First World War was declared.

Article 10 of the Covenant of the League of Nations prohibited aggression and subsequent articles 12-15 prescribed certain procedures for the pacific settlement of disputes. These procedures had to be attempted before Members resorted to war and war was thus not itself outlawed by the Covenant.[11] The Covenant thus introduced a distinction between legal and illegal wars; the latter category comprised conflicts where the formal procedure laid down had not been followed.

However, not even aggression was completely forbidden by article 10 as that article was subordinate to some of the subsequent articles, in particular 15(7) which allowed certain wars to enforce legal rights. Therefore, an invasion could take place in the context of

---

[8]   26 NRGT 2 serie 920.

[9]   3 NRGT 3 serie 360.

[10]   See, for example, the Treaty with Italy, AJIL 1916, suppl. 288; 33 AJIL 1939, Suppl., 86. Numerous bilateral treaties were concluded. See, Brownlie, *Use of Force, op. cit.*, 23 *et seq.*

[11]   Brownlie, *Use of Force, op. cit.*, 57.

a *legal war* under article 15 and then not violate article 10.[12]

On the other hand, article 12 of the Covenant did restrict the right of the members of the organisation to resort to war. The League of Nations condemned the Italian aggression against Abyssinia in 1935[13] as well as the operations of Soviet forces in Finland in the Winter War in 1939,[14] as violations of article 12. But article 12 only prohibited *war*: this gave rise to problems if there was any doubt whether hostilities amounted to such a state of affairs as *war* properly so called. The way *war* was defined at the time[15] left considerable scope for belligerents to avoid disputes being classified as *wars* by their own will, regardless of objective circumstances.

For this reason, there was a good reason for not admitting that war existed for States not to be criticised for illegal actions and for violating article 12 of the Covenant.

The Draft Treaty of Mutual Assistance of 1923,[16] the Geneva Protocol of 1924[17] also restricted, to some extent, the right to use force, as did the Locarno Treaty of 1925.[18]

It was the Briand-Kellogg Act in 1928[19] which finally outlawed aggressive war as well as other types of war waged 'for the solution of international controversies' or as an instrument of *national policy*.[20] This treaty also introduced a duty to settle disputes by peaceful means.

The Briand-Kellogg Pact was reinforced by the doctrine and practice of non-recognition as laid down in the Stimson doctrine of 1932.[21] According to this doctrine the United States declared that it

---

[12]   *Cf.* Miller, 1 *The Drafting of the Covenant*, 1928, 170. For other interpretations, see, Brownlie, *op. cit.*, 63.

[13]   OJ 1935, 1223-6.

[14]   OJ 1939, 539.

[15]   See my *Law of War, op. cit.,* 5 *et seq.*

[16]   LNJO 1923, Spec. Suppl. 16.

[17]   188 LNTS 53.

[18]   154 LNTS 290.

[19]   94 LNTS 57.

[20]   But some dismissed the Act as being 'without value' in international law, see, Undén, Idén om krigets kriminalisering, *Uppsala Universitets Årsskrift*, 1929, 22.

[21]   See, in detail, Brownlie, *Use of Force, op. cit.,* 77, 92-93.

would not recognise situations created by force.[22]

The Treaty to Avoid or Prevent Conflicts between the American States of 1929[23] and the Treaty of Non-Aggression and Conciliation of 1933, the Savedra-Lamas Pact[24] also prohibited force. Some of these agreements were not limited to American States but were ratified by a number of European States as well.[25]

The result of the method employed in these agreements was a conscious recognition of States of an obligation not to wage war as a legally binding rule.[26]

The prohibition of the use of force, and threat thereof, became entrenched in article 2(4) of the Charter of the United Nations, which provides that

'All Members shall refrain in their international relations from the threat or use of force against the territorial integrity or political independence of any State, or in any other manner inconsistent with the Purposes of the United Nations.'

This article has been reinforced by numerous Resolutions of the General Assembly. An attempt to *define* aggression may have proved less successful[27] but other more succinct Resolutions appear to *reflect* what general international law prescribes[28] on the law of force, for example, the Declarations of Principles of International

---

22   *Cf.* the Chaco Declaration by the League of Nations Assembly of the same year, 1932, with similar contents, signed by 19 American States, and 6 Hackworth 45.

23   33 LNTS 26.

24   163 LNTS 393. This Treaty was replaced as between the American States by the Treaty of Bogotà of 1948 which established the Organisation of American States, 30 UNTS 55.

25   See, the Savedra-Lamas Pact which was ratified by Bulgaria, Czechoslovakia, Romania, Spain and the then Yugoslavia, as well as by a series of Latin American States. Many bilateral treaties of Friendship supplement these agreements. As numerous of the ratifying States were communist States the agreements had political overtones which makes it questionable whether they were transmitted to free successor States.

26   *Cf. supra* on Ethics.

27   Resolution on the Definition of Aggression 3314 (XXIX), 1974.

28   See *supra* in Chapter III on the Legal Force of Recommendations.

Law,[29] and the Resolution on Enhancing the Effectiveness of the Prohibition of Force.[30]

b. The Extent of the Obligation

Article 2(4) summarises the prohibition of force - not only war - which binds all international subjects.[31] This is the root provision[32] of the prohibition of force in international society of today, an obligation which is binding on all Members of the UN as well as on non-members, as *accepted as a major obligation* of any civilised State in the modern world.[33] This is not the same as saying that article 2(4) *has passed into customary law* as was argued in the *Nicaragua Case*.[34] No doubt, article 2(4) presented an *innovation* when it was adopted in 1945 and it is clear that the *extent* prohibition of force as laid down in article 2(4) did not apply before the UN Charter.[35] On the other hand, it is also clear that the prohibition *now* comprises all members of international society, whether or not they are Members of the United Nations.

What type of force is then forbidden under article 2(4)? There was, for some time, some doubt whether the article covers economic force.[36] The Brazilian delegation sought to have a proposal adopted

---

[29]   GA Res 2625 (XXV), 1970.

[30]   GA Res 41/22, 1987.

[31]   Not only States; also liberation movements must comply with relevant rules, see further my *Law of War, op. cit.*, 361 *et seq.*

[32]   There is overwhelming literature about article 2(4) of the United Nations Charter. See *e.g.* Waldock, The Regulation of the Use of Force by Individuals States and International Law, RCADI, 1952, ii, 455.

[33]   *Cf.* Verdross & Simma, *Universelles Völkerrecht*, 3rd ed., 1984, § 468 p. 285. *Cf. supra* in Chapter III on Adoption and Parallel Declarations.

[34]   (1986) ICJ *Reports* 1986, 14.

[35]   Judge Jennings, Dissenting Opinion, in the *Nicaragua Case* (1986) ICJ *Reports* 1986, 14.

[36]   Doxey, *Economic Sanctions and International Enforcement*, 1971. *Cf.* Sciso, L'aggressione indiretta nella definizione dell'Assemblea Generale delle Nazioni Unite, *Rivista*, 1983, 253; Barber, Economic sanctions as a policy instrument, *International Affairs*, 1979, 367; St.J. Macdonald, Economic sanctions in the international system, CanYIL, 1969, 69. On similar discussion bearing on the use of force, including economic force, and treaties, see my

at Bretton Woods by which also *economic force* would be covered by prohibition. To forbid such force obviously presents formidable problems and, after some discussion, it was decided not to include such force in the prohibition.[37]

The exact meaning of the article, and of the extent of the contemporary obligation in general, has formed the object of numerous judicial decisions. A special type of force which some have argued should be excluded from article 2(4), or from any general prohibitive rule, is *transitory force*. The United Kingdom thus argued in the *Corfu Channel Case* that force against another State is not forbidden if *individual objectives* are to be reached rather than any permanent impairment of the territorial integrity or political independence of the other State. In the event the United Kingdom had, *i.a.*, resorted to mine sweeping in Albanian waters. The International Court of Justice, without referring specifically to article 2(4) rejected this line of argument and held that forms of self-preservation and self-help are forbidden.

Similarly, the aborted United States rescue mission to fly out hostages from the American Embassy of Teheran was also firmly condemned by the International Court of Justice in the *Hostage Case*,[38] although the Court, in the same case had utterly condemned Iran for holding the persons, all enjoying diplomatic and consular immunity, as hostages, thereby violating one of the most fundamental rules of international law.[39]

The attitude that no form of *transitory force* can be allowed also implies that there can be few cases of valid[40] humanitarian intervention,[41] a mechanism which has notoriously served as a cloak for sovereign self interests of other States.[42] Sometimes States have

---

Independent State, op. cit., 145-163.

[37] See further my *International Law and the Independent State,* 2nd ed., 1987, Chapter III.

[38] (1980) ICJ *Reports* 1986, 1.

[39] *Ibid.*

[40] I mention in my *Law of War, op. cit.,* two examples that *may* constitute lawful action: the action against General Amin in Uganda and against Pol Pot in Kampuchea.

[41] *Cf. infra*, under Intervention.

[42] See further my *Law of War, op. cit.,* Chapter I.

sought to resort to humanitarian assistance *also* on the ground that article 2(4) states that force is forbidden against territorial integrity, or political independence, *or in any manner inconsistent with the Purposes of the United Nations.* They have then sought to argue that this latter ground - which is only a further prohibition - should be interpreted as overriding the other two prohibitions and furnish a reason for *allowing force*.

In the final analysis, article 2(4), concurrently with a general rule of international law, prohibits *all forms of force*, within the parameters indicated above.[43]

The paramount provision of article 2(4) of the UN Charter is supplemented and reinforced by a number of other declarations, conventions and treaties. Among Declarations, we may mention that on Principles of International Law Concerning Friendly Relations and Co-operation Among States.[44] Other important Declarations are the Resolution on Aggression,[45] and the Resolution on Enhancing the Effectiveness of the Prohibition of Force.[46] These Resolutions have, on the face of it as a recommendation of the General Assembly no binding force.[47] Yet, according to our analysis it *reflects lex lata* and is *on that ground* binding.[48] The Declaration was also cited as evidence of the *opinio juris* of States with regard to the binding nature of the obligation to abstain from force in international society.[49]

Among other treaties supplementing article 2(4) the following agreements are relevant: the Inter-American Treaty of Reciprocal Assistance, the Rio Pact, of 1947[50] reiterating the prohibition of the use of force and the threat of force.

The basis for *the protected area* into which other States may not

---

[43]   *Cf.* Jimenez de Arechaga, General course in public international law, 159 RCADI 1978, 9.

[44]   GA Resolution 2625 (XXV), 1970.

[45]   GA Res 3314 (XXIX), 1974.

[46]   GA Res 32/22, 1987.

[47]   See further *supra* in Chapter III under Legal Effects of Recommendations for an analysis of cases where recommendations entail legal effects.

[48]   *Ibid.*

[49]   (1986) *Nicaragua Case* ICJ *Reports* 1986, 14.

[50]   21 UNTS 77.

intervene is found in article 2(7) of the Charter of the United Nations which deals with what has become known as the *reserved domain*[51] and which specifies that States have a certain sphere of *domestic jurisdiction*.[52] This special area of competence comprises *both* the geographical sovereign area of the State[53] *and* the sovereign *activities* in various fields, such as in legislation or general policy.

However, armed force is certainly forbidden under the article, if it is directed against the territorial integrity or political independence of any State or if it is inconsistent with the purposes of the United Nations.[54]

c. Intervention: A Special Case?

Intervention is a special form of the use of force which is of great practical importance in modern international society. The purpose of intervention is usually to make a State do something it would not otherwise do,[55] by force, by direct action, openly or clandestinely.[56]

The term cannot be used for UN action in a territory as intervention implies an act against the will of a State.[57] A definition of the term would be difficult as it covers a number of different and wide ranging acts and any assessment would be coloured by

---

[51]   *E.g.* Rajan, *United Nations and Domestic Jurisdiction*, 2nd ed., 1961.

[52]   *Cf.* the Declaration on the Inadmissibility of Intervention in the Dometic Affairs of States and the Protection of the Independence and Sovereignty, GA Res. 2131 (XX) 1966. Territory and Jurisdiction; Suy, Réflexions sur la distinction entre la souveraineté et la compétence territoriale, *Festschrift Verdross,* 1971, 499;

[53]   See *infra* for delimitations, Chapter V.

[54]   For categorical condemnation of any infringement of State sovereignty see the ex-Soviet writer Tunkin, *Sila i mezhdunarodnoe pravo,* Moscow, 1983, 37, albeit in now somewhat obsolete terms.

[55]   1 Hyde, 69; *cf.* Hoffman, The Problem of Intervention, in Bull, *Intervention, op. cit.,* 9.

[56]   Bull, in *Intervention, op. cit.,* 1.

[57]   Luard, Collective Intervention in Bull, *Intervention, op. cit.,* 160. To such action the States have already given their abstract consent, see my *Law Making, op. cit.,* 322.

ideological differences.[58]

Intervention may mean virtually any type of *interference*[59] in the affairs of another State, by acts ranging from those similar to aggression,[60] to milder acts by, for example, political[61] economic pressure.[62] As appeared in the famous *Nicaragua Case*,[63] a clear distinction should be made between armed attack and armed intervention. But in any event, neither of these activities are compatible with the obligations under article 2(4) of the United Nations Charter. Attempts to define, by enumeration, acts which constitute *aggression*[64] are probably fruitless.

Sometimes the use of *gun boat diplomacy* or the hovering presence of warships offshore[65] has been thought to imply acts of intervention. Even the mere discussion of affairs in another State, for example, in the United Nations,[66] has been considered inappropriate and amounting to intervention. It may now be suggested that such views, earlier not necessarily 'wrong', or at variance with majority views of international lawyers and statesmen, are *now* obsolete.

In this context we may emphasise again that the ambit of article 2(7), that is to say the *reserved domain*,[67] is continuously shrinking. If that privileged domain is now smaller than what it was in 1945, this thus means that an act which in 1945 may have been construed to imply intervention, no longer violates article 2(7). For example, before the disintegration of the Soviet Union, there was a marked

---

58   Thomas, *New States, Sovereignty and Intervention*, 1985, 9.

59   The French term for intervention, *ingérence*, means precisely interference.

60   See my *Law of War*, *op. cit.*, 67-71.

61   For example, the practice of propaganda, my *Law of War*, *op. cit.*, 62, 262, 299.

62   See *supra*, and *cf.* Higgins, Intervention and international law, in Bull, (ed.), Intervention, *op. cit.*, 1985, 30.

63   (1984) and (1985) *Nicaragua v United States*, ICJ *Reports*.

64   See Resolution 3314 (XXIX) of 1974 and, in detail, my *Law of War*, op. cit., 57-61.

65   *Cf.* Calvocoressi, *World Order and New States*, 1962, 17.

66   *E.g.* Vincent, *Intervention*, *op. cit.*, 15.

67   For a Resolution the General Assembly on the context of *intervention* and the *reserved domain*, see GA Res 2131 (XX) on the Inadmissibility of Intervention in the Domestic Affairs of States, of 1965.

trend away from the prohibition of discussion of Human Rights in the USSR in the '40s and '50s, to a defence *on the merits* in the '80s; rather than saying that such discussion of internal policies in the Soviet Union would constitute illegitimate intervention, the USSR would explain that the facts as reported were exaggerated or incorrect.

Certain action amounts to what I have called *patronising intervention*. This is when one State considers that it knows what is *best* for another State, often a weaker State. This attitude explains the behaviour of both superpowers. It explains the recurring intervention by the United States in Central America (and in South America). President Gerald Ford stated in 1974 that there exists a right to *destabilise* a government in certain circumstances.

'It is a recognised fact that historically as well as presently such actions are taken *in the best interests* of the countries concerned.'[68]

The United States has also claimed that

'United States actions are in the exercise of the right, indeed the duty, to engage in collective self-defense with the other Central American States in response to Nicaragua's acts.'[69]

But the mining by the United States of ports of Nicaragua and other para-military action against that State was clearly against international law. The International Court of Justice decided by an injunction in 1984 that the United States should cease such activities[70] but the United States claimed that it was entitled to pursue certain other measures. The United States then decided to withdraw from the Court proceedings and discontinued its acceptance of the Optional Clause.[71]

---

[68]   Statement 16th September 1974 (italics added); Falk, Covert intervention, *op. cit.*, 195. *Cf.* Fatouros, Remarks on covert intervention and international law, *ibid.*, 192.

[69]   *Verbatim Records* CR/84/17, 74.

[70]   (1984) ICJ, *Reports*, 1984, on the interim measures.

[71]   (1986) ICJ, *Reports*, 1986 and *cf. infra*, under Consequential Rules.

It has sometimes been suggested that *humanitarian intervention* should be not only allowed but welcomed.[72] Some now even speak of a *duty to intervene, (un devoir d'ingérence)* in humanitarian matters; such views have, above all, been presented by representatives of the previous French government in the General Assembly. However, the *consent* of the territorial State is of paramount importance.[73] As noted earlier, the form of *aid* by means of humanitarian intervention has, in history, often been used as a cloak for other political motives of States.[74] By speaking of a *duty to give*, in other than moral terms, or a *duty to receive*, merely *obscures the real duties* under international law,[75] to *resolve the political problems*[76] in the receiving State, which have given rise to a situation of crisis. Far from tackling such problems which may *preempt* both humanitarian suffering and floods of refugees, outside States have often even encouraged such problems for their own self-interests.

d. Legitimising Elements

Many forms of the use of force may be allowed and deprived of illegal character provided there is a *legitimising factor* of sufficient importance.

There is an overriding presumption that the UN action is compatible with International Law. But individual States who apply force to another State have to accept a different presumption: that they are deviating from a compelling rule prohibiting force unless they can show a clear legitimising title under international law.

Legitimising elements recognised by the Charter may be self-

---

[72]   *Cf.* GA Res 43/131, 1988 on aid to victims of catastrophies; 45/100, 1990 on corridors for humanitarian aid; SC 733 1992 on Somalia; SC Res 688, 1990 on humanitarian aid to the Kurds.

[73]   See my *Law of War, op. cit.,* Chapter I. *cf.* Dupuy, P-M, *Le droit international public,* 1992, 75-76.

[74]   See my *Law of War, op. cit.,* Chapter I.

[75]   On the notion of *solidarity,* see my *Concept, op. cit.,* 124-127.

[76]   Exceptions must be made for aid in the case of natural catastrophies.

defence under article 51 of the Charter.[77] The wording of article 51 allows for certain exceptions and for certain legitimising factors.[78] Such exemptions and such special circumstances certainly undermine the general prohibition.[79] Much will turn on the facts. Yet, the most problematic side of this are the subjective elements which are incorporated: who will decide on whether force is *directed against the territorial integrity or political independence*[80] of a State? There are numerous situations when border incursions are disputed with regard to number and intensity, when they are perhaps thought to be more serious than they were and when the response sparks off real hostilities. There are many issues: Do you have to be attacked before you strike back?

(i) Self-Defence

According to article 51 of the United Nations every State has the

> '... inherent right of individual or collective self-defence if an armed attack occurs against a Member of the United Nations, until the Security Council takes measures to maintain international peace and security ...'

The article has little meaning beyond 'referring back to general international law or to a general principle of law.'[81]

One form of self-defense has sometimes been called *reprisals* in the past, whereby a State 'pays back' injury suffered by the action of others.[82] Most textbooks speak of reprisals as a special category where the use of force, otherwise condemned, would be permissible. But in view of the fact that only self-defence properly so called, or consent of a State, furnish legitimate ground for the use of force,

---

77   See in detail my *Law of War, op. cit.,* 73-74.
78   See in detail my *Law of War, op. cit.,* 71-81.
79   See my *Law of War, op. cit.,* 124 *et seq.*
80   As the wording of article 2(4) proscribes, *cf supra.*
81   Jimenez de Arechaga, General Course in Public International Law, 159 RCADI 9, 1978.
82   *Cf. infra* on Sanctions in Chapter IX.

reprisals are probably no longer legal in the international society.[83]

The *limits* and *conditions* of self-defence may be summarised in that it must be an *overwhelming situation*

'leaving no choice of means and no moment for deliberation.'[84]

Much guidance may be found in national laws, in comparative of common principles,[85] and in case law of international courts, especially as regards *proportionality*.[86] It is thus vital that self-defence is proportionate to the initial offense.[87]

It is most important that any action for self-defence is taken within a very short time of the first attack.[88] There is also a general condition that a warning, or a demand to restore the situation, should be given before any action is taken.

Much has been said about the condition that a State must have been the victim of an *armed attack*. An *armed attack* must probably be construed widely to encompass any military attack, including the supply of arms coupled with logistical support, and need not involve direct military action.[89]

It is also significant that the Charter, in reflection of general international law, speaks of *an* attack. In other words, there must be a *specific attack*, and one cannot extend the notion of self-defence to imply a right for liberation movements and others subjected to what

---

[83] The right of self-defence does probably not include the right of reprisals. *Cf.* Higgins, *The Development of International Law Through the Political Organs of the United Nations*, 1963, 217; *cf.* Bowett, Reprisals Involving Recourse to Armed Force, 66 AJIL 1972, 1.

[84] *The Caroline* (1837) 29 BFSP, 1137.

[85] See *supra* on General Principles in Chapter III.

[86] *Naulilaa Arbitration* [1928] 2 RIAA 1013. The notion of proportionality has been subject to considerble analysis in the EC Court, see for a general view, Hartley, *The Foundations of European Community Law*, 144; Wyatt & Dashwood, *The Substantive Law of the EEC* 1980, 47. *Cf.* analysis in the European Court of Human Rights, see, for example, the *Lithgow Case* (1986), ECHR *Reports.*

[87] *Naulilaa Arbitration* [1928] 2 RIAA 1013.

[88] On the Falklands War see my *Law of War, op. cit.,* 28, 71 *et seq.*

[89] See Dissenting Opinion of Judge Jennings in the *Nicaragua Case,* (1986) ICJ *Reports* 14.

somewhat pathetically has been called a *permanent aggression* of an oppressive power, with a right to seek to overthrow a government.[90] On the other hand, liberation movements are, in the event of specific situations,[91] entitled, as subjects of international law,[92] to exercise *rights* of self-defence at the same time as they are also subject to congruent *obligations*.

According to the wording of the Charter, all action for self-defence should be taken through the UN. That is, self-defence is only allowed under article 51 of the Charter until the World Organisation can deal with the matter. Therefore, a member State must report to the organisation and then, in special circumstances, take provisional measures if the UN does not act or does not act quickly enough.

The theory of *abstract consent*[93] explains the consequences of *obligation* when Member States agree to delegate powers to the United Nations;[94] the parties to the Charter, and those who later have acceded to it, agreed, beforehand and in the abstract, to certain action by the UN, and such actions include, for example, sanctions[95] which may involve military action, possibly with UN Forces; because of the *abstract consent* such action cannot be held to be in contravention of any rules prohibiting force. Yet, the consent was given *on the condition* that the UN machinery would replace the efficient action by States. If the organisation does not meet those conditions, it would seem the contract with the Member States fails. Therefore, it is probably that only *some* action must be channelled through the United Nations to be legitimate.

It is therefore questionable whether the Charter of the United

---

90   For various arguments put forward by liberation movements to justify the use of force, see Wilson, *International Law and the Use of Force by National Liberation Movements*, 1989, 130-136.

91   The distinction between *rebels*, *insurgents* or even general *dissidents* is difficult to draw, see further my Law of War, *op. cit.* Chapter III. On the other hand, it is clear that the State is obliged to respect *all Human Rights* of *all peoples* present in its territory, and must not suppress any democratically instigated movement.

92   See *supra* in Chapter II and, further, in my *Law of War, op. cit.*, Chapter III.

93   See my *Law Making, op. cit.*, 322.

94   *Supra*, 101 *et seq.*

95   Under article 38, 41 and 42.

Nations actually restricts the right to take action by individual States, more than in marginal situations. An analysis of action by States makes it obvious that the so called right to *collective self defence*, a much liked chapter heading of textbook writers, is nothing more than the parallel individual rights of a number of States.[96] The whole system of 'collective self-defence' under the Charter simply does not exist. Instead, the power to act is usually supplanted by individual States.

If the Organisation is slow to act, as it was in both the Iranian an in the Falkland affairs, an at least temporary right of action may revert to the Member States. It may also be that the UN shows inertia, lack of decision and leadership, which enables Member States to take action by themselves.[97]

Some States have not hesitated to act *in lieu* of the UN,[98] especially in cases when the UN has limited itself to *discussions*.[99] The right to act to defend oneself must not be construed too narrowly: it must be underlined that the operation of the Charter is *deficient* as the foreseen powers in Chapter VII have not been exercised by the United Nations.[100] Thus, an essential element in the Charter is missing and in such a case

'it seems dangerous to define unnecessarily strictly the conditions for lawful self-defence so as to leave a large area where both a forcible response to force is forbidden, and yet the United Nations employment of force, which was intended to fill that gap, is

---

[96] See Dissenting Opinion by Judge Jennings, in the *Nicaragua Case*, (1986) ICH *Reports* 14.

[97] See the previous note.

[98] When both UN and NATO showed themselves powerless, the United States considered itself entitled to bomb attacking positions near Sarajevo on 4th August 1993.

[99] See *e.g.* the Falklands War where there was a problem of time: the United Kingdom could not wait for what appeared at the time to be fruitless discussions in the United Nations and sent therefore a Task Force itself.

[100] See Dissenting Opinion of Judge Jennings in the *Nicaragua Case* (1986) ICJ *Reports* 14.

absent.'[101]

Some States, exposed to what must be considered to be *armed attacks* in the meaning of article 51 have decided *not to react* and *not to exercise the right of self-defence*. This was the curious situation of Sweden in the 1980s, when numerous repeated incursions by Russian submarines were not repelled by self-defence.[102] Instead, for reasons that history will possibly explain, it was considered opportune to declare the submarines, often within shooting range, as *immune*, a misconception[103] of both the right of self-defence - which was never even discussed - and of the notion of immunity.[104]

(ii) Hot Pursuit

International law has, for a long time, admitted the possibility of the vessels of a coastal State to *pursue* an intruder onto the High Seas if the ship has violated the laws of that State when she was in her territorial waters. This right of *hot pursuit* to follow an offender was often invoked in the so called Liquor Cases, that is to say cases which resulted from ships being caught smuggling liquor during the time of prohibition in the United States.[105]

However, numerous cases often quoted in support of the theory are, when closely examined, authorities for the *interest criterion* in jurisdiction,[106] that is proving the right, at times, to intervene on the High Seas for certain crimes against a coastal State. In many of these cases,[107] there has been no pursuit in territorial waters but action has started when the vessel was already outside territorial waters.

---

[101] *Ibid., loc. cit.*

[102] Sweden did not even request payment for the salvage of a Russian submarine, found on a shoal within *internal* waters, within the high security military area of Karlskrona, but towed it to sea without making any claim against the ship or the flag State.

[103] See my article on Foreign Warships and Immunity for Espionage, AJIL 1984, 76.

[104] See *infra* on immunity in Chapter VII.

[105] *The Newton Bay* (1928) 30 F 2d 444; *The Vinces* (927)20 F 2d 164.

[106] See *infra*, in Chapter VII, on principles for jurisdiction.

[107] For example, *The I'm Alone* (1935) 3 RIAA 1619, and *infra* in Chapter VII.

Therefore, the pursuit cannot be classified as *hot.*

On the other hand, the doctrine of *hot pursuit* has given rise to intricate parallels *on land:* is a State entitled to pursue an intruder on land across the border? The limits of this right must be drawn according to what has been considered necessary for self-defence.[108] It is interesting to note the effects of the theory on legal thinking, stretching the concept yet further on land to seek to justify what has been called *anticipatory self-defence.*

(iii) Anticipatory Self-Defence

There is a considerable problem concerning so called anticipatory self-defence, *i.e.* the right that some claim exists to attack *before* one is oneself attacked. To distinguish this category from that of hot pursuit, one may say that anticipatory self-defence is conditioned by an overwhelming *presumed* action which necessitates crossing of a border, whereas hot pursuit is designed to deal with *prolonging* a right of self-defence into other territory.

Naturally, guerilla strongholds across a border will pose considerable threats to the security of a State. Yet, to maintain international peace and stability there must always be a presumption that recourse to anticipatory force is wrongful as otherwise any fear, which after all can only be subjectively assessed and which may be exaggerated, may lead to escalation of hostilities.

(iv) Consent

The consent of a State[109] furnishes a ground for legitimacy. But there are numerous problems concerning the validity of such acts of consent. The problem of consent is particularly difficult in the case of request for assistance to insurgents.[110]

However, consent must be given by *the people* and not only by some puppet government which does not rely on democratic principles. Under the Brezhnev doctrine the USSR claimed that it

---

[108]   See *supra* in the previous section.

[109]   *Ibid.,* 75-77.

[110]   On assistance to insurgents in general, see *ibid.,* 67-68.

was entitled to intervene in other countries to uphold socialist values. In the case of Afghanistan the Soviet Union intervened on the basis of a formal request by the government, a government which did not represent the people of Afghanistan.

However, a government which lacks popular support may be unable to issue a valid *invitation* to other States to intervene. For example, the invitation of the Kabul government to the USSR to 'assist' was held not to be valid by other States which joined a boycott against the Moscow Olympics. But Soviet writers claimed that the USSR was requested to intervene in Afghanistan by the legitimate government[111] and that the United States was acting unlawfully by assisting the rebels. On the other hand, the call from the *people* of Nicaragua to the United States for help was probably a valid invitation as the vast number of the population were those which *should have been represented in the government* and who, therefore, represented the democratic will of the people.

There is thus an important element of democracy in every act of consent and the authentic call from a democratically elected government, representing the majority of the people in the relevant State, must be proven in each individual case. Although self-defence and consent both imply considerable problems, it will, in any given case, be at least reasonably clear on the facts whether article 2(4) has, *prima facie,* been violated.

Other grounds for alleged legitimacy than self-defence or consent are often tainted by political motives (as those two grounds may often be themselves) and may be used by States as a cloak for intervention.

If a State takes action by force in the *interest of another State*, such interference violates, not only the rule prohibiting force, but also the right of self-determination.[112]

On the other hand, there may, on other States and the UN, lie a definite duty to intervene, when there is a valid invitation from a democratically elected government.[113]

Naturally, there will be many instances when it is precisely in question whether there exists such a government, representing the

[111]   Rybakov, *Agressia, op. cit.,* 147.

[112]   See, my *Independent State, op. cit.,* 3 *et seq.*

[113]   *Cf.* Kouchner, *Le droit d'ingérence,* 1990.

people in a specific country. The guide lines must be that there must be a clear and unequivocal demand from a *prima facie* legitimate government, before a State will be held to have given its consent to outside intervention, whether this intervention is to be carried out by the United Nations of by another State.

iii. Piracy: An International Crime[114]

Dubner, *The International Law of Sea Piracy*, 1979: Rubin, *The Law of Piracy*, 1988.

We have seen above that *force* by States, against States, is now forbidden under contemporary international law but that force, in its raw form, was not only allowed but encouraged and admired in earlier history when States conquered or enlarged their territory by wars.[115]

On the other hand, there are some forceful action by *individuals* which has always been condemned. One such form of force is *piracy*, qualified as an international crime. Since time immemorial piracy has been prohibited under general international law

Piracy *jure gentium*[116] can be defined as *any act of violence committed by a private*[117] *vessel, outside the jurisdiction of any*

---

[114]   *Piracy* is one *type* of international crime, conveniently dealt with here *sui generis*. However, there are numerous other international crimes, notably those committed by violations of basic Human Rights, see on this *infra* in this Chapter. For international crimes there exists a right of universal jurisdiction, thus for *piracy* and (tentatively) to *terrorism*, as well as for certain *gross violations of basic Human Rights*. On the universality principle see *infra* in Chapter VI under jurisdiction.

[115]   On conquest and other means of acquiring territory, see *infra*, in Chapter VI. On war in general and the present legal rules of armed conflict, see my *Law of War*, Cambridge University Press, 1987, *passim*.

[116]   Piracy and an *international crime* must be distinguished from what national laws may classify as piracy under municipal law, see, Oppenheim, ed. by Jennings & Watts, I:2 754-755.

[117]   Note that public ships, warships, or insurgents cannot commit piracy, see 1 Calvo paras. 497 *et seq*. Note that violence to further environmental ideas has been classified by national courts as implying a private motive, *Castle John v Macebo*, 77 ILR 537.

State,[118] *against another vessel.*[119] Pirates are said to be *hostes gentium,* enemies of all peoples, and can therefore be tried anywhere.[120] Every State has thus a right over pirates as demonstrated in *United States v Smith* in 1820.[121] There is a trend to compare *hi-jacking terrorists* with pirates.

iv. Terrorism: Force by Groups

Capaldo, *Terrorismo internazionale e garanzie collettive,* 1989.

We have seen how force has been forbidden in international society. States are not allowed to resort to force against each other. Even certain crimes by individuals, such as piracy, are prohibited by international law, as we have seen, from an early date. The non-violence trend in this respect can be seen to be supplemented by emerging rules outlawing international terrorism. Here, the perpetrators who are being subjected to an increasing number of international rules are not always States. More commonly they are groups or individuals. In a sense, one may compare the outlawing of terrorists as a reaction to a modern form of common enemies, comparable to piracy. Terrorism involves by definition force and is classified as an *international crime,* implying a presumption of universal jurisdiction.[122]

---

[118] This qualification excludes territorial waters and the contiguous zone, where States retain jurisdiction, see *supra* in Chapter V, but includes the EEZ and other protective zones.

[119] *Cf.* the definition in i Oppenheim, 8th ed. by Lauterpacht, 614, which also adds the adjective *unauthorised* to qualify the act, and which also includes *mutiny.* In the recent edition by Sir Robert Jennings and Sir Arthur Watts, the more elaborate definition (which excludes mutiny) adopted in the 1958 and 1982 Law of the Sea Convention has been preferred, a definition which adds, *i.a.,* that the act must have been committed for *private ends.* The impossibility of establishing such subjective criteria makes the more elaborate definition in these Conventions less workable. *Cf. supra* in Chapter IV on terrorism.

[120] See *infra* in Chapter VI on the Universality Principle, under Jurisdiction.

[121] 18 US (5 Wheaton) 153, 161.

[122] On principles for jurisdiction, see *infra* in Chapter VII. Another type of offence which is probably emerging as an international crime is *drug dealing,* for which also wide power of jurisdiction is sought by numerous States on a

Terrorism presents the most serious problems of all new disorders in international society. Numerous conventions have been adopted to reduce terrorism. There is a vast number of books and articles on terrorism[123] but few proceed to any legal analysis of the problem. Works focus on incidents, on causes, or on preventive aspects, but often adopts the optique of sociology rather than law.

Terrorism falls into two broad categories, State terrorism and group (and individual) terrorism, as will be seen in the brief analysis set out below.

a. Distinguished from State Terrorism

Since the days of Caligula, and before, there have always been cruel rulers. Some have referred to suppression of *their own subjects in their own territory* by such rulers as *terrorism*; but to include such acts in the definition of terrorism merely obscures the problem.

However, States do resort to violent acts against persons outside their own territory and then their acts may infringe on interests of other States. In such cases some also speak of *State terrorism.*

International instruments often seek to *remind* States that they must not engage in, or condone, terrorist activities directed against other States or persons in their territory, some in the form of resolutions of the General Assembly,[124] others as general statements preparatory to international conventions.[125]

One often refers to the actions of Libya, for example in the alleged attack on a German disco, as terrorism. We encounter, however, difficult problems of evidence. What was, for long, thought to be an example of such State terrorism by Libya proved to have been instigated by Syria. It is therefore essential to reserve assessment

---

solidarity basis, see *infra*, in Chapter VII.

[123] Lasok, *International Terrorism, A Bibliography*, 1987, listing 5,600 entries in the English language alone.

[124] See for example, GA Res 2625 (XXV) of 1970, Declaration of International Law Concerning Friendly Relations and Cooperation Among States; GA Res 2734 (XXV) of 1970, Declaration on the Strengthening of International Society.

[125] ILC Draft of 1954 of Code of Offences Against the Peace and Security of Mankind, ii Yb 1954, 149.

as to who has committed a terrorist act until all facts are clear: it is in the nature of terrorism that the perpetrators do not always work openly. In most cases, it appears that it is not a State, but a *group*, which is behind a so called terrorist attack.

State terrorism could perhaps, as a concept, be used for acts committed by the State outside its territory against the interests or subjects of *other* States. This definition would at least exclude acts whereby a State liquidates one of its own nationals, as in the Bulgarian umbrella murders in the 1970s when agents of that State killed defectors, from the same State, by poisoned umbrellas.

However, it may be that State terrorism is a notion of limited use. It appears preferable to us to relegate all ill-doings of States, both acts against their own citizens, and against others, in their own territory, as well as special violent acts against individuals outside their territory against individuals can be conveniently subsumed under the aegis of other principles and rules. Offences against individuals, citizens or non-citizens in the territory of a State can be dealt with in the context of the protection of individuals in the field of Human Rights,[126] a field where States have specific obligations and where numerous violations are sanctioned.[127] Other violent acts against nationals of other States committed *either* in a State's territory or in the territory of another State, can be dealt with under specific rules concerning diplomatic protection of nationals abroad.

b. Group and Individual Terrorism

In an upsurge against a government violent terrorist tactics can be used. Such violence has, by some, been thought of as a form of terrorism.[128] But throughout history there have been *regicide* and dynastic assassinations as well asoverthrows of governments, and yet, this is not what one today commonly thinks of as a form of terrorism.

Today it is more a question of random attacks against certain

---

126   See *infra* in the next section.

127   See *infra* under Human Rights in this Chapter.

128   Blishchenko, *Terrorism i mezhdunarodnoe pravo*, 1984, 21. This is also the form of action advocated by Lenin as a tactic to overthrow 'bourgois' governments, see Lenin, ii Collected Works, *op. cit.*, 143.

vulnerable targets whereby terrorists make certain demands. There is thus often a triangular relationship between the terrorists the victims and a third party, often a State.[129] It is then often the third party, and not the victim, which is able to grant the demands of the terrorists.

Naturally one can distinguish between terrorism for private ends and terrorism for a cause. If Italian criminals kidnap a German banker called Rolf Schildt, in the mistaken belief that he belongs to the Rothschild banking family[130] and demands ransom from 'his' bank, this is an action for private ends, not much different from what pirates used to do in earlier centuries.[131] Other actions will not be taken for private ends but will be carried out for a *cause*. Such a cause may be the independence of a nation or some other political aim. It is actions like these that constitute the prime core of terrorism as we think of it today. Yet, it is important to consider that the *motive* that a terrorist has is only known to himself and cannot normally be ascertained objectively although his declarations may have certain legal relevance.

Most terrorist acts properly called thus concern acts for a *cause* which often implies a political motive. Some claim that terrorism also, in each terrorist act, must inspire *terror*.[132] But it may be submitted that this is an impossible criterion in view of its subjective nature. Who is to quantify fear? Two people do not, in all likelihood, have the same threshold of fear and one will be 'terrified' when another one will not experience such emotions.

It has also been suggested that *violence* would be an essential ingredient in terrorism.[133] Naturally, terrorist acts are very often violent acts but it may as well be a question of a surreptitious dismantling of an essential part of an aircraft, an act which would not imply, but perhaps result, in violence. Some speak of 'combat' or

---

[129]   See my *Law of War, op. cit.*, 22.

[130]   This is what happened in Sardinia in 1984.

[131]   *Cf. infra* on universal jurisdiction and note that piracy has also taken place this century, see *The Santa Maria* incident, AJIL 1964.

[132]   *E.g.* Wardlaw, *Political Terrorism, Theory, Tactics and Counter-measures*, 1982, 16; Schmid, *Political terrorism, A Research Guide to Concepts, Theories, Data Bases and Literature*, 1983, 111.

[133]   Evans, *Calling Truce to Terror: The American Response to International Terrorism*, 1979, 29.

'surrogate warfare' as if terrorism was a part of actual warfare.[134] Of course, if by terrorism we only mean a type of tactics by treacherous and often simple means, there is ample reason to find a place for the notion in guerilla warfare.[135]

Some claim there must be a *political* target but it is not clear whether this means an actual target or merely a political *motive* for the act.[136] For many terrorist acts there is often a political motive, for example for many, but not all, acts of hi-jacking,[137] where the polticial motive may be to make a valuable plane available to the State which a hijacker has flown. However, one target, which cannot be *political per se* is dangerous installations.[138] These are, for example, nuclear plants, dams and other vulnerable installations. Attacks on these by a simple terrorist attack could obviously cause enormous damage and be used for leverage of terrorist demands. Similarly, terrorist attacks, so far theoretically, could involve weapons of mass destruction and then amount to what has been called *super-violence*[139] or *super-terrorism*.[140]

Apart from these criteria of subjective fear, violence or political motive, which may not be easy to assess in the individual case, there is one element which does seem to recur in what one normally thinks of as terrorist attacks. That is the sporadic nature of the attacks, that is to say the unpredictable nature of their type and location. This sporadic element is, together with the triangular relationship,[141] the

---

[134] See Jenkins, *High Technology and Surrogate War: The Impact of New Technology on Low-Level Violence*, 1975 and my *Law of War, op. cit.*, 23.

[135] See, in detail, my *Law of War, op. cit., loc. cit.*

[136] *Cf.* Arus, Legislación penal y penitenciaria comparada en materia de terrorismo, in *Terrorismo Internacional*, 1985, 113.

[137] Hi-jacking which is a typical terrorist act may also be carried out for private ends, for example, when persons in DDR fled in hi-jacked planes to West Germany. After the demolition of the Wall in 1990 a museum showing various private ingenious escape attempts has been opened at former Checkpoint Charlie in Berlin.

[138] See, in detail, my *Law of War, op. cit.*, 249.

[139] Berkowitz, Frost, Hajic and Redisch, *Super-Violence: The Civilian threat of Mass-Destruction Weapons*, 1972, 9.

[140] Alexander, Super-Terrorism, in Alexander and Gleason (eds.), *Behavioural and Quantitative Aspects on Terrorism*, 1981, 345.

[141] See *supra* and my *Law of War, op. cit.*, 23.

essence of terrorism.

The *effect* of classifying a group as a terrorist movement, may be that they, as guilty of what is an international crime, *loses* the rights they would otherwise enjoy as citizens. For example, the *right of expression,* vital in any State with respect for the Rule of Law, may be *restricted* for terrorists.[142]

c. Conventions and Resolutions to Combat Terrorism

Already the League of Nations emphasised, in many resolutions, the duty of States not to tolerate terrorism within their borders and the corresponding positive duty to do all in their power to repress terrorism. In 1937 the League of Nations drafted a Convention[143] for the Repression of International Terrorism, a Treaty which never came into force.

States have a duty to prevent terrorism *within their borders* under the Declaration of the Rights and Duties of States.[144] The Declaration on Principles of International Law Concerning Friendly Relations and Cooperation Among States of 1970[145] reiterates the obligation. This duty is supplemented by a duty to *refrain from assisting terrorists in other States,* as support for such terrorists may amount to unlawful intervention. This latter aspect was forcefully emphasised by the International Curt of Justice in the *Nicaragua Case.*[146]

There are universal conventions relevant to the reduction of terrorism. They include the Convention for the Protection of International Agents, an agreement designed to enhance the protection

---

142 See *R v Secretary of State for the Home Department ex parte Brind* [1991] 1 ALL ER 720 (HL).

143 LoN Doc C 1937, 222 M 162.

144 This declaration was prepared by the International Law Commission in 1949, see article 4.

145 GA Resolution 2625 (XXV) enacted on 24th October 1970, the twenty-fifth Anniversary of the United Nations.

146 (1986) ICJ *Reports,* 1986, 108.

of diplomats[147] and the Convention Against the Taking of Hostages of 1979.[148]

The Convention to Punish and Prevent Acts of Terrorism of 1971 of the Organisation of American States (OAS) prohibits[149] terrorism on a general scale by a Treaty on a regional basis. The reason for the OAS adopting this Convention was the recurring hi-jacking incidents in the 1960s in the American region, particularly to Cuba.

The first attempt to curb aeroplane hi-jacking on a global scale was made in the Tokyo Convention of 1963 on Offenses and Certain Other Acts Committed on Board Aircraft. This Convention provides that the country of registration exercises jurisdiction over any crime committed on board or against its aircraft. This was done to ensure that hi-jackers are properly brought to trial in a State. Offenses committed on board aircraft registered in a State would be considered as if they had been committed in that State and, if the aeroplane landed in another State, a hi-jacker could be extradited as the Convention made the offense an extraditable crime. Furthermore, certain disciplinary powers are also given to the crew and even to passengers on aircraft.

A more comprehensive attempt to regulate hi-jacking was made in the Hague Convention for the Suppression of Unlawful Seizure of Aircraft of 1970. This Convention applies partly the principle of *aut dedere aut punire*, *i.e.* the principle that a State should either extradite a hi-jacker or punish him itself. Under the Convention States pledge to punish the crime of hi-jacking (which is not given that name) by severe penalties.[150] The Convention also widens the scope of jurisdiction by providing that a State has jurisdiction if the aircraft is registered in that State, or if it lands in its territory or, finally, if the offense is committed on an aircraft which is leased by a company having its place of business in a contracting State.

Extradition, which the Hague Convention sought to ensure in case

---

[147] The full, very long, title of the Convention is the UN Convention on the Prevention and Punishment of Crimes Against Internationally Protected Persons, Including Diplomatic Agents, 1973 13 ILM 1974, 41.

[148] UKTS 1983:81.

[149] Article 8.

[150] Article 1.

terrorists were tried by an arresting State, is at the root of the problem. There have been considerable problems to effect extradition of terrorists for trial. Abu Daoud, who was thought to have been involved in the Munich massacre was not extradited by France but allowed to fly to Algeria. The problem about extradition is that normal extradition treaties usually exclude precisely political crimes. But terrorist acts are usually political and do not therefore fall into the extraditable category. There is thus a need for further specific conventions on terrorism which allow for extradition.

The Montreal Convention of 1971[151] was designed to combat terrorist attacks other than hi-jacking, for example armed attack or sabotage. As not all crimes take place when the aircraft is flying the Convention supplemented the previous 'in-flight' criterion used by the Hague Convention by an 'in-service' qualification covering incidents which occur while the aircraft is on the ground. Although it covers more types of crimes, the Montreal Convention repeats provisions similar to those of the Hague Convention with regard to jurisdiction. The Conventions is supplemented by the Montreal Protocol of 1988 on Suppression of Unlawful Acts of Violence at Airports Serving Civil Aviation.[152]

A special form of terrorism is the *maritime terrorism*, involving attacks on civilians on board ships, or oil platforms, and yet outside the reach of the traditional law of piracy.[153] There have been numerous incidents of this type even after the *Achille Lauro* incident in 1983, which left concerned States without recourse. The Rome Convention of 1988 for general unlawful acts against maritime safety now regulates such violence[154] and its Protocol provides similar rules to protect oil platforms.[155]

For terrorist acts beyond hi-jacking or maritime terrorism there are some regional conventions. The Council of Europe adopted a

---

[151]   UKTS 1974, No. 10.

[152]   27 ILM 1988, 628.

[153]   As defined *supra*, in this Chapter.

[154]   Convention for the Suppression of Unlawful Acts Against the Safety of Maritime Navigation of 1988, 1988, 27 ILM 1988, 672.

[155]   Protocol on Fixed Platforms Located on the Continental Shelf, 1988, *ibid.* 685.

Convention on the Suppression of Terrorism in 1976.[156] However, an escape clause was included in the Convention[157] whereby ratifying States can exclude the operation of the Convention by reserving their rights in the case they consider an offense to be

> 'a political offense, an offense connected with a political offence, or any offence inspired by political motives.'

As a political element often forms an essential ingredient in terrorism, this extremely wide clause undermines the whole operation of the Convention. Sweden, Norway, Denmark and Iceland have all used the right to reserve this right.

v. Human Rights

Ermacora, *Menschenrechte in der sich wandelden Welt*, 1974; Donnelly, *Universal Human Rights in Theory and Practice*, 1989; Sieghart, *The International Law of Human Rights*, 1983; Robinson, *Human Rights and Fundamental Freedoms in the Charter of the UN*, 1946; Robinson, *The Universal Declaration on Human Rights*, 1958; Bridge (ed.), *Fundamental Rights*, 1973; Guradze, *Der Stand der Menschenrechte im Völkerrecht*, 1956; Klecatsky, Menschenrechte, innerstaatliches Rechtsschutz und Volkanwaltschaft, JBl 1985, 577; Sohn-Burgenthal, *International Protection of Human Rights*, 1973; Lauterpacht, *International Law and Human Rights*, 1950; Higgins, Derogations in Human Rights treaties, BYIL 1976/77 281; Walter, *Die Europäische Menschenrechtordnung*, 1970; Sperduti, Protection of Human Rights and the principle of non-intervention in the domestic concerns of States, 63 AnnIDI 1989 i 309; Macdonald, Johnston & Morris (eds.), *The International Law and Policy of Human Welfare*, 1978; Meron, (ed.), *Human Rights in International Law*, 1984; Jacobs, *The European Convention on Human Rights*, 1975; van Dijk & van Hoof, *Theory and Practice of the European Convention on Human Rights*, 1984; Wershof (ed.), *International Human Rights*, Canadian Council on International Law, 1978; Gottlied (ed.), *Human Rights, Federalism and Minorities*, 1970; Glenn, *Le pacte international relatif aux droits civils et politiques et la Convention européenne des droits de l'homme*, 1975; Beddard, *Human Rights and Europe*, 1980; Robertson, *Human Rights in Europe*, 2nd ed., 1977; Nedjati, *Human Rights Under the European Convention*, 1978; Frowein, European Integration Through Fundamental Rights, 18 JL Ref 1984 5; Morrison, *The Dynamics of Development in the European Human Rights System*, 1981.

---

[156]   15 ILM 1976, 1272.
[157]   Article 13.

The power of a State in its own territory is limited in so far as it is bound to afford certain standards of treatment to individuals. This duty is a direct duty of international law itself and it is irrelevant what provisions a State sees fit or not fit to insert in its own legislative rules.

Human Rights can be distinguished and classified according to whether they visualise the protection of specific groups or whether they guarantee certain persons, or all, special guarantees *qua* individuals. Forms of group protection are normally called 'collective rights' as distinguished from 'individual rights.'

(I) COLLECTIVE RIGHTS

a. Self-Determination

The most important rights enjoyed by *peoples* rather than by States is the right of self-determination. The rule that peoples shall govern themselves obviously forms a core of international society and few would nowadays contest that the rule of self-determination constitutes an important Human Right. Self-determination means that individuals have the right to determine the social rules that are to bind them.[158] Self-government to some would mean *moral consensus* and rely on many ideas of, for example, Rousseau.[159] But *which* individuals or groups shall have such right of self-determination?

Some take the view that it is literally a question of a right of single individuals.[160] Marxists say the right belongs to a *class* of people. Others claim that it is a right enjoyed by a *people*. A President of the United States even used those two terms as interchangeable when he wrote to Russia, at the time of the Russian Revolution, that

'No people must be forced under sovereignty under which its

---

[158]   Lively, *Democracy*, 1980, 136 and, further, *supra*, 119.

[159]   Rameau, *Contrat social et discourses*, 1947, 12.

[160]   Rowen, *The Quest for Self-Determination*, 1979, 54-55.

does not wish to live.'[161]

This remarkable message, ignored in international law and in political doctrine, illustrates the role of the United States in the Russian Revolution to the dismay of the free world of which the United States has been the traditional spokesman.

The message implied that the Czarist rule had been a yoke to the Russian people and that the United States was supporting the movement to remove that regime - a regime to be replaced, after Kerensky - by the Bolsheviks who were responsible for countless atrocities. The Bolsheviks were also responsible for Russia's rapid and irreversible economic decline, demoting her, to the delight of Germany and other countries, from being a main competitor, as she had been, in shipbuilding and in other industries. It is possible that the Bolsheviks could not have succeded without the initial support of the United States to remove the Czar.

In the contemporary legal system the right of self-determination needs to be well defined to preempt random fragmentation of States. If the right of self-determination is encouraged, without specific qualification, there is a clear risk of undermining the stability of the international legal order. It is not conducive to peace to allow groups to break away to form their own States which, perhaps, will lack economic viability and which might be politically dependent on other States.[162]

On the other hand, *who* is to decide which unit *deserves* to have its own State? We can not expect the United Nations, or the Great Powers, to play such a role or we will revert to the undesirable order under, for example, the *Concert Européen* during past centuries. The test for new States, therefore, might be what we have suggested in an earlier Chapter:[163] the *consistent and determined will* of the people in the region will be decisive as to whether a new State is to be formed. Only by insisting on such a criterion, coupled with constant

---

[161] Message from President Woodrow Wilson on 16th May 1917 to Russia, see Baker & Dodd, *War and Peace, Presidential Messages, Addresses and Public Papers 1917-1924 of Woodrow Wilson*, 1927, i, 50.

[162] For examples of *puppet States*, see *supra*, Chapter II.

[163] See *supra* under Nations in Chapter II.

reminders of the advantages, in terms of economy, defence and political strength, of federal units, can we arrive at viable State structures in international society.

The legal basis and the detailed rules of self-determination were set out below in the context of the incidents of statehood.[164]

b. Democracy

(i) General Remarks

Another collective Human Right to which has been discussed on several occasions above in various contexts[165] is the right of democracy, the right of peoples to take an active part in the running of their country. Such a right now forms a new condition for statehood and, for those States which are already established, lack of democracy can furnish the ground for introducing important sanctions. It is important to underline that the demand for democratic control and the claim of a Human Right of democracy is quite new.

We shall see the important role played by the notion of democracy in the context of recognition.[166]

(ii) Influence on Decision Making in International Organisations

A specific form of democracy is the recent trend to allow representatives of individuals in the form of 'parliaments' in international organisations to have their voice heard and to contribute to the decision making of the organisation.

As we have seen above,[167] international organisations have normally an *executive organ*, consisting of a few Members, a *legislative organ*, where all Members are represented,[168] as well, at

---

[164]   *Supra*, 58.

[165]   See *supra* under States, and under Recognition, in Chapter II.

[166]   *Supra*, 78 *et seq.*

[167]   See on the structure of organisations *supra* in Chapter II.

[168]   Note that some organisations, like ICAO, gives most decision making power to the Executive, the Council; other organisations, like ILO, UPU and ITU, allow others than Members to vote in the Assembly, see *supra* in Chapter II.

times, as Courts and other organs. A few international organisations have parliaments where individuals play a decisive role.

The Council of Europe has such a parliament where individuals may act although the powers of this body, so far, are modest. The Parliament of the European Community, long thought to be unimportant and ineffective, has now increased its role. It now enjoys important powers in relation to the expansion of the Community and will have a role to play in considering applications for new membership in the Communities.

The reforms of the European Union have also increased the power of its Parliament: the Members of the European Parliament (MEPs) play nowadays an important role to safeguard democracy in EU.

(iii) Minority Rights

Lados-Lederer, *International Group Protection*, 1968; Modéen, *The International Protection of National Minorities in Europe*, 1969; Pircher, *Der vertägliche Schutz ethnischen, sprachlichen und religiösen Minderheiten im Völkerrecht*, 1979; Stone, *International Guarantees of Minority Rights*, 1932; Gottlied (ed.), *Human Rights, Federalism and Minorities*, 1970.

Earlier minority treaties sought to secure minorities in States and protect their interests. Many Peace Treaties traditionally included specific provisions on the treatment of minorities, and such minorities were uplifted to be subjects of international law.[169] After the First World War there was a network of provisions, in the Treaty of Versailles itself and, furthermore, in the Peace Treaties of St. Germain,[170] Neuilly,[171] Trianon[172] and Lausanne,[173] limiting the right of territorial States with regard to minorities. The Peace Treaties after the First World War offered options for the choice of nationality by individuals based on ethnic rather than on geographical

---

[169] *Cf. supra*, on minorities as subjects of law, 119 *et seq.* and, for early examples of treaties, the Treaty of Westphalia, 1648.

[170] On Austria, 28 LNTS 222.

[171] On Bulgaria, *ibid.*

[172] On Hungary, *ibid.*

[173] On Turkey, *ibid.* and *cf.* Romania, Treaty of 1919, UKTS No. 6, 1920; Greece, Treaty of 1920, UKTS No. 13, 1920.

criteria[174] with a system of protection for minorities.

This can be perceived as a development to loosen the State from its territorial base[175] or at least a loosening of the ethnic groups from the framework of the territorial State, giving them special protection as well as some influence in the territory where they live. Certain new States, some of which formed by the decision of the Great Powers, rather than by their own will, also had to assume obligations concerning protection of minorities.[176]

Recently it is particularly minorities that have received benefit from the Convention on Racial Discrimination of 1965[177] which, under an Optional Protocol, allows individual petitions.

Nowadays the interests of minorities often coincide with the groups which wish to exercise the right of self-determination.[178] It is extremely important to effectively safeguard the rights of minorities precisely to avoid the right of self-determination being used in an inappropriate way if a group of minority people do not find their interests adequately protected within, for example, a federal State. It is, as mentioned above, not in the interest of international society to encourage the fragmentation of States and many such break-ups need not occur if statesmen realise their obligation to look after the interests of minorities.

The identification of minority groups is relevant in so far as any attempt to harm minorities is an indication of potential violations of Human Rights of citizens or of aliens[179] by a majority regime.

To sum up the situation: minorities thus enjoy special protection under several headings: (1) under general rules of international law concerning *both* self-determination and basic Human Rights; (2) under special minority treaties or treaty clauses; (3) under the rules allowing the home State of aliens to intervene by *jus protectionis*.

---

[174]   *E.g.*, the Versailles Treaty on 'Czechs' and 'Poles' of 'German nationality'.

[175]   *Cf.* Schätzel, 3 *Internationales Recht*, 1962, 180-186.

[176]   This was the case of Yugoslavia, see Treaty of 1919, UKTS No. 17, 1920.

[177]   Adopted by GA Res 2106 (XX) on the basis of an earlier GA Res on Racial Discrimination 1904 (XVIII) of 1963.

[178]   *Supra*, 119 *et seq.* and 58 *et seq.*

[179]   See, *infra* on *jus protectionis*.

(iv) Majority Rule

Majority rule is another form of collective Human Rights, guaranteeing democratic rule by the rule of the majority.[180] Such majorities are, in their own right, specific subjects of international law, as we have seen earlier in another context.[181]

After the demise of apartheid in South Africa the question of majority rule have taken on a different dimension: it is now of largely historical interest with regard to a country where the black majority for long time was not allowed to form their own government. On the other hand, it is by means certain that similar systems will not develop in other States in the future disallowing the majority their say in the government. However, on balance the problem of denying majority rule as a collective Human Right would appear to be a problem of the past.

c. The Right to Development

Third World countries often claim that they enjoy a right to development. However, as I have had occasion to point out,[182] this is merely a programmatic aim that States can set themselves and a moral duty devoid of legal compulsion. However, there is slowly developing a legal element of this right of development caused by the clear nexus between ethics and legal obligation in this field.

The right of development, like indeed the right to food which is occasionally mentioned as a 'new Human Right',[183] are certainly rights which the international society should consider *de lege ferenda* but, until they are properly formulated and expressed they cannot but confuse rights which are already legally protected. It is important to continue the discussion on the modalities of future legal rights to be accorded to the poorer nations. At times, simple appeal to morality, conscience and compassion may be most effective to promote vague

---

[180] See *supra* under Majorities as Subjects of International Law.
[181] See *supra* in Chapter II under iii f.
[182] *Concept, op. cit.,* 68 *et seq.*
[183] See *supra*, in this Chapter.

notions into the realm of properly secured legal rights.[184]

On the other hand, it may well be that these rights will, in due course, enjoy legal protection, provided they are succinctly defined and limited to clear categories.

(II) INDIVIDUAL HUMAN RIGHTS

a. Basic Human Rights

There is a qualitative difference between the collective rights reviewed above and individual Human Rights. On the one hand, the individual Human Rights are those which, to most persons, would be the most important ones: if there is no right to life and if there is torture, rights like self-determination fade somewhat into the background.

Few, if any, international lawyers doubt that Human Rights, on the individual scale, have developed into legally protected rights. But not all Human Rights have attained this quality. There are few subjects as vague as Human Rights in international law and sometimes insistence on peripheral rights has detracted attention from the viable core rights.[185]

As with most rules in international law, there is here an important question of hierarchy. Thus, there are some Human Rights which are bound to be more important than others. Thus, the right to life, modestly formulated as a right to *avoid genocide*, the right to *avoid torture* or *inhuman treatment* as well as the right to avoid genocide, would appear to apply without treaties binding a State. Although there are now conventions which specifically prohibit genocide,[186] torture[187] and attempts are made to define and prohibit other acts of

---

184   *Catéchisme de l'Eglise Catholique*, 1992, 2437 *et seq*, Justice et solidarié entre les nations.

185   *Cf.* Alston, Conjuring up New Human Rights, AJIL 1984, 607.

186   For the Genocide Convention 1948 see 78 UNTS 278.

187   See the Torture Convention of 1984, the Inter-American Convention on Torture, 24 ILM 1985, 519 and the European Torture Convention 1987, 27 ILM 1988, 1152.

inhuman treatment of individuals,[188] it is clear that such acts are *anyway* prohibited under general international law. Thus, any State which is guilty of such acts may be a target for important international sanctions[189] and even *individuals* who are guilty of such crimes may face prosecution.[190]

These rights are adequately called *natural rights* and States have, in clear unilateral, collective or multilateral acts,[191] accepted that certain basic rights of individuals are protected. Such natural rights form an important part of natural law[192] as discussed in modern writings and which were the result of reaction against excesses during the Second World War. For example, some philosophers[193] designed precisely their theories to show that national laws must, on occasions, be opposed by a higher set of rules, that of ethical standards and of natural law.[194]

It is of special importance that the Universal Declaration, as well as the two UN Covenants on Human Rights, on Civil and Political Rights as well as on Economic, Social and Cultural Rights,[195] all in their Preambles refer to the *inherent dignity of the human person*, a phrase which is meaningless unless we conceive it within the framework of a natural law system.[196]

That numerous Human Rights are protected in international law without being specified in treaties or conventions is furthermore fully proved by the Nuremberg and Tokyo Trials where individuals were held responsible for gross violations of basic Human Rights although there was not a comprehensive treaty system at the time for the protection of violated rights. The defense of the accused individuals,

---

[188] See ILC Draft Code of Offences Against Peace and Security of Mankind, *Yearbook* 1954 onwards; 1982 ii 2 121; and later Reports.

[189] See *infra* in Chapter VIII.

[190] See my *Law of War, op. cit.,* Chapter V, and *cf.* examples of case law, *infra.*

[191] *Supra,* on Recognition of Ethical Rules under Sources, in Chapter III.

[192] See Finnis, *Natural Law and Natural Rights,* Oxford, 1990, *passim.*

[193] See *supra* in Chapter III for numerous references.

[194] Thus Shaw, *International Law,* 1986 49.

[195] On these agreements, *infra,* in this Chapter.

[196] Verdross, *Abendländische Rechtsphilosphie,* 2nd ed., 1963, 257 *et seq.*; *idem, Das Würde des Menschen und ihr völkerrechtlicher Schutz,* 1975; Verdross & Simma, *Universelles Völkerrecht,* 3rd ed., 1984, 824.

that, for example, they had only *followed orders*, was discarded by the prosecution and any reliance on superior orders (*respondeat superior*) was ineffective.[197]

The International Court of Justice has expressly recognised that *fundamental Human Rights* must be respected as part of obligations of Member States under the Charter, or under general international law.[198] The obligations on Human Rights laid down in the Charter, though imperfect with regard to enforcement, are certainly binding on the Member States and constitute proper legal obligations,[199] and their basis are certainly found in general international law. The ICJ also emphasised in the *Hostage Case*[200] that

'Wrongfully to deprive human beings of their freedom and to subject them to physical constraint in conditions of hardship is in itself manifestly incompatible with the principles of the Charter of the United Nations, as well as with the fundamental principles enunciated in the Universal Declaration on Human Rights.'

Numerous internal courts have also recognised the existence of international crimes, regardless of whether there are international treaties on the matter. In the important and widely reported *Filartiga v Pena-Irala Case* a United States Court held that torture gives rise to universal jurisdictional rights as

'the torturer has become - like the pirate and slave-trader before him - *hostis humani generis,* an enemy of all mankind.'[201]

The German Supreme Court spoke in the much commented *Case on*

---

[197] See, in detail, my *Law of War, op. cit.*, 353 *et seq.*

[198] *The Namibia Case* (1971), ICJ *Reports* at 57.

[199] This view was recently confirmed in Oppenheim, *International Law*, edited by the President of the ICJ, Sir Robert Jennings, and the former Legal Adviser to the FCO, Sir Arthur Watts, 1990 i 989.

[200] (1980) ICJ *Reports* 1980, 42.

[201] (1980) 630 F 2d 876, 890 (2d Cir. 1980). *Cf. Demjanjuk v Petrovsky* (1985) F 2d 571, 582 on universal jurisdiction for war criminals.

Botschaftenkonten[202] of the compelling *minimum standard* for Human Rights under general international law. The *Eichmann Case*,[203] also illustrates this point on binding rules under general international law. Although the defendant had probably been seized by illegal means in Argentine,[204] the case shows that a national court found genocide to be an international crime under general international law, regardless of the fact that the Genocide Convention was adopted *after* the Second World War.[205]

Many basic rights have been entrenched by a network of treaties which clarify and reinforce protection of specific rights. This is, for example, the case with regard to *slavery,* where a number of Conventions on both traditional slavery and white slave trade have been concluded.[206] The way prohibitions on slavery are repeated in later documents,[207] however, indicate that the rights are viewed as so intrinsic, so truistic that they are included as a *pleonasm*: even without such inclusion they would be, as amply proved in international practice and case-law, fully effective.

---

[202] (1977) BVerfGE 46, 362.

[203] 36 ILR 5.

[204] *Contra*, Shaw, *International Law,* 1986 135 who claims that international law *permits* a State to exercise jurisdiction 'notwithstanding the illegality of the apprehension', a statement which may be influenced by attitudes in English law to cases like *Entick v Carrington.* Israel's action against Eichmann may illustrate that his actions constituted *international crimes* but does not *per se* legitimise the process against him which had, by his seizure in Argentina, involved a serious infringement of territorial sovereignty, which cannot be condoned by the international legal system.

[205] Even the Israeli law of 1951 under which Eichmann was prosecuted was of a date later than his acts.

[206] For example, the Treaty of London 1841; the General Act of the Congo Conference of Berlin 1885; the General Act of the Anti-Slavery Conference of Brussels 1890 as revised by the Treaty of St. Germain of 1919, 8 LNTS 26; Agreement on Suppression of White Slave Traffic 1904, 1 LNTS 1, and of 1910, 3 LNTS 278; Convention on Suppression of Traffic in Women and Children 1922, 9 LNTS 415; the League of Nations Slavery Convention 1926, 60 LNTS 253; Convention for Suppression of Traffic in Persons and of the Exploitation of Prostitution of Others 1949, 55 UNTS.

[207] For example, article 4 of Universal Declaration; article 8 of the Covenant on Civil and Political Rights; article 4 in the European Convention; article 6 in the Inter-American Convention on Human Rights; on these instruments see *infra.*

It is the Human Rights of life and body that may appropriately be subsumed under the *international minimum standard of treatment*.[208] It is this *international standard* that has been violently attacked in Marxist doctrine, with effect and over-spill in all communist and socialist States, which prefer to stress the *power of the State*, implying a right, or exclusive prerogative, of the State to decide on the level of treatment of individuals in their territory.[209] It is useful if States expressly acknowledge the international minimum standard even if they prefer to raise the level of treatment in their Constitution. However, whether they acknowledge the existence or not of the international minimum standard, States are immediately bound to comply with it, as shown, for example, in the War Crimes cases.

By superficial analysis it may appear that some Human Rights cannot by themselves be universal: one example would appear to be the right of property, a Human Right of obvious ancillary nature as less important than the Human Rights which concern life, physical suffering or physical humiliation. The reason for this special treatment of a specific Human Right, appeared, before the fall of communism, to be that international law is a universal system and must accommodate all socio-economic systems and that it is not for international law to be political and partial. If there was a universal right of property, it could be argued, a State could not become Marxist and nationalise property of its own nationals without compensation.

On this other ideas must now be adopted as it is now clear that no society - as also Plato found in his later writings - can actually function without the right of property.[210] Some minimal right of property, however, is probably, warranted as an indispensable right as a legal system does not appear to function in proprietary vacuum where individuals are deprived of such rights.

---

[208] On the choice between national and international standards for treatment, see in Chapter VII under *jus protectionis*.

[209] Note, however, that the reason for the United States not ratifying the UN Covenants on Human Rights (on these, see later in this Chapter) was that the standard afforded under the US Constitution, with amendments, was considered *higher* than the international minimum standard.

[210] See my *Äganderätten och Europa*, 1992, *passim*.

There are, and have been for some considerable time, clear rules on what a State has to do to pay aliens adequate, prompt and effective compensation[211] for the taking of property. This right now appears to extend *also to a State's own nationals* and thus does appear to constitute a general Human Right. It could also be argued, as it was done in *The Lithgow Case* before the European Court of Human Rights[212] that there are regional rules of general application[213] in Western Europe to pay nationals fair compensation in the event of nationalisation; in all constitutions in Western Europe there are such provisions and it was argued that the same applied in the United Kingdom which does not have a written constitution.

It is now clear, after the collapse of communism/socialism where property rights were demoted to a very low place in the hierarchy of Human Rights, that no economic system can survive unless there is some modest form of private ownership.[214] There is therefore now ground for suggesting that a *minimum right of property*, might be one that must not be displaced, at least not by outright confiscation outside the realm of penal law, or at least not by arbitrary action.

b. General Instruments of Protection

Human Rights have been defined and clarified in specific instruments on Human Rights. Even those which are technically non-binding, as the Universal Declaration of Human Rights which constitutes a recommendation of the General Assembly,[215] does great service to the international legal system by *crystallising* and expressing rules in a document which becomes a point of reference. There is no doubt, furthermore, that the Universal Declaration merely codifies what is already binding under general international law.

Beyond declarations and specific statements which thus may

---

211   See my *Äganderätten och Europa*, 1992, *passim*.

212   *Sir William Lithgow and Others v United Kingdom*, (1986), ECHR *Reports*, 1986.

213   Thus lifted up to international general principles as those mentioned in article 38 of the ICJ Statute; see further, *supra* in Chapter III on the Sources of Law.

214   See my *Äganderätten och Europa*, 1992, *passim*.

215   See on the legal effect of recommendations, *supra* in Chapter III.

clarify and to a large extent *reflect* general international law, there are also numerous treaties and Conventions which, of course may *enlarge* the ambit of Human Rights and penalise violations which are not breaches against general international law. Some such conventions also introduce concrete appeal systems which are not available (yet) under general international law and thus provide concrete means for individuals to introduce specific complaints in special Human Rights courts.

(i) The Universal Declaration

One list of Human Rights embodying those which have been thought important in doctrine and practice is found in the 1949 Universal Declaration on Human Rights, a recommendation of the General Assembly,[216] to which it is often referred.

The Universal Declaration of 1948 may well have legal force as an instrument reflecting standards of treatment of individuals accepted by the majority of States as binding norms.[217]

It is not the fact that the Declaration was adopted as a Resolution of the General Assembly which lends it binding force; it is binding because States have *recognised its precepts as binding legal values.*[218]

(ii) The Universal Covenants

Floretta & Öhlinger, *Die Menschenrechtspakte der Vereinten Nationen*, 1978.

1. THE COVENANT ON CIVIL AND POLITICAL RIGHTS

Nowak, *UNO-Pakt über bürgerliche und politische Rechte und Fakultativprotokoll*, 1989; Tomuschat, Equality and non-discrimination under the International Covenant on Civil and Political Rights, *Festschrift Schlochauer*, 1981, 691.

The United Nations Covenant of 1966 on Civil and Political Rights

---

[216]   *Supra,* 102 *et seq.*
[217]   *Cf. supra*, under Recommendations of the General Assembly.
[218]   See *supra* in Chapter III under D b (iv).

which entered into force in 1976[219] is becoming most important in the safeguard of human rights and is being supervised by the Human Rights Committee in Geneva which has already heard a number of cases in a quasi-judicial capacity.

The Covenant on Civil and Political Rights has proved more important than the second Covenant on economic, social and cultural rights, which demands greater sacrifices by contracting States. The Covenant on Civil and Political Right has thus had a greater impact, for the simple reason that much of what is contained in the convention is already binding under general international law. This instrument contains provisions guaranteeing the right to life,[220] prohibition of slavery,[221] of torture or other degrading or inhuman treatment.[222] Further provisions secure the right of movement,[223] right of privacy with regard to family, home and correspondence[224] and the right of freedom of thought, conscience and religion[225] and freedom of expression and opinion,[226] right of peaceful assembly and freedom of association, such as forming trade unions.[227] The right to marry is specially mentioned[228] and the Covenant stipulates that marriage presupposes free and full consent of the spouses. Children are guaranteed special protection, name and nationality.

Much of the Covenant is devoted to securing fairness of criminal procedure, independence of courts, equality before the courts[229]and prohibition of retroactive law in criminal matters.[230] All those in custody and in prison must be treated with humanity[231] and no one

---

[219] The Covenant has been ratified by 89 States but only 12 LDCs had, by 1990, found it useful to adhere to this instrument.

[220] Article 6.

[221] Article 8.

[222] Article 7.

[223] Article 12.

[224] Article 17.

[225] Article 18.

[226] Article 19.

[227] Articles 21 and 22.

[228] Article 23.

[229] Articles 14 and 26.

[230] Article 15.

[231] Article 10.

must be required to do forced labour.[232] An unusual provision secures rights of aliens: they may not be expelled except in certain circumstances if they are lawfully in the territory of a State.[233] Other provisions specifically secures the right of ethnic, religious and linguistic minorities.

The Covenant on Economic and Social Rights provides for rights to fair wages,[234] equal rights for men and women,[235] with special consideration for mothers, children and young persons,[236] the right to education up to secondary level,[237] the right to form trade unions and to strike,[238] the right to social security,[239] and the right to take part in cultural life.[240] The most important right guaranteed in the Covenant is the right to work[241] but this is also the most controversial right: how can a State with an unemployment problem guarantee work to its citizens?

It is at this stage that we must admit that the Covenant, in many respects, is a proclamation of desired, rather than compulsory, objectives. Naturally, there are substantive obligations in the Covenant to the extent that a State binds itself by ratification to provide a certain specified level of treatment once its nationals are engaged in work. However, the basic right to work itself may not yet exist for the mere reason that it is a right dependent on factual premises beyond the full control of a democratic State.

On the other hand, there is a most important implementation procedure. The Covenant on Civil and Political Rights provides for review by a Human Rights Committee on the basis of written information. The implementation of the Covenant is thus supervised by the Committee, located in Geneva, and, although the Committee

---

[232]   Article 8.
[233]   Article 13.
[234]   Article 6.
[235]   Article 3.
[236]   Article 10.
[237]   Articles 13 and 14.
[238]   Article 8.
[239]   Article 9.
[240]   Article 15.
[241]   Article 6.

is not a judicial body, the impact of its views is substantial. It hears complaints about violations of the Covenant and makes its views known to the State party involved.[242] The Committee may conduct investigations into alleged violations of Human Rights by States[243] whereupon the Committee may lend its good offices to arrive at a friendly solution.

The Committee can receive petitions from one State against another, provided both have agreed to such communications.[244] A mechanism that may become more important, and which has already shown some important results, is the individual right of complaint that individuals may have been given under the Optional Protocol to the Covenant on Civil and Political Rights.[245] However, the Committee cannot take binding decisions nor declarations of violation of the Covenants. The procedure prescribes that all communications must be in writing and all local remedies must have been exhausted.[246]

The procedure for the enforcement of the rights in the Covenant may be deficient. However, the right of petition on a universal scale marks a considerable improvement.

2. THE COVENANT ON SOCIAL AND ECONOMIC RIGHTS

Alston, A third generation of solidarity rights: progressive development or obfuscation of international Human Rights law? NedTIL 1982, 85.

The second Covenant, the Covenant on Social and Economic Rights had by 1990 been ratified by 94 States but the vast majority of these are the industrialised nations whereas less developed States, the LDCs, have found it difficult to accept the obligations laid down in

---

[242] See article 41 of the Covenant on Civil and Political Rights.

[243] This is done on the basis of reports transmitted from the Secretary General at regular intervals.

[244] Article 41.

[245] The Protocol entered into force in 1976. See, for case law, UN Doc CCPR/C/OP, *Selected Decisions under the Optional Protocol*, 1985. Cases are occasionally reported elsewhere, see, for example, *The Bazzano Case*, (1970) 19 ILM 133.

[246] As in all international court and tribunal procedures, this implies that the remedies which might have been effective must have been used to the highest instance of appeal, see *infra* under *jus protectionis* in Chapter VII.

this Covenant: only 13 LDCs have adhered to the Covenant.

The United Nations Covenant on Economic, Social and Cultural Rights, is merely subject to periodic review by the ECOSOC[247] to which the Secretary General submits received reports.[248] Possibly because of its wide and sensitive ambit, this second Covenant, on Economic, Social and Cultural Rights, lacks the mechanisms of the sister Covenant on Civil and Political Rights.

(iii) Other Global Human Rights Conventions

A host of other important conventions on Human Rights exist, providing together a complex and comprehensive network of rules for the benefit of individuals, especially if they also have been ratified by LDCs.

These Conventions prohibit slavery,[249] torture,[250] or forms of racial discrimination,[251] discrimination of women[252] or other forms of discrimination.[253] Other Conventions, of which the International

---

[247] ECOSOC is one of the main organs of the United Nations, see *supra,* 102 *et seq.* After review of a case it may refer a matter to the Human Rights Commission, one of its own subsidiary organs in Geneva.

[248] Reports have been forwarded in this manner since 1970.

[249] The Slavery Convention of 1926 ratified by 34 States of which 9 LDCs. Note that slavery is also prohibited by article 4 of Universal Declaration; article 8 of the Covenant on Civil and Political Rights; article 4 in the European Convention; article 6 in the Inter-American Convention on Human Rights; see *supra.*

[250] The Convention Against Torture and Other Cruel, Inhuman or Degrading Treatment or Punishment 1984 entered into force in 1987, ratified by 50 States of which only six developing countries.

[251] See Convention adopted in 1965 by GA Res 2144 (XXI).

[252] The Convention on the Political Rights of Women of 1952 ratified by 95 States of which 14 LDCs; ILO Convention No. 156 concerning Equal Opportunities for Men and Women Workers, ratified by 16 States of which three are developing countries.

[253] UNESCO Convention Against Discrimination in Education of 1960 ratifed by 77 States of which five developing countries; ILO Convention No. 111 Concerning Discrimination in Respect of Employment and Occupation of 1958 ratified by 111 States and of these 24 developing countries; The Convention for the Elimination of All Forms of Discrimination Against Women of 1979 ratified by 101 States (18 developing countries).

Labour Organisation has been an important catalyst, ensure acceptable working conditons.[254] Also agreements which seek to alleviate the plight of refugees should be mentioned in this context.[255]

(iv) An International Bill of Rights?

Instruments which *together* have been said[256] to constitute an International Bill of Human Rights are the Universal Declaration of Human Rights, issued as a General Assembly Resolution in 1948, the Covenant on Economic, Social and Political Rights and the Covenant on Civil and Political Rights, both of 1966, and, finally, the Optional Protocol to the last mentioned Covenant. The reference to these documents as such a Bill presumably indicates the wide acceptance that rules contained in the documents are binding irrespective of specific adherence; or, in other terms, that the consent of States is *presumed.*[257]

The basic provisions of many of the other global agreements just referred to, could probably also be considered to be incorporated in the generally binding rules.

(v) Regional Agreements

In the field of Human Rights there is now a considerable network of rules binding States and in several cases an individual can now have the right of action against his own State in an international Court.

1. THE EUROPEAN CONVENTION

Among extensive literature, see Cohen-Jonathan, *La Convention européenne des*

---

[254] For example, ILO Convention No. 138 on Minimum Working Age, ratified by four developing countries; ILO Convention No. 29 on Forced Labour ratified by 130 States of which 28 are developing countries.

[255] *E.g.,* the Convention relating to the Status of Refugees of 1951 ratified by 103 States of which 30 are developing countries. Note Protocol relating to the Status of Refugees of 1966. *Cf.* the Convention on the Status of Stateless Persons of 1954; Convention on the Reduction of Statelessness, 1961.

[256] OMCT, *Development and Human Rights*, 1990, 30.

[257] On such construction, see my *Concept, op. cit.*, 97.

droits de l'homme, 1989; Monconduit, *La Commission européenne des droits de l'homme* 1965; Beddard, *Human Rights and Europe,* 2nd ed., 1980; Fawcett, *The Application of the European Convention on Human Rights,* 2nd ed., 1987; van Dijk & van Hoof, *Theory and Practice of the European Convention on Human Rights,* 1984; Robertson, *Human Rights in Europe,* 2nd ed., 1977; Jacobs, *The European Convention on Human Rights,* 1975; Nedjati, *Human Rights Under the European Convention,* 1978.

On a regional scale the European Convention of Human Rights of 1950,[258] linked to the Council of Europe, is of great importance. The Convention guarantees the right of life,[259] prohibits torture and inhuman or degrading treatment,[260] slavery,[261] and entrenches the rights of liberty,[262] and of due process, implying the right of a fair trial.[263] The Convention protects *all persons* present in the territory of a Contracting State, including non-nationals.[264]

A Member State of the Council of Europe which is bound by the Convention may *enter derogations* which has the same meaning as the normal system of reservations to treaties.[265] Derogations are intended to limit the application of the Convention in cases of 'public emergencies threatening the life of the nation'. The right to make a reservation under the Convention is consequently limited to dramatic cases. The United Kingdom has now made such a special derogation with regard to the situation in Northern Ireland, following the condemnation of the United Kingdom in one specific case.[266]

The European Convention is one of the first treaties to allow individuals the *right of petition to a court* and the right has, in practice, played an important role. However, numerous applications to the Commission, which investigates the first stage of a case, prove inadmissible and few are accepted to go through to the Court.

---

[258] 213 UNTS 221.

[259] Article 1.

[260] Article 2.

[261] Article 4.

[262] Article 5.

[263] Article 6.

[264] *Berrehub v The Netherlands* (1989) 11 EHRR 322, concerning a Moroccan citizen in Holland.

[265] See my *Essays on the Law of Treaties,* 1967, Chapter IX.

[266] *Brogan v UK* (1989) 11 EHRR 117 on article 5(3).

Among the more important cases heard by the Court we may mention *The Sunday Times Case*[267] where an English newspaper defied an injunction granted by an English court to draw attention to the dangers of the drug thalidomide; the European Court of Human Rights found that the injunction contravened the right to freedom of expression laid down in article 10 of the European Convention. We may also mention *The Tyrer Case*, again against the United Kingdom[268] where birching was held to be a degrading punishment which violated article 3 of the Convention.

The Lithgow Case, on the law of expropriation, lasting for six years,[269] has been the largest case heard by the Court. As an earlier Swedish case had showed, the *Sporrong and Lönnroth Case v Sweden,*[270] no contracting party of the European Convention may deprive owners of their property or of the use thereof without compensation. This right is enjoyed not only by aliens in a State but also by nationals.[271]

It is particularly important to stress that the rules laid down in the European Convention are held to now form part of the law of the European Community.[272] As part of that law it immediately becomes part of the applicable law of courts in the Member States and investigations concerning the impact of the operation of the European Convention inside Member States must be accordingly adapted.[273]

---

[267]   (1979), *Reports of the European Court of Human Rights.*

[268]   (1978) 2 EHHR 1.

[269]   *Supra,* 252.

[270]   (1982) ILR 1968. This case received considerable international attention, and was reported in the ILR, as Sweden is the only country in Europe which lacks constitutional protection of property.

[271]   See *supra* on a minimum right of property as a Human Right.

[272]   Joint Declaration of the EC Parliament, Council and Commission in 1977, OJ C 103 1; see, for the practice of the EC Court accepting this view, *Johnston v RUC,* (1986) ECR 1651; *Nold v Commission* (1974) ECR 507; *Internationale Handelsgesellschaft mbH v EVS,* (1979) ECR 3727.

[273]   See for example, Drzemczewski, *The European Human Rights Convention and Domestic Law,* 1983.

2. THE CONFERENCE FOR SECURITY AND COOPERATION IN EUROPE (CSCE)

Kimminich, KSZE und Menschenrechte, AVR 1977/78, 274; Meissner & Ushakov, *Probleme KSZE*, 1975; Buergenthal (ed.), *International Law and the Helsinki Accord*, 1977; Bloed & van Dijk (eds.), *Essays on Human Rights in the Helsinki Process*, 1985; Simma & Blenk-Knocke (eds.), *Zwischen Intervention und Zusammenarbeit, KSZE*, 1979; Alting von Geusau, *Beyond Containment and Division*, 1992.

A Conference in Helsinki in 1975 united Western and East European countries to agree on measures to strengthen peace and security. The Final Act,[274] commonly known as the Helsinki Accord or the CSCE Arrangement, marks a landmark in international law both from the point of view of the development of Human Rights[275] as in the field of programmatic resolutions,[276] where it represents an act of considerable practical importance.

One form of measures introduced under the Accord was a system of *confidence building measures*, implying a duty to inform in advance on major military manoeuvres. Another important form of cooperation concerned Human Rights, under what was called *Basket III* to the declaration. Under this system, a participating State may intervene to question another power on national Human Rights problems.

Important advances on the formulation in the basic Accord[277] have been made by ensuing pronouncements under the Accord, by a series of follow-up meetings and special meetings on Human Rights,[278] for example at the Copenhagen meeting in June 1990, the Paris Summit in the autumn of the same year, the Moscow meeting in 1991 and at the meeting in Helsinki in 1992.

Most writers emphasise the non-binding character of the Helsinki Accords and annexed Declarations. Yet, we have seen that statements on Human Rights may often be binding on the basis of another form of obligation, derived not from the document but from general *jus*

---

[274] 14 ILM, 1292.
[275] On the new emphasis on Human Rights see *supra* Chapter II iii d 5(a).
[276] See *supra* in Chapter III.
[277] See Alting von Geusau, *Beyond Containment, op. cit.*, 154 *et seq.*
[278] 29 ILM 1990, 1305 and 30 ILM 1991, 190.

cogens. This is often the case under the CSCE documents.[279]

3. THE AMERICAN CONVENTION

Tomuschat, Interamerikanische Menschenrechtkommission, ZaöRVR 1982, 231; LeBlanc, *The OAS and the Protection of Human Rights*, 1977; García Bauer, *Los derechos humanos in América*, 1987; Buergenthal, Inter-American Court of Human Rights, AJIL 1982, 231 and *idem*. in Meron (ed), *Human Rights in International Law*, 1984, 439 *et seq.*

On a regional scale, again, there is an Inter-American Commission acting under the American Convention of Human Rights of 1969.[280] It has been ratified by thirteen States. The Convention has much in common with the European Convention and there is a Commission and a Court as well as a right of individual petition. But the powers are more vaguely set out and the practical importance of the Convention is reduced by the fact that several countries with a questionable Human Rights record in Latin America have not ratified the Convention.[281]

4. THE AFRICAN CHARTER

Hamalengwal & Flinterman & Dankwa, *The International Law of Human Rights in Africa*, 1988; Welch & Meltzer, *Human Rights and Development in Africa*, 1984; Rembe, *Africa and Regional Protection of Human Rights*, 1985; Kunig & Benedek & Mahalu, *Regional Protection of Human Rights by International Law: The Emerging African System*, 1985.

The African Charter on Human and People's Rights[282] was adopted by the Organisation of African Unity in 1981.[283] It embodies numerous rights laid down in the UN Covenants and establishes a

---

[279] See *supra* on the Legal Value of Recommendations of International Organisations, 183 *et. seq.*

[280] 9 ILM 1970, 673.

[281] The American Convention on Human Rights of 1969 entered into force in 1978.

[282] 21 ILM 1982, 58.

[283] The Charter of the OAU had already emphasised the importance of Human Rights in Africa.

Commission with the power to hear State and individual complaints. When fully operational this entity may furnish increased Human Rights protection in Africa.[284]

5. THE ARAB LEAGUE

Hassouna, *League of Arab States and Regional Disputes,* 1975; An-Na'im, Islamic law, international relations and Human Rights challenge and response, CornLJ 1987, 317.

The Arab League has had a Commission on Human Rights since 1968 but lacks provisions for State or individual petition.

c. The Minimum Standard

Chowdhury, *The Rule of Law in a State of Emergency. The Paris Minimum Standards of Human Rights Norms,* 1989.

It was previously often argued that a national would only have the right to be treated as a State's own subject. This standard is usually called *national treatment.* However, State practice shows that this is not the acceptable level for Human Rights accorded to citizens and others in a State's territory: there is, instead, a binding *minimum standard.* In a few cases, as for example, in the United States, the *national* treatment as under the American Constitution may be *better* than this minimum standard.[285] However, in most countries, the situation would be the reverse, and the national treatment afford *lower* security than what is desirable, and it is useful, therefore, to adopt an international minimum standard as the norm.

The core of Human Rights include, above all, those rights which must not be displaced by agreements of States or in any other way: these are the rules which belong to the *jus cogens,* or the indispositive or peremptory norms of international law. These rules are very few

---

[284] The Charter of Human and People's Right of 1981 entered into force in 1986, ratified by all States in Africa except Ethiopia.

[285] The United States did not ratify the Universal Covenants on Human Rights precisely as it was thought that the Constitution, with relevant amendments, provided a higher standard.

and concern only the fundamental or most basic Human Rights, for example, the right to *avoid*[286] genocide, torture, slavery and apartheid.

These basic rules certain form a body which indicates a *minimum standard* which may not be set aside. In case of grave violations of these fundamental rights, not only the State may be liable but even personal responsibility may follow, as amply illustrated in the War Crimes Tribunals.[287]

The minimum standard only concerns the so called basic rights and does not, for example, include other, more advanced, forms of Human Rights. The minimum standard may be guaranteed, and/or uplifted, by special agreements. Apart from the reviewed global and regional agreements, and apart from the general rights on basic Human Rights, it is important to point out that the *jus protectionis*[288] fulfills certain functions within the field of Human Rights. Thus, when a State protects his own national abroad it is on the basis that this national has certain rights.[289]

vi. Environmental Law

Neuhold & Lang & Zemanek, (eds.), *Environmental Protection and International Law*, 1991; Kiss & Shelton, *International Environmental Law*, 1992; Sand, *The Effectiveness of International Environmental Agreements*, 1992; Dejeant-Pons, *La Méditerranée en droit international de l'environnement*, 1990; Churchill & Freestone (eds.), *International Law and Global Climate Change*, 1991; Springer, *The International Law of Pollution, The Problem of Attribution*, 1983; Klein, *Umweltschutz im Völkerrechtlichen Nachbarrecht*, 1976; Lammers, *Pollution of International Waterways*, 1984; Bothe, Umweltschutz als Aufgabe der Rechtswissenschaft, ZaöRVR 1972, 483; McGonigle & Zacher, *Pollution, Politics and International Law*, 1984; Ruster & Simma, *International Protection of the*

---

[286]   The rights are too modest to be phrased in anything but in a negative way, *i.e.* as the right to *avoid* certain action by others.

[287]   See my *Law of War*, *op. cit.*, 353 *et seq.* To these we can probably add *systematric rape* as ordered by the Serbian High Command in Bosnia in 1992/3.

[288]   *Infra*, under jurisdiction.

[289]   In the past many such cases, where the home State of an individual has intervened by diplomatic means, have concerned cases of expropriation of property, see my *International Law and the Independent State*, *op. cit.*

Environment, 1975; Münch, Umweltschutz im Völkerrecht, AVR 1971, 385; Rauschning, Umweltschutz als Problem des Völkerrechts, EA 1972, 567; Kay & Jacobson, (eds.), *Environmental Protection: The International Dimension*, 1983; Barros & Johnston, *The International Law of Pollution*, 1974; Teclaff & Utton (eds.), *International Environmental Law, Colloque*, 1974; Kiss (ed.), *The Protection of the Environment and International Law, Hague Academy Colloquium* 1973; Quick, *Umweltsaktivität zwischenstaatlicher Organisationen*, 1973; Hargrove (ed.), *Law Institutions and the Global Environment*, 1972; Prieto & Nocedal (eds.), *Legal Protection of the Environment in Developing Countries*, 1976; Land, Haftung und Verantwortlichkeit im internationalen Umweltschutz, *Festschrift Verdross* 1980, 517; van Lier, *Acid Rain and International Law*, 1980; Timagenis, *International Control of Marine Pollution*, 1978; Johnson, *The Environmental Law of the Sea*, 1981; Boyle, Marine Pollution under the Law of the Sea Convention, AJIL 1985, 346; Fitzgerald, Le Canada et le développement du droit international: La contribution de l'affaire de la Fonderie de Trail, *Etudes Int.*, 1980, 393; Starace (ed.), *Diritto internazionale e protezione dell'ambiente marino*, 1983; Timagenis, *International Control of Marine Pollution*, 1980; Hakapää, *Marine Pollution in International Law*, 1981; Tesauro, *L'inquinamento marino del diritto internazionale*, 1971; Ehmer, *Der Grundsatz der Freiheit der Meere und das Verbot der Meeresverschmutzung*, 1974; cf. my article on the Stockholm Conference and its Follow Up, in Groom and Taylor, (eds.), *The General Assembly of the United Nations*, 1989.

a. *Micro and Macro Views of the Environment*

The environment can be understood in an extremely wide way, including any question bearing on the human or animal habitat, on plant life or on the condition of Earth as a planet in the Solar system. It is this macro view that most environmentalists adopt and we shall treat the subject accordingly in this Chapter.

Our analysis is one through a prism that can be inverted. In order to appreciate that, it is important to emphasise that the environment can also focus on the actual micro positions. If a more narrow view is taken of the environment it can thus be understood differently and focus on the situation of the individual and his living conditions.

Adopting a micro view of the environment, special attention is paid to *working conditions* and to the *work place*. In this sense, much improvement has been achieved during this century especially through the conventions elaborated and adopted by the International Labour Organisation (ILO) and, to some extent, through the work of the

World Health Organisation (WHO).[290] Numerous other specific agreements are also relevant to working conditions.[291]

In this work, however, we shall survey rules that apply to pollution, or to other deterioration of the global or regional environment, and to the special problem of dissipation of resources.

The area of environmental studies is representative of the conflict between the interests of the world and the legitimate sovereignty of individual States.

b. Topicality of the Subject

There is increasing concern that the earth's resources are being dissipated and, at the same time, that the resources that are left are being polluted. There is acid rain in Scandinavia, caused by industrial fumes from the Midlands in England and the Ruhr in Western Germany; and this acid rain kills the fish and causes the trees to lose their leaves. *The Death Triangle*, in South West Poland, the northern part of the Czech Republic and Southern East Germany, causes environmental damage far beyond the borders of those countries. The cutting of the Amazon rain forest causes climatic changes in other countries in the region outside Brazil. The accident at Chernobyl affected a major part of Europe; the Laps in Northern Scandinavia had to slaughter their reindeer and children in Switzerland were not allowed to drink milk for weeks. The reduction of the ozone layer has

---

[290]   See on these *supra*.

[291]   See Convention on the Use of White Lead in Painting, Geneva, 1921; Convention on Protection Against Poisoning Arising from Benzene, Geneva, 1971; European Agreement on Restriction of the Use of Certain Detergents in Washing and Cleaning Products, Strasbourg, 1968; Convention on Protection of Workers Against Ionizing Radiations, Geneva, 1960; Convention on Phyto-Sanitary Conditions in Africa, Kinshasa, 1967; Convention on the Physical Protection of Nuclear Material, Vienna, 1979; Convention on Prevention and Control of Occupational Hazards Caused by Carcinogenic Substances and Agents, Geneva, 1974; Convention on Protection of Workers Against Occupational Hazards in the Working Environment Due to Air Pollution, Noise and Vibration, Geneva, 1977; Convention on Occupation, Safety and Health and the Working Environment, Geneva, 1981; Convention on Occupational Health Service, Geneva, 1985; Convention Concerning Safety in the Use of Asbestos, Geneva, 1986.

caused particular concern for the future of the environment in the whole world.

c. *Balancing Legal Interests*

Although environmental destruction has undoubtedly become a major problem in contemporary international society, it is, however, important to balance the importance of *environmental intervention.*[292] The interests of a State to guard its own sovereignty in its own territory precludes any heavy handed intervention from other States, or from foreign private organisations, to direct a State to certain action or to forbid certain activities.

Another development in recent years is the attempt to relinquish international undertakings on the ground that the undertaking is *environmentally unfriendly.* This was the case when Hungary claimed in 1993 that it was not obliged to continue the building of the Gabcikovo Dam on which she had concluded a formal treaty with the Slovak Republic.[293] It is not conducive to international peace and friendship to use environmental pretexts in this way to obtain release from the paramount obligation of *pacta sunt servanda* of international agreements. In other words, it is not correct to ride on the device of environmental interests to displace other obligations.

Nor is it correct to allow environmental interests to become a cloak for interference in the private affairs of other States. It became apparent, in the running up to the Rio Conference on Environment and Development in 1992, that many States felt empowered to order, for example, Brazil to cease any cutting of the Amazon rain forest, as this forest is of major importance to the climate of the world. The reaction to such far reaching claims was, however, that Brazil - which had already changed its policy on the rain forest and, on the whole, had ceased allowing cutting of the forest - strongly resented foreign interference, insisting on her sovereign rights to decide in her own territory. In the end, this attitude, supported by that of many other States, resulted in some much watered down agreements on the

---

[292]   On intervention and its intricacies in general, see *supra*, at the beginning of this Chapter.

[293]   See *infra* in this Chapter under Equitable Use of Water.

environment at the end of the Conference.[294]

The only way forward to protect the global environment is clearly to *inform* the general public as much as possible and induce them to certain behaviour *out of their own free will*. On that score it is possible that certain *exhortations*[295] of international organisations, for example with regard to the so called *standstill principle*,[296] urging conservation of certain areas, will have the approval and consent of States and be adopted[297] for action in certain vulnerable areas. The environment is not an area where is is possible to compel individuals, or the State, to specific behaviour. One should therefore not underestimate traditional conventional techniques of achieving results by treaties.[298]

The interests of protecting the global environment must thus always be balanced against the interests of sovereign States.

d. Basic Rules on Liability

For some time, international law has had rules to deal with some of these situations but, until the last decade, there has not often been reason to apply these rules. Now, however, the destruction of resources has reached such proportions that there is a wide-spread feeling that something must be done. Resources that are dissipated include both natural resources, such as forests and fish, as well as the very historical heritage which is also threatened by pollution and other environmental threats.[299]

---

[294]   There was some general agreements on Climat Change and on Biodiversity in *point form*, similar to the Stockholm Declaration of 1972 (*Cf. supra*), without much substance in terms of legally binding obligations, as well as a Protocol on Forests.

[295]   *Cf. supra*, in Chapter III on the legal effect of such measures.

[296]   UNEP Recommendation 19th May 1978.

[297]   *Cf. supra* in Chapter III on Standards.

[298]   Dejeant-Pons, *La Méditerrannée en droit international de l'environnement*, 1990, 262.

[299]   For Conventions on cultural heritage see, the European Convention on Protection of Archeological Heritage, London, 1969; Convention on Protection of the World Cultural and Natural Heritage, Paris, 1972; Convention on the Protection of the Archeological, Historical and Artistic Heritage of the American Nations, San Salvador and Santiago, 1976.

It is therefore time to revive and develop the rules that international law provides on the topic of environmental protection. The Declaration on the Human Environment at the Stockholm Conference in 1972[300] refers to obligations of States albeit in the form of *principles* of action rather than by laying down exact and detailed legal obligations. Such *principles* have a certain impact on the behaviour of States, but, in legal terms, they present little more than *pacta de contrahendo*, that is to say, agreements concerning future agreements. The legal effect, often watered down and diffuse, of such pronouncements, can be analysed in the context of parallel declarations of States[301] and of recommendations of international organisations or conferences.[302]

On the other hand, apart from guidelines laid down in the Stockholm Declaration, supplemented by new suggestions, for example in the Brundlandt Report, substantive rules on environmental protection are often derived by analogy from national legal systems, have been helpful. Thus, a rule of Roman law, *sic utere tuo ut alienum non laedas,* (use your own (property) in order not to harm (that of) another, has been applied in numerous international cases. For example, in *The Trail Smelter Case,* an arbitration between the United States and Canada, the Tribunal said that

'under the principle of international as well as the law of the United States no State has the right to use or permit the use of its territory in such a manner as to cause injury by fumes in or to the territory of another or the properties of persons therein, when the case is of serious consequence and the injury is established by clear and convincing evidence.'[303]

The question of evidence, as referred to in this leading case, is precisely one part of the problem. How can one prove that the acid rain that affects Scandinavia comes from any specific factories? It may even be that fumes from one factory cause little harm but, in

---

[300]   11 ILM 1972, 1416.
[301]   See *supra* in Chapter III.
[302]   See *supra* in Chapter III.
[303]   (1938) 3 RIAA, 1905.

conjunction with those from another, are responsible for considerable environmental damage.

Pollution is thus often a question of degree. It is also a question of a number of largely unidentifiable actors. On the other hand, all those actors are residents within the area of a given State or within several given States. In some cases then it is that State or those States that will have to bear the responsibility for activities of persons within its territory.

This rule, in environmental terms, is quite an innovation of the normal responsibility of States. A State is not normally responsible at all for damage caused by its nationals unless the State, or any of its organs, had something to do with the damage, either by action or by failing to control an action. In other words, the State must normally have been active in the commission of the act or negligent in the supervision of the actors to incur responsibility under international law for damage caused by its nationals.

In the comments on *The Trail Smelter Case* little attention has focused on this aspect. Few have even noticed that, in the event, Canada itself was held responsible for damage caused to private interests in the United States by a *private* Canadian company. Admittedly, a small strip of government land was affected within the State of Washington but there were other areas too in the United States affected by the fumes from the smelter. But since when does international law, in its traditional form, take into account such damage caused by a *private actor*.[304] According to the traditional textbooks, most of which cite *The Trail Smelter Case* albeit in another context, claim, when they speak of subjects of the international system, that international law is a system between States. But how can it be if it also takes damage of private interests caused by private companies into account?

The Trail Smelter Case ruling was reaffirmed in *The Lake Lanoux Case*, an arbitration between Spain and France.[305] Here the Tribunal said that any State is under duty to take interests of other States into account when preparing any scheme which may have implications for

---

[304]   There was little evidence that Canada had failed in any supervisory duties.

[305]   (1957) 12 RIAA, 281.

312

the environment. *The Rau Arbitration* between Sind and Punjab, two provinces in India. also underlined that

> 'no new project, however beneficent in other ways, should be allowed to impair existing inundation canals without payment of compensation.'[306]

Another important case is *The Corfu Channel Case*[307] where the International Court of Justice emphasised that no State may use its territory to cause damage to others. In this case Albania was held to have had knowledge - at least constructive knowledge - of mines laid in its territorial waters and it was therefore held responsible for damage and injury caused to British warships going through the Corfu Straits.

In the Chernobyl accident it became clear that most States regarded the Soviet Union as having both a duty of warning and a duty of reparation. Although some States, like Sweden, hesitated to make claims, and eventually decided to refrain from doing so, it was clear that most regarded the Soviet Union as having full responsibility under international law for damage and injury caused. The Soviet Union had also committed a breach of the *duty of warning* under international law.[308]

The aforementioned Declaration of the Stockholm Conference in 1972, long thought to be of little legal importance as a 'mere' recommendation[309] of an international conference, has gathered momentum and is now often thought to express international agreement on the duty of States not to cause damage to other States by pollution. Australia and New Zealand also relied on the Declaration as expressing such agreement in *The Nuclear Test Cases* before the International Court of Justice.[310] Furthermore, the liability of States for damage caused to other States by activities within their borders has been further reaffirmed: rules on these matters recur in

---

[306] (1930) AD 1931-1932 No. 124.
[307] (1949) ICJ *Reports* 1.
[308] See my *Concept of International Law, op. cit.*, Chapter II.
[309] See, in detail, on the legal effect of recommendations, *supra* in Chapter III.
[310] (1974) ICJ *Reports* 53.

the Declaration on the New International Economic Order (NIEO)[311] and in the Charter of Economic Rights and Duties of States.[312] As these instruments themselves do not constitute more than formal *recommendations*[313] they still reflect, as we have seen in possible in the case of recommendation, *an underlying legal rule, the genereal principle of liability, binding on another ground.* It may be useful to underline that the said rule on liability also appears in the 1979 Convention on Long Range Transboundary Pollution[314] as well as in the 1982 Law of the Sea Convention where several sections deal with environmental aspects.[315]

Liability is strict for so called ultrahazardous activity where fault or negligence does not have to be proved. Such hazardous activities include Outer Space and nuclear work: for such activities, the State[316] is always and invariably answerable. Conventions may elaborate, in further detail, relevant provisions.[317] Other accidents, involving hazardous material, may also give rise to State liability.[318]

e. Types of Environmental Problems

Apart from the problems caused by pollution and by the reduction of the earth's resources, wildlife has been of particular concern. The Whaling Conventions[319] - read in conjunction with the new Law of

---

[311]   GA Res 3202 (S-VI).

[312]   GA 3281 (XXIX), 1974.

[313]   See *supra* in Chapter III under Legal Value of Recommendations.

[314]   18 ILM 1979, 1442.

[315]   See *infra* under Distributive Rules Territorial Sea, EEZ and the High Seas.

[316]   In the case of Space work it is the State of registration, under the Registration Convention; see *infra* under Outer Space treaties and, in the case of nuclear work, the supervising State.

[317]   See Convention on Third Party Liability in the Field of Nuclear Energy, Paris, 1960 (as amended); Convention on Civil Liability for Nuclear Damage, with Optional Protocol, Vienna, 1963; Convention on Civil Liability for Maritime Carriage of Nuclear Material, Brussels, 1971.

[318]   See *supra* on the Basel Convention on Control of Transboundary Movements of Hazardous Wastes 1989, 28 ILM 1989, 657.

[319]   Convention on the Regulation of Whaling, of 1946 161 UNTS 72. For earlier regulation see the Whaling Convention of Washington, 1931 (as amended), 30 AJIL Suppl. 167. Convention on Whaling, London, 1937, with Protocol

the Sea Convention of 1982[320] which reflects[321] certain accepted general rules - and the activities of the Whaling Commission are of practical importance to the attitudes of particular countries like Japan. A special agreement has been concluded for the Conservation of Polar Bears[322] and there are several conventions on seals.[323]

Numerous Conventions regulate now the management of flora and fauna in the world. There are several Plant Protection Agreements and Conventions[324] and others that deal with wildlife.[325] There is a 1973 Convention on International Trade in Endangered Species which seeks to reduce interest in such trade.[326] The Wildlife Fund and other non-governmental organisations do much to promote awareness of the need to preserve vulnerable species. However, not all wildlife is best preserved as illustrated by the long and difficult efforts to control locusts.[327]

---

of 1938, 34 AJIL 1940 Suppl. 108. A further protocol was concluded in 1944, Cmnd 6510.

[320] Part V, articles 61-65 and note article 120 in Part VII on conservation and management of marine resources.

[321] See *supra* in Chapter III.

[322] Agreement on Conservation of Polar Bears, Oslo, 1973; 1976 CTS No. 24.

[323] See, the Convention on Conservation of North Pacific Fur Seals, Washington, 1957; Convention for the Conservation of Antarctic Seals, London, 1972.

[324] See, the Convention on European and Mediterranean Plant Protection Organisation, as amended, 1951; Convention on Plant Protection, Rome, 1951; Convention on Plant Protection for South East Asia, Rome, 1956; Convention on Cooperation in the Quarantine of Plants and Their Protection Against Pests and Diseases, Sofia, 1959; Convention on Protection of New Variety of Plants, Paris, 1961.

[325] Convention for the Protection of Birds, Paris, 1950; Convention on the Preservation of Fauna and Flora, London, 1933; Convention on Nature Protection and Wildlife Preservation in the Western Hemisphere, 1940; Benelux Convention on Hunting and Protection of Birds, Brussels, 1970 (as amended); Convention on Wetlands of International Importance Especially as Waterfowl Habitat, Ramsar, 1971 with Revising Protocol, Paris, 1982; Convention on Protected Areas and Wild Flora and Fauna in Eastern African Region, Nairobi, 1985.

[326] Convention of Washington, 1973.

[327] See, for earlier Conventions, my *East African Community and the Common Market*, 1969; and the Convention on the African Migratory Locust, Kano, 1962; Agreement on a Commission for Controlling Desert Locust in South

Certain Conventions now also regulate the way non-wild animals are treated, that is to say farming animals and pets.[328] Others, again, deal with provisions that apply to any type of animals, for example to safeguard the way they are treated during transport.[329]

Connected with the concern for animal welfare and protection of endangered species is, of course, the fear that the earth's useable resources are being dissipated and reduced. This concern has expressed itself in a general trend to save energy and to find alternative energy sources. It has also caused some detailed regulation of, for example, scarce forest resources[330] and of marine resources. Numerous agreements now regulate fishing in general,[331] often within wide regional frameworks,[332] or for more specific areas,[333]

West Asia, Rome, 1963; Agreement on a Commission for Controlling Desert Locust in the Near East, 1965 (as amended); Agreement on a Commission for Controlling the Desert Locust in North West Africa, Rome, 1970 (as amended).

[328] For example, the European Convention for Protection of Animals Kept for Farming Purposes, Strasbourg, 1976; European Convention for the Protection of Vertebrae Animals used for Experimental and other Scientific Purposes, Strasbourg, 1986; European Convention for the Protection of Pet Animals, Strasbourg, 1987.

[329] *E.g.*, Convention for Protection of Animals During International Transport, Paris, 1968.

[330] For example, as regulated in the International Tropical Timber Agreement, Geneva, 1983.

[331] For example, the Convention on Fishing and Conservation of the Living Resources of the High Seas, 1958; Agreement on Cooperation in Marine Fishing, Warsaw, 1962.

[332] See, the Convention on Fisheries of the North Pacific Ocean, Tokyo, 1952 (as amended); Convention on North East Atlantic Fisheries, London, 1959; Convention on Conservation of Living Resources of the South East Atlantic, Rome, 1969; Convention on Cooperation on North West Atlantic Fisheries, Ottawa, 1978; Convention on Cooperation on North East Atlantic Fisheries, London, 1980.

[333] *E.g.* the Convention on Fishing and Conservation of the Living Resources in the Baltic Sea and Belts, Gdansk, 1973; Convention on Fishing in the Black Sea, Varna, 1959; Regional Convention on Cooperation for Protection of the Marine Environment, Kuwait, 1978 with Protocol; Convention for the Conservation and Management of the Vicuna, Lima, 1979; Convention on the Conservation of Antarctic Marine Living Resources, Canberra, 1980; Regional Convention for the Conservation of the Red Sea and the Gulf of Aden Environment with Protocol, Jeddah, 1982; Convention on Protection of the

or with reference to rivers[334] or basins.[335] Others may target other resources such as tuna,[336] salmon[337] and lobsters and crabs[338] or regulate methods of catch.[339]

However, the paramount problem is possibly pollution of resources as such pollution appears to be increasing at a rate higher than that of dissipation. In order to improve the environment it is therefore necessary to reduce, in the first place, pollution. Without such measures, there will soon not be adequate resources for human and wildlife survival. There is already problems with regard to drinking water in some areas of the world. Much is attempted but not much is achieved to reduce problems caused by drought.[340] Pollution of the salt water areas also contributes to the dangers posed to wildlife and speeds up ecological imbalances.

There is now a wide network of environmental conventions and agreements to improve living conditions and to prevent deterioration of the human habitat by pollution or by squandering of resources.

Marine Environment of the Wider Caribbean Region, with Protocol, Cartagena, 1983 and Protocol on Wildlife, Kingston, 1990.

[334] *E.g.,* Convention on Fishing in the Danube, Bucharest, 1958; Convention on the International Commission for the Protection of the Rhine Against Pollution, Berne, 1953; Convention on the Protection of the Rhine Against Pollution by Chlorides, Bonn, 1976; Convention on an International Commission for the Protection of the Mosel Against Pollution, 1961; Convention on the Senegal River, Nouakschott, 1972; Agreement on the Action Plan for the Environmentally Sound Management of the Common Zambezi River System, Harare, 1987.

[335] For example, the Convention on Development on the Chad Basin, Fort-Lamy, 1964 (as amended); Convention on the Niger Basin Authority with Protocol on the Fund, Faranah, 1980.

[336] For example, the Convention on Conservation of Atlantic Tunas, Rio de Janeiro, 1966; Convention on an Inter-American Tropical Tuna Commission, Washington, 1949.

[337] For example, the Convention on the Conservation of Salmon in the North Atlantic Ocean, Reykjavik, 1982.

[338] *E.g.,* Agreement on Protection of the Stocks of Deep-Sea Prawns, European Lobsters, Norway Lobsters, and Crabs, Oslo, 1951.

[339] For example, agreements on fishing gear: Convention on the Pohibition of Fishing with Long Drift Nets in the South Pacific, Wellington, 1989.

[340] See, for a regulatory effort, the Convention on a Permanent Inter-State Drought Control Committee for the Sahel, Ougadougou, 1973.

Some Conventions seek to tackle several environmental matters;[341] they can be so general in character and imply few concrete obligations.[342]

Other environmental conventions concern certain regional technical cooperation.[343] Others again, are so comprehensive that one may doubt that their targets can ever be reached as they cover a host of activities but provide no supervision or control mechanisms.[344] Many framework agreements have proved to be of little practical value.[345]

(i) Marine Pollution

Pollution of the environment is perhaps the first type of pollution to cause international worry in the last few decades. It was when the ship *The Torre Canyon* ran aground off the coast of Cornwall in 1967 that the international society was made aware of the dimension of damage caused by oil spillage from oil tankers. It became obvious that the conventional framework, consisting largely then in the 1954

---

[341] See the Convention on the Protection of the Marine Environment of the Baltic Sea Area, Helsinki, 1974.

[342] See the Convention on the Protection of the Environment between Denmark, Finland, Norway and Sweden, Stockholm, 1974; Convention on Conservation of Nature in the South Pacific, Apia, 1976; Treaty for Amazonian Cooperation, Brasilia, 1978; ASEAN Agreement on the Conservation of Nature and Natural Resources, Kuala Lumpur, 1985.

[343] As, for example, the Convention on the Network of Aquaculture Centres in Asia and the Pacific, Bangkok, 1988.

[344] For a comprehensive effort, see the Convention for Protection of the Marine Environment and Coastal Area of the South East Pacific, Lima, 1981, with Agreement on Cooperation Against Pollution, and Supplementary Protocols, Quito, 1983 on Regional Cooperation in the Case of Oil Pollution and on Pollution from Land-Based Sources; and Protocols on Conservation, and on Radioactive Contamination, Paipa, 1980.

[345] For example, Convention on Development of the Marine and Coastal Environment of the West and Central African Region, with Protocol, Abidjan, 1981; Convention on Protection, Management and Development of the Marine and Coastal Environment of the Eastern African Region, Nairobi, 1985; Convention for the Protection of Natural Resources and the Environment of the South Pacific Region, Noumea, 1986, with Protocols on Dumping and Cooperation.

Convention for the Prevention of Pollution of the Sea by Oil[346] was highly inadequate. It had been amended in 1962, and in 1969, after *The Torre Canyon* disaster, and was revised again in 1971, but many States had not ratified the amendments which concerned improved standards for discharge and tank washing; much damage has been caused by oil tankers washing out their tanks near land. The treaty, which prohibited discharge of oil within 100 miles of land was still inadequate. A new Convention, MARPOL, the Convention on the Prevention of Pollution from Ships, was concluded in 1973.[347] This Convention introduced, for example, new ship designs requiring ships to have a slop tank to avoid tank washing pollution.

In a specific way the Nuclear Sea-Bed Treaty is highly relevant to marine pollution although it naturally also safeguards other parts of the environment.[348]

A series of conventions deal with pollution prevention on a regional basis. Among others one may mention the Barcelona Convention on the Protection of the Mediterranean Sea Against Pollution 1976[349] with three protocols of 1976 and 1980, and other agreements on the Mediterranean,[350] the Agreement for Co-operation in Dealing with Pollution of the North Sea by Oil and other Harmful Substances, Bonn, 1983; the Regional Kuwait Convention of 1978 with Protocols, the West and Central African Convention with Protocol of 1981, the Red Sea and Gulf of Aden Environment Convention of 1981 and the Convention for the Protection and the Development of the Marine Environment of the Wider Caribbean Region 1983[351] together with a Protocol of the same year.[352] Some conventions deal specifically with pollution from land-based sources, such as, for example, the Paris Convention for the Prevention

---

[346]   327 UNTS 3.
[347]   1973 12 ILM 1319.
[348]   See my *Law Making, op. cit.*, 91, 147, 196 *et seq.*
[349]   1976 15 ILM 285.
[350]   Agreement on a General Fisheries Council for the Mediterranean, Rome, 1949; Protocol on Mediterranean Specially Protected Areas, Geneva, 1982; Agreement on Protection of the Waters of the Mediterranean Shores, Monaco, 1976.
[351]   1983 22 ILM 227.
[352]   *Ibid.*, 240.

of Pollution from Land-Based Sources of 1974.[353]

The Intervention Convention (or, more fully, the Convention on Intervention on the High Seas in Cases of Oil Pollution Casualties) of 1969[354] expressly allows States to intervene in the high seas to combat or mitigate pollution incidents. It was extended, in 1973, to cover also other chemicals than oil. In *The Torre Canyon* affair in 1967 the British Royal Air Force went out to bomb the wreck to mitigate the flow of oil from the tanker *before* the conclusion of the Law of the Sea and *without* any specific authorisation under any agreement or under any *ad hoc* consent of the parties involved. The flag State, Liberia, never complained of this action. One may therefore assume that the right to intervene in this way outside territorial waters or outside any protection zones is a right founded in *general international law,* as in any legal system, on a right of self-protection. The general right to intervene, enlarged and defined by the Intervention Convention, was also reconfirmed in the 1982 Law of the Sea Convention[355] under which coastal States and port States may enforce international standards.

Under the *Arctic exception clause* in the Law of the Sea Convention, Canada has a special right to prevent, reduce and control the pollution in its region.[356] Although Canada is not mentioned by name in the relevant clause, the article was adopted with that country in mind, and much on the insistence of the Canadian delegation at the Law of the Sea Conference. The reason for this special treatment is that oil dissolves with much greater difficulty in cold water. Therefore, if oil is trapped under ice, serious problems ensue and cleaning up operations are particularly difficult. As the recent Exxon disaster off Canada in April 1989 may show the damage to ecology is considerable in the case of oil spillage in these waters.

Dumping at sea has been a special problem. By not only washing out their tanks but actually discharging large amounts of unwanted remnants of crude oil or, indeed, other substances, ships can cause considerable environmental damage to the marine environment. The

---

[353]   1976 15 ILM 195.
[354]   1970 9 ILM 25.
[355]   Articles 218-219.
[356]   Article 234.

1972 Oslo Convention for the Prevention of Marine Pollution by the Dumping from Ships and Aircraft[357] and the wider 1972 London Convention on the Dumping of Waste at Sea,[358] regulates dumping and lists substances which may never be dumped and modalities for the dumping of other substances.

Liability as such follows from general international law and does not have to be entrenched in any international convention. Yet, it may be pointed out that the 1982 Law of the Sea Convention reaffirms that there is duty not to cause damage by pollution and, if such damage is caused, then the State is responsible and liable to make compensation.[359]

In 1969 a Convention on Civil Liability for Oil Pollution Damage was concluded[360] raising the liability limits. A further Protocol was concluded in 1984.[361] However, since oil pollution risks to cause damage of such dimensions that conventional insurance schemes are insufficient, a special fund was created by the Convention on an International Fund for Compensation for Oil Pollution Damage of 1971,[362] extended by a Protocol of 1984.

Special problems arise when damage is caused by, for example, the breaking up of a privately owned oil tanker and the limits of liability are exceeded. When there is no insurance to cover but a part of the damage and the shipowner's liability is limited who shall pay for the damage? The question was raised in *The Showa Maru Arbitration*.[363] Here, a ship had gone aground in the Malacca Straits where there are treacherous sand dunes which change the contours of the bottom of the Straits to make the depth virtually unpredictable. The ship had hit a sand shoal and broke up causing immense oil spillage in the area. The claims by Singapore and Malaysia far

---

[357]   1972 11 ILM 262.

[358]   1972 11 ILM 1294.

[359]   Articles 194(2) and 235. *Cf.* Convention on the International Fund for Compensation for Oil Pollution, 1971 (as amended).

[360]   1970 9 ILM 45.

[361]   There is also a further Convention on Civil Liability for Oil Pollution Damage Resulting from Exploration for and Exploitation of Sea Bed Mineral Resources, London, 1977.

[362]   1972 11 ILM 284.

[363]   [1979] London Arbitration in Admiralty Chambers, unpublished.

exceeded any sums that could be recovered by ordinary liability rules. Malaysia even sought to close the Straits, an international highway,[364] and threatened to impose a toll for any passing ship or, at least, impose stringent safety standards to prevent sub-standard ships from entering the Straits.

Much damage has, in fact, been caused by sub-standard ships sailing under convenience flag, usually that of Panama or Liberia.[365] It is not unreasonable to propose that the flag State should be ultimately liable for damage once the limits of the shipowner's liability and the insurance, as well as any contribution from any international or private fund, have been exceeded. Such obligations imposed on the States which provide convenience flags would certainly make them less keen to register ships. But is this not perhaps in the interest of international society? As things now stand, such States allow sub-standard ships to be registered and their crew do not have to have the same qualifications as what is required in other countries; furthermore the crew often works under unacceptable conditions.

If the flag States were made responsible for environmental damage caused by ships sailing under their flag (above the limits suggested) this may improve the registration rules at present in force in the relevant countries.[366] A wider rule of liability of the flag State which raises the standards required for ship safety, appears highly warranted.

---

[364] See *infra*, under Distributive Rules, International Straits.

[365] For one of the most recent accidents of great impact see *The Braer* grounding off the Shetland Islands on 5th January 1993, spilling large amounts of oil as she broke up, destroying salmon fish farms in the islands.

[366] Such a rule of liability would, if adopted, furthermore have placed the liability of the flag State on par with what was applicable in the Eastern bloc: there all ships were owned by the State which on that basis is liable for damage and injury. Since a State cannot go bankrupt, another State was then in a better position with regard to its claims for compensation if a ship from the former Eastern bloc caused environmental damage to its shores than if its environment was damaged by a ship from the Western world, including the convenience flag States. Such discrepancy with regard to liability appears absurd. Note that claims of immunity in suits concerning ships from former Eastern Europe were not usually accepted unless the ships were of the official navy, see my *Independent State, op. cit.*, Chapter II.

The International Maritime Organisation (IMO) has been working, for some time, on a further Convention on the Carriage of Noxious and Hazardous Substances at Sea. Within the OECD work is being carried out for a convention concerning the movement of transfrontier hazardous waste. UNEP, the United Nations Environmental programme, which handles numerous environmental questions, has assisted in the elaboration of an agreement, now adopted by numerous States as a Convention on Hazardous Waste, the Basel Convention, of 1989,[367] also of importance beyond the law of the sea.

The Chemical Weapons Convention of 1993, also relevant to the non-marine environment, black lists some chemicals as *super-lethal*, *i.e.* chemicals which are highly toxic and which have no justification on any civilian market; other less toxic chemicals, the 'merely' lethal types, are included in another list of less restricted substances.

Certain rules limiting the liability of operators of Nuclear Ships can be found in the Convention on that matter of 1961.[368] Much work is done in the field of preparing a convention regulating dumping of low-level radioactive wastes which poses particularly serious problems.

(ii) Equitable Use of Water

Every State has the right to use its own water for its own needs. However, when State uses the waters of an international drainage basin, this use must be *reasonable* and *equitable*. The question of subjective assessment - which is common in international law - then becomes relevant. *Who* is going to ascertain what is *reasonable* and *equitable* use? Naturally States will have different views on these subjective criteria.

The two above mentioned cases, *The Lake Lanoux* and *The Rau Arbitration*[369] both dealt with aspects of sharing of water and clarified some aspects as what constitute reasonable and acceptable uses of water.

In numerous cases riparian States have regulated their use of

---

[367]   28 ILM 1989, 657.

[368]   1963 AJIL 268.

[369]   See *supra*.

waters by international agreements. Thus, India and Pakistan have arrived at an understanding on the use of the waters of the Indus.[370] The Nile has also been subject of treaty regulation, first by an agreement between the United Kingdom and Egypt in 1929 when the Nile Waters Agreement was concluded[371] and later, when the Sudan had become independent, by a treaty between Sudan and Egypt in 1959.[372]

The treaties which concern equitable use of water must be distinguished from the numerous agreements which regulate navigational and other rights of communication.[373] Here, we are more concerned with the use of water as natural resources of the States adjacent to those water areas, rivers, lakes or other types of international water basins.

There is widespread agreement that riparians have *some right* to adjacent waters. In the dispute between Bolivia and Chile, for example, concerning the use of the Lauca river, Chile recognised that downstream Bolivia also had certain rights to the river.[374] Similarly, in the Jordan Basin dispute between Israel and the Arab States, both sides acknowledged that they were all entitled to a *reasonable share* of the basin waters.[375] The problem naturally subsists how exactly the waters should be apportioned.

A new dispute between Hungary and the Czech and Slovak republics arose in October 1992 when work started to build a dam on the Danube at Gabcicovo. As the agreement was between the Slovak State and Hunagry to carry out the building work, the dispute is now, after the demise of Czechoslovakia, between Slovakia and Hungary before the International Court of Justice. Negotiations by riparian States may still result in an agreement valid between them but only a Court can decide on a regulation binding or affecting the interests

---

[370]   Treaty of 1960, AJIL 1961, Suppl., 797.
[371]   93 LNTS 46.
[372]   *Khartoum Morning News* 13th November 1959.
[373]   See *infra*, under Distributive Rules, Passage and Transit Through Water.
[374]   OEA/Ser.B./VI.
[375]   SC, OR 1962 Jan-March 87, S/5084.

of other States.[376]

The Helsinki Rules of the International Law Association[377] reject the so called Harmon doctrine which had been put forward by some to claim, for a State, the exclusive use of waters of an international river, and sets out some important criteria. The Helsinki Rules thus suggest that relevant factors for the assessment of what is *reasonable* and *equitable* use of water should include, but not be limited to

a. the geography of the basin, including in particular the extent of the drainage area in the territory of each basin State;

b. the hydrology of the basin, including in particular, the contribution of water by each basin State;

c. the climate affecting the basin;

d. the past utilisation of the waters of the basin, including in particular existing utilisation;

e. the economic and social needs of each basin State;

f. the population dependent on the waters of the basin in each basin State;

g. the comparative cost of alternative means of satisfying the economic and social needs of each basin State;

h. the availability of other resources;

i. the avoidance of unnecessary waste in the utilisation of waters of the basin;

j. the practicability of compensation to one or more of the co-basin States as a means of adjusting conflicts among uses; and

k. the degree to which the needs of a basin State may be satisfied, without causing substantial injury to a co-basin State.

The criterion under heading e. shows the concern nowadays felt for the plight of poorer States. As the rules may apply to any basin in the

---

[376]   For environmental concerns as the ground for this dispute, see *supra* in this Chapter under Balancing Legal Interests.

[377]   ILA *Yearbook* 1966, 488.

Third World that heading must concern the relative economic strength of several countries, all of which may be developing countries and economically weak.

The problem of international water basins is one of major importance; this is indicated by the fact that the subject is at present being studied by the International Law Commission, the body under the United Nations which is in charge of codification of international law.

(iii) Pollution of the Air

Bennett (ed.), *Air Pollution Control in the European Community*, 1992.

The leading case to which we have already referred, *The Trail Smelter Case*[378] was indeed a case on pollution of the air although the fall out from the air later also affected territory. In this case the Tribunal made it abundantly clear that a State is not allowed to carry out activities which have detrimental effects on another country by air pollution. Similarly, *The Nuclear Test Cases* also discussed above[379] concerned atmospheric radioactive fall-out over Australia and New Zealand, the two injured parties in the case, affected by French tests in the Pacific area. Here, the International Court of Justice did not pronounce on the merits of the case after France had stated that tests would not be resumed. However, although the ICJ only ordered interim measures in this case and never dealt with the merits, there is ground for arguing that Australia and New Zealand had a *prima facie* case and that France was violating a general rule of international law on atmospheric pollution.

Some treaty obligations exist to prevent specific types of atmospheric pollution. The Partial Test Ban Treaty of 1963 prohibits nuclear tests in Outer Space and underwater, and the 1971 Treaty on the Prohibition of the Emplacement of Nuclear Weapons on the Sea-Bed and the Ocean Floor widens this prohibition; the two agreements therefore restrict the risk of pollution from this source. Other conventions on nuclear activity are also highly relevant to

---

[378]   See *supra.*

[379]   See *supra.*

environmental affairs.[380]

The 1979 Long Range Trans-Boundary Convention has already been mentioned[381] together with a 1984 Protocol on Financing the Monitoring and Evaluation of Air Pollutants in Europe.[382] Another convention of regional importance is the Nordic Convention for the protection of the Environment of 1974.[383] By unilateral declarations issued by a collective meeting in 1984 numerous parties to the 1979 Long Range convention pledge to reduce sulphur emissions by thirty per cent by 1993.[384] There is a special agreement between Canada and the United States to analyse the extent of North American air pollution. Bilateral cooperation agreement to prevent acidification of the environment have been concluded by the province of Quebec and the State of New York in 1982.[385]

The Vienna Convention for the Protection of the Ozone Layer was adopted in 1985,[386] and later supplemented by the Montreal Protocol of 1987[387] as revised in London two years later. The earlier Environmental Modification Convention (EnMod) of 1977 prohibits special weapons and methods which modify the weather.[388] Of major importance are, naturally, the numerous conventions which prohibit the use of nuclear weapons, for example the Test Ban Treaty of 1963 and the ABM Treaty of 1972.[389] Also the Geneva Gas Protocol of 1925 applies not only to environmental damage by nuclear weapons but also by other chemicals.[390]

The Montreal Protocol of 1987 provides for a reduction of chlor-

---

[380] See The Test Ban Treaty, Banning Nuclear Tests in the Atmosphere, in Outer Space and Underwater, Moscow, 1963; Convention on Early Notification of a Nuclear Accident or Radiological Emergency, Vienna, 1986; South Pacific Nuclear Free Zone Treaty, Raratonga, 1985.

[381] See *supra* and 1979 18 ILM 1442.

[382] 1985 24 ILM 484. A further Protocol was signed in Sofia in 1988.

[383] 1974 13 ILM, 591.

[384] 1984 23 ILM, 662.

[385] 1982 21 ILM, 721.

[386] 26 ILM 1987, 1529.

[387] *Ibid.*, 1550.

[388] See in detail on this Convention, my *Law of War, op. cit.*, Chapter IV.

[389] See further my *Law of War, op. cit.*, 90-92, 199-209.

[390] *Ibid.*, 214-218.

fluor carbons (CFCs) in aerosol cans by 20 per cent by 1993. It is these CFCs which are largely responsible for the damage to the ozone layer. By a special agreement between the Commission of the European Union and the Federation of European Aerosol Manufacturers CFCs in aerosols produced in Europe would have been reduced by 90 per cent by the end of 1990,[391] a target which, like so many environmental undertakings, was not kept. This *voluntary* agreement with the industry was intended to supplement, on a regional basis, the Montreal Protocol. It is particularly interesting to see an agreement of a private character like the one between manufacturers and the EU Commission within the scope of the EU Treaty which supplements an international agreement between States. Here is then another example of the complex nature of rule making in the international society:[392] the implications for the environment are also relevant in this context. On a bilateral scale the United States and Canada operate an Agreement of 1975 on the Exchange of Information on Weather Modification Activities.

The transformation of Eastern Europe, with reconstruction of many plants and factories for heavy industry, implies a new challenge to mitigate air pollution by new environmental technology.

f. Rio 1992: A Failure?

See my article on The Role of States in International Environmental Regulation, Swedish Council for Planning and Coordination of Research FRN (ed.), *International Environmental Negotiations*, 1993.

A major series of international conventions, agreements and unilateral statements were expected at the United Nations Conference on Environment and Development (UNCED) in Rio de Janeiro in June 1992. This Conference sought to bridge the vast areas of the *environment* on the one hand and *development* on the other. As neither of these spheres were appropriately limited or defined, the Conference was, in a sense, about *the world*, as any topic in contemporary international society could fit into either (or even both)

---

[391]   Agreement EC-European Manufacturers of Aerosols, 14th April 1989.

[392]   See *supra*, on Sources of International Law, 166.

of those headings.

The lack of focus diminished the importance of UNCED. Furthermore, high hopes of binding conventions were dashed as States showed themselves unwilling to accept anything except watered out texts without much obligation. Two important Conventions, on Climate Change and on Biological Diversity were adopted, but both contain escape clauses, such as that parties shall undertake to ... *as far as possible* take certain action, a formulation which clearly undermines the legal contents of the provisions; the most important issue of tropical forests did not even form the object of a convention but only of a protocol.

Like the Stockholm Conference in 1972 certain 'points' were adopted as guiding *Principles*. The 27 Principles of Rio all repeat traditional rules on environmental behaviour, or ideas that, at least in the twenty years since the Stockholm Conference had become traditional and accepted. However, even these Principles are undermined in several respects; the nowadays truistic rule that *pollutor pays* is adopted as a rule *in principle* which appear to invite arguments on possible exceptions.

UNCED highlighted the severe conflict between environmental problems and sovereignty: the problems, allegedly caused to the world environment by the cutting of the Amazon tropical forest, are to be solved largely by proposals which the industrialised States will seek to impose on Brazil. This country has, to the extent it binds itself to limit its sovereign rights over the tropical forest, clearly the right to some form of compensation.

It has been thought appropriate to suggest that this compensation could be paid in the form of reduced external debt as Brazil is one of the most indebted countries in the Third World. Yet, there are considerable problems connected with such *debt for nature swaps*, as those to whom Brazil owes the debts, international and national financial institutions, are *not the same* as those who would benefit from Brazil's undertaking not to interfere with the Amazon area: there is thus no identity between those who are Brazil's creditors and those who would benefit from the preservation of the rain forest.

Although there are serious problems connected with the world environment and its use of resources, it is also clear that many fears have been exaggerated. The attention paid to environmental problems represents, to many, an unwarranted deviation from the protection of Human Rights as we have now reached a situation where animals and plants, but not humans, are guaranteed numerous rights under international law. The appropriate attitude must now be to enlarge our understanding of environmental problems and accept that Man must play a central role in the matrix of rules.

CHAPTER VI

Stabilising Rules: Distributive Rules: The Object of Sovereign Functions: Geographical Areas

Stabilising rules is a term which I have chosen to indicate the rules that make up the *framework* for action within international society.[1] The rules that make up this framework do not impose any immediate duty of action: the very term is designed to indicate stable latitudes for action. Some of these rules concern *modalities* of behaviour between subjects, for example treaty making techniques, details of immunity or forms of communication. A crucial group of stabilising rules concern the division of power in territorial and extra-territorial contexts. This group, which we will study in this Chapter, are thus *distributive rules.*[2]

It is interesting to note that most English textbooks focus with inordinate detail on the extent of the territory, land or water areas, over which States exercise their powers. In other countries, like France, more attention is directed towards the more intricate legal questions concerning law making and the emergence of rules. It is obviously important to have the basic rules set out which concern territorial rights. However, the following survey is intended to form a *framework*, where details can be supplemented from the many specialised works that exist on different topics. On the other, an attempt is made in this treatise to view the territorial extent of States in the *context of the rule making process* we have set out earlier[3] and in the *context of prohylactic rules* analysed in the previous Chapter.[4]

Distributive rules, as we call them, represent a special form of

---

[1]   See, further, my *Concept, op. cit.,* 58-67.

[2]   *Ibid.,* 58-63.

[3]   See *supra*, Chapter III.

[4]   However, jurisdictional rights and limitations caused by the duty to respect Human Rights will be discussed in the following Chapter VII.

stabilising rules and concern, as the term indicates, the distribution of functions of a State. The distributive rules, which thus concern the geographical and functional division between the various States of the world, *nowadays* form part of the stabilising rules. The latter term suggests a stable framework: nowadays this framework cannot be displaced by acts of force, acquisition by aggression, or other unilateral expression of military power, to expand a State's territory. However, it is, for historical perspectives, useful to summarise how States previously enlarged their territory and to survey which forms of acquisition may still be viable.

A. ACQUISITION OF TERRITORY

Jennings, *Acquisition of Territory in International Law,* 1963.

i. General Points

Older textbooks always devote considerable attention to the question of acquisition of territory. In contemporary international society, however, the question is one of primarily historic interest. This is intimately connected with the prohibition of force which, as we have seen, has been introduced to prevent States, and also other groups, from legitimately acquiring territory by force.

Historically, there was usually an element of force, or even considerable force by war, which accompanied the process of acquisition of territory. Nowadays, the use of force in international society is no longer permissible.

The way in which Saddam Hussein of Iraq was condemned by international society in 1990 for taking another country, Kuwait, by force, may adequately reflect how repugnant such attempted acquisition of force is to other modern States. The United Nations has continuously condemned Israel's taking of the now *occupied territories.*[5] Argentina's capture of the Falkland Islands, resulted in *war*[6] to restore the islands to British rule. The Serb aggression against Croatia and Bosnia was also universally condemned, although

---

[5]   *Cf.* Resolution of the Security Council 242 of 1981.

[6]   See further my *Law of War, op. cit.,* Chapter I, on typology of wars.

international action to assist victims of aggression was slow.

The last examples may best serve to illustrate that we are here in a field which has greatly changed in international law over the last century. When Captain Cook discovered the Falkland Islands and claimed them for the United Kingdom, territory could legitimately be acquired by force. This is no longer so. Thus, when Argentina, according to its own opinion *retook* the islands, this was wrong in contemporary international law although the taking by Captain Cook had not been wrong.

In the case of the Falkland Islands there was, as mentioned above, a war. But usually States come to a settlement about territorial claims, such as, for example, border disputes as they are aware that nothing can be *legitimately* acquired by force.

It is still useful to set out the different types of acquisition that are historically relevant. A brief analysis of the modes of acquisition will enable a better understanding of present geographical distribution of territory.

ii. Occupation and Discovery

Jèze, *Etude théorique et pratique sur l'occupation comme mode d'acquérir du térritoire en droit international*, 1896.

An early form is obviously *occupation* by which peoples claimed territory as their own. Such territory was then *vacant* and not belonging to anyone else. Such a form of taking, called *occupation*, lies obviously very far back in history before there were competing claims for territory between different groups of peoples, and gradually between *nations*. If the term is reserved for the taking of land which belonged to no one else the category of occupation is clearly a very slim band.

Later, especially when the Nation-States had been established, *discovery* became important as large portions of the world were found by explorers, whose pursuits led to the very knowledge of the spherical shape of a world to be colonised by *occupation*. Here too, however, occupation did not usually imply the taking of no one's land since native tribes were often ousted by the newcomers, in Latin America appropriately called *conquistadores*, that is to say *conquerors* and not *occupiers*.

The International Court of Justice recognised in *The Western Sahara Case*[7] that territories inhabited by tribes with some form of social organisation are not *res nullius*,[8] that is to say vacant territory belonging to no one; these areas are then *not* available for occupation.

On the other hand, an individual can validly acquire territory by occupation providing such territory, at the time of taking, is a *res nullius* and not subject to the restrictions on taking.[9] This was endorsed by Norway's Supreme Court with regard to a part of the island of Jan Mayen, which, at the time, was still *res nullius*.[10]

iii. Conquest, Subjugation and Annexation

Bentivoglio, *Debellatio nel diritto internazionale*, 1948; Schätzel, *Die Annexion im Völkerrecht*, 1920.

It is under the heading of *conquest* and *subjugation* that we ought to consider the form of acquisition by force against an already existing indigenous population; as described above, the pure form of occupation is nowadays extremely rare and, even in the past, there were only isolated instances where territory was genuinely *vacant* and available for occupation. Thus, numerous cases referred to as 'occupation' are, at a closer analysis, forms of *conquest* and *subjugation*.

Annexation is also a secondary way of acquiring territory; the term annexation sometimes evokes connotations of geographical proximity and is often used in the case a neighbouring territory, or adjacent area, has been taken. *Full annexation* is sometimes used as an expression for when a whole State has been conquered and incorporated with another. *Partial annexation* signifies the case where only a part of another State is acquired.

Acquisition by territory by conquest, subjugation and annexation

---

[7]   (1975) ICJ *Reports* 39.

[8]   See *infra* on *res nullius*.

[9]   See *infra*, on prohibitions to acquire territory in Antarctica or in Outer Space.

[10]   *Jacobsen v Norwegien Government*, 7 AD 1933-34 42 (Höjesteret).

are *the most common form of acquisition of territory*, that is in terms of *history*. If we examine the Peace Treaties in Europe over the last 400 years we find that virtually all borders have been settled after wars whereby some countries have lost and some countries have gained territory, precisely through conquest, subjugation and annexation.

Modern international law condemns and forbids such acquisition, which necessarily involves the use of force[11] and which, by definition, excludes consent of the population of the taken country or territory.

These forms of acquisition of territory, *i.e.* conquest, subjugation and annexation, now obsolete in international law, are, however, still of prime importance to all scholars of international law. Unless we are familiar with this past prototype, we will not be able to understand the political framework within which international society now operates: it was largely through such forms of acquisition that the political map of the world was set.

iv. Cession

O'Connell, *State Succession in Municipal and International Law*, 2 vols., 1967.

Cession is commonly used for territory given to another State *voluntarily*. One may question the motives and reasoning behind such free transfer of territory.

If we examine examples given in the usual textbooks of *cession* we find that they come very close indeed to the type called conquest and subjugation, described above. Gibraltar was *captured* by a British-Dutch expedition in 1704 and *ceded* to the United Kingdom under the Peace Treaty of 1713.[12] Is there much difference between such *cession*, voluntary only in name, and the *conquest* of settlements in the Falkland Islands, where territory was claimed, taken and lost

---

[11]   On the prohibition of the use of force, see *supra* under Prophylactic Rules.

[12]   The Treaty of Utrecht, article X, 28 CTS 325.

at repeated intervals?[13] Incidentally, the sale of settlements by the French to Spain in 1767 probably was a form of *cession*, properly so called. Yet, it is important to underline that there is a fine distinction between cession and conquest.

On the other hand, in *contemporary* international law, there may still be valid cases of *cession*, whereas - as mentioned above - territory can no longer be acquired by conquest, subjugation and annexation. The king pin of difference rests on the *consent*, and, in so far as this consent is given by the population in the territory to be ceded, this is another expression for the importance of *democracy* in modern international society.[14]

v. Merger and Absorbtion

On 3rd October 1990 it was demonstrated that an old and previously common form of acquisition of territory still may supply the most spectacular change in the territory of a State. This was the day of the *merger* of the Federal Republic with the German Democratic Republic. Since the merger was not done on a completely equal footing - as the whole political, legislative and judicial machinery of FRG became applicable to the DDR - it may be more correct to speak of a sub-section of merger, or another form of acquisition altogether, namely that of *absorbtion*.

vi. Accretion and Avulsion

Some technical terms of acquisition of territory may be explained. *Accretion* takes place when build-up of, for example, a river, which causes a shift a boundary line between States. *Avulsion* implies the

---

[13]   The islands were taken by the British by force in 1833 after a chequered history: the islands were discovered by Captain Cook in 1592; there were settlements by the French from 1764 and by the British from 1765. The French settlements were sold to Spain in 1767. The British settlements were taken by Spain in 1770, regained by Britain in 1771, but abandoned in 1774. There were Spanish settlements until 1811 when Argentina gained independence; Argentina exercised various forms of sovereignty over the islands and appointed a Governor in 1828, five years before the British re-took the islands by force.

[14]   On democracy see *supra*, in numerous contexts, Chapter II.

shifting of land from one side to another of a meandering river. Such technicalities are not without practical significance. In the *Chamizal Case*[15] an arbitration tribunal held that the United States was entitled to certain areas on the Rio Grande where soil had built up and accretion consequently had taken place. Mexico, on the other hand, was awarded the land, where the river had actually moved and the arbitration thus recognised the change of territory also by avulsion.

vii. Adjudication and Allocation

Cf. infra on the power of courts, under Consequential Rules.
Miele, *L'aggiudicazione di territori nel diritto internazionale*, 1940.

Territory may be acquired through the decision of an international court. We are here concerned with cases before international courts where title depends on argued rights of the parties. Courts, organisations or groups of powerful States may, without referring to any specific justification of title, award territory to one or some of the parties. This can be regarded as a form of derivative[16] acquisition of territory. This mode of acquiring territory is commonly called *adjudication*.

Numerous examples may be given of territories which have been the subject of adjudication, and we may here mention the *Palmas Case*,[17] the *Clipperton Island Arbitration*,[18] *The Eastern Greenland Case*,[19] *The Minquiers and Ecrehos Case*,[20] and, more recently, the case concerning *Burkina Faso v Mali*.[21] Since *water* also forms part of a State's territory, we should possibly also include the cases on maritime territory adjudicated by the International Court of Justice in recent years. The ICJ has had to deal with a number of maritime delimitation cases, especially concerning the continental shelf, in the

---

15   *United States v Mexico*, [1911] 5 AJIL 813.
16   Dahm, i, 603.
17   (1928) 2 RIAA 829.
18   (1932) 26 AJIL 390.
19   (1933) PCIJ Series A/B No. 53.
20   (1953) ICJ *Reports* 47.
21   (1986) ICJ *Reports* 545.

last few years.[22] These cases have by far exceeded those concerning other core problems of international law, perhaps unfortunately for the development of international law which depends only to a lesser extent on principles for the exact delimitation of territory.[23]

The Great Powers sometimes *decided*, often without any form of democratic participation of affected States, on allocation of territory. The Åland Islands[24] were thus allocated to Finland in 1920 although a referendum in the islands had showed that 99.9 per cent of the Ålanders preferred an affiliation with Sweden. Other territory has been similarly distributed.[25]

Conversely, the Great Powers have also in some cases decided that territory must *not* be allocated to other States. This is what was happening in 1992-1993 when the Great Powers, and the United Nations, sought to *forbid* the division of Bosnia, insisting that Bosnia must remain undivided. It may be that the failure of concerted effort on the part of United Nations and of the Great Powers in this respect, marks a step in the decline of the authority of outside Powers with regard to small, or weak, States.

By *arbitration* territory may be allocated to one State by the procedure of territorial adjudication: borders between Guatemala and Honduras were decided by arbitration in 1933.[26] So were the borders between Hungary and Czechoslovakia in 1938.[27]

We may also subsume territorial allocation by Peace Treaties under this heading: the decision in previous decades of the Great Powers have often been dictated in such Treaties.[28]

---

[22] See *Tunisia v Libya* (1982) ICJ *Reports* 18; *Libya v Malta* (1985) ICJ *Reports* 13; *The Gulf of Maine Case* (1982) ICJ *Reports* 3; (1984) *Reports* 246. See further *infra* in Chapter VI.

[23] Naturally, such principles are essential, however, since acts of *aggression* and other acts of *force* may occur precisely in situations when a State considers a part of land is part of its own territory.

[24] See *supra*.

[25] Skutari was given to Albania in 1913; Upper Silesia was divided in 1921; on the Munich Agreement on Czechoslovakia, see my *International Law and the Independent State*, 2nd ed., 1987.

[26] 2 RIAA 1307.

[27] NRG deuxième série XXXVI 662.

[28] See *infra* under Allocation of Geographical Areas, Borders.

viii. Validation of Title

a. The Technique of Non-Recognition and Recognition of Title

For sanctioning of rules forbidding acquisition of territory by force we may note the procedure of *non-recognition,* and, especially, the so called *Stimson doctrine.* By this doctrine, which had been expressed in a letter from the United States to China and Japan, the United States emphasised that it would not recognise any

> 'situation, treaty, or agreement which may be brought about by means contrary to the covenants and obligations of the Pact of Paris[29] of August 27th 1928' ...[30]

The US Secretary for Foreign Affairs, Stimson, wrote the letter to the governments of China and Japan after the establishment of Manchukuo, a Japanese satellite State in China.[31]

The only case when the deficiency of title to taken territory can be remedied is by a procedure of *recognition* of such title. Here we are thus not speaking of recognition in the ordinary sense, of governments or of new States.[32] It is this type of rectification that the *Stimson doctrine* actually reflects: the doctrine was formulated at the beginning of the phase of international law when prohibitions of the use of force were introduced. The doctrine thus indicates that title *can* be 'approved' although, in the specific instance, the United States was not going to 'approve'. In this way, however, it is also clear that should a State from which territory has been wrongly taken *accept* and *recognise* its loss of territory, then title by a *conqueror,* can, even these days, be *validated.*[33]

This is what happened in the case of Goa, the Portuguese enclave in India which was invaded by Indian troops and effectively taken in 1961. In 1974 Portugal recognised India's title to the territory of Goa.

---

[29] The Pact of Paris is commonly called the Briand Kellogg Pact, see *supra.*

[30] 1 Hackworth 334.

[31] See *supra.*

[32] For such recognition, see *supra.*

[33] *Cf.* Jennings, *Acquisition of territory in International Law,* 1963, 62.

Yet, acquisition by conquest[34] must be severely condemned as it threatens the whole basis of international law and security. If States assume that they can legally enlarge their territory by conquest, they may be reminded that *to-day* this is, no longer, possible. The recognition of India's title to Goa by Portugal must be seen as a very rare exception where recognition was presumably based on the special geographical connexity and on the fact that the *mother State* was very far away indeed.

b. Prescription[35]

Verykios, *La prescription en droit international public*, 1934.

In some cases, where there is no clear title, *prescription* may provide, through time, a rectifying factor to enable a State to enjoy full title. This was recognised in the *Dispute about Grisbådarna* before the Permanent Court of Arbitration.[36] In this case both Sweden and Norway claimed territory but Sweden had, for a long time, exercised sovereign rights without any protests from Norway.

The Permanent Court of International Justice and the International Court of Justice have also recognised prescription as a mode of acquiring territory.[37]

It is important to refer to the classification of rules in an earlier Chapter,[38] where it is pointed out that *prescription* is a prime example of *customary law strictu sensu*. For the operation of the principle, there is immediate need of *actual display of sovereignty*.

In most territorial disputes in modern international society, there is a question of claims and counter-claims of sovereignty. We are here not only talking about the *right* to territory, a right which two or more States may claim. We are also considering the actual display of

---

[34] See *supra*, in this Chapter.

[35] For Swedish students, it is again underlined that the Swedish legal term is *hävd*. What in Swedish is known as *preskription* is equivalent to the English term *limitation*.

[36] (1909) 1 Scott 493.

[37] See *Eastern Greenland Case* before the PCIJ, Series A/B No. 53.

[38] *Supra*, Chapter III.

factual acts or expression of sovereignty. Such questions of *effective sovereignty* are often placed, in modern textbooks, in sections under occupation of territory; however, the principle of effective sovereignty is relevant to all forms of acquisition of territory and goes to the root of many disputes. The State that can prove effective sovereignty before, for example, the International Court of Justice, will win his case, provided that no other legal rules prevent the validation of his title.[39]

The question of effective exercise of sovereignty can thus be seen as a *validating* mechanism in certain cases of prescription. Effective exercise of sovereignty can, in cases where a State, without such exercise, would not be considered to have full title, through the lapse of time (prescription) lead to full title.

On the other hand, effective display of sovereignty without any element of time is not sufficient: this is why prescription, implying the laps of time, is highly relevant in all disputes where exercise of sovereignty of one or two States is contested. In other words, prescription need not always be understood as requiring a substantial time element but only *some* time period which, in the case in question, may be regarded as sufficient.[40] In the *Norwegian Fisheries Case*[41] the ICJ held that exercise of sovereign rights during 60 years would suffice for good title. In the arbitration between United Kingdom and Venezuela in the *Case concerning Borders in British Guyana*,[42] 50 years was held to be sufficient. Even a lesser time span may be enough if there are special reasons, for example, geographical inaccessibility.

Display of sovereignty in disputed territory must be *continuous*. This was underlined by the famous judgment in *The Palmas Case*[43] before Judge Huber, of the Permanent Court of Arbitration. The question before him concerned whether the island of Palmas was under the sovereignty of Spain or the Netherlands. The Netherlands

---

[39]   Such legal rules may, for example, concern prohibition of acquisition by force, see further *supra* in this Chapter and in Chapter IV.

[40]   Nor is the term prescription always used.

[41]   (1951) ICJ *Reports* 1.

[42]   NRG, deuxième série, XXIX 583.

[43]   [1928] 2 RIAA 829.

had displayed sovereignty through specific acts of occupation, peaceful and continuous acts over 200 years. On the other hand, only a few and fragmented acts of sovereignty had been displayed.

The *intensity* of sovereign action required may vary according to circumstances. In the case of a far-away island, little may be expected in terms of display of sovereignty, as demonstrated in the afore-mentioned *Palmas Case*. On balance, Netherlands was held to enjoy full title as the *long time* of displayed sovereignty outweighed the lack of full and intense display of sovereign rights, on the ground that *partial exercise of sovereignty* could be justified precisely because the island was so far away from the mother country. This principle of partial expression of sovereignty over far away territories is also illustrated by the *Clipperton Island Case*,[44] where disputed territory was relatively inaccessible; here, almost symbolic exercise of sovereignty was held to be sufficient.

B. AQUISITION OF THE USE OF TERRITORY

i. Leaseholds

Land may be acquired without full title by obtaining the enjoyment of *use of territory* belonging to another State by *leases.* The most famous leases are now probably the leases by China to the United Kingdom for the New Territories in Hong Kong which will now come to an end in 1997. The transfer of the Island of Hong Kong itself acquired by the United Kingdom with full proprietary rights in perpetuity under a *special agreement* with China.

When the Hong Kong leases expire, in 1997, the New Territories will revert to China and the Island of Hong Kong will pass by *cession*[45] to China. The *agreement on leasehold rights*, on the other hand, illustrates a method of acquiring right to *use land,* by agreement, providing for reverting proprietary rights after a certain time.

With legal stringency, it is important to underline that the

---

[44] 2 RIAA 1105.

[45] See *supra*, in this Chapter on cession as a form of acquisition of territory.

sovereign or *ownership* rights never passed, in the first instance with the leasehold agreements, but always remained with the lessor. The leasehold agreements only allowed a *right of use for a certain time.* On the other hand, the exercise of sovereign rights of the United Kingdom, in its colony of the Island of Hong Kong *and* in the leased New Territories, has been of such intensity that, at one stage, it became politically realistic to expect that the Leasehold Agreements would lead to a virtual conversion of United Kingdom rights into permanent title.[46]

ii. Servitudes

Vali, *Servitudes in International Law,* 1958; O'Connell, *State Succession in Municipal Law and International Law*, 1968, ii, 232 *et seq.*

A further method of acquisition of *use of territory* is by *servitudes.* A State may restrict its rights over its territory by concluding an agreement in favour of another state. For example, it may allow another State to establish a military base area in its territory or it may allow grazing rights or transit rights of another state.

Such agreements form part of a special group of treaties that limit the exercise of sovereignty within its own territory. Because of this serious interference with the rights of a State in its own territory beyond what general international prescribes,[47] these agreement need what I have called *continuous consent* of the host State.[48] Thus, the agreements operate only as long as the host State so wishes and they are not transferred to a successor State. In this sense then, the imposed limitations in the territory are no real servitudes: they only operate between the parties (and not *erga omnes, i.e.* vis-à-vis everyone) and they are not *inherited* by or transmitted to a successor

---

[46] There was also a phase, especially before China was admitted, in the place of Taiwan, as a member of the UN, when there were suggestions that the leasehold agreements would be prolonged, or ignored, and that UK sovereignty would be perpetual.

[47] *I.e.*, compelling rules on Human Rights, humanitarian law, Law of War, diplomatic immunity, see *supra* on *jus cogens* in Chapter III and, further, my *Independent State, op. cit., passim.*

[48] See my *Independent State, op. cit.*, 197 *et seq.*, 218 *et seq.*

State.

Some writers, using an analogy of private law, have suggested that, for example, a newly independent State can be fettered by such surviving *servitudes*. But an analysis of practice shows that, in each individual case, the new State has given its consent in one form or other to surviving rights of other States in its territory.[49]

The most useful examples to show that such agreements do not survive State succession, or even a change of government, are *military base agreements*. These agreements *seem* to fulfil many characteristics of servitudes in the conceptual meaning in many national laws. Under these agreements, another sovereign is allowed to exercise certain sovereign, military, functions in the territory of another State. To such agreements certain conditions attach, such as, for example, provisions that the host State must, as mentioned above, give its *continuous consent* to the military bases as they imply a severe encroachment on the exercise of sovereign functions.[50] Yet, the moment a host State wishes to discontinue permission to stay the visiting State will leave,[51] and this is *atypical* for a true servitude, which runs with the land, respective of consent. Furthermore, there can be no successor in title to the host State, nor to the visiting State, in the case of military base agreements and this, again is *atypical* of servitudes properly so called.

A closer analysis of alleged servitudes in international society gives at hand that what is sometimes labelled as such, does not effectively confer any special right *in rem*. A genuine servitude is characterised in most legal system by its link to territory and its independence of the owner: if the owner changes the territory, in municipal law, still has to take the burden of the servitude.

In international law there may be, as we will set out in greater detail,[52] a minimum right of transit over land occasionally confused with servitudes. For example, the right enjoyed with respect to Goa,

---

[49] See *ibid.,* 180-194.

[50] For other similar agreements on exercise of sovereign functions see my *Independent State, op. cit.,* 195 *et seq.* on fettering of judicial and legislative power within the territory of States *infra,* under VII.

[51] See my *Independent State, loc. cit.*

[52] *Infra.*

the former Portuguese enclave in India, was a right of transit but not a servitude: it was a right of transit by necessity,[53] unaffected by any change of regime.[54]

In the *North Atlantic Coast Fisheries Case*[55] it was held that international law knows no firm principle of servitude. *Servitude* is thus used in international law as a term for convenience, devoid of any connotations ascribed to it under Roman law or under various national laws. This is thus yet another term used in international law only *latu sensu*.[56]

C. ALLOCATION OF NATIONAL SPACE: GEOGRAPHICAL AREAS

A State's sovereignty extends over its territory as delimited above with regard to land, water and air space. Over this area the State possesses full sovereignty and may thus enact a host of different laws, rules and regulations and may expect to have such rules obeyed in this geographical area. There is thus a link between a State's sovereign power and the territory which it controls as a State.

The power of a State thus extends within its actual geographical limits, to its land, air and water territory. There are general rules that apply to the delimitation of national boundaries. However, a State may promulgate specific rules as to specific calculation of frontiers, as long as these do not encroach on the territory of another State, or diminish rights others enjoy on the High Seas or other *res communis*.[57]

---

[53]   See my *Independent State, op. cit.*, 234.

[54]   *Ibid., loc. cit.* and *Right of Passage Case* (1960) ICJ *Reports* 6. *Cf.* also Krenz, *International Enclaves*, 1961.

[55]   [1910] Scott 146.

[56]   *Cf. supra*, on customary law *latu sensu*. It is imperative to acknowledge discrepancies in legal terminology in national systems and in international law without thereby alleging that international law would be 'primitive'. On the contrary viewpoint, that international law is a singularly sophisticated legal system see my *Concept of International Law, op. cit.*, Chapter I.

[57]   See *infra* Chapter VIII.

i. Territory

a. Extent of Territory

(i) Borders

Prescott, *The Geography of Frontiers and Boundaries*, 1967; Sharma, *International Boundary Disputes and International Law*, 1976; SFDI, *La frontière*, 1983; De Visscher, Ch., *Le problème des confins en droit international public*, 1969; Sharma, *International Boundary Disputes and International Law*, 1976; de la Pradelle, *La frontière*, 1928; Guilhaudis, Conflits territoriales entre Etats africains, AF 1979, 223; Scherrer, *Zollanschluss Enklave Büsingen an Schweiz*, 1973; Bardonnet, Frontières terrestres et frontières maritimes, AF 1989, 1.

A State exercises its sovereignty within a certain territory and it is naturally important to have clear ideas as to the limits of this land mass. The territory need not be one coherent area, as is shown in the case of Alaska which is part of the United States, or previously by Pakistan and East Pakistan, now Bangladesh. There can naturally be islands which are part of the State territory like Hawaii in the United States, or Gotland and Öland in Sweden. In France there are the *départements outre-mer*, or overseas provinces, which form integral parts of the French Republic.

Some areas may be enclaves near borders, like the German and Italian enclaves in Switzerland. Occasionally, there may be special regulations for similar areas, like for Büsingen (under the Treaty of 1895 between Germany and Switzerland), for Campione, also in Switzerland (under the Treaties of 1861 and 1923 between Italy and Switzerland), for Baarle-Duc and Baarle-Nassau (under the Treaty of 1842 between Belgium and the Netherlands), for Llivia (under a Treaty of 1652 between France and Spain).[58]

On the suggestion of the Pope, the former Spanish and Portugese colonies in South and Central America, adopted the rule *uti possedetis*, implying that the old colonial frontiers would be adopted as they were at the time of independence.[59] The principle, giving priority to actual possession, has been adopted as a general principle

---

[58]   On right of transit see *supra* and *infra*.

[59]   Thus, in 1810 in South America and 1822 in Central America.

of international law[60] as one that is necessary, at least as a presumption, at the independence of any previously dependent territory. The principle is of obvious importance in continents like Africa with large ex-colonial territories[61] The principle of *uti possedetis* was expressly applied by the International Court of Justice in *The Burkina Faso v Mali Case,*[62] which concerned a border dispute.

Frontiers are often decided by treaties. In Europe many borders were decided by earlier peace treaty settlements. In the case of Sweden the Treaty of Brömsebro 1645 the areas of Gotland, Härjedalen and Jämtland were acquired by Sweden and under the Treaty of Roskilde in 1658 Sweden further gained the provinces Scania (Skåne), Halland, Blekinge and Bohuslän. The exact lines of delimitation were laid down by further treaties of 1661 and 1751 for the border with Norway and in 1932 (for territorial waters) and 1983 (with regard to certain islands and the continental shelf) with Denmark.

The whole of Finland was lost under the Peace Treaty of Fredrikshamn in 1809. A further agreement decided on exact delimitation questions.

The Åland Islands lie between Sweden and Finland, but, because of their vicinity to the Swedish coast, and for historical reasons of hegemony, there is a Swedish speaking population. By a League of Nations decision in 1921 the Åland Islands were allotted to Finland in spite of a referendum in the islands where some 99 per cent of the population had declared themselves in favour of a secession from Finland to achieve a merger[63] with Sweden.[64] This is an example of the patronising attitude of the Great Powers this century when borders of strategic importance to them are drawn.

---

[60] See *supra* under General Principles, in Chapter III.

[61] Thus, the Organisation of African Unity gave its express approval by the Cairo Declaration in 1964, IO 1967, 102.

[62] (1986) ICJ *Reports* 554.

[63] On mergers see *supra*, in this Chapter.

[64] This may be seen as one of the last landmarks of the old rule allowing the Great Powers to overrule demands, preceding the requirement of democracy and the rule of self-determination.

Boundary treaties have often been thought to form a special group of agreements which survive state succession. But in *The Case of the Temple of Preah Vihear*,[65] which concerned a boundary Treaty between Siam and France of 1904, the ICJ found Cambodia's consent to the boundary situation essential for it to be effective. On the other hand, it is in border areas that custom has a major role to fulfil and it is here, because of the behaviour of the parties in a territorial connection,[66] a situation rapidly freezes into established international law.

It is for these reasons that boundary treaties are exempt from the provisions in the Convention on the Law of Treaties concerning fundamental change. In other words, no State can argue that a boundary treaty is void, or has lapsed, like some other agreements, only on the ground that there has been a fundamental change of circumstances.[67] The rule on invalidity of ineffectiveness on the ground of a fundamental change of circumstances, is based on the assumption that treaties are concluded with a *tacit clause* a so called *rebus sic stantibus* clause, implying that agreements are concluded only provided there is no major factual change of circumstances.

The theory allowing invalidity or suspension of agreements on this ground has indeed had the most undermining effect on the stability of international treaty relations. Academic opinion, and the Convention on the Law of Treaties, accept that boundary treaties are exempt from the effects of the damaging theory on *rebus sic stantibus*.[68]

Instead of the unhealthy *rebus sic stantibus* theory, it is preferable to allow a rule to abrogate only such treaties which fetter the exercise of sovereign functions in a State's territory.[69]

---

[65]   (1962), ICJ *Reports*, 6.

[66]   This is one of the prime functions of customary law *strictu sensu*, see, *supra*, under Customary Law.

[67]   *Cf. supra*, on Treaties as a source of law, in Chapter II.

[68]   It could be argued, as does the present author, that no treaty is made ineffective on the ground of *rebus sic stantibus*, normally only used by States as a cloak for political interests. See *supra* in Chapter II.

[69]   *Infra*, under Fettering of Sovereignty Under International Treaties, and, further, my *Independent State, op. cit.*, 197 *et seq.*, 218 *et seq.*, on my *doctrine of continuous consent* to treaties which restrict territorial sovereignty.

(ii) Extension or Restriction of Territorial Rights

A State's territory may be extended by the enjoyment of territorial rights in other States or the territory can be conversely restricted by suffering the burden of servitudes or leaseholds of other States.[70]

b. Passage over Land

Already Grotius claimed that there exists a general right of transit across the territory of another State.[71] But modern writers almost all deny this and claim there must be a treaty to enable such transit. Yet, if we examine the actual practice of States we find that numerous routes of transit exist and are often used independently of any treaty arrangements.

(i) Customary Transit

Transit may give rise to a right if there has, as in private law, been consistent use of a route over a certain time. This is a case of customary rules emerging on the basis of a territorial connection,[72] akin to prescription.[73]

(ii) Transit Because of Necessity: Land-locked States and Enclaves

See my own article on Landlocked States and the Law of the Sea, *Scandinavian Studies in Law* 1976; Merryman & Ackerman, *International Legal Development and the Transit Trade of Land-locked States: the Case of Bolivia,* 1969; Palazzoli, De quelques développements recents du droit des gens en matière d'accès à la mer des pays dépourvus de littoral, RGDIP 1966, 667; Sarup, Transit Trade and Land-locked Nepal, ICLQ 1971, 287; Thierry, Les états privés de littoral maritime, RGDIP 1958, 612; Krenz, *International Enclaves and the Rights of Passage,* 1961.

Beyond what rights of passage that has been established by custom, there also exists a general right of transit from land-locked States and

---

[70]   See *supra.*

[71]   *De jure belli ac pacis,* 2, 2, 13; *cf.* Vitoria, *De Indis,* 3, 1.

[72]   See *The Right of Passage Case, Portugal v India,* [1960] ICJ *Reports,* 6.

[73]   See, on prescription, *supra,* in this Chapter, and in Chapter II.

from enclaves for civilians and goods. In many cases such transit has been regulated by treaty. Conditions may be imposed and it may be assumed that only existing routes, and the shortest ones may be used. Transit must furthermore be innocent and peaceful, implying prohibition of military transport of equipment or personnel.

State practice shows that the territorial State preserves a large latitude to control and limit such traffic. It is also politically unrealistic to expect hostile neighbours to allow transit across their State territory.

On the other hand, it may be that international society has some duty to provide alternative trade routes. For example, when Rhodesia closed its border to Zambia in 1973, numerous States hastened to provide and/or finance alternative routes. Zambia also claimed that international society should bear the costs incurred when it was cut off from the shortest transit route to the sea. On May 21 1973 the United Nations Secretary General furthermore gave assurances on a programme for developing alternative trade routes.

The proclaimed interests of land-locked States would indeed be without any value unless the right of access to the sea were coupled with a minimum right of transit overland to reach the sea.

Another group of areas from which there probably exists a right of transit irrespective of treaties are enclaves; but in most cases, at least in Europe, transit is guaranteed by special agreement.[74]

(iii) Transit Under *ad hoc* Permission

In this group we may note the extensive use of transit facilities used by Soviet TIR vehicles throughout Sweden throughout the '80s and early '90s. Such traffic depended on a permission *in casu*, given freely by the then socialist government without even any routing requirement and without any supervision whatsoever. It is important to note that there was not even any requirement of reciprocity: Swedish lorries could certainly not travel where they wished in the ex-Soviet Union. One would have expected transit traffic through Sweden, which posed far greater security threats than the submarine

---

[74]   See, *supra*, on *e.g.* Campione and Büsingen.

incidents,[75] to be curtailed at least by certain conditions. On the other hand, if this traffic had any other purpose than legitimate trading, similar operations could be carried out by hired lorries which would make supervision more difficult.

Since the ex-Soviet Union, and present day Russia, is not land-locked, however, and since it has ample other alternative routes to the continent of Europe, it has no right under international law to transit Sweden without express permission in each individual case.

Consent to transit, when given on an *ad hoc* basis, must be freely given by a government representative of the democratic views of the people in the country.[76]

(iv) Transit under Treaties

See my *International Law and the Independent State,* 2nd ed., London, 1987.

Some general conventions allow free right of transit through other countries. Under article V of GATT[77] contracting parties acquire such a right but only along *the most convenient routes* in the territory of other contracting parties. If Russia adheres to GATT, as has recently been suggested, it will acquire such a right of transport but only on the basis of reciprocity by opening up its own country to transit traffic.

Other major conventions for transit on road are the Road Traffic Conventions of 1949 and 1968, the Convention on Land-Locked States of 1965, and, although they also cover other forms of transit as well as far reaching rules on establishment, the agreements of the European Communities.[78]

Numerous bilateral agreements regulate the need of adjacent

---

[75] On this *infra,* under Innocent Passage, and see in further detail my article on Foreign Warship and Immunity for Espionage, AJIL, 1984, 53.

[76] It may be that, in a war situation, a territorial State may be deprived of any possibility to deny transit when it is placed under military threats: see, for example, the action of Sweden to allow German troops through to and from Norway. In the event, this transitory traffic was limited, or at least so it is alleged, to allow German soldiers to go on leave.

[77] *Cf. supra.*

[78] See my *Independent State. op. cit.,* Chapter IV.

States, like the transit arrangement of 1958 between Afghanistan and Pakistan, or between investing States and their contracting parties where a right of establishment is usually supplemented by a right of access and transit.

As mentioned earlier, transit from enclaves is usually regulated by treaties on a bilateral basis[79] although one could argue that here, a right of transit to the mother State must be implied.

Transit by rail requires express consent laid down in a treaty, both for the construction of the fixed installations and for rail transit.[80] Numerous agreements exist on these matters. Certain rights are laid down in the Barcelona Convention on Communication and Transport of 1921 concerning rail traffic and in the Geneva Convention of 1923 which also deals with certain aspects of electric power. Many bilateral arrangements regulate transit between adjacent States where it is not unusual that trains have to cross over short stretches of another State's territory. For example a Treaty of 1895 between Germany and Switzerland allows trains crossing from Schaffhausen to Zürich to be exempt from German customs handling when trains briefly transit through German territory. Similar arrangements exist between Czechoslovakia, now the Czech Republic and Slovakia, and Poland.[81]

An important Treaty is the one forming part of the dissolution arrangements of the Swedish-Norwegian Union in 1905, allowing transit of Swedish iron ore along a railway line to Narvik in Norway.

In the Third World there are also numerous treaties regulating rail transit, for example the network of treaties concerning the Benguela railway in Africa.[82]

For other fixed installations like the transmission of electric power, express treaties are also necessary. The Geneva Convention of 1923 deals - together with rail questions - also with transit of electric power. Other earlier conventions regulate certain aspects of telephone and telegraph installations within the framework of the International

---

[79] *Supra,* on Büsingen and Campione.

[80] See in further detail, my *Independence, op. cit.,* Chapter II.

[81] UNTS 34.

[82] See my *The East African Community and the Common Market,* London and Nairobi, 1970, Chapter I.

352

Telecommunications Union (ITU).

International pipelines also require explicit treaty authorisation. On agreement regulates, for example, a pipeline between Brazil and Bolivia,[83] another one of 1957 a pipeline between Chile and Bolivia. One pipeline was constructed when other transit traffic proved impossible. This was the case when Rhodesia closed its borders to Zambia in 1973 - in retaliation for harbouring guerillas - Zambia constructed an oil pipeline in conjunction with Tanzania and the Italian company AGIP. Another important pipeline agreement is the Treaty between Canada and the United States concerning the pipeline from Alaska to the United States through Canadian territory.[84] Special provisions here allow for the use of access roads. Nothing in the agreement is, as specifically stated, to derogate from the domestic law of Canada in its own territory.

In some cases pipeline regimes are governed by national common carrier legislation in which the pipeline is treated as a national common carrier of the State in which the actual section is situated. Concession regimes apply especially in the Middle East where the pipeline is usually the property of an affiliate of a petroleum company and carries exclusively the products of that company.

ii. Waters and Shelves

On delimitation of the water territory see: McDorman & Beauchamps & Johnston, *Marine Boundary Delimitation, Annotated Bibliography,* 1983; Jagota, Marine Boundaries, 171 RCADI 1981 ii, 81; Voelckel, Apercu de quelques problèmes techniques concernant la determination des frontières maritimes, AF 1979, 693; Apollis, *Les frontières maritimes en droit international,* 1979; O'Connell, ed. Shearer, *The International Law of the Sea,* 2 vols, 1982.

a. The Status of the Law of the Sea Convention

We shall refer to this Convention, finally signed in 1982 after nine years of elaborate negotiations, from time to time in this Chapter. Therefore, it might be useful to tackle here the repeated claims of

---

[83]   51 UNTS 256.

[84]   206 UNTS 93; 99 UNTS 223; 11 UNTS 325.

UNCLOS as a source of law.

The very status of the Law of the Sea Convention should not be overestimated. It must be underlined that the Convention has not been ratified by the great seafaring nations but only by small or, from the point of view of their fleet, small countries, many or most in the Third World.

The United States which had diligently taken part in the numerous and lengthy preparatory Conferences, backed out at the last minute, unwilling to accept any duty of sharing *know how* expertise to exploit assets on the Ocean Floor to which only technologically advanced countries can have access. The United States was also unwilling to accept any world Authority for Law of the Sea questions, and opposed the powers given to the proposed organ under the Convention. To the extent that the Convention does not reflect already binding rules,[85] it certainly does not bind States that have not ratified it. Suggestions that the mere signing of this Convention would entail any duties is also against any accepted rules of the law of treaties.[86]

Many States behave, especially within the institutions of the United Nations, as if the Convention was already fully binding upon the whole world and it is thought quite appropriate to organise further, often costly, work to prepare the functioning of the Authority, which is reminiscent of the determined efforts to simulate an already binding Maastricht Treaty.[87]

Until there is world wide ratification of the 1982 Convention it is the 1958 Law of the Sea Conventions which are binding. Naturally, many rules contained in these have been superseded by other rules tacitly tolerated without protests or expressly acknowledged by international society. Some such rules undoubtedly concern the permissible width of territorial waters. Others regard the connected question of a patrimonial sea, or what now is called an Exclusive Economic Zone or other protection zones.[88]

---

[85]   *Cf. supra.*

[86]   *Cf. infra.*

[87]   *Cf. supra.*

[88]   See *infra* in this Chapter.

b. Inland Waters

We shall first set out the basic rules for the delimitation of the water territory of the State, bearing in mind a distinction between what is *inland* waters and *internal* waters which are adjacent to the territorial waters.[89] The State comprises, if its geographical position so permits, any relevant water areas.

Inland waters are those which lie inside a State's territory, like lakes and national rivers. These waters have the same status as a State's territory and come therefore entirely under the competence of the territorial State.

On the other hand, there may be a right of transit of non-military goods and persons, from land-locked countries or from enclaves.[90]

(i) National Rivers

When a river is a national one, that is to say one which only flows through one State, it may still, in special circumstances be open for such navigation. This could be the case if it is navigable to the open sea and it is indispensable to international commerce or the only way of access of a land-locked State to the open sea. The right of all States to an equal right to the high seas becomes illusory unless such land-locked states are also granted access to the sea.

It has thus been suggested by Colombos, the nestor of the law of the sea,[91] that the arbitrator in *The Faber Case* was 'wrong' then he held that Venezuela possessed the right to prohibit altogether navigation in the Catatumbo and Zuila rivers, two of its internal national rivers, even to sea-going vessels carrying goods for transport over the oceans.

(ii) International Rivers

Colliard, Evolution et aspects actuels du régime juridique des fleuves internationaux, 125 RCADI 1968 iii, 337; Gidel, Le régime des fleuves internationaux, 1948; Baxter,

---

[89]   *Cf. infra.*

[90]   See *supra* on transit arrangements, in this Chapter.

[91]   *International Law of the Sea,* 1967, 236.

The Law of International Waterways, 1964; Zacklin & Caflisch (eds.) *The Legal Regime of International Rivers and Lakes,* 1981; Wegener, *Die internationale Donau,* 1951; Gorove, *Law and Politics of the Danube,* 1964; Pichler, *Donaukommission und die Donaustaaten,* 1973; Scheuner, Rhein, VW iii, 117.

A river which flows through one country and thus forms part of its inland waters may also flow through another State. It is these rivers, those which flow through several States, that we call international rivers. Some such rivers are essential to international society as international communications and transport have become dependent on their status as international waterways. This has naturally happened more frequently in regions where the need for river transport is pronounced, or where the size of the river is such that its uses for international communication is obvious. In most cases, however, the internationalisation of large rivers that flow between several States has been regulated by treaty.

Treaties which have imposed limitations in the sovereignty of a territorial State with regard to internal waters are, for example, the convention of 1804, further elaborated at the Congress of Vienna in 1815 which internationalised the Rhine. The Treaty of Mainz 1831 and the Convention of Mannheim 1868, supplemented these agreements. The Treaty of Paris of 1856, together with the later Treaty of Berlin of 1878 and the Treaty of London of 1883, internationalised the Danube.

The river regimes of the Rhine and of the Danube have been subjected to important River Commissions with important regulatory powers.[92] We may even perceive, in this context, some of the first European efforts to issue binding international regulations, adopted by majority votes. Some of the riparian States of the Danube have concluded a competing Convention of Belgrade of 1949[93] to which also Austria has acceded. This Convention can, however, not alter the

---

[92]   For the Rhine, see Part XII of the Versailles Treaty of 1919 and Convention 1936 7 Hudson, 290 and the 1963 Convention; *cf. Van Eysinga, La Commission centrale pour la navigation du Rhin,* 1935. For the Danube Commission, see Convention of 1921, 26 LNTS 174, and the Peace Treaties 1947 41 UNTS; *cf. Advisory Opinion on the European Danube Commission,* (1927) PCIJ Series B, No. 14.

[93]   33 UNTS 181.

contractual relationship between the original parties, especially since the initial relationship had established a special territorial regime,[94] amplified by the regulatory power of the Commission.

The river Elbe was internationalised by the Treaty of Dresden of 1821. The rivers Meuse and Escaut, which had been subjected to a regime of free navigation by a unilateral declaration of the French provisional executive in 1792, were further internationalised by the Treaty of London of 1839. The Versailles Peace Treaty of 1919 and the Barcelona Convention of 1921[95] reconfirmed the right of free navigation on principal European rivers.

Great rivers, in other continents have also been internationalised. In Africa, the Congo and the Niger were internationalised by the General Act of the Berlin Conference in 1885. In South America, agreements were concluded in 1850 to grant free navigation to all on the Rio Grande, the Amazon and the Rio de la Plata. A Treaty of 1854 opened the St. Lawrence river in North America to international navigation.

It is nowadays clear that a right of free navigation exists, for merchant shipping, but not for men of war, on rivers whose navigable waters pass through the territory of more than one State, or which form a boundary between two States.[96] In the latter case, the waters are apportioned along the middle of the channel or along the so called *Thalweg*. Such a right of navigation appears to exist irrespective of the aforementioned international agreements. In other words, a general rule in favour of merchant shipping has grown out of the practice and use of such rivers over a long period of time. Here is thus another example of a customary rule of international law which has grown out of practice within a territorial context.[97]

---

94   The original treaty will bind the original parties and later agreements may operate as an inter-se agreement, see my *Essays on the Law of Treaties*, 1967; on regimes, see my *Concept, op. cit.*, 38-40. *Cf.* the discussion on the Maastricht Treaty, for example, in the English and Danish Parliaments in 1992/1993, considering *opting out* mechanisms.

95   7 LNTS 35.

96   See ILA Helsinki Rules, *Report* 1966, article XIV.

97   See *supra* in Chapter II under the discussion of certain valid claims of existing customary law *strictu sensu*.

(iii) International Canals

Baxter, *The Law of International Waterways,* 1964; Wehser, Die Durchfahrt durch die interozeänischen Kanäle, DGVR 1975, 55; Böhmert, Kanäle, WV iii 237; my *International Law and the Independent State,* 2nd ed., 1987.

For international canals State practice show a number of examples where use has been regulated by agreement. The Hay-Pauncefote Treaty,[98] between the United States and the United Kingdom of 1901, and the Hay-Bunau-Varilla Treaty[99] of 1903 internationalised the Panama Canal, revised in 1955 and 1959. Two later Treaties of 1977[100] provide for the reversion of control to Panama. The Convention of Constantinople of 1888 internationalised the Suez Canal[101] and the Kiel Canal was opened to international use by article 380 of the Treaty of Versailles in 1919.[102]

Occasionally, a right of passage can be acquired to pass through internal waters outside provisions of a treaty. This has, for example, happened in the case of the Corinth Canal. This artificial canal lies entirely within Greek territory but has, since it was opened in 1883, consistently been used by foreign merchant vessels. Here is another example how custom can give rise to an international legal rule provided there is a territorial connection.[103]

c. Internal Waters

(i) Definition of Internal Waters

For literature, see *supra,* on Delimitation of Water Territory under ii, Water and Shelves.

Depending on their geographical position, some States will have a

---

[98]   3 Moore 366.

[99]   31 NRG deuxième série 1905, 599.

[100]   16 ILM 1977, 1021.

[101]   *Cf.* Statement by the Egyptian Government 24th September 1957, 15 NRG deuxième série 1891, 557.

[102]   *Cf. The Wimbledon Case* [1923] PCIJ A No. 1.

[103]   See further my *Concept, op. cit.,* 115-116 and *supra* on Customary Rules.

coastline and therefore additional water areas.

Internal waters are the waters between the dry land mass of a State and the base line from which the territorial waters are calculated. Internal waters are thus necessarily in a State which has a coast line. Switzerland, for example, has thus inland waters but no internal water areas.

Internal waters include harbours, estuaries and bays up to the width of 24 nautical miles as well as historic bays[104] which do not fulfil the qualifications of other bays. Furthermore, internal waters also include waters like rivers, lakes and canals. Over these waters, the coastal State exercises sovereignty as over its territory. If, therefore, another State seeks privileges,[105] in territorial waters, a specific treaty, or other special clear consensual act of the coastal State, is necessary to limit sovereignty over these areas in favour of the other State. Few general rules of international law infringe on the total power of a State in these areas, *unless* the State has consented to certain limitations by clear acts of consent.

(ii) Access to Ports

Laun, Le régime international des ports, 15 RCADI 1926, 1.

Ports and roadsteads are wholly within the sovereignty of the territorial State. A State thus enjoys full jurisdiction over ships in its harbours although many States often refrain from exercising this jurisdiction as a gesture of international courtesy: for example, as demonstrated in the cases of *The Sally* and *The Newton.*[106]

No foreign ship can insist on going into foreign ports as of right. But in most States merchant vessels have a right to expect that non-military ports are open and that they will be able to enter. If a ship is in distress a coastal State is probably under duty to allow her into any port. The right of access to ports may be incidental to a right of

---

[104]   See *infra.*

[105]   Not even *innocent passage* which is enjoyed in *territorial waters, cf. infra.,* is enjoyed in internal waters.

[106]   [1806] French Conseil d'Etat, Bulletin des Lois 1806, No. 126, 602; for Italy, *The Albissola* [1930] AD 1929-1930, 105.

transit: if there is free navigation along an international river there must also be some minimum access to a port at the mouth of the river. Such a view is confirmed by the judgment of the Permanent Court of International Justice in *The Case concerning Jurisdiction of the European Commission of the Danube.*[107] The same Court came to a similar conclusion in *The Oscar Chinn Case* although other complex questions such as the interpretation of an international convention were also at stake.[108]

The minimum right of access to ports that merchant vessels have under international law implies that a coastal state may, at any rate, not abolish this right without warning.[109]

(iii) Access to Bays

Bouchez, *The Regimes of Bays in International Law,* 1964; Strohl, *The International Law of Bays,* 1963.

Bays come within the internal waters of a State provided they fulfil certain criteria. These criteria were basically laid down in the 1958 Geneva Convention and provide the following. If the distance between the low water marks of the natural entrance points of a bay does not exceed 24 miles, a straight base line may be drawn to enclose the bay as internal waters. If, on the other hand, the points are wider apart than 24 miles, then a straight line should be drawn further inside the bay to enclose as internal waters what is nearer to the coast along that line.

Furthermore, in exceptional cases *historic bays,* for example Hudson Bay,[110] may be recognised when an area over a long period of time has been treated as a bay although it does not fulfil these criteria.

A new category of *vital bays*, has been adopted by some

---

[107]   (1927) PCIJ B No. 14.

[108]   (1934) PCIJ Series A/B No. 34.

[109]   See *The Portendinck Incident*, in Laun, Le régime international des ports, 15 RCADI 1926, 1.

[110]   More questionably, the Gulf of Aqaba.

authorities.[111] This concept implies bays too wide for the traditional criteria and not qualifying as historic bays, but which are *necessary*, involving *non-negotiable national interests*. These qualifications seem to indicate a certain new way for States to *insist*, before international tribunals and courts, that an area of a bay is *indispensable* for national interests. The development appears to reflect an unhealthy trend towards self interest and determined insistence, all expressions of subjective views rather than what can be established by reasonably objective legal criteria. It is also a development that would appear to favour the strong, determined and territorially ambitious State at the expense of the law abiding, reasonable and meeker State.

With regard to access to bays, sections which qualify as internal waters are wholly excluded from international use unless specific consent is given, under treaties or under special authorisation or by acquiescence. Thus, no vessels can claim any right of access or passage within these areas, subject to what has been said above about access to ports.

d. Territorial Waters

Walker, The Cannon Shot Rule, BYIL, 1945, 210; O'Connell, BYIL, 1971, 1; Kent, The Historical Origins of the Three Mile Limit, 48 AJIL 537.

(i) The Notion of a Territorial Sea

The territorial sea comes under the full sovereignty of the coastal State, under general international law as reflected in both the Territorial Sea Convention of 1958 and in Law of the Sea Convention 1982. The notion of a territorial sea has its origins in the need to protect a coastal state from attacks and to provide a costal buffer zone.

(ii) The Width of the Territorial Sea

As the territorial sea has its historic origin in the defense needs of a coastal State, the width of the territorial sea was initially determined

---

[111]   i:2 Oppenheim (ed. Jennings and Watts) 1992, 631.

to be that of the length of a cannon shot: it was this width of the territorial water belt that the coastal State could effectively defend by cannons on the shore, and conversely, it was through this belt that foreign ships with cannons could attack the coastal State. As territorial waters were at first claimed to protect themselves, so was the width thus set in defense terms. On the other hand, States did not claim more water areas than they could effectively protect.

The width of the territorial sea was explained and elaborated in these terms by the Dutch lawyer Bynckershoek in the early eighteenth century.[112] Historically, the normal limits were often three miles. However, in Scandinavia the Scandinavian league, *i.e.* four miles, was in general use. Denmark and Norway proclaimed a zone of four miles in 1745 but this implied a reduction of earlier claims of the whole ocean between Norway and Iceland. The reduction was made in order to effectively protect a narrower belt as neutrality waters. Similarly, Sweden reduced, during the First and Second World Wars, its territorial waters from four to three miles as a special neutrality water margin.

The two principles, of three and four miles, were confronted when French privateers captured two British ships off Denmark in 1761, within an area outside three but inside four miles, Denmark protested to France as the ships were within the zone proclaimed by Denmark as territorial waters. However, France insisted that Denmark was not entitled to more than three miles, *i.e.* the possible range of a cannon shot. Denmark did not yield to the pressure from France and successfully continued to claim a zone of four miles. In 1779 Sweden, also adopted the four mile limit.

On the other hand, some other States claimed a greater limit: Spain claimed six miles (1760) and argued in 1862 that United States ships unlawfully interfered inside its six mile limit around Cuba, a limit which was not unreasonable in view of the increased range of a cannon. Czarist Russia claimed, at different times, three or twelve miles.

As weaponry was modernised the old short limits became obsolete but States still used them and did not expand their water zones

---

[112]   For detailed references to Bynckershoek and ancillary historical classics, see my *Bibliography of International Law*, New York (Bowker), 1976.

according to greater military capacity. The zones claimed, remained for several hundred years and, as we shall see, were only changed through the influence of the 1982 Law of the Sea Convention.[113]

It is useful to revert briefly to the historical background and note that coastal water zones were soon used for different purposes. Some States did not distinguish between territorial waters and other zones for jurisdiction and claimed, like, for example, Portugal, six miles for territorial waters and another adjacent zone of another six miles. The United States, and Canada, claimed six miles together with a six mile adjacent *contiguous zone.*[114]

At the Codification Conference in 1929 most English-speaking countries, together with France and Germany, accepted the three mile limit; the Scandinavian countries still insisted on four miles; most Spanish speaking countries, together with Italy, claimed six miles; and Portugal claimed twelve miles or six miles plus and adjacent zone.

The 1958 Convention on the Territorial Sea reached no agreement on the matter but in State practice larger claims were increasingly made, especially after the Truman Declaration on the continental shelf.[115]

There has been an increasing tendency towards twelve miles. Some States claimed twelve miles. The Soviet Union and a number of newly independent nations claimed twelve miles by the 1960's.

Certain States in Latin America had long sought enormously wide territorial water belts, usually to protect their own fishing rights. In South America many States early claimed larger territorial seas, often up to 200 miles, usually under persistent protests by other States.

Under the Santiago Declaration of 1952 Chile, Ecuador and Peru thus claimed 200 miles. Similar 200 mile claims have come from Argentina (1966), Panama (1967), Uruguay (1969), Brazil (1970). African States have also claimed 200 miles like Sierra Leone (1971). Guinea has claimed 130 miles (1967) and Nigeria, Ghana and Mauritania 30 miles (1972).

The claims of coastal States in adjacent waters were confirmed by

---

[113] See *infra* in this Chapter.

[114] See, *infra,* in the section on the Contiguous Zone.

[115] See, *infra,* under The Continental Shelf.

the Montevideo Declaration in 1970[116] and by the Lima Declaration issued the same year.[117] However, neither of these Declarations mentioned any specific width of the territorial sea. The Yaoundé Declaration of 1972[118] voiced the concern of some African States and insisted that coastal states need a *patrimonial sea* of 200 miles if they were to keep their territorial sea at twelve miles.

A similar statement, the Santo Domingo Declaration, came in 1972 from some Latin American and Caribbean states.[119]

Some of the protection sought by South American and African States for fishing interests and which had prompted their proclamation of wide belts of territorial sea have been satisfied by the new notion of an Exclusive Economic Zone (EEZ) under the 1982 Law of the Sea Convention.[120]

Now it is clear that other forms of adjacent zones will cater for the need of coastal States with regard to fishing and other economic interests. The territorial sea can therefore be kept relatively limited, that is less extensive than the previous Latin American and African claims, but more extensive than the modest limits of other States.

The 1982 Law of the Sea Convention, the first agreement to fix a general limit for the territorial sea, sets the limit to twelve miles. Some claim that the South American territorial sea zones of 200 miles are invalid as the 1982 Law of the Sea Convention explicitly limits the territorial sea to twelve miles. But it is important to remember that the Convention has not been ratified by the countries in question.

Secondly, it may be that specific needs of the States in the Third World are such that wider zones may be permissible, especially in view of geographical factors. In South America it would often seem reasonable to allow extensive territorial sea in view of the isolated

---

[116] The Declaration was signed by Argentina, Brazil, Ecuador, El Salvador, Peru, Nicaragua and Uruguay.

[117] This Declaration was signed by Mexico, Colombia, Honduras, Guatemala and the Dominican Republic.

[118] Signed by Algeria, Cameroon, Dahomey, Egypt, Equatorial Guinea, Ethiopia, Ivory Coast, Kenya, Mauritius, Nigeria, Sierra Leone, Tanzania, Togo and Zaire,

[119] This Declaration was signed by Columbia, Costa Rica, Dominican Republic, Guatemala, Haiti, Honduras, Mexico, Nicaragua, Trinidad and Tobago and Venezuela.

[120] *Infra*, under The Exclusive Economic Zone.

position seaward of the States in question. Why should their zones have been limited to enable the Onassis fishing fleet to fish off their shores? Why should persistent protests by certain developed nations be allowed to the detriment of the development of Third World States?

Thirdly, it must be emphasised that the Law of the Sea Convention has not been ratified by the great sea faring nations and is of little formal legal significance.[121]

On the other hand, the freedom of the high seas must always be weighed against those of a coastal State. If the fishing interests of coastal States are taken care of by zones with other names, for example, by the EEZ,[122] there is certainly less need to allow considerations concerning the needs of developing nations to play a role in this particular case.

The earlier series of declarations and forceful claims from Latin American and African countries undoubtedly had a considerable impact on the contents of the 1982 Law of the Sea Convention and these non-binding unilateral statements illustrate how a final text is coloured by informal pressures from States and non-State sources prior to the formal acceptance by ratification. It is far fetched to claim that it is the Law of the Sea Convention which entails any binding obligations *before* final ratification.[123] What the new legal situation illustrates, however, is rather a clear example of a *general rule adopted by States as binding.*[124] but the legal rule of permissible width certainly changed by uniform State practice, in the 1980's.

One may claim that the normal limit of territorial sea is now admitted as twelve miles and numerous States, even those which have not adhered to the 1982 Convention, have uniformly adopted this limit by their own national legislation. Sweden adopted this limit even

---

[121]   *Cf. infra.*

[122]   See, *infra,* in detail under The Exclusive Economic Zone.

[123]   Some thus argue that State must not undermine the 'spirit' of the Convention after signature. Such claims of any *legal obligation* are fictitious and do little to advance international law. On the other hand, it is more realistic to claim that States *have adopted a new rule.*

[124]   See *supra* in Chapter III on this category.

before signing the convention.[125] The breadth of the territorial sea is of particular importance to ascertain where a coastal State is under duty to allow foreign merchant ships to pass.

(iii) Calculation of Territorial Waters

Voelkel, Lignes de bases, AF 1973, 820; Gihl, *Utgångspunkten för territorialhavets beräkning*, SOU, 1965, 1; O'Connell, Mid-Ocean Archipelagos, BYIL, 1971, 26; Sorensen, The Territorial Sea of Archipelagos, *Liber Amicorum J P A François*, 315.

To apply the modern rules of the width of the territorial sea, it is obviously essential to know the starting point for any calculation of the breadth of water belt to lay down its exact extent off the shore of a State. The inner line of the territorial sea is drawn from the low water marks along the coast. If the coast is very irregular *straight base lines* may be drawn to follow the *general direction* of the coast, as ruled in *The Norwegian Fisheries Case*.[126] However, such a general direction depends somewhat on the scale of the map of the area and there will be an element of arbitrariness.

Bays are closed by straight lines provided they have an opening of less than 24 miles or are admitted as historic bays.[127]

Archipelagos are also enclosed, at least under the 1982 Law of the Sea Convention, as internal waters by straight base lines drawn from the outer islands; this may be done under article 46 provided the group of islands form a geographical, economic or political unit or historically have been regarded as such. One example of such an archipelagic state is Indonesia.

e. The Contiguous Zone

Oda, The concept of the contiguous zone, ICLQ 1962, 131.

Article 24 of the 1958 Geneva Convention on the Territorial Sea and the Contiguous Zone specified that, within a stretch of water outside the territorial sea, a State may exercise certain sovereign functions to

---

[125] Law of 1966 as amended 1978.

[126] (1951) ICJ *Reports*, 116.

[127] See further *supra* in this Chapter.

prevent and punish infringements of its customs, fiscal, immigration or public health regulations. Such a zone is, under the 1958 Convention, not to extend further than twelve miles; under the 1982 Law of the Sea Convention this limit has been extended to 24 miles.

Passage in this zone can be seen as passage on the high seas restricted by certain rules of the coastal State; or it can be conceived as a form of diluted sovereignty exercised in a belt offshore where a State still has certain control.

f. Special Protection Zones

Andrassy, Mésures internationales contre pollutions maritimes, IDI, 53 Annuaire i 1969, 547; Alexander, (ed), *The Law of the Sea: Offshore Boundaries and Zones,* 1967.

Canada declared a special protection zone in 1970 by a unilateral measure, the Arctic Waters Pollution Prevention Act. Within a distance of 100 miles offshore Canada held itself competent to lay down regulations and standards of construction and navigation and to intervene against ships violating the Act. The reason for this legislative action interfering with what had been the high seas, was the threat of pollution in Canadian water and of Canadian territory. In icy waters, such as those near Canada, oil spills do not break up as easily as elsewhere and oil slicks may be caught under ice and preserved to cause considerable damage as pollution fighting equipment is unable to reach the spills.[128] There were very few international protests against this legislation, although the United States questioned the Canadian measures.

It is probably in full accordance with international law to enact such protective measures for environmental reasons. In a zone of this type there is a right of passage only on the conditions as laid down by the coastal State.

A special protection zone may often be subsumed under the above mentioned contiguous zone: this special zone may cater for needs of customs control and may specifically refer to customs and fiscal regulations.

---

[128]   *Cf. supra* on Environmental Law in Chapter IV.

Sometimes a special customs zone has been declared in adjacent waters independently of other regulatory power in this belt. Thus, Sweden proclaimed by Law of 27th November 1925, a special zone of 12 miles to prevent the smuggling of alcohol into the country. The United States has claimed a similar zone, of four leagues, since 1790, reinforced by the Anti-Smuggling Act of 1935. The United Kingdom had similar so called Hovering Acts in operation between 1736 to 1876.

g. Fishery Zones

Rodriguez, *La zona exclusiva de pesca en el nuevo derecho del mar,* 1977; Kehden, *Die Inanspruchnahme von Meereszonen und Meeresbodenzonen durch Kustenstaaten,* 2nd ed., 1971.

The main purpose of the extended claims by, for example, South American States[129] was to protect fishing. Sometimes States have not labelled such zones as territorial waters but as explicit fishery zones. This was the case of Costa Rica which, since 1955, has claimed a fishery zone of 200 miles.

Iceland declared unilaterally a fishery zone of 50 miles whereupon United Kingdom filed a suit in the International Court of Justice claiming that this extension of fishery limits was contrary to international law. Under an earlier agreement between the United Kingdom and Iceland of 1961, the United Kingdom had promised that it would no longer object to an extension of fishery zones to 12 miles by Iceland but the agreement also provided that the Icelandic Government would continue to work for the implementation of a resolution of the Icelandic parliament regarding further extension of the whole of the continental shelf, some 50 miles off shore. This could be construed to indicate that the United Kingdom was put on notice and agreed to further extensions. But the International Court of Justice held in 1974 in *The Icelandic Fisheries Case*[130] that Iceland was not entitled to exclude United Kingdom fishing vessels from an area between 12 and 50 miles off shore or unilaterally impose any

---

[129]   See *supra.*
[130]   [1974] ICJ *Reports,* 2.

restrictions.

This decision appears anachronistic some 15 years later when international developments show that most States, whether they have ratified the 1982 Law of the Sea Convention or not, all claim 200 miles wide Exclusive Economic Zones, (EEZs),[131] zones which are especially designed to protect fishery rights of the coastal States; the EEZs now absorb the category of fishery zones. The United Kingdom itself, a non-party to the Convention, also claims such a zone.

On the other hand, some[132] have argued that the development of extensive zones constitute a questionable development, infringing on the character of the High Seas as *res communis omnium.*

h. The Exclusive Economic Zone (EEZ)

O'Connell & Shearer, *The International Law of the Sea,* 1982 i 552; Conforti (ed.), *La zona economica exclusiva,* 1983; Extavour, *The Exclusive Economic Zone,* 1976; Attard, *The Exclusive Economic Zone,* 1985.

The 1982 Law of the Sea Convention allows for a special Exclusive Economic Zone (EEZ) of 200 miles, rapidly accepted by numerous States in their practice although the 1982 Convention has not been ratified by any of the major seafaring States. The background of the EEZ were the claims of a *patrimonial sea* made by certain countries largely in the southern hemisphere and claims to fishery zones elsewhere.

The initiative of forming a cohesive group during the negotiations of the new Law of the Sea Convention was taken in 1973 by Australia and the group included Argentina, Brazil, Canada, Chile, Iceland, India, Indonesia, Kenya, Mexico, New Zealand, Norway, Peru, Sri Lanka, Trinidad and Tobago, Tunisia and Venezuela. This was the New York group which encouraged the conference to adopt a notion which became known as the EEZ and incorporated in the 1982 Convention. Within the EEZ coastal States have the right to fish and to enjoy any other economic rights to the exclusion of others.

There is an unlimited freedom of passage through the EEZ, both

---

[131]   See further *infra* in the next section.

[132]   Verdross & Simma, *Universelles Völkerrecht,* 3rd ed., 1984, 698.

for merchant vessels and for warships, as on the high seas. But no ships are allowed to stop and fish in these waters which, for the purposes of fishing and other economic rights, come under the sovereignty of the coastal state.

As mentioned earlier in this Chapter with reference to the change of rules concerning the width of the territorial sea, there is here too, a rapid change and reversal of rules relating to the extent of fishery zones, now absorbed by the EEZ. What is particularly striking about the development of rules relating to the width of an economic zone is that the new rule emerged only some eight years after the *Iceland Fisheries Case*,[133] a case where the United Kingdom argued that the Icelandic claims to a fishery zone of 50 miles was *excessive* and not allowed in law.[134] The rules relating to the EEZ also clearly illustrates the mechanism of adoption of States of new general rules on a specific matter.[135]

The International Court of Justice held in *The Tunisia v Libya Case*[136] that the EEZ now forms part of general international law and is not dependent on adherence to the 1982 Convention.

On the other hand, the suggestion in the 1982 Law of the Sea Convention that delimitation of the EEZ between opposite and adjacent States is effected by agreement, is a clause which is not, by itself producing any legal obligation: it is a mere *pactum de contrahendo*, that is to say, and agreement that a future agreement should be reached. It is, however, *useful*, for the international order, if States do conclude such agreements.[137]

j. The Continental Shelf

Klemm, *Die seewärtige Grenze des Festlandssockels*, 1976; Rigaldies, La delimitation du plateau continental entre états voisins, CYIL 1976, 116; Finlay, The

---

[133]   *United Kingdom v Iceland* (1974) ICJ *Reports* 1974

[134]   *Cf. supra*, under Fishery Zones.

[135]   See further *supra* in Chapter III under Adoption of Rules.

[136]   (1982) ICJ *Reports*, 18; *cf. Tunisia v Libya (Interpretation) Case* [1985] ICJ *Reports*, 1; *Libya v Malta* [1985] ICJ *Reports*, 1.

[137]   See Dissenting Opinion by Judges Oda and Evensen in the *Tunisia v Libya Case* (1982) ICJ *Reports*, 18. *Cf. Guinea v Guinea Bissau Arbitration* (1985), 77 ILR 636.

outer limit of the continental shelf, AJIL 1970, 44; Auguste, *The Continental Shelf,* 1960; Mouton, *The Continental Shelf,* 1952; Ruster, *The Rechtsordnung des Festlandssockel,* 1977; Scelle, *Plateau continental et le droit international,* 1955; Vallat, The continental shelf, BYIL, 1946, 333; Gidel, A propos des bases juridiques des prétensions des états riverains sur le plateau continental, ZaöRVR, 1959, 81; Oda, A reconsideration of the continental shelf doctrine, *Tulane Law Review,* 1957, 21; Dupuy, R-J., Droit de la mer et communauté internationale, in *Mélanges Reuter,* 1981, 224; Bardonnet & Virally (eds.), *Le nouveau droit international de la mer,* 1983; Vallee, *Le plateau continental dans le droit positif actuel,* 1971; Kunz, Continental shelf and international law, AJIL 1956, 828. Colson, UK - France Continental Shelf Arbitration, AJIL 1970, 562; Oellers-Frahm, Festlandssockel Tunisien-Libyen, ZaöRVR 1982, 604.

A State has a right to exclusively exploit the resources of its continental shelf, if there is such geological configuration off its coast. This is the submerged land mass between a State's territory and the open sea. The portion under the territorial waters comes in any event under the full sovereignty of a coastal State but, although the coastal State may have the right to certain jurisdiction and to certain economic right in the waters of the contiguous zone and of the EEZ, it has not *ipso facto* acquired any exclusive right to the submerged shelf. Such a right is derived from another rule of international law which has developed in recent years.

Through the Truman Declaration of 28th September 1945 the United States claimed for itself the resources of the continental shelf up to one hundred fathoms, *i.e.* about 200 metres. Numerous States followed the United States by similar declarations and the Geneva Convention on the Continental Shelf incorporated the same limit which, at the time, was the only depth technically feasible to exploit, and added, as alternative outer limit, the depth which admits the exploitation of the area.[138] This *'exploitability'* criterion is, however, dependent on whether there actually is a shelf; the geomorphological environment thus decides, ultimately, on the rights of exploitation of a coastal State.

The Convention of 1958 used three criteria to identify the Continental Shelf. The shelf has to be *adjacent* to the coast of the claiming State; it must be *above a depth of 200 metres*; and it must

---

[138]   Article 1.

be *possible to exploit* the shelf. These criteria all present problems; the question of what *adjacent* means gave rise to the *North Sea Continental Shelf Case* before the International Court of Justice where it was held that this was a *general* expression referring to the *natural prolongation* of a State.[139] On the other hand, a rift in the shelf, like the one off the coast of Norway, does not necessarily break the continuity of the shelf under national jurisdiction.

The 1982 Law of the Sea Convention has adopted a complicated formula for the delimitation of the continental shelf. Under article 76 the shelf may extend to the continental margin and thus, in some cases, out to a distance of 350 nautical miles.

The 1982 Convention marks a regression with regard to the *clarity* of the status of the continental shelf. The formulation and definition of what is now to be considered the continental shelf is so complicated and so convoluted that the Rule of Law in maritime matters is seriously put at risk: no one can be exactly sure as to whether or not a particular area forms part of the Continental Shelf. The Convention adopts no fewer than seven criteria, three general rules[140] and two sub-rules[141] and two special cases[142] to define the continental shelf. The Convention also provides for a Commission which would certify existing claims to the continental shelf.

The 1977 draft, negotiated during the discussions leading up to the 1982 Convention, was considerably simpler and it is indeed remarkable that not more States objected to the formulation in the final 1982 text which, in this part, reflects the incompetence of the government negotiators to indicate clear guidelines of demarcation for the shelf.

---

[139] (1969) ICJ, *Reports,* 1969.

[140] The main rules are: coastal States can claim a continental shelf up to 200 miles distance even if the shelf is smaller than this distance (art. 76(4)(a); in certain cases, depending on geological calculations, a further distance may be claimed if the shelf is larger than 200 miles; in certain cases the limit may be fixed at 60 miles, under article 76(4)(a)(ii).

[141] These rules provide that in no case may exploitation take place further than 350 miles from the base line *or* at 100 miles beyond the isobar of 2,500 metres, under art. 76(5).

[142] The special cases concern configuration in the shelf affecting the calculations, under article 76(6).

As the 1982 is not binding on the most important seafaring nations,[143] the earlier Convention is still of great importance. Furthermore, there are certain general rules of importance. The Continental Shelf Convention of 1958 provides in article 6 that delimitation of the shelf should be carried out along a rule of equidistance unless *special circumstances* warrant another type of delimitation. However, the International Court of Justice held in *The North Sea Continental Shelf Cases*[144] that the rule of equidistance did not form part of general international law. Germany, which had not ratified the Convention, was therefore not bound by this rule. The Court said that delimitation must be carried out by agreement of the parties along equitable principles, leaving to each party as much as possible of the continental shelf which constitutes a *natural prolongation* of its land. As the continental shelf is also the natural prolongation of the other party, such delimitation may not always be easy to achieve.

Recent cases before the International Court of Justice have concerned precisely delimitation of the continental shelf. In *the Tunisia v Libya Case,*[145] *Libya v Malta,*[146] and *The Gulf of Maine Case,*[147] the Court abandoned any thought of equidistance principles and sought instead *equitable solutions* whereby the court functioned as *an independent surveyor* drawing the necessary dividing lines. In *The Gulf of Maine Case* and *The Libya v Malta Case* the Court was careful not to be influenced by relative economic interests lest a solution discarding such values become *radically* inequitable. In this sense the Court reversed the earlier trend set in *The Icelandic Fisheries Case.*[148]

Numerous agreements have now been concluded between adjacent States to delimit continental shelves, for example in the Persian Gulf and in the North Sea and in the Baltic (e.g. agreements between UK

---

[143] *Cf. supra.*
[144] [1969] ICJ *Reports* 27.
[145] [1982] ICJ *Reports* 18.
[146] [1985] ICJ *Reports* 1.
[147] *Ibid., loc. cit.*
[148] See *supra.*

and Norway 1965;[149] between UK and Denmark 1966;[150] UK and the Netherlands 1965;[151] Sweden and Denmark;[152] and between Sweden and Finland, 1972.[153]

k. Passage Through Water

(i) Innocent Passage

Baldoni, Les navires de guerre dans les eaux territoriales étrangères, 65 RCADI 1938, 185.

Under general international law a rule has evolved that certain ships, on certain conditions, are allowed *innocent passage*. The rules were originally elaborated in article 14 of the 1958 Territorial Sea Convention and, further, by article 19[154] of the 1982 Law of the Sea Convention. However, innocent passage is enjoyed only by merchant ships under established international law. For warships, numerous, if not most, States require prior notification of passage of warships. The United States claimed that this is even a rule of law in its Memorial in *The North Atlantic Fisheries Arbitration*,[155] and there is much support for this opinion. Lately, the United States has interpreted the criterion *innocent* as implying that a ship has already obtained permission to go into an American port and thus limited innocent passage to mean passage between a port and the high seas. The Soviet Union also insisted[156] on previous authorisation, not only *ad hoc* notification, of any passage of warships through its territorial waters. Exceptions may always be granted in the case of genuine distress.

For passage to be *innocent* it must not be detrimental to the interests of the coastal state. Thus, it must not involve the landing of

---

149 Cmnd 2526.
150 Cmnd 2973.
151 Cmnd 2830.
152 SÖ 1969 No. 3.
153 SÖ 1973 No. 1.
154 *Cf.* article 17, 21 and 25.
155 [1910] Hague Court *Reports* 1 141; 1 Hackworth 646.
156 Russia's and Ukraine's position in this respect is not yet clear but it appears that they are adopting a similar approach.

spies and agents; it must not involve smuggling, to be transferred to other boats or to be retrieved later. Furthermore, ships must not engage in radio pirate broadcasts or pollute waters or shores. Nor must any fishing take place during transit. Submarines must, at no times, be submerged during passage.

Passing ships may not engage in any coastal trade (*cabotage*) without specific agreement of the coastal State.

(ii) Transit Passage in Straits

Brühl, *International Straits*, 1947; Reisman, Regime of Straits and National Security, AJIL, 1982, 532; Sorensen, Bruckenbau and Durchfahrten in Meerengen, *Festschrift Menzel*, 1976, 551; See the series on Straits of the World, especially Leifer, on the *Malacca, Singapore and Indonesia Straits*, Morris on *Magellan Straits* and Pharand, on *The North West Passage*, 1976.

We have hitherto considered the right that the coastal State has in its own waters and what rights ships of other States may have to pass and enter. International straits form a special category in the sense that they are technically part of the high seas and must, as such be open to all ships. Yet, their shores will belong to coastal States and, in many cases, international straits cannot be navigated without passing through the territorial waters of one or both (or all) coastal States. The right to go through straits is thus an extended right of passage. This right is even more pronounced nowadays when the extension of territorial waters to twelve miles had reduced the open channel, and in many cases eliminated it, in the numerous international straits of the world.

The negotiators of the Law of the Sea Convention of 1982 envisaged a *package deal* in the sense that the powers which attach importance to passage through straits for their blue water navies, *i.e.* the superpowers, would *allow* an extension of the normal width of territorial waters to twelve miles *in return* for secured free transit for all vessels, including warships and submerged submarines, through the waters in international straits which would become new territorial waters under the extension.

Somehow developments overtook the negotiators. After having taken these positions on the width of the territorial sea and on transit rights one of the superpowers decided not to ratify the Convention.

The United States thus felt that the rules on deep-sea mining would not favour the only experts in the field, the United States firms, and the proposed Authority would have too much power. Following the United States most of the large seafaring nations also declined to ratify the Convention. What was left? Some smaller States and most of the Third World, anxious to benefit from technological transfer and other benefits under the Convention. But somehow States suddenly all adopted the twelve mile territorial limit by their own unilateral legislation[157] but not at all as a *package deal* as had been proposed but by clear *promissory unilateral announcements,*[158] whereby they claimed the wider territorial sea but said nothing about rights of transit for warships in straits enclosed by the extended territorial limits.

From the point of view of law making, the announcements and their isolation from any *quid pro quo* is certainly interesting. It is a good example of how rule making in the international society has little to do with *custom*[159] and how easily and quickly rules emerge when there is a need for them. Even though States said little on the transit right it is probably clear that such rights must subsist through international straits as *international highways.*

There is thus a general right of transit through international straits; submarines do not have to be submerged. International straits are indeed *international highways* as emphasised in *The Corfu Channel Case.*[160] As emphasised in this case, international straits do not even have to be the *necessary* way for ships; it is sufficient if they provide a *useful* route.

The 1982 Law of the Sea Convention extends the previous rule of *innocent passage* through straits to a *right of transit.* This latter right is more substantial and implies the right for warships to pass unhindered. Except for certain special straits (articles 36 and 38(1), there is free transit through straits; warships may pass and submarines

---

[157] On the discussion of the *adoption* mechanisms see *supra* in this Chapter and in Chapter III. On the 200 EEZ zone, see *infra.*

[158] See my *Concept, op. cit.,* 100-101 and *supra.*

[159] Unless there is a territorial connection there is rarely any customary legal rules *strictu sensu,* see, *supra,* under Customary Law.

[160] [1949] ICJ *Reports* 4.

may be submerged if this is their normal mode of transit (article 39(1)(c)). In a sense, international straits are as free as the high seas themselves. International conventions can, however, restrict the right to pass, as is the case in the Dardanelles under the Lausanne Convention of 1923. But now, under the 1982 Convention, there is another very important distinction between the regime of the high seas and that of straits: under part XII of the Convention the coastal State has considerable powers to prevent or mitigate pollution.

The right of transit in straits under the 1982 Convention must be coupled with the extension of territorial waters. This was part of the so called *package deal* which meant, on the one hand, that territorial waters were enlarged provided that straits did not become enclosed as a result. Calculations had envisaged that the extension of the territorial waters limit would make 133 straits in the world come within such waters. Then, it became necessary to ensure that a free channel through which such international straits was preserved.

As mentioned before the Law of Sea Convention of 1982 has not been ratified by the important seafaring nations of the world. Yet, it has, in parts, been treated as if its rules already formed part of general international law. This has not been done by any nebulous customary law function but rather by unilateral acts of acceptance of part of the regime.[161]

An accident involving the ship *The Showa Maru* in the Malacca Strait in 1975 raised the question whether a coastal State is able to limit the right of passage near its shore in the case of risk for pollution by oil or other agents. Malaysia, which had suffered much damage through the breaking up of the vessel, claimed that it could impose special rules, or even a toll, for international supertankers which pose a particular risk to the environment

On the one hand, it may not be permissible to stop traffic through international straits. No toll can legitimately be imposed nowadays for the passage through international straits.[162] On the other hand, it is hardly possibly to deny coastal States to take certain safety measures to minimise the risk of considerable environmental damage caused by

---

[161] See *supra*, 180 *et seq.*

[162] Note the payment of a certain lump sum to Denmark in 1857 under the Treaty of Copenhagen in return for the abolition of the toll system in Öresund.

oil carrying supertankers. It is thus possible to insist that a master can show that his ship is not sub-standard and that the crew is sufficiently trained to handle the ship. Standards are imposed by an increasing number of international agreements, such as the SOLAS (Safety of Life at Sea) Conventions.

Other restrictions may possibly be imposed in time of war. Chile prohibited, for example, transit during the night through the Magellan Straits in 1941 and did not allow its lighthouses to display light at night although the Treaty of 1881 had opened the strait to all nations.

Coastal States are thus not entitled to prohibit traffic through international straits altogether but may impose rules with regard to modalities of transit.[163]

Such control by coastal States is increasingly taking the form of traffic separation schemes which are designed to minimise risk of collision and shoaling. Some such schemes are imposed by national legislation but others are enforced by the International Maritime Organisation (IMO).

iii. The Air Space of a State

Bin Cheng, *The Law of International Air Transport,* 1962; De la Pradell, P., Les frontiers de l7 air, RCADI 1954 iii 121; Goodhuis, Frontiers of Outer Space and air space, 172 RCADI 1982 i 366; McWhinney & Bradley, *Freedom of the Air,* 1969; Benzien, *Unerlaubter Einflug in fremdes Hoheitsgebiet,* 1982; Hailbronner, Freedom of the air and the Law of the Sea, AJIL 1983, 490; *idem, Schutz der Luftgrenzen,* 1972; Fauchille, Le domaine aérien et le régime juridique des aérostats, RGDIP 1901, 414.

a. General Remarks

For a long time State sovereignty was thought to extend *usque caelum et infernum,* that is to say both as far as the universe and down to the centre of the earth. As far as the depth to which State sovereignty extends it is now obvious that minerals and other natural resources do

---

[163]   *Cf.* Institut de Droit international, article VI, Measures concerning accidental pollution of the seas, *Annuaire* 1969.

belong to States.[164] On the other hand, the question of how far State sovereignty extends upwards has caused great difficulty; the reason for this has been the rapid development of aviation and Outer Space activities during this century.

The claims to sovereignty in airspace were soon modified once it became possible to use the air space by aeroplanes. Yet, at the beginning of the century some insisted that the air was *free*.[165] As the importance of air transport grew States were only said to have preserved a right to protect their *security*.[166]

A State's right to remain isolated and without contact with other States is obviously severely undermined if its activities can be observed from the air. The problem is obviously aggravated once we consider activities carried out in Outer Space from which the territory of a State can now be accurately observed.[167] There are therefore two problems: what right does a State have to prevent overflight through its airspace, and conversely, which right do other States have to overfly other States' territory? Secondly, what are the rights in this respect with regard to overflight in Space? In this section we shall deal with the first question, obviously linked to the question as to how far State sovereignty extends.

In 1902 the *Institut de droit international* proposed that the status of the air, above a certain limit, should be assimilated to that of the High Seas. A Convention was eventually concluded in Paris in 1919, after the First World War in which aeroplanes had played a vital role.[168] This Convention is based on the full sovereignty of States over their airspace and the Convention underlines in its very first article that the Contracting Parties recognise that each State has complete and exclusive sovereignty over the airspace over its own territory. The Treaty allows, however, a defined right of *innocent*

---

164   However, States are, of course, free to grant the right to citizens and to others to exploit these resources. On the special case for compensation in the case of taking natural resources, see under Nationalisation.

165   *E.g.* Fauchille, Le domaine aérien et le régime juridique des aérostats, RGDIP 1901 414.

166   Fauchille's Report to the Institut de Droit international 1910.

167   See, *infra*, under Outer Space.

168   There had been an effort in 1910 to conclude a relevant Convention after Blériot had overflown the Channel, an event which illustrated the potential of airtravel.

passage,[169] over non/military areas in peace time.[170]

The Paris Convention provided, while emphasising the sovereign right of each State to its air space, that non-scheduled civil aircraft would have the right of innocent passage through this space. Transit may only take place through certain specified zones and certain areas may be closed to foreign aircraft. For scheduled flights or landing rights special agreements were necessary. A special body, the *Commission internationale de la navigation aérienne* (CINA) was established to assist in the implementation of the agreement.

In 1928 American States concluded the Havana Convention. However, in 1944 a new worldwide Convention was concluded and this Treaty, the Chicago Convention, replaced the earlier Paris and Havana agreements. The Chicago Convention recognises, as did the previous agreements, that State sovereignty extends to the air-space above its territory. Chicago Convention entered into force in 1947 to provide for special regulation between certain States.

Both the Paris Convention and CINA were replaced by the Chicago Convention which established the International Civil Aviation Organisation (ICAO). The minimum provision on transit in the ICAO Convention is supplemented by the International Air Services Transit agreement, (the so-called Two Freedom Agreement) also of 1944 and the international Air Transport agreement (the so-called Five Freedoms agreement), equally of 1944.

The *five freedoms* include the right to

1) fly across foreign territory (of a Contracting State) without landing);
2) land for non-traffic purposes (*technical landing*);
3) disembark in a foreign country from a flight originating in the home State of the aircraft;
4) pick up traffic in a foreign country to return to the home State of the aircraft; and
5) carry traffic between two foreign (contracting) parties.

The *two freedoms* are then the first two of these five rights. The

---

[169] *Cf.* on Innocent Passage under the Law of the Sea.

[170] 27 States concluded the Convention in 1919 and it entered into force in 1922; Germany adhered in 1929 when the Convention was revised. From 1933, there were 53 Contracting States.

ICAO Convention and these agreements are also supplemented by the Paris Convention of 1956 on Transit Rights for Scheduled Transport Flights and the Convention on Commercial Rights of Non-Scheduled Air Services, also concluded in Paris in 1956. The latter Convention concerns, *inter alia,* right of transit for planes for humanitarian or rescue purposes. Numerous bilateral agreements supplement these agreements, some often concluded by an airline and a State and not by two States.

The Chicago Convention is supplemented by the Eurocontrol Convention of 1960, concluded between certain European countries, which include the original six members of what is now the European Union, France, Germany, Italy and Benelux, as well as the United Kingdom, but this Convention was of little practical importance. The Chicago Convention is also supplemented by the Warsaw Convention on Liability, by the Tokyo, the Hague and the Montreal Conventions on Hi-Jacking[171] and by the Convention on Montego Bay, the 1982 Convention on the Law of the Sea, which regulates certain issues of overflight.

The most important implementation of the Chicago Convention is carried out through the regulatory function of the International Civil Aviation Organisation (ICAO) which adopts rules for navigation through the airspace. This organisation has considerable regulatory power which contracting States have accepted, by their *abstract consent.*[172] Furthermore, the Regulations are adopted by majority votes by the Organisation and this not by the plenary body, the Assembly, but by the Council, the executive organ, where not all States are represented.[173]

The ICAO Regulations are adopted in the form of Annexes to the Convention. The rules adopted concern rules of air traffic, nationality marks, registration of aircraft, customs and airport facilities, accident inquiries and transport of dangerous goods etc. The most important

---

[171] See *supra* under the Use of Force in Chapter V iv.

[172] See, on this concept adopted in my *Law Making, op. cit.,* 322 and *supra,* under Formation of Rules.

[173] It is important to emphasise this to Swedish students who are often taught that adhering to the European Community would imply a 'new' rule on binding decisions adopted by majority votes.

rules concern undoubtedly the rules of the air where standardised methods of communication have been adopted, facilitating landing and take off all over the world and contributing to the safety of air travel.

b. The Limits of the Air Space

Where are now then the limits of a State's airspace? Unless we ascertain this limit we will not know at what stage we have the right to complain about overflights without special permission, *ad hoc,* or under a treaty.

The airspace of a State extends to the air above its territorial waters. In this air strip there is no general right of passage unless the waters also form part of international straits.[174] But the air above fishing zones, the EEZ or special protection zones are not included unless they form part of special *air identification zones* currently claimed by, for example, the United States, Canada and the Philippines. In the case of the United States, there is duty to report at least one hour from the coast which obliges a Concorde flight to report in the mid-Atlantic.

The vertical delimitation has caused some problems. Neither the Paris Convention of 1919 nor the ICAO Convention imposed any fixed upper limit of a State's airspace. The Outer Space Treaty of 1967, The Rescue Agreement of 1968 and the Liability Convention of 1972 as well as the Moon Treaty of 1971 are all silent on the matter.

The first Sputnik, launched in 1957, made clear that, for assessing the outer limits of a State's airspace, at least the *usque ad caelum* rule could not be right.[175]

One suggestion was that a State's airspace extends as far as an aeroplane is able to ascend. The problem was difficult to solve as certain vehicles had proprieties of both spacecraft and airplanes, such as the X-15 which could attain a height of 47 miles but still had some characteristics of an aircraft. Some high-altitude aeroplanes were increasingly used for surveillance and espionage. This was the case

---

[174] On the regime of straits, see *supra.*
[175] See *supra.*

of the U-2, shot down over the USSR in 1960 with its pilot Captain Powers who was convicted to a ten year sentence for espionage but later released.[176]

Another theory was that airspace is equal to *atmospheric space*. There are traces of oxygen up to an altitude of 10,000 metres. But, whatever the virtue of this theory, it is unconfirmed by State practice. One idea has been to say a State's airspace is what a State is able to control; but in that case the limits of a State's airspace will shift all the time as technical capabilities improve. Another idea, put forward by Soviet scholars, is that the airspace is what a State *needs for national security*. But this theory too is unconfirmed by State practice. On the contrary, States have not protested when high capability observation satellites are put in orbit, satellites which can observe far more clearly than Captain Power's U-2 what is going on on the Earth's surface.

The most acceptable theory concerning the limit between a State's airspace and Outer Space is the Karman theory which claims the limit of a State's airspace should be set at about 53 miles, where an object travelling at 23,000 feet per second loses its aerodynamic lift and the centrifugal force takes over. This theory, at least, takes into the actual physical differences between the propulsion of aircraft and the operation of satellites and does provide reasonable guidelines.

It is important to conceive the regime of airspace and in Outer Space[177] as complementary and supplementary: in both fields of regulation it is important to safeguard legitimate interests of sovereign States and, at the same time, the reasonable interests of the international society as a whole.

c. Innocent Passage in Air Space

Aircraft have probably a right of overflight in emergency situations, analogous to that which exists, with regard to ships in distress at sea. Before the International Court of Justice Israel claimed that Bulgaria, which had shot down an El Al plane in 1955 killing 58 people, did

---

[176]   See in detail my article on Foreign Warships and Immunity for Espionage, AJIL 1984 76.

[177]   See on Outer Space, *infra*, in Chapter VII.

not enjoy any right of exclusive sovereignty which could prevent the innocent passage of a civilian aircraft in distress which had 'inadvertently' intruded into Bulgarian airspace before Bulgaria had adhered to the Air Transit Agreement.[178] On the other hand, Israel itself did not concede that any such right of innocent passage of an aircraft in distress existed when a Libyan plane was shot down over Israel-occupied Sinai on 21 February 1971 killing 109 people, in spite of Israel being a party to the Air Transit Agreement.

The problem of allowing innocent passage to aircraft is possibly that their *innocence* is difficult to ascertain: overflights are often used for reconnaissance purposes even if such flights are becoming increasingly rare as States prefer to surveillance by satellite. But until such sophisticated systems take over there is certainly a great number of 'inadvertent' deviations from flight routes; as there were 116 such deviations in a few years over Czechoslovakia where one has reason to assume a lack of innocence and the pursuit of espionage.[179]

d. Broadcasts in Air and Space

In connection with freedom of transit in air space one should mention the new and important right to broadcast radio waves, either direct from a State or via a satellite in space. Some have, perhaps for political reasons, contested this obvious right but most opponents to freedom of broadcasting have now taken the view that technical developments cannot be hindered. The problem obviously does not lie so much on the broadcasting side as on the receiving side: some States, especially socialist States in Eastern Europe, have, in the past, sought to prevent their own citizens from listening to Western broadcasts which have been construed to imply *propaganda*. Broadcasts can even be seen as interfering with the *reserved domain*

---

[178]   ICJ, *Aerial Incident of 27 July 1955, Pleadings.* This case was settled. Note, for numerous allegations of 'inadvertent' overflights and 'inadvertent' intrusions of submarines, my article on Foreign Warships and Espionage, *American Journal of International Law,* 1984, 76.

[179]   *Cf.* the Soviet submarine claiming to have been 'lost' in the military area of Karlskrona, see my article on Foreign Warships and Espionage, cited in the previous note.

and violating article 2(7).[180] Now that communism/socialism has fallen, States in Eastern Europe take quite different attitudes and are as anxious as those in Western Europe to allow freedom of broadcasting.

Not many such objections are heard to-day.[181] Naturally, a State may have an interest to control certain reception of broadcast for reasons of State security or to protect public interests, such as to protect children from being exposed to pornography,[182] or to prevent certain subversive activities. However, there must always be a heavy presumption in favour of free speech as only unhampered freedom of expression is compatible with democracy.[183]

The most staunch objectors in Eastern Europe have, as mentioned in different contexts earlier, changed many views on values and no longer object to broadcasts which were previously jammed. This should be seen against the general transformation of their societies where earlier prohibited types of art and music is now allowed. As values have changed, so have the previous objections to domestic reception of international broadcasts also lost most of their foundation.

---

[180]   See further Frowein & Simma, Das Problem des grenzüberschreitenden Informationsflusses und des *domaine reservé*, 19 *Berichte* DGVR 1979, 1.

[181]   But note the objections of a representative of the Ministry of Education in Sweden who at a doctoral dissertation of a thesis on Space Law at the University of Stockholm in 1990 insisted that the 'sovereignty of the State' implies complete right to control all broadcasts.

[182]   This is partially being achieved through Broadcast Convention adopted by the Council of Europe in 1989.

[183]   On democracy see *supra* in Chapter I.

CHAPTER VII

Distributive Rules:
Objects of Sovereign Functions:
Persons

Specific distributive rules govern the relationship between a State and individuals. Here, we are thus no longer concerned with geographical allocation[1] but with ties between a State and its nationals, a *relationship* which also has geographical aspects as ties are derived from the territorial competence of the State: its nationals are primarily persons born and living there, although there are numerous exceptions allowing nationality to be conferred in other ways.

Another form of relationship than nationality is the *function* exercised by States over individuals by its right of *jurisdiction*. *Jurisdiction* is a term which is often lightly used by lawyers to imply a host of different functions: it can thus mean *factual power* over territorial space[2]; it can also mean the *right to enact rules and exercise judiciary powers* over individuals,[3] either because they are the State's nationals, or because they are present in the State's territory, or - a proposition which is more tenuous - that their actions in some way concern the State's interests. It is *jurisdiction* in this sense that we will analyse in this Chapter.

This jurisdictional function, to enact laws, make decrees, take administrative decisions and adjudicate, is a function obviously related to the geographical spaces we have analysed above[4] and thus applies within specific territorial contexts. The jurisdictional power is exercised over certain *persons*, the *nationals*, which are the *subjects*

---

[1]   See the preceding Chapter.

[2]   As discussed in the previous Chapter on Geographical Spaces.

[3]   *Cf.* Mann, The doctrine of jurisdiction in international law, 111 RCADI 1964; Beale, The jurisdiction of a sovereign State, 36 HarvLR 1923.

[4]   See *supra* Chapter VI.

and *citizens*[5] of the State.

It may be emphasised that the jurisdictional function is a *power* that *may* be exercised by a State: there is thus *normally no obligation* to use that power. A State has naturally a duty under international law to provide minimum rules to uphold order in its State; apart from this general obligation there is no duty to *legislate*. With regard to *judicial power*, there is again no obligation to deal with matters in the courts. Exceptions to this general rule are made in situations where the interests of an alien has formed the object of specific diplomatic complaints from another State when a State must fulfil its duty to justice or be guilty of *denial of justice*;[6] but there are few other instances where a State is under *duty* to adjudicate.[7]

A State is wise, however, to remember that the *exercise of jurisdiction* must be seen in the context of comity and competing jurisdictional claims by other States. As an American court expressed it

'When foreign nations are involved ... it is unwise to ignore the fact that foreign policy, reciprocity, comity, and limitations of judicial power are considerations that should have a bearing on the decision to exercise or decline jurisdiction.'[8]

Jurisdiction is exercised, when the State so wishes, on the basis of certain links with the case. The most important link is the *nationality* of persons. It is for its nationals that a State enacts most of its rules

---

[5]   Note that under the complicated nationality legislation in the United Kingdom, under the Immigration Act of 1971 and the British Nationality Act of 1981, a difference is now made between *British citizens* who have a *right of abode* in the UK and *British subjects* who, in general, lack such a right. The distinction was made to curb immigration from former colonies.

[6]   Fitzmaurice, The meaning of denial of justice, BYIL 1932; de Visscher, Le déni de justice en droit international, 52 RCADI 35; see also, Freeman, *The Responsibility of States for Denial of Justice*, 1938.

[7]   A duty may furthermore exist under treaty obligations, for example, to prosecute and convict under a *aut dedere aut punire* clause for terrorists and hi-jackers. A similar obligation probably exists for international crimes, such a piracy and gross violations of Human Rights, see *supra* in Chapter IV.

[8]   *Mannington Mills Inc. v Congoleum Corp.* (1979), 595 F 2d 1287.

and it is for them that the State has a paramount interest in judicial powers. Of course, the *territoriality* principle is, as we shall see, of primordial importance, as it is in a State's own territory that its own powers are most intense. However, with regard to jurisdiction over persons who are not nationals, the interests of the State is usually limited to ensuring obedience of penal laws rather than any general interests as the State displays towards its own nationals. We shall therefore first survey the rules which tie persons to a State by their nationality as it is over these nationals that the State exercise its main jurisdictional powers. As we shall see, it is not for the State alone to decide what rules are to be enacted as international law provides certain compulsory parameters for State action.

A. NATIONALITY

i. Establishment of Nationality

A link of State authority is the nationality of individuals which, together with territory furnish the power base of a State. Although a State must have a population in order to be a State, *nationality* is not related to this condition. Nationality is a *consequence* of statehood and not a *condition* of a territory being a State.[9]

a. Nationality of Individuals

Nationality can be acquired, as in the United Kingdom before 1979, by the fact that someone is born in a certain area; anyone born in the United Kingdom before that year was automatically a British citizen with the right of abode in the United Kingdom. This is the extreme form of the *jus soli* (law of the land) rule which still applies in the United States and in some other English-speaking countries. The rule in continental Europe has, by tradition, been to follow instead the *jus sanguinis* (the law of the blood) and let nationality depend on the nationality of the parent(s).

Nationality can also be acquired by marriage, both in the

---

[9]   Cf. Crawford, *The Creation of States in International Law,* 1979, 77 *et seq.*

(predominantly) *jus soli* and in the *jus sanguinis* countries. In many countries nationality is automatically acquired by a wife by marriage, which leads to a family having the *same nationality*, as the children, by *jus sanguinis*, also follow the nationality of their father and their mother who may have the same, but derived, nationality. There is trend against the acquisition by nationality by a wife by the sole virtue of her marriage and this is sometimes seen as an expression of the inequality of the sexes. On the other hand, it is important to view the *jus sanguinis* rule, including its limb which endows a wife with derived nationality, for what it is: a rule that safeguards *the unity of nationality of the family*.

State succession, that is to say, when a new State replaces another one, or breaks away from a larger unit, can also give rise to new nationality of persons.

A passport[10] is only *prima facie* evidence of a person's nationality. In Sweden a passport is not even sufficient to prove a person's identity for certain bank transactions as this country's passports have proved easy to forge.[11] This highly unsatisfactory state of affairs has provoked little reaction from either the general public or from the authorities and is unparalleled in the practice of other States which take a far more serious view of the function of a passport.

A person must freely apply for nationality in a State or indicate by clear actions that he is willing to become a citizen, for example by entering State employment in that State. On the other hand, a State is free to offer nationality to any person it so wishes: such an offer must normally include wife/husband as well as children who have not reached the age of majority, all this to preserve, as far as possible, the

---

[10] A *passport* means a document which grants the right to enter, stay and leave *other* countries. A person thus should not really need a passport to reside or to return to *his own country*. Further permission in the form of a *visa* may be required for persons from certain countries, especially for persons from the Third World. Visa restrictions were also introduced during several years in the 80's for Swedes wishing to visit France to mark France's disapproval of the numerous terrorist bases in Southern Sweden, tolerated by the Swedish authorities.

[11] A new type of passport was introduced in 1989. However, this type, too, is apparently easy to forge.

family unit.

Nationality gives rise to a two-sided legal relationship between a person and the State. On the one hand, the new national is under obligation to pay *allegiance*[12] to his country, that is to say be loyal in any of his actions and, if asked to do so, he must perform military service or other public tasks imposed on him. On the other hand, the State acquires a duty of protection of the individual and must resort to any reasonable means of ensuring his safety if he approaches a consulate abroad for help; any cost for such assistance, however, may later have to be repaid by the individual. The State has also a *duty of protection* of an individual should he be captured by terrorists or by a liberation movement. But naturally, the State has great latitude in deciding what action should be taken as these are delicate matters.[13]

In the case of double, or multiple, nationality one often finds one prevailing point of attachment, *i.e.* the *effective nationality*. In case of doubt, guidance is often found by establishing where the individual in question exercises his rights as a citizen, that is to say where he votes.

Some have claimed that there is a general requirement that any relationship created on the basis of nationality constitutes a *genuine link*. Only if there is such a link would, they claim, the other duties of the State be activated, *i.e.* the particular *jus protectionis*[14] to protect its citizen abroad: this was demonstrated in *the Nottebohm Case*.[15] But such views have no support in general State practice[16] and have a most dubious foundation.[17] We must here rely on the rule that nationality is conclusive. Any rule which limits the link based on nationality and seeks to assess, *in casu*, where a person is resident and what his links and feelings are about his home country will lead to inevitable insecurity in international society.

---

12 See *infra* under Jurisdiction and the *Haw-Haw Case* in this Chapter.
13 See, *supra*, on Liberation Movements.
14 On *jus protectionis*, see *infra* in this Chapter.
15 ICJ, (1955) ICJ *Reports* 4.
16 For a contrary trend see, *The Flegenheimer Case* (1958) 25 ILR 91; *Cf. The Salem Case* (1932) 2 RIAA, 1161.
17 See discussion in *The Mergé Claim* (1955) 22 ILR 443.

b. Nationality of Legal Persons

In the case of a company an analysis of its nationality should focus on the *country of incorporation;* the headquarters of management; on the centre of activities or on the nationality of those who control the company. The latter test would depend on the *piercing of the veil* of the company, as was suggested in *The Barcelona Traction Case.*[18] This is allowed, and perhaps necessary in the case of multinational companies. Yet, the ICJ came to the conclusion that even in that case - where there were a number of Belgian shareholders and where Belgium sought to protect their rights against Spain - only Canada, in the opinion of the International Court of Justice, enjoyed the right of protection as the country where the company was incorporated.

There is now a possibility of having *European companies* under the treaties of the European Communities. Such companies will be truly international, unlike other companies specifically incorporated in the Member States.

c. Nationality of Ships, Aeroplanes and Spacecraft

Nagendra Singh, International law of merchant shipping, 107 RCADI 1962; Rienow, *The Test of Nationality of a Merchant Vessel*, 1937.

A ship is a national of its flag State, that is to say where it is registered, and subjected to its laws.[19] Efforts to equate a ship flying the flag of one State to being one of the State where she is *managed* or *controlled,* or of which the *owners are nationals,* have not yet succeeded in international law.[20] If, however, a vessel is no longer registered anywhere she is considered to have the nationality of her owners,[21] but this is a contingency rule which cannot displace the nationality of the flag State, if there is one.

By registering ships in countries like Panama or Liberia

---

[18]   (1964) ICJ *Reports* 1964 6 and [1970] ICJ *Reports* 1970, 3.

[19]   *Oteri v Oteri* (1976) 69 ILR 159.

[20]   *Cf. The I'm Alone* (1933) 3 RIAA 1609. Note 1:i Oppenheim ed. Jennings & Watts 1992, 513, note 8 that some owners of the ship were nationals of a *defendant* State.

[21]   See, for example, *The Chiquita* (1927) 19 F 2d 417.

shipowners often avoid stringent rules of ship safety or standard or working conditions of the crew; this is not in the interest of the international society as sub-standard ships. There has already been a great many accidents, some of them causing considerable and serious environmental damage, by such ships, sailing under what is called a *convenience flag*.[22] Occasionally there have been boycotts in ports to offload such ships when the crew has endured unacceptable social conditions. To realise the implications involved, one may only mention the incident involving the supertanker *The Amoco Cadiz*, registered in Liberia, a ship which caused a major disaster off Britanny in 1977, or the *The Braer*, also flying a convenience flag, a super-tanker carrying oil breaking up off the Shetland Islands in 1993.

In April 1990 there was an outrage in Sweden when it was revealed that the ship *The Scandinavian Star*, which was set on fire by a pyromaniac killing at least 180 people, was manned by incompetent crew, recruited for the ship which was flying a convenience flag.

I have suggested that it may be a useful idea to make States of convenience flags liable for damages for pollution damage, over and above the limit of the shipowner, of the insurers and of the International Fund for Oil Pollution Damage.[23] It could be suggested that such convenience flag States should also contribute in the case of other disasters. Some may say that such liability would inevitably make the convenience flag States introduce a system whereby it became more expensive to register ships in their countries; they would obviously have to do this to recuperate costs. Then fewer shipowners would find it attractive to register their ships in these countries. But this may not be a bad thing. It is important to ensure that ships and crew keep a certain standard so that loss of life and damage by pollution are avoided.

The 1958 High Seas Convention incorporated a criterion of a *genuine link* in order to reduce the hazards of ever increasing

---

[22] Even land-locked States have the right to provide ships with their flag, see the Barcelona Convention 1921, 7 LNTS 74.

[23] See my article on Supertankers och internationella sund (Supertankers and international straits), in *Svensk Rätt i Omvandling*, 1976, 97.

convenience flags.[24] But the International Court of Justice declined to attach importance to any such requirement of a genuine link in the ICJ *Advisory Opinion concerning the Inter-Governmental Maritime Consultative Organisation (IMCO)*,[25] now the IMO - the International Maritime Organisation. The Court held that what is decisive for membership in one of its Committees was the size of tonnage and on the basis of this both Panama and Liberia would qualify for membership although, in most cases, there is no genuine link between the flag State and the ships. If that is the position in present international law as *lex lata*, it is, however, important to note that, *de lege ferenda* it may be desirable to insist on such a connection. One can also compare this situation with the nationality of an individual, to activate all duties of protection and allegiance, should also rest on a *genuine link*.[26]

Aeroplanes have the nationality of the country of registration. Here it is more questionable whether one can require any genuine link. The question was discussed when a French aeroplane, owned by a Moroccan company, and carrying the Algerian liberation fighter Ben Bella, was forced to land.[27]

Aircraft of joint operating agencies are to be registered in one of the participating States or included in a joint register. An aircraft does not have to be registered in the same country as its mother company. It is to be noted that, for example, the Scandinavian Airline System, is functioning as a *Scandinavian company* but it is not incorporated in any of its participating States, nor elsewhere.

It is important to establish the nationality of an aircraft as many rights and duties flow from this concept. Thus, the right of jurisdiction under the Tokyo, the Hague or the Montreal Conventions on hijacking[28] depend in part on the nationality of an aircraft.

Space objects are also registered in one State and this nationality may decide jurisdiction over the object (Outer Space Treaty 1967, article VIII), liability for damage under the Liability for Damage by

---

24   Article 5; *cf.* Law of the Sea Convention, 1982.
25   (1960) ICJ *Reports* 1960.
26   *Cf. supra* on the *Nottebohm Case* in this Chapter.
27   AF 1958, 282.
28   *Supra*, under Terrorism.

Space Objects Convention of 1971, or duties under the Convention for Recovery of Astronauts of 1968.

ii. *jus protectionis*

Ress, Mangelhafte diplomatische Protektion und Staatshaftung, ZaöRVR 1972, 420; Leigh, Nationality and Diplomatic Protection, ICLQ 1971, 453.

The protection of a national[29] abroad is covered by what is called the principle of *nationality of claims,* precisely based on the link between the claim and the protecting State through the intermediary of the nationality of the injured interests.[30] The right of a State to protect its own citizens when they reside in or visit another State is commonly referred to as the *jus protectionis.*

A national enjoys thus right and has the right to expect certain action on behalf of his home State if his rights are violated in another State. It is probable that international law *forbids* any contracting-out of such rights of protection. There was earlier a tendency in Latin America to allow a so called *Calvo* clause[31] in contracts which ousted any diplomatic protection of the home State and bound the party to content himself with local laws; the reason for this clause had been unwarranted use of diplomatic protection to *intervene*[32] in the domestic affairs of a State. There is considerable authority that such a clause is not compatible with international law[33] and therefore void.[34]

An injured party must, in order to be able to address his own

---

[29] On the question as to what is a 'national', see, *supra* and *The Nottebohm Case,* (1955) ICJ *Reports* 1955, 4.

[30] For specific instances, see *The Mavrommatis Palestine Concessions* (1924) PCIJ Series A No. 2 12; *The Chorzow Factory Case* (1928) PCIJ Series A No. 17, 25; *The Panevezys-Saldutiskis Railway Case* (1939) Series A/B No. 76 17.

[31] i Calvo, *Le droit international théorique et pratique,* 5th ed., 1896, 322. The clause was allowed to have at least limited effect in, for example, *The North Dredging Co. Case* (1926) 4 RIAA 26.

[32] See *supra* in Chapter IV on intervention.

[33] *North American Dredging Co. v Mexico* (1926) 4 RIAA 26.

[34] For a detailed and clear analysis of the legal effects of the clause, see, ii O'Connell, *International Law,* 2nd ed., 1970, 1059-1066.

diplomatic missions for help in the matter, have exhausted the local remedies, that is to say he must have sought to obtain justice himself in the local courts and appealed, if appeals were allowed, to the highest tribunal or court. The *local remedies rule*[35] constitutes a procedural impediment[36] to any action of diplomatic protection.[37] A complainant is, however, only under duty to use what has been called *effective local remedies*, *i.e.* those which were able to rectify the situation about which he complained,[38] and he is not obliged to have presented every argument.[39] The country where interests have been injured has, on the other hand, a duty to provide legal redress or it will be guilty of what is called *denial of justice*;[40] infringements of such duties will lead to international responsibility with ensuing duty to make compensation to the home State of the person in question.

iii. Allegiance

Nationality forms the link between a State and its nationals. It is on the basis of nationality that important legal consequences follow. The allegiance by a subject to a State is derived from this link. The duty to do military service,[41] if or when such duty is activated by a State, is also dependent on this link.

---

35   Cancado Trindade, *The Application of the Rule of Exhaustion of Local Remedies*, 1983; *cf.* Fachiri, The local remedies rule in the light of the Finnish Ships Arbitration, BYIL 1936.

36   Amerasinghe, The formal character of the rule of Local Remedies, ZaöRVR 1976, 727;

37   See *The Interhandel Case* (1959) ICJ *Reports* 1959, 46 *per* Judge Córdova.

38   On what are *effective remedies* see, *The Finnish Ships Arbitration* (1934) 3 RIAA 1479. If the State *deliberately frustrates the claim*, the applicant may be considered to have exhausted remedies: see Preliminary Objections in the *Barcelona Traction Case* (1964) ICJ *Reports* 6; *The Brown Case* (1923) 6 RIAA 120.

39   See *Elletronica Sicula Case* (1989) ICJ *Reports* 15.

40   See *supra*, at the beginning of this Chapter on the duty to adjudicate.

41   A number of States have abolished the duty to do military service and rely instead on professional armies. The United Kingdom thus decided at the end of the 50's to abolish conscription. However, the duty can, at any given moment, for example at the time of crisis, be re-activated.

It is interesting to note the practice of the United States during the Vietnam war to call up also other residents, even students on temporary visits to the country, for military service; this practice is probably not in conformity with international law. It is nationality which is the link between a State and its subjects and it is this link which, as a rule, has enduring effect and which proves, above all, the allegiance aspects.

For an analysis of *allegiance* to a State one can turn to interesting remarks in *The Lord Haw-Haw Case*.[42] In this case it was stated that there has to be some link of allegiance for a person to be punished as a traitor: only if some allegiance is due is the link strong enough for penal prosecution. Conversely, the *von Herder Case*[43] before the Supreme Court of Sweden showed hesitation to punish a German spy in Norway, spying against Sweden during the War: the German officer von Herder *owed no allegiance* to Sweden. This important case shows that, until 1946, Swedish Courts *applied directly rules of general international law*.[44] It is interesting to note that this case has been consistently overlooked in *all* postwar Swedish textbooks on international law. Yet, this case is singularly important to assess the implications of allegiance.

iv. Nationality and Domicile:
Connecting Factors for Jurisdiction

It is only in civil law countries that *nationality* is the relevant link for certain specific matters of jurisdiction: in case law countries like the United States and England, as well as the whole of the British Commonwealth, far greater reliance is placed on *domicile*.

Domicile, in the sense it is used by lawyers in England, in the Commonwealth but less so in the United States,[45] means far more

---

42   *Joyce v DPP* [1946] AC 347 and *infra; cf. R v Casement* [1917] 1 KB 98; *R v Newman* [1949] 3 SA 1238.

43   NJA 1946 65. *Cf. infra* under Jurisdiction, in this Chapter.

44   *Cf. supra*, under Monism and Dualism and in other contexts in Chapter III as well as later in this Chapter.

45   The United States has a less stable conception of domicile, see, *e.g.* Nussbaum, *Principles of Private International Law*, 1943, 135.

than habitual residence or even permanent home. Everyone is born with a domicile of origin[46] and strong evidence of factual residence as well as of intention is demanded for any rebuttal of this domicile of origin in favour of a *domicile of choice*. Domicile implies - if we simplify the complex issues involved - factual residence as well as the intention to stay until retirement or death.[47]

Domicile is highly relevant for certain aspects of tax legislation and the fortunate person who can prove that he has a family tomb in another State, a country to which he presumably would wish to return during his last days, will find himself in quite a different tax situation, by his links to the other country, than to the person who cannot supply such evidence. The Inland Revenue authorities in the countries which apply the domicile principle are, on the other hand, most severe in their investigation of evidence and seek to bar any *related transaction* as well as any contrived establishment of domicile.

Jurisdiction in civil matters depend on whether the Court finds a sufficient link between itself and a claimant. States phrase their rules in different ways but the mechanisms fall into two groups: some States (the civil law countries) attach a number of legal consequences to the *nationality* of a person whereas countries which apply the English legal system attach such effect to *domicile*. However, since the English conception of domicile is as stable, or as some say *more* stable than nationality,[48] the situation before courts becomes similar in all these legal systems.[49]

The connecting rules, which attach importance to nationality or domicile, are said to form part of conflict of laws system, or the *private international law*, which, many writers (and Courts) claim form part of the respective national legal system.

Yet, most States apply very similar rules in this respect and,

---

[46]   English law assigns to a child, at birth, the domicile of the father, to an illegitimate child, the domicile of the mother: *Udny v Udny* (1869) LR 1 Sc & Div 441, 457.

[47]   Intention may be referred from the fact: *Munro v Munro* (1840) 7 Cl & Fin 877.

[48]   i Rabel *The Conflict of Laws*, 1945, 110.

[49]   There is a trend to *harmonise* conflict of law rules whereby *domicile* is increasingly used as connecting link, see *infra* on harmonisation, in this Chapter.

bearing in mind the division between the *jus soli* and the *jus sanguinis* countries, one is justified in claiming that most of the so called conflict of law rules also form part of the *international legal system.*

B. JURISDICTION

i. Restrictions of Jurisdictional Sovereignty

Territorial sovereignty is limited, as set out above, by special rules of transit, occasionally existing without the need of any specific treaty, in favour of other States. Secondly, the power of the territorial State may be limited by further treaties it has concluded, and these treaties may concern a variety of matters. Finally, a State's sovereignty in its own territory may be hampered by general rules which a State has to accept by the very fact that it is a member of international society to which rules it thus may not have specifically expressed its consent or to which its consent may be presumed.[50]

Certain limitations to a State's sovereignty in its own territory are caused by rules concerning basic Human Rights which a State is under duty to respect under general international law, even outside the framework of treaties. The right of jurisdiction of a territorial sovereign does thus not imply any unlimited right to enact rules, take executive or administrative decisions, or adjudicate within the so called *reserved domain.*[51] Article 2(7) of the UN Charter which codifies general international rules on the right of States to decide on *most* matters within their territory, must be understood to concern a notion that may *change* with time:[52] the reserved domain is thus now more circumscribed than when the Charter was drafted and States and precluded by clear rules of international law to, for example, infringe basic Human Rights.

Such *basic Human Rights* may be very modest and very few but still most important and they *prevail* over whatever a State chooses

---

[50]   *Cf. supra*, on the relevance of consent to norms of international law, in Chapter III.

[51]   See *supra* on this notion in Chapter IV.

[52]   *Nationality Decrees in Tunis and Morocco* (1923) PCIJ Ser. B No. 4.

to legislate. They can perhaps be summed up as being the right to avoid genocide, the right to avoid torture and slavery and the right to avoid apartheid.[53] It is gradually clear that also the important right of expression must qualify among these *basic rights*, as the right to criticise State structures are excluded from comment.[54]

Formulated in this modest way, it is not even suggested, with regard to genocide, that a State has to refrain from imposing the death penalty, although there is a marked trend towards an international convention on this matter. The formulation merely suggests that - as in philosophical terms - quality changes with quantity. There is thus a difference between inflicting the death of one, or several, citizens and the extermination of a group.

The prohibition of torture, outside the 1980 Torture Convention, follows the trend towards humanisation of the treatment of prisoners and would now cover both prisoners-of-war, as already guaranteed under the 1949 Geneva Conventions and detainees under the 1977 Protocols but also ordinary citizens under general rules of international law.[55]

Although the trend towards the prohibition of apartheid has been long and slow, it is clear that such treatment of individuals is not compatible with international law. On the other hand, it is not possible to criticise the system of apartheid unless one admits that there is a general rule of international law prohibiting such treatment of individuals, a rule which does not have to be incorporated in a State's internal system (as it notably has not been incorporated into

---

[53] See, further, *supra*, under *jus cogens*, 150, 159 *et seq.*

[54] Limitations of this fundamental right of expression can only be allowed for pornography, and other publications which offend public morals, along similar lines as those laid down in the case law of the European Court of Human Rights, see its *Reports of Judgments.*

[55] *Cf.* my *Law of War, op. cit.*, 286 on reprisals against prisoners of war: the Soviet Union had pledged in 1942 that reprisals would not be taken against German prisoners of war even when these soldiers had themselves committed crimes against the Law of War; the Soviet Union was, at the time, not bound by the Geneva Conventions. Note that a duty, even as perceived and recognised by a State, is not always fulfilled; in the event the Soviet Union no doubt exposed the taken prisoners to maltreatment or even torture and execution.

the laws of South Africa).[56]

Most States, except the most totalitarian regimes, now accept in their practice and in their doctrine, certain limitations of a State's internal sovereignty. This does not mean that any such basic Human Rights would be *inherent* or in any way dependent on any natural law. All it means is that States have accepted[57] an *international minimum standard of behaviour* which States, or their internal power organs, officials and authorities must show individuals present in their territory.

There is considerable hesitation in Sweden[58] with regard to the effectiveness of international rules in this country. On the other hand, Sweden is not enabled to displace binding international rules. The Supreme Court of Sweden held in the *von Herder Case*,[59] that no prosecution could be brought in Sweden against a foreign spy who had carried out his actions in a foreign country, even though Swedish interests had been harmed, as such prosecution would be contrary to general principles of international law which, according to Swedish law, must be applied in Sweden.[60] This judgment is now ignored.[61]

It is, however, clear in State practice that States do not hesitate to criticise regimes which refuse to allow immediate application of basic Human Rights. There is ample evidence that criticism of the Amin regime in Uganda did not, in the opinion of other States, or of the United Nations, imply any interference with the *reserved domain* in the meaning of Article 2(7) of the United Nations Charter. Nor was criticism of the Pol Pot regime in Cambodia/Kampuchea perceived as such interference; nor was the criticism of the regime in Argentina which allowed hundreds of opponents to 'disappear'; and, indeed, nor of South Africa, where, as mentioned above, the conduct of the authorities is entrenched precisely in internal law. Sweden, herself

---

56 *Cf. supra.*

57 Even the ex-USSR explicitely accepted this rule shortly before the demise of communism, see *supra* in Chapter I.

58 *Cf. supra*, under *jus cogens*, in Chapter III.

59 NJA 1946 65; *cf. von That* NJA 1946 B 1014. *Infra*, Chapter VII on Effect Principle. *Cf.* Chapter III on Sweden's reluctance to accept *jus cogens*.

60 See further on *the Alabama Arbitration*, in Chapter III.

61 See, *supra*, under *jus cogens* in Chapter III.

denying the efficacy of general rules, is a staunch critic of South Africa.

There has thus been a trend away from emphasising the rule laid down in Article 2(7) of the United Nations on the reserved domain. This used to be, and still is, the sphere inside a State into which other States must interfere. But from this sphere the aforementioned basic Human Rights are thus exempted showing, yet again, the dynamic nature of international law as evolving and changing its own rules.

The territory of a State is the framework within which the State exercises its competence: the territory could even be said to furnish the very title of that competence. To have a territory is one condition of statehood and one of the main differences between a State and an international organisation. Many international organisations today exercise functions remarkably similar to those of a State: a law-making function as well as executive and judiciary functions.[62] Some organisations have, as we have seen, extremely far reaching powers, like, for example, the European Community. But however developed the Community may be as an international organisation, there is one criteria for statehood which it does not fulfil: it does not have a territory over which it exercises exclusive and general functions.

ii. Jurisdiction by Legislature and Administration Distinguished

Jurisdictional competence can be understood also to mean something wider than the competence of Courts: it may imply the reach of the legislature or of the executive. The latter form of the concept of jurisdiction is then concerned with the extraterritorial effect of laws or administrative decisions of a Sate.

With regard to the problem of extraterritorial application of laws, similar considerations as with jurisdiction of courts can be made in this context. The normal rule is thus territoriality: the laws of a State apply within its territory, including territorial waters if the laws so prescribe.[63] In other cases, the basis for application of the laws of a State, becomes more questionable.

---

[62]   *Cf. supra* in Chapter II.

[63]   *Cf. R v Keyn* [1878] 2 EX D 63 and *supra* in Chapter I on *Comity. Cf.* also *supra*, in Chapter I and VII on Foreign Judgments and Awards.

Many older textbooks staunchly deny that laws of one State have any effect in another. Especially *public laws* would, traditional writers say, be deprived of any such effect. If one looks at actual practices and at case law in several countries, however, this is obviously not at all true. There are numerous situations when foreign public laws are applied by courts in another country or allowed to take effect there by the State authorities.[64] To sum up the most important aspects: it is for the *forum* country, *i.e.* the State where the court is, or for the government of that country, to decide to what extent foreign laws are to operate, that is to say, on the mechanism of *operation*. However, the underlying duty to consider such application is derived from general public international law and the duty of comity.[65] The reason for applying foreign laws is obviously that States are mutually interdependent in international society and, on the basis of reciprocity, they may need to rely on the cooperation of other States, especially when non-political matters are in issue.

Also when political issues are at stake there are, as we shall see, many situations when a State may apply public laws of another State, for example under Freezing Orders issued in the interest of international society[66] or under the (technically) non-binding Co-com rules of the United States on limitation and prohibition of certain exports to the former Soviet Union and its satellite States.[67]

There are also other situations when a State is clearly entitled to extend its own rules beyond its borders. One such common situation is that concerning the operation of a passport.[68]

---

[64] For a detailed analysis, see my article on Extraterritorial Application: Private International Law Aspects of Comity in *Svensk Juristtidning* 1988. For an English case refusing the right of defence based on the *Act of State doctrine* (on this *supra*, in Chapter I), to avoid foreign public acts see *William and Humbert Ltd. v W.H. Trade Marks Ltd.* [1986] 1 AC 368.

[65] See *supra* on *comity* in Chapter I.

[66] For example, *The Freezing Assets Affair*, where the United Kingdom applied a United States Decree to freeze Iranian funds in American banks in London, see further, *infra*, under Sanctions.

[67] See *infra*, on jurisdiction over Persons, in this Chapter.

[68] *Cf. supra*, and *infra* in the following section, in this Chapter on the functions and characteristics of a passport..

iii. The Basis of Sovereign Jurisdiction

States have the prerogative in the international society of being competent and able to legitimately bring matters before their courts. To do this, there must obviously be a link between an action and an actor who is to be asked to present himself before a court.

If the act took place within the State, there is such a right of jurisdiction in all States unless the State in question or its authorities waive this right. But the question as to where an act was carried out is, as all tort and criminal law specialists know, a very difficult question: an act might well have started in one State and had its effect in another.

In civil matters there are few limits set down by international law although special rules do apply within the law of admiralty. In criminal matters, on the other hand, international law usually accepts a four-fold basis for jurisdiction.

a. The Territoriality Principle

(i) General Remarks

Every sovereign State has *full and absolute territorial jurisdiction* within its allocated area.[69] We have already demonstrated that there are certain limits to the full competence of a State to decide on all matters within its territory: there are rules of international law, for example on Human Rights, which always must be respected. However, it is certainly true that, as a general rule, a State enjoys the right of jurisdiction in its territory. In effect, such jurisdiction is a direct result and consequence of State sovereignty.

On the other hand, there are certain geographical limits to this power. In other words, the jurisdiction of a State may, according to the territorial principle, also end where the territory ends. For that reason a court may not apply its own laws or its own tests of legality to activity beyond its own territory. In *American Banana Co. v United Fruit* the Supreme Court of the United States said that

---

[69]   *The Schooner Exchange* (1812) 11 US 7 Cranch. 116, 137.

'The general and almost universal rule is that the character of an act as lawful or unlawful must be determined wholly by the law of the country where the act is done ... For another jurisdiction, if it should happen to lay hold of the actor, to treat him according to its own notions rather than those of the place where he did the act, not only would be unjust but would be an interference with the authority of another sovereign, contrary to the comity of nations, which the other State may justly resent.'[70]

For reasons of comity the Court in that case refused to apply United States antitrust law to activities of an American company abroad. It is interesting to note that in that case the activities abroad had even repercussions and considerable effect in the United States.

The territoriality principle has, in practice, the following consequences. If an actor, who perpetrated the act, is present within a State, there is a ground for jurisdiction of that State. For the purpose of knowing whether the actor is *within* the State, it is obviously important to know the geographical extent of the State as set out above. This is also important to know in case the person committing the crime is to be subject to extradition, or as some such procedures are called within the Commonwealth, to rendition.

It is usually not sufficient that the actor is within the jurisdiction but the act should also have taken place there. There are numerous exceptions to this rule in all the modern hi-jack conventions and anti-terrorism agreements which all extend the jurisdictional basis to a wide circle of contracting parties. We should also perhaps consider the notion of *hot pursuit* as precisely one that *extends* the territorial span to cover certain fleeing criminals.[71]

We must also be aware of 'artificial' extensions of the territoriality principle which enables courts to accept cases when an individual, or a corporation, has assets in the jurisdiction.[72] Even if such a person is not connected with a specific country, by nationality, domicile or residence, or it is, in numerous jurisdictions, still possible

---

[70] (1909) 213 US 347, 356 and *supra*, on Comity.

[71] See *supra* in Chapter VI on *hot pursuit*.

[72] See on *Mareva injunctions, infra,* and *cf.* Bowett, Jurisdiction: Changing patterns of authority over activities and resources, BYIL 1982, 1.

to take action against him if the person has movables (including money in a bank) or real estate in that country.

(ii) Vessels and Aircraft within the Jurisdiction

Fedozzi, La condition juridique des navires de commerce, 10 RCADI 1925; Sack, The doctrine of quasi-territoriality of vessels and the admiralty jurisdiction over crimes committed on board national vessels in foreign ports, 12 NYUnivLQR 1934-35.

The jurisdictional powers of a State extends to its water space.[73] Even if the laws of the flag State are those which normally operate with regard to the vessel, a ship is not *only* subjected to the laws of the flag State but must also respect, for example, legislation of coastal States when passing through territorial waters[74] and, like nationals of other States, a ship must respect all laws of the territorial State when she is in a foreign port.[75] On the other hand, for all accidents or incidents on the High Seas, the law of the flag State is of paramount importance.[76] In cases of distress, for example, when a ship involuntarily enter a port, the territorial right of jurisdiction of the port State for crimes committed on the High Seas probably cedes to the law of the flag State.[77]

On the other hand, the territorial State is entitled to exercise its jurisdiction if a crime is committed on board a vessel in one of its ports especially in cases where a person who is not a citizen of the flag State is involved or where the general order of the territorial State is affected.[78] Jurisdiction is naturally often exercised if a crime

---

[73]   *The Cristina* [1938] AC 485.

[74]   See *supra* in Chapter VI on innocent passage and *infra*, in this Chapter, on Vessels in National Waters.

[75]   *The Tempest* (1859) 1 Dalloz 88 where the French Cour de Cassation held that only matters of discipline and administration are left to the flag State; a case of murder will be dealt with by territorial jurisdiction if the ship is in port.

[76]   See article 97 of the 1982 Law of the Sea Convention, codifying general international law.

[77]   *Hallet & Browne v Jenks* (1810) 3 Cranch 210.

[78]   *Chung Chi Cheung v R* [1939] AC 160, *per* Lord Atkin, rejecting Oppenheim's idea that a ship if a 'floating portion of the flag State'. On the rejection of the proposition that a neutral vessel is neutral territory for

is committed ashore.

The position of foreign warships involve similar considerations. Allegations that such warships are generally *immune* are misconceived. They are, like other vessels subject to local laws and regulations also as far as navigation, anchorage and public health are concerned. On the other hand, they are exempt from the executory proceedings by the host State: *The Schooner Exchange v M'Faddon*.[79] But the Supreme Court of the United States, which adjudicated *The Schooner Exchange* case held in *The Girard Case* held that

> 'a sovereign nation has exclusive jurisdiction to punish offenses against its laws committed within its borders unless it expressly or implicitly consents to surrender its jurisdiction.'[80]

There is thus no automatic immunity but a presumption in favour of the jurisdiction of the territorial State unless evidence of consent to waive jurisdiction is produced. The authorisation to allow foreign forces to visit the territory of another State commonly implies such a waiver but covers only

> (i) acts committed on board a warship, on an aircraft or within barracks or foreign military area provided there are no effects for the receiving State (the local interest criteria);
> (ii) acts relating to the discipline and internal administration (the functional criterion); and
> (iii) acts against the sending State alone (the general interest criterion).

Division of jurisdictional competence in this field is often divided by treaty. In other words, the presence of warships in the first place depend on the consent of the territorial State either under a general agreement on visiting forces or on an act of consent *ad hoc*. Without

---

purposes of jurisdiction see *The Newton and the Sally*, (1806 Bull. des lois 126, 602.

[79]   [1821] 1 Cranch 116.

[80]   (1967) 354 US 524.

such consent the foreign warships have no right to be in port and its illicit presence can lead to demand for compensation or damages.

Sweden chose not to exercise this right of redress when a Russian submarine, *The U-137*, was found on a shoal inside the military area of Karlskrona in 1983. The salvage cost should, under normal international rules, have been borne by the offending State, together with compensation for the intrusion. Submarines are, with specific permission, able to go through territorial waters, and may then not be submerged. If they go into the territorial waters without permission, the coastal State may claim damages. Such a claim will be enhanced as to its amount if the warships transgressed, as far as *internal waters,* or, as did submarine *U-137* of the USSR did in Swedish waters, as far as an islet or shoal in internal water *within a specifically prohibited military protection zone.*

(iii) Mandatory Restrictions on Jurisdiction

A limitation imposed on a State's internal sovereignty by general rules on immunity of diplomats, or other persons or entities endowed with immunity under international law, is mandatory. Such restrictions of jurisdiction therefore operates whether or not a State has acceded to relevant conventions on the immunities. For example, even if a State has not ratified the Vienna Convention on Immunities of Diplomats of 1969, it may not infringe the liberty of diplomatic agents duly accredited in its territory. The Iranian hostage crisis, resulting in a case before the International Court of Justice[81] and the ensuing *Frozen Assets Case* in the High Court of London[82] show that a State is not able to rid itself at will from obligations to respect general rules of international law.

(iv) Duplicated Jurisdiction

There is occasionally a case for duplicated jurisdiction. A State's jurisdiction follows, in many cases, its nationals abroad. If it seeks to

---

[81]   (1979) and (1980) ICJ *Reports*, 1970 and 1980.

[82]   Settled and unreported. See, further, *supra*, under Freezing Orders.

claim jurisdiction over a national abroad this will then, if accepted by the territorial State, be seen as a limitation in the usual jurisdictional power of that State over its territory. But often the two powers exist side by side.

b. The Nationality Principle

Most States only claim jurisdiction[83] over its own citizens in other States for certain specific crimes, such as treason, terrorism or specific crimes committed in direct violation of international law or of binding Resolutions of the Security Council.[84] In most cases other States will resent the application of the laws or decrees of another State within its territory unless it has bound itself by treaty to do so, or in case it gives its consent in the individual case, for example in the case of offenses against the bases of international society.

In matters of criminal law it is not unusual, however, that States claim jurisdiction beyond its territory.[85] Such power is often coupled with the duty of allegiance which a citizen owes to his own country. This is what was argued in the *Blackmer Case*[86] where the court also held that a State has the power to demand the return of a citizen to the country

> 'whenever the public interest requires it and to penalize him in case of refusal.'[87]

Numerous States claim jurisdiction by the nationality principle extending its powers over its own citizens wherever they may be.[88] However, there may be limits under international law to the actual

---

[83] See *supra* on *jus protectionis* for other rights a State may exercise in favour of a national and the *Nottebohm Case* (1955) ICJ *Reports* 1955, 4.

[84] For Sweden see the UN Act 1971:171.

[85] For example, (1952) *Steel v Bulova Watch Co.* 344 US 280, 282. Such power may also belong to the States of the United States provided that such juridiction does not conflict with acts of Congress, *Skiriotes v Florida*, (1941) 313 US 69, 77.

[86] (1932) 284, 421.

[87] *Ibid., loc. cit.*

[88] See, for example, Swedish Penal Code (*Brottsbalken*), 2:2.

powers of a State in this respect. On the one hand, it may well be that a court can hear a case as to the behaviour of nationals abroad. But on the other hand, it is questionable whether a State has the right to demand the return of its own citizens. Unless there is a clear extradition treaty enabling a host State to hand over a person in certain circumstances it is difficult to see how a citizen can be brought back to his home State against his own will. It is generally accepted that a State cannot *expel* its *own citizens*.[89] This rule was put in serious doubt when several hundred Palestinians, all Israeli citizens, were expelled from Israel in 1993 and when the Supreme Court of Israel decided that they had no right to return.[90]

It may well be that claims of extra-territorial jurisdiction conflict with rules of general international law and especially with rule on Human Rights. If a States claims a national back for alleged *crimes* such crimes may well be of a political nature in which case if may be highly undesirable to assist the other State in having its citizen back. In any event it is often uncertain whether a person is or is not a *criminal*, since he must always be presumed innocent until proven guilty. It is therefore excessive to allow claims of States to have a citizen returned on the suspicion of a committed crime unless there is an extradition treaty in operation.[91]

c. The Passive Personality Principle

In some cases jurisdiction is founded on the nationality of the victim and not on the offender. Then, there is some indication in rather hesitating State practice that the offended State - whose national has

---

[89]   This is a rule of general international law; see also, the Hague Convention on Certain Questions Relating to the Conflict of Nationality Laws 1930, 179 LNTS 89.

[90]   Decision 27th January 1993.

[91]   Such a treaty would often exempt precisely political crimes although it is difficult to identify such acts. Conventions on terrorism, for example on hijacking, which focus on crimes for political motives, fill a similar function in the context of extradition. Note that numerous countries, for example, Brazil, have few extradition treaties. Biggs, one of the Great Train Robbers, thus escaped British justice by fleeing to Brazil from where he could not be extradited.

suffered damage or injury - can rely on the *nationality of the victim* as a ground for jurisdiction.

The principle with which we are concerned in this context has often been called the *passive personality principle*. However, it would seem more appropriate to rename it the *passive nationality principle* since it is nationality, rather than any other connecting factor that has been decisive in the few cases where the principle has been allowed to operate.[92]

The leading case on this aspect is *The Lotus Case* before the Permanent Court of International Justice.[93] Here a Turkish ship, *The Boz-Kourt* had been hit, on the high seas, by a French mail steamer, *The Lotus*. The Permanent Court held that Turkey had jurisdiction to try the officer on duty on the French ship for manslaughter. However, this judgment has been severely criticised. Already when it was delivered Judge Moore wrote a strong dissenting opinion and, later commentators have usually expressed doubt whether the passive nationality principle, on which the Court did not clearly pronounce, should furnish ground for jurisdiction.

d. The Effect Principle

Many States thus claim jurisdiction if an act produces *effects* in its territory. *The Lotus Case* before the Permanent Court of International Justice in 1927,[94] just discussed, illustrates how near the effect principle comes to the passive personality rule. The Court held that Turkey had not violated principles of international law by asserting criminal jurisdiction over a French officer on a French ship on the high seas after the French vessel had collided with a Turkish ship. The Court argued in a *negative* way by searching for a rule of international law that would limit the right of Turkey to extend it criminal jurisdiction in this way. Thus, the Court did not look for or find a rule *allowing* or *endorsing* such claims but applied a rule which *forbade* such extensive claims.

As has been mentioned above, the case has been much criticised

---

[92]   See *supra*.

[93]   (1927) PCIJ A No. 10.

[94]   PCIJ Ser. A No. 10, and *supra*.

over the years for widening rights of jurisdiction of the home State of a victim. Similarly, we may have apprehensions about any rule that eliminates the freedom of expression on this ground. To grant to a coastal State a right to jurisdiction over unauthorised sound and television broadcasting offshore, as suggested in the 1982 Law of the Sea Convention,[95] appears to be such a overambitious restraint of legitimate rights.

If an act is contrary to the economic interests of a State it may also claim jurisdiction under the effect principle. It is on this ground that some States have unduly sought to extend their rights into the territory of other States by inland revenue rules, rules against investment or anti-trust laws. The United States has, at recurring intervals, been criticised for applying the effect principle to its anti-trust legislation. In the case concerning *The United States v Aluminium Co. of Americas* the Court allowed United States anti-trust legislation to bind a Canadian company operating in Switzerland where it had taken part in a cartel arrangement. The Court did not refuse far reaching claims on this basis as

'any State may impose liabilities, even upon persons not within its allegiance, for conduct outside its borders that has consequences within its borders which the State reprehends; and these liabilities other States will ordinarily recognise.'[96]

The Court sought to justify its claim to jurisdiction by arguing that American interests were affected and that extra-territorial actions had produced effects in the United States.

In many cases the situation can be perceived to concern the question of extraterritorial application of national economic laws. Harmonisation of rules in the economic field may provide a possible solution for some cases where the use of jurisdictional powers has caused irritation.[97]

---

[95]   Article 109.

[96]   *US v Aluminium Co. of America* (1945) 148 F 2d 416; 148 F 2d 416 2d Cir 1945. *Cf. British Nylon Spinners Ltd. v ICI* [1953] Ch 19 (CA).

[97]   Lowe, Problems of Extraterritorial Jurisdiction: Economic Sovereignty and the Search for a Solution, ICLQ 1985, 724.

It must also be noted that the Court of the European Community does exceed the boundaries of binding international law when it extends its jurisdiction to firms in non-Member States, using the blue print formula of the United States in anti-trust cases.[98]

In other fields, the effects principle is particularly inappropriate and shows lack of respect for comity[99] and the jurisdictional powers of other States. The *von Herder Case* before the Swedish Supreme Court,[100] concerned a German officer for espionage against Sweden from his posting in Norway. It was claimed that jurisdiction could be exercised by Sweden over von Herder on the ground that he had injured Swedish interests. But the Swedish Supreme Court emphasised that principles of international law precluded the application of Swedish criminal law in the instance and that, therefore, von Herder's actions were not punishable in Sweden.[101] This case, and many others in other countries, tend to show that there is, at present, no rule in international law which permits jurisdiction over a non-resident foreigner for an act committed out of the country of the forum.[102]

It is to be noted that under the present provisions in Swedish law,[103] Sweden does use an extensive effect principle[104] and claims jurisdiction for crimes committed by foreigners, on foreign

---

[98]   *Re Wood Pulp Cartel: Ahlström Osakeyhtio v EC Commission* (1988) 4 CMLR 901. The Court's argument was that jurisdiction was based on a 'territoriality' notion, meaning the 'territory' (of the EC) where effects were produced.

[99]   See in detail *supra* in Chapter I.

[100]   NJA 1946 65. *Cf., supra*, under Restrictions of Sovereignty Over Individuals.

[101]   For present legislation in Sweden see The Penal Code (*Brottsbalken*) BrB 2:7 which provides that the application of Swedish law and the competence of Swedish Courts may be limited by general rules of international law but with the proviso that such rules will be effective only *beyond what is here prescribed.* In other words, the provision for extra-territorial jurisdiction seeks to override international law. *Cf.* provisions in *ibid.* 2:2 and 2:3.

[102]   Note, that in the field of anti-trust matters for which United States claims jurisdiction, protests of other States have gradually subsided; on the other hand, and the United States now restricts claims for jurisdiction to cases where actual effects have occurred in the United States: *Restatement (Third) Foreign Relations Law of the US* (1987), 415.

[103]   See BrB 2: and 2:3.

[104]   And even the universality principle, see *infra* in this Chapter.

soil, if such crimes are directed *against Sweden, Swedish municipality or other group of individuals*[105] *or Swedish public institution.* Such juridictional claims are not in conformity with international law and with comity[106] owed to other nations. For there to be jurisdiction on any ground in such a case there must be *other factors* which link the defendant to the forum State. Such a link can perhaps be found if it can be proved that he owes some form of allegiance to the offended State. This was, for example, argued in the *Lord Haw-Haw Case,*[107] where a person was prosecuted for broadcasting anti-British propaganda during the Second World War.

Claims of jurisdiction under the effects principle are, as has been mentioned, excessive and unwarranted; they lack justification in international law.

e. The Protective Principle

In *United States v Pizzarusso* an American Court held that jurisdiction could be justified to cover

> 'conduct outside its territory that threatens its security as a State or the operation of its governmental functions, provided that the conduct is generally recognised as a crime under the law of States that have reasonably developed legal systems.'[108]

In the event, an alien had made false statements at an American consulate in Canada for the purpose of a visa application.

The difference between this principle and the one we just examined, the *effect principle*, is that under the *protective principle*, a State claims jurisdiction *before* any effects have been suffered, thus if certain behaviour threatens the interests, or the security, of the State. In a sense, jurisdiction under this heading is designed to *preempt* such deterimental effects.

There is less objection to extended jurisdiction for *security*

---

105   In Swedish *'menighet'*.

106   See *supra* under Comity.

107   *Joyce v DPP* [1946] AC 347 and *supra*.

108   (1968) 388 F2d (2d Cir 1968), cert. denied, 392 US 936.

reasons under this so called *protective principle* than for other general interests, but, again, there are better avenues to entrench State security than by jurisdiction of the Courts. The same reasoning which clarifies that jurisdiction on the basis of an interest criterion,[109] apply with the same force with regard to protective jurisdictional claims.

f. The Universality Principle

Another principle is alleged to furnish ground for jurisdiction to try a non-national for any act he has committed *anywhere*. Such a rule would, in its raw form, be rejected by all jurists. Yet, if, on the other hand, the universality principle is qualified to concern *certain international crimes* and is limited to certain *serious violations of the fundamental rules of international society* we will find that it is, in fact, a workable principle of jurisdiction, a principle which has often been used and with justification.

The universality principle is thus a principle which in this modified form has been approved by all nations for *specific international crimes*. Thus, when we consider the power all States have, in history, claimed over *pirates* it is precisely on the basis of the universality principle that jurisdiction has been exercised. Piracy *jure gentium*[110] can be defined as *any act of violence committed by a private*[111] *vessel outside the jurisdiction of any State*[112] *against another vessel.*[113]

---

[109]   *Supra.*

[110]   Piracy as an *international crime* must be distinguished from what national laws may classify as piracy under municipal law, see, I:i Oppenheim, ed. by Jennings & Watts, 754-755.

[111]   Note that public ships, warships, or insurgents cannot commit piracy, see 1 Calvo paras. 497 *et seq.* Note that violence to further environmental ideas has been classified by national courts as implying a private motive, *Castle John v Macebo*, 77 ILR 537.

[112]   This qualification excludes territorial waters and the contiguous zone, where States retain jurisdiction, see *supra* in Chapter V, but includes the EEZ and other protective zones.

[113]   *Cf.* the definition in i Oppenheim, 8th ed. by Lauterpacht, 614, which also adds the adjective *unauthorised* to qualify the act, and which also includes *mutiny.* In the recent edition by Sir Robert Jennings & Sir Arthur Watts, the more elaborate definition (which excludes mutiny) adopted in the 1958 and

Pirates are *hostes gentium,* enemies of all peoples, and can therefore be tried anywhere. As international law *lacks the mechanisms* to prosecute and punish pirates, it is a power[114] and possibly, if seen in the context of the solidarity between nations,[115] a duty,[116] for States to take necessary action against pirates who come into their jurisdiction.

It is also on the basis of the universality principle that recent treaties on jurisdiction over the new form of piracy, the hi-jackers and the terrorists, have been concluded. Under these treaties,[117] jurisdiction can be exercised, or must be exercised, by any contracting party on whose territory the accused person is present, regardless of where the action took place and regardless of his nationality.

The universality principle is thus the basis for jurisdiction that every State has over pirates as demonstrated in *United States v Smith* in 1820.[118] The basis for jurisdictional claims of this category is both recognised and accepted in modern international society for cases concerning severe violations of international law.

Apart from piracy, we may refer to cases concerning violations of Human Rights. In the important and widely reported *Filartiga v Pena-Irala Case* a United States Court held that torture gives rise to universal jurisdictional rights as

'the torturer has become - like the pirate and slave-trader before him - *hostis humani generis,* an enemy of all mankind'.[119]

1982 Law of the Sea Convention has been preferred, a definition which adds, *i.a.*, that the act must have been committed for *private ends.* The impossibility of establishing such subjective criteria makes the more elaborate definition in these Conventions less workable. *Cf. supra* in Chapter IV on terrorism.

[114]   *The Lotus Case* (1927) PCIJ Series A No. 10, 70; *Re Piracy Jure Gentium,* [1934] AC 586; *Bolivia v The Indemnity Mutual Marine Assurance Co.* [1909] 1 KB 785.

[115]   See my *Concept, op. cit.,* Part Four: III 124-128 on Solidarity Rules.

[116]   But there is certain latitude concerning consequences: *cf.* Oppenheim, ed. Jennings & Watts, I:2 753-754 on that it is for the courts of the State which has seized the vessel to determine the penalties.

[117]   See, *supra,* under Terrorism.

[118]   18 US (5 Wheaton) 153, 161.

[119]   (1980) 630 F 2d 876, 890 (2d Cir.1980). *Cf. Demjanjuk v Petrovsky* (1985) F 2d 571, 582 on universal jurisdiction for war criminals.

It is probable that also *war crimes* form such a category for which there may be a right of universal jurisdiction. It would seem logical that the State most affronted by such crimes would enjoy the right to adjudicate. But if we consider the *Eichmann Case*[120] where Israel did claim such a right, and if we overlook the fact that Israel was not a State when the crimes were committed, there is still *no right to violate the territorial sovereignty of another State* in order to exercise that right of universal jurisdiction. In the event, Israel, which has never denied this action, kidnapped Eichmann in Argentina; such intrusions in order to bring someone to justice cannot be condoned and does not further the international legal order however justified a nation's anger may be about relevant crimes.

The advent of new crimes, such as terrorism or drug dealing, has made this principle more acceptable for new *international crimes*[121] for which there is a tendency to seek *universal* jurisdiction.[122] This was demonstrated in *United States v Yunis*,[123] where a Thai drug dealer was lured into international waters where he was arrested by United States agents and later prosecuted in the United States for terrorist acts which were not connected with the United States. Similarly, in *Liangsiriprasert v United States*[124] a Thai drug dealer was persuaded to go to Hong Kong where he was arrested whereupon the United States asked to have him extradited. The Privy Council in England held that

'in this century crime has ceased to be largely local in origin and effect. Crime is now established on an international scale and common law must face this new reality. Their Lordships can find nothing in precedent, comity or good sense that should inhibit the common law from regarding as justiciable in England inchoate crimes committed abroad which are intended to result in the commission of criminal offences in England ...'

---

120   83 (1961) 36 ILR 5.
121   See *supra* on this qualification in Chapter IV.
122   See on this *infra* in this Chapter.
123   (1988) 681 F Supp 896.
124   [1990] 2 All ER 866 (PC).

It may be that the Privy Council's attitude is more a reflection of a protective principle.[125] Yet, by assisting the United States future prosecution, and by specifically referring to the internationalisation of crime - and making references to terrorist activities - it would seem the universality principle for specific crimes, like drug smuggling, was at the root of the decision.

The universality principle thus applies to *crimes against international society*, either to *piracy*, or (tentatively) to *terrorism* and *drug dealing* and furthermore to certain *gross violations of basic Human Rights*. The universality principle must, however, be strictly limited to such serious international crimes, which, along with piracy and torture, warrant such wide jurisdictional powers.

Surprisingly enough, Sweden, probably unnoticed by other States, claims, however, unlimited and universal jurisdiction for *all crimes*, covering an unqualified number. These excessive Swedish claims to jurisdiction, and in conjunction with this, claims to apply Swedish law, extend beyond the interest criterion and demand universal application: Sweden thus claims rights over *any person,* for *any crime,* committed *anywhere* provided only the penalty is more than four years in prison.[126] If the *government of Sweden so orders* even *foreign public agents, civil servants or Ministers*, or *officials of international organisations* can be prosecuted in Sweden according to Swedish law for any crime committed outside Sweden.[127] Apart from disregarding general rules of international law on comity, Sweden seems to have overlooked entrenched rules on immunity of both agents of foreign States and of officials of international organisations.

Such absurd claims to universal jurisdiction, except for piracy, war crimes, gross violations of Human Rights, like, for example, torture, or for terrorists and drug dealers, as set out above, must be firmly rejected by international lawyers as an affront to the

---

[125]   *Supra.*
[126]   Swedish Penal Code (*Brottsbalken*), 2:3,7; Lag 1990:416.
[127]   BrB 2:7a, Lag 1985:518.

sovereignty of other nations and of the principle of comity.[128]

iv. Extraterritorial Application of Judgments, Laws and Decrees

a. Foreign Judgments

Foreign judgments may easily operate in other countries with a minimum of action to re-activate their effects in another jurisdiction than where they were delivered. There is a special network of rules facilitating recognition and operation of foreign judgments within the British Commonwealth[129] as under the Brussels Convention on Jurisdiction and Enforcement of Judgments in Civil and Commercial Matters, which applies between EC/EU Member States.

Twenty years after that the original EC members had concluded the Brussels Convention on Jurisdiction and Enforcement, and after the EU Court had decided in more than fifty cases on the interpretation of the Convention, there was a response to the aforementioned Brussels Convention by the Lugano Convention of 1988, the so called *Parallel Convention* by the countries in Europe which do not belong to the European Community but to the European Free Trade Association (EFTA). EFTA is a slowly dying organisation with weak powers,[130] which Austria will soon leave to join the European Community. Sweden, too, has announced that it will apply for membership of the European Community[131] which will leave few Contracting Parties of the Lugano Convention. This Convention also seeks to obtain rapid effectiveness of judgments delivered in a

---

128   See *supra* under Comity. It is not to protect such Human Rights that Sweden introduced an unqualified universality principle. On the contrary, it is such basic Human Rights that Sweden does *not* recognise to bind Sweden unless there are specific treaties on the matter, see *supra* under Monism, Dualism in Chapter III and under Human Rights in Chapter IV.

129   See further the Commonwealth Convention.

130   See my Aspects institutionnels de l'Association Européenne de Libre Echange (AELE), AF 1960.

131   The planned transitory arrangement involving a new organisation, European Economic Space (EES), will, in the opinion of this writer never come into effect as it is contrary to the adopted policies of the European Community. Like Austria, Sweden should have applied for unconditional membership.

number of other States as well as within the European Union.[132]

Even outside these contractual treaty systems, it is, as any barrister knows, relatively easy to obtain a new judgment on the basis of an already existing judgment or decision of a foreign court, a much underestimated mechanism of private international law.

In this field the *theory of comity*[133] has been supplanted by the *theory of obligation*.[134] This theory of obligation implies that, if a competent[135] foreign court, has imposed a duty on the defendant to, for example, pay a specific sum an action of debt can be brought in another country.[136] What has occurred, in terms of law, after the judgment, is that *a new contractual right* has accrued to the party in whose favour judgment was given and *a new duty* has accrued to the losing party. There is thus, at least an *implied promise* of the losing party to pay the adjudicated sum.[137] For this new undertaking, an action can easily be brought in a number of jurisdictions.

This second type of suit, that of an action of debt, comes very near an *executionary* action, as the defendant in this way will eventually be obliged to pay, provided he has assets in the jurisdiction. Numerous Swedish firms, with assets in England, have painfully learnt that, on this ground, a Swedish judgment can be enforced in England, regardless of whether the previous textbooks on private international law in Sweden reassuringly suggest that no judgment can be enforced elsewhere unless treaties or conventions so provide.

Older textbooks on Conflict of Laws, especially in Scandinavia, tend to treat recognition of judgments as something which can only have practical importance if a State has ratified a treaty obliging it to give effect to judgments of foreign States.

Yet, anyone who has practised as a barrister knows that it is often

---

[132]   The so called Lugano Convention of 1984.

[133]   See on this in detail *supra* in Chapter I.

[134]   Piggott, *Foreign Judgments and Parties out of the Jurisdiction*, 3rd ed., 1908, i 11.

[135]   'Competent' is then used as a condition that the court has exercised proper jurisdiction according to the general jurisdictional rules set out above, in this Chapter.

[136]   *E.g. Russel v Smyth* (1842) 13 M & W 810.

[137]   *Slade's Case* (1602) 4 Co 912; *Grant v Easton* (1883) 13 QB 302.

with relative ease that actions can be brought in another country, on the basis of a judgment obtained in another State; treaties only seem to be relevant in so far as they facilitate and make this process even easier. The ease with which even summary judgment can be obtained, for example, in England, on the basis of a Swedish judgment, should not be underestimated, although this may be done outside any form of treaty relationship.[138]

Naturally many criteria must be satisfied before a Court attaches any importance to a foreign judgment: it must have been rendered by a competent, properly constituted Court. To establish whether a foreign Court is competent, an English Court, as other Courts within the Commonwealth, will attach special importance to whether rules on natural justice have been observed, *i.e.* the two-fold rule[139] stating both that *audiatur et altera pars*, *i.e.* that both parties must have been heard and the rule *nemo judex in causa sua*, that is the rule that no one may be a judge in his own case,[140] essential maxims in all countries with respect for the Rule of Law.

Once a Court is satisfied that a foreign judgment has been issued by a competent Court it will have effect in so far as the underlying facts may be accepted by the Court that considers the case. If, for example, a certain sum has been found to be due by a foreign Court, an English Court may find that a legal obligation arises from the foreign judgment on which an action of debt can be maintained in England.[141] The basis for this reasoning is that a party to a foreign suit has acquired a right under a foreign judgment and it is to this acquired right that the *forum* court gives effect. Some cases even emphasise that this rule has become viable by itself, and applies without relying on the principle of comity although comity certainly gave rise to the rule.[142]

The acceptance of acquired rights and/or underlying facts may

---

138 See, also *supra* on these Conventions.
139 The concepts have been particularly well developed in English administrative law, see *infra*.
140 See, further, *supra* 34 *et seq.* under Public International Law and Conflict of Laws and *infra* 49 note on the concept Natural Justice.
141 *Williams v Jones*, 13 M/W at 633 per Parker B.
142 *Hilton v Guyot*, 159 US 113, 233 per Mr Justice Gray.

thus be the consequence of foreign judgments. In *Bradstreet v Neptune Insurance Company*, the Court held that

> 'If a civilised nation seeks to have its sentences of its own courts held of any validity elsewhere, they ought to have a just regard to the rights and usages of other civilised nations and the principles of public and national law in the administration of justice.'[143]

Foreign arbitral awards may also have immediate effect under specific treaties and here there is a particularly important network of rules. The 1958 New York Convention on the Recognition and Enforcement of Foreign Arbitral Awards[144] has numerous parties, for example the United States,[145] a State which has not found it useful to adhere to convention on the recognition of judgments; it is thus easier and quicker to allow the operation of a foreign arbitration award in the United States than of a foreign judgment. This should be noted as a arbitration tribunal, neither by its structure nor by its rules of procedure, is as strictly supervised as that of a Court.

b. Conflict of Laws Situations

(i) General Points

Laws of another country are frequently applied in *conflict of laws* situations. It is useful to view basic conflict of law principles in the context of the concept of comity analysed earlier in this treatise.[146]

The situation of competing claims of jurisdiction is clearly a consequence of the splitting up of jurisdictional sectors for each State, some separate, some overlapping and some seeking to oust others.

Once one accepts that the numerous States in the world have an *equal* right to have their laws applied to situations of special interest

---

[143] 3 Summer 600

[144] 330 UNTS 3.

[145] The United States adhered, in 1986, also to the Inter-American Convention on International Commercial Arbitration 14 ILM 336.

[146] See in detail *supra,* Chapter I.

to them, and once one accepts that, therefore, there must be a question of *sharing* and *dividing* this jurisdictional competence, one can perceive clearly certain common principles for such division between courts of different States.

When there is a situation of *overlapping* of competence one frequently speaks of a collision[147] or of a *conflict* of laws. Regardless of whether or not these expressions are appropriate, the term *conflict of laws* has gained foothold in international law to designate the area of problems associated with a court's decision to accept a case with international connotations and with its choice or decision to apply a specific law to the case.

The discipline of conflict of laws appears to fit in, from the point of view of a homogeneous system, as a sub-branch of general international law, rather than a set of parallel national subjects. Thus, national legal rules on these matters have more in common than what divides them and merit to be viewed as a common discipline of international law, consisting of both public international law and of conflict of laws, often called private international law.

One reason for this global way of perceiving the interwoven relationships between public and private international law is that private international law shows numerous internationalised trends and features, obtained both by the common sense approach in many countries which often arrives at similar solutions, and by positive efforts to conclude treaties and conventions to harmonise rules on numerous questions.[148]

The connecting factors for *jurisdiction of courts* and *choice of law* are vaguely the same in most countries and can be tentatively summarised in a basic set of rules. Naturally, national scholarship is required to elaborate and elucidate intricate operation of complex issues under different systems of law. In order to deal with any specific case it is necessary to look into exact provisions under the national law in question and into recent case-law. However, such analysis may be furthered by an internationalistic optique of relevant problems.

---

[147]   In Swedish and Scandinavian literature the word *kollisionsnormer* are often used.

[148]   See in detail *supra* in Chapter I.

It is also our contention that the system of conflict of laws is no autonomous discipline, to which each State has a right to adopt its own attitude. Far more, the subject appears to be a sub-section of general international law, apportioning various fields of competence to individual States.

For areas, where rules are not yet harmonised, it is clear that *comity*, as discussed in detail earlier in another context of the structure of the international system,[149] is at the basis of the division of jurisdictional power of States and also of the division of their right to apply their own laws. The *link* that every State preserves with regard to its nationals, is thus *either* expressed in the way a 'foreign law' may be applied to that person in a 'foreign court' *or* indicated in the way that a State preserves the right to protect that national, when he is in a 'foreign State' by the *jus protectionis,* discussed earlier.[150] That right alone, the right to protect a citizen abroad, may prove the close *nexus* between public and private international law.

(ii) Harmonisation of Rules

In many fields the risk for conflict of laws situations to arise is minimised by the trend to *harmonise* rules on certain topics which leads to that many courts, in many jurisdictions, apply the same or similar rules. Substantive laws have now been extensively harmonised and there is now a detailed network of rules which are common to many States. In some cases this is because the substantive internal laws of these States have been developed along similar lines or have been harmonised by specific conventions and treaties. Apart from unification or harmonisation of substantive rules there is an on-going process in international society to harmonise the formal conflict rules of various States. Numerous co-ordination efforts and many conventions deal with both substantive harmonisation or unification of laws as well as with specific conflict of laws solutions.

Important Conferences were held in the Hague in 1893, 1894, 1900 and 1904 which resulted in a series of Conventions on Validity

---

[149] See *supra* in Chapter I.
[150] See *supra* under A., in this Chapter.

of Marriages of 1902, the Effects of Marriage of 1905, on Divorce and Separation of 1902, on Guardianship of 1902, on Interdiction of 1902, on Civil Procedure of the same year. Further Conventions concluded under the auspices of the now permanent Hague Conference include the Convention on Maintenance of Children of 1956. Even States which have not acceded to these Conventions, or which adhered and subsequently denounced them, have, in their internal laws, been greatly influenced by the Conventions. The Hague Conference on Private International Law, made permanent in 1951, has since also made significant contributions to the unification of national private law as well as to uniform conflict solutions.

Some attempts towards greater uniformity have been greatly assisted by institutions like UNIDROIT, established by the Italian Government in Rome as an institute of the League of Nations for the Unification of Private Laws, and UNICITRAL, administered on the international level as a United Nations Committee, have both contributed to further harmonisation of substantive rules. UNIDROIT elaborated together with the Hague Conference the 1964 Convention on the International Sale of Goods. UNICITRAL has drafted a further Convention now adopted as the United Nations Convention on Contracts for the International Sale of Goods of 1980.

Sometimes efforts are coordinated because States experience similar problems in the private law sphere. Thus, in the field of foreign investment there is often approximation of substantive rules of internal laws.[151] More common, however, is that States adhere to specific legal tradition and for such reasons find it natural to adopt similar rules.

In this way, some unification efforts result from previous historical factors. For example, States which earlier formed part of the British Empire still often apply rules which are similar to those of English law.[152] In Latin America, a common heritage of similar laws from colonial times coupled with efforts under regional treaties have resulted in early cooperation to adopt similar or identical rules in many areas.

---

[151] See, for example, my *Finance and Protection of Investment in Developing Countries*, 2nd ed., 1987.

[152] Fawcett, *The British Commonwealth in International Law*, 1963.

Efforts have concerned not only approximation of internal laws but also specific conflict of laws mechanisms. Conventions on such devices and conflict of laws solutions have been adopted by the Contracting Parties to multilateral Conventions in Latin America. Conventions like the Montevideo Conventions of 1889 and 1940, the Havana Convention of 1928 and the famous Código Bustamante[153] have been of great practical importance.

Within the European Community a far reaching program of harmonisation have contributed to similar rules on a number of matters.[154] Conventions on coordinating conflict of laws rules have been adopted, for example, the Convention on Contractual Obligations of 1980. On the whole there is continuous assimilation of conflict of law rules within the European Community, now the European Union,[155] for example the Brussels Convention on Jurisdiction and Enforcement of Judgments in Civil and Commercial Matters of 1968 with its Protocol of Interpretation of 1971. This Convention was amended in numerous sections to provide for British, Irish and Danish accession, which took place in 1978, five years after they had joined the Community.

In Scandinavia there are long-standing Conventions on similar substantive rules as well as close cooperation under the auspices of the Nordic Council.[156] Some efforts only concern loose co-operation in the legislative field whereas others have resulted on specific conflict of laws Convention. Treaties range from questions like bankruptcy regulated in a Convention of 1933 and a series of agreements in the field of family law. In the latter area special

---

[153] For cooperation in detail see, for example, Parra-Aragueren, RCADI iii 1979, 55.

[154] See, for example, article 100 of the EEC Treaty which empowers the Council to issue Directives 'for the approximation of such provisions laid down by law, regulation or administrative action in Member States as directly affect the establishment or functioning of the common market'. Directives are, according to article 189, *binding as to the result to be achieved* but leaving to individual States the 'choice of form and method'.

[155] Jayme and Picchio Forlati, *Guirisdizione e legge applicabile ai contratti nella CEE*, 1990; cf. Fletcher, *Conflict of Laws and the European Community*, 1982.

[156] Anderson, *The Nordic Council: A Study in Scandinavian Regionalism*, 1967.

problems have been caused by the fact that only Denmark[157] currently follows the principle that the law of domicile governs questions of a personal nature whereas the other States have adopted the more current European approach of using nationality as the decisive element.[158]

The Nordic Convention of 1931 on unification of rules on marriage, adoption and guardianship rests on the agreement to use the law of the domicile, or habitual residence, for relationships between citizens of the Contracting Parties, *i.e.* Sweden, Norway, Denmark, Finland and Iceland, but allows the Contracting Parties to still use their traditional methods for deciding conflict of laws matters with Third States.[159] Another inter-Nordic Convention of 1934 regulates matters like succession, wills and administration of estates.

A Scandinavian Convention on Economic Rights of Spouses of 1912 also provided for choice of law solutions based on habitual residence at the time of the marriage. The Act of 1912 implementing this Convention in Sweden has now been replaced with a controversial Act of 1990 which provides that, after a time limit of five years Swedish citizens abroad, even in ethnically quite different areas, will have their financial rights under the marriage governed by the local law where they live.

Between the various *blocs* of countries adopting a similar approach to private law matters there have been further bridges built by specific conventions. As one example, one may refer to the carriage of persons or goods by aircraft under the Warsaw Convention of 1929 as amended,[160] which provides uniform rules both with regard to substantive law to be applied,[161] and with respect to

---

[157]   Note, that *domicile* in Danish law is an entirely different concept to the English notion of domicile. The Danish understanding of domicile comes near to what in England is called *habitual residence*.

[158]   See, further, *infra*, on Connecting Elements.

[159]   It is worth noting that the law of domicile, used in a less technical sense than in English law and more corresponding to habitual residence, is increasingly adopted in Swedish legislation. Note also *supra* on the Danish use of the domicile rule, albeit in a weaker form than the English.

[160]   Revised by the Hague Convention of 1955 and supplemented by the Guadalajara Convention of 1961.

[161]   Contracting Parties even undertake not to amend these uniform rules.

jurisdiction. Another example is the Brussels Convention of 1924 on Maritime Law, *inter alia* on the carriage of goods, incorporated in England in the 1924 Carriage of Goods by Sea Act of the same year. The similar Convention on Carriage by Rail, the Berne Convention of the same year was only adopted by States in continental Europe, and not by the United Kingdom.

The Geneva Conventions on Uniform Bills of Exchange of 1930 and on Unification of the Law Relating to Cheques of 1931, have both been widely adopted by numerous countries in Europe, as well as by the former Soviet Union, Brazil and Japan, but has not been ratified by the United Kingdom, most countries in the Commonwealth or by the United States, which adhere to a different legal tradition. The Conventions still have real practical impact, although the United States, United Kingdom and other members of the British Commonwealth have not adhered. The reason for this practical importance is that international business cannot be carried out unless businessmen within the Anglo-American system also adapt to rules used by other partners.

A bridge between the systems of the Geneva Conventions and the Anglo-American approach, as far as Bills of Exchange are concerned, was achieved by the United Nations Conventions on International Bills of Exchange and International Promissory Notes of 1988.

A further influence on the harmonisation of national conflict of laws attitudes is exercised by the International Court of Justice (ICJ). This was demonstrated in, for example, the *Boll Case*[162] on guardianship of children, often referred to as authoritative on general guardianship rules. The judgment of the Court's predecessor the Permanent Court of International Justice, PCIJ, in the *Serbian Loans Case*[163] also illustrates this point as numerous national Courts followed and adopted the interpretation of the PCIJ of a gold clause in a loan agreement.[164]

Although private international law rules are primarily found in internal laws, they are thus harmonised, unified and interpreted by international efforts and thus, themselves, become increasingly

---

[162]   *Reports* 1955.

[163]   (1929), Series A., No. 20.

[164]   *Cf. The Case of Brazilian Loans* Series A., No. 21.

international.

It is safely suggested that the delimitation between so called 'public international law' and 'private international law' is now continuously eroded by the process of harmonisation of conflict rules.

(iii) Common Concepts

Conflict *principles*, such as the notion of public policy or *ordre public*, although applied in private international law with different implications depending on the local setting, may not necessarily operate as a fragmenting force but as a harmonising and unifying principle *by its very existence* as an internationally accepted principle. An international tribunal may thus interpret a treaty in the light of such national public policy, without undermining a harmonised and uniform manner of interpretation.[165] Other such commonly accepted notions, usually understood and interpreted in similar ways, concern the question of *renvoi*, of *further* reference to another legal system, on *classification* (also called *qualification* or *characterisation*), which concerns the allocation of a question to a specific legal category.

(iv) Jurisdiction: Conflict Principles

Most countries apply a two-fold approach to conflict of law matters and ask, first, whether a specific Court is competent from the point of view of *jurisdiction*, and, if that question is answered in the affirmative, the Court will proceed to the second question which concerns a question of *choice of law*, that is to say, which law shall be applied to the specific dispute. It may thus be helpful for students to set out the following basic rules.

We have examined some of the problems related to extraterritorial jurisdiction, *i.e.* some of the problems which concern the aspects of

---

[165] See, *The Boll Case, (Guardianship of Infants),* (1958), 72-73 for this point as discussed by Judge Spiropoulos; *cf.* 120 *et seq.*, for views of Lauterpacht; 102 *et seq.* for Moreno Quintano and 74 *et seq.*, for Badawi; for a view that such regard for *ordre public* is misplaced, see Spender at 120 *et seq.*, and Córdova at 140 *et seq.*

428

comity,[166] and in the context of specific *jurisdictional principles*.[167] We can perceive certain common rules respected or applied by national courts in various States with regard to accepting a case.

Because the jurisdictional sharing process between States is a matter of obligation under international law, the sets of conflict of laws cannot be merely a matter for national law, as often suggested by conflict of laws writers.

The power to exercise jurisdiction in *criminal* matters is, as has been shown, limited to certain sectors and must be founded on *nationality* or specific *territorial links* unless there is a rare case of a crime against the fundamental principles of international law, where the *universality* principle may have some room.[168] In this sense, jurisdictional competence concerns the reach of the *criminal* courts.

With regard to the reach of courts in *civil* matters, *i.e.* when courts are competent to adjudicate in litigation concerning, for example, contracts or tort, other rules apply. In this area, most States leave a considerable latitude of decision to the parties involved and often accept cases if there is a specific choice of jurisdiction by both parties or there is some other *genuine* link with the court.

Some courts resent what has been called *forum shopping* and declare, when there is little or no connection with the *forum* country at all that it is a *forum non conveniens*.[169]

It is a useful rule for counsel to consider that it is of little avail to sue a party in a jurisdiction where he has no assets. Such considerations also explain that many countries allow suits to be brought in civil cases when the defendant has material possessions in that jurisdiction. There may even be special facilitating measures to allow such a suit by what in English law is called a *Mareva*

---

[166]   See *supra* in Chapter I.

[167]   See *supra* in this Chapter under the Basis of Sovereign Jurisdiction.

[168]   See *supra* in the preceding section, for crimes like genocide, torture, piracy and other flagrant violations of international law.

[169]   See further *supra* under Comity in Chapter I.

injunction[170] which thus allows the immediate freezing of certain assets while the case is being brought before a court.

In family matters courts often take into account the interests of non-parties, for example of children, in proceedings for divorce or separation; these are situations where some States perceive also a *social* interest in the matter before the court.

With regard to jurisdiction in *property matters* most States respect a strict rule that only the country where the property is has jurisdiction[171]

One area is exceptionally difficult to map for general rules, applied by different countries. That area, bankruptcy, may be a fruitful field for future studies of others. At this stage, there appears to be numerous different and incompatible approaches with regard to the right of jurisdiction and to the proper *forum concursus*, the court or administration which ought to deal with a bankruptcy. For obvious reasons, many bankruptcy suits are instigated at the forum of the *domicile* of the debtor.

Some have put forward ideas of *unity of bankruptcy* which requires considerable international cooperation of administrators, something which does not occur in international society.[172] In practice, courts appear to consider it possible and desirable to have separate and independent bankruptcies in different jurisdictions, and the doctrine of *universality*, also forwarded by many,[173] whereby all movable assets abroad are brought into the bankruptcy, may also overestimate the efficacy of bankruptcy proceedings.

(v) Jurisdiction: Refusal to Hear Cases

On the other hand, some minimum link is usually required for a court to hear a case which has ties to other jurisdictions. In some cases it

---

[170] An injunction in English law (or, indeed, in international law before the ICJ) is a preliminary or provisional measure pending the decision on the merits of the case. It is to be noted that the possibility of obtaining such an order in a case before a Swedish court, as in the courts of former Eastern Europe, is extremely limited or non-existant.

[171] See further *infra* under Choice of Law.

[172] Westlake, ed., Bentwich, *A Treatise on Private International Law*, 1925, 163.

[173] For example, authorities like Cheshire, *op. cit.*, 8th ed., 549.

may see itself as precluded from dealing with the case. Indeed, it may be required by the legislation of its own State to do so, very often enacted for political or economic reasons.

1. Blocking Statutes

Blocking Statutes can be applied to stop a litigant suing in the jurisdiction. For example, in the United States, this device has been used in order to comply with international comity. This was done in the famous *Laker Cases* where a Protection of Trading Interests Act was promulgated to allow the British Government to prohibit compliance with judicial or administrative proceedings in other countries if such proceedings might threaten the trading interests of the United Kingdom.[174] Canada was quick to react and adopted similar legislative arrangements and now an Act authorises the Attorney General to prohibit disclosure of evidence to courts in other countries if such courts are exercising, or proposing to exercise, jurisdiction in a manner that adversely affects 'Canadian interests in relation to international trade or commerce', or, even 'likely to infringe Canadian sovereignty'.[175]

In a sense, blocking statutes represent a further degree of allowing the extraterritorial effect of foreign public laws: blocking statutes are designed to effectively implement foreign policy directives in the laws of another State to show *solidarity*,[176] especially in trade matters, between politically allied States.

2. *forum non conveniens*

In some cases a court may decline to deal with a case as the link tying the parties to the jurisdiction are too weak. As indicated earlier in this work it is certain *comity* which lies behind the doctrine of *forum non conveniens* - a conflict of laws rule that a Court should not hear a case with which the Court's country or the litigant has no

---

174   Protection of Trading Interests Act 1980, ch.11, 21 ILM 1982, 834.

175   The Canadian Extraterritorial Measures Act of 1985.

176   On this notion see my *Concept, op. cit.,* 124 *et seq.*

connection.[177]

It has, for some time, been attractive to bring suits - even with the most tenuous links with that country - in the United States as Courts there are thought to be particularly generous to a winning party. Thus, Lord Denning said in the case *Smith, Kline & French Laboratories v Bloch*[178] that

> 'As a moth is drawn to the light, so is a litigant drawn to the United States. If he can only get his case into their courts, he stands to win a fortune ... The Courts in the United States have no costs deterrent as we have. There is also in the United States a right to be tried by jury. These are prone to award fabulous damages. They are notoriously sympathetic ... All this means that the defendant can be readily forced into a settlement. The plaintiff holds all the cards.'[179]

In *Piper Aircraft Co. v Reynolds*[180] the United States Supreme Court said that there was little reason to assume that the choice of going to United States Courts really suited the plaintiff's interest: essential witnesses were all in the United Kingdom and the Courts of Scotland had a 'very strong interest' in trying the case. In this case British citizens domiciled in Scotland had been killed in an air crash. The Scottish heirs sought to sue in California; the case was transferred to Pennsylvanian Courts, in the State where the aircraft had been manufactured, but the Pennsylvania Federal Court dismissed the action on the grounds of *forum non conveniens*.[181] Thus, a right to sue in the United States may not exist.

A Court can couple the dismissal on the ground of *forum non conveniens* with specific order to assist the plaintiff in just demands

---

[177] On the comity aspects see *supra* in Chapter I.

[178] [1983] 2 All ER, 72, 74.

[179] *Loc. cit.*

[180] [1981] US 235.

[181] *Ibid., loc. cit. Cf. Gulf Oil Corp. v Gilbert* [1947] 330 US 501; *Cf. Koster v Lumbermen's Mutual Co.* [1947] 330 US 518.

for appropriate forum. Thus, in the *Bhopal Case,*[182] the Federal Court for the Southern District of New York dismissed the case which concerned compensation for a poisonous gas disaster in India which had killed over 2000 people. The Court held that India was the proper forum for the action but ordered that Union Carbide, the United States mother company, to agree to submit to jurisdiction in India and to comply with the ensuing judgments of the Indian Court as well as with the discovery rules[183] that apply in the United States when the cases were heard by Indian Courts.

United States Courts, and also Canadian Courts, have recognised the usefulness of a *forum non convenience* doctrine. Scottish Courts had no problems either whereas the House of Lords unanimously rejected the theory, at least as a general doctrine, in *The Atlantic Star.*[184] But Lord Diplock emphasised in a later case that, by 1984, 'judicial chauvinism had been replaced by judicial comity'[185] and this more positive approach was endorsed in a later case,[186] where the doctrine *forum non conveniens* was recognized as a useful devices to stay an action.

(vi) Choice of Law

Once a court has decided it has jurisdiction in a case with international connotations it will proceed to the question as to *which law is to be applied.* This decision of the court lies behind the very term of *choice of law* and, on the face of it, the court is free to choose any law it wishes. The law, once chosen, is commonly referred to as the *lex causae,* that is to say the law of the (specific) case.

Initially, a few words may be said about the *type of law* that may be selected by a court to apply in the specific case. That law may be

---

182   *Re Union Carbide Corporation Gas Plant Disaster at Bhopal* (1986), 54 USLW 2586.

183   These, as those in England, are designed to allow both parties access to all relevant documents within specified times.

184   [1974] AC 436 at 453-454.

185   *The Abedin Daver,* [1984] AC, 398 at 411.

186   *Spiliana Maritime Corp. v Consulex Ltd.,* [1986] 3 All ER 843.

part of the Civil Code or other collection of private law of another country. However, in many cases it may also be a public law. On the other hand, many such foreign public laws are excluded by means of a device known as *public policy* or *ordre public*.[187] Yet, in some instances such public policy interests operate to ensure the application of foreign public laws.

1. FOREIGN PUBLIC LAWS AND PUBLIC POLICY

In a number of civil cases courts apply foreign *public laws* - regardless of the fact that writers in various countries pretend that this should not be done. The limits set for such application is that foreign public laws (nor any other laws) must be applied if they violate *public policy* of the *forum* State.[188] On the other hand, it is also well settled that a court will not lend its assistance to a foreign country to collect, for example, taxes.[189] It is also well settled that a court, in criminal matters,[190] will always apply *its own law*, and that therefore there can never be a question of application of foreign penal laws. Whether we view these exceptions as falling under the general heading of *laws repugnant to public policy* or as specifically excluded by other choice of laws principles, is less important. What is important to note is that courts in numerous States do apply foreign public laws, including revenue laws,[191] *unless* they are *penal* or *confiscatory*.[192]

---

[187] The French term does not have exactly the same meaning as the English expression. However, space does not allow for details of definition, for English Law see Dicey, *Conflict of Laws* and for French law consult, for example, Batiffol, *Droit international privé*, in their latest editions.

[188] See on this problem, in detail, *supra* in Chapter I.

[189] *Holman v Johnson* (1775) 1 Cowp. 341 at 343.

[190] Further *infra*, in this section.

[191] *Re Claim by Helbert Wagg & Co.* [1956] Ch. 323. See further on this, and other relevant cases, my *Finance and Protection of Investments in Developing Countries*, 2nd ed., 1987, 97 *et seq.* and *infra* under Nationalisations, in this Chapter.

[192] Where this limit is drawn may be the subject of some dispute: the foreign laws applied in *Kahler v Midland Bank* [1950] AC 24 were certainly of *confiscatory effect* and the judgment has been much criticised for this reason, see F.A. Mann, *The Legal Aspect of Money*, 2nd ed., 1953, 372 *et seq.* On the

434

Foreign public laws are sometimes, but not always, excluded on the ground of public policy. In *Re Liebl's Estate*[193] a New York Bank, holding certain bank books and stock certificates, allegedly held for account of a Czechoslovak Bank, did not release these assets to their owners, heirs of a Mrs Liebl, as no transfer permission, as required under Czechoslovak law, had been obtained. In this case it was held that

'There is no principle of international comity which would be binding on this State to accord such laws recognition as to evidences of ownership which are transmitted for liquidation. Rather, it seems to be the rule that the public policy of this State, based upon the necessity of protection of the rights of domestic creditors, distributors and legatees of estates, is paramount.'

A careful survey of German exchange control regulations during the 1920s shows that foreign public laws, at least exchange regulations, were consistently applied *unless* there were serious public policy considerations to exclude their application.[194] Thus, a Berlin Court in the '20s held specifically that in the case concerning the *Polnische Landesdarlehnkasse*[195] that a German Judge is under obligation under article 30 of the Civil Code to apply all foreign law unless they conflict with good morals (*guten Sitten*) or with the 'aim' of a German law. The case concerned Polish exchange control regulations which, in the event, were thought to be 'immoral' as the regulations sought to upgrade a Polish Mark - as it then was - at the time worth 5 German Pfennig to the level worth 100 Pfennig.

Thus, there is consistent trend to apply foreign public laws, unless

---

other hand, the judgment must be seen in the light of the political situation of 1950 with different attitudes than now to the former East-European legal systems. *Cf. infra* under Nationalisations, in this Chapter.

[193]   (1951) NY Surr. Ct. 106 2d 705, 711.

[194]   See in greater detail my article on Extraterritorial Application of Foreign Exchange Control Regulations, *Nordisk Tidskrift for International Ret*, 1987.

[195]   (1922) OLG Berlin 25.2. 1922 398.

they offend against public policy.[196] Public policy may demand that application of foreign laws is refused if allowing such laws, or relevant regulations, would lead to activities deemed criminal in a country. If a loan would support a revolution in another country there is thus room for applying public policy to refuse application of foreign regulations, or other measures relevant to such a loan.[197]

Domestic labour laws may not necessarily apply to situations before a Court involving foreign elements. Courts may sometimes deplore the lack of mandatory legislative provisions enabling it to apply the forum labour laws in such situations,[198] especially if it considers its own labour legislation 'superior' as being more protective of workers' interests. If the Court is unable to find such mandatory provisions, and it still considers the internal laws of its own State *more appropriate*, it may avoid the application of foreign law by resorting to the notion of public policy as a ground for application of such laws. In all matters, however, there are clear limits concerning the ability of States to *avoid* the application of international law, for example to respect the international minimum standard.[199] The field of *jus cogens* indicates further restrictions in this respect.[200]

Public policy has even been used as an instrument to *ensure* the application of foreign laws. It was used in the settled *Frozen Assets Affair* before the English Courts in 1980 when England was precluded from arguing that United States exchange control regulations should not apply on the basis of public policy as the United Kingdom had

---

[196]   *Ibid., loc. cit. Cf. Pan American Securities Corp v Friedrich Krupp AG*, NYSp Ct. 1938, aff'd App. Div. 1939, 6 NYS 2d 933, 10 NYS 205, 39 B 361; *De Wutz v Henricks* [1824] 2 Bing. 314; *Foster v Driscoll* [1929] 1 KB 470 CA; *Regazzoni v KC Sethia* [1958] AC 301; *Kahler v Midland Bank* [1950] AC 57; *De Beesche v South American Stores* [1935] AC 178; *St. Pierre v South American Stores* [1937] 3 All ER 349; *Catz & Lips v SA Union Versicherung)* TC Antwerp 21.1.1949 J (1953) 808; *Sucres v Schweizerische Kreditanstalt*, EG 21.9. 1937; *Lorenzen v Lydden & Co.* [1942] 2 KB 202; US v Pink, Sup. Ct. 1942, 315 US 203.

[197]   Trib. Seine 2.7. 1932 S 1934 2.73; *cf. Foster v Driscoll* [1929] 1 KB 470.

[198]   *Windward Shipping v American Radio Administration* [1974] 415 US 104, 110.

[199]   See *supra* in Chapter V.

[200]   On *jus cogens* see *supra* in Chapter III. On other aspects of Human Rights, see *supra* in Chapter V.

ratified the Bretton Woods Agreement setting up the system operated by the International Monetary Fund with regard to such special regulations.[201]

2. OTHER APPLICATIONS OF PUBLIC POLICY

Connected with such reasoning is the conflict of laws rule which denies parties to carry out an action or perform a contract which is illegal by the laws of another country. The root of this rule is to be found in public international law and it leads to clear rules of behaviour of parties to contracts with international elements.

> 'If I in England promise to do that in France which the law of France does not suffer there to be done, then the respect which independent nations are bound to pay to each other's sovereign forbids the law of England to contemplate a performance which the ruler of France has by the law of nations, authority to prevent.'[202]

Thus, an English Court will not require a party to commit an act which is illegal by the *lex loci solutionis,* that is to say in the country where the transaction is to be fulfilled.[203]

In some cases courts have not even allowed arguments that a foreign law should be excluded on the basis of public policy. In the *Joe Stoich Case*[204] the court did not allow any argument on public policy: if a State, for example, has adhered to an international convention such adherence precludes its courts from later allowing public policy to exclude what follows from the implementation of the Convention. In other words,

---

[201] This was especially so as the International Monetary Fund had specifically confirmed that the United States regulations complied with the IMF rules. This case which concerned - and ensured the release of - the American Hostages in Teheran, was settled in January 1981.

[202] Westlake, *Collected Papers on International Law,* 1914, 303.

[203] *Ralli Bros. v Co Naviera Sota y Aznar* [1920] 2 KB 287.

[204] *In the Estate of Joe Stoich* 1959 (1960) 349 P2d 255.

'Courts should respect the 'international public policy' laid down in a treaty.'[205]

This shows that there is here a close link between the problems now discussed and the relationship between international law and internal law.[206]

In numerous cases the concept of public policy as used by the courts in a country like, for example, England, may reflect what is considered to represent certain minimum notions necessary in any country with respect for the Rule of Law. Pronouncements on public policy may in such cases reflect international norms.

3. LEGALITY OF FOREIGN LAWS

(a) Nationalisations

Wortley, *Expropriations in Public International Law*, 1959; White, *Nationalisations of Foreign Property*, 1962; Münch, Les effets d'une nationalisation à l'étranger, RCADI 1959 iii 416; Lillich, (ed.), *Valuation of Nationalisations*, 1980; Nwogugo, *The Legal Problems of Foreign Investment in Developing Countries*, 1965; and my own *Finance and Protection of Investments in Developing Countries*, 2nd ed. 1987.

Extraterritorial problems can be caused by nationalisations. Here there is often an *administrative act* which constitutes the actual *taking* of property, but this is normally done under the authority of a *nationalisation law* which provides for the general framework of the taking.

Numerous problems have been caused by the alleged extraterritorial effect of nationalisation laws: in other words, should other States respect the taking and the passing of ownership from a private owner in another State to the State itself? Should courts pronounce themselves on whether the taking is legal under international law? Furthermore, what effect do such nationalisation laws have when nationalised goods have left the taking country and are perhaps being freighted across the oceans?

---

[205]   ii Rabel 591.

[206]   See *infra* 218 *et seq.* under Monism and Dualism.

The problems, which are many and to which there are not always clear answers, are now largely historical, although new and different political theories will emerge which, in different shapes, may re-iterate the ideas adopted by now collapsed ideologies.

If we examine taking in the historical light we will see that there have been different waves of nationalisations. The first wave of takings, after earlier historical precedents like the French Revolution, concerned the nationalisations in Russia after the Revolution in 1917; then came a number of nationalisations in Spain under the Catalan government in connection with the Spanish Civil War in 1936; then came another wave of socialist nationalisations in Eastern Europe after the Second World War; and, a quite different type of a number of nationalisations of oil in Iran in 1951-4, sugar in Cuba in 1960, oil in Algeria in 1965, copper in Zambia in 1966, copper, cobalt and zinc in the Congo in 1966, copper in Chile in 1971, oil in Libya in 1971 and numerous other later examples.

It is obviously important, in many circumstances, to verify who enjoys, for example, title to specific goods. Only if an administrative decision to nationalise (under a general nationalisation law) is effectively recognised by other States will a new nationalised corporation possess full legal title to assets and products in other countries. In other cases the old owner, the person whose assets have been nationalised will, in the eyes of foreign courts, still enjoy title. Complications arise if the assets are no longer in the expropriating State, for example, in the case of consignments of oil which have left the country.[207]

In the oil and mining sector the problem has been considerable as numerous nationalisations have taken place in countries with such industries. If, for example, an oil company is nationalised in one country, it can still contest the title to oil from an expropriated field when that oil reaches another country. One hardly needs to emphasise the practical importance of these matters after the wave of nationalisation of large oil companies in Third World States.

The large oil company British Petroleum Company Ltd. (BP) declared in December 1971 that it would sue any customer who

---

[207] Such a distinction would explain attitudes in *Re Helbert Wagg,* [1956] Ch 323.

bought Libyan oil. The basis for this claim was that title had allegedly not validly passed from BP Exploration Company (Libya), to the Arabian Gulf Exploration Company, as the nationalisation had been illegal under international law. The Basrah Oil Company made a similar declaration in 1972 and stated that it would sue anyone who bought oil from its expropriated oil fields in Rumalia in Iraq.

The standard of compensation may be variable. The international stadard of compensation may be different depending on the nature of the nationalised assets.

Nationalisations of natural resources such as oil and copper, as listed above, were often accompanied by other *socialist* measures like expropriation of other types of private property, such as under Allende in Chile after 1971. But contrary to the global nationalisation measures after the Russian Revolution in 1917, nationalisations during the last few decades have been *primarily* measures to nationalise *natural resources.* These efforts to nationalise must be seen in the context of the trend to emphasise the right that States have to their own resources.[208] The United Nations has given much emphasis to this rule by numerous forceful resolutions, in particular Resolution 1803 (XVII) of 1962.[209] Some suggest that this particular Resolution represents an *agreement by States about a general principle,*[210] although it may be conceptually more attractive to subsume this agreement under the heading of *adoption of a standard.*[211]

I have previously suggested that a special tariff may be applied for the valuation of expropriated *natural resources,* a tariff lower than for expropriation of other assets such as industrial plants or factories. This is because it is virtually impossible to grant *full* compensation for such types of nationalisations and also because such assets, after all, *belong* to the State in quite a different way than other private property, or even land. The nexus between a State and the assets in

---

[208] See Rosenberg, *Le principe de souveraineté des Etats sur leurs ressources naturelles*, 1983, 149-225.

[209] For an analysis of this Resolution see my *Finance and Protection of Investments in Developing Countries,* 2nd ed., 1987, 54 *et seq.*

[210] Rosenberg, *Le principe, op. cit.,* 197.

[211] See *supra,* for my classification, in Chapter IV.

its ground, such as minerals or oil, is thus different from the nexus between private individuals and their possessions, chattels or land, as the case may be.

In the same way as there may then be a special, possibly lower, tariff for compensation for deprivation of holdings in natural resources, it could also be argued that the act of State doctrine operates differently with regard to the different types of cases. Thus, it is absurd for Courts to give heed to arbitrary legislation depriving nationals of their private possessions without compensation under a socialist system especially if the possessions have already left the expropriating country;[212] some may argue that it seems less objectionable to give effect to nationalisation acts that focus on natural resources, especially if they are still present in the expropriating country. The view that there ought to be a special tariff for natural resources, as sketched above, does not imply any right to deprive oil companies of lawful (adequate, prompt and effective)[213] compensation, but merely suggests an arguable right of States, particularly in the Third World, to assess compensation at a *slightly lower level for natural resources* than for investments in industry or for holdings in land.

Problems connected by *nationalisation* are now largely overshadowed by questions concerning *privatisation*. One can distinguish two *waves* of nationalisation of property: first, in the communist/socialist countries; secondly, in certain Third World countries which, for a while, adopted Marxist ideas for survival reasons. Now, that it has become clear that such political ideas leads to gradual poverty, numerous States attempt to *reverse* to privatise a number of enterprises, an attempt which we already know is far more difficult, and costly, than the simplistic taking by States by nationalisations.

---

212   As, for example, in the above mentioned *Princess Paley v Weiss* [1929] 1 KB 718 and *supra*.

213   See *infra* on the quantum of compensation under Objects of Sovereign Functions, Property, Nationalisations.

(b) The Act of State Doctrine

A special facet of the problem of extraterritoriality of laws concerns the so called *Act of State doctrine*, widely accepted and certainly much discussed both in the United States and in England.

The act of State doctrine implied traditionally that an English Court is not empowered to pronounce on the legality of the acts of the Crown. Later, the act of State doctrine was extended to include a similar prohibition with regard to foreign acts of State, including their laws.[214] In later years, the doctrine became particularly concerned with the question whether foreign *expropriation* or *nationalisation* laws should have effect in another country. In a similar way as problems discussed in the preceding section, the act of State doctrine concerns the extraterritorial application of foreign laws. But contrary to the questions dealt with in the previous section, the act of State doctrine concerns more specifically an alleged prohibition of courts to look into the *legality* of foreign legislative *or* executive acts.

English Courts affirmed the doctrine in cases like *Luther v Sagor*[215] and stated that an English Court would not look into the legality of Soviet legislation depriving Russian citizens of their property: even when such property was no longer in the Soviet Union, the deprived owner had no longer any rights of ownership in the opinion of the English Courts: *Princess Paley v Weisz*.[216] Such cases are, at least to some modern writers, abhorrent to Human Right rules on private property[217] and it is remarkable that English Courts were so swift to lend support to the questionable measures of the Bolshevik regime under the guise of this regime having been recognised[218] *de facto* as being in power. Arguments that criticism of foreign acts of State would 'embarrass' the executive in reaching

---

[214] Note the conceptual difference between *examining* foreign laws from the point of view of their *legality* and *applying* foreign laws in a conflict of laws situation, see *infra*, this Chapter, under g and under iv.

[215] [1921] 1 KB 456.

[216] [1929] 1 KB 718.

[217] See, *infra*, on Human Rights.

[218] Further on recognition of States and regimes, see Chapter II, *infra*.

a diplomatic settlement[219] were advanced but would seem highly inappropriate.

What is also remarkable is that these cases are referred to in a majority of English textbooks on international law as representing the *law* on this matter, without any reference to the fact that courts of numerous other countries take a weary view of allegations that courts should be precluded from looking into the legality of foreign acts and from measuring them against yardsticks on Human Rights and/or against other generally accepted norms.

In the countries where it has been applied, such as in England, the act of State doctrine is now limited to disallow the defence based on the doctrine to avoid the application of foreign public acts.[220] Other cases, like *The Rose Mary,*[221] show that the doctrine is not applied by British Courts in respect of expropriated property belonging to persons who are not subjects of the expropriating State. Moreover, the United States has specifically repealed the doctrine by the *Second Hickenlooper Amendment* of 1964,[222] to the United States Constitution, providing that

'Notwithstanding any other provision of law, no court in the United States shall decline on the ground of the federal act of State doctrine to make a determination on the merits giving effect to the principles of international law in a case in which a claim of title or other right to property is asserted by any party including a foreign State (or party claiming through such State) based upon (or traced through) a confiscation or other taking after 1 January 1959, by an act of State in violation of the principles of compensation and the other standards set out in this sub-section ...'

---

[219] So Brownlie, *Principles,* 4th ed., 1990, 322. *Cf.* the arguing in *Bandes v Harlow,* (1983) US Distr. Ct, SDNY, 18th July 1983, ILR 1983, 571.

[220] *E.g., Williams and Humbert Ltd. v W. and H. Trade Marks Ltd.* [1986] 1 AC 368.

[221] *The Rose Mary,* Supreme Court of Aden, ILR 1953, 316. But see hesitation on this point in *Re Helbert Wagg* [1956] Ch 323.

[222] See, further, my *Finance and Protection of Investments in Developing Countries,* 2nd ed., 1987, 90 *et seq.*

This amendment was introduced after the doctrine in specific cases led to unacceptable and absurd results.[223]

But the act of State doctrine has been curiously limited to England and the United States, although now largely discarded in the latter country. On the other hand, we are not here concerned with any rule of *international law:* the act of State doctrine is largely unknown and is not applied in many European countries.[224] There are numerous cases showing that a court will apply public policy to avoid the recognition of effects of foreign laws interfering with private property: thus, the Court of Appeal of Paris refused, in *Compagnie Nord de Mouscou v Phoenix Espagnol,*[225] to give any recognition to foreign expropriations without compensation as such an act was contrary to the respect for private property laid down by the French legal system. Indeed, to give effect to expropriatory or confiscatory measures of another State of private property, is to allow considerable infringement of clearly accepted Human Rights, and cannot be justified on the cowardly ground that States cannot *sit in judgment* of another, or *par in parem non habet imperium.* Of course, this rule must not be taken as an excuse for violating lawful rights of individuals.

In some cases courts have measured the legality of foreign expropriation laws against other yardsticks. In the *SUPOR Case,*[226] an Italian Court, the Court of Rome, held that Iranian nationalisation laws could be applied in Italy as their legality had been confirmed by Resolution 626 (VII) of the General Assembly.[227] The Court had also checked the validity of the relevant Iranian laws against the

---

[223]   *Banco Nacional de Cuba v Sabattino* (1964) 376 US 398.

[224]   See, for Belgium, *Taco Masdag v Heyermans,* CC 23.5.1898; for France, *Soc. Cementos Resola v Larrasquitu et Etat Espagnol,* CA Poitiers 20.12.1937; for Germany, OLG Hamburg 10.7.1948; for Sweden, *Herzogliche Steueramt v Lundberg,* NJA 1909, 638.

[225]   AD 1927-1928, 66. *Cf. The Ropit Case, ibid.,* 67 and *Soc. Potasas Ibericas v Nathan Bloch,* AD 1939, 150.

[226]   *Anglo-Iranian Oil Company v SUPOR Co., Unione Petrolifera per l'Oriente,* ILR 1955, 23.

[227]   It is questionable whether the General Assembly has such competence, see, *infra,* under the Legal Value of Recommendations of International Organisations.

provisions of the Italian Constitution and against rules of international law. In case foreign laws do not meet the yardstick of such rules, Italian courts have not hesitated to apply public policy to mitigate the result.[228] Swiss Courts have taken a similar stand.[229] The act of State doctrine is also alien to Austrian Courts which use the public policy mechanism to avoid the application of foreign expropriation laws.[230] Belgian Courts have refused to apply foreign expropriation laws, occasionally without mentioning public policy, but merely referring to its own Constitution which, no doubt, reflects public policy.[231] German case law is more hesitant and Courts have, in some cases, allowed the effects of foreign expropriation laws, but then on the basis that the facts in the case did *not* violate German public policy.[232] In other words, the Court saw itself free to examine the validity of the foreign law against certain *national standards*.[233]

Whether or not the textbooks claim that a State should never sit in judgment of laws or of decisions of the executive or of the administration in another country, courts have not hesitated to do so. Courts have thus considered themselves competent to look into whether the nationalisation in question was compatible with the standard required by *international law,* for example, whether *adequate,*[234] *prompt*[235] and *effective*[236] *compensation* was paid as required by international law and whether there was no discriminatory practices or lack or patent lack of public purpose, which, again, would have violated rules of international law.[237]

---

228 *E.g. the Miriella,* ILR 1955, 19.

229 *E.g., Rey v Jaccard* BG 13 2 1906.

230 *E.g.,* OGH 9 7 1948.

231 *Lowis v Banque de la Société Générale de Belgique,* PB 1939, 505 and my *Finance, op. cit.* 99 *et seq.*

232 *E.g.* Bremen 21 8 1959.

233 *Cf. infra* 275-282 on Standards.

234 This implies that compensation is 'fair'.

235 This means that compensation is paid within a reasonable time-limit.

236 This signifies that compensation is paid in a useful currency, for example one that can be taken out of the country.

237 See further my *Foreign Investment of Investments in Developing Countries,* 2nd ed., 1987, 92 *et seq.*

Courts have furthermore found themselves competent to measure the compatibility of a nationalisation order against *international law as incorporated in municipal law* of an expropriating State,[238] or against the *municipal law of the forum country*,[239] against the *provisions of General Assembly Resolutions* as part of accepted international law,[240] against *the public policy* of the *forum* State,[241] or, finally, against the *laws of war*.[242]

One reason for contesting the validity of a nationalisation is thus when the *international standard* has not been respected, *i.e.* when the taking State has failed to give an alien adequate, prompt and effective compensation.[243] Nowadays, one can even argue, with considerable support in State practice, that the international standard also obliges States to pay compensation to their own nationals.[244] Thus, it appears that a minimum Human Right of property is actually one without which no society can survive.[245]

On the general proposition that the courts of a State cannot pronounce themselves on laws of another State if they violate international law it must be said that this must be a matter of the

---

238   See my *Finance and Protection, op. cit.,* and cases cited there as, for example, *The Rose Mary* (1952) ILR 1953, 316 (Supreme Court of Aden).

239   *Ibid.,* 98 *et seq.* and, for example, *Compagnie Nord de Moscou v Phoenix Espagnol* AD 1927-1928 66 (Court of Appeal of Paris).

240   *Cf. supra* in Chapter III under the Legal Effect of Recommendations, and see my *Finance and Protection, op. cit.,* 98-99 and, for example, *Anglo-Iranian Oil Co. v SUPOR, Unione Petrolifera per l'Oriente* (1954) ILR 1955, 23, on GA Resolution 626 (VII) (Court of Rome).

241   See my *Finance and Protection, op. cit.,* 96-102 and, for example, *Société Potasas Ibericas v Nathan Bloch* (1939) AD 1939, 150 (French Cour de Cassation).

242   See my *Finance and Protection, op. cit.,* 102 and my *Law of War, op. cit.,* Chapter VI and, for case law, for example, *NV De Bataafsche Maaschappij and Others v the War Damage Commission* ILR 1956, 810 (Singapore Court of Appeal).

243   For specific details on the conditions and meaning of the standard see my *Finance and Protection, op. cit.,* 67 *et seq.*

244   See my *Äganderätten och Europa,* SIRIL, 1992, Chapter II.

245   See *supra* on Human Rights in Chapter IV and the reference to Plato, in his later writings.

degree of the violation.[246] If there is a *gross violation* of a *clear* and *important* rule of international law by the law or decree of another State, it would be to the detriment of the international legal system if a national judge did not have the courage to pronounce himself on this incompatibility.

4. CONFLICT PRINCIPLES: THE STATUTE THEORY

Numerous principles are respected by most States, making the application of a foreign law appear to be appropriate and just. In this context too - as in the field of jurisdiction - there is an obvious need for respect for foreign laws which are perhaps intimately linked to the case before a court and comity may require that another law than the *lex fori*, that is to say the law of the court's own State, is applied. *Justice of the parties* also often requires that a court takes into account a foreign law.[247]

With regard to the *choice of law*, a court in most countries applies, once jurisdiction has been accepted, certain clear principles. Some of these can only be understood with a certain knowledge of the so called *statute theory* used since the fall of the Roman Empire. It was at this time in history when the Goths, the Burgundians, the Franks and the Lombards had founded their own kingdoms in what had previously been the Roman Empire, that it became *normal* and *natural* to allow each member of each *nation* to insist on having his *own law* applied to him, at least in personal matters.[248]

The full-scale statute theories may have had flaws when they required a rigorous division into personal, real or mixed statutes, for personal matters, matters concerning real property and for those questions which could not easily be referred to either category and therefore would be subsumed under a mixed statute.

---

[246]   *Cf.* Dupuy, P-M., *Droit international public*, 1992, 324 on '*une violation manifeste*' and the importance that the international legal rule is *clear*.

[247]   *Cf. e.g.* Cheshire, 17th ed., Introduction.

[248]   See Bishop Agobardus, statement on Different Laws. The statute theory was mainly developed by Bartolus of Sassoferrato (1314-57). A complementary theory was devised by Savigny at the middle of the last century, *System des modernen römischen Rechts,* 1848.

However, a modified statute theory is certainly not only warranted but positively helpful. The *statute theory* explains the necessary territorial limitation of laws and how some laws are designed, and appropriate to *follow* a certain person or a certain matter. Viewed in this limited context, the statute theory comes near what Savigny also proposed at the middle of the last century - although he claimed to discard the statute theory - by finding an *appropriate local law for every legal relationship.*[249]

It is interesting to note that Sweden does accept the statute theory in all recent books on private international law.[250] It is clear that a noticeable and recent application of the statute theory was necessary to enable foreign consuls to assume jurisdiction in China under the Capitulations Treaties, as explained elsewhere in this treatise.[251]

A modified statute approach is useful as it furnishes *presumptions*[252] - we are here only concerned with the *fixing of applicable law* in a specific situation, that which concern certain, but not all, matters. To speak of a *statute* in such cases is not unwarranted. Therefore, the statute theory, or a form thereof, should not be easily discarded, as it has been by some writers in some countries.[253]

If the statute theory is understood as a set of rebuttable presumptions, the mechanisms of conflict of laws can be more easily explained. Indeed, the whole history and development of conflict of

---

[249] Savigny, *op. cit.,* 98.

[250] That Swedish textbooks on private international law are still based on the statute theories is surprising in view of the fact that, in other fields, Sweden discards, as has been noted in this work, most of the values and principles of the *Corpus juris,* especially any remnant of the natural law doctrine. Yet, the *Corpus juris,* which is no longer studied in Swedish universities in History of Law, was the law by which the emperors Gratian, Valentinian and Theodosius sought to compel Roman citizens to observe the Christian faith. This was done by means of the statute theories which accorded only limited territorial application of various laws.

[251] See *infra* under Fettering of Sovereignty, under C. iii. (i), on Judicial Competence, in this Chapter.

[252] See further *infra* on such tentative presumptions, in this section.

[253] See, for example, the full-scale condemnation of the theory by Cheshire in the Introduction of the 8th edition, 23. Cheshire over-reacts when he so scathingly condemns the whole statute theory.

laws is impossible to understand without recourse to the statute theory.

5. APPLICABLE LAW IN CRIMINAL CASES

For *criminal* cases, one of the aforementioned principles of jurisdiction are used to claim competence of a national court. If a court is held competent (by itself!), the Court will then apply *the law of its own State,* that is to say, the *lex fori.*

6. APPLICABLE LAW IN CIVIL CASES

If, on the other hand, the court is faced with a *civil* case, it will, again, once it has established that it has jurisdictional competence - in *ordinary* civil cases, for example, those concerning *contracts,* apply *the law indicated by the parties*, or, if the parties have not agreed on any such law, or are not *allowed* to agree on such a law, as, for example, in family matters, the court will normally apply *the law with which the matter has the closest connection*, and seeks thus a law founded on a *link* with the parties or with the situation, established by various methods.

(a) The Link: The Proper Law of Contracts

In such civil matters, such as contracts, most States thus look for some connection between their courts and a contractual dispute in much a similar way as a *genuine link* is demanded for nationality of ships.[254] In England we speak about the *proper law* question which implies a weighing of various elements to assess where the contract has its weight; a similar system[255] is used in a very different legal system in Sweden where Courts also seek to find the natural attachment of a contract in a specific legal system by a similar process.

---

[254]   *Cf. supra*, see in detail, Dicey ed. Morris, ed. 1993.
[255]   The 'individualising method'.

(b) Negotiable Instruments

Negotiable instruments may often be conceived as containing a number of different contracts. Here, there is often no unlimited right for the parties to select the law they wish to apply to these different contracts.

To facilitate the task of courts facing questions regarding negotiable instruments, such as bills of exchange, several international conventions have been adopted, for example on Bills of Exchange and Promissory Notes of Geneva of 1930.[256] In this area it is more difficult to perceive general rules applied by several countries, although the principle regarding place of payment, the *lex loci solutionis*, that is to say the law where an obligation is to be performed, may furnish considerable guidance.[257]

(c) Bankruptcy

The applicable law in bankruptcy cases is, if one may generalise and simplify a difficult and much discussed problem, probably always the *lex fori*, possibly as every bankruptcy has over-riding elements of administrative procedure.[258]

(d) Family Matters

For civil cases concerning, for example, *family matters*, including separation, affiliation and succession issues, most States choose, the *personal law of the claimant*, and this personal law is assessed as being the one of nationality or domicile, depending on whether the Court is in a *jus soli* or a *jus sanguinis* country.[259]

The rule indicated is, of course, modified and amplified by sub-rules, for example, on the assessment of *whose* personal law is relevant (testator's law; the husband's law etc.). Furthermore, other

---

[256] See *supra* in Chapter I. The Convention has not been ratified by the UK.

[257] For England, see *e.g. Rothschild v Currie* (1841) 1 QB 43.

[258] See *infra* under Formalities, in this Chapter, on *lex fori* for all procedural questions.

[259] See Cheshire, 17th ed., Introduction.

sub-rules specify *relevant time* of assessment: the personal law for numerous purposes in family law may thus be the law of the husband *at the time of the marriage*; for the purposes of inheritance, it is often that of the deceased person *at the time of death.*

(e) Tort Cases

Most countries apply the *lex loci delicti* for tort cases, or even for paternal suits, that is to say the law where the damage or injury occurred, or where the relevant act took place, much by analogy to criminal cases.

(f) Real Property and Proprietary Questions

With regard to real estate,[260] as well as with regard to third parties,[261] in the case of contractual or other questions of obligation, most States tend to use the *lex rei sitae*, that is to say the law in the place where the object in question is situated. Naturally, in this case, there are some very difficult questions - becoming more and more common as trade is internationalised - with regard to goods in transit (*res in transitu*) when it is not always clear which law is to be decisive for ownership. Questions in this respect are made particularly difficult by the fact that the common law countries and the civil law countries take different views as to the merit of acquisitions in good faith: in civil law countries, such as all the States of continental Europe, a purchaser who is in good faith can validly acquire goods from a thief who lacked ownership, whereas in, for example, England, he cannot.[262]

7. FORMALITIES

Choice of law questions are supplemented by *formal* considerations and Courts readily use the *lex loci contractus*, that is to say the law where a contract was made, or a marriage celebrated, or a will made

---

260 In the Swedish legal system *fast egendom.*
261 In Sweden, *sakrättsliga frågor.*
262 There are exceptions, however, in the case of purchases at public auctions.

out, to decide on all questions of *form*, and this rule operates often in a subsidiary way to validate a specific transaction.

Procedure is regulated by the law of the court itself, *i.e.* by the *lex fori*. It is occasionally contentious whether a question is *procedural* or *material*.[263] On the whole, however, procedural matters can clearly be distinguished from the merits of the case.

c. *Extraterritorial Effects of Administrative Acts*

Not only foreign laws may be *applied* in other countries and not only foreign judgments may produce effects in other jurisdictions than where they were delivered. Also *foreign administrative acts* produce effects in other countries. We may, in this context, illustrate this proposition by some examples.

(i) Passports

A State cannot normally legislate to protect nationals abroad. The issue of a passport, however, is an *administrative act,* in most countries by delegated power of the executive under the framework of a law enacted by the legislature. This administrative act results in a travel document which, in effect, seeks to ask *other States* to respect the status of a person as a subject of another State. Some passports still provide a sentence to remind other States that the bearer is one of its subjects. Thus, the British passport still states that

> 'Her Britannic Majesty's Secretary of State requests and requires in the Name of Her Majesty all those whom it may concern to allow the bearer to pass freely without let or hindrance, and to afford the bearer such assistance and protection as may be necessary.'

This type of passport will soon disappear as the British passport is redesigned to comply with EC regulations on a standardised form of passport. But the implications are still there. All passports have such

---

[263]   For Sweden see the *Gold Clause Case*, NJA 1930, 30.

a tacit clause: such call for letting a bearer pass is the essence of a passport. Albeit often neglected by international lawyers, it is also the prime example of the extraterritorial application of an executive decision of a State.

Naturally, States retain the power to exclude visitors to its country and may qualify their entry by prescribing visas. Recently Swedish citizens were subject to such controls even in Europe as France sought to draw the attention of the Swedish authorities, and of international society, to the numerous terrorist bases in Sweden. As the point was made and, to some extent, taken by the Swedish government, the visa requirements were rescinded. Many other States require visas, *i.e.* specific permission to enter a country above the *ad hoc* admission by passport alone. Such countries, were, above all, those in the Eastern bloc, which preferred themselves to keep an exact check on who entered and who left their territory by stringent visa requirements. Another group is found among those exposed to large immigration, such as the United States. Many countries in Europe also maintain visa requirements to curb the flood of immigration from other non-European densely populated States.

In spite of the aforementioned visa requirements, a passport implies, as a whole, a document acknowledged by all States to allow a person to enter and a passport is, in a number of countries, sufficient for permission to enter and exit. A passport also serves as the most important piece of identity for a variety of purposes.[264]

(ii) Freezing Orders

In the *Iranian Hostage Affair* President Carter of the United States ordered the freezing of Iranian assets all over the world as an economic sanction to force the Iranians to give up the hostages they had taken in stark violation of one of the most fundamental rules of international society, that of immunity of diplomats.[265]

It was in London, in American banks, that most of the Iranian

---

[264] But note, as mentioned earlier, that a Swedish passport is not, because of risk of forgery, sufficient to withdraw money from a Swedish bank; a special identity card is necessary.

[265] *Infra* under Immunity.

funds were held. The International Court of Justice had already condemned the actions of Iran by a decision on Interim Measures issued in December 1979 ordering Iran to hand over the hostages.[266] When this Order was defied by the Iranian regime the United States resorted to its own action and froze all Iranian assets in American banks. Iran sued seven American Banks that held large funds in London. The Bank contested the action and prepared their defence for the action in the High Court. The Iranian funds were effectively blocked by the Freezing Order of President Carter. But how could the United States decree on the freezing of assets to take effect in, for example, London?

This problem obviously concerns the question of extraterritorial effect of laws and of administrative decrees. The laws of one State are normally not operating in another country. American banks must naturally obey a United States decree. But we are not concerned with *American banks* in the ordinary sense of the word. The *American banks*, certainly owned to a large extent by American interests, were *incorporated under English law* and, as such, technically subject only to English law.

It must be noted that in this case the United States could not have forced the application of United States decrees to these banks. But, in the event, there was a question of a reaction to an extreme violation of a fundamental rule of international society - that concerned with the immunity of diplomats - and, for these reasons, other countries displayed their solidarity[267] with the United States whose diplomats had been the target of illegitimate action by Iran. In other words, the United Kingdom *allowed* the United States decree to operate within its territory. Thus, the extraterritorial application of the United States decree was effected through and by the consent of the State within which it operated. However, since there was a question of a violation of one of the most fundamental rules of international society, the United Kingdom was probably under some duty, as other States also would have been, to respect and give effect to the United States decree which sought to remedy the serious violation by unilateral

---

[266]   (1980) ICJ *Reports.*

[267]   See my *Concept., op. cit.,.* 124 *et seq.,.* on solidarity as a basis of obligation.

sanctions permitted under the United Nations system.[268]

The case in London was settled[269] and it is considered by some that it was this very case that secured the release of the hostages. There was an agreement between the banks and the regime in Teheran that the funds would be released if the hostages were released and there was a close chronological link between the timing of a telex to Teheran, that the funds had effectively been released and the freeing of the hostages. There was indeed, a condition that the lifting of the freeze would secure the release of the hostages. The case is highly interesting as an example of sanctions by freezing assets to secure compliance with rules of international law of fundamental importance to all States. The International Court had also emphasised, in its case, that rules concerning the immunity of diplomats belong to the most important rules of international society; it is clear that without these rules international society cannot function.[270]

v. Immunity of States and of International Agents

Equality of States implies that one State cannot sit in judgment of another or, as the Latin expression has it, *par in parem not habet imperium*. This means then that a State, or its organs, or its agents, for example, diplomats and consuls, cannot be impleaded in the courts of another State.

This is a general rule. On the one hand, the rules on immunity are, as the International Court of Justice remarked in *The Hostage Case*,[271] the most fundamental rules of international society. On the other hand, it is important to set out in detail the limits of immunity to avoid anachronistic complications in the modern world of communication and commerce.

One commonly distinguishes between the immunity of the State and diplomatic immunity. We shall first analyse State immunity.

---

[268]   *Infra* under Sanctions.

[269]   The case is therefore unreported. A large team of barristers and solicitors worked for one year on the defence in the action.

[270]   See ICJ *Reports* 1980 and my *Law of War, op. cit.*, 75.

[271]   (1980) ICJ *Reports* 3.

a. State Immunity

Bouchez, The nature of Scope of State immunity from jurisdiction and execution, NYIL 1979, 4; Sucharitkul, *State Immunities and Trading in International Law*, 1959; Allen, *The Position of Foreign States Before National Courts*, 1933; Loening, *Die Gerichtsbarkeit über fremde Staaten und Suveräne*, 1903; Gmur, *Gerichtsbarkeit über fremde Staaten*, 1948.

The immunity of a State is of two types: immunity *ratione personae* and immunity *ratione materiae*, We have already dealt with immunity *ratione materiae*, in so far as it concerns certain *acts* of other States, earlier in this treatise in other contexts[272] and we shall here devote some time to analyse the implications of State immunity *ratione personae,* and the specific immunity *ratione materiae* which attaches to State *property*.

(i) Sovereign Immunity *ratione personae*

Immunity *ratione personae* concerns a specific circle of persons who, according to international law, enjoy immunity on the basis that they represent the State. The circle of persons who enjoy immunity under this heading are, in the first place, the Head of State,[273] members of the government, above all the Minister of Foreign Affairs,[274] as well as other organs of the State.

State immunity, or *sovereign immunity* which it is sometimes called, implies that a foreign State may not be sued in the municipal courts of another State. Immunity under this title is enjoyed by the Head of State, as he (or she) can be supposed to enter a foreign territory only under express licence, or in the confidence that the immunity belonging to his independent sovereign station, though not expressly stipulated, is reserved by implication and will be extended

---

[272] This type concerns special acts of another State, as, for example, legislation and governmental decrees; these acts are immune in the sense that the competence of courts in other countries may be restricted with regard to these acts. *Cf. supra* on the Act of State doctrine in Chapter I.

[273] See, for example, Berber §39.

[274] i Berber §40.

to him.[275]

State immunity is occasionally said to endow certain persons with special protection, beyond what even diplomats enjoy. This is said to be the case if a delegation includes the Head of State of the Foreign Minister.[276]

Immunity, which extends to the family of Heads of State,[277] and of other State representatives, appears to cover, in general, commercial transactions to purchase, for example, official medals or decorations,[278] and other activities connected with the functions of a Head of State.

Immunity objections have, in the past, also been successful in cases concerning private commercial transactions. King Farouk of Egypt was also held to be immune for debts incurred for the purchase of private jewellery for his wife Narriman.[279] The immunity extended to a foreign Head of State in this way has been held to cover *all* private acts, as illustrated in *Mighell v Sultan of Johore*[280] where the Sultan, using another name, had promised to marry a Miss Mighell and then changed his mind; at the time breach of promise of marriage was actionable.

State organs, *i.e.* bodies connected to the State and under its full control, also enjoy State immunity; the criterion here is whether the entity is an *alter ego* of the government.[281] An entity may enjoy immunity although it has been established by separate legal incorporation. It is not the organic criterion as much as the degree of control by the State which is relevant.[282]

At the same time, it is important to remember that courts in

---

275   *The Schooner Exchange v McFaddon* [1812] 7 Cranch 166 11 US 74; *Le Parlement Belge* [1880] 5 PD 197; *The Christina* [1838] AC 485.

276   *Chong Boon Kim v Kim Yong Shik*, 58 AJ 1964, 186.

277   *Kilroy v Windsor (Prince Charles, The Prince of Wales et al).*, US *Digest* 1978, 641.

278   *Case Concerning Emperor Maximilian*, Trib. civil Seine, 1917 Cl 44 1465.

279   *Lefour v King Farouk*, (1947) Trib. civ. Seine. But *cf. see Re Honnecker* (1984) 80 ILR, 365.

280   [1894] 1 QB 149.

281   *Mellenger v New Brunswick Development Corp.* [1971] 2 All ER 593.

282   *Krajina v Tass Agency* [1949] 2 All ER 274; *Baccus SRL v Servicio Nacional del Trigo*, [1957] 1 QB 438.

different countries have not had the same views of the extent of immunity to be granted. Thus, in numerous cases in Italy, France and Germany immunity has been refused for private acts or for commercial activity; but Anglo-Saxon courts have taken a far more generous view and allowed immunity for all acts. Secondly, the test as to whether an entity is an organ of the State has also been solved differently in different States. Thus, courts in continental Europe[283] often found that Soviet agencies like TASS should not enjoy immunity whereas, again, Anglo-Saxon courts showed other, and more generous, views.[284]

In the 1970s United States and English views on immunity changed, almost abruptly. Legislation was introduced, both in England[285] and in the United States.[286] In internal law in the United Kingdom the situation changed with the adoption in the United Kingdom of the 1978 State Immunity Act,[287] adopted to implement the 1972 European Convention on State Immunity of 1972,[288] which had entered into force in 1976. That year, in 1976, the United States also adopted a State Immunity Act.[289] This Act sets out commercial and private acts which are considered to be acts *de jure gestionis*. A similar enumerative approach has been taken in the Canadian State Immunity Act of 1982.[290]

The European Community had, a little earlier, adopted a

---

[283]   See the survey in my *Independent State, op. cit.*, 234 and add, for France, *Chemins de fer Iraniens c Levant Express,* 73 RG 1969, 883; for Germany, *Petioner v Central Bank of Nigeria,* 16 ILM, 1077 501; for Italy, *Mercantile v Greece,* 22 ILR 1955, 240; for Belgium, *Dhellemes v Central Bank of Turkey* (1963), 45 ILR, 85; for the Netherlands, *Krol v Bank of Indonesia* 26 ILR, 1958 180.

[284]   Minor encroachment on the solidly applied absolute rules of immunity in English Courts were made in *The Christina* [1938] AC 485; *Sultan of Johore v Abubakar* [1952] AC 318; *Rahimtoola v Nizam of Hyderabad* [1958] AC 379 per Lord Denning; *Thai-Tapioca Service Ltd. v Pakistan* [1975] 3 All ER 961.

[285]   UK State Immunity Act, 1976.

[286]   US State Immunity Act, 1978.

[287]   1978 c 33.

[288]   1972 11 ILM 470

[289]   90 Stat. 2891, 1976 15 ILM 1388.

[290]   SC 1980-81-82 c 95

Convention on Immunity[291] and the new legislation in the United Kingdom was, it was stated, introduced to implement this EC Convention.

The Tate letter from the Acting Legal Adviser to the State Department in the United States to the Attorney General in that country stated that the United States, as a matter of policy, would adopt a *restrictive theory of immunity,* refusing immunity for commercial transactions, and abandon the *absolute theory.*[292]

The changes which have recently taken place in English and United States law as well in the law of some Commonwealth countries concern new attitudes above all to commercial activity. Until recently, courts in these countries, contrary to other courts in Europe, had held that a State is immune for all activities. Continental courts accepted, for decades, only a very limited version of immunity whereas English and American courts appear to have ignored the immense volume of case law in civil law countries.

We are here also concerned with an important matter of principle. Why is it that all textbooks in the English language rely so heavily on exclusively English, Commonwealth and United States cases when they set out rules on immunity? Are they not, as when they deal with other matters in other chapters, setting out what can be applied all over the world? Naturally, immunity has also internal aspects in the sense that, for example, English students who read such textbooks to pass exams in England and to later work as barristers, judges or have other legal appointments, must naturally know what entities can or cannot be sued in English courts. In this respect the question of immunity forms part of English law and has internal relevance in England. But this is far from saying that international law on immunity has a similar content. Why should a Japanese court take any such rules or views into account? Where are, in fact, the Venezuelan, Chinese or Portugese cases which could give some symmetry to all the cases lined up in English textbooks on international law?

These comments concern many other areas of international law as well but it is in the field of immunity that English cases are

---

[291]   Convention of 1972.
[292]   1952, 26 Dept. of State Bull. 984.

predominant.[293] On the other hand, when English judgments on international law are succinct and clear, they have certainly an important impact on international legal theory.

In 1979, in England, the influencial judge Lord Denning hesitated to grant immunity for commercial transactions and said that

'If the dispute concerns ... the commercial transaction of a foreign government (whether carried on by its own departments or agencies or by setting up separate legal entities) and it arises properly within the territorial jurisdiction ... there is no ground for granting immunity'.[294]

Here, it was emphasised that if the State behaves like a businessman, it must be treated like one, and not enjoy immunity for transactions of a commercial nature.

What is now seen as a major 'new' development in English and United States courts is to some extent, only an alignment with what many courts in Europe had already found. Thus, numerous courts outside the Anglo-Saxon world had already refused immunity for private or commercial acts and they had also been far more restrictive than English and United States courts when they decided what entity is an organ of the State.[295] The latter question, was, of course, of major importance in any dealings with the Eastern bloc[296] where an extensive version of immunity made almost everything immune since the State owned and controllled all commercial entities. Such an extensive theory and corresponding practice of immunity was hardly in the interest of the former Eastern bloc States: who would trade with entities who can never be sued for non-payment?

National legislation will help to make the immunity rules of international law more uniform. It is also to be noticed that although

---

[293]   Even the English form of citing cases is imposed on the few civil law cases that are ever studied: the editors of international law reports *assume* that that cases must have 'names' as they do in England wheras the normal listing in France and Germany is by indication merely of court and date.

[294]   *Rahimtoola v Nizam of Hyderabad* [1958] AC 379.

[295]   See my *Independent State, op. cit.*, 234.

[296]   *Cf.* Boguslawski, NTIR 1970, 167.

immunity, as a matter of principle and tradition, rests on reciprocity, there is provision, for example in the UK Act, to apply the immunity provisions to all States, whether parties to the European Convention or not. This is also a novel development.

The hesitation to allow immunity for commercial transactions grew but now there was another ancillary and most important problem. How do you assess the nature of an act? What is a sovereign act and what is a commercial act? Or, as most expressed it in its Latin form, how do you know when the State acts *de jure imperii* (in its sovereign capacity) and when it acts *de jure gestionis* (in its commercial capacity)? To the problems in hand was added the difficulty to assess, what was thought to be relevant and decisive, the *purpose* of the act.

Suppose the purpose changed? A State can intend to purchase a shipload of boots for its army and, for some reason, change its intention to sell the boots on the market. And what if this change of plans takes place before the boots are sold, say, when the ship carrying them is on the high seas? Does this mean that the State is immune until the moment when it displays a different intention or does it mean that the State was never/or is always/ immune?

It soon became obvious that the extent of immunity must be assessed in some other way than by a *purpose* criterion. If commercial activity is to be excluded it would obviously make sense to qualify the acts on the basis of their nature (which is a fairly objective criterion) rather than the purpose of the acts (which is entirely subjective, existing only in the mind of the decision makers). Still, it took until 1977 when Lord Denning stated this clearly in the now leading case on immunity in England: *Trendtex Trading Corp v Central Bank of Nigeria.*[297] We have referred to this case above in the context of expanding jurisdiction to include commercial activities of a State. But the second important implication of this case, is that it shows that the *purpose criterion* is obsolete and requires to be replaced by the criterion of the *nature of the transaction*.

In this case, it was established that the Central Bank of Nigeria

---

[297] [1977] QB 529.

was not an organ of the State.[298] However, said Lord Denning (and Lord Shaw) *even if* it had been organically linked to the State, that was irrelevant since, in any event, there could be no question of immunity in a commercial situation. If the relevant transaction was one which, *by its nature*, was a commercial transaction, then there could be no question of immunity.

In this important case, a third important aspect is worth underlining. The Court stated that international law knows of no *stare decisis* doctrine.[299] This means that English courts which treat general principles of international law as part of law of the land must take changes in international law into account and thus apply a new rule which has emerged in international society as part of the law of England. It is thus a question of applying the most recent rule of international law. This decision has been followed in a number of cases.[300]

In this context it may be useful to recall the *rationale* of sovereign immunity: the very purpose which such immunity is intended to serve is to facilitate international contacts between States. Such interests are hardly served by undermining confidence in State parties to business contracts by allowing a loophole of immunity for a State, unwilling to pay for a commercial transaction. Similar considerations may have played a part in restricting rules on State immunity to exclude business transactions.

(ii) State Immunity for Property *ratione materiae*

State property forms a special category in sovereign immunity cases. The general rule is that no property of other States may be taken, impounded or sequestrated in any case before courts of other States. The plaintiff has the burden of proof to show that certain property

---

[298]   *Cf. supra.*

[299]   This rule, applied in most English speaking countries, is derived from Roma law and is designed to secure stability in case law by obliging a court to follow earlier decisions on similar matters. The doctrine is alien to theories of law in most countries in continental Europe. Even the ICJ is not bound by its previous decisions although it has become a practice for the Court to make clear when its decisions deviate from previous rulings.

[300]   For example, *1er Congreso del Partido* [1983] 1 AC 244.

either does not effectively belong to the State or, alternatively, that the property is not designed to be used for State purposes. There is, however, a heavy presumption that all State property has been acquired, or kept, precisely for State purposes.

Courts have conceded the possibility of adjudicating on property belonging to *State companies* when the plaintiff has been able to prove that the property did not effectively belong to the State.[301]

As distinct from the normal test about the character and *nature* of acts which exclude immunity for *commercial transactions*, we employ, in sovereign immunity cases not bearing on *transactions* but concerning *property*, the simple test as to whether or not the property is designed for use of a State.[302] Thus, if State property is *not* used for State purposes it can, in certain special circumstances, be sequestrated.[303] A most important Swedish Case in this context is the case of the *Sequestrated Ships*,[304] where the Swedish Supreme Court stated that property belonging to other States cannot be sequestrated in Sweden. The judgment of the Supreme Court, acknowledging the rules of immunity in international law, has been severely criticised on the ground that the Court should have come to the obvious conclusion on immunity without making, as it did, this immunity *dependent* on certain conditions. It has thus been remarked that this immunity, in any event, is *absolute and unconditional* and cannot be limited by the decisions of national courts.[305] It is thus often underlined that immunity must not be subjected to conditions and that such attitudes violate international law.[306]

One distinguishes mainly between *jurisdictional immunity* and *immunity for executionary action*, *i.e.* in matters concerning, for example, the implementation of decisions of judgments of a court.

---

[301] Delapenna, *Suing Foreign Governments and their Corporations*, 1988, 375; Schreuer, *State Immunity*, 1988, 143; for specific instances see, *e.g. Iran c Eurodif*, Cass., Paris, 20.3.1989, GP 1989; 326 892; *Iran c Framatome*, JDI 1990, 1004;

[302] *C.f.* Verdross-Simma, *Universelles Völkerrecht*, 3rd ed., 1984, 771.

[303] *The Botschaftenkonten Case*, BGH 1982.

[304] *Fallet om Kvarstadsbåtarna*, NJA 1942:342.

[305] Gihl, Staters immunitet vid främmande domstolar, SvJt 1944, vid 289.

[306] ii O'Connell, 965.

Some State property is exempt from any executionary measures, for example monies held in a bank used to defray expenses of a diplomatic mission.[307] Some States have enacted legislation to clarify what type of State property may be used to satisfy a Court Order.[308] It may be a rule of general international law that recourse may be had to property which is *no longer* used for diplomatic purposes,[309] although fairly conclusive proof must be required for such qualification.

Immunity of execution can only be restricted by specific international conventions. The European Convention of Immunity of 1972,[310] expressly forbids executionary measures but obliges a losing State to *fulfill* assumed obligations.

b. Diplomatic Immunity

It is mainly diplomats who, in international society, are concerned with international relations, and their *immunity,* without which these relations cannot be maintained,[311] has, in numerous cases before international courts and tribunals, been held to constitute *the core of international law* and most important part, forming the basis of the whole international legal systen. This attitude was demonstrated, for example, in the *Case concerning the Hostages in Teheran.*[312]

From the comprehensive immunity of the State one distinguishes thus *diplomatic immunity,* which, in many respects is more far-reaching.[313]

Diplomatic immunity is commonly used to describe the type of

---

307   *Alcom v Colombia* [1984] 2 WLR 750.

308   See, for example, the UK State Immunity Act 1978, which refers to assets used for 'commercial purposes'.

309   *Westminster City Council v Iran* [1986] 3 All ER 284.

310   BGBl.II 34, 1400; *cf.* Karczewski, Das Europäisches Übereinkommen über Staatenimmunität vom 16.5.1972, 54 *Rabels Zeitschrift* 1990, 533; Kronke, Europäisches Übereinkommen über Staatenimmunität, in the *Praxis des Internationelen Privat- und Verfahrungsrechts* 1991, 141.

311   *Cf.* Merle, *Sociologie des relations internationales,* 4th ed. 1988, 211.

312   ICJ *Reports* 1980.

313   Also *consular immunity,* on which see further *infra,* is usually conceived as a sub-section of diplomatic immunity.

immunity which cover other agents of a State and which can be distinguished from State immunity. This type of privilege is granted not only to diplomats, but also, in certain circumstances, to consuls and international agents.

(i) Diplomats

Satow, *Guide to Diplomatic Practice*, 5th ed., 1979; Denza, *Diplomatic Law, Commentary to the Vienna Convention*, 1976; Hardy, *Modern Diplomatic Law*, 1968; de Mello, *Tradado de derecho diplomatico*, 1953.

1. THE REASONS FOR DIPLOMATIC PRIVILEGE

The right of active and passive legation, *i.e.* the right to send and to receive envoys, follows from the *sovereignty* of the State.[314] Accompanying such right of legation is the privilege for envoys to enjoy *immunity* so that they can travel and return unhindered to their own sovereign. The legal ground for all immunity is, as already mentioned, the rule of *par in parem non habet imperium*, that is to say that one State cannot sit in judgment of another.

The force with which diplomatic immunity is upheld in international society is explained by the force of *reciprocity*.[315] The State which places itself outside this system of rules cannot expect that the integrity of its own envoys is respected: States must have complete confidence that their diplomatic agents are fully protected.

There were, earlier, views that diplomatic immunity depended on, or was rooted in, a notion of *extraterritoriality*, that is to say the embassy of a State was regarded as a piece of the home territory. This view has now been abandoned[316] as well as one which relied on *sovereign substitution*, *i.e.*, that the envoy *replaced* the State that

---

[314] See my *Independent State, op. cit.*, 10.

[315] *Cf.* my *Concept, op. cit.*, 66.

[316] From the present position in law, that the embassy is *not* extra-territorial, flows the consequence that an embassy has no right to grant asylum to refugees in the building. When such a right has been claimed, as it often has in South America, this has been based, not on a general rule of international law, but on a local rule of limited application, see The Asylum Case, ICJ *Reports* 1953.

sent him. Nowadays, the basis for diplomatic immunity is thought to be the very *function* he fulfills in international society.[317]

Diplomats enjoy immunities by virtue of their functions in the international society where they are sent as envoys from one government to another.

The immunity of diplomats is, as underlined in *The Hostage Case*,[318] at the root of relations between States and forms part of the fundamental rules of international society. For as long as there have been States, there has been a need for diplomatic immunity: there has been a need to send a messenger from one State and have him back, unharmed, to report his news from the other State. The reason why this rule has worked better than many others in international society is naturally that this system relies on *reciprocity*. Mutual respect for the rule of diplomatic immunity has thus reinforced and entrenched the rule.

2. DEVELOPMENT OF DIPLOMATIC IMMUNITY

As international law itself can be traced to relations between early States, such as between the Greek city States Athens and Sparta, and to earlier kingdoms,[319] so we can trace the gradual development of diplomatic immunity, to early history, forming the core of early international law.

As international law expands as a system at the rise of the nation-States in the 16th and 17th centuries so do the rules of diplomatic immunity expand, in a dramatic fashion, at the same time. The reason for this parallel development is precisely that the rules of diplomatic immunity forms the centre, or basis, of international law itself. International law is a system of law primarily between the powerful units of States (but note we have showed there are numerous other subjects or actors).[320]

---

[317]   ii O'Connell, 965. *Cf.* UK *Report on Diplomatic Immunity*, Cmnd 8460 1952, para 3.

[318]   (1980) ICJ *Reports* 3.

[319]   See, for example, the Peace Treaty between Rameses II of Egypt and the Hittites of 1270 BC.

[320]   See *supra*.

Communications between States depended earlier on the use of diplomats. It was they who declared war and it was they who made peace. It was they who negotiated and concluded treaties.[321] It was diplomats, again, who relayed messages of importance from one sovereign to another. It is therefore natural that the functions, and immunities, of diplomats should develop in a parallel way to the growth of international society itself.

Historically, the first embassies were *itinerant* and followed the envoy on his occasional journeys to various destinations. Gradually, during the 16th century, *permanent missions* were established where the Ambassador took the place of representing his sovereign at the Court of another sovereign.[322] Naturally, diplomatic relations have taken on other dimensions with the rapid increase of modern communications and the increased mobility of Ambassadors and other diplomatic agents.[323] In a sense, the practice on special missions[324] has made history revert to the *itinerant diplomats*.

3. THE GROWTH AND DECLINE OF DIPLOMATIC FUNCTIONS

In one sense, the importance of diplomatic relations has *increased* with technical development and, at the same time as many communicatons are transmitted by telephone, telefax or telegram,[325] the *functions* of the diplomat have also been widened to be that of an *intermediary*, a *representative* and an *observer*.[326]

---

[321] But see *supra* on ratification, in Chapter III.

[322] It is this relationship which explains the *equality* of ambassadors and which is at the root of their immunity: no State can sit in judgment of another (equal) State.

[323] Note the earlier delays: it took one year for Ambassador Lesseps to go from Russia's Pacific coast to Versailles in 1787/88. *Cf.* Colliard, *Institutions, op. cit., loc. cit. Cf.* Merle, *Sociologie des relations internationales*, 4th ed., 1988, 211.

[324] See further *infra* in this section.

[325] *Cf.* Merle, *Sociologie, op. cit.*, 212.

[326] *Cf.* Colliard, *Institutions des relations internationales*, 9th ed., 1990 No. 188 page 208. It is important to retain the *main* characteristic of a diplomat, that of *representing his own sovereign to another sovereign*. This is why foreign ambassadors in London are still called *ambassadors at the Court of St. James's*.

It would be reasonable to expect that the more States there are, the more diplomats there will be to keep up communications between these units. One would even expect even further growth when international organisations are established which obtain the right to send and receive diplomats. On the other hand, *because* of the technical facility for one Head of State to contact another, the importance of diplomats has also *decreased* as there are numerous occasions when Heads of State have preferred to speak to each other directly on the telephone,[327] or have recourse to supersonic flights to personally speak to another leader of another country.[328]

We must also be aware of the frequent use in the past of *personal leaders*, long before such meetings were justified by modern communications.[329] In this way, world leaders have always preferred personal meetings, dispensing with the services of diplomats, for particularly important matters. The reason for having diplomats in the first place was, as mentioned above, the need to communicate. As postal systems are introduced with later telephone and telegraph systems, the need for diplomats thus diminished as Heads of State and their ministries start to communicate with greater ease in other ways.

International organisations, which, at one stage, contributed to the expansion of the number of diplomats, also caused a reduction of such agents by furnishing permanent fora for discussion: in these fora government representatives of States could meet and discuss on a multilateral basis rather than relying on endless networks of bilateral communications through diplomats.

In recent times, States resort more and more, not only to top level meetings but also to special missions, at a lower level than Head of

---

[327] But the use of the so called *hot line* is much exaggerated. It is more useful to point at specific agreement reached by personal contacts, as for example, the agreement between the United States and the USSR in 1963 in Geneva, see, Colliard, *Institutions, op. cit.,* No. 190 210.

[328] *Cf.* Merle, *Sociologie des relations internationales,* 4th ed. 1988 211.

[329] Thus, Cavour went in 1858 to Plombières to see the Emperor and Bismarck went, for the same reason, to Biarritz in 1865. Queen Victoria went personally to see Louis Philippe in 1843 at St. Leu and the French King returned the visit at Windsor in 1844. The Czar and the Sultan had meetings for talks in 1867 in Paris, see Colliard, *Institutions, op. cit.,* No. 188 208.

State, to negotiate and agree on specific matters.[330]

4. THE EFFECT OF DIPLOMATIC PRIVILEGE

The rules about diplomatic immunity are included in the *corpus* of rules which is called *jus cogens* and from which, as has been set out above,[331] States may not derogate by agreement or by unilateral legislation. The International Court of Justice underlined in the *Hostage Case* that all States are *obliged* to safeguard diplomatic immunity.[332]

As immunity is rooted in *jus cogens* of general international law it is *irrelevant* whether States promulgate national legislation on immunity as the privileges are rooted in the international legal system from which States cannot deviate by internal acts.[333] On the other hand, it is naturally helpful when States legislate to make provisions on immunity more precise and enable all national authorities to respect such rules.[334] Therefore, rules on immunity cannot be displaced by national courts as these rules for part of *jus cogens*.[335] This has also been confirmed by the Supreme Court of Sweden in the famous *von Herder Case*.[336]

The immunity of an envoy is *taken for granted* in international society as demonstrated in the cases *Don Pathelon Sa*,[337] *Pole's Case*,[338] *Marche's Case*,[339] and in *Pilkington v Stanhope*.[340] As underlined by the International Court of Justice in the *Hostages Case*

---

[330] See i Oppenheim 9th ed. Jennings & Watts, part I: 2. Colliard, *Institutions, op. cit., loc. cit.*

[331] See in detail *supra* in Chapter III.

[332] See, ICJ *Reports* 1980 where the Court mentioned the importance of the *inviolability of diplomatic envoys*, para. 38.

[333] *Cf. supra* in Chapter I on this point of supremacy of international law.

[334] See for Swedish legislation on immunity Lag 1976:661, re-issued in SFS 1984:341.

[335] On this see *supra* in Chapter III.

[336] NJA 1946.

[337] (1654) 5 St.Tr. 462.

[338] 4 Co. Inst. 153.

[339] 3 (1615) 1 Rolle Rep. 175.

[340] 1694 2 Vern. 217.

all States are *obliged* to assist in the protection of rules on diplomatic immunity.[341] This is a further expression of the special *duty of solidarity*[342] which flows from the membership of international society and which binds all States, whether or not involved in an actual dispute concerning diplomats and whether or not they have acceded to conventions and treaties on diplomatic privilege.

The rules of immunity are clearly derived from the *equality* of States;[343] any deviation from such legal equality engages the responsibility of States and lead to responsibility for offences of the international legal order.[344] To deny a diplomat his immunity is thus a serious violation of international law.[345] Persons who have taken part in the arrest of a diplomat may, in many jurisdictions, be prosecuted themselves for this offence which, in turn, engages the responsibility of the State vis-à-vis another State for which the offended State may demand compensation. *The Case about the Russian Ambassador in London.*[346] In another case those who had taken part in the indictment and execution against an envoy were themselves punished.[347] The wording of the International Court of Justice in the *Hostage Case,*[348] where Iran was condemned for not respecting diplomatic immunity, is also a guide as to the serious nature of any effort to deny diplomats their protection under international law.

5. THE SPECIFIC IMMUNITIES OF DIPLOMATS

Immunities and privileges enjoyed by diplomatic agents are, in

---

341   (1980) ICJ *Reports* 1980.

342   See on this duty as a fundamental obligation of States, my *Concept of International Law, op. cit.,*127-128.

343   See *supra* in this Chapter.

344   See *infra* in Chapter VIII on Consequential Rules.

345   Genet, *Traité de diplomatie et de droit diplomatique*, 1931-2, 487; *cf. Nikolaus Hjelmeland v Kristin Biong*, 87 Clunet 1960, 512.

346   Martens, *Causes celèbres* 47.

347   Process of Sequestration 22 USC 252 according US Act 1790 1 Stat 117. The American Act of 1790 is held to reflect what applies under general international law: ii O'Connell 965.

348   (1980), ICJ *Reports* 1980.

principle, those set out in the Vienna Convention 1961 which, in principle, reflects general international law.[349]

Diplomatic privileges and immunities are enjoyed, to the full, by members of an embassy or a special mission.[350] *All* diplomats and other employees at the mission enjoy these immunities. Diplomatic immunity has, through history, extended to the diplomat's family and to his suite. There are some recent restrictions in this respect in some States as *private acts* of family members have been subjected to court proceedings, at least in isolated instances.[351] Furthermore, servants and domestic staff are, if they are citizens of the host country,[352] excepted in so far as they are only immune for acts in their official capacity.[353] Undoubtedly, the independence of the diplomat is substantially curtailed by these exceptions, especially with regard to actions of his own family and it is questionable whether such jurisdiction of a host State is warranted.

Diplomats in general, except the domestic staff who are nationals of the receiving State, thus enjoy far-reaching privileges both for their official and for their private acts.

A diplomat enjoys immunity from the moment he has been accepted in the receiving State: the act of acceptance is expressed in a formal *agrément* for the Head of a Mission and such *agrément* can be denied without giving any reasons. Other members of the mission

---

[349] But see on this point *infra* in this Chapter on instances where the Convention goes beyond general international law in denying full immunity for private commercial acts.

[350] See further *infra* under Travelling Envoys and Special Missions in this Chapter.

[351] *Empson v Smith* [1966] 1 QB 426.

[352] Note that in many States citizenship is automatically lost if a person expressly seeks other nationality by application or by entering into the service of a foreign State. This is, for example, prescribed in Sweden by the Act (1950:382) on Swedish Citizenship, as revised by Act 1970:139. In a case where a Swedish national takes up employment at a foreign embassy, the person should automatically lose his Swedish citizenship. This rule does not seem to be implemented by Swedish authorities. There appears at least to be an exception, overriding the wording of the Act, as far as concerns lower echelons of employment of service, such as that of secretaries and domestic staff.

[353] *Cf.* article 37(3) and (4) of the Vienna Convention.

need only be notified[354] to the receiving State and here too, the receiving State may have objections and may give a message to the sending State that a person is not welcome. However, the mode of acceptance is extremely informal, apart from the Head of Missions who formally presents his letter of *agrément* to the sovereign, and acceptance can be implied in numerous actions taken by the receiving State, such as the simple inclusion in the Diplomatic List, which, in many countries is conclusive for immunity enjoyed by *permanent diplomats*. Other diplomats may, as mentioned be received more informally, and will still be guaranteed their full immunity. The reason for these informal procedures is that the receiving State, at any time, may, again without giving any reasons, declare a diplomat *persona non grata* and demand that he leaves the country at once.

Not only the Foreign Ministries of other countries are bound to respect the immunity enjoyed by envoys under international law but also, and perhaps, especially, the courts of foreign nations. This is demonstrated by a number of cases in various jurisdictions[355] as well as by international tribunals.[356]

The *details* of immunities are laid down in the Vienna Convention of 1961. However, this agreement merely reflects *lex lata* and all rules on diplomatic immunity therefore derive their legal force from general international law, and apply irrespectively of whether or not a State has ratified the Vienna Convention.[357] This is also recognised in case law.[358] However, the Convention *clarifies* what is already binding and is a convenient instrument for the codified

---

[354] See article 10 of the Vienna Convention.

[355] For example, *The Case of the Sequestrated Ships (Fallet Rörande Kvarstadsbåtarna)*, NJA 1942, 342 and further *infra* in this section.

[356] *Cf. The Hostages Case*, before the International Court of Justice, cited above.

[357] Dahm, 1 *Völkerrecht*, 1958, 311, writes three years before the Vienna Convention that rules on diplomatic immunity do not *need* to be codified as they are so entrenched in the international legal system: 'Heute sind Normen, die sich auf die Rechtstellung der Diplomaten beziehen, wohl so allgemein anerkannt, und sie stellen einen so gesicherten Bestandteil des allmeinen Völkerrechts dar, dass es in der Gegenwart der vertraglichen Sicherung kaum noch bedarf.'

[358] *E.g. R v Pentonville ex parte Teja* [1971] 2 QB 272. There are forceful authorities from numerous countries on this point, see, for example, Satow, *passim*.

rights and privileges of diplomats.[359]

Under the Convention, as under general international law, diplomats enjoy full immunity from *criminal* and all *civil jurisdiction* of the receiving State and from civil and administrative jurisdiction except for recovery of personal immovable property and questions of succession.[360] A diplomat enjoys a *higher standard* of protection than representatives of foreign governments in general.[361] His immunity is *complete*[362] and includes *official acts* as well as *private acts*. As the immunity of diplomats is *comprehensive* and covers all acts, there is no need to investigate whether a specific act was an official act or a private act as, in neither case, there can be any question of jurisdictional competence of another State in civil *or* criminal matters.[363] The few instances when courts have assumed jurisdiction, there have been severe international protests and the responsibility of the State of the court which has instigated a suit against a diplomat is engaged.[364]

A diplomat does not have to attend court proceedings to give evidence in actions where he is not involved.[365] A diplomat is exempted from all judicial and administrative procedures, from execution and other compelling measures. *Even* if a court proceedings in a case is validly brought against a diplomat, as if, for example, an ambassador has given his special *consent* to this for a lower employee at an embassy, this does not mean that the receiving State would *ipso facto* be entitled to take executionary measures. Any such measures

---

[359] There are instances, see *infra*, where the Convention appears to go further than general international law.

[360] Article 31 of the Vienna Convention. The Convention also mentions actions relating to private commercial activities but it is questionable whether any action in these fields can validly be brought against a serving diplomat; all case law point to full immunity for such activities.

[361] O'Connell, ii 1965, 965.

[362] See further *infra*, in this Chapter.

[363] Colliard, *Institutions, op. cit.,* No. 194, 213.

[364] See *ibid., loc. cit.*

[365] Article 31(2). The Ambassador can restrict this immunity for himself, (which would be rare) with agreement from his home State, and by his own decision for any member of his staff.

are thus *distinct* from the questions bearing on jurisdiction.[366] As the immunity of a diplomat also covers private acts, there can be no question of execution even for private debts.[367]

Immunity includes also all immunity against fiscal payments or any other tax.[368] The reason for this is that the payment of taxes is an expression for allegiance[369] and loyalty and the equality of States cannot accept that a diplomat, in this way, is subjected to taxes.[370] The diplomat must furthermore not be arrested, interrogated by customs police or by any other authorities, have his right of movement curtailed,[371] or in any way have his various rights of communication hampered.[372] The right of movement, and freedom from legal process, is probably the most important privilege of a diplomat as all his functions depends on this freedom of action. It is also this freedom which explains that there can be no distinction between official and private acts. O'Connell expresses this in the following words:

'(The envoy) must be allowed such freedom from the legal process of the receiving State as is necessary to ensure that he will be undisturbed in his freedom to represent his sovereign and report back to him. Under modern conditions it may prove difficult or even impossible to distinguish the private from the public activities of a diplomat, and even if such distinction is possible it may be that legal process in respect of private functions will jeopardise freedom of action with respect to public.

---

[366]   *Cf.* article 23 of the European Convention on Immunity of 1972 and Crawford, Execution of judgments and foreign Sovereign Immunity, 75 AJIL, 1981, 820.

[367]   *The Case of de Wrech* (1772) Hackworth ii 110.

[368]   Colliard, *Institutions, op. cit.,* No. 195 211.

[369]   On this see *supra* in this Chapter.

[370]   See article 34 in the Vienna Convention and Nguyen Quoc Dinh & Dailler & Pellet, *Droit international public,* 1987, 665.

[371]   But it is obviously in accordance with international law to restrict the access of diplomats to prohibit access to certain areas, installations or buildings. It is more questionable to limit the area for diplomats to a radius around the capital of a certain mileage, as did the Soviet Union, during the communist era.

[372]   Colliard, *Institutions, op. cit.,* No. 191-3, 211-212.

A diplomat, for example, who is in danger of having distraint levied on his property, who is required to appear in court to defend himself to give evidence, is, to this extent, incapacitated in his freedom of movement. The law thus tends towards complete immunity of the diplomat from any process and it allows him greater privilege than it appears to allow to the sovereign he represents.'[373]

Members of the mission, have the right to use ciphers and have the absolute right to send and to receive communications, documents, or objects necessary for the service.[374] According to many writers the privilege to send *the diplomatic bag* only entails a privilege by politeness (*courtoisie*)[375] which, according to them, would not be technically binding but only grated as a gracious concession. Yet, all State practice uniformly shows that this privilege is consistently respected and it is difficult to see why this would, by now, have crystallised into a legal binding rule. At least it is our opinion that that is the case.[376]

Diplomats also enjoy other privileges beyond what has been set out above under special conventions enhancing their protection in modern international society. A series of conventions thus protects diplomats from *terrorist attacks:* they have in the last few decades been the target for terrorism. Diplomatic agents represent their home State and that therefore they provide a good bargaining position for blackmailers. Thus, a diplomat may be taken hostage and held until his home State, or for that matter another State or an organisation, or a private entity, carries out what the kidnappers demand. The German Ambassador von Spreti was eventually killed and found in a car boot in Central America after one such drama; he was just one of many diplomats who had to give his life in the chain of terrorist attacks.

---

[373] ii O'Connell, 965. *Cf.* UK *Report on Diplomatic Immunity*, Cmnd 8460, 1952 para 3.

[374] *Cf.* Reuter and Combacau, *Institutions, op. cit.,* 161.

[375] To be distinguished from *comity*, see, in detail, *supra*, Chapter I.

[376] *Cf.* Reuter and Combacau, *Institutions, op. cit.,* 161.

6. TRAVELLING ENVOYS AND SPECIAL MISSIONS

Travelling diplomats enjoy immunity when they travel through a third country on their way to their embassy where they are, or are to be, accredited. Also other travelling diplomats *rely,* if we analyse actual State practice, on such privileges when they travel to any destination for any purpose and considers himself as a *special mission.*[377]

It is important to specially mention special missions as many functions of diplomats are nowadays carried out by such direct negotiations. Full immunity is enjoyed by all envoys and other diplomatic agents as well as by special envoys and other plenipotentiaries sent on separate missions. If this was not so, a State would not venture to send persons to negotiate treaties, or attend conferences. Only if someone is *sent on a secret mission* can the person in question be indicted before a foreign court.[378]

For such missions to enjoy immunity the agreement of the host State is required; on the other hand, this agreement can be given informally and is certainly *implied* in any invitation or in any granting of a special diplomatic visa.[379] Consent can even be given *retrospectively* when a receiving State recognises that failure to grant immunity to a foreign envoy will violate rules on equality of States. This point was illustrated in the *Tabatabai Case,* in which an Iranian person had been indicted in Germany for crimes which were not connected with any official acts. Germany had not been notified until at a later stage that the person was sent on an Iranian mission as special emissary. As soon as this became clear the court proceedings were immediately stopped.[380]

Once the mission arrives it must be accorded full diplomatic privileges. If this was not so States would not send *ad hoc* diplomats

---

[377]   *Cf.* Bartos, 108 Recueil 1963 i 438; ILC Yb 1960 ii 108; 62 ii 155; 63 ii 151.

[378]   *The Quirin Case,* AD 1941-42, 168. *Cf.* the expert advice *Gutachten des Eidgenösissischen Politischen Departements vom 31. Januar 1979,* 36 SchwJIR 1980, 210. *Cf.* my article about Immunity and Espionage, *American Journal of International Law,* 1984, 76.

[379]   Sen, *A Diplomat's Handbook of International Law and Practice,* 1979, 177. On special visas grated by Sweden see, Utlänningsförordningen (1989:574) UF 1989:4 §2(7).

[380]   *The Case of Tabatabai,* 1983-86, ILR 80, 389.

to negotiate matters.[381] Immunity must be granted as soon as a travelling diplomat enters the State.[382] An exception is probably made for a diplomat who travels *incognito,* as demonstrated in *US v Rosal.*[383] *E contrario* it may be said that *if* a travelling envoy makes his presence and his status known to the relevant authorities, he will also be able to rely on specific privileges.[384]

A Convention on *Special Missions,* elaborated by International Law Commission and adopted by the General Assembly Resolution GA Res 1787 (XVI).[385] was concluded in 1969. Other agreements have also elaborated the rules applicable to special missions. Although this Convention has clarified immunities enjoyed by special missions, it is important to underline that special envoys, in any event, already enjoy immunity and far-reaching privileges under general international law.[386] There are thus numerous rules of general international law which operate irrespective of this agreement.

7. IMMUNITY OF EMBASSIES AND ARCHIVES

The *Embassy* itself is immune but this does not apply when the Ambassador *asks* for assistance.[387] Apologies are made if police enter 'inadvertently'.[388] The embassy enjoys immunity together with its *archives.*[389] However, evidence once seized may be used in proceedings.[390]

---

[381]   *Cf.* Reuter and Combacau, *Institutions et relations internationales,* 4th ed., 1988, 159.

[382]   *Cf.* Vienna Convention on Special Missions article 43:1.

[383]   ILR 1960 31, 389

[384]   *Cf.* article 40 of the Vienna Convention concerning transit to State of accreditation.

[385]   *Cf.* the Havana Regulations of 1928..

[386]   Rivier i § 44.

[387]   *Fatemi v United States* (1963) ILR 34.

[388]   *The Dorf Case* (1973) ILR 552 in Norway; *The South African Embassy in the Hague* (1986) 86 NTIR 181.

[389]   Article 24.

[390]   See *R. v Rose* [1946] No. 76, on a cipher clerk spy at the Soviet Embassy in Canada and, further, my article on Foreign Warships and Immunity for Espionage, AJIL 1984, 76.

The Embassy is particularly protected and the host State has a duty to provide adequate police (or army) protection, especially in the event of potential *demonstrations*. The question of immunity of the Embassy building itself arose in the Libyan drama in London in 1986 when a woman police officer was shot from the window of the Libyan Bureau, the name given to its Embassy. A Foreign Office Select Committee reaffirmed the principle of immunity of an embassy and of diplomats. Yet, it would have been in place to emphasise the role of self-defense: it cannot be possible to construe immunity to preclude a state from taking protective action when its subjects, in a crowd, are exposed to firearm attacks by diplomats shooting from an embassy.[391]

8. WAIVER AND LIABILITY

Immunity from prosecution or action is not the same as immunity from liability. In other words, diplomats are exempt from local jurisdiction but may still be legally liable.[392] The distinction is important as *waiver of immunity* may allow the diplomat to be taken to court: such a waiver may be effected by the Ambassador or the head of mission or by the home state.[393] In most cases there is naturally consultation with the sending state. The reasons for waiver may, for example, be that the offense is such that it would lead to embarassment if the diplomat was not brought to court.

Any waiver must be explicit and clear as shown in ample case-law.[394] Furthermore, waiver to jurisdiction does not *ipso facto* imply waiver to execution.[395]

The social dimension of diplomatic relations have increasingly contributed to the practice of waiver or, as is the alternative, the recall

---

[391]   *Cf.* It would have been more appropriate to draw an analogy with the treatment of illegally entering foreign submarines: there is a question of self-defense, see my article Foreign Warships and Immunity for Espionage, AJIL, 1984, 53.

[392]   *Cf. Dickinson v Solar* [1930] 1 KB 376 at 380.

[393]   Article 32(2). *Cf. infra* in this Chapter on Temporary Jurisdiction.

[394]   *E.g. Dame Nzie v Vessah*, CA 17.3. 1978, DI 1978, 605, Note Kahn..

[395]   For executionary proceedings, a special, additional waiver is required: *In Re Suarez* [1918] 1 Ch 176.

of diplomats. It has become unacceptable to insist on immunity for minor offenses and diplomats of most countries are currently instructed to pay, for example, their parking fines. The police in cities like London, in a country which has been traditionally generous with regard to immunity,[396] now put wheel clamps on diplomatic cars which are parked in contravention of parking regulations. Authorities in many States also remove the keys from diplomats who attempt to drink and drive.

There is even stronger resentment to allow immunity if the diplomat has abused his privilege in any more serious way. Thus, an Algerian diplomat was arrested at Schipol airport in Amsterdam when he was found to have a suitcase packed with handgrenades, explosives and letter bombs. When he was allowed to go it was not, according to the police because of his *immunity,* but because they *could not prove* he had full knowledge of the contents of his luggage.[397]

A diplomat has to be accepted by the host State to which he presents his letters of accreditation. Should he no longer be held acceptable to the host State, he can be asked to leave as a *persona non grata,* that is to say, a person who is no longer welcome in the host country. For this, he need not necessarily be given any explanation.

9. IMMUNITY AS IMPEDIMENT TO JURISDICTION

(a) Temporary Jurisdiction

As set out above, a diplomat enjoys full immunity in all civil and criminal proceedings as well as in all administrative of fiscal matters in a receiving State. In certain rare cases a sending State, or an Ambassador may decide to waive diplomatic immunity.[398] However, Courts can only assume *temporary jurisdiction* which remains effective if the plaintiff has *proved* that the defendant has *waived*[399]

---

[396]   *Supra.*

[397]   *The Times* 26th October 1972.

[398]   See *supra* under Waiver.

[399]   See further *supra* on waiver in the Section in this Chapter.

his immunity, as shown in *Filius v Lot Airlines*.[400]

(b) Intervening Immunity

As immunity is rooted in *jus cogens* of general international law, it implies an *imperative impediment* to jurisdiction.[401] In case the *status* of a person is altered during the court hearing, the court is obliged to take action *ex officio* to inhibit the proceedings. For example, if a person who is indicted is created an ambassador or other high ranking diplomat, the case against him cannot continue. This occurred when the Consul General of Venezuela - taken to court for private acts for which he, as a consul was not immune[402] - was nominated as Minister Plenipotentiary of Venezuela at the United Nations. The case had to be stopped because of the *intervening immunity* of the defendants *perpetuatio fori*,[403] as the court would no longer be competent and barred because of immunity,[404] as the right of jurisdiction has been extinguished. [405]

10. THE FUTURE OF DIPLOMATIC PRIVILEGE

The role of diplomats is likely to diminish as many of their tasks are taken over either by direct contacts of Heads of State or by the growing body of international civil servants. Furthermore, many of the new nations, both in Europe and in the Third World, are increasingly questioning the value of the expense of large embassies. However, as long as diplomats operate as State agents, they enjoy full immunity for their actions. On the other hand, such immunity can only make sense if it also comprises, as it used to do several hundred

---

[400] 1990 2nd cir. 29th June 1990.

[401] Objections based on immunity can also be raised in cases concerning, for example, bankruptcy, see Bogdan, *Internationell konkurs- och ackordsrätt*, 1984, 93.

[402] See on immunity of consuls, *infra*, in this Chapter.

[403] On *perpetuatio fori* see Dennemark, *Om svensk domstols behörighet i internationellt förmögenhetsrättsliga mål*, 344 et seq.

[404] *Arcaya v Paez* (1956) 145 F Supp 464.

[405] In this context Dennemark cites a series of authorities such as Riezler, 98; Praag, 82, 189; Walker, 106; Neuner, 44; Kann, 24; Pagenstecher, 353-7.

480

years ago, the *ad hoc* travelling emissary.

(ii) Consuls

Lee, *Consular Law and Practice*, 1961; Bodin, *Les immunités consulaires*, 1899; Ferrarra, *Manuale di diritto consolare*, 1936.

The Vienna Convention on Consular Relations of 1963 provide for immunity of consuls. This immunity is restricted to official acts of consuls.[406] The reason for consuls having less wide immunity is to be found in their functions. Diplomats represent a government to another government and therefore a diplomat cannot be tried for any action; it would be as if one state sat in judgment of another as the diplomat is an agent and a representative of his own *sovereign* to another *sovereign*. Consuls, on the other hand, are in charge of assisting their own nationals in commercial or cultural matters and they also provide visas for visitors to their home country.

Because of their functions being on another level, assisting nationals rather than being a representative to another Head of State as diplomats are, the immunity of consuls is correspondingly circumscribed to include only acts on duty or official acts. Difficult questions of evidence arise, however, with regard to proof whether an act was committed on duty or not as demonstrated in case law: in the case of *Bigelow v Princess Zizianoff* an American consul in Paris refused to issue a passport to a former citizen of Russia and telephoned newspapers saying that the applicant was a Russian spy. The Federal Court held that the consul was immune for refusal to issue a passport as this was an act in the line of duty but not for slander for which he was personally answerable. In the defamation proceedings, therefore, the consul was held liable for slander: the telephone call to the newspapers was not an act carried out in the course of his duties.[407]

---

[406] Article 43(1). See my *Independent State, op. cit., loc. cit.*
[407] RGDIP 1929 77 and my *Independent State. op. cit.*, 120-121.

(iii) International Organisations

International organisations enjoy in their own right immunity under international law but this immunity is *defined* by the Headquarters Arrangement that is concluded with the host State.[408] Lately, the immunity of organisations has taken on other dimensions as the question has been debated whether the organisation itself assumes all obligations and debts on behalf of the entity and, consequently, debtors have no recourse to the Member States[409] which stand *behind* the organisation. In a sense, it is almost that the organisation, by its very *personality*[410] is *shielding* the Member States from any action against them, almost as in a case with a limited company.[411]

Details of provisions on immunities of international organisations are often interpreted by analogy with diplomats: rules of inviolability of embassies are thus applied *mutatis mutandis* to the headquarters of international organisations.[412] On the other hand, the written text of a Headquarters Agreement has considerable weight in the case of disputed immunity of an international organisation and little is left to general rules of international law.

(iv) International Civil Servants

Crosswell, *Protection of International Personnel,* 1952; Kunz, Privileges and immunities of international organisations, AJIL 1947, 828; Ahluwalia, *The Legal Status, Privileges and Immunities of the Specialised Agencies and Certain Other International Organisations,* 1964; Cahier, *Etude des accords de siège conclus entre les organisations internationales et les Etats ou elles resident,* 1959; and my *Law Making of International Organisations,* 1965, 123 *et seq.*

Those employed by an international organisation also enjoy immunity if their post is one of those included in the Headquarter Agreement

---

[408] See my *Law Making by International Organisations,* 1965, Chapter II.

[409] *Standard Chartered Bank v International Tin Council* [1987] 1 WLR 641.

[410] See *supra* in Chapter II under International Organisations and my *Law Making, op. cit.,* Chapter I.

[411] *The Tin Council Cases* [1988] 3 All ER 257, [1989] 3 All ER 523.

[412] On the International Tin Council, see *Shearson Lehman Bros Inc. v Maclaine Watson & Co. Ltd.* (No. 2) [1988] 1 WLR 16.

which allows for immunity and privileges.[413]

Although the immunity of international civil servants conceptually figure as a variation of diplomatic immunity, it is to be emphasised that their immunity, like that of consuls, is limited to *official acts*. Official acts are furthermore possibly construed to have even less ambit than the similar category for consuls and may not cover any traffic offences: not even the chauffeur of the Secretary General was held to enjoy immunity for speeding when driving the Secretary General to an official function.[414] Secondly, the immunity even for official acts may be restricted under the Headquarters Agreement to exclude certain employees, such as secretaries who are employed for certain administrative duties.

United Nations soldiers enjoy, as staff of subsidiary organs of either the General Assembly[415] or of the Security Council,[416] immunity as employed by the UN.[417]

The Judges of the International Court of Justice are also, technically speaking, employed by the UN, although they act, by reason of their appointment in their individual capacity. They are immune as officials of one of the main United Nations organs.[418]

c. Visiting Forces

The view that visiting forces would have any *general immunity* is generally considered as obsolete and is now generally rejected.[419]

Under special Visiting Forces Agreements it is common to grant immunity to forces for certain acts. This type of immunity is derived from the immunity of State agents.[420] Special questions arise in the

---

[413]   On such agreements in detail see my *Law Making, op. cit.*, 128 *et seq. Cf. supra.*

[414]   *Westchester v Ranollo* (1946) 67 NYS 2d 31.

[415]   Like, for example, UNEP in the Suez Crisis in 1956.

[416]   This has been the rule in later cases.

[417]   The Secretary General usually leaves disciplinary responsibility to the force commander.

[418]   Article 19 of the Statute of the Court reaffirmed in the agreement with the Netherlands.

[419]   See i:2 Oppenheim, ed. by Jennings & Watts, 1992, 1157.

[420]   *Cf. supra*, in this Chapter.

context of jurisdiction unless there are clear provisions in such agreements.[421]

C. FETTERING OF SOVEREIGNTY UNDER TREATIES

i. General Remarks

States may be bound by international treaties with regard to the internal exercise of their sovereignty. We have given some examples of fettered States in the context of *subjects* of international law.[422] In this context we shall make some further references which have a special bearing on the limitation of jurisdictional power in the State's own territory. Some such limitations may result from general rules but most limitations are usually laid down in specific treaties.

It is not unheard of that even the constitution of a State is laid down in an international treaty. The constitutions of Rumania and of Bulgaria were both laid down in the Final Act of the Congress of Berlin in 1878. The Constitution of Cyprus of 1960 provides that the Constitution of the Republic of Cyprus may not be altered without consent of the treaty making parties, which did not even include Cyprus itself. The Austrian State treaty of 1955 imposes some far reaching obligations on Austria with regard to protection of minorities.

However, once a State has come into being it flows from its statehood that internally it can act freely. Whatever limiting treaties provide, it follows from the very notion of sovereignty that the State can *amend its own Constitution* and such apparently encroaching treaties must, in that respect, be considered as void. As we shall establish, also other undertakings may be void, or at least require the *continuous consent* of the territorial State, and such undertakings concern *limitations of the exercise of sovereignty in the territory of a State.*

On the other hand, any other treaty or engagement that the State has taken upon itself will necessarily bind the State and must be

---

[421] *Cf.* my article on Foreign Warships and Immunity for Espionage, AJIL 1984, 76. See also the NATO Agreement of 1951, 199 UNTS 67.

[422] See *supra* in Chapter II under Fettered States.

subsumed to the important principle of *pacta sunt servanda, i.e.* all agreement must be faithfully kept. Obligations can normally be subjected to re-negotiations by a subsequent treaty which modifies the rights and obligations of the parties.

However, certain obligations assumed under treaties cannot be freely discarded; there is, at least, one notable case where assumed duties with regard to Human Rights, cannot be abolished and cannot even be subject to re-negotiation of conventions to *reduce* rights already granted. This was illustrated in the case of treaties on minority rights in Austria.[423] It thus appears that such Human Rights can only be uplifted and not reduced once they have been granted.[424]

A special category of treaties, those which restrict sovereign functions within a State's territory, may be subjected to special rules of denunciation, either if there is no adequate *quid pro quo*, or merely if there is a national interest to resume the sovereign functions restricted under such treaties.

In any event, such a right to rid oneself of a treaty which encroaches on the exercise of sovereign right is to be preferred to one general right to dismiss a treaty on the basis of a *fundamental change of circumstances* (the so called *rebus sic stantibus* rule) which certainly undermines international security of law in the sense that no State can clearly know whether a treaty is in force or not if any State is at liberty to dismiss treaties that lightly.[425]

ii. Delegation of Sovereignty

Certain sovereign functions may be transferred by a State to an international organisation: this certainly does not imply a delegation in perpetuity of a portion of sovereignty, as has been argued by some in the case of the European Community, now the European Union. There is no question that a Member State could, although it may

---

[423] *Supra.*

[424] See *infra.*

[425] See, the right to denounce treaties restricting territorial sovereignty under the doctrine of continuous consent, my *Independent State, op. cit.,* 231, a doctrine to replace the rebus sic stantibus rule as one of more restricted ambit.

economically be a costly operation, renounce its membership in the European Union and retrieve these sovereign functions.

A State may validly agree to the exercise of sovereign functions in its own territory by another power. This consent may concern, for example, legislative acts of an organisation (like those of the European Union),[426] judicial acts of foreign agents (like the power exercised by consuls in China under the Capitulations Treaties)[427] or power exercised under a foreign military base agreement. But the State also reserves the right to rid itself of any such limitations of sovereignty in its own territory and can denounce any such agreement: such agreements are not only subjected to the initial consent of the parties but by continuous consent of the territorial State.[428]

The legal ground for retrieving sovereign functions would then be the fact that any State which allows limitations of its sovereignty in its own territory is entitled to denounce the relevant agreement as an incident of statehood, by what I have called an exercise of the *eminnent domain*.[429] This does not mean that any other agreements can be denounced: treaties affecting *territorial sovereignty functions* thus form a special class of agreements.[430]

iii. Spheres of Interest

The position of certain *satellite States* does not imply that their independence is diminished. Under the so called *Brezhnev doctrine* the Soviet Union considered itself entitled to interfere in any of its *satellite States,* the other socialist States in the region, whether or not the government of the day so wished. Any such *patronising*

---

[426] See my *Law Making, op. cit.,* Chapter VI.

[427] See my article on Unequal Treaties, in *International and Comparative Law Quarterly,* 1966, 72.

[428] See my *Independent State, op. cit.,* 231.

[429] See my *Finance and Protection, op. cit.,* 61 *et seq.*

[430] Nor does this mean that *jus cogens, supra* Chapter III, can be displaced.

intervention[431] is certainly contrary to international law as the international reaction to interferences in Hungary in 1956 or in Czechoslovakia in 1968 well illustrate. The United States has been criticised as well for resorting to similar intervention, albeit by more intermittent interference, in Grenada in 1983 or in Nicaragua between 1983 and 1986. The International Court of Justice condemned the action of the United States in *The Nicaragua v United States Case*[432] after having also been ordered to cease certain interfering activities by interim order of the Court.[433] It was in this case that the United States claimed it could waive its already given consent to submit to jurisdiction.

After the demise of communism, the spheres of interests have changed. The United States still exercises great influence in Central and South America whereas all influence of the former Soviet Union has disappeared, a particularly noticable development in the Third World and, of course, in the former satellite States which have now loosened themselves from political and trade ties. However, it is to be expected that new bloc building will occur, with new alliances and combinations, as earlier history shows has always been the case after major political upheavals.

a. Limitation of Sovereignty in a State's Own Territory:
Presumption in Favour of the Competence of the Territorial State

There is a heavy presumption of the full power of a territorial State within its own borders unless a clear rule can be shown as having been laid down in a treaty or in a general rule of international law. In any proceedings before a court or in arbitration proceedings this becomes a question of a burden of proof.

This burden of proof in proceedings rests on the party which

---

[431] See my *Law of War, op. cit.,* 80-81. The situation in Lithuania in 1990 was quite different: here, the Soviet Union appeared to 'intervene' in its own country. Other considerations than 'patronising intervention' are then relevant, *e.g.* on the role and right of a 'nation', and on the question of self-determination. See, *supra,* under Incidents of Statehood.

[432] (1985) ICJ *Reports* and *supra.*.

[433] (1984) Interim Order ICJ *Reports.*

alleges that there is a limitation of the territorial sovereignty. The same applies for any claim of extending territorial jurisdiction.[434]

In *The Right of Passage Case*[435] the International Court emphasised that it was Portugal which had the burden of proof to show that it had the right of passage over Indian territory from and to its colonial enclave Goa in India. Here, the Court avoided the question whether there was any general rule in international law concerning enclaves but held that Portugal had a right of passage derived from bilateral custom. This is one of the few situations where customary rules have a role to fulfil because of the territorial context.[436]

The derogation from territorial sovereignty was also tested in *The Asylum Case*.[437] In this case, the Court underlined that no right of diplomatic asylum - which itself limits the territorial sovereignty of a State - can be allowed unless a legal basis is established in the individual case.

There is thus a strong presumption against the limitation of sovereign power in a State's own territory. On the other hand, in the face of clear rules, for example on *jus cogens*.[438]

b. Types of Limitations

A State may conclude a treaty to limit its internal exercise of sovereignty. There are different forms of limitation of sovereignty, not only with regard to the extent of the restriction of sovereign power, but also with regard to the *type of function* involved. Thus, in the latter case, there can be as many types of limitation of sovereignty as

---

[434]   Thus, in *The Lotus Case*, (1927) PCIJ A No. 9-10, the Permanent Court of Justice held that there was no clear rule of international law which allowed Turkey to exercise jurisdiction over a French ship outside its territorial waters even though the French ship had caused damage to a Turkish vessel and injury to its crew. The fact that the ship had gone into a Turkish port did not, by itself, grant Turkey jurisdiction for an incident which had occurred on the high seas.

[435]   (1960) ICJ *Reports* 6

[436]   *Cf.* my *Concept, op. cit.*, 116-177.

[437]   (1950) ICJ *Reports.*

[438]   *Supra*, in Chapter III; *cf.* Chapter V on Human Rights.

there are types of sovereign functions: thus, there can be limitation of *judicial* functions, as well as of *legislative* or *executive* functions, as well as of the power to keep *armed forces*.

(i) Judicial Competence

A treaty may, as did the Capitulations Treaties in China, give judicial powers to foreign consuls who are empowered to hear cases involving their own nationals.[439]

In the European Community, Member States limit their own judicial competence in certain matters in favour of competence of the European Court.

(ii) Legislative Competence

Treaties, such as those establishing and enlarging the European Community, may allow for the exercise of legislative functions inside a State's territory; the same Treaties even allow the exercise of sanctions over individuals in the territories of the member States.[440]

(iii) Power to Keep Armed Forces

Other treaties, again, permit foreign States to keep armed forces in the territory of another State. Because of their importance, such restrictions are invariably granted by explicit treaties.[441]

(iv) Passage or Grazing Rights

Other positive restrictions may involve, for example, grazing rights or rights of passage. Occasionally, rights of passage may, as we shall see, be claimed under general international law in the absence of treaties.

Certain restrictions are of a negative type and imply that a State

---

[439]   See my article on Unequal Treaties in *International and Comparative Law Quarterly* 1966, 1069.

[440]   See my *Law Making, op. cit.,* 258 *et seq.*

[441]   See, in detail, for military base agreement my *Independent State,* 200-219.

is bound to refrain from certain activities in its territory. Such negative duties may concern the duty to refrain from certain pollution or misuse of common waters or from other activities that endanger the global environment. In this field there is increasing pressure on States to accept not only responsibility in tort for damage incurred by other States, but also a duty, which we shall elaborate further below, not to cause damage in the first place by, for example, industrial activities which are detrimental to the environment.

CHAPTER VIII

Distributive Rules:
Areas Outside Sovereign Jurisdiction

The rules on distribution of competence between States, both in geographical and in functional terms, apportion tasks between them, albeit with some conflict of competence in some cases. Whole areas are, however, outside the competence of States at least in the sense that States may not use these areas exclusively.

One can visualise areas like the High Seas, or Outer Space as belonging to Mankind *in general*. But the cliché of the *common heritage of mankind*, so often used with environmental connotations, is too often a cloak for forcing others to share when they do not wish to share: as we have established, there is no *legal rule* that States must share, and help, other States.[1]

By leaving the question of *sharing resources* to an area of free will one might encourage statesmen to take a considerate and compassionate perspective with peoples in poorer, or less advantaged States; but if we *force* others to share, if this were at all legally possible, we know from the experiments in Eastern Europe, that we will merely preempt effective resource management. *Attitudes* to help freely are always more dynamic and effective than *constraints*.

Furthermore, precisely because only a few States are capable of exercising powers in Space, the question whether there is a *common heritage of mankind* in Space has been largely avoided, although some claim that this notion has contributed to the avoidance of appropriation of areas in Space for any particular States at the outset of spatial activities in the 1950s and 60s. I do not mean to say that the notion common heritage has not played a role in the phrasing of

---

[1]　　See my *Concept, op. cit.*, 69-70 on the distinction between sharing *common resources* and sharing *national resources;* and between absence of *duty to share* and presence of a *duty not to appropriate.*

provisions in treaties relevant to Space.[2] The usefulness of the notion is even more unrealistic with regard to Space than when it concerns the open seas or the Ocean Floor: it may sound attractive to *share all resources* but those who have the technology will not see things that way without some financial benefit to them. Nor is there any *duty to share* in any other field.[3]

Furthermore, the necessary organisation is lacking to administer any *heritage of mankind* on the High Seas or in Space. Therefore, and the legal situation in Space at present is probably only that of areas not belonging to anyone, based on the simple rule of international law on non-appropriation

It is also noteworthy that the unrealistic insistence on the nebulous concept of a *common heritage of mankind,* entailing nebulous legal consequences, especially in the field of *sharing* and in by the *subjection to an international Authority*, is actually the reason for the collapse of the UNCLOS Treaty of 1982[4] as well as of the Moon Treaty:[5] not one of the Great Powers, seafaring on the High Seas, exploiting the Ocean Floor, or active in Space, could accept these principles. Therefore, what had an emotional appeal especially to many environmentalists, proved to have devastating abortive effects in modern treaty negotiations.

Rather than seeing the areas outside sovereign States as a *common heritage*, some thus consider them to be *res nullius*, or the property of no one.[6] On the other hand, *res nullius* has one unacceptable legal consequence attached to it: it also implies a right of appropriation. But even the Romans used another category for the Open Seas, a notion which also lends itself to application in Outer Space, that of

---

[2]   It is expressly provided in the Outer Space treaty that exploration of Space is carried out for the benefit of all humanity, art.1 (1); the Moon Treaty adds to this that the Moon and its natural resources constitute a part of the common heritage of mankind.

[3]   *Cf.* my *Concept, op. cit.,* 69.

[4]   *Cf. supra* in Chapter V, on the Law of Sea Convention of 1982.

[5]   See *infra* in this Chapter.

[6]   See, Friedheim, *Negotiating the New Ocean Regime,* 1993, 12. *Cf.* Dupuy, R.J., Réflexions sur le patrimoine commun de l'humanité, *Droits,* 1985, 63.

res communis.[7] Under this notion, which was only distorted and corrupted by the common heritage concpet, the High Seas were considered as *exempt from appropriation but open to everyone's use*. No other rights or duties can be implied or derived from the notion which makes it a useful realistic concept for modern international society.[8]

On the other hand, a status of *res communis* need not mean that responsibility would not follow upon misuse or pollution, or that there would be any freedom to monopolise such resources. On the contrary, it is already established and known that no State can appropriate these areas - even if it has not adhered to any treaty on the matter. It is also clear that responsibility of States will be engaged for deliberately or accidentally polluting the open sea, for dumping hazardous material on the High Seas or for operating a satellite which falls down: in all these cases there is often responsibility and ensuing compensation without fault,[9] although we must naturally discard certain consequences under a *de minimus* rule.

A number of conventions and treaties have been concluded both with regard to the High Seas and with regard to Outer Space. But even outside these treaties States are bound to behave with a *duty of care* to these open areas. This is a legal rule for which we need not resort to the nebulous *heritage* notion.

Negligence or *fault* is not always required for liability under international law: in Space or in the nuclear field there is often *general responsibility* because of certain ultra hazardous activities that are carried out and that only may be carried out under State supervision.

I have also suggested that the duty of supervision that States have over ships flying their flag on the open seas should be extended to ensure that the ships, and the crew, are not sub-standard,[10] and that

---

[7] Dig 8.4.L.13.

[8] *Cf.* Verdross & Simma, *Universelles Völkerrecht*, 3rd ed., 1984, 698.

[9] See *The Showa Maru Arbitration* 1977 and my article, Supertankers och internationella sund, *Svensk rätt i omvandling*, 1976. For an example regarding Outer Space, note the compensation paid by USSR to Canada for space objects accidentally falling down in Canada.

[10] *Ibid., loc. cit.*

any environmental damage is compensated by the flag State, above the limits of the shipowner, the insurance, and the various international funds for damage by pollution of oil or other matters.[11] If there were such a duty of flag States, this would, on the one hand make shipowners less inclined to sail under a convenience flag. On the other hand, such a rule of responsibility would have a real beneficial effect on safety at sea and would effectively reduce particularly the danger of oil pollution by sub-standard ships.

It is necessary to recognise that responsibility of States for damage to these open areas ensues, without fault, for certain activities, such as for ultra-hazardous activities, and, as I suggest, for pollution disasters.[12]

Strict responsibility or *responsibility without fault* is the rule for *ultra-hazardous activities* in international society such as nuclear work or missions in Space. In many States such activities may only be conducted by the State and under a number of Conventions.[13] States must, at least supervise such activities.[14]

A view that areas outside sovereign States are *res communis* is also compatible with a sensible regime for the oceans[15] and especially for the Ocean Floor. Shipwrecks and minerals cannot easily be shared out. Yet, those who find, for example, minerals, and those who explore and exploit the Ocean Floor for other purposes, must obviously do so with a heightened duty of care.

i. *res communis*

a. *The Arctic*

Pharand, *The Law of the Sea of the Arctic*, 1973; *idem.*, and Legault, *The North West Passage Straits*, 1984; Dosman (ed.), *The Arctic in Question*, 1976.

---

[11] On these funds, see *ibid., loc. cit.*

[12] In this case a duty of the flag State to compensate above the limits indicated above.

[13] See, for example, the Outer Space Treaty, article 11.

[14] On duties flowing from obligations under general environmental law, see *supra* in Chapter IV.

[15] This is also the view of international relations scholars in recent works, see, Friedheim, R.L., *Negotiating the New Ocean Regime*, 1993, 12.

494

Contrary to the South Pole,[16] which has been subjected to numerous appropriation claims, [17] the Arctic does not form any land mass but is only open sea. As such it does not belong to any nation and is part of *res communis*. As it consists entirely of ice, which is merely frozen water, it consequently forms part of the High Seas and, as such, it belongs to no specific State or States.[18]

b. The High Seas

Ehmer, *Grundsatz von Freiheit im Meere und Verschmutzung*, 1974; Caflisch & Picard, Legal regime of marine scientific research, ZaöRVR 1978 848; Buzan, *Seabed Politics*, 1976; Bernhardt & Rudolf (eds.), Schiffahrtfreiheit, Ber.DGVR 1975, 15; Anand, *Legal Regime of the Seabed and Developing Countries*, 1975; Paolillo, Institutional Arrangements for International Seabed, 188 RCADI 1984, 135; Vitzthum, Recht unter See, *Festschrift Stödter*, 1979, 355; Wildberg, *Internationales Meeresbodenbehörde*, 1979.

On hot pursuit: Martens, H.L., *Das Recht der Nacheile zur See*. 1937; Williams, The juridical basis of hot pursuit, BYIL 1939, 83; Massin, La poursuite en droit maritime, 1937.

The High Seas form an area which falls outside the control and sovereignty of States. Grotius proclaimed in his famous work *de mare liberum* published in 1609 that the High Seas are open and free for all seafarers. One may think that Grotius had a clear vision of what was right for what is nowadays referred to by the hazy notion of a *common heritage of mankind* implying a right for everyone to share in common resources. But Grotius had a different motive: he was asked by his government to prove that the seas were free so that the Dutch could oust the Portugese from their advantageous trading position in the Far East. This may be a good reminder that the world

---

16   Antarctica consists of land covered with Ice, and which has been appropriated by a specific agreement of 1959 which at least precludes new proprietory claims, On Antarctica, see *infra*.

17   See *infra*.

18   The placing of flags on the North Pole has thus, in history, only had moral significance to claim the feat of having reached the Pole and has not implied any appropriation, as elsewhere, of the flag State. On acquisition of territory see above in Chapter V.

is not built on fairness alone, but sometimes, perhaps often, on the self-interests of States. It is also a good reminder that international lawyers, given an appropriate brief by a State, may encourage a biassed development of international law.

The delimitation of the High Seas is drawn from the end of claimed Economic Exclusive Zones. In this context we may remind ourselves that 'The High Seas', as a notion, is undergoing considerable changes: the *High Seas* claimed off Iceland for the United Kingdom fishermen as late as in 1974 in a case against Iceland before the ICJ, have been absorbed into the first *quarter* of Iceland's economic zone; the *High Seas* claimed by Mr Onassis against the wishes of numerous Latin American States which, according to the traditional textbooks, had made *absurd* claims of 200 miles territorial sea, now have those areas safely incorporated in their Exclusive Economic Zones, now set at 200 miles under UNCLOS and under general international law.[19]

States are not, under general rules of the Law of the Sea, allowed to do what they want on the High Seas: above all there are stringent rules preventing military installations under different agreements.[20] Furthermore, ships on the High Seas are subject to the law of their flag State.[21]

Duties may subsist under general international law for certain behaviour on the High Seas, for example with regard to duty of care to other ships or to the environment. Certain such rules apply in all waters, as extended beyond what general international law requires and including the High Seas. Rules of this type may concern safety at sea, as, for example under the SOLAS[22] Conventions which prescribe rules on lifeboats and other equipment, under the Load Line Convention,[23] which deals with the limit to which it is safe to load

---

[19]   On this development, see *supra* in Chapter V.

[20]   Treves, Military Installations on the Seabed, AJIL 1980, 808 and my Law of War, *op. cit.* 147, *et seq.*

[21]   *Supra* under Jurisdiction..

[22]   The first Safety of Lives at Sea (SOLAS) was concluded after *The Titanic* sank in 1912.

[23]   The first Convention was concluded in 1930, 135 LNTS 303.

ships, or under ILO Conventions regarding working conditions.[24]

There is also a right to intervene in the case of threatened environmental pollution, against any ship on the High Seas. This right is accorded, under general international law and may be extended under international conventions. This is, for example, the case of the Intervention Convention.[25]

There is also a right of *hot pursuit* if a ship leaves the waters of a coastal State and proceeds to the High Seas.

c. The Ocean Floor

Kronmiller, *The Lawfulness of Deep Sea Mining*, 3 vols., 1981; Post, *Deep Sea Mining and the Law of the Sea*, 1983; Brown, *Sea Bed Energy and Mineral Resources*, vols. 2 and 3, 1964-1986; Hauser, *Das rechtliche Gestaltung des Tiefseebodens nach der Seerechtskonvention*, 1982; Treves, (ed.), *Lo sfruttamento dei fondi maritimi internazionali*, 1982.

Resources of the Ocean Floor may be exploited although few States are technically able to carry out such work because of the considerable depths involved. Reluctance to accept the far-reaching provisions in 1982 Law of the Sea Convention concerning transfer of technology to assist other States, particularly those in the Third World, to exploit the Ocean Floor, was one of the reasons why the United States,[26] and many other seafaring States, refused to ratify the Convention. It should be discussed whether the insistence to *share* such technology with LDCs, as administered by a fairly independent international 'Authority', was worth the demise of the whole Convention.

On the other hand, numerous rules have, as we have seen above,[27] been accepted by States outside the contractual framework of UNCLOS as binding rules of general international law.

Assets on the Ocean Floor do not merely consist of mineral and

---

[24] *Supra* under International Labour Organisation.

[25] See *supra* under Environmental Rules on the intervention Convention and on the rights afforded under UNCLOS, in Chapter V.

[26] *Cf. supra* on the Ocean Floor and UNCLOS, in Chapter V.

[27] See *supra* on norm creation by adoption in Chapter III and on recognition of the UNCLOS rules in Chapter V.

other natural deposits. There may also be shipwrecks. That shipwrecks in international waters[28] do not necessarily lose their nationality (and certainly do not become any *res communis*) is illustrated by the *Nakhimov incident* when *The Admiral Nakhimov* was found in the open seas of the Straits of Japan. The Russian accused Japan of piracy[29] and claimed sovereign immunity for the ship; the United Kingdom did the same with regard to *The Birkenhead* which had sunk off South Africa.[30]

The highly questionable *Moratorium Resolution*[31] issued by the General Assembly in 1969,[32] pretends to limit the right to exploit the Ocean Floor and its Subsoil and sought, the following year, to repeat this obligation for States to remain passive in this area by another reminder of the *common heritage of mankind.*[33]

d. Outer Space

Matte (ed.), *Space Activities and Emerging International Law*, 1984; *idem, Aerospace Law*, 1977; *idem, Treatise on Air-Aeronautical Law*, 1981; *idem,* Aerospace Law, Telecommunications Satellites, 160 RCADI 1980 i 119; *idem, Droit aerospatial: Les télécommunications par satellites*, 1982; Jasentuliyana (ed.), *Manual on Space Law*, 4 vols., 1983; McDougal & Lasswell & Vlasic, *Law and Public Order in Space*, 1963; Christol, *The Modern International Law of Outer Space*, 1982; *idem, Space Law, Past, Present and Future*, 1991; Gorove, International Space Law in Perspective, 181 RCADI 1983 iii 349; Marcoff, *Traité de droit international public de l'espace*, 1984; Böckstiegel, (ed.), *Studies in Air and Space Law*, 1977; *idem*, (ed.), *Weltraumrecht*, 1991; Martin, *Droit des activités spatiales*, 1992; Delbruck, *Direkten Satelliten Rundfunk und nationaler Regelungsvorbehalt*, 1982; Malanscuk, Das Satellitendirektfernsehen und die Vereinten Nationen, ZaöRVR 1984, 257; Rudolf & Abmeier, Satellitendirektfunk und Informationsfreiheit AVR 1983 1; Reijnen, *Utilisation of Outer Space and International Law*, 1981; Hagelin, Prior consent to the free flow of information over international satellite radio and television, Syracuse JIL, 1981, 265; Back-Impallomeni, *Spazio cosmico e corpi celesti nel ordinamento internazionale*, 2nd ed., 1993.

28	See Münch, Schiffswracks, AVR 1982, 183; Engert-Schüler, *Eigentum an Wracks auf Hohen Meer,* 1979.
29	*Sea Changes,* 10 1989, 46.
30	*Ibid.,* 47.
31	GA Res 2574 (XXIV) 1969.
32	See *supra*, for critical comments, in Chapter IV.
33	GA Res 2749 (XXV) 1970.

(i) The Spectrum of Space Law

Outer Space activities now occupy an important place among practical problems which must be addressed by lawyers. It is no longer a question of mere academic argument.

The main difference between jurisdictional questions in terrestrial areas and in Outer Space is undoubtedly that in Outer Space it is *activities* which are regulated, rather than spatial *areas*. The way in which such activities are regulated is furthermore only fragmentary and there are many contradictions between the way certain actions are viewed by relevant space nations.

Apart from certain general principles on non-appropriation of *res communis*,[34] important sources for Space Law are found in specific treaties, especially the Outer Space Treaty of 1967. The Moon Treaty of 1979,[35] which could have implied significant development of detailed Space Law, has proved unacceptable to most States, by its insistence on the notion of *common heritage*[36] and on extensive powers of an international *Authority*.

1. DEMILITARISATION OF SPACE

Jurisdiction of States in Space is limited by the pledge, by agreement and possibly by general rules, not to militarise Outer Space. On the other hand, the demilitarisation of Outer Space does not go as far as one may be led to believe.

The Moon and other celestial bodies are demilitarised[37] but, as we are well aware of, the important space between celestial bodies is only subject to the prohibition, by treaty, concerning nuclear weapons.[38] It is important to note that, although the Partial Test Ban Treaty of 1963 and the Outer Space Treaty of 1967 both forbid the

---

[34] See *supra* in Chapter III.

[35] This Treaty entered into force in 1984.

[36] See *supra* in this Chapter and Moon Treaty, article 11:1, 11:5 and article 18.

[37] See the Outer Space Treaty of 1967 as supplemented by the Moon Treaty of 1979. See further my *Law of War, op. cit.,* on the implications of demilitarisation.

[38] Under the Outer Space Treaty.

testing and use of nuclear weapons in Space and thus leave open whether *other weapons of mass destruction*, for example, laser weapons may be used,

Any weapons can be used in Space to immobilise, for example, satellites which are extremely vulnerable targets for any hostile action. As satellites fulfil numerous functions, such as Early Warning, weather information and telecommunications, the deliberate harming of satellites can have serious consequences. Kinetic energy is inexpensive and, by standing in the path of a satellite a 'thing' can thus effectively become an ASAT, the use of which is not technically forbidden.[39]

Does *peaceful* mean merely *non-aggressive* or does it mean *non-military*? For years there was an intense dispute on this between the United States and the Soviet Union: the United States claimed that *no aggressive weapons* may be placed in Space whereas the USSR held that Space must be *entirely demilitarised.*

The question concerns different demarcations between *aggressive* and *defensive* weapons.The United States obviously argued the point in order to justify the Strategic Defence Initiative (SDI or *Star Wars*)[40] which involved the placing of a system of laser beams, direct energy and kinetic weapons, controlled partly by satellites, as a shield over the United States. The former Soviet Union rejected the right to do this under international law but was, at the same time, working on a similar system to be placed over, *i.a.*, Moscow.

A heightened duty of care applies with regard to arms in Space as no State is expected to use weapons in Space considering the impact such weapons would have on Earth itself. The Strategic Defence Initiative (SDI)[41] illustrates the difficult legal rules which, on the one hand allow States to defend themselves, but, on the other preclude a *dominant position* in the real sense of the word, for any State in Space with regard to development of technology.

A special question is concerned with the ABM Treaty of 1972,

---

[39] See my Paper on Anti-Satellites, for the Swedish Delegation to the Conference on Disarmament, 1987.

[40] See my *Law of War, op. cit.,* 144.

[41] See *supra.*

which prohibited certain long range anti-ballistic missiles.[42] There is a problem as to whether the Treaty should be interpreted extensively or restrictively to respectively include or exclude advanced technology as that used in the SDI. It would, however, seem that SDI, on balance, as directed as a shield against attack, does not violate the rights of other States in Space.

The question is now almost historic but may be revived with new force in another coalition or system of alliances and counter-alliances.[43] After the demise of communism, States succeeding the former Soviet Union, are in no position to show strength in military control of Space. However, after the greatest re-shuffle of the map of Europe after the Congress of Vienna in 1815, the recent drastic developments in 1990-1992 may, and is indeed very likely, to result in new bloc building of unexpected and unforeseeable alliances which may change the power situation in Space.

2. NON-APPROPRIATION OF SPACE

The Outer Space Treaty of 1967 provides[44] that Space cannot be appropriated by individual States by occupation nor by use.[45] The Outer Space Treaty is based on the free use and free exploration of Outer Space. The Treaty is of primordial importance to Space law. But its statement that Space cannot be appropriated by individual States does give rise to certain problems as certain States already appear to monopolise Space by their *advanced technology*; but many States are *not able* to exploit Space and to launch or operate satellites.

The distinction between the 'have' States and 'have-not' States in Space Law is evocative of the parallel, and related, distinction with regard to nuclear weapons and ballistic missiles: the same States as have superiority in one of these fields, tends to display superiority in the other area as well.

---

[42] This important Treaty was concluded by the United States and the Soviet Union at the height of the Cold War. See further my *The Law of War, op. cit.*, 144 *et seq.*

[43] On alliances and their effect, see my *Law of War, op. cit.*, 87 *et seq.*

[44] Article II. *Cf.* the Moon Treaty of 1979.

[45] On occupation see *supra.*

(ii) The Components of Space Law

1. GENERAL INTERNATIONAL LAW AND TREATY LAW

International Law, as such, has been formally incorporated into Space Law, *i.a.* by Article III of the Outer Space Treaty. In this context, we are compelled, however, to point out again [46] that States cannot avoid obligations under international law by referring to their internal national law.[47] This rule takes on special significance in Space matters.

The Swedish Act on Space Activities[48] can therefore only have limited effect. In so far as it deviates from general international law it will be devoid of effect and may even give rise to valid claims by other States. This Act prescribes that all signalling to Space must be subjected to consent of Swedish authorities. As the signalling activities are not subjected to any qualification, they obviously also include the signalling of a boy scout, with a torch, to his friend in a tree house. To formulate an Act of international importance in such a casual way would be embarrassing to the legal stringency one may have the right to expect from the Ministry of Justice which must have scrutinised, if not even drafted the law.

Numerous other basic rules of international law apply with great cogency in Space. Thus, rules concerning the use of resources and rules concerning pollution are of utmost practical importance in Space; these rules may be perceived as to some extent limiting the right of action in Space.

Rules relating to property - of utmost importance in Space - are also pertinent and Article VIII of the Outer Space Treaty consecrates the usual rule well known to all civilised systems of law, that ownership, in the event of a space object, is not affected by where it is situated. In this respect, registration[49] is *prima facie* proof of ownership, although it is the launching State - and not necessarily the actual owner - which takes care of registration. In any event,

---

[46]   See *supra* in Chapter I.
[47]   *Alabama Case Arbitration* [1872], Hudson 665.
[48]   *Lag om rymdverksamhet* 1982:923.
[49]   Under the Registration Convention of 14th January 1975, Article 2.

ownership is not affected by the presence of a space object in Outer Space or, after return to Earth, *beyond the limits of the State Party on whose registry they are carried.*

General rules on communications, such as the right of transit and passage,[50] operate with respect to space objects in various geographical contexts.

Furthermore, rules on Human Rights[51] and humanitarian law in war, or in warlike situations[52] also form specific boundaries of action in Space.

In tort situations general rules on responsibility, applicable in international law,[53] apply to assess duties of reparation.

2. RULES BY INTERNATIONAL ORGANISATIONS

Rules enacted for - or by - international organisations also form important parts of Space Law. Thus, rules emanating from organisations are, for example, those included in the basic treaties of the European Space Agency (ESA), the International Telecommunications Union (ITU), the International Civil Aviation Organisation (ICAO), the International Meteorological Organisation (IMO) or INTELSAT, INMARSAT, EUTELSAT, as well as rules enacted and contracts entered into by these organisations.

3. NATIONAL LAWS

National law may also form part of Space Law. National regulatory mechanisms affect actors of relevant nationality or domicile in their activities in Space. National rules may also be incorporated in contracts relating to Space.

With regard to national law it is important to underline, as mentioned above, that the law of a State must never be used as a

---

[50]   See *supra* in Chapter V.
[51]   See *infra* on the European Convention.
[52]   See in detail my *Law of War, op. cit.,* 271 *et seq.*
[53]   See, Catalano Sgrosso, *Responsibilità sulle ogetti spaziale,* 1990. *Cf.* my *Law of War, op. cit.,* 352 *et seq*

vehicle to avoid obligations under international law.[54] National legal systems may often be used to exclude the practical application of the international legal rules relating to Space, for example, to exclude the reception of foreign satellite broadcast. It is questionable whether such restrictions are compatible with general rules on freedom of information and freedom of expression.[55]

(iii) Harmonisation of Rules

There is a progressive harmonisation of national rules on Space and this within a host of different fields: in constitutional, administrative, civil, criminal, labour and commercial law as well as in the field of rules relating specifically to investments.

(iv) A Distinct Body of Law

The substantive rules of Space Law are found in international agreements, in national laws and in national and international contracts. These rules are supplemented, to a considerable degree, by general substantive rules applicable to Space activities, by other general rules applied *mutatis mutandis* to Space matters, by general rules on property and ownership rights,[56] by rules on international responsibility and tort, as well as by general conflict rules relevant to Space relationships.

Space law could then be said to be a conglomerate of international, national rules and some rules *sui generis*; various rules private international law are embodied, to the extent they are relevant. Space law is thus a *mélange* of various norms and rules, much in the same way as the *lex mercatoria*, the existence of which scholars disputed for a considerable time but now admit as a viable legal

---

[54]   See above on this point and *The Alabama Case*, cited above.

[55]   See *infra*.

[56]   This point may be illustrated by the fact that Article VIII of the Outer Space Treaty specifically underlines that ownership rights are not affected by where an object is situated. *Cf.* analogies with the Law of the Sea and the application, for example, of Article 12 of the Chicago Convention to the High Seas.

504

system.[57]

Space Law would appear to consist of all rules *necessary*[58] to regulate the behaviour of actors in Space and in Space matters in general. There is no question that this body of law is now a distinct body of law. It is obviously a highly dynamic legal system which is continually being expanded and developed. However, there appears to be sufficient foreseeability of relevant rules to ensure the Rule of Law (*sécurité de droit; Rechtsicherheit*).

As in the case of *lex mercatoria*, private actors play a significant part in the norm creating of Space Law. States, and/or international organisations, are by no means the only instigators or adopted rules, although States always retain their ultimate power of control of this norm forming activity.[59] In a sense, therefore, Space Law could be said to be *transnational*[60] where private actors play an increasing role commensurate with the commercialisation and privatisation of Space,[61] not only with regard to radio and television broadcasting,[62] but also with regard to future potential air transport.[63]

Specific parts of Space Law may not be commonly available, such as the practice reflected in private and commercial contracts which are not divulged to the general public.[64] Other rules are not generally available as these rules bear on national security of States.

Certain rules of the body of Space law are not easily accessible.

---

[57] See my *Law Making, op. cit.* 184-186, arguing the existence of a *lex mercatoria* and of a 'international private law' at a time when many disregarded such a body of law; and, later, Lando, *Lex mercatoria, Scandinavian Studies in Law,* 1976.

[58] *Cf.* He Quizi, *Legal Aspects of Commercialization of Space Activities,* IISL 58.

[59] *Cf. supra,* Chapter III, on the latent power of States with regard to rules adopted by other entities; see also my *Concept, op. cit.,* 96 *et seq.*

[60] *Cf.* DeSaussure, The Unification and Development of Transnational Space Law, IISL 1989, 253.

[61] See, for example, Catalano Sgrosso, International Legal Aspects of Commercialisation of Private Space Activities, IISL 1987, 251. *Cf.* Bordunov, IISL 1986, 154.

[62] See on this below under Restrictions of Jurisdiction.

[63] See, for example, Frenandez-Brital, Legal Problems of Commercial Space Transportation, IISL 1990, 30.

[64] *Cf.* Martin, *Droit des activités spatiales,* 1992.

Such rules may be included in contracts on supply or launching of satellites or referring to their modes of operation. This situation is not much different from that of national rules on contracts, where rules on validity and form of contracts are clear but the *contents* of contracts is not disclosed in situations of commercial competition.

Again, other rules relating to Space may be suppressed from the general public for national security reasons the situation in Space law is similar to those rules within a State which concern the organisation of defense where also many rules are not commonly available as they are held to be militarily sensitive.

(v) Basic Problems in Space Law

1. ISSUE AND PLACE ORIENTATION

Contrary to many other fields of international law, Space Law is specifically *issue orientated*. This means that rules tend to apply differently and tend to have different substantive contents depending on which subject is regulated. Rules are therefore often variable according to whether the matter concerns launching, navigation, pollution, right to intervene, research, broadcast and reception of television and radio information, testing objects and crew, ASATs and their testing, building in Space, construction and use of permanent stations, proprietary and intellectual rights, rights and obligations under labour law etc.

The differentiated treatment of space objects/subjects also relate to where the object/subject is situated (*place orientation*): if a space craft has landed (or its astronauts) in the territory other than the registration State, this has important legal consequences in so far as the objects are treated as if still in Space and under the jurisdiction of the registration State.[65]

The main difference between jurisdictional questions in terrestrial areas and in Outer Space is undoubtedly that in Outer Space it is activities which are regulated, rather than special geographical areas. The way activities are regulated in Space is furthermore only

---

[65]   See Articles 2 and 5 of the Rescue Agreement of 14th January 1975.

fragmentary and there are many contradictions between the way certain action is viewed by relevant space nations.

Special questions concern jurisdiction in Space or the power of States to regulate, by their own laws, behaviour in Space. Jurisdiction is closely tied to the notion of responsibility. For example, the Moon Treaty prescribes in article 12 that States retain their *jurisdiction* over spacecraft and personnel on the Moon. By such regulation, States also become *responsible* for any actions even if their operations are carried out together with international or national bodies.

2. DEFINITION OF SPACE OBJECTS/SUBJECTS

It is useful to consider a definition of the term *Space object*, possibly coupled by *Space subjects*. Many have already ventured into various attempts to define at least Space objects and proposed various criteria; it may be that a simple approach is preferable.

It is expedient to retain a wide definition of the term Space object, implying any object, launched or present in Space, except the celestial bodies themselves.

Any object, present for any (even short) length of time in Space thus qualifies as a space object. This means that also rockets and ballistic missiles are space objects *during the time that they are present in Space.*

Astronauts, who according to the terminology of many also are Space 'objects', could conveniently be called *Space subjects* to lend some dignity to man, and to distinguish astronauts from ordinary matter. Rules, however, applicable to Space objects operate, in their relevant parts, with regard to such space subjects.

Objects present in Space through involuntary or accidental action, such as space debris, are also included in our classification of space objects.

It could be argued that objects on Earth designed and intended for launching into Space are also space objects. By using a subsidiary purpose criterion (was the object made to function in Space?) one could possibly arrive at a pragmatic solution to delimit the category of objects made for presence in Space. Yet, it appears unnecessarily complicated to extend the realm of space objects beyond those which are actually present in Space and there does not seem to be actual need to extend the meaning of Space objects to this category.

Space objects have the *nationality* of the registration State. Space objects are registered in one State and have thus a *nationality*, very much in the same sense as persons, legal persons, ships and aircraft. This *nationality* will lead to a State's *jurisdiction* of the space object.[66] Furthermore, liability for damage may be linked to this nationality of the space object,[67] and this nationality may give rise to rights and duties, *i.a.* with regard to astronauts.[68]

The method of deciding whether a Space object actually comes under the jurisdiction of a specific State is, to some extent, defined by the Registration Convention. This Convention may be decisive in the sense that, if a spacecraft has been registered by a particular State, the ensuing nationality of the spacecraft will be taken to be that of the registering State. The consequences of this 'linking' of a spacecraft to a particular State are of wide economic and political importance. For example, the statement, or the assessment, that a spacecraft comes under the jurisdiction of the United States leads to the inference that patent rules will apply as if the object had been situated in the United States and the United States rules on joint and several responsibility will apply. This is indeed a matter of great practical importance.

(vi) Activities Regulated by Space Law

1. BROADCASTING

The organisation of telecommunications[69] of each State is still a matter for national decision. This is indeed sometimes called a *sovereign right*.[70] For these reasons, international regulation has sometimes been resented.[71]

---

66   Outer Space Treaty 1967, Article VIII.

67   Convention on Liability for Damage by Space Objects 1971.

68   Convention on the Recovery of Astronauts 1968.

69   Matte, *Droit aerospatial, Les télécommunication par satellites,* 1984.

70   ITU Convention 1947, Preamble, as amended; *cf.,* Codding, *The International Telecommunications Union,* 1952, 7; *cf.* my *Law Making, op. cit.,* 223 *et seq.*

71   See, for example, Hondius, Internationasl Control of Broadcasting Programs in Western Europe, in McWhinney (ed.), *The International Law of Communications,* 1971, 69.

Fixed installations for telecommunications are, on Earth, subjected to territorial jurisdiction and control. Radio transmissions themselves are, according to the older theory, also *subject to national law* of the area where they are broadcast, if such space comes within the territorial areas of another State.[72] According to another opinion *the air is free* and, therefore, no State can claim jurisdiction over radio transmissions.[73] A further opinion has been put forward that the air is a *condominium,* or, alternatively, forms part of a *common heritage of mankind,* and States should therefore share jurisdiction and rights with regard to broadcasting.[74] A fourth view is that, although the air does not belong to States, nor forms part of a condominium, its *use* should be open to all.[75]

A General Assembly Resolution 37/92 of 1982 lays down certain principles for television broadcasts from satellites but, among the truistic principles which no one would contest on, for example, peaceful settlement of disputes, we find a remarkable suggestion that States would be obliged to inform affected States and, after consultation, obtain their agreement. That such procedure would violate the freedom of information and freedom of expression and would, as a legal principle, lack general support, is fairly clear.

A certain regulatory network now exists and we may refer to the Directive on Coordination of Radio Broadcast Activities within the European Community[76] without specific Space reference European Convention on Transfrontier Broadcasting of 1989, open to non-European partners, which has still not entered into force and which only two States (one of which was San Marino) had ratified after two years. The Convention rests above all on the assurance that article 10 of the European Convention on Human Rights which guarantees freedom of expression. The Convention may have its deficiencies[77] and, as no distinction is made between direct broadcast from satellites

---

[72]   Guggenheim, 1 *Lehrbuch des Völkderrechts,* 1951, 396.

[73]   Fauchille, La télégraphie sans fil et le droit des gens, RGDIP 1906, 58.

[74]   Alexandrowicz, *The Law of Global Communications* 1971, 28.

[75]   This view would then distinguish between proprietory rights and rights of usage.

[76]   L 298/23, JO 17 10, 1989.

[77]   See on this Martin, *Droit des activités spatiales, op. cit.,* 164-167.

(SFS) and transmission through intermediaries (RDS) in the Convention,[78] one may deduce that the Convention was negotiated without much access to Space law expertise. A revision of the Convention is therefore desirable and, if there is a genuine interest in obtaining ratification by major States, such revision is to be expected.

We have earlier already dismissed the use of the notion of a common heritage of mankind, at least as any legally definable concept.[79] As far as broadcasting is concerned, there are also problems connected with any view that the air is a condominium, as State practice rather points at clear recognition of broadcasting rights as being *independent of any proprietory rights* in Space.

In other words, States regard themselves as competent and as having the right to broadcast *anywhere*. This development is not contested by any States, after the demise of communism in Eastern Europe and the decline of sovereignty centered socialist ideas elsewhere, as in Cuba and in China. Recent views on freedom of information compatible with new attitudes concerning the true and viable attributes of sovereignty are also in line with the fact that most broadcasts do not pass only through *air* but largely through areas of *Outer Space,* through satellite communications.[80] With regard to Outer Space we have already demonstrated that its use is free for all - except for military purposes.

As shown above with regard to overflight of satellites, and emphasising that these flights must be conducted with *due regard for the sovereign rights* of States, there are also pronouncements that *broadcasts* must be conducted on the basis of *respect* for sovereign rights of States.[81] As suggested above in the context of information

---

[78]   *Ibid.,* 165.

[79]   *Supra* in this Chapter and in Chapter V.

[80]   For example, Courteix, Aspects juridiques internationaux de la diffusion par satellite d'émission de télévision, *Droit et pratique du commerce international,* 1990, 550. On shortwave broadcasting see Samara, Space Law and the Development of International Business: Implementing a Satellite Sound Broadcasting Service, IISL 1990, 74.

[81]   See, for example, Principles II and IV of the UN General Assembly Resolution 41/65 adopted on 22nd January 1987, referring to Article 1 of the Outer Space Treaty for guidance and emphasising that broadcasting activities must be conducted on the basis of respect for sovereign rights of all States.

collected by overflying satellites, here to, in the context of transmitting activities, States have no right to interfere or control such broadcasts. In effect, the two activities are *linked*, as the information collected by satellite, or information sent to a satellite from an earth station,[82] is often relayed through broadcast activities. These days, when the free word is appreciated in all quarters of the world, all broadcasting activity is free and should be freely accessible in all States.[83] Restrictions can only be allowed with regard to undesirable broadcasts offensive to public morals, and which are, for example, harmful to children.[84]

The right to broadcast cannot be analysed without a comment as to the *possibility* to broadcast. This latter quality demands two *abilities*: the ability to have the technical resources to transmit and, secondly, the ability to access a band for broadcast. With regard to transmitting, there is already substantial transfer of know-how to developing countries, not all devoid of commercial interests.[85] As far as access to broadcasting bands, these are allocated by the International Telecommunications Union (ITU), one of the oldest international organisations.[86] Naturally, the interests of developing States in this allocation must be safeguarded.[87]

---

[82] For stations on land there may be restrictions imposed by the territorial State, see *supra*, in this section.

[83] See, for example, Colliard, La télévision directe par satellites, SFDI, 1977 143; Cohen-Jonathan, La libre circulation international des information par satellite, RUDI 1990, 313.

[84] Broadcasting gives rise to give and take situations where the interests of many sides must be taken into account. Naturally, clear international regulation is desirable. The recent European Convention adopted by the Council of Europe seeks to balance the interests of public morals with the general right of freedom of information.

[85] Nor is it 'wrong' that developed States and their private enterprises should develop communication networks in the Third World without proper business perspectives. The international legal order can only benefit from such action enabling developing countries to have their own broadcasts.

[86] See, in detail, for its regulatory powers, my *Law Making, op. cit.*, Chapter IV.

[87] *Cf.* article 33 of the International Telecommunication Convention as amended in 1973 and 1982, reflecting the need of developing countries to equitable access to spectrum orbit; and Article 10 of the International Frequency Registration Board; Appendix B WARC ORB. World Administration Radio Conference 85, 1988.

2. REMOTE SENSING

There are now numerous satellites crowding the geo-stationary orbit.[88] In 1976 a number of equatorial States over whose territory such satellites fly protested and requested that the spatial route was one of their *common natural resources* to which they, under numerous other agreements and declarations, have an inalienable right.[89]

Here we find an interesting juxtaposition, and conflict, of two principles equally propagated in modern international law: the principles of free use of Space and the principles of permanent sovereignty over natural resources.

The transfer or collection of information from satellites raises a number of interesting questions of sovereign power and control. For some time, there was a continuing discussion as to whether transmission of information from one country violated the legitimate interests of another State to its own *reserved domain* as understood and guaranteed in the UN Charter article 2(7).[90]

Two types of developments have changed the situation: on the one hand, article 2(7) is now understood to imply a much less wide area than when the article was drafted in 1945.[91] Secondly, the free form of information has been accepted as a natural and normal form of modern life. This latter trend has been accelerated by the advent of telecommunication satellites, as well as by the increased use of relay stations and transmission discs.

As mentioned above the notion of prior consent has been abandoned in the field of broadcasting in favour of full freedom with certain responsibility to other States. The formula prevailed longer, as

---

[88] This is the most convenient orbit for a number of satellites at the distance of 35,000 miles from Earth.

[89] Statement 8 December 1976 by Colombia, Brazil, Congo, Zaire, Uganda Kenya, Indonesia and Equatorial Guinea. On common heritage see *supra*.

[90] *E.g.*, Simma, Grenzüberschreitender Informationsfluss und *domaine réservé* der Staaten, 19 *Berichte der Deutschen Gesellschaft für Völkerrecht* 1979. 39 *et seq.* On the *reserved domain* in general, see *supra* in Chapters I and IV.

[91] See *supra* in Chapters I and IV.

a guide light, in the field of remote sensing.[92] One can only say this tentatively as no international obligations exist so far in the realm of remote sensing; an agreement in COPUOS in 1986 is merely a preliminary measure.[93] The concept of sovereignty has been used to explain a right of States to avoid the abuse of information about conditions in its territory: according to a well known Resolution of UNESCO[94] operation of satellites all collection of information must be done with *strict respect* for sovereign rights. This implies that overflown States should have *some* right to avoid information about their territory being collected and, on the other hand, that they should have *some* right to access to the information collected, whether or not this information concerns precisely their country.

On the other hand, these rights have not been formulated or expressed in terms that have any concrete legal contents,[95] and may reflect sovereign ambitions. Furthermore, the relevant information cannot be readily *located*, nor can the actors who collected the information be *identified*. The main problem in the field of remote sensing is thus that the power of States to prevent such interference with jurisdiction is even more limited than with regard to broadcasting; in the case of broadcasting it is, for example, nearly always clear *who* is broadcasting and it is relatively easy to at least propose talks or to forward protests; in the case of remote sensing, a State need not even be aware that it has been exposed to such activity and even less aware as to who carried it out.

It is unrealistic to expect States and/or and private enterprises

---

[92]   Christol, The 1986 Remote Sensing Principle; Emerging of Existing Law, IISL 1987, 268; Cocca, Legal Principles on remote Sensing from 1970 to 1986, IISL 1987, 276; Bourély, Legal Problems Posed by the Commercialisation of Data Collected by the European Remote Sensing Satellite ERS-1, *Journal of Space Law* 1988, 129; Gorove, UN Principles on Remote Sensing, Mélanges Matte, 1989, 105; Sybesma-Knol, Negotiating the UN Principles on remote Sensing of the Earth, IISL 1987, 394.

[93]   See, on this, Bordunov, IISL 1986, 154.

[94]   Res. A 2916 (XXVII).

[95]   See *supra* in Chapter III on problems connected with *crystallisation of rights and duties*.

which explore Space to collect information of various kinds, to *share*[96] the information collected with others. Without reimbursement for their costs, and possibly with some commercial gains, States and private enterprises which collect information from Space about conditions on Earth, are unlikely to let others have access to this information. As the legal situation now stands, therefore, the alleged rights of States to information about their territory in data material collected by others, are indeed hollow rights.

The conclusion must inevitably be the right States have to information from above their territory is *restricted* to a right of intervention against any plane or object in their *airspace.*[97] As for information from Outer Space, however, there exists no viable legal right for States to prevent others from collecting or publishing such information. This is an immediate consequence of the rapid technical development: as a parallel development to the territorial sea which developed symmetrically with the actual power of States to defend it, so do the legal right of States above their territory diminish with their lack of their actual control of Space.

The role of private or quasi-private actors in the field of remote sensing is striking. This has developed into an important commercial activity where French companies like SPOT-Image, or American EOSAT, and even Russian Soyuskarta, are active.

In the field of remote sensing international regulation would be welcome and useful but so far there is only the Moscow Convention of 1978 which applies between the ex-communist countries. Contrary to what one would have expected with the communist attitude to State sovereignty and prior consent, the Convention is based on Open Skies policy and full freedom of information. With regard to this Treaty there are some particularly important aspects of State succession as the treaty may not, in its integral shape have been taken over by the States in new Eastern Europe, with regard to rights and obligation.

It is now clear that States have *tacitly accepted*[98] the principle

---

[96] On lack of a duty to share, see *supra* in Chapter V and my *Concept, op. cit.,* 69-70.

[97] On the limits of the airspace of States, see *supra* in Chapter V.

[98] '... ont tacitement accepté', Reuter and Combacau, *Institutions et relations internationales,* 4th ed., 1988, 252.

514

of reciprocal surveillance of their territory by 'hostile'[99] satellites; it was this form of control that made it possible to conclude international agreements on disarmament. But, at the same time, the use of satellites also created a fear that States, and others, by an illimited use of satellites would 'impose' their culture on others.[100] Agreements on division of wavelengths have only partially resolved this question; the fears still subsist.

(vii) Sovereign Links in Space: Jurisdiction

It is common to think of jurisdiction as applying to *a sovereign territorial area*.[101] It has even been suggested that if no sovereignty is exercised over an area, then a national may be treated as if he was still in his home country.[102] On the other hand, it is now sought to establish artificial sovereign links with satellites and since 1984 American Courts tend to perceive a specific *sovereign connection between ground stations and satellites*.[103]

There is also a specific link perceived between broadcasting satellites and the territory of States and, in this second case, there is not so much a question of claims of active jurisdiction as a claim that transmissions *interfere* with jurisdictional rights of a territorial State.

Enhanced sovereign links now exist with regard to Manned Space Stations. It is obvious that once an artificial territorial construction exists, sovereign claims and sovereign competence can be more readily exercised than in the case of mobile and time-limited excursions of specific space vehicles. The Agreement for Cooperation

---

99   Reuter calls them 'adverses', *ibid., loc. cit.*

100   *Ibid., loc. cit.*

101   See further above on the connecting factors for jurisdiction.

102   *Martin v Commissioner of Internal Revenue* [1969] cited by Martin, *op. cit.*, 196-197, and his comments on this case which concerned a American seeking tax exemptions for having resided in Antartica; this residence could not, said the Court qualify as 'abroad' as the question of sovereignty in Antarctica is unsettled.

103   See further Martin, *op. cit.*, 197 on *Communications Satellite Corporation v Franchise Tax Board* [1984], and note in *Journal of Space Law* 1985, 185.

on the Manned Space Station[104] (IGA) contains provisions whereby the contracting States seek to extend their jurisdiction to the part and functions to which they have contributed, as well as to their own personnel. The agreement thus extends the jurisdiction of the participating States. *Jurisdiction*, in the text, appears to be used both in the meaning of judicial and legislative competence. New rules have been introduced for both crimes and for intellectual property; patents and copyright obviously form an important area of legal issues which are now *actual* and not merely *potential*.[105]

A certain discrepancy is found between the competence given to each State: all contracting States, except the United States, have agreed to exercise their criminal jurisdiction over their own nationals. But the United States, retaining its affection for the *effect principle*,[106] has managed to obtain the privilege that in addition to this competence of trying its own nationals, the United States may exercise criminal jurisdiction over non-US citizens if their acts have endangered the space station or its crew. There is no condition that specifically American interests should have been jeopardised or damaged. The extension of American extra-territorial jurisdiction caused considerable protests, especially on the part of the Canadian

---

[104] Agreement Among the Governments of the United States, of the Member States of the European Space Agency, the Government of Japan, and the Government of Canada on Cooperation in the Detailed Design, Development, Operation and Utilisation of the Permanently Manned Civil Space Station, signed in Washington 29th September 1988. On this see, for example, Lafferanderie, Les accords relatifs à la station international RGDIP 1989:2 311; Bourély, Les organisations de l'espace, *Jurisclasseur* DI, 1981 -.

[105] See the American Patents in Space Act of 1990 and Martin, Legal Regime of Inventions in Outer Space, IISL 1990, 74; Osterlink, The Intergovernmental Space Station Agreement and Intellectual Property Rights, *Journal of Space Law*, 1989, 23; Lafferanderie, The United States Proposed Patent in Space Legislation, *Journal of Space Law*, 1990, 1; Catalano Sgrosso, International Legal Aspects of Commercialisation of Private Space Activities, IISL 1987, 251.

[106] See *supra* in detail, on the American attitude to the effect principle, and for criticism of extended rights of jurisdiction, in this Chapter.

516

Government.[107]

In a sense, regulation of American jurisdictional competence under the Manned Space Station Agreement, goes even further than the effect principle and approximates a *stewardship principle.* In other words, the United States claims to be speaking *for all* in the case of damage or injury suffered by *anyone.*

In terms of international legal theory, the stewardship notion is most interesting. In a sense, the role of a *steward* comes near the field of *common heritage of mankind* and its administration.[108] However, as we have seen above, the common heritage notion is vastly exaggerated and has too often served as a cloak for sovereign interests of one or some State(s). Even if we do not recognise any general notion of a common heritage of mankind - or allow such a notion to have a strictly limited contents - the stewardship notion could be linked to another concept of great importance in international society, namely that of *international solidarity.* There is a distinct similarity of thinking in terms of *speaking for international society*, as a *steward*, and *international solidarity* which, according to our own theory, may form one of the legal basis of obligation of rules of international law.[109]

Thus, a breach of any *fundamental rule* of international law appears to trigger an obligation on behalf of *all States* to condemn the State that violated the rule. *Any* State is thus entitled to protest and a duty for all States *to recognise the illegality of a situation* may be activated.[110]

---

[107]   On this see Dubois, Mouvements transfrontières: biens, personnes et technologies, *Report to the Government of Canada,* 1991, 18 and, for the Canadian position on extra-territorial jurisdiction, Fried, L'application extraterritoriale des lois et les politiques canadiennes et américaines en matière d'extraterritorialité, 3 *Revue québecoise de droit international* 337; Stern, Quelques observations sur les règles internationales relatives à l'application extraterritoriale du droit, AF 1986, 7.

[108]   See above on the relationship of this notion and Outer Space.

[109]   See my *Concept, op. cit.,* 124-128.

[110]   *Ibid.,* 128 and *The Namibia Case* [1971] *Advisory Opinion* ICJ *Reports* 54 and the *Frozen Assets Case* settled in 1980 where it was argued that a duty to condemn violations of immunity of American diplomatic personnel was incumbent on all States; *cf. Hostage Case* [1981] ICJ *Reports* 1.

It is possibly warranted that the United States, with its considerable input in Space activities, both with regard to funding and to technical expertise, should have a decisive role to play with regard to jurisdiction. It may have looked more attractive if a stewardship role had been granted to an agency, (even to NASA),[111] or to an international organisation, or at least in conjunction with some other State or States, rather than to an individual government. On the other hand, it may be in the interest of all that there is sufficient basis for exercise of jurisdictional competence in the case where other participating States might waive rights of jurisdiction.

(viii) Institutional Cooperation

Jurisdictional competence which States would otherwise enjoy, may have been curtailed by the actitivies of an international organisation to which States have already delegated certain powers.

In some case, however, bodies set up by States have a mere consultative role and are deprived of any power of decision or of any operational powers with regard to the launching or operation of space objects. One such 'weak' body is, within the United Nations, COPUOS. This Committee may have contributed to a certain extent to the interest in peaceful space activities. However, its work has not left any noticable mark, nor does it appear to have given any particular incentive to carry out research.

The Chicago Convention under which the International Civil Aviation Organisation (ICAO), exercises its regulatory powers, only concerns the *atmospheric space* and is thus not applicable to Outer Space objects. In itself, the Organisation could form a model for a future regulatory international organisation for Outer Space. ICAO may have extremely wide powers[112] it decides, for example, about the extent of its own competence.[113] Yet, its activities so far have proved extremely successful as a model for a technical organisation designed to provide efficient cooperation between States. The way ICAO exercises its regulatory function is a model for an anti-

---

111   *I.e.* to the United States national agency for space matters.

112   See, my *Law Making, op. cit.*, Chapter IV, on the powers of ICAO.

113   See article 12 of the Chicago Convention.

bureaucratic and efficient use of powers, yet submitted to checks and crosschecks to ensure that organisational competence is not abused.[114] The ICAO for model appears suitable in the field of Space Law. A similar organisation to ICAO could possibly contribute to convenient regulation of certain space activities.

The European Space Agency, (ESA), on the contrary, has taken a special interest in analysis of space activities from a legal point of view and, by its creation of the European Space Law Centre (ESLC), actively promoted interest in Space Law.

Other organisations, like Intelsat, Inmarsat and Eutelsat, are, as indeed ESA itself, largely operational agencies, devoted to launching and operation of space objects.

A special position in Space matters is occupied by the International Telecommunications Union, (ITU), which is charged with certain distribution of wavelengths of paramount importance to the communication systems between satellites and Earth stations as well as the operational bands that satellites use for the path through Space.[115]

ii. *res communis* Subjected to National Claims: Antarctica

Watts, *International Law and the Antarctic Treaty System*, 1992; Dupuy, R.J. & Mouton, The international regime of the Polar regions, RCADI 1963 iii 175; Guyer, The Antarctic system, RCADI 1973 ii 149; Battaglini, *La condizione dell'Antarctico nel diritto internazionale*, 1972, Bermejo, *L'Antarctique et ses ressources minerales: le nouveau cadre juridique*, 1990; Beurier, Le droit de la mer dans l'Antarctique, RevJurEnv 1989, 5; Peterson, M.J., Antarctic implications of the New Law of the Sea, Ocean Dev & ILJ 1986 1; Van der Essen, Les régions arctique et antarctiques, in Dupuy & Vignes, *Traité du nouveau droit de la mer*, 1985, 463; Orrego Vicuna & Infante, Le droit de la mer dans l'Antarctique, RGDIP, 1980, 340; Luard, Who owns the Antarctic? ForAff 1984, 1175; Labouz, Les aspects strategiques de la question de l'Antarctique, RGDIP 1986, 3.

On the various treaties see, Watts, cited *supra* and on the Treaty of Washington, Dupuy, R-J., AFDI, 1960, 111; Simmonds, JDI 1960, 669; Van der Essen, Des réunions consultatives dans l'Antarctique, RBDI, 1980, 20; on the Convention of Canberra, Vignes, AFDI 1980, 741; on the Convention of Wellington, Couratier,

---

114   See my *Law Making, op. cit., passim.*

115   See my *Law Making, op. cit., loc cit.*

AFDI 1988, 764.

Although the High Seas and Outer Space lend themselves as areas to be conceived as belonging to no one, Antarctica appears to be an area held in common by numerous States. The area does not by any means *belong* to these States, or to any other States. However, some States, or their explorers, had some early interest in this area and, after a certain time, it would seem reasonable to allow these States some priority.

Antarctica represents a twentieth of the earth; it also represents nearly 60 per cent of the freshwater supplies in the world. The land mass under the ice is known to contain vast deposits of valuable minerals. This may explain why Antarctica is of considerable strategic and economic importance.

The importance of Antarctica is reflected by the Falklands War which was conducted, at least partially, to safeguard certain claims to Antarctica. The United Kingdom sector of the South Pole is calculated precisely with reference to the position of the strategically important island of South Georgia, which played a key role in the Falklands War.

Various theories have been invoked to substantiate territorial claims to Antartica. Before the Congress of Berlin in 1885 *discovery* was the most common form of title to new territory.[116] After this date, the theory of discovery was abandoned, and another theory, that of *effective occupation* introduced. Some States adopted other ideas, mainly for their own self interest: so would Chile rely on its territorial rights in Antarctica because of a theory of *contiguity*[117], implying that the claimed territory is geographically near the claiming State.

In Antarctica, a special theory of *sectors* has evolved and this solution is based on partition according to earlier interest areas. Both the sector idea and the theory of discovery were used in 1955 when the United Kingdom took Argentina and Chile to the International Court of Justice over territorial claims in Antarctica. But neither of the defendants recognised the jurisdiction of the Court and the ICJ

---

[116] See *supra* in Chapter V.

[117] Note that similar ideas were adopted by Argentina to defend claims to the Falklands Islands.

struck off the action. During the later years of 1950's there was some considerable tension among States interested in the area as there were more and more discoveries (or assumptions) of wealth in the area. Eventually it became obvious that territorial claims had to be regulated by a forceful treaty.

The Washington Treaty on Antarctica was concluded in 1959 and entered into force in 1961. The original Contracting Parties were Argentina, Australia, Belgium, Chile, France, Japan, New Zealand, Norway, South Africa, the Soviet Union, United Kingdom and United States. The Treaty provides for partial internationalisation of the area. It is partial only in so far as it applies between the contracting parties and not *erga omnes*, that is to say in relation to third parties in general.[118] The system essentially grants privileges to States having territorial claims themselves in Antarctica. The Washington Treaty, which was concluded for thirty years, introduced a static regime which prohibits new claims of sovereignty during the validity of the Treaty. The territorial regime was thus, in for the region appropriate words, effectively *frozen*.

States are, under the Treaty, not permitted to rely on activities during this time to substantiate further any territorial claims. In other words, the claims will rest as they were when the Treaty entered into force, and will last beyond the validity of the Treaty. In this sense, later agreements have taken over the attitude that little must change in Antarctica.[119]

Furthermore, Antarctica is, under the Washington Treaty, demilitarised. This regime of demilitarisation survived through what some called 'The Second Cold War'[120] between the Superpowers, as well as the *Beagle Channel Dispute* between Chile and Argentina[121] and the Falklands War in 1983.

The Treaty provides specifically for cooperation in the field of

---

[118] For the benefit of Swedish students: the Swedish equivalent would be *med sakrättslig verkan*.

[119] See *infra* on, for example, the Treaty of London.

[120] See Halliday, *The Second Cold War*, 1986.

[121] This affair gave rise to famous Arbitration where Pope John Paul II mediated in 1978 between the two sides to obtain a mutually satisfactory settlement signed in the Vatican in 1984. *Cf. supra*.

research. However, obligations are undermined by the safety catch that apparent duties must be carried out *in so far as this is possible*, a formula which leaves complete freedom to do nothing to cooperate. There is, in this respect, not much loyalty between the treaty Parties.

On the other hand, the Antarctica regime is a *closed system*: it is not open to other States unless they have the approval of the earlier Contracting Parties to join. Six States have been added to the original States since 1959, namely Germany, Poland, Brazil, India, China and Uruguay. The privileged parties, that is to say the original twelve and the additional six States, vigorously defend their interests and have so far refused to allow a more open regime where more States participate. The General Assembly eventually took note of the tension and, hoping for wider settlement, adopted a Resolution[122] in 1983 to ask the Secretary General for further studies on the question.

The Treaty of Washington is supplemented by the Treaty of London of 1972 which concerns the protection of seals and which reserves the hunting right of the Contracting Parties. New States can adhere but, in this regime too, the original parties must all consent.

The Washington Treaty is also supplemented by the Treaty of Canberra of 1980, which mainly concerns the marine flora in Antarctica.[123]

With regard to the rigid distinction of the 'haves' and the 'have-nots', the Antarctica regime is reminiscent of the Nuclear Proliferation Regime[124] by which the circle of those which have atomic weapons cannot be enlarged. Considering some geographical absurdities - that give far away countries priority to Antarctica - it may be suggested that the Antarctic Treaty should be re-negotiated giving some lee way to some States which are neighbours of Antarctica, to make claims on the basis of geographical connexity.[125]

---

[122] Resolution 33'77.

[123] This Treaty establishes an international Commission to elaborate further proposals for the protection of living species.

[124] Under the Nuclear Proliferation Treaty of 1968 see my *Law of War, op. cit.,* 91 and 201 *et seq.*

[125] Such theories are sometimes resisted by the United Kingdom on the ground that such ideas may encourage Spain to make renewed claims to Gibraltar or (before the Hong Kong Treaty) of China to Hong Kong. It is better, however, to tackle such a theory head-on and acknowledge that by allowing some claim

In a sense, the Antarctic regime is somewhat anachronistic, allowing claims made long ago by States in other parts of the world, in an almost colonial context. The only difference between colonisation in other parts in the Third World is that Antarctica lacks a population which is dominated by the occupying States. In Antarctica the only object of claims is the territory - and the minerals which are expected to lie under the ice.

on the basis of geographical connexity one may actually safeguard other positions.

CHAPTER IX

Consequential Rules

Consequential rules are those which safeguard the application of other *binding* main rules. Thus, consequential rules ensure that *prophylactic* and *stabilising* rules are maintained in the international society. There are serious shortcomings in the formal settlement of disputes in so far as States may not be forced to appear before Courts unless they have at some stage agreed to do so. However, there are other ways of applying pressure on law breakers in the international society, for example by applying sanctions. On the other hand, more and more States now agree to submit to the jurisdiction of the International Court or to arbitration.

i. The Nature of the Obligation

See my own *Concept of International Law*, 1987, Part IV; Verdross, Die *bona fides* als Grundlage des Völkerrechts, *Gegenwärtige Probleme des Internationalen Rechts, Festschrift für Laun*, 1952, 20; *idem*, Le fondement du droit international, 16 RCADI 1927, 247; *idem*, Zum Problem des völkerrechtligen Grundnorm, *Festschrift Wehberg*, 1956, 385; Walz, *Wesen des Völkerrecht und Kritik der Völkerrechtsleugner*, 1930; Finnis, *Natural Law and Natural Rights*, 1980; Manning, *The Nature of International Society*, 1962; Le Fur, La théorie du droit naturel depuis le XVIIe siècle et la doctrine moderne, 18 RCADI 1927, 259; Allott, Language, Method and the Nature of International Law, BYIL 1971, 79; Bos, *Methodology of International Law*, 1984; *cf.* McDougal and Reisman, *International Law in Contemporary Perspective*, 1981; Schachter, Towards a theory of international obligation VirgLR 1968, 300; Brierly, *The Basis of Obligation in International Law and Other Papers*, 1958.

Because international law is binding, certain consequential rules will be activated *in case of a violation of an obligation under international law.*

The *basis of obligation*, that is to say the *reason* why there is an obligation at all, appears to be *variable.* Thus, the basis of obligation in the case of treaties may well be merely contractual, as it is in the case of ordinary situations under national laws; parties then rely, in all legal systems on the maxim *pacta sunt servanda*, that is to say agreements must be kept, without which rule no legal system can function.[1]

With regard to other rules, however, the basis of obligation may be found elsewhere. The reason why the rule *pacta sunt servanda* itself is binding is, I have suggested, because of simple logical necessity;[2] no legal system can function without the simple maxims.[3]

Other rules of international law, like those forbidding force and other *prophylactic rules*, like those which deal with Human Rights, might be binding because, I have proposed, *social necessity*, as no legal society can survive unless such rules carry legal obligations and engage consequential rules in case of violation.[4]

If we then establish that international law is *binding* and that the basis of obligation is *variable*, the next focus is to consider what *types of violations* that may occur in international society. It appears that there are a number of variations. An act may involve the violation of the interests of another State in which case that State may be willing to excuse the violation or to settle the matter in some amicable way, or alternatively, agree on certain conditions with regard to compensation or other requests. A similar situation arises when the act of a State has infringed upon the legal interests of several States.

If, on the other hand. the violation is of a general rule, for example, concerning Human Rights, no other single State, and no other group of States, is competent to exculpate or excuse such a violation. This is so for the mere reason that there is no necessary identity between victims and potential exculpators. In other words, violations of fundamental Human Rights offend the dignity of specific individuals and the harm done cannot be wiped out by a State, or some States, condoning what has happened.

A crime involving violation of fundamental Human Rights is thus opposable *erga omnes*, that is to say, there has been a violation of the very fabric of the legal system to such an extent that the violation is

---

[1] See my *Concept, op. cit.,* 49 on the maxim and 122 *et seq.* on A Variable Basis of Obligation.

[2] My *Concept, op. cit., loc. cit.*

[3] See *supra*

[4] My *Concept, op. cit.,* 122.

held committed against *everyone*.

The consequence of this is that, in the case of such serious violations of international law, all States have a special duty of *solidarity* to uphold and defend the international legal system.[5]

The International Court of Justice has emphasized the importance of solidarity in several cases and has, on numerous occasions, underlined that fundamental rules of international law are binding *erga omnes:* let us here mention the *Namibia Case*[6] and the *Barcelona Traction Case*.[7]

We shall see that certain specific consequential rules are activated when and if there is a violation of international law. These rules are of two kinds, the first group concern the administration of justice in the formal sense: these rules provide how and by which means international disputes can be settled. The second group of rules concern material consequences, *i.e.* sanctions or punishment which will incur to rectify an illegal situation.

It is most important, however, to insist that the operation of the international legal system and the nature and force of legal obligations under that system is in no way dependant on the existence of effective sanctions. We may compare the situation to a national legal system; even if it not always possible to arrest a murderer, this does not imply that murder is not forbidden. In the same way, in international society, there are instances when culprits are not punished and when States, or individuals have violated international law, without seemingly having incurred any consequences. In this context, however, it is worth noting that such consequences may come late, and there are also many non-legal consequences which may ensue and by which a law breaker may find itself to have, for example, lost, as a consequence of his ill-doings, any willing trading partners.

The violation of international law normally results in a *dispute* between another State, or other States, and a State that has broken the

---

5   See my *Concept, op. cit.,* 124.

6   (1971) *Advisory Opinion* ICJ *Reports* 1971, 54; and, further, my *Concept, op. cit.,* 124 *et seq.*

7   (1970) (Second Phase) ICJ *Reports* 1970, 3 at 32; *cf. Hostages in Teheran Case* (1980) ICJ *Reports* 1980, 26; and, further, my *Concept, op. cit.,* 127.

law. In many cases, all parties to a dispute have violated their obligations under international law. In other cases, again, there is a dispute before any rule has been violated. In this case prompt settlement of the dispute may preempt that force is used or other obligations violated. However, even if rules have already been broken, amicable settlement will prevent escalation of the problem. Therefore, rules on settlement of disputes are among the most important provisions of international law as they comprise important peace preserving mechanisms: once a dispute is settled the *raison d'être* of war or other hostilities or unfriendly acts is diminished.

ii. Peaceful Settlement of Disputes

Reuter, Obligation de négocier, *Hommages Morelli* 1975, 711; Bedjaoui, Règlement pacifique des différends africains, AFDI 1972, 85; Basdevant, La place et le rôle de la justice dans les relations entre Etats et à l'égard des organisations internationales, AE 1958, 331; Dupuy, *Présentation systématique de la justice internationale*, IHEI, 1966; Stone, *Legal Controls of International Conflict*, 1954; Bailey, *Peaceful Settlement of Disputes*, 1971; Waldock, (ed.), *International Disputes*, 1972; Delbez, *Les principes généraux du contentieux international*, 1962; Bowett, Contemporary Developments in Legal Technique in the Settlement of Disputes. RCADI 1983 ii 169.

Under the Charter of the United Nations, Members are obliged under article 2(3) to settle their disputes peacefully so that international peace and justice are not endangered. This provision no doubt reflects general international law.[8] Some have, however, interpreted this obligation to imply that Member States must, if they settle disputes, do so peacefully, but that they are not obliged to settle disputes at all.[9] However, that conclusion is to deprive the provision of its *rationale*: surely there is, albeit vague, undertaking by Member States of the United Nations to take some steps towards settling their disputes. It may be conceded though that the legal obligations to do so is severely undermined by the way the article is phrased, much along the hollow contracts or conventions which stipulate that something must be done 'as far as possible'.

Certain concrete mechanisms are obviously helpful when States

---

[8]   See *supra* in Chapter III.

[9]   Dixon, *Textbook, op. cit.*, 161.

do decide to settle disputes and the very existence of a convenient machinery can sometimes encourage precisely that States do take some positive action.

a. Fact Finding Commissions

Politis, Les commissions internationales d'enquête, RGDIP 1912, 149; Hyde, The place of commissions of inquiry and conciliation treaties in the peaceful settlement of international disputes, BYIL 1929, 96; Al-Baharna, Fact Finding Missions of the UN Secretary General in Bahrain, ICLQ 1973, 541; Bar-Yacoov, *Handling of International Disputes by Inquiry,* 1974.

Fact-finding commissions, established under an already existing treaty, or created *ad hoc*, can be of great importance to *preempt* a full-scale conflict. Many times the parties to a potential dispute will, in the face of objective facts and reports brought to their attention, be ready to find a speedy and reasonable settlement. The duties of lawyers in this respect are considerable: here we are not speaking of individuals who consult a lawyer on a private matter but we are speaking of States, which, with their war machines, can resort to armed force and cause great loss of life, at the advice of the international lawyer.

b. Negotiation

Bindschedler, Obligation zu Verhandlungen und Konsultationen, *Festschrift Huber* 1981, 533.

Parties involved in a dispute, whether or not this be a dispute about a matter laid down in a treaty, are under a basic duty in international law to negotiate to resolve the dispute and come to a settlement. The duty of *negotiation* flows from the obligations under the Charter, and under general international law, to solve disputes with peaceful means. Naturally, the parties involved in a dispute are best equipped themselves to come to a mutually acceptable settlement.

A duty of *negotiation* is also a consequence of treaties falling behind technical or political developments which make a *revision*

528

necessary.[10] Numerous textbooks refer to an alleged rule that a *change of fundamental circumstances* or the rule *rebus sic stantibus* may entitle a State to withdraw from a treaty.[11] This spurious rule has been introduced in recent history to enable States to retract, somewhat dishonourably, from their legal engagements. This rule has thus been used as a cloak for unwarranted claims of States not to honour a treaty. Yet the actual position in law is that no treaty is void under the clause *rebus sic stantibus* but that this clause is merely a ground to demand *revision by negotiation*: consequently, there is pronounced duty of re-negotiation of texts.[12]

c. Mediation, Conciliation and Good Offices

Wehberg, Die Vergleichkomissionen im modernen Völkerrecht, *Festgabe Makarov*, 1958; Schücking, Das völkerrechtliche Institut der Vermittlung, 1923; Virally, La médiation de M. Enrique Iglesias sur l'application par années 1988-1992 de l'accord de pêche franco-canadien du 27 mars 1972, AF 1987, 807; Ricsti, La médiation, Thèse Paris, 1939.

Evremoff, La conciliation internationale, RCADI 1927 iii; Neuhold, *Internationale Konflikte, Verbotene und erlaubte Mittel ihrer Austragung,* 1977; Rolin, L'heure de la conciliation comme mode de règlement pacifique des litiges. AE 1957 iii 3; Vulcan, *La conciliation dans le droit international actuel,* 1932; Revel, Rôle et caractère des commissions de conciliation, RGDIP 1931, 564; Cot, *La conciliation internationale,* thèse Paris, 1965; *Cf.* Colliard, Le règlement des différends dans les organisations intergovernementaux de caractère non-politique, *Mélanges Basdevant,* 1952.

Bindschedler-Robert, Bons offices en politique étrangère suisse, in Riklin (ed.) *Handbuch des schweizerischen Aussenpolitik,* 1975, 679; Pechota, *The Quiet Approach, A Study of the Good Offices Exercised by the UN Secretary General in the Cause of Peace,* 1972.

---

10   See my *Essays on the Law of Treaties,* 1967, 99 and *supra.*

11   The argument is that every treaty is concluded with a silent clause that, should fundamental circumstances alter, the parties are no longer bound. The argument falls on the subjective qualification as to *who* is to decide that there has been such a radical change since the conclusion of the treaty, see *supra* under Treaties, in Chapter III.

12   See further *supra.*

In many cases a dispute situation is too infected for the involved parties to negotiate directly with each other to find a settlement. In such cases, a third party may be of assistance to make contacts and to propose an acceptable solution.

Mediation and *conciliation* are terms which are often used as synonyms in international law. If there is any nuance between *mediation* and *conciliation* it is possibly that *mediation* concerns a mere go-between function whereas *conciliation* implies actual positive efforts to bridge differences between the parties involved in a dispute.[13]

A settlement proposed by a third party by mediation or conciliation is not by itself legally binding. A proposal made by a third party must be seen in the light of such a party having offered its *assistance* by proposing a concrete and practical solution. It is the lack of obligation of a proposed settlement which is the hallmark of mediation and conciliation. It is this feature which distinguishes mediation and conciliation from binding arbitration or other forms of judicial or quasi-judicial settlement.[14]

Good Offices, on the other hand, is not a type of substantive settlement but rather a form of *mechanism* or *method* used to obtain results in the form of a settlement by mediation or conciliation. There are other forms of contacts in order to secure such an aim, such a diplomatic *démarches*[15] or offer *notes*. In other words, a third party may use its own initiative and offer his Good Offices to mediate.

Mediation can often successfully be carried out through a neutral third party. States which could have exercised this function have sometimes been most reluctant to be involved and have not accepted the responsibility. Whereas Switzerland often has volunteered its mediation, Sweden has not, to the disappointment of those who knew matters could have been resolved, had that neutral country taken a more courageous stance.

States have, on the whole, been keener to send representatives of

---

[13]   One may suggest that the *consultation* procedures in GATT, under article XXII are reminiscent of conciliation procedures, for which GATT provides *panel.*

[14]   See further *infra.*

[15]   See Seidl-Hohenveldern, *Völkerrecht*, 1987, 366 No. 1709.

the United Nations, or of the European Community, to mediate. Naturally, a Secretary General of the calibre of Dag Hammarskjöld, could be most successful in such negotiations. However, we have seen some disastrous results when other officials have not been capable of taking on the task that States had given them.

Mediation may be *prospective*[16] to preempt a possible dispute but it would, in relation to fact finding commission, intervene at a chronologically later stage and when the dispute has deepened into a two-sided entrenched conflict.

Organisations may designate not only their own officials but also third parties to mediate. In the case of the United Nations, for example, a cousin of the King of Sweden, Count Folke Bernadotte, was invited to mediate in Palestine by the Secretary General.[17]

The Pope has, throughout history, often acted as a mediator. One of the most successful mediations in modern international law was the proposed settlement of Pope John Paul II in the aggravated and protracted *Beagles Channel Dispute* between Chile and Argentina in 1978.[18]

d. ad hoc Arbitration

Raeder, *L'arbitrage international chez les Hellènes*, 1912; Carlston, *The Process of International Arbitration*, 1946; Nantwi, *The Enforcement of International Judicial Decisions and Arbitral Awards in Public International Law*, 1966; Lammasch, *Die Schiedsgerichtbarkeit in ihrem ganzen Umfänge*, 1914; Sohn, The function of international arbitration to-day, 108 RCADI 1963 i.

The *ad hoc* settlement of disputes by arbitration was common in the

---

[16]   *Cf.* Virally, La médiation de M. Enriques Iglesias sur l'application pour années 1988-1992 de l'accord de pêche franco-canadien du 27 mars 1972, AF 1989 807.

[17]   Count Bernadotte was subsequently tragically murdered in Palestine, an event which gave rise to the famous *Reparation for Injuries Case*, (1949), ICJ *Reports* 174. *Cf. supra* under Jurisdiction, in Chapter VI.

[18]   See Dustin & Pire, *La Politique selon Jean Paul II*, 1993, 131, also on mediation in the Falklands War; *cf.* Brouillet, AFDI 1979, 47. *Cf.* mediation by Pope Leon XIII with regard to the dispute between Germany and Spain on the Caroline Islands in 1885 and *supra*. *Cf. supra* in Chapter V on the *uti possedetis* principle.

Middle Ages, often by one single arbitrator. During the 19th century numerous treaties were concluded to resume this practice, and now often to include three arbitrators, often appointed by each of the parties and the third one by the two already elected.

During the era of frequent semi-institutionalised arbitrations of the last century, arbitrators either functioned *ad hoc* or were members of a specially constituted Mixed Commission for a series of similar cases. Numerous agreements to settle disputes by arbitration were concluded after the First and Second World Wars. Some dealt with claims resulting from war damage and others have been concerned with compensation claims for nationalisation. In recent years, numerous arbitrations have dealt with investment disputes or disputes about nationalisations.[19]

An arbitral award is binding[20] and, unless the parties have agreed or submitted to appeal procedures,[21] final. There may be ways to introduce actions for nullity for procedural anomalies.[22] Although it is not always possible to execute an arbitral award, it is striking that inter-state arbitration by *ad hoc* tribunals are normally implemented.[23]

e. Arbitration by Permanent Courts

Bastid, S., L'arbitrage international, JC 245; de Taube, Les origines de l'arbitrage international, RCADI 1932 iv; François, La Court Permanente d'Arbitrage, 87 RCADI 1955 i 457; Brintzinger, Die Tätigkeit des Ständigen Schiedshofes in Den Haag, JIR 1961-1962, 264.

At the Hague Peace Conference, convened by Czar Nicholas II in 1899, a Convention on the Pacific Settlement of Disputes, was adopted. A Protocol was added at the subsequent Peace Conference

---

[19]   *Texaco v Libya* (1977) 53 ILR 389; *Aminoil Case* (1982) 21 ILM 976; *Jalapa Railway Claim* (1948) 8 Whiteman 908; *Amoco Finance Case* (1987) 15 US CTR 189.

[20]   *Interpretation of the Treaty of Lausanne* (1925) PCIJ Series B No. 12.

[21]   As in the *Irish Sea Arbitration* (1987), see Zoller, AFDI 1978 327.

[22]   See *Guinea Bissau v Senegal* (1991) ICJ *Reports* 1. *Cf. The King of Spain Award Case* (1960), 192.

[23]   *Cf.* conclusion by Dupuy, P-M, *Droit international public*, 1993, 387.

in 1907. Under these agreements a Permanent Court of Arbitration was established to which States could submit their differences for legal settlement. But the Court is *permanent* only in name: it functions on the basis of a list of arbitrators that may be selected in individual cases; the list is administered by a secretariat. The Court is thus permanent only in terms of an existing flexible framework.

It is to be noted that the International Bureau of the Permanent Court of Arbitration issued Rules for arbitration (or conciliation) for disputes where one party is not a State.[24] This is a useful reminder of many other entities than States are actors in international society and in need of settlement of their disputes on the same level as States.

On the basis of a separate arrangement between Iran and the United States provided for numerous cases to be settled by a *special arbitration tribunal*, the United States-Iran Claim Tribunal, in the Hague after the Hostage Crisis in 1980. This Tribunal has already adjudicated in thousands of disputes, and there are still thousands of cases pending.

Some organisations provide a *setting* and a *mechanism* for arbitration, of which parties can avail themselves when they so desire. One example of such arrangements is the International Chamber of Commerce in Paris[25] and the Centre for the Settlement of Investment Disputes.[26]

f. Judicial Process by Courts

(i) The Judicial Function

The difference between arbitration tribunals and courts is not easy to draw. It may be suggested that a court is designed to decide questions by continuous reference to a full legal system, whereas arbitration tribunals are requested to decide matters by the limiting terms of

---

[24]   See my *Finance and Protection of Investment in Developing Countries*, 2nd ed., 1985, 124.

[25]   See my *Finance and Protection, op. cit.*, 124-125, on details concerning types of claimants and types of disputes before the ICC.

[26]   *Ibid.*, 123, 127.

reference of the parties.[27]

International law is marked by its absence of a legislator, an executive and a judiciary.[28] However, what Scelle called the *judicial function*[29] is execised by a number of important courts.

The judicial function is exercised by a number of courts. In the field of individuals, the role of the European Court of Human Rights, safeguarding the respect for Human Rights in Europe, is of paramount importance.[30] International organisations have their own administrative tribunals dealing with staff matters.[31] The European Community has a court with such intense out-flow of cases that the legal relationship of Member States, firms and individuals, within its ambit is continuously illuminated by finer and finer nuances.[32]

The actions of these courts are interrelated and often one court will cite the award of another. The Court of the European Community (EC), now the European Union (EU), has, for example, expressly integrated all the case-law of the European Court on Human Rights to form part of EU law, under judgments of the EU Court.[33]

This is not the place to describe the detailed functioning of these courts and tribunals. However, to view the impact of the work of the World Court, the ICJ, to which we shall give some attention, its position must be seen against other judicial organs, which all, with appropriate respect, rely on various statements, judgments, and opinions of the ICJ as laying down what international law provides.

(ii) The International Court of Justice (ICJ)

McWhinney, *The World Court and the Contemporary International Law-Making Process*, 1979; Mosler & Bernhardt (eds.), *Judicial Settlement of International Disputes*, 1974; Waldock, Aspects of the advisory jurisdiction of the International Court of Justice, BYIL 1974; Rosenne, *The Law and Practice of the International*

---

[27] But note that the ICJ can be asked to make a *'compromis'*, very much on the same lines as if it were an arbitration tribunal, see *infra* under the ICJ.

[28] See further in Chapter I.

[29] *Précis de droit des gens*, 1932-34.

[30] See *supra* under the Council of Europe in Chapter II.

[31] See my *Law Making, op. cit.*, Chapter II.

[32] See *supra* on the EC in Chapter II.

[33] See *supra* under Human Rights in Chapter IV.

Court, 1965; *idem, The World Court,* 3rd ed., 1973; Fitzmaurice, The law and practice of the International Court, BYIL 1950 1; 1951 1; 1952 1; 1953 1; 1954 371; 1955-1956 20; and 1957 203; Dubisson, *La Cour internationale de justice,* 1964; Lissitzyn, *The International Court of Justice,* 1951, reissued 1972; on the Optional Clause, see Waldock, The decline of the Optional Clause, BYIL, 1956, 244.

On the procedure, see Lachs, The revised procedure of the International Court of Justice, in *Essays in Memory of Panhuys,* 1980 21; Oellers-Frahm, Die Verfahrungsordnung des Internationalen Gerichtshofes vom 14. April 1978, ArchVR 1979-1980 309; on interim measures of protection, see Oellers-Frahm, *Die einstweilige Anordnung in der internationalen Gerichtsbarkeit,* 1975; *eadem,* Interim Measures of Protection, 1 Encyclopedia 1981 69; Elkind, *Interim Measures of Protection,* 1981.

On enforcement, see Nantwi, *The Enforcement of International Judicial Decision and Arbitral Awards in Public International Law,* 1966; Oellers-Frahm, Zur Vollstreckung der Entscheidungen internationaler Gerichte im Völkerrecht, ZaöRVR 1976 654; Schachter, Enforcement of international judicial and arbitral awards, AJIL 1960 1.

1. THE ROLE OF THE COURT

The Permanent Court of International Justice (PCIJ), established under the League of Nations in 1919, was replaced after the Second World War by the International Court of Justice (ICJ). Contrary to the Permanent Court the ICJ forms an integral part of the World Organisation and is thus one of the principal organs of the United Nations; the PCIJ never formed part of the League of Nations. The International Court of Justice is, under article 92, of the Charter one of the principal organs of the World Organisation entrusted with judiciary functions. By adhering to the Charter the Member States are thus contracting parties to the Statute of the Court. Non-Members of the UN can, under article 93, adhere to the Statute separately.

Even though it is now acknowledged through the decisions of the ICJ itself that there are other subjects than States in the international society,[34] it is only States that can bring regular cases before the Court. However, the main reason for this is that the ICJ is a Court set up by States for States and does not by itself have any specific

---

[34] *The Reparations Case* (1949) ICJ *Reports* 174, see *infra* in this section and *supra* in Chapter II under Personality of Organisations and under the United Nations.

consequences.

It is sometimes thought that the rulings of the ICJ are not essential to issues on peace and security as some States, usually not parties in any dispute, treat the Court with little respect. On the other hand, it must be remembered that the Court exercises important functions as an impartial and authoritative body in a number of cases and that States that appear before the Court normally comply with what is required of them. It is also important to remember that Libya, often criticised as a 'terrorist' State, is a State which, in recent years, has agreed to be taken to the ICJ and also, itself, has taken cases to this Court, presenting itself before the Court to argue the cases and abiding by its rulings.[35]

2. THE COMPOSITION OF THE COURT

The ICJ consists of 15 independent judges whom are elected for nine years by the General Assembly and the Security Council according to fairly complicated rules, according to which the main legal systems in the world must be represented. If there is no judge on the Court of the nationality of one of the litigant parties in a dispute, such a party may then nominate his own additional judge who will serve *ad hoc* only in that dispute.

Member States of the United Nations are automatically members of the Court's Statute. Also non-members of the UN can adhere to the Statute, as, for example, Switzerland has done.

Until 1983 the ICJ worked, at all times, as a plenum court. The Court then established a Chamber system to handle disputes; the parties have no influence on the composition of such Chambers.

3. FORM OF CONSENT TO JURISDICTION OF ICJ

As in the case of arbitration, or even mediation, the contentious jurisdiction of the ICJ depends on *explicit consent* of the parties to a

---

[35]   *Tunisia v Libya* (1982) ICJ *Reports* 18; *Libya v Malta* (1985) ICJ *Reports*.

case.[36] This consent may have been given by members of the UN, or of non-members who wish to use the Court for a dispute.

Consent is necessary not only of the parties but also of any third State, if its interests will be affected by the outcome of the case, as demonstrated in the *Monetary Gold Case*.[37] In this case, gold belonging to Albania had been seized by German forces in Rome in 1943 and taken to Germany. The US, UK and France agreed in 1946 that the gold should be given to the UK in partial satisfaction of the damages awarded in the *Corfu Channel Case*.[38] In the meantime, an arbitrator had decided, between Italy and Albania, that the gold should be given to Albania. Italy sought to have the case heard by the ICJ but, in the absence of Albania's consent, the ICJ found itself precluded from dealing with the case on the ground of the lack of consent of an interested third party, a third party with vital interests in the outcome of the case.[39]

Consent to jurisdiction is even required for Advisory Opinions[40] as illustrated in the *Interpretation of Peace Treaties Case*.[41]

(a) The Optional Clause

The consent[42] of States to allow the Court to hear cases involving them is given when a party signs, in advance, the so called Optional Clause in the Statute of the ICJ. This clause is laid down in article 36

---

[36]   The Permanent Court said in the *Eastern Carelia Case* (1923) Series B No. 5 that 'It is well established in international law that no State can, without its consent, be compelled to submit its disputes with other States either to mediation or to arbitration, or to any other kind of pacific settlement.'

[37]   (1954) ICJ 24 *Reports*, 19.

[38]   (1949) ICJ *Reports* 4.

[39]   ICJ *Reports* 1950, 10.

[40]   On these see *infra*, in this section.

[41]   (1950) ICJ *Reports* 65. This case, decided at the height of the Cold War, concerned allegations that a number of East European satellite States had violated Human Rights and there were demands to establish commissions of inquiry under the Peace Treaties, which lead to certain questions of composition of such commissions. The refusal to give consent to an Opinion on these matters may be regarded as (now) violating what is (now) *jus cogens* and it is not clear that the ICJ would take the same view today.

[42]   See my *Law Making, op. cit.*, 322.

of the Court's Statute and provides that a State can bind itself in advance to present itself before the Court.

(1) The Legal Effect of Consent Under the Clause

The consent to let the Court hear an action given under the Optional Clause implies that consent is given for all future cases. This type of consent is akin to what I have called *abstract consent* when States allow, in advance, organisations to bind them by certain acts.[43]

Consent to the Optional Clause also binds a subsequent government of a State. There have been problems to apply the Optional Clause when a new regime has taken over a country. Thus, Iran was unwilling to admit jurisdiction of the Court in the *Hostages Case*[44] when the United States sought to retrieve the diplomatic personnel from Teheran. However, the fact that Iran withdrew must be seen as a violation of the duties it had to respect Iran's undertaking under the Clause. On the other hand, it was the United States, having criticised Iran on this ground, that withdrew itself a few years later in the *Nicaragua Case*, alleging a right to do so under a reservation.[45]

(2) Reservations to the Optional Clause

To a declaration under the Optional Clause a State may append reservations, sometimes seriously restricting the possibility of adjudication by the ICJ. Well known problems have been caused by the so called Connolly Amendment by which the United States adhered to the Optional Clause with the reservation that

'... this declaration shall not apply to ... (b) disputes with regard to matters which are essentially within the domestic jurisdiction of the United States of America *as determined by the United States of America.*'[46]

---

[43]   See my *Law Making, op. cit., passim.*

[44]   (1980) ICJ *Reports* 1980.

[45]   See the following section.

[46]   ICJ *Yearbook* 1981-1982, 92.

This form indicates an obvious *subjective* right to determine *what* comes 'essentially' within the domestic jurisdiction of the United States; there is no control as to whether such claims of domestic jurisdiction are *objectively* warranted.

The United States withdrew from the case that Nicaragua had brought against it for Paramilitary Activities in 1984, using *inter alia* the Connolly Amendment to escape the Court's jurisdiction.[47] The withdrawal of the United States in *The Nicaragua Case*[48] on the basis of a dubious interpretation of its obligations under a signed Optional Clause has deprived the Court, and perhaps more, the United States, of some respect. The United States had criticised Iran, only a few years earlier, in *The Iranian Hostage Case*[49] for not presenting itself before the Court to answer a case; Iran had signed the Optional Clause and had been bound to appear. In *The Nicaragua Case* it was the United States which behaved in this way: although the United States had first appeared before the Court, something which Iran had never done in *The Hostage Case,* the United States decided later to withdraw, denouncing its own adherence to the Optional Clause.[50]

(b) Consent *ad hoc*

Consent to ICJ jurisdiction can thus also be given in casu for the hearing of a specific dispute, or by one party when the other State is bound by the Optional Clause. Non-Members of the United Nations may also give such *ad hoc* consent to the Court's jurisdiction. The Federal Republic of Germany brought two cases before it became a member of the United Nations: *The North Continental Shelf Cases*[51] and *The Icelandic Fisheries Case*[52], an action started just before the

---

[47]   (1984) ICJ *Reports* 1984. The argument was that matters in issue allegedly came within the domestic jurisdiction of the United States.

[48]   (1988) ICJ *Reports* 1988.

[49]   (1980) ICJ *Reports* and *supra.*

[50]   The ICJ held that this could not be done with immediate effect: *Nicaragua Case (Jurisdiction)* (1984) ICJ *Reports* 392 at 419. *Cf. supra* under various types of Unilateral Declarations, in Chapters III and IV.

[51]   (1969) ICJ *Reports* 192.

[52]   (1974) ICJ *Reports* 192.

FRG became a member of the United Nations in 1973.

(c) Jurisdiction by Special Agreement

Parties to a dispute may *by special agreement* between them submit the matter to the International Court. By such an agreement, the parties to a dispute can *limit the terms of reference* of the Court, as shown in the *Minquiers and Echrecos Case*.[53]

An agreement may also be designed to allow the Court to act in accordance with its usual parameters as shown by the agreement in the case concerning *Frontier Lands*.[54]

(d) ICJ as *forum prorogatum*

Consent to refer a dispute to the Court can be inferred from behaviour or implied acts. Such acts may be construed to imply consent to jurisdiction. This happened in the *Corfu Channel Case*,[55] where a letter to the Court by Albania indicated that she would appear before the ICJ was accepted as sufficient display of consent to jurisdiction.[56]

4. INTERIM MEASURES

In the case of actions where a court ruling cannot wait the ICJ may grant an *injunction,* or so called *provisional* or *interim measures*.[57] This has been done in a number of cases, including the *Hostage Case* itself.[58] Such measures are intended to preserve the *status quo*, or, as in the *Serbian Genocide Case*,[59] prohibit certain acts of a State.

---

[53] 1953) ICJ *Reports* 47.

[54] *Belgium v Netherlands* (1959) ICJ *Reports* 225.

[55] (1949) ICJ *Reports* 1.

[56] But a primilnary objection to jurisdiction, like that of Iran in the *Anglo-Iranian Oil Case* (1952) ICJ *Reports* 93.

[57] For an analysis, see Oellers-Frahm, *Die einstweilige Anordnung in der internationalen Gerichtsbarheit,* 1975, *eadem,* Interim Measures of Protection, 1 Encyclopedia 1981, 69; *cf.* Elkind, *Interim Measures of Protection,* 1981.

[58] Interim Order 15th December 1979, ICJ *Reports* 7.

[59] *Bosnia v Serbia-Montenegro*, ICJ *Reports* 1993.

5. INTERVENTION IN CASES

There are procedural possibilities[60] to intervene in a case before the Court but the ICJ has declined to allow such requests in many cases,[61] demanding a high degree of evidence that the third party's legal interest are affected by the dispute. The ICJ has only been satisfied on this ground in one case[62] where it was found appropriate to allow a third State to intervene.

6. THE PHASES OF A CASE

The case before the ICJ is, as is the rule before many courts of national jurisdiction, divided into matters dealt with by way of introduction, where a defending State may make *preliminary objections*[63] to contest the competence of the Court. If such objections does not lead to the ICJ finding that the case is to be struck out, the Court will go on to decide on the *merits,* that is to say the substance of the case.

7. INTERPRETATION OF AWARDS

If a judgment is not clear a party can ask for interpretation of its terms. Tunisia did this in the dispute with Libya in *The Tunisia v Libya (Interpretation) Case.*[64] A judgment which interprets and, in a sense, supplements the original judgment must obviously be *subsumed* under the original award and not exceed its parameters: it is in essence only clarifying the original text.[65]

---

60 Article 62 of the ICJ Statute and article 81 of the Regulations.

61 See *Tunisia v Libya* (1981) ICJ *Reports* 19, request by Malta refused; *Libya v Malta* (1984) ICJ *Reports* 1, request by Italy refused.

62 *Honduras v Salvador* (1990) ICJ *Reports* 92, request by Nicaragua before a Chamber of the Court.

63 Article 36(6) of the Statute.

64 (1985) ICJ *Reports.*

65 See *The Chorzow Factory Case* (1927) PCIJ Series A No. 13, 11; *Interpretation of the Judgment of the Treaty of Neuilly* (1925) PCIJ Series A No. 4, 7.

8. CONSULTATIVE POWERS OF THE ICJ

Under article 96 of the Charter of the United Nations the General Assembly or the Security Council may ask for an *Advisory Opinion* of the Court. An opinion may, strictly speaking, only be asked for a *legal question*, as opposed to questions of fact. Initially, during the time of the PCIJ, the Court adhered strictly to this limitation of its competence and interpreted the condition in a very narrow way.[66] In recent years, however, the Court has relaxed this condition, or expressed differently, has interpreted the category *legal questions* much more widely.[67]

Among those introduced by the UN there are some of the most important decisions of the Court, such as the *Reparations for Injuries Case*.[68] This case was caused by the murder of the United Nations mediator in Palestine, Count Folke Bernadotte.[69] Before bringing an action for compensation against Israel which had exercised control in the new part of Jerusalem where the murder took place, the UN had to show that it had personality to bring an action. The ICJ made it clear that this was the case and that the UN could act in its own name for compensation. This case has been important to show that States are not the only subjects of international law; a number of other organisations and entities are now often able to act in their own name.[70]

Another case, important to the functioning of the UN is the *Conditions for Admission Case*.[71] The UN has also, for example, asked the Court to advise on the extent of its immunities.[72]

A similar power to request Advisory Opinions is granted to the specialised agencies.[73] A number of actions have been referred to the

---

[66]   *Eastern Carelia Case* (1923) PCIJ Series B No. 5.

[67]   *Western Sahara Case* (1975) ICJ *Reports* 12.

[68]   (1949) ICJ *Reports* 185 and *supra* in Chapter II, under Personality of Organisations.

[69]   *Cf. supra* on Mediation.

[70]   See my *Concept, op. cit.,* 19-34, *cf. supra* on Subjects, in Chapter II.

[71]   (1948) ICJ *Reports* 52.

[72]   *Applicability of Article VI section 22 of the Convention on the Privileges and Immunities of the UN* (1989), 177.

[73]   On these see *supra* in Chapter II.

ICJ by these agencies,[74] especially in matters concerning their competence.[75]

Certain advice has been needed, both by the UN,[76] and by the specialised agencies,[77] with regard to the UN Headquarters Arrangements[78] with a host State. Other matters of special importance to the functioning of an organisation, such as budgetary questions,[79] have also formed the object of important Advisory Opinions.[80]

9. THE EFFICACY OF THE AWARD

The execution of an award is somewhat secured by a provision in the UN Charter that each Member of the UN 'undertakes to comply' with decisions of the ICJ in cases to which a State has been a party. If any State fails to comply with a judgment, the other party 'may have recourse to the Security Council' which may make 'recommendations' or 'decide' on measures to be taken.

This bland formula is of little consolation to a State which has won a case before the ICJ when the other party refuses to execute the judgment. The scant provisions on execution of judgments must,

---

[74] *Constitution of the Maritime Safety Committee of IMCO* (1960), ICJ *Reports* 150; *Administrative Tribunal of the ILO* (1956) 77.

[75] It may be noted that contentious cases between parties in ordinary cases before the Court may also clarify powers of the specialised agencies, see, for example, *Appeal Relating to the Jurisdiction of the ICAO Council (India v Pakistan)* (1972) 46. As some of these agencies are older than the United Nations, certain cases bearing on the power of, for example, ILO were delivered by the PCIJ, *Competence of the ILO to Regulate Agricultural Labour* PCIJ (1922) Series B No. 2 and 3, 23; *Competence of the ILO to Regulate the Work of Employers* (1926) Series B No. 13, 6.

[76] *Applicability of the Obligation to Arbitrate under secion 21 of the Headquarters Agreement of 1947* (1988) 12.

[77] See *Interpretation of the Headquarters Agreement of 1951 between WHO and Egypt* (1980) ICJ *Reports* 73.

[78] On such arrangements and their importance as *primary matters* of an organisation, see my *Law Making by International Organisations*, 1965, Chapter I.

[79] On such matters, too, as being what I have called *primary matters*, see my Law Making, *op. cit., loc. cit.*

[80] *The Expenses Case* (1962) 150.

however, be seen in the light of the *normal* practice to implement of awards, perhaps reinforced by the fear of public opinion in case of flagrant disobedience,[81] *and* in the light of the *self-help* - albeit prohibited by international law.[82] Certain measures, which at first sight may appear to constitute illegal self-help, may be legitimate reactions against an offending State which has also lost a case before the ICJ. For example, the *freezing* of Albanian assets to secure payment awarded in the *Corfu Channel Case*,[83] may not be unwarranted and would appear to be in violation of any rule of international law.[84]

iii. Sanctions

Kunz, Sanctions in International Law, AJIL 1960, 324; Kelsen, The Nature of International Law: International Delicts and International Sanctions, in *Principles of International Law*, ed. Tucker, 1966, 3; Brierly, Sanctions, in *Basis of Obligations in International Law and Other Papers*, 1958, 201; Brown-John, *Multilateral Sanctions in International Law*, 1975; Coplin, The Enforcement of International Law: The Operation of Sanctions, in *Functions of International Law*, 1966, 19; Kuyper, *The Implementation of International Sanctions*, 1978; Hsu Mo, The Sanctions in International Law, 35 *Grotius Society Transactions* 1949, 3; Picchio-Forlati, *Le sanzioni delle Nazione Unite*, 1984.

On economic sanctions see Doxey, *Economics Sanctions*, 1981; McDonald, Economic Sanctions in the International System, CYIL 1969, 61; Barber, Economic Sanctions as a Policy Instrument, *International Affairs*, 1979, 367; Mersky, *Transnational Economic Boycotts and Coercion*, 1978; cf. my *Finance and Protection of Investments in Developing Countries*, 2nd ed., 1987, 71.

In international relations one often talks about *sanctions* in most general terms to indicate some form of forceful measures in response to certain undesirable action by another State. But the term should be more clearly defined in order to be studied and analysed. So what are sanctions? In the abundant literature sanctions are usually thought to enforce international law.

---

81   See *infra* under Sanctions.
82   *Supra* in Chapter IV.
83   (1949) ICJ *Reports* 1.
84   But see also *supra* on the *Monetary Gold Case*, in this section.

In basic terms sanctions can be said to be measures which enforce international law. Contrary to municipal law there are no centrally organised sanctions in the international society. Yet, the *function* of sanctions is required in any legal system.[85] There are effective ways of exercising such measures in the international system.

It must be emphasised that the legal character of international law is not affected by the absence of organised sanctions.[86] The question of the basis of obligation is thus distinct[87] and not necessarily dependent on the presence of sanctions although the presence of such coercive measures are likely to strengthen the basis of obligation whichever we conceive that to be in a specific event.

In a more precise sense writers seem to use the term in different ways: sanctions means either a *penalty* for a wrongdoing and/or some measure imposed to make a State *cease* certain behaviour. This seems to indicate a two-fold nature of sanctions.[88] Thus, sanctions in international law imply measures taken to induce a subject of the international system to cease breaking legal rules of that order, or, to punish the subject for acts in the past.

Sanctions can thus be either intervening as primarily corrective measures, with a *preemptive function,* in the midst of illegal acts taken by a subject to change the flow of events from a certain point and compel that subject to act lawfully in the future; or sanctions can intervene *ex post facto* when the acts no longer occur; in this latter case sanctions have a largely *punitive function,* although they will, of course, also have deterrent effect.[89]

In criminal law under most systems one distinguishes between *individually and generally preventive aspects.* The first category indicates the concern to prevent the individual offender from

---

[85]   *Cf.* Scelle, *Principes de droit international,* 1944, 29.

[86]   *Cf.* Krüger, in *Festschrift Spiropoulos,* 1957, 265 on the normative force of factual situations. *Cf.* Fitzmaurice who states that the foundation of authority of international law resides in the fact that states recognize the system as binding and the legal order does therefore not have to be coupled with sanctions to be binding. See Fitzmaurice, The Foundations of the Authority of International law, MLR, 1956, 1.

[87]   See my *Concept, op. cit.,* 112.

[88]   See my *Concept, op. cit.,* 86.

[89]   *Ibid., loc cit.*

repeating a crime; the second one focuses more on the need to deter members of society in general from committing the undesired act. Sanctions in the international society have similar effects.

Certain concepts are indispensable to allocate blame and responsibility in the international legal order. Thus, one would normally lead an action back to its instigator by *imputation* and then allocate responsibility.[90]

Naturally, certain sub-rules come into operation in many fields, such as in the context of armed conflict when often the responsibility has to be taken by a superior officer according to the rule *respondeat superior*.[91] There are also numerous rules to decide for which organs a State is responsible. To summarise some such rules, a States thus normally incurs responsibility for all *State organs,* even if they act *ultra vires.*[92] The State is also responsible for damaging acts of individuals if these are acting on orders of the State,[93] or if the State has failed to do what it could to prevent the injury.[94]

In all these instances just mentioned, we can perceive an element of *either organic connection* with the State *or* an element of *fault.* There are, however, some further areas where the State will be *strictly liable* for anyone in its territory, including individuals, who are engaging in certain *hazardous activities.* The *rationale* behind such strict responsibility is that such activities require close supervision by the State because of their inherent dangerous character. Such activities include exploitation of *nuclear material* or of *Outer Space.*

In a sense, however, responsibility is a non-subject as it cannot be conceptually explored in any rational way *except* by an inversion of the duties and obligations a State, and others, have under international law. Thus, the violation of *any* rule of international law will give rise to *responsibility.* However, the *mechanisms* of that responsibility in any individual case are impossible to predict except for the basic notions just referred to, like imputation, assessment of fault, qualification of certain areas for strict responsibility etc.The ILC

---

[90]   *Cf.* ii O'Connell, *International Law*, 2nd ed., 1970 942.

[91]   See in detail my *Law of War, op. cit.*, Chapter V.

[92]   *Youman's Claim* (1926) 4 RIAA 110.

[93]   *The Zafiro Case* (1925) 6 RIAA 160.

[94]   *Janes Claim* (1926) 4 RIAA 82.

546

has laboured for years over a draft on State responsibility; their time might have been better spent on investigating the *obligations* of international law, for responsibility is nothing more than the consequence of any breach of any given norm. The only intricate question, is where to pitch the standard of fault and to assess whether there, in any cases, should be vicarious responsibility.

If we consider how much international law has in common with internal law, as a structural legal system, it is also symptomatic that we do not study responsibility for our law degrees; we study tort, breach of contract or criminal law, at all times keeping our focus on the obligation, the breach of which entails consequences in the form of responsibility.

It is important to consider these general questions before we address the problem as to *how* to react against a wrongdoer, in other words, by what form of *sanctions*.

a. Sanctions and the Use of Force

See the references *supra* under iii. Sanctions and further, Derpa, *Das Gewaltverbot der Satzung der Vereinigten Nationen und die Anwendung nicht-militarischer Gewalt,* 1979.

Sanctions in International law cannot be viably studied unless they are set in relation to the use of force.[95] The use of force has been outlawed in international law but it may still be permissible to resort to force in order to respond to a violation of international law. In other words, a right to resort to sanctions preempts the illegitimacy of the use of force.

It is clear from a number of practical instances as well as from the overwhelming evidence of the doctrine that there are certain clear limits to the use of forceful sanctions. They must be *proportionate* to the initial violation, they must allow the other State to amend its ways and *not* be imposed *without warning* and they must be imposed *with reasonable speed* after the initial violation of a rule.[96] Naturally,

---

[95] On prohibition of the use of force, see *supra* under Prophylactic Rules.

[96] *The Naulilaa Arbitration* (1928) 2 RIAA 1949 1011; The Air Services Agreement Arbitration (1963) 16 RIAA 5.

there is considerable latitude in assessing any of these limitations. Thus, the Task Force was thought to have been sent 'immediately' from the United Kingdom in the Falklands War although it took a month for it to arrive.

Forceful sanctions should be channelled through the Security Council of the United Nations but it is evident that if that organisation, or that organ, does not act with required speed, a State, or, indeed, another organ of the UN, may take it in its own hands to take necessary action.

It was on the ground that the United Nations was too slow that the British Government thought itself competent to act with a forceful response in the Falkland emergency. It was on the ground that the Security Council was too slow to act that the General Assembly took action in the Suez Crisis.

This last mentioned lack of action even caused a *de facto* transfer of power from the Security Council to the General Assembly; there was an informal shifting of power during the Suez crisis under the earlier *Uniting for Peace Resolution*[97] when the General Assembly set up an Emergency Force, a decision, which technically, under the Charter, should have been taken by the Security Council.[98]

With regard to non-forceful sanctions States have considerable latitude to ensure compliance with a desired pattern by other forms of *pressure*.[99] It may be that it is only when such pressure constitutes the response to breaches of international law that we should be speaking of sanctions properly so called. But the line is fine, difficult to trace, between that which a States desires for general foreign policy reasons and that to which it is entitled under international law. This is especially so since many breaches, or alleged breaches, depend on assessment of facts *in casu*. In other words, the case will often, if not always, *turn on the facts*. In the absence of objective analysis by a third party, the views of a State of a possible breach of international

---

[97]   Adopted during the Korean crisis in 1950, see *supra*, in Chapter IV. *Cf.* on the structure of the UN and the competence of the General Assembly in Chapter II.

[98]   On the *de facto* revision of the Charter by this act see my *Law Making, op. cit.,* 34 *et seq.*

[99]   On reports to organisations, see *infra*.

law are intertwined and interlinked with its foreign policy attitudes.

b. Typology of Sanctions: The Subjects and Objects of Sanctions

The intervention of sanctions presupposes that an international legal rule has been violated. When such a violation has taken place the international system allows for certain counter measures to be taken. Sanctions are thus immediately linked to the specific question of *responsibility*.[100]

The first question that must be answered before sanctions are introduced is thus: What was the offence? Was it an offence? Who is responsible for the damage and/or injury?

The allocation of blame will be assessed by means of *imputation*, a notion which is indispensable to the international legal order[101] and to this end it is necessary to refer to the different subjects we have identified in this work: it is desirable that responsibility is assessed, and sanctions directed, in relation to these subjects.

The State is itself responsible for damage it has caused itself, and that has been caused by its organs and agents.[102] The State is also responsible for all *ultra-hazardous* activities which must always be authorised and supervised by States, and in most cases, such activities are also carried out by the State. Typical examples of such activities are *nuclear fission* or *launching of satellites*.

The State cannot absorb all responsibility and it is not desirable for the effectiveness of the international legal order that the State shields misdeeds of others. There are thus cases where, for example, individuals are personally responsible for their acts, especially if such acts have involved gross violations of international law.[103] On the other hand, there are cases when a State, for environmental reasons, *ought* to take the responsibility for certain activities it has *authorised private individuals to carry out*, for example, for pollution damage

---

[100]   *Cf.* Verdross, *Die völkerrechtliche Kriegshandlung und der Strafanspruch der Staaten*, 1920.

[101]   *Cf. supra. Contra*, Brownlie, *Responsibility. op. cit., loc. cit.*

[102]   *Cf. supra* under the State and its organs in Chapter II and under immunity for State agents in Chapter VI.

[103]   *Cf. infra.*

caused by sub-standard ships flying a flag of convenience of the State in question,[104] and for pollution damage caused to the territory of another State by insufficient safety rules for certain factories or smelters.[105]

The type of sanctions allowed by the international legal order[106] will obviously depend on what type of rule was violated. Furthermore, the subjects and objects affected by international sanctions will again depend on which type of norm was violated.

Certain sanctions may be taken by States but international organisations and even individuals may play a role in the system of sanctions. Again, the typology shows also that numerous sanctions are directed against States, and others have international organisations or, in some instances, individuals as targets. The classification below is based on the *target of sanctions*.

(i) States

The type example of sanctions may well be the measures taken by a State in retaliation against another which has broken international law. Such measures will often take the form of reprisals.

1. MILITARY REPRISALS AND RETALIATION

The normal type of sanctions exercised by a State against another State is characterised by the fact that it may comprise measures which would otherwise be illegal under international law.

The definition of reprisals is that it is the response to an illegal act by another an act which itself would have been illegal under international law had it not been a justified counter measure.

It is also important to note that the term *reprisals* is often used in armed conflicts as measures taken, not against States, but *against the civilian population*[107] and then are measures intended to lower

---

[104]   *Cf. supra* on flags of convenience in Chapter VI.
[105]   *Cf. supra* on Environmental Rules and the *Trail Smelter Case*, in Chapter IV.
[106]   *Cf.* von Bardeleben, *Die zwangsweise Durchsetzung im Völkerrecht,* 1939; Keller, *Die nicht-kriegische militäre Gewaltsmassnahme,* 1934.
[107]   See my *Law of War, op. cit.,* 254 *et seq.*

moral and to force the home State of such victims to certain concessions. In this form, reprisals are prohibited by international law as unlawful attacks against the civilian population.[108]

The general type of reprisals, however, implying action, or reaction, *against a State* which has violated international law is not only permissible but represents *measures essential to the safeguard of the international legal system.* Such measures may then include a form of use of force that would otherwise be forbidden.

Reprisals are thus usually distinguished from other retaliatory measures in the sense that reprisals involve measures which would otherwise be illegal whereas other milder acts would not be tainted in that way. In the same way as self-defence, reprisals will thus legitimize certain use of force which otherwise would have been forbidden.[109]

The wording alone indicates the dangers when evaluation, as is normal in international relationships, turns on the facts. Who is to assert that an illegal act took place in the first place? Was there in intrusion across the border? Did the others start to shoot first? Was the behaviour actually illegal?

The response by force, like that in the Falklands Affair, is a prime example of sanctions by the use of military force. Yet, the action, or reaction, of the United Kingdom to the attack of Argentina on the islands, could also be conceived, from the point of view of conceptual analysis, as *self-defence*.[110]

The last mentioned qualification illustrates that sanctions is an ambiguous term: a *reaction* to a breach of international law may take the form of self-defence on an attacked party. Over and beyond the immediate defence of own positions, a State or some State(s), may proceed to 'punish' a State which has broken international law. As such 'punishment' nowadays may not take place unless authorised by the United Nations: any form of *self help* is thus precluded by the prohibition of the use of force in the Charter. The term *sanctions* must then probably be reserved for the action of the United

---

[108]   *Ibid.,* 241 *et seq.*
[109]   See my Law of War, *op. cit.,* 65, 75 *et seq.*
[110]   See *supra.*

Nations.[111]

2. ECONOMIC SANCTIONS

See *supra* and especially, McDonald, Economic Sanctions in the International System, CYIL 1969, 61; Doxey, Economic Sanctions, 1981; Mersky, *Transnational Economic Boycotts and Coercion,* 1978; *cf.* my *Finance and Protection of Investments in Developing Countries,* 2nd ed., 1986.

Economic sanctions can be most powerful. Such sanctions may concern, for example, the banning of exports, and may be recommended or ordered by the United Nations.

Economic sanctions were tried, without much success, against Rhodesia[112] and in numerous later cases, when most leading States and many organisations, wished to expressly *condemn certain behaviour.*

There is always a problem of considering the impact on the economy of the exporting sanctioning States vis-à-vis the effect on the economy of the target State. There is, as in the case of South Africa, an almost embarrassing question whether sanctions actually had a healthy effect on the economy of the target State.

It may be questioned whether trade sanctions are largely more effective against poorer States and less appropriate against States with developed and sophisticated economies and which are *also* rich in natural resources, for example South Africa.[113] The ban on exports of arms to South Africa[114] had the effect that South African started

---

[111] Possibly including its organs, for example, the International Court of Justice.

[112] For sanctions against Rhodesia, e.g., GA Resolutions 2024 (XX) 1965; 2151 (XXI) 1966; 2262 (XXII) 1967; 2383 (XXIII) 1968; 2505 (XXIV) 1969; 2652 (XXV) 1970; 2769 (XXVI) 1971; 2945 (XXVII) 1972; 2946 (XXVII) 1972; 3115 (XXVIII) 1973; 3116 (XXVIII) 1973; 3297 (XXIX) 1974; 3298 (XXIX) 1974; 3396 (XXX) 1976; 3397 (XXX) 1976; 31/154 A and B, 1976; 32/116 A and B, 1977; 33/38 A and B 1978 and 34/192 1979.

[113] See, for sanctions in general, for example, GA Resolution 36/172 B and D 1981.

[114] For sanctions banning arms trade with South Africa, *e.g.* SC Arms Embargo Resolution 569 (1985) and 591 (1986); See also, for example, GA Resolutions on arms embargo Resolution 418 (1977)) and 37/69 1982. *Cf.* 31/6 K 1976, 32/105 K.

producing its own arms, and is now an exporter of arms all over the world.

Other measures of persuasion may be warranted: many deplored that, with regard to South Africa, for example, there was a ban on UK university lecturers delivering lectures in that country. After all, since the Crusades it has been obvious that it you wish people to change their mind and adopt other basic views, you must establish and maintain contacts rather than resort to isolationary measures which only seem to entrench adopted attitudes.

Other economic sanctions than trade sanctions can be highly effective, especially a *freezing of assets.* This is a course of action open, for example, when a State patently does not respect fundamental rules of international law, or a judgment of the International Court of Justice.[115] One efficient way of reacting against major deviations from international law is thus a blocking of bank accounts, like the one ordered by President Carter in 1979 of all Iranian assets in American Banks worldwide. This case obviously involves several fascinating aspects: the extraterritorial application of a US Decree,[116] the intricacies of the operation of article VII 2(b) on *exchange contracts* of the International Monetary Fund and the practical operation of the Euro-dollar market, as well as the question whether other States are bound by solidarity to reinforce action taken when the initial violations, which concerned the arrest of diplomats, go to the foundations of international society. The case also amply illustrated the effectiveness of economic freezing sanctions.

In the event, the World Court had, as often before, showed itself powerless, whereas the economic sanctions of freezing produced the release of the hostages. A case was prepared in the High Court of London where Iran had sued the England-based Banks for the release of its money: a telex notifying the release of the frozen money was followed within minutes by a telex from Iran confirming that the

---

[115] See, for example, the *Freezing of Albanian Assets* in London following the unpaid damages awarded in the *Corfu Channel (Assessment) Case,* (1949), ICJ *Reports* 244.

[116] See my article on Extraterritorial Application of Exchange Control Regulations: Private International law Aspects of Comity, *Nordisk Tidskrift for International Ret,* 1987.

hostages had been released. The causation chain was largely obscured in the media where various statesmen claimed 'credit' for the release of the hostages, who had effectively been *bought back*, using the (blocked) funds of the State, Iran, that had taken the hostages.

The case in Iran also illustrates the level of non-permissible forceful sanctions. The United States was condemned in most quarters, including by the International Court of Justice, for having organised a special squad rescue mission which was foiled. Yet, the mission was curiously similar to the Entebbe raid where few, perhaps considering the atrocities of the Amin regime, had questioned the legality of the rescue mission.

We may note the remarkable decision of the Security Council in October 1992 to 'take' Serb assets outside Serbia to defray UN expenses for the UNPROFOR[117] in 1992. This action goes further than *freezing of assets*. A formal action for war crimes seems now a likely course to claim responsibility for serious violations of international law, *i.a.* the prohibition of aggression, as well as serious violations of the Law of War, of humanitarian law and of Human Rights. It might have been more appropriate to proceed to the *taking* of assets for reparation after the judgment in such War Crimes Trials but the taking of assets at an earlier date reflects the serious view taken *prima facie* as to the numerous violations by the Serbs in an expansionist war.

3. RETORSION

Many stretch the category of responses to include another dubious candidate, that of *retorsion*.[118] This term could be said to indicate an act of response which would itself not be *illegal* but merely *unpleasant*. Yet, one wonders what good such a category will do considering that States have no legal duty to be *pleasant* to each other. It appears to be yet another one of the expressions of extreme *Begriffsjurisprudenz*.

On the other hand, there are measures taken by a State which fall

---

[117]   The United Nations Protective Force operating in Croatia and Bosnia (but not in the attacking country, Serbia).

[118]   *E.g.*, Rapisardi-Mirabelli, *La ritorsione*, 1919.

into a group of acts of foreign policy, all designed to ensure a certain behaviour of other States. The spectrum of these acts range from showing disapproval by breaking or altering the level of diplomatic relations,[119] to decisions not to take part in the Olympic Games.[120] The most common action, apart from reduction of diplomatic contacts, appears to be restrictions of exports and other trade relationships, banning the fishing of another State's ships in a State's waters, prohibition of transfer of technology, curtailment of flights, or the traditional cancellation or restriction of consular relations.[121] Another form of reaction is to prescribe that most-favoured-nation status shall cease. The United States chose this way to react against Rumania's new law to make emigrés repay debts and expenses for education in 1982.

4. LOSS OF PRIVILEGES

Other modes of imposing sanctions on States which fall out of the accepted framework for action in international society is to withdraw certain privileges from the failing States.

Although the right of legation, to send and to receive envoys, is not an absolute right but one that depends on the consent of the receiving State, that consent may be suspended to mark the displeasure of the receiving State at certain action. In this sense, the

---

[119] For example, Peoples' Republic of China recalled its Ambassador from the Hague to protest against the sale of Dutch submarines to the Republic of China (Taiwan), and replacing him on a *chargé d'affaires* level. If a country does not have diplomatic relations it can still *restrict contacts*: Japan restricted all official contacts with North Korea after the murder of South Korean Ministers in Burma allegedly engineered by North Korea.

[120] As the action against the Games in Moscow in 1980 following the invasion by the USSR of Afghanistan.

[121] The United States took all these measures against the USSR in 1980. After the introduction of martial law in Poland in 1984 the United States barred new licences for the exports of certain oil and gas equipment and high technology equipment, curtailed flights, prohibited fishing by Polish ships in the EEZ, required 14 (instead of four) days' notice for ships to go into US ports and refused new export credit guarantees.

renouncing of the right for an embassy to remain, or for a specific envoy to stay, implies a certain type of effective sanction.

When Argentina invaded the Falkland Islands, one of the first actions of the United Kingdom was to order the Argentinean Embassy in London to close. Diplomats employed at this embassy were given a short time delay by the Foreign Office to leave the country.[122]

Another effective measure is to order a specific diplomat out of a receiving State as *persona non grata* as a sanction after certain non-acceptable action has occurred. This was thus a way of dealing with spying diplomats or diplomats who carried on activities incompatible with their diplomatic status.[123]

5. EXPOSURE: SUSPENSION OF MEMBERSHIP

As another type of sanctions, we may mention measures imposed by international organisations on States to ensure compliance with various rules.[124] There are different types of such measures: one is the type of sanctions imposed to ensure that the *operative acts*[125] of an organisation, that is to say sanctions which entrench and safeguard the goals for which the organization has been set up: a particularly wide type of sanctions would thus be those imposed by the United Nations to secure world peace and security.

Another type are those which ensure that primary acts, that is to say the acts which all concern the very administration of an organisation, are fulfilled.[126] Organisations may impose sanctions on

---

[122] For the practice to ask another State to be caretaker of certain interests, see *supra* under Diplomats, in Chapter VI.

[123] For numerous examples and for the retaliating practice to counter-expel other diplomats, see my Foreign Warships and Immunity for Espionage, AJIL 1984, 76.

[124] On these see my *Law Making, op. cit.,* 309 *et seq.*

[125] *Ibid.,* 319 and *supra* in Chapter III.

[126] For the terminology see my *Law Making, op. cit.* 320, and *supra.* Note that many organisations, for example, the EC, has adopted much from French law, both with regard to the functioning of administration as a whole and with respect to staff.

556

States to ensure both operative and primary acts.[127]

Organisations may produce compliance with operative acts by *exposure* of the behaviour of Member States to others in reports which are distributed for general circulation. This is the system of the Committee of Experts of the International Labour Organisation (ILO), a Committee not provided for by the Constitution of the organisation, but which in practice has taken upon itself to control the implementation of rules by Member States. The international Monetary Fund (IMF) has a similar report system under articles XII(8) and XIV(4). A specially severe case of *exposure* to bring a failing State back to the fulfilment of international duties is if court proceedings are instigated. This may happen, for example, if there is an argument as to what a State is obliged to finance under the budget of an organisation.[128]

A special form of *exposure* is the indictment of a State in Human Rights proceedings in the Council of Europe, where the first step is an investigation by the Commission and then, in many instances, a fullscale hearing by the Court of Human Rights. Some governments have even attempted to silence reports on such cases, and made vigorous attempts to obtain settlement out of court to avoid publicity. It is of considerable concern that Sweden has, by far, the highest complaint rate *per capita* for violations of Human Rights before the European Commission of Human Rights.

Suspension of membership is an effective and often embarrassing sanction, provided the organisation from which a failing State is suspended is of sufficient interest to that State. If, for example, a State has been considered to have violated the rules which forbid aggressive force, as Israel is said to have done when it bombed a nuclear installation in Iraq, it could be excluded from the relevant international organisation. This is the action which was thought appropriate after the bombing raid in Iraq and Israel was suspended

---

127 For a list of examples, see *Law Making,* 309 *et seq.* Note the sanctioning measure of expulsion if membership dues have not been paid.

128 For example, see, *The Expenses Case* (1963), ICJ *Reports,* 5.

from the International Atomic Energy Agency (IAEA).[129]

6. EXPOSURE: WORLD OPINION

As we have propagated a theory whereby the individual is conceived as a subject of international law it follows that individuals are capable of exercising a number of rights, if not all rights, under the international system. One such right is the right to impose limited sanctions on other subjects of the international legal order.

The most compelling type of sanctions exercised by individuals is doubtlessly that of *world opinion*. World opinion, signifies the views of large numbers of individuals in various States, including public figures such as charismatic leaders.[130] Even if unaccompanied by positive action the mere condemnation of a State's action by world opinion or by the views of influential groups of individuals may often induce that State to change its policies.

This world opinion, which is not as nebulous and difficult to assess as sometimes claimed, is clearly assisted by the action of numerous non-governmental organisations (NGOs) which have taken an interest in the matter. One scholar has also insisted that public opinion, as one of the most efficient types of sanction, is the result of the *tension* between what people perceive as desirable in the international legal system and the actual lack for adequate provisions on that specific question.[131] Some will not be interested in taking part in this pressure making process, like what he calls the 'masses' whereas the 'militants' will and the 'governments', the third element in this scenario, will gradually move to another position.[132]

It was thus mere *condemnation* of apartheid which gradually caused a change of State policy towards South Africa, even if

---

[129] This Agency is based in Vienna and is primarily concerned with safety standards for nuclear installations. It is unclear what actual disadvantages entail a suspension from membership beyond that of a *stigma*.

[130] This expression is normally used to signify persons who have the factual power to lead and inspire large number of people; it is important to underline that the expression is *neutral* and implies no information as to whether the person has good or less laudable motives.

[131] Merle, *Sociologie des relations internationales,* 1988, 437.

[132] *Ibid.,* 425-442.

sanctions chosen were not, as noted, above, particularly appropriate or effective.

Other shifts of policy caused by world opinion, for example, in the field of Human Rights, or in the field of the Law of War, show the very strong sanctioning power of world opinion. In both these areas, world opinion has suggested *limitations* to a State's sovereign power in its own territory:[133] obligation to abolish apartheid[134] and obligation to refrain from cruel behaviour in war, or from the use of certain weapons; in other words States have been encouraged to pledge *negative action.*

Public opinion has been particularly noticeable with regard to recent development within environmental affairs. The whole new concern for an improved Earth, with less pollution and with a more effective resource management is to be attributed to growing world opinion. Here too, action has sought to induce States to refrain from certain action but, on the whole, States have been encouraged to *take positive action* with regard to environmental matters.

World opinion may start from small groups in a relatively few countries[135] and then grow to catch on a larger audience and numerous supporters. But even isolated efforts of expression of personal views may contribute to changing of State policy. Thus, manifestations in Paris against the CAP, the Common Agricultural Policy of the European Community, are probably far more effective with regard to the contents of future regulation than any other State negotiations. Demonstrations against the Maastricht Treaty[136] are, again, more influential than expert opinions of government advisers.

Individuals voicing their opinion may not even be acting entirely on their own without State support. To give one example, the measures announced by a Soviet trade union in 1984[137] to take action against Western business interests, were also a form of pressure of individuals. Such expressions of opinion, rare in the ex-Soviet

---

[133] See my *Independent State, op. cit.,* 125 *et seq.*

[134] On some time schedule as negotiated with relevant parties.

[135] On the role of Non-Governmental Organisations (NGOs) see *supra* in Chapter II.

[136] *Supra.*

[137] *The Times,* 31 October 1984.

Union, might have been endorsed, and consequently much reinforced, by the State.

(ii) International Organisations

One situation is that an organisation is the target of sanctions. This may be the case when the organisation has overstepped its authority or mismanaged its funds or in some other way has behaved in a way which is unacceptable to the member States. The United States thus withdrew from UNESCO in 1983, followed by the United Kingdom in 1984, after accusation that the organisation had *anti-Western attitudes* as well as questionable budget policies. Particularly the withdrawal of the United States was most effective to make the organisation change its policies: the United States contributed 25 per cent to the budget.

The United States had earlier witnessed the effectiveness of withdrawing from another organization. In 1977 it had left the International Labour Organisation (ILO), charging it with violation of the tri-partite rules which ensure the representation of States, employers and employees, as well as charging the organisation with running questionable Human Rights policies. It rejoined in 1980 after the ILO had made substantial changes.

(iii) Individuals

Individuals can also be the object of sanctions. The type example is the case when a compelling rule on Human Rights has been violated. Individuals can then not escape personal liability.[138] Thus, if a person commits an act which is a veritable crime under international law, and perhaps a crime of a flagrant type, he may be personally liable. The rule *respondeat superior*, implies that a commanding officer, or commanding civilian, is normally responsible for what has been done by his subordinates. However, a subordinate soldier cannot claim the normal *respondeat superior* defence in cases of *gross violations of fundamental Human Rights*. In other words, he cannot

---

[138]   See my *Law of War, op. cit.,* 352 *et seq.* and my article on Foreign Warships and Espionage, AJIL, 1984, 53.

argue that he, perhaps as a soldier, was 'merely' obeying orders or that he, perhaps as a diplomat, was ordered to act as he did by his home Government. If he oversteps that line in international law which distinguishes a mere violation of a rule from that of a gross crime, he and perhaps his superiors as well, will be all personally liable.

This rule is thus *suspended* with regard to gross crimes for which *individual responsibility* ensues.[139]

There are obviously extremely few cases when this may happen. One type of act which is one of the few which we know will engage such personal responsibility is that of genocide or crimes against the Law of War.[140] Although the right of life is not adequately entrenched in international treaties or in general rules of international law we know that a certain quantitative and qualitative excesses will entail such consequences in law. An emerging area where rules are gradually crystallised include also rules prohibiting torture and, probably, apartheid. Other lesser violations of Human Rights, however unjustified they may be, would not have such consequences. However, by increased awareness of the need for protection of human dignity the circle of rules safeguarded by personal responsibility may be described as elastic and may well comprise new categories in a few decades' time.

c. *Reasons for Sanctions*

If we then briefly consider in what situations states resort to sanctions in the modern international society we notice that, if we leave the specialised field of international organisations, there are two main fields. The matter of sanctions, as it were, seem to concern either violations of Human Rights - such as sanctions against Rhodesia or South Africa - or against the illegitimate use of force of a particular State - such as sanctions against the Soviet Union for the invasion of Afghanistan.

Yet, as mentioned above, the whole question of legitimacy of the sanctions themselves will often turn on facts alone, especially in the

---

[139]   See my *Law of War, op. cit.*, 357-359.

[140]   See *supra* on the planned War Crimes Trials of Serb leaders for aggression and for atrocities.

case of the use of force. South Africa rarely denies that it has adopted an apartheid policy, but claims it has the right to have such a policy. The Soviet Union claimed that it was requested by the 'legitimate' government in Kabul to intervene and 'help'. President Reagan also claimed that he was 'helping' Nicaragua, although he had not been asked by the legitimate government he was helping those, the Contras, who, in his opinion, *ought* to have formed the government.

In this sense, the legitimacy of action may often turn on the facts and each party may be convinced that they are acting not only according to their desirable foreign policy they wish to pursue but in accordance with international law.

With regard to Human Rights, the other main field of sanctions, it may be noted that until recently such matters remained largely within the *reserved domain* of a State, and, under article 2(7) of the United Nations Charter, it was not for others to comment on these matters. However, in later years this domain has become more and more restricted and now States consider themselves allowed to impose sanctions even to bring about *democratically elected government*,[141] indicating that the right for States to chose their own form of structure is increasingly limited.

It may be suggested that sanctions represent a multi-faceted type of measure in international society which may contribute to the gradual development and entrenchment of worthy international rules. However, there is a problem area where States often use measures under the guise of sanctions to justify certain forceful acts they anyway wish to see executed for their own particular interests. It is an area where qualifications and distinctions therefore should be of essence.

---

[141]   See my *Law of War, op. cit.,* 24 *et seq.*

Index

564